# THEY BUILT THE WEST

THE COUNCIL BLUFFS CROSSING ON THE OVERLAND TRAIL

James Linforth, *Route from Liverpool to the Great Salt Lake Valley,* 1855. Engraved after a drawing by Frederick Piercy. Courtesy of the Salt Lake City Free Public Library.

# THEY BUILT THE WEST

## *An Epic of Rails and Cities*

BY

GLENN CHESNEY QUIETT

D. APPLETON-CENTURY COMPANY
INCORPORATED
NEW YORK                    LONDON
1934

TO

S. B. K.

# PREFACE

TWO gigantic bridges are being thrown across the Bay of San Francisco to make one great metropolis of the cities around the Bay. Across the deserts of Southern California an elongated caterpillar of steel is slowly creeping from Boulder Dam to Los Angeles. Through it will flow the water that has fallen on the slopes of the far-away Rockies and has rushed away to the lowlands cutting out the Grand Cañon in its swift advance. Trains are now running through the Moffat Tunnel, which pierces the stony barrier of the Rockies at its most formidable point and gives Denver a place on a quick, direct transcontinental railroad route. In eastern Washington the waters of the Columbia are being impounded by the Grand Coulée Dam to furnish power, and ultimately irrigation, for a new empire. In Oregon there is being built at Bonneville, near tide-water on the Columbia, a huge dam to harness the river for the making of electricity.

So do improvements on a tremendous scale go forward in the West, overcoming barriers, harnessing natural resources, making the land more fruitful, the cities more populous. All these enterprises, carried on by state or municipal or Federal authority, are the logical culmination of the earlier achievements of the individual industrialists and capitalists who built the West.

The age of rugged individualism is over. No longer will it be necessary to look to a few hardy, far-sighted, and perhaps unscrupulous individuals for the planning and execution of the vast schemes needed to develop the resources of the West. Undoubtedly there will be some such in the future, but there now seems to be neither necessity nor opportunity for individual exploitation on a large scale such as marked the building of the first transcontinental railroads and the first large industrial enterprises.

Bold, shrewd, courageous, grasping, tenacious—yes, some of them even dishonest,—these giants of another day played their parts well. They were cast in the rôles of builders, and they built. They built for themselves first and the rest of the world second. If they recognized that they had any responsibility to society, it was only an occasional vagrant flash of thought in their weaker moments of idleness. And it was quickly discarded when they returned to their work, driving to completion those projects which made them exultant and rich. It was a personal matter with them. They were there to scheme and manipulate and profit, and whether planning or building or operating, the motto of many of them, implied if not expressed, was the same as that attributed to Commodore Vanderbilt—"The Public Be Damned."

Now that same public has stepped in and asserted its rights. Little by little, through regulation and legislation it has enmeshed its gigantic corporations in a maze of restrictive control. It has made them do an about-face and declare their main purpose to be public service. And, finally, it is apparently on the way to further control by taking over the railroads as a public charge. When, as, and if this is done, let us hope that something of the best of the old qualities of character that pioneered in these precarious undertakings will be preserved. It would be a pity to lose from American life the shrewd planning, the daring execution, the dogged determination of these exploiters and buccaneers of the nineteenth century. If we are lucky, we shall find some way to carry it over into the public service in some newest of new deals which brings out all the best of the old qualities of leadership and business ability for public instead of exclusively private good.

Curiously enough, after long lives of ruthless exploitation, some of these early builders began to see that they owed something to the world that had made them rich—or perhaps it would be better to say that they discovered a new and extraordinary pleasure in giving away their money for the public good. So from these Western barons of rails and land came princely gifts to the people of the Pacific— Leland Stanford Junior University, the Henry E. Huntington Library and Art Gallery, Reed College, the Sutro Library, and many a lesser benefaction. And in the minds of some of them there grew up a belief that perhaps they had a responsibility, not only to society, but to the laborers who shared with them the hard work and the dangers of their projects.

In the later days of even such a hard master as Collis P. Huntington, there is some inkling of a will to do right by his men—not a settled, orderly, social philosophy, but a dim realization that there was something here to think about. Before he died, this regal democrat declared that "the aristocracy of labor is my aristocracy," and he stopped his private car at El Paso to go down to pay a social call on an old hack-driver who lived there. And General William J. Palmer, the suave and genial exploiter of the Rockies, actually distributed among his employees a million dollars from the profits of a railroad deal with George Gould at a time when such generous conduct was almost unheard of.

They had the minds to grasp great problems, these hard-headed, hard-fisted men, the hands that wrought mighty works. Their ethics were in tune with the ethics of the day. They saw the possibility of a steadily growing prosperity through the exploitation of apparently illimitable natural resources, and they felt that any wise man who saw such opportunities would be a fool not to take all he could get. It was a game to them—intricate, crafty, subtle,—always rewarding in satisfaction if well played, increasingly rewarding in profits as their skill grew. If the trend of the day's thought had been more strongly toward social betterment, some of these giants might have grasped it, appropriated it, triumphantly led it to new achievement.

We in America ought to understand these builders. We should be able to share in the joy of conquest that they felt and in their satisfaction of accomplishment. For we are young and aggressive still, even if a little tired. And we have been a part of this gigantic enterprise of building and exploitation. We have witnessed within the lifetimes of our old people the conquering of the wilderness, the pushing back of the frontier, and the building there of cities of delight. And we must now realize that whatever the natural advantages favorable to growth may be, the prime factor in the building of cities was and is _men_. Location, transportation, natural resources are necessary; but it is wise, aggressive, determined men who turn the weight of the scales of fortune in favor of one place or another. Men made an important center of Denver, which might have been a way-station on a branch line. Men built Los Angeles, in an unfavorable location, battling for her harbor, her water supply, her place in the sun. Men tore down the hills of Seattle to make room for a metropolis. And wherever there are men with far-sightedness and grasp and a love of accomplishment and a belief in their own destiny, cities will grow, to-day as yesterday.

This book is about the accomplishments of some of the leaders in the building of the West, the men in the lime-light, the men at the top. But the story would not be complete if it did not tell also about the part played by the men at the bottom—the men who sweated and struggled and worked for a pittance to build the West we know. There were Chinese in basket hats living on rice and tea; hardy, whiskey-drinking Irish; Poles and Swedes and Americans, who laid rails and built cities by the sweat of their hands. It is this same army of men who to-day fill the dingy employment offices and watch the jobs listed

on the black-boards on the Occidental Avenues and the Burnside
Streets and the Howard Streets of the West. Strong young men, broken
old men, unkempt, unshaven, sometimes drunk, wearing clumsy
shoes and sweat-shop suits, satisfied if they have enough money for
meals at a frowsy restaurant and a room in a cheap hotel. They are
the workers in the army; they are the privates without whose strong
backs and capable hands the generals would have issued orders in vain.
Our western cities and the steel trails that bear us swiftly to them
are built on the bodies and spirits of these men. Let us not forget
them when we pay tribute to the builders of the West.

G, C, Q.

# ACKNOWLEDGMENTS

MANY people have helped write this book. When a writer who is not a professional historian attempts an historical subject, he must ask for much help and advice from those who are. The first of those who offered counsel and encouragement was the late Archer Butler Hulbert, who, out of his long experience and wide knowledge of early trails and transportation and life on the Western frontier, was able to give invaluable assistance. He freely opened his library of books and manuscripts at Colorado College and read and corrected the first five chapters of this book. Bubbling over with enthusiasm, full of plans for writing more about the history of the West, and anxious to help others to do such writing and research, he was one of the most lively and vivid of American historians. His recent death brought a severe loss to the West and to his friends.

The collections of the Colorado State Historical Society were drawn upon in writing about Denver, and the assistance of the Secretary, LeRoy R. Hafen, was helpful on this chapter as well as upon everything connected with early stage-coach and pony-express lines, on which he is an authority. He very kindly read the chapter on Denver. A. E. Ellsworth of the Denver Chamber of Commerce also provided information. Miss Louise Kampff of the Colorado College Library assisted in collecting the material used and in checking various points. Considerable information about General Palmer was contributed by his former associate, William W. Postlethwaite of Colorado College. James F. Willard, professor of history at the University of Colorado, and the publishers of the Greeley *Daily Tribune* were helpful in collecting material on Greeley.

California is fortunate in having a State Library at Sacramento which is unequaled for the speed, accuracy, and completeness with which historical information is supplied. To Miss Mabel R. Gillis, librarian, my compliments. And the same to Miss Dorothy Huggins of the California Historical Society, who also supplied information. The officers of the Society of California Pioneers were most agreeable in opening their fine collections of books and pictures. The most valuable material on California was obtained from the manuscripts of the Bancroft Historical Library at Berkeley, which Herbert I. Priestley very kindly made available. This included manuscripts concerning the builders of the Central Pacific which had been collected by Professor Bancroft himself. Stuart Daggett, professor of transportation at the University of California, was helpful, as was also Robert P. Scripps of San Diego, who provided material about his father. The publishers of the San Francisco *Examiner* very kindly opened their files of clippings. Assistance was also given by Mrs. W. C. Morgan and Miss Clara Helen Brooks of the Friday Morning Club Library.

Charles Caldwell Dobie, author of *San Francisco Pageant,* read the chapter on San Francisco, and Professor John Walton Caughey of the University of California at Los Angeles read the chapters on Southern California.

Oregon has a splendid historical library in its State Historical Society in Portland, and Miss Nellie B. Pipes, librarian, was untiring in her assistance. George Himes, secretary of the Society, contributed much by way of reminiscence. Miss Amanda Otto, librarian of the *Morning Oregonian,* Simeon Reed Winch, business manager of the *Oregon Journal,* J. C. Ainsworth, president of the United States National Bank of Portland, and Dr. Arthur J. McLean all gave assistance in collecting information about Portland.

W. P. Bonney of the Washington State Historical Society read the chapter on Tacoma; Mrs. Roberta Frye Watt, author of *The Story of Seattle,* read the chapter on Seattle; Cornelius J. Brosnan, professor of American history at the University of Idaho, read the chapter on Spokane. Thanks are also due C. E. Johns of the Seattle Chamber of Commerce, W. G. Oves of the Spokane Chamber of Commerce; the staffs of the public libraries of Tacoma and Seattle; and Miss Margaret Prosser.

Various services were rendered by Carl R. Gray, president of the Union Pacific Railroad, W. N. Willard of the Atchison Topeka and Santa Fe, and officials of the Nippon Yusen Kaisha Steamship Company.

James Blaine Hedges, professor of history at Brown University, read the material concerning Henry Villard and the Northwestern railways; John Leeds Kerr, railroad economist of Young and Ottley, New York, read much of the manuscript and offered the use of some of his unpublished writings; Mrs. Senah Baylor Keenan of Los Angeles read and helpfully criticized the entire manuscript. For the valuable suggestions and painstaking editing of F. G. Wickware the author is deeply grateful.

Thanks for permission to quote is due the following publishers: the Grabhorn Press, San Francisco, *The Diary of Johann August Sutter;* Frye and Smith, San Diego, *The Man John D. Spreckels;* the Macmillan Company, New York, Hamlin Garland's *A Daughter of the Middle Border;* the Bobbs-Merrill Company, Indianapolis, J. R. Perkins, *Trails, Rails and War;* the Viking Press, New York, Will Irwin's *The City That Was;* the Arthur H. Clarke Company, Glendale, California, LeRoy Hafen's *The Overland Mail;* the Lewis Publishing Company, Chicago, Jerome Smiley's *History of Colorado;* the S. J. Clarke Publishing Company, Chicago, the histories of Spokane, Tacoma, and Seattle; Houghton Mifflin Company, Boston, Bret Harte's "That's What the Engines Said" and George Kennan's *Life of E. H. Harriman;* the Ronald Press, New York, Stuart Daggett's *Chapters in the History of the Southern Pacific;* James F. Willard, Boulder, Colorado, *The Union Colony at Greeley;* Smith-Brooks Publishing Company, Denver, J. Max Clark's *Pioneer Days;* the Greeley Tribune Press, Greeley, David Boyd's *Greeley and the Union Colony.*

G. C. Q.

# CONTENTS

# ILLUSTRATIONS

# MAPS

THEY BUILT THE WEST

# THEY BUILT THE WEST

## CHAPTER I

### THE ROUTE FOR THE FIRST PACIFIC RAILROAD

ON a September morning in 1859, nine months before Abraham Lincoln was nominated for the Presidency of the United States, he climbed to the top of a high cliff at Council Bluffs, Iowa, and looked westward across the plains. At his back was American civilization—the busy cities, the rich commerce, fertile farms, and comfortable homes of the young Republic. Before him was a sparsely peopled land, beginning with the bare flood-plains of the Missouri, through which the broad, sluggish, muddy river twisted and cut its way. Close at hand, in the fields of wild grass and sunflowers below him, a few lonely, scattered cabins sent their columns of smoke drifting upward. And away to the west stretched the open country, flat, unbroken, interminable as a becalmed sea.

As he looked over those wide-spreading plains that morning and watched the meandering river which found its sources a thousand miles to the north and west, Abraham Lincoln symbolized America. For America, too, was looking to the West and dreaming of its future. Her eyes and thoughts had crossed the Mississippi two generations before, in 1803, when Congress purchased the vast territory of Louisiana from France. Four decades later she had looked to the southwest and, in 1845, acquired the plains of Texas. Next year she ended a long dispute with Great Britain over the western fur trade and added Oregon, reaching north along the Pacific to the 49th parallel of latitude. In 1848, by cession from Mexico, came golden California; and in 1853, with the Gadsden Purchase of a strip of Mexican desert, her territory was solidly completed from Atlantic to Pacific.

Gold was discovered in California in '49, in Colorado in '58; there were rich farm-lands waiting for the plow in green Oregon valleys; the plains of Texas swarmed with fat cattle. The fever of adventure spread

through New England, the Mid-West, the South, and men by the
thousands set out on the long overland journey to the land of romance
and riches. For years a stream of covered wagons had been struggling
across the broad plains over which Lincoln now stood, to California
and Colorado and Oregon. The early emigrants encountered hard travel,
tortuous roads, and hostile Indians to hold them back. Wagons stuck
in the mire, costly heavy equipment abandoned by the roadside, and
the blanching bones of men and animals were visible signs of the
rigors of the overland trail. Men paid a high price for the privilege of
making that pilgrimage in search of the pot of gold at the foot of the
rainbow.

All these things Lincoln knew, and he knew more. He knew of the
titanic struggles in Congress over the political alignment of those new
territories; he knew that they were ready for orderly colonization by
larger numbers of people than the covered wagon could ever carry;
that the things now needed for the development of the cities, towns,
and resources in the vast new empire were men and money; and that
the first step in opening up the Western country must be the building
of a railroad.

Where should it go? No one doubted that the riches of the West
must be brought to the doors of the East; the only question was, which
doors? The South would have the rails extend westward along the 32d
parallel of latitude from Texas to California, draining the commerce
of the new country to the port of New Orleans at the mouth of the
Mississippi; St. Louis interests favored the 35th-parallel route, going
somewhat southward from their city to California; Kansas wished the
railroad to run straight west between the 38th and 39th parallels over
the hump of the bear's back of the Rockies at its center near Denver
and on to San Francisco; Chicago favored a line between the 41st and
42d parallels to unite the Missouri River at Council Bluffs and Omaha
with the harbor of San Francisco; and the most northern route of all
was that projected between the 46th and 48th parallels to join Lake
Superior with Puget Sound and the Columbia River, and to connect
with the East by means of steamers across the Lakes to Detroit. Each
of these routes had its determined advocates, who were ready to battle
uncompromisingly; for each meant commercial advantage to the section of the country it would traverse.

As one who had represented Illinois in the Congress of the United States and had been invited to be Governor of Oregon, Lincoln was, of course, interested in the northern route favored by Chicago and the route from St. Louis favored by southern Illinois. When a political speech took him to Kansas, he took the Missouri River boat from St. Joseph to Council Bluffs in order to study the railroad question further, and one evening, on the big front porch of the Pacific House, he had a chance to get first-hand information. From among the group of citizens who gathered to meet him, his friend W. H. M. Pusey picked out a dark young New Englander and brought him over to Lincoln's chair by the porch rail. "This engineer knows more about railroads than any two men in the country," he said. And so Lincoln began to question the 28-year-old railroad surveyor, Grenville M. Dodge, as to the best route for a railway to the Pacific.

Dodge knew his subject thoroughly; in addition to his own surveys, he had read the reports and opinions of Frémont and the pioneer surveyors, Stanbury's studies of Salt Lake, and other government documents. And he knew the 42d-parallel route so well that he had made a map for emigrants which, he said, "gave an itinerary showing each camping-place all the way to California, giving the fords, and where water and wood could be found. This map was published by the citizens of Council Bluffs for the purpose of controlling emigration; and, as it was one of the first maps of the country giving such information, it had greater influence in concentrating a large portion of the Oregon and California emigration at Council Bluffs after 1854."

So sure was Dodge that the 42d-parallel route was the predestined and logical way to the West that he took up a government claim on the Elkhorn River, 30 miles west of Omaha, and began his fight for the proposed Pacific railroad to pass through his property and go up the valley of the Platte River. Soon afterward, the covered wagons, usually twenty in a train, having outfitted at Council Bluffs, began to roll past the Dodge cabin and to use his land for camping, since it was just far enough west of Omaha to afford a first-night halting-place. All the information he had gained from his own investigation and from the experiences of others who had made the trip west, the young engineer of the Chicago, Rock Island and Pacific now put at Lincoln's disposal. "He shelled my woods completely," Dodge said later, "and got all the information I had collected for my employer in less than an hour."

From Dodge, Lincoln learned that the 42d-parallel route was the most practical and economical; that buffaloes, Indians, and Mormon emigrants had already proved the trail up the Platte River valley to the Rockies to be the natural route to the West; that Council Bluffs was the logical starting-place because of the railroads building to that point from Chicago. For the young surveyor believed that "there was never any very great question, from an engineering point of view, as to where the line, crossing Iowa and going west from the Missouri river, should be placed. The Lord had so constructed the country that any engineer who failed to take advantage of the great open road out the Platte valley, and then on to Salt Lake, would not have been fit to belong to the profession."

Perhaps Lincoln was further influenced in favor of the 42d-parallel route by the fact that his manager in the Douglas debates, Norman Judd, already owned Council Bluffs real estate and was asking him for a loan of $3,000 on it. At any rate, when he boarded the river-boat that evening and watched the sun-scorched village and its yellow cliffs recede in the twilight, he had ample reason to believe that the Pacific railroad should be built on the central route and find its terminus at Council Bluffs. As to the necessity of building Western railroads he had never any doubt. Long ago, in an election campaign, he had registered his belief when he said, "Whether elected or not, I am for distributing the proceeds of the sale of public lands to construct the railroads."

Heavy battles had yet to be fought before the route of the first Pacific railroad could be settled, but when the decision was finally made, by President Lincoln, that the terminus of the Union Pacific should be at Council Bluffs, the course of the economic development of the nation was profoundly influenced. By this one act, impetus was given to the commercial ascendancy of Chicago as opposed to St. Louis and Cincinnati, the building of the cities of Omaha and Denver was made possible, the position of San Francisco was strengthened, the South was definitely deprived of benefit from Western trade, and the early economic development of the Northwestern states was assured.

Congress and the country had long before recognized that railroad-building and community development must go hand in hand, and

Stephen A. Douglas, Representative from Illinois, had urged the organization of the Territory of Nebraska so as to provide for the settlement of the country through which a railroad might pass and the development of its resources in order that business and traffic might be created for the railroad. Asa Whitney had made the first proposal to Congress for a Pacific road, to be aided by a grant of land 60 miles wide, extending from Milwaukee through unsettled public lands to the mouth of the Columbia; but he was opposed by Douglas, who favored the route from Chicago. Since Whitney's line would have to connect with the East by the water route across Lake Michigan to Detroit, Douglas objected that it would be out of commission four months a year because of ice; he maintained that Whitney's plan conferred too much land and power on one man, and that the logical place of convergence for Eastern and Western railroads was Chicago.

In the jockeying for commercial ascendancy that followed, the routes of both Whitney and Douglas were opposed by the Southern states, and when Jefferson Davis became Secretary of War, it looked as if the Southern states would win. He ordered the survey of the southern Pacific route through what is now Arizona, estimated the expense of construction to be much less than by any other route, and caused the United States to make the Gadsden Purchase of a strip of Mexican desert below the Gila River to provide this Southern railroad with easy access to the Pacific through American territory. His plans had been furthered by the Mexican War, which gave New Mexico and California to the United States, and by the settlement with Great Britain of the Oregon question, which removed the cause of pressure for the immediate building of a northern Pacific railroad.

Douglas, who, in anticipation of success, had bought 70 acres of land at Chicago, now mustered his forces for the selection of the northern central route. In 1853 he again introduced the measure for the organization of Nebraska, but, in order to give Chicago a better chance, he changed the bill to provide for the organization of the two territories of Nebraska and Kansas instead of only one. Historians have usually assigned the reason for this split to a desire to compromise with the South by permitting slavery in one new territory, Kansas, to balance the prohibition of slavery in the other, Nebraska. But a representative from Iowa stated the reason thus: "The interests of our state

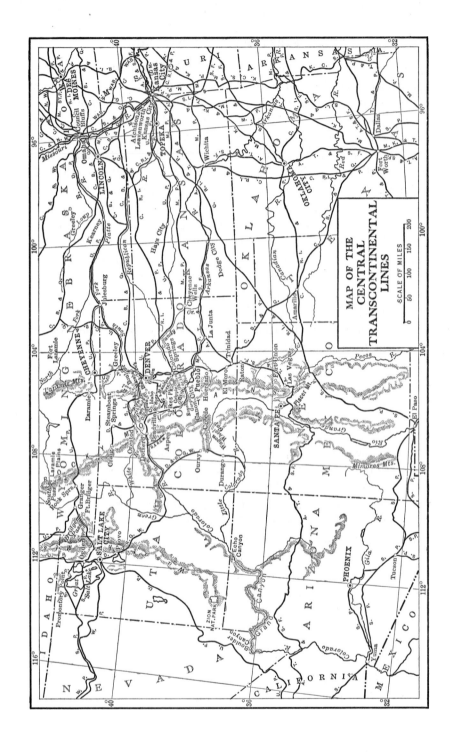

MAP OF THE
CENTRAL
TRANSCONTINENTAL
LINES

SCALE OF MILES

0    50    100    150    200

demanded two territories; otherwise the seat of government and leading thoroughfares must have fallen south of Iowa."

To Douglas, one territory meant aid to the central route; two territories meant an equal chance for the northern route from Chicago. Hence, he championed the Kansas-Nebraska Bill, which was to mean so much to the development of certain parts of the West. Professor F. H. Hodder of the University of Kansas, who has made a thorough study of the matter, has this to say:

The organization of Kansas and Nebraska was the outcome of a project that Douglas had formulated nine years before and for six years had been actively promoting. Not feeling very strongly on the subject of slavery and believing sincerely that it was not likely to invade this region, he was willing even to repeal the Missouri Compromise in order to accomplish the great purpose of his life. There is a saying: "You cannot see the mountain near." There is point in the proverb, but it is equally true that you cannot see anything else when you are near the mountain. Our fathers were so near the mountain of slavery that they did not realize the importance of the great movement of population of which they were a part and of the building of the railways, which was its controlling factor. Our generation has been making history out of partisan diatribes of the past. It is time to take account of the forces that made for nationality and union as well as those that made for sectionalism and separation.

In 1854, when the Kansas-Nebraska Act was passed, the Southern route was permanently blocked, and with it Jefferson Davis' plan for the ultimate absorption of Mexico into the United States. It is probable, also, that the Act saved California to the Union, for had that state been joined to the South by ties of commercial interest, it might well have seceded along with the Confederacy. Like the Middle-Western states, whose sympathies had passed from the South to the North when northern railroads had carried their trade away from New Orleans to New York, the new state of California now found its interests definitely allied with the North against any movement for secession. Thus did purely commercial considerations change the history of the United States and chart the course of empire in the West.

Cataclysmic events followed Lincoln's trip to Council Bluffs. He was nominated and elected to the Presidency; the South seceded, removing its insurmountable opposition to the granting of government aid to building a northern railroad to the Pacific; and the North could not build through the states in secession. The Union Pacific Railroad was chartered July 1, 1862, and Congress left the fixing of the eastern terminus to the President of the United States. Lincoln issued an executive order establishing it at Council Bluffs, Iowa, and Grenville M. Dodge, the young man he had met on the porch of the Pacific House, was soon helping to build the first railroad to the West. From Omaha, Nebraska, across the Missouri River from Council Bluffs, the road began to send its shining bands of steel westward to meet a second road, the Central Pacific, building east from Sacramento. And although the project moved slowly for several years and the tracks became covered with rust, they were a visible promise of the fulfilment of that roseate dream of Senator Thomas H. Benton of Missouri, who thrilled Congress with his romantic predictions of the railroad that would change the whole world. "Let the great line be adorned with this crowning honor," said he in a burst of enthusiastic oratory, "the colossal statue of the great Columbus, whose design it accomplishes, hewn from the granite mass of a peak of the Rocky Mountains, overlooking the road, the mountain itself the pedestal, and the statue a part of the mountain, pointing with outstretched arm to the western horizon, and saying to the flying passenger, 'There is the east!' 'There is India!'"

As yet no sculptor has carved Senator Benton's heroic Rocky Mountain Columbus, but if this should ever be done, the doughty Genoese should be surrounded by a host of other figures, equally bold, and some of them almost as visionary, the men who bore the sweat and heat of the day in pushing the rails across the continent, completing the circle of world trade-routes and creating that new and opulent civilization in the West of which Benton dreamed.

With the laying of the first rails, the way was finally opened for the building of the West. The day of the covered wagon and the pony express and the straggling train of weary and beleaguered emigrants was over. Now great hordes of colonists would make the western trip quickly and easily in a few days, and the crops and goods they produced in the new country would be speedily transported back to the centers of population in the East. As the rails pushed westward, the buffalo and the Indian would vanish. As the country became more and more cultivated, cattle would be driven from the free open range, mountains would be rifled of their coal and ore, waters of their fish, forests of their trees. Smoke would arise from great industrial plants, factory-whistles would blow, dollars would jingle, and busy cities would spring up as the beneficiaries of the new order of things. The way was now made ready for the second string of pioneers—the builders, business men, industrialists, promoters, who would bring those two prime necessities, money and men, to exploit the resources, and build the cities, and create America's new empire in the West.

They form a bridge, those determined, practical men of affairs, joining our own prosaic age with those romantic days when the moccasin-shod hunters and trappers first softly padded through the Western forests and along the Western rivers; when the early missionary priests stilled the war-cries of the Indian with the upheld cross and beguiled him into Christianity with the picture-story, "The Catholic Ladder"; when the stage-coach, surrounded by a cloud of dust, lurched into primitive mining camps with letters a month old from the East; when bearded prospectors first panned and dug the gold. Invading the waste places, bringing with them the iron horse, the city, the farm, the factory, the construction gang, they were not so fascinatingly exotic as their predecessors, but they were just as vitally necessary to the country. And they brought to their task notable qualities of daring, strength, energy, determination, and practical powers of translating ideas into actualities which have built the West we know to-day.

# CHAPTER II

## THE SURVEYORS WHO CLEARED THE WAY

WHEN the first transcontinental railway, the Union Pacific, was finally completed as a railroad system, it comprised two routes from the Missouri to the Rockies: the first and main line extended from Council Bluffs through Cheyenne, Wyoming, to Ogden, Utah; the second and subsidiary line, built later as a rival road, known as the Eastern Division of the Union Pacific and also as the Kansas Pacific, paralleled the main line at the south and extended from Kansas City to Denver. Grenville Mellen Dodge was the chief figure in the surveying and engineering development of the first line, and William Jackson Palmer occupied a similar position on the second. The engineering work of both had been interrupted by active service in the Civil War, and when they returned to civil life, each had attained the rank of brigadier-general in the Federal Army. In their long lives of exploration, surveying, construction, and financing, these two men well represent the engineering and constructive genius that took the first step in the building of all the railways of the West. They knew the hardships and pleasures of exploring the new country and determining the routes over which the iron horse should travel, the thrill of discovering unknown passes through forbidding barriers of mountain ranges, the delight of viewing vast expanses of unpeopled territory and dreaming of how it might be developed for the uses of man. They had the driving power and dogged determination which kept surveying parties on the march and construction gangs laboring under burning suns and in the bitter cold of winter, which pushed the rails steadily westward, day by day, despite hostile Indians, unfavorable weather, and natural barriers. They knew the difficulties and rewards of financing large projects, of colonizing farms and cities, of developing the resources of the country, and of upbuilding its communities.

On the 1st of May, 1866, at the age of 35, Grenville M. Dodge was made chief engineer of the Union Pacific. At the outbreak of the Civil War he had abandoned his surveying work to organize companies of infantry in Iowa. He was soon given the rank of colonel, and later that of brigadier-general, and he rose to such importance that he was assigned the task of keeping open the line of communications in the Union descent on Vicksburg. Grant considered him the ablest officer in the field in railroad work and said of him:

General Dodge, besides being a most capable soldier, was an experienced railroad builder. He had no tools to work with except those of the pioneer —axes, picks and spades. Blacksmiths were detailed and set to work making the tools necessary in railroad and bridge building; axemen were put to work in getting out timber for bridges; car builders were set to work repairing the locomotives and cars. Thus, every branch of railroad building, making tools to work with and supplying the workingmen with food, was all going on at once and without the aid of a mechanic or labor except what the command furnished. General Dodge had the work assigned him and finished in forty days after receiving his order. The number of bridges to rebuild was 182, many of them over deep and wide chasms; the length of the road repaired was 182 miles.

And Sherman once remarked to Grant during a critical campaign, "Dodge is two weeks ahead of us as usual."

All this military experience stood Dodge in good stead when he returned to the engineering problems of the Union Pacific, and his friendship with Grant and Sherman and acquaintance with Lincoln procured him frequent favors at their hands. Since the building of the Union Pacific, aided by government grants of land and funds, was regarded at this time not only as a commercial desirability but as a military necessity, positively essential in binding together the East and the West, Dodge was able to draw heavily upon the military establishment for troops for the protection of his parties against Indians. He also found it to his advantage that most of his men had seen service in the Army and were, therefore, trained in military discipline.

The surveying parties that went out for Dodge were made up of from eighteen to twenty-two men, all armed, all inured to hardship, all keyed to a life of daring adventure. Each party had a chief engineer and two assistants, several young men with engineering training to act as rodmen and linemen, some herders and axmen, and often a hunter to bring in game for the party's larder. When they entered a country occupied by hostile Indians, they were furnished with a military escort of from ten men to a company, under a competent officer, to protect them in camp and at work. In the field this escort would usually station itself on hills commanding the territory and would watch the party and the surrounding country so as to head off sudden attacks by the Indians. Notwithstanding this protection, the parties were often attacked, their men killed or wounded, and their horses stolen.

From daylight till dark the engineers labored. They would set out at the crack of dawn, and by night they would have advanced from eight to twelve miles if they were working on preliminary surveys in open country, three or four miles if on the more careful work of final location. In the mountainous country, however, the obstacles were so many that they frequently made no more than a mile a day. The chief engineer reconnoitered ahead, laying out the preliminary survey which indicated the streams to follow and the controlling points of summits and river-crossings, and the party of location followed him, carrying forward the maps and profiles and endeavoring to obtain a line of the lowest grade and least curvature.

In 1867 Dodge had sent four parties into the field, the first to revise the location of the route at the eastern base of the Rockies, the second to make a final location through the Laramie Mountains, the third to examine the Wyoming country between Fort Sanders and Green River, the fourth to examine the country between Green River and Salt Lake and as far north as the comparatively unknown Snake River. But plans made for surveying the wild West in those days were subject to change without notice, and life itself was a matter of luck. Six miles east of Cheyenne, when his work was only well begun, the chief engineer of the first party was surrounded by hostile Indians and killed. The second party completed its work without mishap, and the third was proceeding well when the chief engineer, Percy Brown, for whom the Union Pacific station Percy, Wyoming, is named, was surrounded by a band of nearly 300 Indians at Bitter Creek, east of Rock Spring. Although he fought them off successfully from noon until dark, he was finally shot through the body and mortally wounded. After suffering these two losses, Dodge was compelled to split up the fourth party to supply the losses of the other three, and himself to take the field in direct charge of all the surveying.

It was evident that the Indians had attacked all along the line, picking off members of the escorting parties as well as the engineers, and even the graders in the construction gangs. Consequently, the work was virtually broken up and the morale of the surveyors shattered, and Dodge had the task of reviving courage as well as of reorganizing parties and plans.

Some idea of the problems of the engineer can be had from the work he did on this trip. Accompanying him, as he left the end of the track, at Julesburg, Nebraska, was a Mr. Blickensderfer, who had been assigned by President Lincoln to the duty of determining the eastern base of the Rocky Mountains, so as to fix the amount of subsidy per mile that the Government would grant for building the Union Pacific Railroad and its branches. Dodge intended to help decide this delicate problem of the point where the mountain construction work would begin. They pushed by rapid marches up the Lodge Pole Creek valley, examining the line, and pitched camp at what is now the city of Cheyenne. Massi C. E. Fontanero said he was with General Dodge when the latter rode ahead to locate Cheyenne. At the end of the day, sore with riding, the General slid painfully from his horse, and as he sank his hatchet into the ground, he said, "By God, Cheyenne will be right here."

At Cheyenne Dodge took over the work abandoned when the surveying parties were driven out by the Indians. After making the difficult location of the road between Cheyenne and the Laramie Mountains, he entered the Laramie Plains to the west. Here, because of heavy snows in winter and the lack of water in parts of the country, Dodge found it necessary to carry his line through at the lowest possible elevation on the Plains; so, clinging closely to the watercourses, he obtained a line away from the high mountains, unexposed to drifting snows, and accessible to the coal-fields near Rock Creek. He then examined the country to the north and south, after which he struck west, to seek water and a crossing of the divide farther north, taking the old Cherokee Trail. Here he met one of his parties which had got into the Red Desert and had been wandering about without water for three days. Several men had nearly died from drinking poisonous water which they found in a stagnant lake. But this was only an incident in the life of the Union Pacific engineers. Water finally reached the men, hauled in by their wagons, and Dodge pushed on, endeavoring to find the outlet over the western rim of Red Basin that would lead to Bitter Creek with the shortest possible route between running water and running water. The task of examining, or, as Dodge referred to it, "developing," the country proved to be so heavy that he left a party for that purpose, a party which wandered among the cliffs and rocks seeking the most feasible line during the whole fall and early winter. Though they endured hardship and suffering, often being without water for days and without fire or wood, Dodge says they nevertheless did the work fully and successfully—that their chief "met the question and solved it."

Those terse words might well be the epitaph of many an engineer who blazed the trail for the first Western railroads: *He met the question and solved it.* No matter what the difficulties and obstacles these men faced, there was no turning back. Rough, dangerous, deadly the life, baffling the problems, but the surveyors seldom flinched or failed. The chief engineer of each party was a man of natural courage and ability, and to him was given complete authority. One of the instructions ordinarily given in the field was that the chief must absolutely command his men and at all times be ready to fight. And from chief to humblest axman every man could be counted on to sweat and strain and give the best that was in him to push the line on to the West. Dodge, as chief engineer, might well have contented himself with sitting in a swivel-chair in a far-away city and directing his men to do the dirty work. But, like Palmer and the other leading engineers of the Western roads, he was always ready to abandon comfortable living in the city and get down into the muck with his men. He was equally at home riding in his carriage in the Bois de Boulogne, seeking to enlist the financial aid of Paris bankers, or sleeping in a pup tent pitched in the arid hills, eating beans and bacon from a tin plate and working 14 hours a day in the rough and tumble of mountain surveying. Theodore Judah, the engineer of the Central Pacific in California, was a similar example of versatility, who alternated the luxurious life of a lobbyist in Washington with the hardships of surveying in the high Sierras. During his early surveys he had so little money at his disposal that his wife used to catch trout for the meals of his crew, counting it not only good sport but a valuable contribution to the party's supplies. To all these early engineers the building of the railroad was the only thing that mattered, and they cheerfully adapted themselves to whatever the circumstances of the moment might require.

In these years as chief engineer, Dodge benefited from his previous Army explorations. He had been assigned to the Department of the Missouri in 1865 and 1866, charged with the Indian campaigns, with command from the Missouri River to California; during this time he had had reports made by all troops and scouting parties concerning the resources and topography of the country, and later these were of much assistance to him in his railroad work. It was on one of the trips of this period that he accidentally discovered the pass through the Laramie Mountains over which the Union Pacific was finally routed. J. R. Perkins tells the story dramatically in his interesting biography of General Dodge, *Trails, Rails and War*: *

All the way up the Chugwater, Dodge had scanned, through powerful glasses, the slopes of the Black Hills looking not for Indians but for some indications of an undiscovered pass through which a railroad might be built down into the Laramie Plains on the other side. Nothing had come of his observations, so he decided to ascend Cheyenne Pass, gain the summit of the range and follow the divide on southward, keeping his eyes open for a possible break through the granite slopes. He knew that on the western side of this range there was a grade not to exceed ninety feet to the mile, but on the eastern side, where he traveled, no pass had ever been discovered with a grade less than one hundred and sixteen feet to the mile, which made it impossible for the locomotive of that day to ascend with freight. For three hours Dodge and his thirteen men had crept along the ridge of the mountains when Leon Pallady reined in his horse and, pointing down the eastern slope, said:

"Indians, and a lot of 'em."

Dodge lifted his glasses and looked. A large band of Crows had worked in between him and his train.

"How many?" he asked.

" 'Bout three hundred," Pallady responded.

"Do they see us?"

"They've likely followed us all day, and aim to close in at night," was the guide's cheerful conclusion.

* J. R. Perkins, *Trails, Rails and War* (copyright, 1929). Quoted by special permission of the publishers, the Bobbs-Merrill Company.

Dodge was certain that the Crows were hostile, so he dismounted his men, placed the horses on the west side of the ridge and moved slowly down the summit. When they came to fuel, they lighted a fire, for he had arranged signals with the remainder of his escort. But the distant train toiled on along the base of the mountain, unaware that the commander and his little escort were in danger.

The skirmishing soon began and Dodge quickly made the comfortable discovery that his rifles carried farther than those in the hands of the Crows. But the Indians began to creep from rock to rock, narrowing the semicircle they had formed, and getting to where their fire might be effective; moreover a band of about fifty started to scale the mountains with the obvious intention of cutting off retreat either north or south. Leon Pallady tumbled a venturesome Indian with a well-directed shot and two others had horses shot from beneath them. This caused greater caution on the part of their foes, who now began a slow and increasing accuracy of fire from more concealed places.

Dodge's anxiety increased as the shadows began to lengthen down the slope, so he selected a strong position, built another great signal-fire and waited. The Indians crept closer and the spat of their bullets sounded against the boulders behind which the white men crouched.

"Our men—the cavalry," Leon Pallady unexpectedly cried, pointing toward a ravine that lay below them.

Dodge's troops at last had seen his signal-fires and were making their way up the mountainside. The firing of the Crows suddenly ceased, and thirty minutes later Dodge and his little escort were surrounded by seasoned soldiers and Indian fighters.

"Boys," Dodge said, as he gazed down a slope that seemed to lower gently to the plain, "I think we've discovered a pass through which we can build the Union Pacific."

The men were about as much excited over this as they had been over the proximity of the Indians, and crowded around him for explanations. He pointed out to them that the Crows had fled down a slope to a creek— a slope that looked as if it had a grade of less than one hundred feet to the mile. Ordering his troops to follow, down the slope he plunged, and, sure enough, it led, not to a great drop-off as might have been expected, but to a gentle depression. Crossing this depression, the company found a gradual descent to the plain and to their camp. The grade and pass thus discovered did not exceed ninety feet to the mile. Dodge marked the place by a lone tree, and over this ridge the Union Pacific was finally built.

Because of his use of the surveyor's instruments the Indians called Dodge "Long Eye" and considered that he had miraculous powers. His mysterious telegraph wires also awed them. Of this marvel he wrote:

When the overland telegraph was built, they were taught to respect it and not destroy it. This was done after the line was opened to Fort Laramie by stationing several of their most intelligent chiefs at Fort Laramie and others at Fort Kearny, the two posts being 300 miles apart, and having them talk to each other over the wire and note the time sent and received. Then we had them mount their fleetest horses and ride as fast as they could until they met at Old Jule's ranch, at the mouth of the Lodge Pole, this being about half way between Kearny and Laramie. Of course this was astonishing and mysterious to the Indians. Thereafter you could often see Indians with their heads against the telegraph poles, listening to the peculiar sound insulators. They thought, and said, it was "Big Medicine" talking.

Although, as an Army officer and an engineer, he was continually called on to make war against the Indians—both the fierce Indians of the Plains and those tamer specimens near Iowa who could be beaten off with a hoe-handle, Dodge's view of the Indian problem was not untouched with kindliness:

There is not a tribe of Indians on the great plains or in the mountain regions east of Nevada and Idaho but which is warring on the whites. The first demand of the Indian is that the white man shall not come into his country; shall not kill or drive off the game upon which his subsistence depends; and shall not dispossess him of his lands. How can we promise this, with any hope or purpose of fulfilling the obligation, unless we prohibit immigration and settlement west of the Missouri river? So far from being prepared to make such engagement with the Indians, the government every day is stimulating immigration. Where under such circumstances is the Indian to go? It is useless for the government to think of undertaking to subsist large bodies of Indians in remote and inaccessible districts. Whatever may be the right or wrong of the question our past experiences in America reveal that the Indian must for the most part be dispossessed. The practical question to be considered is how the inevitable can be accomplished with the least inhumanity.

Beset by hostile savages, impeded by rugged mountain-ranges and great stretches of country without water, Dodge and his surveyors continued to seek the shortest, easiest way to the Pacific. But this was only part of their work. Besides the problem of easy grades and direct route, they had to consider the commercial possibilities of the country. Where was coal to be found? Where were the fertile farm-regions, the deposits of iron, gold, silver? What were the resources of timber, stone, and water-power? All these varied matters had to be investigated and reported upon by the trail-blazers.

In his Report of 1868 Dodge covered these questions: There were 2,000,000 acres of farm-land within 200 miles west of Omaha ready for settlement; there were 1,152,000 acres on the Platte River between Fort Kearny and Julesburg that could be irrigated without much expense to the company, 1,000,000 acres more on the Laramie Plains, and 2,000,000 acres in the Green River valley. On the tributaries of the Green River were fine forests of pine, hemlock, and spruce. There was limestone for building west of Cheyenne. There were 5,000 square miles of coal-lands, bearing lignite, "which burns with a bright red flame, giving off a fair degre of heat, leaving scarcely any ashes, quite desirable for domestic purposes." There were beds of iron scattered along the route which, with the coal, could bring the West the wealth and industry that the same thing brought Pennsylvania in the East. There was much gold and silver in Colorado, the Black Hills, and Utah. After his survey of the country's resources he concluded:

As soon as completed, the traffic over the Union Pacific railroad will be limited only by the capacity of the road. California, Washington, Oregon, Nebraska, Idaho, Montana, Utah, Wyoming, and Colorado will soon fill up. Their precious metals, their rich soil and unequalled climate, will inaugurate a business and a trade that will soon demand another track, and which no man to-day can even estimate. Without the Union Pacific railroad, the country west of the Missouri river would be a burden to the government, and almost an uninhabitable waste; with it, it will soon be an empire, and one of our principal elements of power and strength.

It was upon such data as these that the directors of the railroad, sitting around a table in New York, could raise money to finance operations and lay plans for the development of traffic. From those laconic reports they could visualize the empire that was to be, with its checker-boards of waving grain and pasture, its irrigated orchards, its coal-mines and factories, its thriving cities and prosperous people. Surely the whole fate of the enterprise as an engineering project, as a commercial success, and as a factor in upbuilding the country depended on the judgment, skill, and personal force of a few hardy and intrepid engineer-builders such as General Dodge.

No less versatile was that other engineer-soldier, General William J.

Palmer, the man who was one of the leading figures in the building of the Kansas Pacific and who afterwards conceived and constructed the railroad system that follows the base of the Rockies, the Denver and Rio Grande. General Palmer began his career as a surveyor of railroads in Pennsylvania, and he accompanied President J. Edgar Thompson of the Pennsylvania Railroad as secretary when that official was sent abroad to investigate European railroads. He organized troops at the beginning of the Civil War, became colonel and brigadier-general, and was ranked by General George H. Thomas, "the Rock of Chickamauga," as the best cavalry officer in the service, bar none. At the close of the war he was ordered to pursue Jefferson Davis to the ends of the earth, and he finally drove the President of the Confederacy into the arms of the Union officers by whom he was captured. His "Reports of Surveys" for the Kansas Pacific cover not only the route from Kansas City to Denver, but also the southern 32d- and 35th-parallel routes to the Pacific now followed by the Southern Pacific and the Santa Fe.

Included in General Palmer's surveying party was a young Englishman, William A. Bell, Master of Arts and Bachelor of Medicine from Cambridge University, who joined as a photographer and, knowing nothing of photography, prepared himself for the post remarkably well by the "cramming" process, studying with professional photographers in New York the elaborate technique then necessary. He saw the country with the fresh eyes of a foreigner, and he wrote so well of his experiences that he was made a Fellow of the Royal Geographical Society. His book *New Tracks in North America,* published in London in 1869, is the most complete informal story available of the Palmer surveys and gives a colorful picture of the life of the surveying parties of his day. After several months with one party as photographer Bell joined another as "doctor," and thus he saw the country from the Mid-Western plains to San Francisco with a side trip through Mexico. He later became one of Palmer's most trusted business associates and a lifelong citizen of Colorado.

This is the typical routine of Palmer's railroad surveyors moving across the Western plains, as described by Bell:

Two days previously, the line of survey had been run across this country for six miles, so that, as soon as our wagons came to the end of this line, the engineer corps commenced work, and continued it onward as fast as possible. The ground had to be measured, stakes driven in at regular intervals, and every undulation of the surface had to be accurately determined by means of proper instruments; and this had to be done through an Indian country, which was, moreover, so dry that it was probable we should not find a drop of water along the whole seventy-two miles. The greatest possible expedition was therefore required on the part of the surveyors, and their achievements across this country were really wonderful.

There were under General Wright, at that time, three parties or divisions, each capable of running a line independently. At Fort Wallace, the transit-man, leveller, and topographer of each division, had obtained mules, and one of the wagons had been emptied of its contents, and devoted, for a time, to the surveyors. One division commenced work, and the men were soon spread out into line a mile long, upon the plain, measuring and taking observations at every point. On one side of this line came the wagons, following each other closely, and guarded by a small body of the escort. The remainder of the cavalry moved with the surveyors—some in front, others in the rear, and the greater number in the centre, so that, being between this body of cavalry and the wagon train, the long line of surveyors was well protected. The transit-man, carrying his instrument on his shoulder, and riding a mule at a gallop, would suddenly stop, jump off, arrange the transit, wave to the flagman ahead, wait until satisfied of the correctness of his observation, then back into the saddle, shoulder his transit, and gallop away again. Behind him came the rodmen and levellers, mounted in the same way, and advancing with a like rapid accuracy. It was very hard on the mules, but by five o'clock that evening fifteen miles had been chained, located, and levelled—no chance nor guess-work, but an accurate preliminary survey.

Under a July sun this activity could not possibly be kept up indefinitely; so, about every two hours, when one party was tired, those in the emptied wagon would relieve them, while the men who had been working would get in and rest. In this manner the day passed by, and evening came. After working until it was too dark to see any longer, we halted; and, too tired for the most part to pitch tents, threw our blankets on the ground, and soon fell asleep. Our day's march was twenty-one miles, but of these, six had been surveyed before. . . .

During the next day our tired animals toiled along over the endless undulations of the dreary, arid plain, occasionally crossing dry water-courses, but nowhere was there a drop to drink. About five o'clock, far away on the horizon, a number of black specks came in view. At first, even with the glasses, we could not make them out; though they were evidently moving and coming towards us. In half an hour we could plainly see that they were a herd of over one hundred buffalo. At this sight our hopes of finding water were greatly revived; for at eventide so large a herd would certainly not be found far from it. I could not resist a chase, although early that morning I had had a successful one. On my way towards the herd I saw evidence of a heavy local rain, and on my return found our party camped within half-a-mile of some large pools of water. Since morning we had travelled twenty-one miles, and the engineers had surveyed a line the whole of the way. In a very few minutes our clothes were thrown off, and, like shouting school-boys, we were splashing each other in the sparkling water. These pools were all transitory, and probably in less than a week afterwards had disappeared into the sandy soil.

Next day—long before the streak of pink and gold, so beautiful in this region, had begun to appear in the east, the heavy sleepers were roused. By five o'clock the engineers were at their transits and levels; and as General Wright was desirous that the train should accompany the surveyors, the unfed animals were slowly pulling the wagons through the yielding earth. As the day advanced, the mules of the engineers began to give out; still the party, both mounted and on foot, kept bravely on through the scorching heat, until twenty-three miles of the desert had been staked, levelled, and chained. By this time the sun was setting; and the hot wind coming from the south, sent up clouds of dust. As no Sand Creek came across our path, I started on a-head about four o'clock with the chief wagon-master to search for it, and, if possible, to find water to camp by. We kept a little to the right, and after a ride of ten miles came to a broad arroyo, or dry bed, which we thought might be Sand Creek. This we followed for four miles; but not finding a trace of water, returned at sundown to camp. Two or three tents were being pitched, while several of the party, from the top of a lofty undulation, were intently viewing through their glasses a distant row of trees, and a long silver thread, winding away to the eastward. Could it be water, or only a mirage? Perhaps a bank of shining sand in some dry water-course!

As the setting sun lit up the horizon, there seemed to be no doubt, from its breadth, that, if it were water, it must be the Arkansas. General Wright consulted his maps, and concluded that this was impossible, as the Arkansas River could not be less than thirty-two miles distant. So we halted for the night. All our stock were suffering terribly for want of water. The horses stood motionless on three legs, with ruffled coats and drooping necks, now and then snuffing the dry parched grass, and refusing even to look at their corn. The mules, as is their wont, did manage to eat up their corn, but they made the night hideous with their frightful cries. A hundred mules uniting their voices at intervals in chorus, louder and more frequent as the night changes into morning; kicking at each other, and rattling their chains, in vain efforts to escape and quench their burning thirst: these form perhaps the most diabolical combination of sounds that ever broke the slumbers of a worn-out traveller. Such was the conclusion I came to, as I watched with impatience the first streak of day.

In the middle of the summer 1867, at about the time when the young Englishman had become acclimated to the life of the surveying party, it was joined by two new members who shared his tent, General Palmer and his aide, Captain W. F. Colton. Palmer had gained such a reputation for his qualities of leadership and executive ability that he had been elevated to the office of secretary-treasurer of the Kansas Pacific and had been active in its negotiations for financial aid. He now came west to supplant General W. W. Wright, who had been active head of the surveys. Although he was a man who peculiarly enjoyed a life of luxury and ease and who moved in the best circles of Philadelphia society, he also found pleasure in roughing it and was thoroughly at home in the field. As he had written his friend Isaac Clothier, a young man who later became head of one of Philadelphia's large department stores, when he was surveying for the Pennsylvania Railroad,

I am in the field nearly all the time, from early in the morning till late in the evening, tramping over hills and across valleys, through woods and through fields of grain. Nothing stops us—for a railroad line must be a straight one—a locomotive is not a proficient in turning corners. So a locating party travels in a bee line—it cannot avoid a hill or go round a pond or choose its own walking. It must tramp right over the one and ford the other and walk by the points of the compass. We sometimes get pretty rough fare too—we stop once in a while at a roadside inn where they pack the whole corps—engineers, rodmen and axemen in the same sleeping apartment—and that one apartment none of the best.

And later, when urging Clothier and other friends to join him in the Army, he said:

Now, all you "light, active, and hardy young men" in Penna. who desire special service, I give you fair warning. If you join the Anderson cavalry, you must expect to behave as soldiers, to fare as soldiers, and to be treated as such. There is no special service in this army that I know of which exempts a trooper from cleaning his horse, or from living on hard crackers and pork occasionally, and sometimes more frequently. The service is healthy to a sedentary man, interesting, and if performed well, highly honorable—but there is no exemption with this Regt. from the usual fatigue, hardships and dangers of a cavalry man's life. How'd you like to join?

At this time Palmer was still under 30, though, as Bell says, "active service in the war, and the responsibility of being the moving spirit of a great company, have added a few years, in moral influence at least." Under his guidance there now began a series of explorations which added immeasurably to his knowledge of the West, its potentialities and its needs, and which probably directly determined the part he was to play in the upbuilding of the Rocky Mountain section.

The first trip of the three men, in advance of the slow-moving surveying parties, was to Santa Fe. They set out with a Mexican guide, one servant, and a wagon carrying luggage and provisions drawn by two weedy Mexican mules. Says Bell:

A poor crippled Mexican as driver, who had at one time barely escaped from the Indians with his life, completed the outfit, the best we could get at Las Vegas, but one which broke down, as might have been expected, at the first difficulty we encountered. We carried no tents; Palmer, Colton and the guide were on horseback, I had to content myself with a mule, an animal by no means to be despised in the Far West provided he be a good one. Our spirits were high and our hearts light, as we felt the freedom of travelling quite independently, and we watched with all the interest which the great object of our trip inspired, the general features of the beautiful country as they opened before us at every step.

Difficulties beset them. Their wagon stuck in the Rio Pecos, and they were forced to empty it and carry each piece of luggage across the rapid river, with the water above their waists; after which they put themselves in the harness and dragged the wagon through. Raids of Navajo Indians were reported, and a close watch had to be kept. Their diet was decidedly limited until they reached the Pecos valley, where they rejoiced to find a Mexican farmer who brought them fine large. watermelons, onions, eggs, and fowls. Since their search was for coal- and mineral-lands as well as for railroad routes, they detoured to the Placer Mountains and entered a barren country of disordered grandeur between the Placers and the Santa Fé Range, so wild as to fill them with awe. It was a good introduction to their southwestern explorations—a waste of crags and cañons, deep-red cliffs, and precipices whose sides were striped with rocks of every hue, appearing to have been burned in some fierce furnace. "It seemed as if, having left purgatory behind, we had at last come to the gate of hell. The wag of our party remarked that here the devil must have frizzled all the Christians in the land, so that it was no wonder we so seldom came across any."

In the Placer Mountains, which were nearly all covered by two Spanish land-grants owned by Americans, the party found old gold- and galena-mines, which had been worked by the early Spaniards and later stopped up by the Indians, and coal that "has a beautiful lustre, fractures easily into blocks and does not blacken the fingers when touched." They agreed that if it should be found well suited for smelting the iron ore of the neighborhood, its value would be great; indeed, the destinies of the country when tapped by a railroad, they thought, could hardly be conjectured. Traveling among the hospitable, easy-going Spanish, they noted the soft and religious names that had been given to mountains, rivers, and towns—*El Sangre de Cristo* ("Blood of Christ"), *Santa Fé de San Francisco de Asís* ("City of the Holy Faith of St. Francis"), *Trinidad* ("Trinity"), and they contrasted these with the harsh names of the mining towns of Colorado—Cash Creek, Buckskin Joe, Fair Play, Tarryall, Strip-and-at-him Mine. In these names was manifested the contrast between the rough, virile Anglo-Saxon pioneer and the indolent, religious-minded Mexican, expressing the last stand of the old Spanish civilization which was already being absorbed and overshadowed by the new American. But however decadent the civilization, it had ample charm, and the travelers rejoiced to reach the old Spanish town of Santa Fe, where they settled down to a few days of rest and entertainment.

Their visit was enlivened by a Mexican dance and the climax of a political campaign, which Bell describes:

The ball was a strange sight. In a room sixty feet long by twenty wide, was collected at about nine o'clock a very considerable proportion of the youth and beauty of the town, which, however, is not paying the fair sex present any particular compliment. They wore roboses, often gracefully thrown over their heads, gay coloured dresses, big brooches and pendant earrings, smoked sigarettas incessantly, and sat quietly on forms placed around the room, waiting for any one who should choose to ask them to dance. The band occupied a platform, and consisted of a clarionet, a French horn, and three large brass instruments which groaned out the bass. At the other end of the room, slightly partitioned off, stood the bar, and it was customary at the conclusion of every dance to take your fair charmer to the counter and pay an exorbitant sum for sweetmeats, fruit, wine, or cocktails, as the case might be. In fact the luxury of each dance represented half a dollar, which, being interpreted, means "one-and-six"; thus, although no admittance is paid at the door, a reckless votary to the giddy dance would find his evening's amusement rather expensive. The dancing, however, was well worth watching; for those sunburnt brunettes glide most gracefully through the languid and suggestive movements of their Spanish dances. An occasional quadrille was formed in honour of the Americans present; and thus the evening passed away with—quadrille, drinks—slow waltz, drinks—Spanish reel, drinks—mazurka, drinks—and so on, with sigarettas ad libitum.

The Delegate to Congress for New Mexico was elected during our visit, and caused for the time a great deal of excitement. The inhabitants here know or care very little either about the squabbles between North and South, the nigger question, or the fundamental difference between a Copper-head and a War-Democrat. Mr. Clever represented the American Party, whose motto was, of course, *Progress*. Mr. Chavez, his rival, was a Mexican, and advocated the individual interests of the large landowners, who felt the raid against peonage, and the increased price of labour, caused by the developing influence of the new-comers, to be greatly prejudicial to their interests. The American party, for the first time, carried the day, and their victory was commemorated by a ball to Clever and Progress, and other appropriate rejoicings. Some of the young ladies who were present we had met before at Fort Union; they did not consider a hundred-mile drive at all too long for so great an occasion as the Santa Fe ball. In this I quite agreed with them.

During the festivities General Palmer found time to collect information about the country to the west and the best route for the railroad to the Pacific. He held a continuous levee in his rooms, which were always crowded with men either interested in the railway or well acquainted with some portion of the country to the westward. Indeed, so much conflicting testimony was given concerning the relative merits of the 32d- and 35th-parallel routes that the General finally decided that both routes must be examined. So more surveyors were sent for, and five parties were organized, two going south on the 32d parallel below the Gila River and three following the 35th-parallel route through northern Arizona. Bell went with one of the southern parties; Palmer took charge of one of the northern.

One of the tasks set Bell's party was to find a new pass through the Mimbres Mountains. The only route then in use was known as Cooke's Pass, but Palmer had heard at Santa Fe that another pass existed more to the north, that a train of wagons had once passed over it, and that it was practicable for a railroad. They now set to work to find this pass. The Mexican guide had never even heard of it; but, nothing daunted, as Bell reports,

We started at daybreak next morning, a little party of six, up into the mountains. By twelve o'clock we were resting our panting horses and surveying the peaks all around us from a grass-covered eminence. Looking westward, we saw, a few miles distant, a deep break in the mountains, and a cañon, or narrow arroyo, leading to it. This we followed. Every mile it became better and smoother, and opened straight upon the plain without any precipitous descent. Our delight was great; so we determined to turn back, and trace the cañon, if possible, across the median line of the mountains, and see if it opened upon the eastern plain from which we had come. After riding all day, we came in view of the eastern plain, just as sufficient light remained to see it, and to prove that our labour had not been in vain. We were still far from camp; mountains were all around us; the sun had set; there was no moon; and darkness soon covered everything. We could not so much as see the face of our compass, and had to keep in the closest single file, for fear of losing each other.

It was in such a predicament as this that the wonderful faculty of locality, which is peculiar to the semi-civilized man, shone out conspicuously. Not one of us could tell even the direction of camp; yet the Mexican guide brought us straight to it, after a three hours' ride, over country he had never traversed before, and this, too, in pitch darkness. It was nevertheless a rough ride, for, regardless of obstacles, we went straight over everything, walking, climbing, and riding in turns, until the sight of our watchfires gladdened our hearts. Our poor horses were quite worn-out, for they had travelled at least fifty miles over the pathless mountains.

Next day they continued the survey and discovered the entrance to what they named Palmer's Pass, the summit of which was 5,854 feet high; the average grade was less than 100 feet per mile on the surface, which, they estimated, could be lessened to about 75 feet on construction. After this Bell continued, with varying vicissitudes, through southern Arizona and Mexico, suffering the hardships of traveling through an unpeopled desert, and finally reached the Gulf of California, whence he took passage for San Francisco by boat.

General Palmer, exploring the 35th-parallel route westward, passed through the mountainous country of northern Arizona that is now traversed by the Atchison, Topeka and Santa Fe. His diary recounts how he scrambled among the mountains for weeks, having parted from tents and wagons, and found some of the country too rugged even for pack-animals, which are popularly supposed to hold their footing anywhere. Again and again his strong mules, struggling along some precipitous Indian trail, slipped, rolled over, and fell to death. All around him were signs of Indian occupancy—the "wicky-up" wigwams of bunch-grass and branches; the mescal heaps, where they had been roasting their winter supplies; the earth ovens, which they climbed into to sweat themselves when sick. Although they saw no Indians, they felt sure that the Apaches were on their trail and were waiting to surround them. Let Palmer tell what happened:

The dread moment finally came, when the party was in a deep cañon strewn with fragments of red sandstone, from the size of a church to that of a pebble, over which we dragged our foot-sore animals very slowly. We had made some eight miles when, as it seemed, at the roughest part of the whole way, where nature had made a sort of waste closet at random for all the shapeless blocks and sharp-cornered masses of rock and washed-out boulders that she had no time to work up and wished to hide from sight, we suddenly heard a shot from the brink of the cañon at our rear, and the dreaded war-whoop burst upon us. Then we looked up to the right and left, ahead and to the rear; but the walls seemed everywhere as tall as a church-steeple, with scarcely a foot-hold from top to base. They had looked high before, and the chasm narrow, but now it seemed as though we were looking up from the bottom of a deep well or a tin-mine, and no bucket to draw us up by. Soon the shots were repeated, and the yells were followed by showers of arrows. We staggered and stumbled, about as fast as a very slow ox-team, along the rocky bed, till we came to some bushes, and then stopped.

Some of the Indians had got on the edge of the cañon ahead of us, whose yells answered those from the rear; and the whole concatenation of sounds echoed among the cliffs till it seemed to us that every rancheria in Arizona had poured out its dusky warriors to overwhelm us. It was a yell of triumph—of confidence. It appeared to say, "Oh, ye wise and boastful white men, with your drilled soldiers and repeating guns, and wealth and power, who came out to hunt the poor Indian from his wigwam, look where we have got you! We have only been waiting for you to make some blunder; now we shall take advantage of it, and not let any of you escape. It shall be worse than at Fort Kearny, for not even one shall be spared to tell the story. It will be a good place to bury you; in fact, you are already buried in as deep a grave as you could wish. We shall only leave you there, that is all, ha! ha! What are your Spencer carbines worth, and your soldiers with their fine uniforms and drill? It is only the old lesson we are teaching you: our forefathers taught it to Braddock, and it has been repeated many times since; but we shall drive it into you deeper than ever it has been before, ha! ha! You thought we had all gone, but our eyes were never off you; and now we are gathering our warriors from every hiding-place. This is the way we call them out—whoop! whoop! whoop! and they are lining the edge of the cañon before and behind you. You can take your time. It is only ten miles to the mouth; and the farther you go, the deeper the cañons get. Perhaps you wish to retreat? It is only eight miles back, and you know what sort of a path it is. From the cedars on the brink we will pick you off at our leisure, and you shall not see one of us. This country belongs to us—the whole of it; and we do not want your people here, nor your soldiers, nor your railroad. Get away to where you belong—if you can, ha! ha!" It was not all this in detail, but the sum and concentration of it, that flashed through my mind as I listened to those yells, now rising clear and wild on the breeze, and now dying away in the distance.

The contest between the surveyors and the Indians continued for days, each side trying to outmanœuver the other. When the Indians rolled great rocks down from the top of the cliff, the party deployed, and Palmer headed a group which set out on the dangerous task of scaling the cliff. Amid a fire of protecting shots from the rest of the party, war-whoops of Indians, and shouts and calls from the men below, the seven men finally reached the top exhausted, wet with perspiration, hands cut and bleeding and boots nearly torn off, and the Indians disappeared for the time being. They had to descend other cañons, however, in constant fear of the redskins; and they made their way by night through the underbrush and over the boulders of a ravine, fording the stream twenty times yet being unable to light a fire to warm themselves for fear the Indians might see it. After traveling the equivalent of 60 miles on level ground they scrambled out over the top, faint from hunger and fatigue and with no hope of escaping the Indians, when they were surprised to see the welcome smoke of their own camp in the near distance, half a mile away. But so exhausted was the General that at this unexpected good fortune his legs refused to carry him the short distance remaining; so he made a fire, lay down to sleep, and sent his servant for food and whiskey.

Such hardships were typical of the long exploratory trip General Palmer made through the Grand Cañon country of northern Arizona and into California, a trip which resulted in a "Report of Surveys" which is a classic, summarizing the terrain and advantages of the various routes from the Rockies to the Pacific—routes which are now occupied by great transcontinental railways. From September to February Palmer and his companions continued their difficult, rough journey to the coast. William Bell, at San Francisco, had had no news of them and impatiently waited their arrival.

At the end of the seventh week, my own party arrived by sea from San Pedro; two days later, another came in from the 35th parallel; and the next morning, when I went from my hotel, the Cosmopolitan, to hear the latest news at the Occidental, in came five of the shabbiest-looking fellows I ever saw. Their coats were torn, their caps washed into shapeless mushrooms of felt, their faces tanned and bearded, and their figures covered with mud; these were Palmer, Colton, Calhoun, Parry, and Willis; all my old friends had arrived together. What congratulations we had! How we startled the Frisco dandies who were languidly perusing the morning papers; with what determination they (Palmer and party, not the dandies) sat down to breakfast while the waiters covered the table with the choicest fare of the best hotel in the States; and how they enjoyed that first square meal of civilization.

By his dangerous, rough-and-tumble journey Palmer had cleared his mind on the problem of routes to the Pacific. He had found that easy grades could be maintained through northern Arizona over what is now the Santa Fe route, and that there was little advantage in the 32d-parallel or southern Pacific route so long and enthusiastically touted by Jefferson Davis. His final conclusions were that although the western half of the continent was not an agricultural paradise, it was far from being a desert as many had supposed. He had found that it was everywhere inhabitable and that there were frequent areas good for farming, while to the grazier it offered a vast, almost uninterrupted belt of superior pasturage, extending from Kansas to the Pacific Ocean, on which horses, mules, cattle, and sheep could be raised in countless herds as cheaply, perhaps, as anywhere in the world. Moreover, the mildness of the climate would enable more than one crop to be raised in a season, permit stock, without care, to fare as well in winter as in summer, and add grapes, cotton, and other semitropical fruits or products to those of the temperate latitudes. Good wheat could be grown, and if thorough methods of cultivation were adopted, irrigation would not be necessary in many sections. As to minerals, the hills and mountains contained an amount of mineral wealth of all kinds, the useful as well as the precious, which could be considered practically inexhaustible. From the Arkansas River to the western spurs of the Coast Range, near San Francisco, a distance of 1,500 miles, the mountains, never out of sight, might almost be said to possess continuous deposits of one kind or another of valuable minerals. Palmer concluded his report on the territory he had explored by saying, "When it is remembered how little and how carelessly this vast territory, the home of savage Indians, has been explored by white men, and that, even in the small and old-settled district of Cornwall, where mining was carried on before the Christian era, and where the earth has been burrowed for ages at a great depth, new discoveries are still made of tin and copper lodes, we may well wonder at the amount of hidden treasures which the few disclosures already made would indicate."

As to the other benefits of his long trip, General Palmer further wrote that a little experience of hardship such as he had suffered

enables you to determine a number of nice problems which otherwise might never have been solved, to say nothing of the new phases in which it exhibits the character of your comrades; the test of their true-heartedness, their pluck, perseverance, and generosity. There are also some important minor questions to which it supplies accurate solutions. For instance, how would a man ever know whether a smooth boulder of lava or a flat sandstone slab would make the best pillow, until such occasions had induced him to test the matter practically at frequent intervals during the same night? And how could he ever ascertain the durability of a pair of Santa Fe boots under active service, until a trail of this kind had placed it forcibly before his observation? And while he might hitherto have had a theoretical appreciation of the value and excellence of a slice of fat pork with "hard tack" for dessert, it is doubtful whether he would ever comprehend the essential sweetness and delicacy of these dishes until, after twenty-four hours' fasting, he had watched with a field-glass across a cañon until they should start out towards him from a camp two miles distant.

It was such first-hand knowledge as this trip produced that enabled the young engineer to understand the future possibilities of the West and to determine in his own mind that there must be a railroad north and south at the foot of the Rockies to tap this rich country from Wyoming to Mexico and feed the transcontinental railroads. When, later, his suggestion to this effect was turned down by the Kansas

GRENVILLE M. DODGE         OAKES AMES
GEORGE FRANCIS TRAIN
WILLIAM J. PALMER         DAVID F. MOFFAT

Dodge, courtesy of the Union Pacific Railroad; Ames, from H. H. Bancroft, *Chronicles of the Builders of the Commonwealth;* Train, from the collection of Frederick Meserve, New York; Palmer, courtesy of the Colorado Springs Chamber of Commerce; Moffat, from William N. Byers, *Encyclopedia of Biography of Colorado.*

A SURVEY PARTY ON THE KANSAS PACIFIC ROUTE

William A. Bell, *New Tracks in North America*, 1869.

Pacific, he resigned as secretary-treasurer of the company and began the project himself by organizing the Denver and Rio Grande Railway.

As he and Bell and Colton journeyed back to Denver by stage, Palmer was probably mulling over these things in his mind and making the plans for development of the Rocky Mountain country and its railroads which afterwards brought him fame and fortune. But the trip back was a merry one and a welcome relaxation after the months of roughing it. Bell recounts that

When Palmer, Colton, myself, and another passenger, had seated ourselves and packed away our wraps and blankets, to use whenever any great increase of elevation should make it very cold, the agent called out for Mr. Leland of the Occidental Hotel, San Francisco, and as Mr. Leland did not respond to the summons, he had forcibly to be conducted from the bar-room by his friends (to whom he had been saying good-bye in the usual manner nearly all the morning), and pushed with difficulty, blanket, coat, and all, through the door of the mud-wagon; then came half-a-dozen blankets to match the coat, and sealskin boots reaching to the hips; then a large bag, labelled muck-a-muck, which he soon informed us was food for the journey, should we need anything between times; then came a gallon keg of whiskey, then a second ditto, then a third, a fourth, and, lastly, a demijohn of the same. Bang went the door! "All aboard? Whoops!" shouted the driver, as he cracked the whip over the leaders; and thus, amidst a chorus of cheers from our new acquaintances, and a long string of messages to Tom, Dick, and Harry from the stentorian voice of Leland, as he bid them good-bye, we bumped and rattled through Virginia City. The whiskey was all finished before we reached Salt Lake; and, although it was at times a nuisance, and notwithstanding the fact that the owner of it drank with every one along the road, whether they wished or not, it was, nevertheless, a source of great amusement, and probably helped the horses, through the driver, out of many a tight place.

Four kinds of conveyance were required to make the 1,350-mile trip from San Francisco to the Laramie Mountains, over which Pullman cars would soon travel: 124 miles were covered by steamboat, 92 by rail, 250 by sledges, and the rest in "mud-wagons." The ride from Cheyenne to Denver brought out the full beauty of the mountain country. "The Rocky Mountains lay in full view of us all the way, gradually increasing in grandeur as we neared Denver," writes Bell; "the moon was very brilliant, and the view over the plains to the eastward presented an endless expanse of undulating whiteness; upon which the moonlight played like phosphorescence on the sea. The complete solitude, the vastness of the expanse on all sides, the clatter of the four-in-hand as they dashed along at a gallop, the keen sharp air, and the refreshing influences of a long night's rest made this drive inexpressibly delightful." This ride must have been balm to Palmer's spirit, for the beauties of the Rockies he never tired; he wrote and talked of them all his life, the climate and the scenery being equally important, in his mind, with the commercial resources. As he once wrote his friend Isaac Clothier, pointing out the value of the traffic in timber, coal, gold, and silver that would accrue to the railroad at the base of the Rockies, "The weather is quite exhausting here in Washington, and I long once more to be in the Rocky Mountains. I often find myself doubting that a kind Providence ever intended man to dwell on the Atlantic slope." Perhaps it was on this moonlight ride to Denver that Palmer made up his mind to cast his lot with Colorado and her glorious mountains for the rest of his life.

# CHAPTER III

## THE BUILDERS OF THE RAILROADS

WHEN General Dodge, on leave of absence from the Army, took charge as chief engineer of the actual building of the Union Pacific in 1866, he found a chaotic, blundering, and utterly ineffective organization, or, rather, lack of organization. The construction and the operation of the railroad were being carried on separately under orders from different groups of officials in New York, none of whom knew anything about building a railroad across the plains; there was no head of the work west of the Missouri; the New York office men quarreled among themselves; the route had not been finally fixed, and engineering parties were roaming aimlessly around the prairies, some of them unpaid for months; while the road itself consisted of two streaks of rust jutting out into the Territory of Nebraska, which were likened to the man in the song who said, "I don't know where I'm going but I'm on my way."

Knowing full well from his Army experience the dangers of a divided command, and being aware of the difficulties involved in constructing a railroad through a territory with neither law nor order, Dodge had told Thomas C. Durant, vice-president and general manager, that he would accept the post of chief engineer only on condition that he be given absolute control in the field, without interference from any officials in New York or elsewhere. Having spent $500,000 and produced just 40 miles of track, over level prairie land, Durant, despite his itch to manage the project himself, was ready to turn it over to the one man who could confidently be expected to make it succeed. It was said that about half of the $500,000 had gone into Durant's own pocket, and he probably thought that pocket would not be comfortably filled with Union Pacific money again unless the railroad should actually be built. So Dodge was given the job.

A month later he had organized the building of the Union Pacific along lines of military efficiency with all departments under his own unified command; and surveying, Indian-fighting, and track-laying were going forward simultaneously. Within two months more Dodge had the two Casement brothers, General Jack S. and Daniel, at work with a thousand men and a hundred teams laying track at furious speed. His formula for pushing the construction work was simple. He selected the two men best qualified for the job, gave them ample supplies, and to the track-layers, who were "ex-Confederate and Federal soldiers, mule skinners, Mexicans, New York Irish, bushwhackers and ex-convicts from the older prisons of the East," he said, "Boys, I want you to do just what Jack Casement tells you to do. We've got to beat that Central Pacific crowd."

Thus the elements of a contest entered into the building of the Union Pacific, for a second road, the Central Pacific, was now pushing its tracks east from California as fast as it could. And this spirit of rivalry combined with a sense of loyalty to General Dodge to give these hardy laborers incentive to excel in speeding the tracks towards the Pacific. It was a rough-and-ready, happy-go-lucky crowd of Paddies, troopers, and toughs who laid the tracks of the Union Pacific. The preponderance of men who had been in the Army, the leadership of General Dodge, General Casement, and other military men, the use of troops to protect the workers against the Indians, all gave the enterprise something of the racy flavor of war without all its dangers. Moreover, there was freedom such as soldiers seldom know, for there was plenty of money in circulation and plenty of opportunity to spend it with the collection of gambling-games and dance-halls that followed the construction camps and received the euphonious title of "hell-on-wheels."

Altogether, it was a rough, dangerous, dirty, sweating, hard-working, hard-drinking, free-spending life that this army of track-layers lived as they pushed the steel rails across the plains. They worked long hours under a fiercely burning sun in summer and in bitter cold in winter, for the plains climate ranged the extremes of heat and cold. A day's routine would read something like this: In the morning the men are up early in the boarding-train, wash in tin basins, eat a hearty breakfast, and set out to the job. Heavy work at plowing, shoveling and grading, or placing ties, carrying and spiking rails, keeps up till noon, when everybody knocks off an hour for a heavy dinner. Pitchers of steaming coffee; pans of soup; platters heaped with fried meat, roast meat, vegetables, potatoes; iron dishes of cold, watery canned tomatoes; condensed milk diluted with water; canned fruit, cakes, and pies make up the hearty menu. Little conversation enlivens the meal; the men are there to eat, and they make a business of it. In 15 or 20 minutes they are out of the cook-house, sitting around their bunks, smoking, sewing on buttons, or taking a little "shut-eye"—and when was sleep ever so sound or so efficiently refreshing as the half-hour snatched from heavy, muscle-straining work in the middle of a long, hard day?

At one o'clock the walking boss routs them out, herds them back to the job, and for an hour or so spurs them on to their labors with exhortations and profanity so as to overcome the noontime lassitude. Cy Warman, in his *Story of the Railroad*, gives this picture of the walking-boss foreman:

He has his eye constantly upon the men. In ferocity he approaches nearer to the ideal sea captain than any man on the work. If a man is caught soldiering, he is jacked up; the next time he is jacked up a little higher; and with the third offence the walking boss calls the time-keeper, whom he orders to give the man his time, adding, for the enlightenment of the others, that this is not a Salvation Army, but a grading outfit. As a parting shot to the discharged man, he advises him to buy a drum if he wants to be a soldier. This little incident has a good effect. A hundred whips crack, and at the end of an hour each of the one hundred teams has brought in an extra scraper of dirt. At twenty cents, five scrapers to the yard, this means, for a hundred scrapers, five dollars; and that is where the skill of the walking boss comes in, and it counts.

In the late afternoon, "time" is called again, and the men have an hour to rest before supper, a more leisurely meal, after which they return to the bunk-house cars, where card games are soon in progress and the air is thick with pipe smoke and murky with talk, perhaps talk somewhat akin to the "railroad talk" of later years, which was said to consist entirely of "whiskey and women and higher wages and shorter hours." Or maybe they sing "Poor Paddy he works on the railroad," or "The great Pacific railway for California hail; bring on the locomotive, lay down the iron rail," or that favorite ditty:

Then drill, my Paddies, drill,—
Drill, my heroes, drill,—
Drill all day, no sugar in your tay,
Workin' on the U. P. railway.

If the money from the last pay-day is not all spent, the men will probably wander into the town, that moving "hell-on-wheels," for a night of bad whisky, gaudy dance-hall belles, crooked card games, and a morning-after headache. Of the raw night-life of those camp towns it was written, "They counted that day lost whose low descending sun, saw no man killed or other mischief done." One of the worst of these moving towns was that at Julesburg, Nebraska, where the gamblers took possession, occupied the land Dodge had set aside for shops, and took the law into their own hands. Dodge ordered General Casement to take charge and restore order; three weeks later, when he returned, the following conversation took place between Dodge and Casement:

"Are the gamblers quiet and behaving?"

"You bet they are, General. They're quiet and behaving out there in the graveyard."

As to the actual methods of work that produced such speedy building as was done on the Union Pacific, an anonymous contemporary journalist has this to say:

One can see all along the line of the now completed road the evidences of ingenious self-protection and defense which our men learned during the war. The same curious huts and underground dwellings which were a common sight along our army lines then, may now be seen burrowed into the sides of the hills, or built up with ready adaptability in sheltered spots. The whole organisation of the force engaged in the construction of the road is, in fact, semi-military. The men who go ahead, locating the road, are the advance guard. Following these is the second line, cutting through the gorges, grading the road, and building bridges. Then comes the main line of the army, placing the sleepers, laying the track, spiking down the rails, perfecting the alignment, ballasting the rail, and dressing up and completing the road for immediate use. This army of workers has its base, to continue the figure, at Omaha, Chicago, and still farther eastward, from whose markets are collected the material for constructing the road. Along the line of the completed road are construction trains constantly "pushing forward to the front" with supplies. The company's grounds and workshops at Omaha are the arsenal, where these purchases, amounting now to millions of dollars in value, are collected and held ready to be sent forward.

The advance limit of the rail is occupied by a train of long box cars, with hammocks swung under them, beds spread on top of them, bunks built within them, in which the sturdy, broad-shouldered pioneers of the great iron highway sleep at night and take their meals. Close behind this train come loads of ties and rails and spikes, &c., which are being thundered off upon the roadside, to be ready for the track-layers. The road is graded a hundred miles in advance. The ties are laid roughly in place, then adjusted, gauged, and levelled. Then the track is laid.

Track-laying on the Union Pacific is a science, and we pundits of the Far East stood upon that embankment, only about a thousand miles this side of sunset, and backed westward before that hurrying corps of sturdy operatives with mingled feelings of amusement, curiosity, and profound respect. On they came. A light car, drawn by a single horse, gallops up to the front with its load of rails. Two men seize the end of a rail and start forward, the rest of the gang taking hold by twos until it is clear of the car. They come forward at a run. At the word of command the rail is dropped in its place, right side up, with care, while the same process goes on at the other side of the car. Less than thirty seconds to a rail for each gang, and so four rails go down to the minute! Quick work, you say, but the fellows on the U. P. are tremendously in earnest. The moment the car is empty it is tipped over on the side of the track to let the next loaded car pass it, and then it is tipped back again; and it is a sight to see it go flying back for another load, propelled by a horse at full gallop at the end of 60 or 80 feet of rope, ridden by a young Jehu, who drives furiously. Close behind the first gang come the gaugers, spikers, and bolters, and a lively time they make of it. It is a grand Anvil Chorus that those sturdy sledges are playing across the plains. It is in triple time, three strokes to a spike. There are ten spikes to a rail, four hundred rails to a mile, eighteen hundred miles to San Francisco. That's the sum, what is the quotient? Twenty-one million times are those sledges to be swung, twenty-one million times are they to come down with their sharp punctuation, before the great work of modern America is complete!

It was fortunate that Dodge had insisted on complete control in building the Union Pacific, for within the next year he was faced with so many and so varied obstacles that only an indomitable fighter clothed with absolute powers could have overcome them. When the road had been extended 200 miles west of Omaha, a band of Indians swept down on one of the freight crews, captured the train, and held it; and this was the beginning of 20 months of bitter and continuous warfare. Personal conflict developed between Dodge and Durant, when the vice-president attempted to assert his powers as general manager and interfere with Dodge's work and plans. The final location of the route had not yet been determined, and consequently Dodge was compelled to spend much time in the field exploring the country. Snow blockades stopped work and traffic in the winter, and in spring great floods swept through Nebraska tearing out miles of track and telegraph poles.

When Dodge wrote General William T. Sherman that he proposed to reach Fort Sanders, 288 miles west from the head of the tracks, in another 12 months and that he needed 5,000 soldiers east of the mountains and north of the Platte to give the men confidence and ensure the success of his plans, Sherman was astonished. "It is almost a miracle to grasp your purpose to finish to Fort Sanders in 1867," he wrote, "but you have done so much that I mistrust my own judgment and accept yours. I regard this road as the solution of Indian affairs and of the Mormon question, and I will help you all I can. You may rest easy that both Grant and I feel deeply concerned in the safety of your great national enterprise."

But, despite the sending of additional troops, the Indians were more than a match for the Union Pacific. From the Laramie Mountains they swooped down on the line, pulled up the surveyor's stakes, stole the horses, and drove the workmen away; they attacked another section near Laramie, stole the supplies, and burned everything in sight; they routed engineering parties; they killed a soldier and a tie-hauler and burned the stage stations on a 50-mile front. They tried to wreck an engine by stretching a rawhide lariat across the track with thirty braves on each side; as retaliation for the resulting carnage, they raided a near-by railroad station next evening, captured one man, and killed him by building a bonfire on his breast. General Dodge wrote Sherman that he was beginning to have serious doubts of the ability of General Christopher C. Augur, who had charge of the troops, to campaign against the Indians in the Powder River country and at the same time protect the railroad mail-routes and the telegraph. So dangerous was the situation that Dodge traveled in a private car which was in reality an arsenal, with only enough space for a bed and a table which served alternately as a dining-table and a desk.

The raids had become so frequent that Dodge had difficulty in hiring workmen; but Congress refused to allow military campaigns against the hostile Indians who infested the country to the south of Dodge's line near the Republican River, and the military protection from the marauders of the north and the west was inadequate. The situation indeed looked hopeless. At this time, however, the Government sent three commissioners from the East to the end of the track to examine the road. They had just finished their task and were standing on a hill overlooking the work, talking to Dodge, when suddenly more than a hundred Indians swooped down and attacked the workmen at lunch. For the first time government representatives heard the war-whoops and the spatter of bullets, saw the wild savages, and felt the chill fear of death and scalping. Although there was a company of infantry a mile away, it could not reach the scene until after the Indians had finished their swift attack; the workmen ran for the shelter of the box-cars and fired not a single shot; Dodge left the commissioners standing on the hill, drew his revolver, berated the fleeing workmen, and then, returning, told the commissioners, now thoroughly frightened, "We've got to clean the damn Indians out or give up building the Union Pacific. The Government can take its choice." Convinced, now, that Indian warfare was a desperate matter and not mere cattle-stealing and annoying interference, the commission went back to Washington and obtained more troops from Congress for the protection of the railroad-builders, and the danger from Indian attacks was materially lessened.

But Dodge had other battles to fight. Some of the government commissioners recommended that he stop work for six months, awaiting stronger military detachments, and he wrote in protest to President Oliver Ames in New York, "I'll push this road on to Salt Lake in another year or surrender my own scalp to the Indians. If we stop now, we may never get started again." Small wonder that Dodge was loath to stop now, for he had made a splendid record in pushing the road westward. His report of progress says that "the first surveys were made in the fall of 1863. The first grading was done in the fall of 1864. The first rail was laid in July, 1865. Two hundred and sixty miles were built in 1866, 240 in 1867, including the ascent of the first range of mountains to an elevation of 8,235 feet above sea-level."

In his insistence that construction should continue uninterrupted, Dodge had the support of President Ames, but Vice-President Durant, irked by his loss of power, started intriguing to regain the control that Dodge had taken. Since the line had been pushed through the difficult stretch of Laramie Mountain country, Durant felt he could now get along without Dodge. So he began his bid for authority by attempting to change the location of the line and by declaring that the mountain-division headquarters would be at Laramie instead of Cheyenne. When he heard this, Dodge left Washington, where he was lobbying for the railroad, and started west. At Cheyenne he bluntly told the citizens that Durant had lied and that the railroad shops and headquarters would remain in their city. In May, 1868, he hurried on to Laramie, where a powerful gang of gamblers and whisky-venders were determined to make Laramie the division headquarters and were threatening with violence the men on the construction work between Laramie and Cheyenne.

Dodge's biographer, J. R. Perkins, tells colorfully of his spectacular visit: *

The "Big Tent" was up and doing a thriving business the evening Dodge arrived. It was the town's social and civic center and it was just a little bigger and a little tougher than it had been at the other points. From a platform a German band played noisily; and while the mule-whackers, miners and railroad workers danced with the strumpets, scores of others crowded the gambling tables, played monte, faro and rondo coolo; and against the long bar, with its background of cut-glass goblets, ice pitchers and high mirrors, leaned those who drank hard whisky and sang the sentimental songs of their childhood back in the older states.

Dodge's visit to Laramie City was a dash of cold water.

"The shops will remain at Cheyenne," he said. "And if the gamblers and saloon-keepers here don't let the railroad employees alone, I'll have General Gibbons send down a company of soldiers and we'll proclaim martial law. Take your choice."

Then he hunted up Thomas C. Durant, and the meeting was far from pleasant. "Durant," Dodge said in his deliberate way, "you are now going to learn that the men working for the Union Pacific will take orders from me and not from you. If you interfere there will be trouble—trouble from the government, from the army, and from the men themselves." He turned abruptly and left Durant standing in the dusty Main Street of Laramie City, and the rails of the Union Pacific began to be laid faster than ever before.

* J. R. Perkins, *Trails, Rails and War* (copyright, 1929). Quoted by special permission of the publishers, the Bobbs-Merrill Company.

Dodge had long since told Oliver Ames that Durant was in the way and had received in return this statement from the president: "It shall be the duty of the chief engineer of the Union Pacific to take charge of all matters pertaining to the construction of the road." But now a battle royal loomed. Sidney Dillon wired Dodge that Durant had secured large powers from the company, and asked Dodge to hurry east to a meeting arranged by Durant with Grant, Sherman, railroad officials, and government commissioners to confer on the completion of the building of the road. At this meeting, July 26, 1868, Durant accused Dodge of selecting impossible routes, squandering money, and ignoring the judgment of his associates. He also declared that the road had not yet been located into Salt Lake. As Perkins tells the story: *

"What about it, Dodge?" General Grant inquired, leaning back in a cane-bottomed chair and smoking vigorously.

"Just this," Dodge began deliberately; "if Durant, or anybody connected with the Union Pacific, or anybody connected with the government changes my lines, I'll quit the road."

There was a tense pause; Grant shifted his cigar, Sherman's seamy face was immobile, but the others were ill at ease. Durant's delicate fingers pulled at his Van Dyke beard; he glanced at Colonel Seymour, his henchman, but said nothing. Grant finally broke the silence.

"The government expects this railroad to be finished," he said slowly. "The government expects the railroad company to meet its obligations. And the government expects General Dodge to remain with the road as its chief engineer until it is completed."

It was a dramatic moment; it was even a critical moment in the building of the first great transcontinental road. Durant looked at the man who would soon become President and doubtless did some quick thinking. Anyhow, whatever he thought, he turned to Dodge and said:

"I withdraw my objections. We all want Dodge to stay with the road."

With the question of absolute control finally settled, Dodge turned all his energies to the race with the Central Pacific and, with Dillon, hastened to Salt Lake. The Central Pacific had originally been chartered by the Government to build east through California to the Nevada line, where, it was supposed, it would join tracks with the Union Pacific. But the wording was vague, and under the influence of the Central Pacific lobbyists Congress amended the act to declare

* *Ibid.*

that the two railroads should continue construction until their rails met. Just where this was to be was not stated, and since every mile of track meant thousands of dollars in subsidies, each road was anxious to build as long a line as possible. Moreover, each looked covetously upon the traffic of the Salt Lake basin country, controlled by the Mormons, and each was anxious to earn the favor of the American public as the aggressive and dominant Western road.

When officers of the Central Pacific saw that the Union Pacific was going to beat them to the western shore of Salt Lake and so cut them off from this rich traffic, Collis P. Huntington of the California road, who spent most of his time lobbying in Washington, induced President Johnson's Cabinet to believe that the Union Pacific had been poorly built and was not up to government specifications. He filed the location of the line of the Central Pacific 300 miles in advance of actual construction, partly over a line already graded by the Union Pacific east of Salt Lake; and then he obtained an order from the Secretary of the Interior restraining the Union Pacific from building west of the eastern end of this 300-mile survey. Since the Union Pacific had also filed its line west far beyond Salt Lake, as permitted by law, the question of which road should have the cash subsidies from the Government was a difficult one; and it appeared that, under the law, both could ultimately collect, or try to collect.

In Washington the Central Pacific lobbied to secure the support of President Johnson's administration; in the field Dodge told his story to sympathetic General Grant, who was soon to succeed Johnson as President. When the two roads were about the same distance from Promontory Point, on Salt Lake west of Ogden, Dodge proposed to Durant that they agree to meet there, but Durant, with his eye on the $30,000 a mile subsidy, refused to consider any such negotiations. So both roads pushed forward as fast as they could.

In the meantime Dodge was having his troubles with the Mormons. When he announced that his surveys showed that the road should be built north of Salt Lake City to Ogden, the officials of the Mormon Church were furious. Since Brigham Young had already told his followers that the Lord had revealed to him that the Union Pacific would build directly to Salt Lake City, he now called the Faithful together and preached a scorching sermon against this impious engineer and his railroad which defied the Divine Will by leaving Salt Lake City off the main line. So strong was the feeling in the Mormon capital that Dodge's life was threatened, but fortunately the Central Pacific engineers decided that their road too must go north of the Lake. Informing Brigham Young of the decision of the rival road, Dodge promised him that his company would build a branch south from Ogden into Salt Lake City; if the Mormons would not support this arrangement, the Union Pacific would block the Central Pacific from building such a connection. Thereupon the Prophet called together his twelve apostles, and it was decided that Dodge had more to offer than the road that the Church of Latter-Day Saints was then supporting. Consequently, in a great Tabernacle meeting, Brigham Young told his followers of the plans of the railroad to build into Salt Lake City from Ogden and revealed that "the Lord, in another vision, had commanded the Mormons to help the Union Pacific."

Having solved this difficulty, Dodge was called upon to take the hardest blow of all. For now the Central Pacific played its trump card. Huntington obtained from President Johnson, the day before his Cabinet went out of office, an order on the Treasury to issue $1,400,000 in bonds to the Central Pacific in payment of the government subsidy on its line from Echo Cañon to Promontory Point, Utah, a line which had been filed by the Central Pacific but was already actually graded by the Union Pacific. Meanwhile, the Union Pacific had no money: the Government withheld its subsidies; Jim Fisk, the stock-plunger, had secured a large block of its shares and tied the company up in litigation; Oliver Ames wrote, "We may have to quit." But Dodge pushed construction forward through the worst snow-storms in years and reached Ogden in March of 1869. With the final blow of the issue of government bonds to the Central Pacific it appeared that the Union Pacific could get no money for construction west of Ogden. Nevertheless, Dodge kept his crews at work and communicated with his friend Grant. He was rewarded for his tenacity when the new President of the United States annulled the former President's order and prohibited the issuance of bonds to either road until the affairs of both companies should be investigated.

Under the Congressional Act of 1862 the Union Pacific had been empowered to build to the western boundary of Nevada and the Central

Pacific to the eastern boundary of California, but there was an am-
biguous clause permitting the Central Pacific to aid the Union
Pacific in completing its tracks to the western boundary of Nevada.
An amendment in 1866 permitted the two roads to continue construction until their rails met and allowed each road to locate its line 300
miles in advance of construction. Dodge suggested informally that the
roads meet at Promontory Point, Utah, but the Central Pacific officers,
who were anxious to build into Ogden and capture the Salt Lake trade,
refused to agree, and Durant, who wanted to get the government subsidies for every possible mile, insisted that the Union Pacific build as
far west as it could. Consequently, while pushing the tracks on toward
Promontory Point, Dodge began locating the line, grading, and laying
ties west of this point. And the Central Pacific began to grade a line
from Ogden to Promontory Point paralleling that of the Union Pacific.

As Dodge continued westward and the gradings of the two roads
began to parallel each other, fights between the crews were frequent.
But, with the support of President Grant, Dodge had the upper hand,
and he told Huntington that if they did not agree on a meeting-point,
the Government would undoubtedly step in and take charge of both
railroads. This powerful argument settled the matter; they agreed to
meet, as Dodge had originally suggested, at Promontory Point, Utah,
west of Ogden; and the Union Pacific agreed to sell the Central Pacific
its graded right of way from the west at Echo Cañon into Ogden.
Ultimately the Union Pacific received from the Central Pacific more
than a million dollars for this construction work, as well as the government subsidies.

Even after agreement had been reached, there was still spirited, if
not bitter, rivalry between the two roads, however; and the newspapers
began to print reports of the race. It was pointed out that a day's
work often resulted in more miles of track being laid than an ox-train
could travel in a day over the old overland trail. The papers would
report that the Union Pacific had laid six miles of track one day; and
next day the Central Pacific would make an extra spurt of speed and
lay seven miles. In order to speed construction the Chinese track-layers
of the Central Pacific were supplemented by championship crews of
stalwart Irishmen; as a result, Thomas Durant lost a $10,000 wager
that the rival road could not lay 10 miles of track in a day. As the

roads neared Promontory Point, another crisis loomed when a general strike was threatened if the Union Pacific workmen were not paid their overdue wages immediately. They had already shot one foreman, hanged another, and kicked a contractor out of his own camp because they were not paid, and finally Durant, on his way west for the final construction ceremonies, was seized by workmen and held for ransom, the ransom being payment in full of all wages. Dodge wired Ames of the desperate situation, requesting one million dollars in cash. Fortunately, the president was able to obtain this, Durant was released, and the Union Pacific completed its tracks into Promontory Point.

On May 10, 1869, the rival roads came together, and grimy workmen leaning on their shovels joined with state officials and railroad officers, Mormon Saints, Indians, frontiersmen, and camp-followers in the celebration that marked the end of five years of toil. Leland Stanford, Governor of California and one of the backers of the Central Pacific, came out with his party on a special drawn by an engine christened "Jupiter," the party including Collis P. Huntington, Mark Hopkins, Charles Crocker, and others; the Union Pacific party included, among others, Dodge, Durant, Dillon, and the Casement brothers. There was a spirited controversy over whether Durant or Stanford should drive the Golden Spike, but finally the Union Pacific crowd sulkily yielded this honor to the Governor.

Although the project of the Pacific railway had seemed to many a wildcat scheme, the recent race between the roads had filled the newspapers with stories of the magnitude of the project, its future possibilities, and its importance to the nation. Hence the whole country was agog over the driving of the last spike. When a clergyman from Pittsfield, Massachusetts, had concluded his prayer, the telegraph flashed, "We have got done praying"; and the reply came back, "We are all ready in the East." Now came the great moment. Every town in the nation got the message, "Hats off," and Governor Stanford with a silver sledge drove the golden spike home, into a tie of polished laurel, touching an electric wire attached to the spike which sent its impulse over the telegraph wires of the nation and told the world that the Pacific railroad was completed. In New York, Trinity Church was thrown open at midday. The Te Deum was sung, and an address was delivered by the Reverend Dr. Vinton before a large crowd "united

to tender thanks to God for the completion of the greatest work ever
undertaken by man." In Philadelphia bells were rung and cannon fired.
At Buffalo thousands gathered to hear the telegraph signals, sing "The
Star-Spangled Banner," and listen to speeches by distinguished citizens.
A hundred guns were fired in Omaha, and Chicago showed its feeling
in a parade four miles long and a mass-meeting at night. Business was
entirely suspended in San Francisco; buildings and ships were decorated with bunting, bells rang, whistles tooted, and the town was in a
furore for days.

When their engines stood head-on at the end of their respective tracks
that day, the Central Pacific had constructed 690 miles of railroad east
from Sacramento, the Union Pacific 1,086 west from the Missouri.
Each engineer broke a bottle of champagne over his rival's engine,
and the day ended in speeches and feasting. And Bret Harte was inspired to write his poem, "What the Engines Said," * which read, in
part:

> What was it the Engines said,
> Pilots touching,—head to head,
> Facing on a single track,
> Half a world behind each back—?
>
> .    .    .
>
> With a prefatory screech,
> In a florid Western speech,
> Said the engine from the WEST:
> "I am from Sierra's crest;
> And if altitude's a test,
> Why, I reckon, it's confessed
> That I've done my level best."
>
> Said the engine from the EAST,
> "They who work best talk the least.
> S'pose you whistle down your brakes;
> What you've done is no great shakes,—
> Pretty fair,—but let our meeting
> Be a different kind of greeting.
> Let these folks with champagne stuffing,—
> Not the engines, do the *puffing*."
>
> .    .    .

* Quoted by permission of the publishers, Houghton Mifflin Company.

A UNION PACIFIC CONSTRUCTION TRAIN AND CREW

From a photograph of 1868. Courtesy of the Union Pacific Railroad.

THE OLD AND THE NEW IN OVERLAND TRANSPORTATION

The special train, drawn by "Jupiter," bearing Leland Stanford to the last-spike ceremonies meets a covered-wagon train of emigrants bound for California a few miles west of Promontory Point. Courtesy of the Southern Pacific Company.

THE MEETING OF THE LOCOMOTIVES AT PROMONTORY POINT

Joining hands are the chief engineers of the two systems, S. S. Montague, of the Central Pacific, on the left, and Grenville M. Dodge, of the Union Pacific, on the right. Courtesy of the Union Pacific Railroad.

That is what the engines said
Unreported and unread
Spoken slightly through the nose
With a whistle at the close.

How well Dodge's work was done, despite the speed at which it was finished, we can judge from the final report of the government commission of engineers:

Taken as a whole, the Union Pacific Railroad has been well constructed. The general route for the line is exceedingly well chosen, crossing the Rocky Mountain Ranges at some of the most favorable passes on the continent, and possessing capabilities for easy grades and favorable alignments unsurpassed by any other railway line on similarly elevated grounds. The energy and perseverance with which the work has been urged forward, and the rapidity with which it has been executed are without parallel in history. In the grandeur and magnitude of the undertaking, it has never been equalled, and no other line compares with this in the arid and barren character of the country it traverses, giving rise to unusual inconveniences and difficulties, and imposing the necessity of obtaining almost every requisite of material, of labor, and supplies for its construction, from the initial point of its commencement.

Another project of considerable magnitude was the building of the Kansas Pacific Railway from Kansas City to Denver, which later was absorbed as a branch of the Union Pacific. The leadership of this enterprise also depended, to a large extent, upon one man, William J. Palmer, and it involved him in such varied activities as the superintendence of construction, assisting in the raising of money to finance the road, securing the coöperation of other business interests, and lobbying in Congress for government support. In the furtherance of this project there came prominently to the fore that rare combination of qualities which marked General Palmer as it marked General Dodge—practical driving force at pushing construction, executive ability, and leadership. As a contemporary journalist said:

At the time of entering upon the work of construction of the Kansas Pacific railroad, no material was in sight and yet General Palmer graded the road bed, procured ties and rails, laid the tracks and constructed the bridges for one hundred and fifty miles of road in ninety-two days. This masterly achievement in railroad building was accomplished in the face of serious obstacles other than those placed by impersonal forces, as the workmen were greatly harassed by hostile Indians, and eight of their number including the principal contractor were scalped. In order to accomplish this work in the time desired he was compelled to inspire his men with his own earnestness and determination, pushing them to the very limit of their strength, but with such courtesy and tact that they remained willing workers to the last and were his friends as well as his workers. This was but a forecast of what he was to accomplish on almost a national scale.

Various complicated financial and political difficulties had beset the Kansas Pacific, with the result that in the late Sixties it was a "stalled" road, jutting out into the Kansas prairies with no prospect of completely successful operation until it could extend itself to transcontinental proportions or tap the Central Pacific so as to get into California. One or the other of these things it proposed to do, as its comprehensive surveys under the direction of General Palmer indicated. Originally chartered by Congress to join the Union Pacific at the 100th meridian in central Nebraska, it had succeeded in changing its route to parallel the Union Pacific across Kansas and Colorado, and it had negotiated with Denver for aid in reaching that city. But the $2,000,000 it needed was too much for the little city on the Platte, and the citizens decided to get a transcontinental outlet by building their own road, the Denver Pacific, straight north to meet the Union Pacific at Cheyenne. This decision left the Kansas Pacific stranded on the prairies two hundred miles from Denver, looking forlornly westward.

In July, 1868, General Palmer, lobbying in Washington to secure additional government aid, wrote his friend Isaac Clothier:

The only hope I have left is of getting additional aid for about 76 miles to a proper point of divergence for New Mexican and Denver trade. This point is called Cheyenne Wells—and there is abundant water there. Congress will not give us through aid at this session because of political timidity. Our Radical Senators and Representatives would be willing to jeopardize the most important practical interests of the Country, rather than run the slightest shadow of risk to their political schemes. Being selfish, they are consequently narrow and do not know that these measures are more popular than anything else with the people. ... It will be necessary for our Road to reach the base of the Rocky Mtn's before it will be very profitable or have a flourishing traffic. The business this year has not, I believe, been proportionately so large as last. If we had reached the mtns.—we should have had an immense amount of coal and timber to carry—besides supplies for the gold and silver mines.

The financial deadlock was broken when Congress passed a bill permitting the Kansas Pacific to transfer its rights and lands to the Denver Pacific, granting each road alternate sections of land on both sides of its track and authorizing them to borrow $32,000 for each mile of the route to be covered. With this support both roads were able to negotiate large loans, and General Palmer came to Denver in 1869 to perfect the arrangements whereby the two companies would work harmoniously together. In these negotiations he proved to be most diplomatic, smoothing out all difficulties between the two roads and enabling construction to go forward rapidly, both north and east. Grading and track-laying on the Kansas Pacific was started east from Denver at once, and within three months there was only 10 miles of trackless section remaining. Palmer and the contractors then decided to make a spectacular play by building the remainder of the track in 10 hours; and though there were many scoffers to say it could not be done, the 10 miles of track was actually built in that time, equaling the speed that the Central Pacific had made in its most spectacular day's work.

It was while the Kansas Pacific was being built that young William F. Cody acquired his proud title of "Buffalo Bill." Cody and some other plainsmen were hired by the railroad company to provide buffalo meat for the construction crews. He was paid five hundred dollars a month to kill an average of twelve buffalo a day, to oversee the dressing and cutting of the meat, and get it to the construction camps where the 1,200 men of the Kansas Pacific were working. The pay was high because the buffalo were already disappearing; they had deserted the route of the railway and had to be hunted farther out on the plains. Once, when a herd of buffalo was sighted on the prairie, Cody mounted his trained buffalo horse, Brigham, and galloped away with his breech-loading needle-gun to provide the day's meat supply. When he reached the vicinity of the herd, he found five Army officers from Fort Harker waiting for the herd to pass. They told him that they would shoot the animals but wanted only the tongues and a chuck of the tenderloin and that he could have the rest. He thanked them, and when the herd arrived, he ran from the party and advanced on the buffalo from the rear. There were eleven in the herd, and with twelve shots he picked them all off before the Army officers had a chance to put their guns into action. So astonished were the officers at the prowess of this young plainsmen that they dubbed him "Buffalo Bill," a title which he bore ever afterward.

The Kansas Pacific did its part toward the destruction of the buffalo by running excursion trains filled with hunters from the Middle West, and it was not many years until the thundering herds had entirely disappeared. When the Grand Duke Alexis of Russia toured the West, Buffalo Bill was hired to be his guide in a buffalo hunt, receiving $1,000 a month for his services. Needless to say, the Grand Duke shot his buffalo. In 18 months Cody killed 4,280 buffalo for the Kansas Pacific construction crews.

Although General Palmer completed the road straight west into the city of Denver, this route was selected against his advice. He had recommended that the road reach the Rockies 100 miles south, at Pueblo, and proceed north from there to Denver, thus occupying the valley of the Arkansas and the base of the Rockies from Pueblo to Denver, so that the mining country could be tapped and branch lines built wherever new mining properties were discovered. Since the directors of the Kansas Pacific refused to adopt this plan, General Palmer lost no time in carrying out the project himself. In September, 1870, when the Kansas Pacific was completed and operating into Denver, he resigned; and showing his usual speed and energy, within a month he had organized his own road, the Denver and Rio Grande, to follow the base of the Rockies south and ultimately, he planned, to enter Southern California and Mexico.

The building of the Denver and Rio Grande by General Palmer is a fascinating story of faith and achievement; for it was built through an almost unpeopled territory with no great center of population at either end, a territory which had considerable wild beauty of rocks and mountains but was also characterized by arid plains which would not yield easily to the arts of the farmer. There were as yet few gold-camps, no trading-centers, and fewer than 500 people between Denver and Pueblo, while the whole state of Colorado south of Denver contained less than 10,000 inhabitants, and the only transportation from Denver to Colorado City was a triweekly stage which averaged five passengers a trip. But Palmer had faith in the future of this country—in the minerals that could be dug from its mountains, the cattle to be raised on its grazing-lands, and the cities that could be built through the exploitation of its resources. All this was far in the future, and few could have sensed these possibilities. Indeed, even such experienced men as the directors of the Kansas Pacific had failed to do so.

In completing his system of mountain railways the construction problems Palmer faced were tremendous, and time and again his engineers declared, "It's no use trying. You can never carry freight and passengers over those mountains to any advantage." On one such occasion he gathered his surveyors together in their camp and stopped all dissent with the statement, "The decision is made, gentlemen. It's going to be done!" But it was no wonder the engineers demurred, for before it was completed, the railroad company encountered nearly every kind of difficulty that engineering science had had to meet. It went through mountain-ranges two miles high and into cañons half a mile deep; it crossed and recrossed the Continental Divide with a grade of 211 feet to the mile in an intricate maze of meandering lines and abrupt curves; it zigzagged over dizzy pinnacled heights where "men plied picks and shovels amid the clouds that floated around the spinal column of the continent." One observer described a typical scene of construction activities in Animas Cañon:

The smooth vertical wall was 1,000 feet deep. From that height were seen hanging spider-web-like ropes, down which men seeming not much larger than ants were slowly descending while others perched upon narrow shelves in the face of the cliff, or in trifling niches from which their only egress was by dangling ropes, sighted through their theodolites from one ledge to the other, and directed where to place the dabs of paint indicating the intended roadbed. Similarly suspended, the workmen followed the engineers, drilling holes for blasting, and tumbling down loose fragments, until they had won a foothold for working in a less extraordinary manner. Ten months of labor were spent on this cañon-cutting—months of work on the brink of yawning abysses and in the midst of falling rocks and yet not one serious accident occurred.

And the chief engineer said, "Often it seemed as if another hair's breadth or a straw's weight would have sent me over the edge."

It was this perilous construction work that later earned for the Rio Grande the title of the world's most scenic railway route—this and the 25 years of artistic press-agentry of Major S. K. Hooper, who "started out in life as a ship blacksmith and in that school learned to fit and join, and also the virtues of constant pounding. On these lines, he conducted a publicity campaign for the Rio Grande that was at once the admiration and despair of his fellow craftsmen. 'Always in the lime light' was his motto for the road and he made the Royal Gorge and the rest of its scenery known wherever print was read."

For several excellent reasons General Palmer adopted the narrow gage for the initial stages of his railroad-building. Since he received no subsidies from the Government (and his was the first Western road so built), but only a right of way 200 feet wide and 20 acres for station purposes in each 10 miles, all the money he used had to be raised privately. Consequently, the saving of 37 per cent of the construction cost achieved by using the narrow gage was well worth considering. Moreover, it was especially adapted to the rough country and precipitous grades, since it could loop the loop when necessary and turn around on the brim of a sombrero. Before deciding the exact gage, in 1870, he visited with Dr. William A. Bell the Fastiniog Railway in Wales, which used a two-foot gage, and he consulted the London engineers Fowler and Strachey, who had built a successful railroad in India one meter wide. As a result of these investigations Palmer finally adopted a three-foot gage, and it was said that his miniature coaches and equipment were a delight to look at and to ride in, being beautifully made and fitted with extraordinary care. Later, when funds were available, his lines were made standard-gage by the addition of a third rail.

It was while building the Denver and Rio Grande in the late Seventies that General Palmer engaged in one of the most spectacular building and operating contests in the entire history of American railroads. By this time his "baby railroad" was growing with the speed and hardiness of a wild blackberry-vine, pushing out from its main trunk various winding offshoots which penetrated the mountains at the west to the places where rich mines were to be found. It was still in the precarious early-development stage and could not compare with the Union Pacific in importance or length—or even width, but "the little road" already represented a substantial achievement in planning, engineering, building, and financing. Although burdened by its heavy program of construction and hampered by the fact that it was built entirely with private capital, the Denver and Rio Grande had aspirations to become a transcontinental road. Its original plans, filed with the United States Government when it secured a Federal charter, called for construction westward through the only easily available pass in the Rockies in Colorado, the Grand Cañon, or Royal Gorge, of the Arkansas River, a little west of Pueblo. And Palmer had always intended to extend another line straight south into Mexico, so as to tap its riches for the benefit of his Rocky Mountain empire.

Palmer considered his position secure in Colorado, particularly in southern Colorado, and was leisurely planning to build south, when he suddenly found that he had an adversary worthy of his mettle in Vice-President and General Manager William B. Strong of the Atchison, Topeka and Santa Fe. For this road, which had built westward across the Colorado line from Topeka, Kansas, now threatened to extend branches north and south to drain off the traffic of the Denver and Rio Grande. Before Palmer realized what was happening, Strong had moved into the only available pass to the south, at Raton, New Mexico, a route already surveyed and virtually occupied by Palmer's road for its proposed extension to Mexico. Strong's chief engineer, A. A. Robinson, having seen General Palmer and officials of the Denver and Rio Grande on a train going to this pass, surmised that construction work was about to start there; he immediately assembled a crew of several hundred men, and at dawn next morning, when the Denver and Rio Grande forces arrived, the Santa Fe was in armed possession, thus effectively shutting off Palmer's entry into southern territory. This *coup de main* occurred on the 26th of February, 1868, and Palmer resolved that any further advantage to be obtained by the Santa Fe would not be without a struggle.

In April the warfare between the two roads was fiercely resumed when both sought to occupy the pass to the west, the Grand Cañon of the Arkansas, so as to penetrate westward through the mountains. This narrow gorge was so deep a defile that neither man nor beast had ever passed through it. Its perpendicular walls were 2,000 feet high and only 30 feet apart. When railroad construction was finally begun, the workmen had to start at the top and split the granite walls downward for hundreds of feet. Lowered by ropes suspended from the edges, they hung midway of the opening above the bed of the river until a foothold was secured by drilling and splitting. Jagged and irregular masses of rock overhung the roadbed 100 feet, and below the cooped-up Arkansas rushed by, a narrow thread of boiling water, imprisoned in a crack so deep that the sun seldom reached it.

The Rio Grande people, having possession of the telegraph lines, discovered that the Santa Fe was about to make a sudden dash into this cañon, and a spirited scramble for priority ensued. Strong of the Santa Fe was at El Moro when he heard that Palmer's engineers were moving to cut him out and that a gang of a hundred men had been despatched to begin work in the Royal Gorge. He instantly made application to the Rio Grande for a special train to convey him to the spot but was met by refusal. He then telegraphed to one of his surveying engineers at La Junta, ordering him to take an engine and run with all speed to Pueblo and thence to beat the Rio Grande force to Cañon City. Following this order, the surveyor arrived at Pueblo at three o'clock on the morning of the 19th of April; he asked the Rio Grande management for a narrow-gage locomotive to carry him to Cañon, but this likewise was refused. Unable to procure steam-power, this bold engineer mounted the swiftest horse he could find and struck out under whip and spur for the mountains. It was a ride of 45 miles, and the desperate emergency demanded that horse and rider should be strained to the uttermost. The Santa Fe engineer, Morley, felt that he must at all hazards beat the Rio Grande men into Cañon City, and as he had a few hours start, to do so was simply a matter of endurance. When he was within a few miles of the goal, however, his horse fell dead; but without stopping he picked himself up and ran at top speed the remainder of the way. Arriving in the town, where the sympathy of the people was given most heartily to the Atchison cause because Palmer's railroad had recently built to the rival town of El Moro, Morley quickly gathered a force of sympathetic helpers. These he rushed to the mouth of the cañon, two miles distant, and by the time the Rio Grande men arrived, half an hour later, the Santa Fe engineer had full possession.

But the Rio Grande forces, not to be foiled and never for a minute considering giving up the Royal Gorge to the stronger road, took possession a few miles above where the Santa Fe had begun working, erected armed forts, and began construction on their own account. Both roads now began to pour men and grading-teams into the Cañon and to fortify various points; and the men indulged in so many fights

SHOOTING BUFFALO ON THE LINE OF THE KANSAS PACIFIC
*Frank Leslie's Illustrated Newspaper, 1871.*

### THE GRAND CAÑON OF THE ARKANSAS

The Royal Gorge, for which the Denver and Rio Grande and the Santa Fe battled. The 1,260-foot suspension highway bridge now spanning the gorge is the highest bridge of any kind in the world, being 1,053 feet above the floor of the cañon. Courtesy of the Denver and Rio Grande Western Railroad.

that arrests were made daily. Palmer meanwhile carried the battle to the state courts, and within a week he had won his first legal victory in the struggle for possession of the Cañon by securing an injunction to stop the Santa Fe's work. Ten days later he had the injunction transferred to the Federal court, where, after several preliminary skirmishes, the judge finally permitted both roads to go forward in the Cañon, "neither to obstruct the other," though how this was to be done in a narrow gorge hardly big enough for one, the learned court did not say. Palmer then appealed the case to the United States Supreme Court.

But financial difficulties now pressed so heavily against the little Rio Grande road, and the Santa Fe, which had earned nearly $4,000,000 the previous year, was so much more powerful, that Palmer finally was forced in December, 1878, under pressure from the bondholders, to lease his road to the Santa Fe for 30 years, with the proviso that the Santa Fe should make no discriminations against Denver in its freight-rates. This was a bitter pill; but even with the completed tracks of the Rio Grande in the possession of the Santa Fe, Palmer was not licked. The great silver-mine center of Leadville was booming, but it had no rail outlet; and the General was determined to build a road into it and capture its rich traffic. For he had had frequent advices from his general freight-agent, Colonel David Child Dodge, concerning the huge shipments in prospect. Twelve thousand teams were freighting into the town, and they were already hauling 50,000 to 100,000 pounds of silver bullion a day, charging $18 a ton to Colorado Springs. And Dodge made such reports as these: "The Gallagher mine promises twenty-five tons of ore a day after May 1st"; "Harrison reduction works could ship 100 tons a day if they had the transportation. Want to contract for shipment of 100,000 pounds of ore and bullion." With such good prospects Palmer quietly and energetically set about trying to interest outside capital, and so successful was he that he secured funds for the construction of the railroad into Leadville despite the somewhat precarious financial position of the Denver and Rio Grande. Meanwhile, litigation over the right of way to the Grand Cañon of the Arkansas continued, for this had not been affected by the lease.

A new factor now entered the complex situation, when it began to be apparent that the Santa Fe was discriminating against Denver in its operation of the Rio Grande railway system. Freight-rates from Denver to the south had been immediately raised, and it was evident that Strong intended to favor the shippers of Kansas City and thus to cut off Denver's jobbing trade. Since this was a violation of the lease, General Palmer began efforts in the courts to get his property back. Moreover, the Santa Fe was accused of permitting the road to deteriorate, removing the rolling-stock, assisting a rival line to build into Leadville from Denver, and, in the opinion of Palmer, attempting to ruin the property. For these reasons he had the general support of the business interests of Colorado in the fight he now waged.

In March of 1879 the General began to send armed men back into the unoccupied stone forts he had built above the cañon of the Arkansas, where the Santa Fe was continuing its construction, while the Santa Fe armed its own men for defense. Under the leadership of a cool and daring engineer, De Remer, the Rio Grande work went forward. In April, with his men, he climbed down the cliffs and swam the Arkansas to a point near where the Santa Fe had built a bracket bridge, and there they began work for the Rio Grande. At Cañon City, at the mouth of the Gorge, there were twenty deputy sheriffs with orders to bring him in dead or alive, but not one dared adventure into the deep cañon where he had established himself and his party. One day a member of the party who was sent into Cañon City to get the mail and to arrange for food supplies was arrested. De Remer immediately went into town to arrange for bail, and Sheriff Ben Shaffer, who knew he was coming, determined to arrest him. But as the Sheriff came into the justice's court, De Remer dashed out, cut the reins of the Sheriff's horse with one slash of his knife, mounted him, and headed for the mouth of Royal Gorge, pursued by a yelling squad of officers and citizens. At the mouth of the Cañon he dismounted, turned the Sheriff's horse loose, and was soon safe among the crags and peaks, where none cared to follow him.

Another day, it is said, "De" was working with his men on Stonewall Point, when Holbrook, the Santa Fe engineer, brought in his gangs and began a flanking movement which, unless headed off, would gain his party a position farther up the cañon, above the Denver and Rio Grande. The only way De Remer could reach this point and head him off was by swimming. So he offered $20 apiece to every man who would follow him, darted down the crags, and plunged into the boiling river.

Not one man followed, but De Remer headed off the Santa Fe party and saved the location for the Rio Grande. He built seventeen forts and established a dead-line at the twentieth mile-post beyond which the Santa Fe men could not go. They built to that point, and the Denver and Rio Grande built beyond.

Each road thought the Supreme Court decision would be in its favor; but on April 21 the Santa Fe builders, who had completed 20 miles of track, were stopped by De Remer. With fifty armed men he forcibly held up the Santa Fe work, and when asked by whose authority he did so, he replied, "By the authority of the United States Supreme Court and these fifty men behind me." He had received word that the Court had at last decided in favor of the Rio Grande, giving it the sole right to build a road through the Cañon, and he compelled the Santa Fe to withdraw. This victory was quickly followed by a second, when, in June, General Palmer won his next legal advantage by obtaining a court order abrogating the Santa Fe lease and turning the road back to the Denver and Rio Grande.

Armed with writs to sheriffs in every county on his line, Palmer now began a systematic campaign of seizure of the property, as coolly and calculatingly as if he were still "the best cavalry officer in the Army, bar none." A group of armed men was mobilized in East Denver, marched to the general offices of the railroad in West Denver, broke open the doors with a tie for a battering-ram, and occupied the place with Denver and Rio Grande employees. A passenger train then made up by the new management triumphantly proceeded southward, systematically capturing stations all along the line and taking the captive station-agents aboard. At Colorado Springs the sheriff took possession of the railroad property and turned it over to General Palmer, while state cavalry preserved order. At Cucharas two Santa Fe men were reported killed and two wounded. At Pueblo the Santa Fe had imported Bat Masterson, famous sheriff of Dodge City, the toughest town in Kansas, to defend its property. This crack-shot sheriff had recruited a band of fighting-men and posted them in the railroad roundhouse ready to pick off the Palmer men as fast as they appeared. But the practical and suave treasurer of the Rio Grande, Robert F. Weitbrec, was aboard the train; reasoning that hired assassins could become peacemakers if offered a higher wage, he waved a flag of truce and succeeded in negotiating a cessation of hostilities with the truculent Bat. The last stronghold, the despatchers' office in Pueblo, fell when ex-Governor Alexander Cameron Hunt, a director of the Rio Grande and a "whirlwind of energy and indiscretion," proceeded up the line from El Moro with 200 armed men and stormed the office with much shooting but no loss of life. The doughty Governor then dashed on to Cañon City, where news of his imminent arrival had caused the Santa Fe employees hastily to escape on a locomotive, and took the place without a struggle. General Palmer must have felt like an old war-horse sniffing the smoke of battle as he surveyed his complete triumph and ordered timber forts to be erected around the depot at Pueblo and a garrison of armed men posted. It was reported that a virtual reign of terror existed in Pueblo, El Moro, and Trinidad, armed men patrolling the streets and outlets to the city, and that no one dared utter a word in favor of the Santa Fe for fear of death.

Upon appeal of the Santa Fe next day, the Rio Grande injunctions were transferred to the Federal court, and two weeks later the Rio Grande was ordered to return the property to the Santa Fe. And since a receiver was appointed for the Rio Grande who was favorable to its interests and those of Denver business men, this was peaceably done. Palmer had now won out in obtaining the right to build through the strategic Royal Gorge and also to have his road operated in a manner favorable to himself even though it was under lease to his rival. In January of the next year, 1880, the final decision was handed down, giving the Rio Grande the rights through the Royal Gorge and ordering the Santa Fe to turn over its tracks there to the Rio Grande upon suitable payments. Next month a treaty was signed at Boston whereby the Rio Grande agreed not to build to St. Louis or El Paso, the Santa Fe agreed not to build to Denver or Leadville, and the Santa Fe received $1,400,000 for the track it had laid.

Thus ended the most exciting episode in Western railroad-building. It was virtually a fight between the two individuals, Palmer and Strong, a campaign "which was much like the strife between feudal lords supported by their respective phalanxes." Palmer's victory was at least partly due to the loyalty of these phalanxes—his employees; for he had always conducted the affairs of the Denver and Rio Grande in such a way that it was considered a good railroad to work for, and his men liked him. When there was an opportunity to show what they thought of him and his road, they responded with a will, and there never was any doubt as to which management the employees of the road favored. Perhaps one underlying reason for Palmer's success as a railroad man was that deep down in his complex, many-sided personality there was a love of the physical fact of railroading which brought him close to his men—an appreciation quite distinct from building, or planning, or managing, a sheer delight in the engine as a living creature, a boyish love of riding with the engineer in his cab. Witness this letter to his Quaker friend, Clothier, when he was working for the Pennsylvania:

I thought that thee would enjoy the scenery in crossing the Alleghenies and in cutting through the Laurel and Chestnut Ridges with the gradually increasing Conemaugh, and finally in leaping across the rolling country that intervenes between Blairsville and Pittsburgh—to be set down at the portal of the West, on the site of old Fort du Quesne. But did thee relish any of it as much as our night ride up the mountain on the "Blue Ridge" locomotive the evening thee spent at Altoona? I find car-travelling quite tame now and one can certainly get tired in half the time boxed up in a long passenger car, that he would on the engine, watching the flame in the furnace, or the black smoke wreathing out of the chimney, and talking with the engineer and fireman of the wonderful machine which they control with such facility. In addition there is the wide open view over hill and valley—and "Kittanning," and "Allegrippus" and "Whippoorwill" (sealed volumes to the inside passengers) become as familiar to you in every outline, as the walls and ceiling of your own room at home.

And again:

You desire me to tell you what is new about Altoona. Suppose I do. Engine "156" has been fitted up with a fire brick deflector, and on being tried up the mountain yesterday, performed with great satisfaction. Her bonnet and spark-arrestor having been taken off her, she ran with a straight stack, and made steam much more freely with a 3⅞ nozzle than she did before with one of 3⅝ of an inch. This, of course, was extremely satisfactory—so also was the fact of her producing very little smoke and an inconsiderable amount of dirt, although using the gaseous Pittsburgh coal. Mike, the engineer, was of the opinion that she would bear a 4 inch nozzle—But on the trial being renewed in the afternoon, with Broad Gap Coal, it was found impossible to sustain the pressure. From some unaccountable cause, either bad firing, or the character of the fuel, the steam sank down and down, until it reached 75 lbs. and it was feared that we would come to a halt. This was all the more vexatious, as we had Mr. Scott the Superintendent along, with two young ladies, who, as they rode on the locomotive, could see everything that was going on. Moreover, in consequence of this great reduction in the draught of the engine, much more smoke was produced, and the ladies had their pretty faces tolerably well blacked—while the Superintendent was kept pretty busy with his fingers pulling the upper lid of his eye over the lower, to remove sparks. When they got off at the Tunnel (to descend in a hand car), the party looked very much as if a dexterous Bootblack had been manœuvering with his brush over their countenances.

I could tell you that 207 is having Gill's improvement applied to her; and that the variable exhaust on 114 is doing well, and has already saved, the engineer estimates, a half cord of wood in the round trip; and that the new turn-table in the Round House is finished, and works to a charm— and that the Vandevender Bridge has only her piers half-way up although the Boiler makers finished the trusses some time ago—but I feel doubtful whether these things will interest you. Nevertheless, they form the staple of the conversation here, and as a faithful correspondent, I must depict things as they are—not as we would have them. If you want to learn here what any one thinks of the Patent Brake, you can quickly get it. But if you want to know what is thought of the last article of the "Autocrat," you will have considerable difficulty.

Once Palmer had won his fight with the Santa Fe, he put aside the vagaries of legal wrangling and the heady delights of armed conflict and whole-heartedly applied himself to the extension of his railway system. Without any delay, he pushed the road on to the rich prize of Leadville, which he had eyed so longingly and long, there to be met with the enthusiastic and prodigal welcome of the mining Crœsus Horace A. W. Tabor. The first Denver and Rio Grande train to reach Leadville bore none other than the former President, General Ulysses S. Grant, just returning from a tour around the world; and Tabor, though invited to be a passenger on this train, hastened from Denver to Leadville by stage-coach so as to meet the General with all the pomp and glory possible as ruler of his own silver kingdom. When the first train arrived, 30,000 people filled the streets of Leadville, and the little frame station almost gave way with the crowd—and General Grant. General Palmer and Grant rode down the main street in an open barouche flanked by miners in buckskin waving bottles and flags. At the Tabor Opera House a group of miners sprinkled gold-dust on the backs of the four black horses as a symbol of Leadville's prodigality. Grant, after making a short speech from the balcony of a hotel, retired to listen to the incredible story of Leadville's inexhaustible riches as told by the irrepressible "Haw" Tabor, who punctuated his recital with much back-slapping of the ex-President as the high-balls and champagne made them all one big family. Thus the Denver and Rio Grande made its triumphal entry into the world's greatest bonanza silver-camp, from which over $2,000,000,000 worth of precious metals was to be taken, with the auspicious omen of an ex-President of the United States as an honored guest.

Now that he had won his fight for the Rio Grande, even if he had lost his opportunity to push south to Mexico, Palmer carried on with extraordinary vigor his projects for developing his railroad empire in Colorado. Five new branches were completed in three years, after which he finished a subsidiary road, the Rio Grande Western, to Salt Lake City, establishing a connecting link with the Union Pacific. So well had he carried out his original plans that within 13 years from receiving his charter he had completed every unit in the comprehensive project as first outlined with the exception of the road to Mexico and Southern California.

The completion of the Denver and Rio Grande Railroad system marked an epoch in the building of the new West, and it was a personal tribute to the genius of the one man who conceived it and constructed it and fought its battles and developed its territory. His monument will always be this great railroad threading the precarious passes of the Rocky Mountains, the central section of the steel arch which crosses the Continental Divide to connect two oceans.

# CHAPTER IV

## EARLY RAILROAD FINANCING

LOOKING back on the building of the first Western railroads, it is easy and natural to say that the promoters of each of them had a "sure thing," a bonanza which, without effort on their part, poured a steady golden stream into their strong-boxes. When we consider the rich, fertile, populous country through which these roads pass; the profitable traffic that has been theirs; the vast sums given by the Government as subsidies for building them; the manipulations by which further vast sums were caused to accrue to their backers; the various deals, often far from ethical, by means of which huge profits were made and legislative action influenced, we wonder if the whole early era of Western railroad-building was not simply a wild orgy of get-rich-quick speculation for the profit of a few favored insiders.

There is no question that enormous fortunes were made by the backers of these railroads. Congressional investigation cast some light on the millions amassed by Oliver and Oakes Ames and others from the building of the Union Pacific. General Palmer began life as a man of small means and, after his operations in the limited field of Colorado railroads, ended it living regally in a Tudor castle adjoining the Garden of the Gods, to which he imperially summoned all the members of his old Army regiment from Pennsylvania, providing special trains and weeks of princely entertainment. Thomas C. Durant's horses were the pride of Central Park and the admiration of New York. We need only contrast the humble beginnings of Collis P. Huntington and Mark Hopkins, partners in a Sacramento hardware store, of Leland Stanford, dealer in groceries and miner's supplies, and of Charles Crocker, peddler, iron-maker, gold-miner, and trader, with their financial preëminence after they built the Central Pacific to realize that their touch on the steel rails was the touch of Midas.

But what we have difficulty in realizing to-day is that, at the time these railroads were first proposed, they were regarded as wildcat schemes; that even with heavy government subsidies few capitalists wished to have anything to do with them; that without the possibility of most extraordinary gains no one would have touched the railroad enterprises.

When the engineer Theodore D. Judah conceived the idea of building the Central Pacific east from California and had made his preliminary surveys, he went to the established San Francisco capitalists for aid. But they told him that no railroad could be built if Congress did not pass a Pacific-railroad act, which was doubtful, and even if it did, the road could not be completed for 10 or 20 years; they therefore declined to participate in any such uncertain project. Judah, who thought he could finance the road by getting a million subscriptions of $100 each, then went to Sacramento to try to get funds to make further surveys, and he held public meetings, at which nobody subscribed very much, "some a barrel of flour and some a sack of potatoes." If it had not been for the willingness to gamble of the four Sacramento merchants, Huntington, Hopkins, Crocker, and Stanford, he would not have been able to continue his surveys, and four vast California fortunes would never have been made. These men, with a few others, agreed to share the expenses of Judah's work across the Sierras, estimating that it would probably cost them $15,000 or $20,000 apiece. And so the great Central Pacific–Southern Pacific railway system, which came to monopolize the traffic of California, had its beginning.

When General Palmer initiated the Denver and Rio Grande, he gathered a few friends of himself and William A. Bell around him, obtained subscriptions in England through Bell's acquaintances and in Philadelphia through his own contacts, and began the project of building a road from Denver, population 4,800, to Pueblo, population 500, without government aid and with no visible means of support. Adequate financing of the road could come only through his own clever manipulations, and its support had to rest entirely on his own faith, enthusiasm, and personality.

As to the deep and devious devices used to finance and extract profits from the Union Pacific, it need only be said that, despite enormous land-grants and heavy subsidies made by the Federal Government for the building of the road, New York capitalists would not put money into it; that the friends of Durant were so doubtful that they refused to increase their small initial subscriptions until he made himself personally responsible for three-fourths of the $2,000,000 needed; and that the much-criticized building contracts entered into by Oakes Ames and other insiders could not be sublet to outside contractors at any price and were characterized at the time by Horace Clarke, Cornelius Vanderbilt's son-in-law and a director of the New York Central, as "the wildest contracts he ever knew to be made by a civilized man."

When such risks were undertaken, it is not surprising that those who took them felt they had a right to large, even exorbitant, returns. The favorite device by which the financial backers of the Western railroads obtained their first and largest profits was through the organization of contracting companies. Once money was procured by the railroad company for the building of track, a second company would be organized by the insiders to contract for the construction, at highly profitable figures. The backers of the project, sitting as the board of directors of the railway, would enter into a contract with themselves, as directors of the contracting company, to build the road at so much a mile, and when the trackage was completed, the large profits would be divided. The Union Pacific carried on these building operations through the Crédit Mobilier and other subsidiary organizations; the Central Pacific, through Charles Crocker and Company and the Contract and Finance Company. The financial details of the transactions of the Crédit Mobilier came to light through a Congressional investigation, which rocked the nation, smudged a number of Senators and Representatives with the tar of bribery, and caused the official censure of Oakes Ames, member of Congress and brother and partner of the president of the Union Pacific. There is no reason to believe that the profits of the Contract and Finance Company were proportionately any less; but the books of the company having providentially disappeared, no detailed analysis of its operations was ever made public.

The Pacific Railroad Act of 1862 provided that the Union Pacific could build from Omaha to the California state line and the Central

Pacific from San Francisco to the Nevada line with a government subsidy of one-half the land in a strip 20 miles wide on either side of the track, a total of 33,000,000 acres. To provide ready money the Government agreed to turn over to the railroad, as certain sections of the tracks were completed, official bonds of the United States as follows: east of the Rockies and west of the Sierras, sixteen $1,000 6 per cent 30-year bonds per mile; from the base line of the Rockies through the mountains, three times this subsidy, or $48,000 per mile; for the plateau region between the Rockies and the Sierras, $32,000 a mile. Thus the Government offered $61,000,000 for the building of the Pacific railroad, not as a gift, but as a loan to be repaid from earnings.

It would seem that, with these rich subsidies, capital would have leapt at the chance of sharing in the enterprise. Yet the stock-subscription books of the Union Pacific were opened throughout the country in 1862 with the discouraging result that only thirty-one shares of $1,000 each were subscribed and $17,300 paid in. Capitalists felt that the project was too much of a gamble; prices of labor and materials were too high; the country was distraught by the war and most of the able-bodied men were in the Army; there was a long gap between the Eastern railways and Omaha, making it necessary to transport supplies by the Missouri River. Hence, few wanted to invest in so hazardous and costly an enterprise. Had it not been for visionary faith or business shrewdness, or a combination of both, on the part of Vice-President Thomas C. Durant, the building of the Union Pacific would have been postponed indefinitely. But he was so anxious to proceed, at all hazards, that he made stock subscriptions of his own and worked assiduously to secure others from his friends. By dint of much effort and by promising to buy stock back should the original purchasers wish to withdraw, he obtained $218,000 from a group which included August Belmont, of New York; J. Edgar Thompson, president of the Pennsylvania Railroad, of Philadelphia; and Joseph H. Scranton, of Scranton, Pennsylvania. Ground was immediately broken at Omaha, on December 2, 1863, some $200,000 or $300,000 was borrowed, and the road was constructed for 40 miles; when, all funds being exhausted, the company began to sell its materials and cars to raise money.

No further support from eastern capitalists could be obtained until Congress passed the Act of 1864 doubling the government land-grants, permitting the railroad to issue bonds to the same value as the government bonds, and relegating the government loans to the rank of second mortgages. Even then it was hard for the road to get money, but $2,000,000 was finally subscribed and the contracting began. Now the original backers began to see a way to get their first profits. A committee of the board entered into a contract with one H. M. Hoxie to build 100 miles of track at $50,000 per mile, later extended to 247.45 miles and to cost a total of over $12,000,000. Hoxie was assisted in his contracting operations by being exempted from paying more than $85,000 for any one bridge; the cost of iron above $130 a ton at Omaha was to be borne by the Union Pacific; if cottonwood ties had to be "Burnetized" to make them more durable, 16 cents apiece was to be paid. The contract also provided that Hoxie should cause to be subscribed $500,000 of capital stock of the railway at par, which, as a matter of fact, was worth only 30 per cent of this amount at the time. However, Hoxie was never called upon to do any of these things, because, according to agreement, he obligingly assigned his contract to persons designated by Vice-President Durant. To take up the contract $1,600,000 was subscribed, and the greater part of this liability was divided as follows: Thomas C. Durant, $600,000; C. S. Bushnell, $400,000; H. W. Gray, $200,000; Charles A. Lambard, $100,000. Only one-fourth of the subscriptions was paid in, however, and with this $400,000 the partners started in to execute the Hoxie contract. But even with the prospect of large profit it offered, some of them grew so worried that they were willing to lose their first payments and refused to pay the second instalment. Consequently Durant had to look for more and new capital, and to this end he succeeded in interesting the brothers Oakes and Oliver Ames, of Easton, Massachusetts.

Oakes Ames, who, with his brother, was to become the ruling power in the Union Pacific, was described as follows by a contemporary writer:

Mr. Ames's reputation as a financier stood high throughout the country. His business life had been commenced by the manufacture of shovels on an enormous scale; he was the King of Spades for the whole land. The failure of a firm, the largest in the world, engaged in the manufacture of agricultural implements, and on whose stock he held a mortgage, had made him and his firm the fortunate owners of other factories at Worcester and Groton Junction. Starting from one of the small homes of New England, he had become a millionaire before he arrived at middle age. As years rolled on and wealth increased, his business reputation lifted him into Congress. In that body he was a prominent member of the Pacific Railroad Committee, and must have been thoroughly cognizant of these great offers, if he did not, as is most probable, actually inspire them. He was honest, as the world reckons honesty; his word was perfectly good, nor were his plans above or below the morality of Wall Street. He well knew the commercial value of a reputation for integrity, and made that value his standard. So clear-headed was he, that doing a private business of millions of dollars a year, though guiding the affairs of a large firm, carrying on three separate factories, attending Congress, and building more than one railroad, he kept no books and employed no bookkeeper for his private affairs; nothing but dates was ever forgotten by this capacious brain. He had no dread of large sums; no objections to taking a contract for forty-seven millions of dollars provided the margin for profit was sufficiently large; and he testified that he never once saw the books which kept the account of his contract for that amount. He believed to some extent, in the integrity of men, but acted on their selfishness; and he worked for profit rather than for patriotism. He would have the road built for the good of the nation; but he took hold of it for his own advantage.

It soon became evident that large capital could not be raised under the scheme first used by Durant, that of assigning contracts to a group of partners, for under this arrangement each member was liable to the extent of his property. So it was decided to form a corporation with wide powers of operation and limited liability. Such a corporation, the Pennsylvania Fiscal Agency, was discovered already organized but inactive. It had been modeled after the Crédit Mobilier of France, and to it, as agent of Durant and Ames, went George Francis Train, famous as an eccentric and promoter, who purchased its charter for $26,645. When this charter was taken to New York, the corporation was rechristened the Crédit Mobilier of America, and each large stockholder of the Union Pacific subscribed for the same number of shares of its stock, at $10 each, as he owned in the railroad company. Durant took 6,041 shares; Oliver Ames, 3,125; and Oakes Ames, 900 shares.

Now the operations that later drew the fire of Congressional investigation were begun. The Hoxie contract was assigned to the Crédit

Mobilier, and $2,500,000 was subscribed for its stock. Meanwhile, the bonds advanced to the Union Pacific by the Government were sold for what they would bring, and about $4,000,000 of the Union Pacific bonds were used for borrowing at an annual interest of 14 to 15 per cent. But all funds were soon exhausted, and a meeting was called at the Fifth Avenue Hotel to increase the capital stock of the Crédit Mobilier by 50 per cent. Even at this stage of the game it was necessary to hold out special inducements to get stockholders to increase their subscriptions; so it was voted to give the holders of stock a $1,000 railroad bond for every $1,000 they subscribed to the Crédit Mobilier. Since the Union Pacific bonds were then selling at 90 cents or more on the dollar, the Crédit Mobilier stock could thus be obtained for five or ten cents on the dollar. Nearly all stockholders accepted the offer. But even after the terms of the profitable Hoxie contract had been extended to cover 58 additional miles of work, at $50,000 a mile, the finances of the Union Pacific and the Crédit Mobilier were still strained, and capital was hard to get. It was so difficult to interest investors that C. S. Bushnell, one of the directors, was commissioned to undertake the sale of a large block of first-mortgage bonds on which the road was borrowing money at the rate of 14½ per cent. Only by means of a widespread advertising and selling campaign did he succeed in disposing of these bonds, but his publicity effort brought in $10,0000,000 and raised the price of the bonds from 90 to 95.

After several minor contracts had been arranged, the railroad entered into what has been called the largest contract ever made, up to that time, with one man. It was with Oakes Ames for the construction of 667 miles of road, at prices varying according to the character of the country, and it aggregated $47,915,000. The contractor was to receive payment as follows: 100 miles at $42,000 per mile, 167 at $45,000, 100 at $96,000, 100 at $80,000, 100 at $90,000, and 100 at $96,000. The prices were high for the eastern sections, but not exorbitant for the western sections; and here again considerable risk was involved, for the contract stated that if proceeds from the mileage bonds were not sufficient to pay for the building of the difficult portions of the road, the contractor must himself subscribe for enough stock at par to furnish money for meeting the deficit. By complicated legal arrangements this contract was assigned to the Crédit Mobilier, and a third contract was made with James W. Davis to build the road from the 935 mile-post to Ogden.

Undoubtedly, the cost of the road was high under these contracts, and there was considerable juggling of business arrangements, so that in at least one case (that of the Boomer contract) duplicate payments were made by the Union Pacific to two contractors for work that had been performed by only one. But the fact remains that up to the fall of 1867, when the Ames contract was let, the Union Pacific project was still so precarious that it was obliged to borrow money in New York at the ruinous rates of 18 and 19 per cent, and the stock of the Crédit Mobilier had never had any market value.

Moreover, this was no ordinary building effort. The actual cost of the construction of the road was greatly increased by reason of the necessity of completing it quickly, and the saving of six years of the time allowed for building by the Government doubled the cost to the contractors. If the work had not been completed until the time-limit fixed, July 1, 1874, the weight of interest on borrowed money, with no income from traffic to offset it, would have crushed the Union Pacific. Consequently, speed was made the essence of the building contract: four or five miles of track were laid per day, and the cost of this one item of labor rose accordingly from $600 to $1,500 a mile. Work stopped neither summer nor winter, and Dodge declares that in winter the cost of blasting the frozen earth was sometimes as great as that of blasting rock, as high as $3 a cubic yard. He says:

We laid the track over the Wasatch Range in the dead of winter on top of snow and ice, and I have seen a whole train of cars, track and all, slide off the bank and into the ditch as a result of a thaw and the ice that covered the banks. We built almost as rapidly through the winter as we did during the summer, notwithstanding the short cold days and long nights, but it was at an immense cost. We estimated that the work during that winter made an extra cost to the road of at least $10,000,000.

The Government further increased expenses by stipulating that only American iron could be used, increasing the cost $10 for every ton of rails laid. The government commissioners interfered constantly, requiring, for example, against Dodge's advice, that a cut be made through each rise in the Laramie Plains, making the track a dead level instead of conforming to the contour of the land; between $5,000,000 and $10,000,000 was spent following out this order, and it was then found that snow blockaded the cuts in winter, so they all had to be refilled. The Government required that machine-shops be built at the crossing of the North Platte, and although these were worth nothing to the company, they cost $300,000. Finally, one of the commissioners demanded $25,000 before he would approve the work done by the railroad, and this blood-money was paid. Moreover, although the Ames contract looks juicy to-day, the risk involved in building the more difficult portions of the road was so great that it was impossible to sublet the work to any established contractors. And there was a time in the progress of the enterprise when it would have been delayed for years if Oakes Ames had not sacrificed his personal fortune, saying, "We must save the credit of the road. I will fail."

In the days when money was hard to collect for the Union Pacific, Durant even went so far as to enlist the coöperation of his old enemy, General Dodge, in attempting to lure the dollars from the pockets of recalcitrant investors. In 1866 he organized a party of "150 prominent citizens, capitalists and ladies to see the railroad and the country." This party, dubbed the "joy-riders of 1866," included Sidney Dillon, John Duff, John Sherman, Senator Wade, Joseph Medill, George M. Pullman, Robert Todd Lincoln, Monsieur Odilon Barrot, Secretary of the French Embassy, Marquis Chambrun, and "Mr. and Mrs. George Francis Train and maid." In addition, there were certain government directors of the Union Pacific—the Hon. W. M. White, General Simpson, and General Curtis, who rode in a coach which had been built for Abraham Lincoln, the one that also bore his body to Springfield.

J. R. Perkins tells the story in his biography of General Dodge: *

When Durant and party arrived in Omaha their equipment resembled an old-fashioned traveling show. There was a band, a caterer, six cooks, a photographer, three tonsorial artists, a sleight-of-hand performer, and a printing press. They had provisions enough to feed a regiment and of a kind that a regiment never ate. One of the menus included, beef, mutton,

---

* J. R. Perkins, *Trails, Rails and War* (copyright, 1929). Quoted by special permission of the publishers, the Bobbs-Merrill Company.

roasted ox, broiled ham, corned beef, roasted antelope, Chinese duck, Roman goose, peas, tomatoes, asparagus, salad, potatoes, cheese, pickles, pineapples, strawberries, damsons, peaches and cherries, to which should be added, as representing the principal feature of the unpublished wine-list, Verzenay, Ve Max Sutaine Et Cie, T. W. & G. D. Bayaud, Sole agents of the United States and Canada.

From Omaha the excursionists went out over the new Union Pacific Railroad to the camp Dodge had prepared on the Loup Fork River, and, after a big supper, a bonfire dance and a musical program, they retired to their tents. At three o'clock the next morning Dodge took an engine and crossed the river to where Major North was camped with his Pawnee scouts, loaded them on the coal-tender, the pilot, and wherever an Indian could cling, and at dawn backed across the river to the camp of sleeping easterners. The Pawnees, following instructions to the letter, stole into the camp fully dressed in their war trappings and began to whoop at the top of their voices. The surprise was so complete that for the next minute great excitement prevailed and a couple of the ladies found it convenient to faint. But the whole affair ended in a friendly dance around the fire followed by breakfast, and the Indians left the camp laden with gifts. Dodge conducted the excursionists on to the end of the road, and there were hunting parties in which buffalo and antelope were rounded up in droves so great that the amateur hunters could not miss them, and many Union Pacific bonds were negotiated over the fires that roasted the meat, just as the shrewd vice-president of the road had planned.

In 1867, however, when it became fully apparent that the line was to be a success and that huge profits were to be realized from its building, there was no further difficulty in securing funds, and stock in the Crédit Mobilier suddenly rose from nothing to a premium. Those who held it, for the most part, refused to sell, but the few sales recorded were for such fancy prices as $260 a share.

As to how much profit was actually pocketed in building the Union Pacific, estimates differ. One writer of the period makes the following appraisal:

### What It Cost the Nation

| | | |
|---|---|---|
| Hoxie Contract | .......... | $12,974,416.24 |
| Boomer " | .......... | 1,104,000.00 |
| Ames " | .......... | 57,140,102.94 |
| Davis " | .......... | 23,331,768.10 |
| Total | .......... | $94,650,287.28 |

### What It Cost the Crédit Mobilier

| | | |
|---|---|---|
| Hoxie Contract | ........... | $ 7,806,183.33 |
| Boomer " | ........... | 0,000,000.00 |
| Ames " | ........... | 27,285,141.99 |
| Davis " | ........... | 15,629,633.62 |
| Total | ................. | $50,720,958.94 |
| Profit | ................. | $43,929,328.34 |

On the other hand, Henry Kirke White's economic study, *The History of the Union Pacific Railway*, published by the University of Chicago in 1895, after exhaustive calculations of the value of the stocks and bonds given in payment for the work, reaches the conclusion that "the total profit appears to be $16,710,432.82, or slightly above 27½ per cent of the cost of the road. Considering the character of the undertaking and the time when it was carried through, this does not seem an immoderate profit."

But in the Seventies, that drab period of discouragement, hard times, and disillusionment following the war, there was fertile soil for the muck-raker, and the affairs of the Union Pacific received ample attention. To its own ethical lapses, which were serious enough, were added other imaginary sins of omission and commission until it became a symbol of all that was depraved and corrupting in public life. As the New York *Sun* remarked, "The public has long known in a vague sort of way that the Union Pacific railroad was a gigantic steal." An investigation was started by Congress, and Oakes Ames, Representative from Massachusetts, was given a vote of censure, being accused of trying to bribe every member who was found holding Crédit Mobilier stock. As a matter of fact, his crime seems to have lain in selling them that stock at a price below market value when it was rising fast, not to influence any specific vote, but to get friends for the road among influential Congressmen. The result was that many political fortunes were ruined, including that of Oakes Ames himself.

General Dodge sums up his ideas on the profits made thus:

The capitalization of the contracting company was only $1,000,000 at first and that company had to raise and expend $55,000,000 to build the road so when you apply the profits of those days to that large sum of money, it was small, but when you apply those profits to $1,000,000 of capital it was very large; and everybody took it that the simple investment of $1,000,coo carried these great profits to those men, when, in fact, they had to raise the $55,000,000 and go under obligations and take chances that very few would touch when the opportunity was presented to them.

However distrustful of the Union Pacific conservative investors might be, in the end even the most sanguine hopes of its promoters were realized. At the request of the directors Dodge had estimated that the earnings might be $5,000 a year per mile, and to arrive at this figure he had boldly claimed all the traffic between America and Australia, Japan, and China, as well as the transcontinental trade. Yet within 10 years the earnings rose to nearly $12,000 a mile, and the road that "had cost three times as much as it was worth came to be worth many times more than the three times as much as it cost."

Out in California, those sanguine small-town merchants, Hopkins, Huntington, Stanford, and Crocker, found equal difficulty in inducing capitalists to believe that any money could be made out of such a crack-brained scheme as the Central Pacific Railway. The bankers knew that the Sierra Nevada Mountains, 150 miles wide, offered an almost impregnable barrier, requiring an ascent from Sacramento of nearly 7,000 feet in a distance of 105 miles; that from November to January the mountain trails were impassable because of snow; and that the prices of supplies were exorbitant because of both the war and the difficulty of getting them to California from the East without a railroad. Nevertheless, the Central Pacific Railroad Company was organized, in 1861, by these dealers in hardware, groceries, and miner's supplies, with a capital stock of $8,500,000 divided into $100 shares, of which each of the four merchants and the chief engineer, Theodore Judah, subscribed 150 shares. So slowly were funds collected, however, and so difficult were the surveying problems encountered, that it was not until 1863 that ground was broken for the railroad. On January 8, with a band playing in the rain and a crowd standing on bundles of straw to keep their feet dry, Leland Stanford, who had by this time become Governor of California, lifted the first shovel of dirt, on the river levee of Sacramento, and Charles Crocker called for nine cheers for the Central Pacific Railroad.

The first Pacific Railroad Act, that of 1862, was substantially influenced by the lobbying of Judah; but though it granted large subsidies of land and loans to the Central Pacific, as to the Union Pacific, it did not induce purchases of the stock of the railroad. The subscription books were kept open in San Francisco, in an office at the corner of Bush and Montgomery Streets, during November and December, 1862, and February, 1863, with a net result of fifteen shares sold. Crocker personally went to Virginia City and tried to sell stock. Of this experience he said: "They wanted to know what I expected the road would earn. I said I did not know, though it would earn good interest on the money invested, especially to those who went in at bed rock. 'Well,' they said, 'do you think it will make 2 per cent a month?' 'No,' said I, 'I do not.' 'Well,' they answered, 'we can get 2 per cent a month for our money here,' and they would not think of going into a speculation that would not promise that at once."

There was little sale for either stock or mortgage bonds, and Stanford says he bought back 2,300 shares of Central Pacific stock to accommodate a disgusted stockholder at 10 cents on the dollar. Even with the amended Pacific Railroad Act passed in 1864, which doubled the subsidies offered by the Government, it was apparent that the Central Pacific could not be built quickly without additional help. Accordingly the partners started a vigorous campaign for local aid. The arguments used were that the railroad would increase land-values, give wider markets, denser population, higher wages, lower prices, and greater prosperity. An advocate of subsidies to the road in Tulare County stated his reasons thus:

It costs for passage to San Francisco from Visalia $25 and consumes generally a day and a half. By rail the trip could be made in eight hours, at a cost of $10, thus saving $15 and nearly a day in time. If on the average, each adult makes one visit per annum to the upper country, and taking 1,300, the number of registered voters, as the adult population, it costs every passenger for the round trip $50 in cash and three days in time—excess over railway fare, $30; board for two extra days, $4; value of time at $2 per day, $4; total excess $38; total loss to 1,300 passengers, $49,400. I contend, therefore, that the people of Tulare County are now actually paying, in addition to the loss or inconvenience resulting from isolation from market, the sum of $77,780 per annum, for the privilege of being without a railroad.

The result of this propaganda of the partners was that they finally obtained from San Francisco a donation of $650,000 on which they realized $475,000; from Sacramento, a subscription to stock yielding $190,000; and from Placer County, $160,000. Later they secured from the State of California the assumption of 7 per cent interest on 20-year bonds, amounting to the sum of $1,500,000. But all these funds were a long time coming, and meanwhile the company struggled to meet expenses.

One of the first things to be done was to erect an office building for the railway enterprise, and Judah proudly came forward with a design which he said would cost "only twelve thousand dollars." Huntington snorted, took up a piece of chalk, and drew on the floor of his hardware store his design for the building. It was completed that same day and cost $150. Thus did the partners watch the expenses of the great railway enterprise as carefully as their own invoices of spades and shovels and cases of tomatoes. It was only thus that they could meet the bills for building their road, for none of them was wealthy, and, in the early stages of construction, credit was hard to get. Stanford's wholesale grocery store was assessed at $32,900. Huntington had a personal tax assessment of $7,222, and his partner Hopkins of $9,700, while their store was rated at $34,115. So cautious were these partners that they never bought a dollar's worth of stock in a mine, though mines were all around them. They never speculated in any form, never had a branch house, never sent out a drummer to get business, never gave more than $500 credit to anyone, never sued for a debt, and made it a cardinal rule never to sell any but good articles at the highest price they could get. And in the first meetings of the associates at 54 K Street, Huntington laid down the rule, soon to be prodigally violated, "We will pay as we go and never run a dollar in debt. If we can't pay a hundred workmen, we will pay fifty; if not fifty, ten; if not ten, one. We will employ no more than we can pay."

The work did not stop even though it was hard for the merchants to meet the pay-roll. In 1864 they sent Judah east to try to sell their franchise; but he died of fever crossing the Isthmus of Panama, and they had now gone so far that they could not turn back. The only thing to do, if they expected to recover their original investment, was to keep on putting in more. Fortunately, Eastern capital would now buy the government bonds, even if it shied away from Central Pacific stock, so they were able to keep on. But expenses were terrific. Iron rails cost $91.70 per ton at the mill, with $51 added for transportation across Panama. Blasting-powder cost as much as $6 a pound, hay was $100 a ton, and Stanford says that he sold a potato for $2.50. Huntington tells of inspecting the line and meeting some teams carrying ties in the mountains, and one can imagine how his merchant's heart bled at what he saw:

They had seven ties on that wagon. I asked where they were hauled from, and they said from a certain cañon. They said it took three days to get a load up to the top of the Wahsatch Mountains and to get back to their work. I asked them what they had a day for their teams, and they said $10. This would make the cost of each tie more than $6. I passed back that way in the night in January, and I saw a large fire burning near the Wahsatch summit, and I stopped to look at it. They had, I think, some twenty-five ties burning. They said it was so fearfully cold they could not stand it without having a fire to warm themselves.

It did not take the partners long to come to the conclusion that if they were to profit largely from the building of the Central Pacific, they would have to take over the building contracts. After a few contracts had been let to outsiders, Charles Crocker resigned from the directorate, organized Charles Crocker and Company, and began the building of the road. Various arguments were publicly advanced for this policy: "The independent contractors got to bidding against each other for laborers, and thus put up the price; the smaller contractors quarreled with each other, and tried to 'scoop' labor from each other; they did not finish their sections in consecutive order, they did not hurry, and could not be sufficiently controlled." In June, 1865, Hopkins made a report to the president and directors of the Central Pacific which dwelt upon the necessity of rapid construction to capture the passenger and freight traffic between Sacramento and Virginia City and to comply with the acts of Congress and the state legislature. As Professor Stuart Daggett of the University of California states it, in his *History of the Southern Pacific*: "Persons of large capital, he said, seemed unwilling to bind themselves to construct the road as rapidly as necessary. Charles Crocker and Company, on the other hand, had pushed and were pushing the work with extraordinary vigor and success, and had in all cases complied with the orders and directions of the officers of the company. He recommended, therefore, that arrangements be continued with that firm, at rates specified in an accompanying resolution."

These rates were not by the mile but according to the class of work, such as clearing, grubbing, and rock-excavation, and Charles Crocker was left to make his classifications as he saw fit. Payments were to be made partly in cash and partly in stock valued at 30 cents on the dollar. The Central Pacific purchased the cars and locomotives needed and charged them to Crocker at cost. Under this contract the total payments made to Crocker were $23,654,828.15. This amounted to an average of $69,210 a mile, although he accepted his first contract out of Sacramento at $13,800 a mile. From this it appears that the profits were considerable, and these he undoubtedly shared with his associates, though just how is not clear. Despite the favorable contract, heavy risk was still involved, and Crocker says of his situation at this time, "It was decided that I should go on immediately and see what I could do. I did go on until we got tied up in suits and I had to stop. I could not get any money. They had all the money I had, and all I could borrow. That was the time that I would have been very glad to take a clean shirt, lose all I had, and quit."

In 1867, when the road had reached the Nevada state line, the partners decided that it would be best for Charles Crocker and Company to retire. They needed to attract outside capital, they said, before tackling the rest of the line, so they organized the Contract and Finance Company with a capital of $5,000,000. With this as an inducement, they again tried to interest leading capitalists of New York and San Francisco, but the effort was a failure, and the associates had to take up the stock themselves. As with the Crocker contracts, the Central Pacific provided the equipment and iron used and billed it to the Company at cost. There is no evidence to show that the partners paid any money for their stock. They gave their notes and then, as individuals, loaned money to the Finance Company to carry on its operations. The first contract was for 552 miles of track at $86,000 per mile, half in cash, half in Central Pacific stock. Combining the Crocker contracts, the Central Pacific paid out to these two contracting companies a total of $33,761,992.72 in cash, $3,000,000 in bonds, and $38,437,710.32 in stock. As to the profits, Professor Daggett has this to say:

If the conclusions of the United States Pacific Railway Commission are to be relied upon, and they were made by engineers relatively soon after the completion of the road, the builders of the Central Pacific were able to accomplish their contracts with the cash and the proceeds of the company's bonds that were turned over to them, and to retain their Central Pacific stock as a clear profit. If we compare this stock surplus with the probable cash investment in the road, taking the shares at any reasonable valuation, say at $15 or $20 per share, the profit does not seem excessive. If we compare it with the contributions of the associates, however, and this is the more reasonable because the associates received the full benefit of the difference between cost and receipts, it represents, on the most conservative calculation, 500 or 600 per cent for an investment which probably did not exceed $1,000,000, over a period of six years. To this should be added the proceeds of the land grant and of the local subsidies.

Whatever may be said of the extent of the profits, it is equally true that the risk was also great. Daggett says that "at the time when the construction of the Central Pacific Railroad was finished the private property of every one of the directors of the company was mortgaged up to the limit of all his individual credit would possibly allow and bear. The notes of the four associates were outstanding everywhere, many of them bearing interest rates as high as from 10 to 12 per cent, and the statement is made that Leland Stanford alone upon one occasion had his account at the bank overdrawn to the extent of $1,300,000."

Yet we can hardly agree with the speech Stanford made when the golden spike was driven to join the Central Pacific and Union Pacific at Promontory Point. He criticized the Federal Government for its interference with the project, which was doubtless irritating enough at times, and in a burst of arrogance he declared that the subsidies granted the Central Pacific by the Government were more of a hindrance than a help. Dan Casement, the contractor, probably reflected the feelings of all present when he climbed on the shoulders of his brother and shouted to Stanford, "Mister President, if this here subsidy has been such a big detriment to the building of your road, I move you, sir, that it be returned to the Government with your compliments."

Whatever criticism may be leveled against it, the financing of the building of the Central Pacific and the Union Pacific was simple and childlike in comparison with the complicated operations that were indulged in later. Lawyers, business geniuses, and financiers combined their talents to create a complex financial structure for the railroads of the country which permitted the insiders to reap enormous profits and often to squeeze out other investors for large losses. The owners of the larger railroads controlled smaller roads which they leased to the larger at exorbitant rentals, turning surplus earnings into deficits. The directors also often made it a point to own the companies that made the repairs on the railroads, built and owned the bridges, operated the connecting ferries, sold the coal and supplies; and every operation was apt to turn profits into their pockets. New issues of stocks and bonds flowed forth from the printing-presses in bewildering variety, part being sold to investors, part being freely bestowed on the insiders, with the result that the capital structures, upon which interest and dividends had to be paid, were highly inflated. To meet the charges on these watered securities freight-rates had to be raised to inordinate heights, farmers and producers suffered, and the consumer had to pay the bill. When the bill grew so staggeringly heavy that it could no longer be borne, one after another of the railroads went through bankruptcy, receivership, and reorganization, with consequent loss to the owners of the stock, particularly the small owners. And the outcome was a continual tightening of the regulations by which the Government sought to control these servants of the public.

# CHAPTER V

ONE important source of revenue that was open to the backers of the early Western railroads was the building of cities. The fact that transportation facilities are of first importance in the development of centers of population had long been recognized in America. In 1792 Philadelphia interests spent the then enormous sum of $465,000 to build a 62-mile stone highway, the Lancaster Turnpike, and it quickly paid for itself by the trade it brought into the Quaker City. The Erie Canal poured the freight of the North and West into the Hudson and built the imperial city of New York. Washington had made its bid to bring traffic from the Middle West by way of the Chesapeake and Ohio Canal, a project to cost millions of dollars. Baltimore, determined to hold on to her commercial supremacy, countered this move with the most revolutionary and spectacular scheme of all—the building of America's first railroad, the Baltimore and Ohio.

In the West, St. Louis calmly and majestically occupied her position as Queen City of the Mississippi, her hundreds of river-boats drawing in traffic from as far away as St. Paul, 740 miles to the north; New Orleans, 1,200 miles south; Council Bluffs, 677 miles west on the Missouri; and Pittsburgh, 1,160 miles east on the Ohio. Disdainfully she looked at the little muddy, windy settlement at the foot of Lake Michigan, to the north, until she found that the men who lived there had made an important discovery. They had found that they could beat her in the race for commercial power by making their town a magnet for steel rails and centering there the transportation system of the country. And St. Louis was distressed to see that these shrewd and aggressive business men, disregarding all obstacles, were by sheer determination building a great city at Chicago. It was then that the editor of the *Missouri Republic* cried in anguish:

Have these people greater enterprise than ours? They do not appear to have greater industry or greater economy. They haven't greater natural advantages or acquired capital, yet whenever anything is to be done for the good of Chicago, someone is found to do it; whether to build a railroad or an elevator or a cattle pen or to prevent others building them for the advantage of some other place, there Chicago is, to do or to hinder the doing, as may be to her interest. Keen, sharp-sighted and long-sighted, quick and bold to the verge of audacity, persistent and, the censorious say, unscrupulous, they rush on, rejecting doubts and conquering difficulties, to triumphant prosperity.

In uttering his cry of protest against the stripling city that was taking the railroads and commercial supremacy away from St. Louis, this newspaper man expressed the formula that has been successfully followed again and again in city-building: natural advantages plus transportation facilities plus aggressive men make cities. Since most places that men select for the sites of their communities have some natural advantages and the coming of transportation is a matter that can be influenced by individuals, the formula can almost be reduced to the simple phrase, Men make Cities. Given the leadership of aggressive and far-sighted men and a tolerably favorable site for a city, transportation will come, business will come, population will come. Astute railroad-builders early realized that this was to be the story of the building of the great commercial centers of the West, and they acted upon it to their own advantage.

The Central Pacific crowd played one existing California settlement against another in their effort to raise funds. As a member of the California Constitutional Convention of 1879 put it,

They start out their railway track and survey their line near a thriving village. They go to the most prominent citizens of that village and say, "If you will give us so many thousand dollars we will run through here; if you do not we will run by," and in every instance where the subsidy was not granted, that course was taken, and the effect was just as they said, to kill off the little town. Here was the town of Paradise, in Stanislaus County; because they did not get what they wanted, they established another town 4 miles from there. In every instance where they were refused a subsidy, in money, unless their terms were acceded to, they have established a depot near to the place, and always have frozen them out.

The Union Pacific people took a proprietary interest in Cheyenne and the other towns that were to be their division points, and they also played communities against each other, beginning with their encouragement of the fight between Council Bluffs, Omaha, and smaller communities for the eastern terminus. For all practical purposes the terminus was set at Omaha, which became a large city, but legally it was fixed, in accordance with Lincoln's order, at Council Bluffs. To-day travelers can see on the plains of the Missouri, near Council Bluffs, a solitary brick building known as the Union Pacific Transfer. Once the center of great activity, it is now merely a lonely sign-post marking the spot of the legal eastern terminus of the railroad. From 1857 to 1864 Omaha was only a struggling village, but when the Union Pacific came, it suddenly bloomed into the liveliest city in the country. Since this was the supply-center for all the railroad operations to the west, the Union Pacific built immense car- and engine-houses and machine-shops, and by 1866 five or six hundred substantial buildings had been erected, one brick block costing $100,000. Business was rushing; one grocery house had sales of $500,000 a year, and the pioneer merchants were making fortunes. The railroad spent a quarter of a million dollars a month in Omaha, and business lots sold for as much as $5,000.

The Union Pacific associates profited from the development of Omaha and the other towns on their line through the organization of the Crédit Foncier, a corporation in which George Francis Train was the moving spirit and which was "clothed by the Nebraska legislature with nearly every power imaginable save that of reconstructing the late rebel states." It erected rows of cottages in Omaha for the workmen and sold them at a profit, and its real-estate operations assisted Mr. Train in profitably disposing of his own property in Omaha, 500 acres of land which cost him only $175 an acre. This internationally known genius in real-estate speculation and railroad promotion, whose American schemes were to extend from the Missouri to Puget Sound, had risen from sweeping out a counting-house to the headship of a Boston shipping firm with a branch in Liverpool. Subsequently he became a commission merchant in Australia, and he astonished the natives with an office containing Brussels carpets and marble counters, where he served free champagne lunches daily for all customers. In later years he made the circuit of the world, inspiring Jules Verne's story of globe-trotting, fought British prejudice against street-railways, made audacious speeches on Fenianism, and was jailed in Dublin. He is credited with inventing the perforations on postage stamps (which used to be cut apart with scissors), erasers on pencils, folding carriage-steps, and tilting coal-wagons, as well as the fashion of wearing a flower in the buttonhole. Of him Albert D. Richardson said,

Curiously combining keen sagacity with wild enthusiasm, a man who might have built the pyramids, or been confined to a strait jacket for his eccentricities, according to the age he lived in, he observes dryly that since he began to make money, people no longer pronounce him crazy! He says Chicago and San Francisco have more men of brains than any other cities in the world—men who would know what to do in an earth-quake, a fire, or a shipwreck—a definition of brains worthy of Fosco. He drinks no spirits, uses no tobacco, talks on the stump like an embodied Niagara, composes songs to order by the hour as fast as he can sing them, remembers every droll story from Joe Miller to Artemus Ward, is a born actor, intensely in earnest, and has the most absolute and outspoken faith in himself and his future.

Train and the Crédit Foncier were intimately connected with the building of all the early towns on the Union Pacific. They had the inside track on developments, but the whole course of the building of the Pacific railway was marked by contests between towns, banking interests, and real-estate groups to secure advantage from ownership of property along the route. Of the Cheyenne enterprise General Dodge says,

In the winter of 1867-68 the end of our track was at Cheyenne. During the winter there had assembled a very large number of people; possibly it was the greatest gambling place ever established on the plains, and it was full of desperate characters. The town of Cheyenne we had claimed, laid out and leased the lots to occupants, and organized the local government. There was then no title to be obtained to the town, but we treated it as all the towns, claiming it for the company, laying it out into town lots and not allowing anyone to locate there without taking an agreement from us allowing them to occupy it and agreeing to deed it to them when we got the title.

What sort of communities did the early Western railway-builders find already established? In Kansas there was, for example, Ellsworth, at the end of the cattle-trail from Texas, of which Bell says in his report of General Palmer's surveying party,

We passed through Ellesworth, a wonderful place, having seven or eight stores, two hotels, fifty houses of other kinds, occupied by nearly a thousand persons, and yet just one month old. Six weeks ago the wild buffalo was roaming over its site, and the Indians scalped a foolish soldier whom they caught sleeping where the new school-house now stands. The day of the buffalo and Indian have passed for ever; never again will the one graze, or the other utter a war whoop on this spot.

In Colorado there was the more or less Mexican town of Trinidad, of which Bell wrote,

It consists of a main street lined on either side by adobe houses of one story, with flat roofs and few rooms. Many of these were stores belonging to American traders, and well stocked with goods; two of them were billiard-saloons, and two were boarding-houses—all American innovations. There was no public-house proper, but strong drinks were sold at every one of these establishments, and, so far as I could make out, at every house in town. "Liquoring up" seems to be the sole amusement of the inhabitants. It commences before breakfast, goes on all day, and begins again with renewed vigour at sunset.

At Trinidad General Palmer held a railroad meeting

at which everything was said that could be said to enlighten the populace, and to explain to them the wonderful results to be expected when "El cameno de fiero caril" should traverse the territory. The speeches had all to be re-delivered in Spanish by an interpreter, and so impressively was the subject put that none could help seeing that their fortune was only a matter of time provided the railway passed near enough to their properties. This difficulty was easily overcome by promising any number of branch lines, and thus the meeting ended most auspiciously, and all the resolutions were in due form carried unanimously.

To the south there was Albuquerque, later to be reached by the Santa Fe, but included in General Palmer's surveys. And there Bell observed that the prime characteristic of all the early Western settlers was the ambition to make money:

Money-making is, of course, the great desideratum which attracts the white man to so out-of-the-way a country, far from home, and often also from all that is dear to him. Once here, he cares little what he does provided it pays. The most entertaining man of the evening at Albuquerque was a young Southerner, who kept us in roars of laughter with his droll stories, while he did the honours of the evening with the most delightful ease and good breeding. At parting, he told us that we should be called early next

morning to visit some of the fruit gardens and take an early breakfast—
breakfast No. 1—of grapes and peaches. "You must come and see me on
your way," said he; "I am the butcher of Albuquerque, and as the people
must have their chops, you must excuse my absence." So next morning, as
we were being conducted to the vineyards, we recognized our friend—with
blue blouse and paper cap—knife in hand, performing wonders in dissec-
tion upon his slaughtered sheep. Two hours later, on our return to the
hotel, we stopped at the office of the Albuquerque Chronicle. At the door
we met the editor and proprietor, who, to our great amusement, was no
other than our facetious host of the night before, the butcher of Albuquerque, and now, bereft of blouse, the energetic editor of the daily paper.
Is not a lesson to be learned from this little sketch of western life? I
would at least respectfully recommend it to the consideration of our
would-be emigrants.

Last and most exciting of all the communities to greet the railroad-
builders was the mile-high city of Denver, which the gold-camps of
the Rockies, particularly the Gregory Diggings at Central City, were
making a center of business, industry, and dissipation. Even the modern Western movies could hardly improve on this wild and woolly
capital of the Rockies, where every fifth building was a saloon and
every tenth a gambling-hell and every inhabitant carried "at least a
revolver and perhaps a knife suspended from his belt."

These towns were typical of what the early railroad-builders found,
but they were more interested in making towns of their own than in
cultivating the few communities already established. Whether the railroad officials wished it or not, there was always the moving hell-on-
wheels at the head of the tracks, ready to take the money of the
free-spending laborers; and in some cases, as at Cheyenne, these lurid
trains of camp-followers were converted into permanent settlements
through the establishment of the division points of the railroad system.
In later years, when the Northern Pacific was being built, one of the
towns at the head of the rails in eastern Washington was christened
Hell-to-Pay. But when the country had become more settled and it
was necessary to include the name on dignified time-tables, the railroad officials felt they must make the title more high-sounding and
respectable; so they changed the spelling to make it read Eltopia,
and so it remains.

For a contemporary picture of the town-making along the early

Western railroads, we must again become heavily indebted to that witness with the keen eye and colorful pen, William A. Bell.

Wholesale town-making may not be a romantic theme, or one capable of being made very attractive to the general reader; but it is the great characteristic of this part of our route, and is only to be seen to perfection along the line of these great railways. On the Platte, where the central line across the continent often advances at the rate of two miles a day, town-making is reduced to a system. The depot at the end of the line is only moved every two or three months; and as rich valleys are far scarcer in this section of country than in Kansas, the town usually moves also, while nothing remains to mark the spot where thousands lived, but a station, a name, and a few acres of bare earth. Last winter, Cheyenne was the terminal depot on this route, and increased in size to 5,000 inhabitants. A man I met at Denver, who had just come from Cheyenne, told me that while he was standing on the railway platform, a long freight train arrived, laden with frame houses, boards, furniture, palings, old tents, and all the rubbish which makes up one of these mushroom cities. The guard jumped off his van, and seeing some friends on the platform, called out with a flourish, "Gentlemen, here's Julesburg." The next train probably brought some other city, to lose for ever its identity in the great Cheyenne....

Thousands of dollars are daily won and lost all along the line by speculating in town lots. A spot is chosen in advance of the line, and is marked off into streets, blocks, and town lots, sometimes by the railway company, sometimes by an independent land company. As the rails approach it, the fun begins, and up goes the price of the lots, higher and higher. At last it becomes the terminal depot—the starting-point for the western trade—where the goods are transferred from the freight vans to the ox trains, and sent off to Denver, to Santa Fe, Fort Union, and other points. It then presents a scene of great activity, and quickly rises to the zenith of its glory. Town lots are bought up on all sides to build accommodation for the traders, teamsters, camp-followers, and loafers, who seem to drop from the skies. This state of things, however, lasts only for a time. The terminal depot must soon be moved forward, and the little colony will be left to its own resources. If the district has good natural advantages, it will remain; if not, it will disappear, and the town lots will fall to nothing. Salina, when we were there, was just at this zenith stage of existence; so I shall describe it as we found it.

On the open grass land between the Smoky River and the Salina Fork several broad streets could be seen, marked out with stakes, and crossing each other like a chess-board. The central one was deeply cut up with cart-rucks, and strewn with rubbish. There had been heavy rains, and the mud was so deep that it was almost impossible to move about. On each side of this main street were wooden houses, of all sizes and in all shapes

EARLY OMAHA

Lithograph after a drawing by H. Lambach, 1867. From the Stokes Collection, New York Public Library.

A DESERTED RAILROAD TOWN IN KANSAS
*Harper's Weekly*, 1874.

IN THE GARDEN OF THE GODS
Courtesy of the Colorado Springs Chamber of Commerce.

of embryonic existence. Not a garden fence or tree anywhere to be seen. Still paddling about in the mud, we came to the most advanced part of the city, and here we found three billiard saloons, each with two tables, and the everlasting bar. Then came the ice-cream saloon; then a refreshment saloon. Next—we could scarcely believe our eyes—appeared the office of the Salina Tribune (I will not vouch for the name). All these institutions, as well as a temporary school-house, and several small well-stocked shops made of wood unpainted, evidently represented first principles—the actual necessities, in fact, of Western life. Opposite was a row of substantial stores, having their fronts painted. The builder here was evidently a rash speculator. He did not look upon Salina as a Julesburg, but intended to tide over the stage of depression. Each of these houses was already inhabited and piles of unpacked goods lay fronting them in the streets. On each side was an hotel, at the door of which—it being just mid-day—the landlord was ringing furiously a great bell to announce to the inhabitants that dinner was ready. And what a dinner!—fried fish, fried mutton, fried eggs, fried mush (a great luxury), fried potatoes, and fried pudding—all swimming in grease; bad coffee without milk, dough cakes without butter, and muddy water out of dirty glasses. Trying to escape up a side street, we discovered the Methodist Chapel, the Land Agency Office, labelled "Desirable town lot for sale," the Masonic Hall (temporary building), and the more pretentious foundations of the Free School, Baptist Chapel, and Episcopal Church. The suburbs consisted of tents of all shapes and forms, with wooden doors; shanties, half canvas, half wood. These were owned by squatters upon unsold lots. All around were scattered the empty tins of the period, labelled in large letters, "desiccated vegetables," "green corn," "pears," "peaches," "oysters," and other untold luxuries.

Still farther from the centre, dotted here and there, white and glistening in the sun, we could see the camps of the bull trains, each made up from ten to twenty huge wagons, covered with white canvas, coralled sometimes in the form of a square, sometimes of a circle, so as to form a place of protection if attacked by Indians. An unusually wet season, and the fearful depredations caused by the red-men further west, detained an unusual number of these trains at that time around Salina. Partly shutting out the horizon on two sides, was a continuous belt of rich green trees. These might have been the commencement of a fine forest; but alas! as we came up to them, we found only two rows—one on each side of the river; and beyond, the same broad sea of grass, the undulating plain, relieved only by some distant bluffs. The grass was rich and abundant—a very fortunate circumstance; for everywhere were to be seen the droves of oxen, mules, and horses belonging to the wagon trains, feeding and fattening on their idleness. About the railroad station, and on each side of the line for some distance, lay pile after pile of the munitions, not of war but of peace—

iron rails, oaken ties, cradles and pins, contractors' cars, little houses on wheels, trucks innumerable, both empty and full; while at the opposite side to the town, our picturesque little camp of twenty wall tents, formed in a square, and flanked by our wagons and ambulances, lay peaceful and cool on the short greensward.

But the railroad-builders were not the only ones who profited from the building of towns in the West. As the tracks pushed forward over the prairies, that boom psychology which has ever been an outstanding characteristic of the West and of Westerners began to put forth its gorgeous blossoms. While the most solidly founded town developments were made by the railroads themselves or their subsidiaries, there were plenty of independent real-estate promoters who were willing to guess where the roads were to establish division points and to dream rosy dreams of the future possibilities of any city site where land could be obtained, however unfavorable it might be. It was no trouble to build new cities on paper. Land was cheap. The Homestead Act permitted an actual settler to take up 160 acres of government land which he could purchase for a nominal sum by "preëmpting." Although this was designed to apply only to persons who intended to make their homes on the land, it was customary for any one interested to ride into the interior, select a claim, erect four posts around a hollow square on the ground, and file a notice in the land-office that he had laid the foundation of a house and begun settlement. In 30 days the homesteader could "prove up" his claim, in the meantime having erected a cheap slab house, unfit to live in but giving the appearance of a building, or, perhaps, having only four logs and posts to mark the site. A witness would swear that a habitable dwelling had been erected, and, having paid $1.25 an acre for the land, within a few months the homesteader would receive a government patent to his claim. Usually the new owner's connection with his homestead ended at this point, and he sold his land. When the homestead racket was at its height, claims used to be preëmpted by the use of houses on wheels, which were rented and hauled from one claim to another as necessity dictated; and it was not unusual to find a windowless shack with a window-sash hanging inside on a nail, this luxurious adjunct enabling the witness to swear that the homesteader's house "has a window in it," as required by the land-office.

Once the land was patented, it could be sold to an incorporated town-site company, which itself could stake out 320 acres of government land as a town-site and by adding surrounding homestead claims could increase its holdings to a thousand acres or more. Then the land would be cut into building-lots, usually 25 by 125 feet, and a selling campaign begun. If the town was a success, the promoters grew rich; if it failed, little was lost, for the land cost but a trifle. In 1867 there were a number of such towns in Kansas: Wyandotte, four months old, population 400, with shares of ten building-lots selling for $1,800; Doniphan, 1,500 acres, population 300, with shares selling at $500; Geary City, where shares had advanced from $250 to $400 within a week. And the residents of each embryo metropolis, as well as the promoters thereof, could give unanswerable arguments as to why their community was to be the future St. Louis of the territory.

Of the land-boom at Osawkee, Kansas, Albert D. Richardson writes in *Beyond the Mississippi*:

In July one hundred thousand acres of public lands were sold at Osawkee, Jefferson county. Theoretically to the highest bidder; actually each quarter-section to its occupant at its appraised value: from one dollar and fifty cents, to four dollars and fifty cents per acre. The "settler," who lived fifty or a hundred miles away, had built a cabin or driven a stake upon his claim, and could therefore swear that he was a bona fide resident! The constructive squatters respected each others' rights and protected their own. The first man who ventured to bid against one of them was instantly shot down; so there was no further competition. Many sold their newly-acquired lands to speculators at double the cost within an hour after bidding them off. But hundreds borrowed money at five per cent. a month, and invested it here. I knew a Tennessean who loaned funds at this rate to forty-five young men, taking the Government title to each tract in his own name, but giving a bond to deed it back to the actual purchaser upon the payment of principal and interest. Two years later, he told me that he still held every one, as not a single note had been paid. Money abounded and times were flush. One evening I borrowed one hundred and fifty dollars from a total stranger, to aid in purchasing a quarter-section; for I had not escaped the universal mania. When I offered a mortgage as security, he replied: "It would be some trouble to have the papers drawn, and cost us five or ten dollars. Just send me the money by express within two or three weeks."

David's covetousness for the wife of Uriah, was no stronger than the lust of the frontier Yankees for territory. Town shares and quarter-sections passed as currently as bank-notes or gold dollars. It was history repeating itself; for in the early days of Tennessee, people in trading used to say: "I will give you a three-twenty," or "I will take a six-forty." Six hundred and forty acres near the present city of Nashville, once sold for three axes and two cow-bells. "The circulating medium of Europe is gold, of Africa, men, of Asia, women, and of America, land." Two thousand people attended the sales at Osawkee. In this interior town of a dozen houses, a huge hotel had been erected; every building was crowded, and hundreds of strangers lived in tents, or slept on the grass in the open air. Streets were filled with blinding dust, and heated like furnaces by the July sun; gambling and drinking booths stood upon every corner; reeking odors poisoned the air, and a new Coleridge might have sung of this mushroom Cologne:

> In Colin, a town of monks and bones,
> And pavements fanged with murderous stones,
> And rags, and bugs, and hideous wenches,
> I counted five and seventy stenches.

When Themistocles at a feast was asked to play upon a musical instrument, he replied: "I cannot fiddle; but I know how to make a small town a great city." Every Kansan thought himself a Themistocles. Nearly all transactions were cash, and money was plentiful, though commanding from three to five per cent. a month. Shares often doubled in price in two or three weeks. Servant girls speculated in town lots. From enormous buff envelopes men would take scores of certificates elegantly printed in colors, representing property in various towns, and propose to sell thousands of dollars worth, certain to quadruple in value within a few months! If you declined to purchase, they might ask to borrow six shillings to pay their washerwoman, or twelve dollars for a week's board. Three days later, meeting you again, they would cancel the debt from pockets burdened with twenty-dollar gold pieces, and offer you five hundred or a thousand dollars for a few days, if it would be the slightest accommodation. This pantomime of actual life began with beggars clothed in rags. But the genie of real estate speculation touched them with his wand, and lo! the tatters were gone, and they stood clothed in purple, adorned with jewels, and weighed down with gold. Young men who never before owned fifty dollars at once, a few weeks after reaching Kansas possessed full pockets, with town shares by the score; and talked of thousands as if they had been rocked in golden cradles and fed with the famous Miss Kilmansegg's golden spoon. On a smaller scale was repeated the story of that Minnesota wood-sawyer who accumulated half a million in half a year.

On paper, all these towns were magnificent. Their superbly lithographed maps adorned the walls of every place of resort. The stranger studying one of these, fancied the New Babylon surpassed only by its namesake of old. Its great parks, opera-houses, churches, universities, railway depots and steamboat landings made New York and St. Louis insignificant in comparison. But if the newcomer had the unusual wisdom to visit the prophetic city before purchasing lots, he learned the difference between fact and fancy. The town might be composed of twenty buildings; or it might not contain a single human habitation. In most cases, however, he would find one or two rough cabins, with perhaps a tent and an Indian canoe on the river in front of the "levee." Anything was marketable. Shares in interior towns of one or two shanties, sold readily for a hundred dollars. Wags proposed an act of Congress reserving some land for farming purposes before the whole Territory should be divided into city lots. Towns enough were started for a State containing four millions of people.

It was not a swindle, but a mania. The speculators were quite as insane as the rest,—"Themselves deceiving and themselves deceived." Any one of them could have turned his property into cash at enormous profits. But all thought the inflation would continue; and I do not remember a single persons who sold out, except to make new investments. Much eastern capital was sunk in these paper cities. When the collapse came it was like the crushing of an egg-shell. Again the genie waved his wand, and presto! the spangles and gold disappeared, and the princes of an hour were beggars again. The shares had no more market value than town lots in the moon. Cities died, inhabitants deserted, houses were torn down.

But among the real-estate operators of the early West there were a few men, like General William J. Palmer, who built cities that were permanent. Perhaps no one had a keener eye for the scenic and commercial possibilities of a site than General Palmer; certainly no one was more far-sighted in mapping out the future development of territory, and none excelled him in ability to pull the wires of diplomacy and business intrigue. Building his Denver and Rio Grande Railway without state or Federal aid, he had to depend for his profits on intelligent and far-sighted exploitation of all its possibilities, and he achieved this with noteworthy success. To him town-building and business maneuvering and railroad construction were all parts of a game in which skill and shrewdness received high stakes as their reward. The love of manipulation was in his blood. At the tender age of 17 he wrote as follows to a young friend of an elaborate scheme he had invented to procure the autographs of distinguished persons, and this project was a presage of his later activities in business:

I got them not by merely writing to them and requesting their autographs. A little chicanery was necessary. I doubt if a written request for their signatures would bring them. The modus-operandi was as follows— Taking advantage of that inherent quality in the souls of our great statesmen, Ambition, and being aware of that love of distinction and that desire for office which characterizes all our politicians, myself and another interesting juvenile formed ourselves into a society for the diffusion and perfection of the intricate science of wire-pulling. This much being premised, what follows is plain. At a meeting of the members of the Sewardambian Society of Philada. for the promotion of the political and much to be lauded art of wire-pulling, Hon. Wm. H. Seward was unanimously elected an honorary member of the same with the privilege of participating in the discussions, and with all other privileges guaranteed to active members. In a few minutes a letter is dropt in the P. O., that goes post haste to Washington and into the Senate chamber—informing the Honorable member from N. York, as he sits at his congressional desk, of his election to such a desirable post. The next mail brings with it a franked letter to Wm. J. Palmer, corresponding Secretary of the Sewardambian Mutual Improvement Society of Philad. The two ingenious members constituting the latter corporation, chuckle over the contents that evening and laugh at the very easy manner in which our Representatives are gulled. But meanwhile another letter is despatched informing the Hon. Henry Clay of his election with but two dissenting voices to the post of Honorary member of the Claytonian Society of Philad. and another franked letter from the Disappointed aspirant for the Presidency thanks the Society for the honor conferred upon him and for the kind affable manner in which Mr. Wm. J. Palmer, the corresponding secretary, has informed him of the proceedings of the meeting. And the two ingenious members chuckle again as they add another document to their pile of literary morceaux. And so on till you've caught as many as will bite. Then the Society makes a move at one of its stated meetings to dissolve—the move is seconded—the President puts it before the meeting with all due formality and it is unanimously adopted— the members divide the plunder, separate, and find themselves possessed of a nice parcel of autograph letters from distinguished people. This is the way, and now you and Josiah Chapman can form yourselves into a society for the purpose of fillibustering or extending the Union indefinitely or for any other object. To be sure, the acting members would be small but the Honorary department would, I hope, be well filled and that would be sufficient.

A mind that was capable of evolving such a plan before 17 might confidently be expected to be an adept at the arts of diplomacy and manipulation by the time it reached maturity. At 22 Palmer organized a series of antislavery lectures in Philadelphia and, though the meetings were threatened by armed mobs of Southern sympathizers, carried them through successfully. In preparation for these lectures he showed his grasp of the fine details of the situation and his understanding of how to deal with people when he wrote Clothier, "You must not let the Murphy protest die by inanition, but keep a sharp look-out on the different members of the committee as they return to the city and take a decided move at the earliest moment. I was anticipating some such difficulty in the way of carrying out the close resolution of the subscribers that you mention." At about this time he showed his flair for the bold and unusual by suggesting that the Philadelphia and Cincinnati chess teams play a series of games by telegraph.

General Palmer's genius for organization appeared further when he formed the Anderson Troop of Cavalry, "a picked body of young men of respectability selected from nearly every county of the State to be attached to General Anderson for the performance of any special service required by him involving delicacy or danger." To recruit this corps he wrote men of influence throughout the state, asking them to nominate for their own county and each adjacent county "five young men, or any less number, aged between 18 and 30 years (the younger the better), of unusual intelligence and trustworthiness, endowed with nervous energy and courage and patriotic spirit. The men to be light, active, hardy—and more or less accustomed to riding—and the names to be mentioned in your list (with their addresses) in order of your preference, so that in case all the counties respond, the best may be taken from each." As a result of this plan an unusually fine body of cavalrymen was selected, which later came under Palmer's own command.

When Palmer looked over the field in Colorado in 1870, he mapped out the main opportunities for immediate development that would bring money to investors and create profitable traffic for the Denver and Rio Grande. Since there was no town in the 100 miles between Denver and Pueblo and no apparent reason for one, the General, with characteristic audacity, decided to build a city some place along the line. Having noted the beauties of the strange red rock-formations at the foot of Pike's Peak—the Garden of the Gods—and the Manitou mineral springs a few miles distant, he determined on this locality as the site for the city of Colorado Springs, and, staking out his town-site on the bare prairie, he exploited all its attractions of scenery and climate so thoroughly that within a few years it was nationally famous as a resort and residence city. He saw near the Royal Gorge at Cañon City great deposits of coal, and he determined to develop them profit-ably on a large scale. At Pueblo there was iron and more coal, and he saw in his mind's eye the great industrial development that later became the Colorado Fuel and Iron Company.

To initiate his plans, Palmer secured, from his friends in Philadel-phia and those of Dr. Bell's father in London and Holland who had subscribed to build the first 76 miles of the Denver and Rio Grande Railway, initial subscriptions of $300,000 to the Mountain Base In-vestment Fund. With this as a nest-egg he set out to develop his whole comprehensive scheme. His first move was to organize the National Land and Improvement Company with the proceeds of the $300,000 stock of the Mountain Base Investment Fund as its cash capital. The purpose of this company was to buy, but not to develop, property. It immediately purchased twenty-five tracts of land between Denver and Pueblo, a total of 5,445 acres, costing an average of $7.88 an acre. It also bought a half-interest in 9,300 acres of land at and near the site that Palmer had selected for his city of Colorado Springs. Lastly, it purchased a large tract of coal-land at Cañon City, near the Grand Cañon of the Arkansas River, and town property around Cañon City. The route of the Denver and Rio Grande Railway, of course, was not announced until the land company had purchased all the property it wanted at the appropriate locations. The company then gave the railroad $75,000 of its capital stock in return for the agreement of the railroad to put its stations on land-company property, to provide all necessary railroad facilities, and to relinquish to the land company the profitable business of making towns along the railroad line.

To provide for the development of the coal- and iron-lands, a second company was now formed, the Central Colorado Improvement Com-pany, with capital stock of $3,500,000 and bonds of $1,500,000. A total of $1,305,500 was subscribed to the stock and bonds of this company, $884,000 being paid in cash. The company then proceeded to purchase $1,040,000 worth of the 7 per cent first-mortgage bonds of the 75-mile section of the Denver and Rio Grande Railway that was to run through the property it intended to acquire, paying $561,000 in cash. It then paid $247,000 for 436,766 acres of land, an average of 56 cents an acre, including 350,000 acres of timber- and pasture-land, 83,584 acres of valuable farm-land, 1,800 acres of Cañon City coal-land, 1,062 acres of iron-ore land, and 320 acres in the Grand Cañon of the Arkansas River to secure water- and power-rights. To this company the National Land and Improvement Company conveyed all its coal and iron property, being paid actual cost plus 7 per cent interest, or $33,000, in the bonds of the Central Colorado Company, with a bonus of nearly six times that amount in stock, or $187,500.

The third concern organized was the Colorado Springs Company, with capital stock of $300,000, for the development of a city at the foot of Pike's Peak. To this company, in return for 77 per cent of its stock, the National Land and Improvement Company conveyed its interest in the property at the Colorado Springs site. The Colorado Springs Company acquired additional interest in the lands at the town-site, bringing the total of its property to some 10,000 acres, paying for this land and for the improvements on it with $60,000 of its capital stock.

This was the capital structure of the first group of companies, all closely interlinked with the Denver and Rio Grande Railway, by which Palmer and his associates intended to develop, and receive the profits from, the natural resources of Colorado along the line of the railroad. How sound were his schemes we can see by observing the steady growth and profits of the various corporations through the years. Through the varying vicissitudes of "hard times" in 1873, invasion of grasshoppers and trade exhaustion in 1877, collapse of Colorado's main support, silver, in 1893, the National Land and Improvement Company and the Colorado Springs Company went steadily ahead, sometimes paying as much as 20 and 30 per cent dividends and averaging about 7 per cent up to 1908. They also largely increased the value of their investments and fostered various subsidiary developments. How much Palmer and the other insiders indirectly got out of the operation of these concerns, it is impossible to say, but certainly the ordinary stockholders had nothing to complain of, for they received a steady return on their investments and realized a heavy increment in the value of their properties over a period of years.

To a man as sensitive to natural beauty and as much a lover of the outdoors as General Palmer, the country at the foot of Pike's Peak had deep appeal; so it is not strange that he decided to build a city at what is now Colorado Springs. He had always been fascinated by mountains; the mountains of Pennsylvania were the first love of his youth, before he had seen the Rockies. On a Sunday morning in 1859 he had written from Altoona, Pennsylvania:

If the Reverend War Horse, Chambers, who preaches here to-day, would mount a racer, and lead his congregation, big and little, from the little Presbyterian Altoona Church up the rugged road, inadmissible for carriages, to Wapsunnonnack and from that solid pulpit point out to them the sublime scene before them, I think they would be more impressed with the insignificance of man and the greatness of God, than ever they could be, if Calvinism were steam-hammered into them diurnally for a life-time.

Man has to go to the mountains for health, and he must go there likewise, if he would get a true insight into things. There is a refraction in the atmosphere of cities and low lands like that the traveller meets with on the desert or in the equatorial seas, when a long coast line or a city with steeples and turrets loom out of the horizon—to vanish the next day into vapor.—Mankind as a general thing cannot see through brick walls. To be sure I have gazed myself through an instrument hawked about our Philada. streets by an individual whose conversational powers were tolerably developed—the object of which was to enable one to see through a brick. But the majority of minds are not furnished with cameras, and it were better to take the brick away and look straight and clear. This they can do in the mountains.

And again, the same year, he wrote:

Come up to Cresson, where health and strength are wafted from the swaying boughs of the pine trees, and well-up in the transparent springs of pure water. All the children on the Allegheny Mountains are Venuses and Adonises—in my rides up and down the side of it I see faces which no painter would hesitate to transmit to his canvas in connection with the finest scenery of Allegrippus or Kittanning. What is this due to—what but the fresh, invigorating mountain air in which they roam about hatless and bonnetless, and the unsurpassable water?

In the shadow of Pike's Peak, therefore, at an altitude of 6,500 feet, where the gently rolling plains, changing from delicate green to brown with the seasons, rise up to the foot of the gigantic Rockies, he planted his city. Here there was no especially favored farming-country, though the soil could be tilled fairly well, no mines of any consequence, no prospect of any great population, no commercial reason for building a city except that there was a pass over the mountains into the South Park mining-country over which considerable traffic might be expected to flow. But Palmer felt that the superb, rugged mountain-peaks, the pure water, the mineral springs, and a climate which was cool in summer, exhilarating, sunny, and free from heavy snows in winter, would be sufficient attraction to build Colorado Springs into a city of homes and a pleasure- and health-resort. On his first visit to the Manitou mineral springs and the Garden of the Gods he had written in his diary, "I am sure that there will be a famous summer resort here soon after the railroad reaches Denver." Later, in 1869, when he was traveling in advance of his Kansas Pacific railroad-building party, accompanied by Cyrus W. Field and Nathan C. Meeker, agricultural editor of the New York *Tribune,* who later founded the town of Greeley, he took them to this favorite spot, and of their visit he wrote, "The whole party was in the finest possible humor. Pikes Peak never looked grander, and the Garden of the Gods fascinated my companions of the eastern slope so that they bubbled all over with enthusiasm resembling the soda Springs whence we drank great quaffs, as Dr. Bell and I had done only a month before."

Of the benefits promised by his scheme of building Colorado Springs and other towns along the line of the railroad, General Palmer declared that many of the first drawbacks to immigration might be counteracted by the formation of land companies with capital enough to construct irrigation ditches, lay out farms and towns, plant trees, aid the building of hotels and dwellings, while selling tracts and lots to arriving colonists on small annual payments distributed over several years. By such a system, he felt, the colonization of the country could be greatly stimulated, the railroad earnings increased, and "the work of twenty years to be concentrated into ten."

As soon as the money for the Denver and Rio Grande was assured, therefore, everything was ripe to organize. On June 26, 1871, in Denver, the Colorado Springs Company held its first meeting, elected officers, authorized the construction of roads, bridges, and a hotel, and on the next day the whole party, with Colonel Greenwood, the chief engineer of the railroad, started from Denver to lay out the new town, appraise the lots, and begin business. The company at once subdivided part of its property into 616 residence and 480 business lots and put the remaining acreage into farm and garden tracts of from 4 to 40 acres. Residence lots sold for $100, business lots for $175, outlying land for $30 an acre; and the company proposed to subdivide other business and residence lots as needed. All the lands at Colorado Springs and Manitou were classified as either "white" or "red." The "white" lots, which constituted two-thirds of the property, were to be sold conditionally upon satisfactory improvement by the purchaser within one year; the proceeds were to be used, first, to reimburse the company for the cost of the land (which was only about $16 an acre), and second, to pay the cost of laying out and improving the city, salaries, and other company expenses. The "red" lots, which were checker-boarded among the "white" lots and therefore received the benefit of all the surrounding private improvements, were to be retained by the company and sold later, when they had increased in value, to provide a profit for the stockholders. Another company, the Fountain Colony, was organized, but not incorporated, to take care of such profitable parts of the town-making business as the parent corporation wished to turn over to it.

The first stake was driven on July 31, 1871, and the railroad reached the town on October 23. By the end of the year 159 structures had been built and various improvements had been made, all at a cost of $160,000. The first move General Palmer made to insure the success of the colony was to employ as manager General Robert A. Cameron, who had occupied this position with great success at Greeley, Colorado, in the initial stages of the colonization project there. Since he intended to make Colorado Springs a residence center which would attract well-to-do people from all over the country, Palmer decreed that it should be as different as possible from the wild and woolly Western towns of the day. Culture and refinement were to sit as the twin goddesses that presided over this infant community; there were to be schools, parks, colleges, art-galleries, and a public forum, but no saloons. Of this exclusion Palmer wrote:

The liquor restriction had already been adopted by Mr. Meeker for his Greeley colony. In the early summer of 1871, while we were making arrangements with General Cameron and some of his confrères to interest themselves in our new enterprise, I was asked by them whether we would adopt a similar restriction for the proposed Fountain Colony. Having had some experience with the railroad towns of the day in the new West, especially those whose generally short but always lively existence punctuated the successive stages of advance westward by the Kansas Pacific and Union Pacific railroads, I answered "Yes." At Sheridan, especially, on the former road, where I had the privilege of a residence of some eight months in 1870-71, while directing the construction of the railroad to Denver, the most noticeable suburban feature, notwithstanding the salubrity of the air and the brevity of the settlement, was a fat graveyard, most of whose inhabitants, in the language of the 100th meridian, had died "with their boots on."

So, under General Cameron, "a man in ten thousand to take charge of a young and feeble settlement of colonists," Colorado Springs began to build itself into "a city of beauty and refinement, a city that fascinates not only by the beauty of its surroundings but by its health-restoring climate." Six months after the railroad arrived, Cameron was able to report that the new city had 350 people, a passenger-office, freight-depot, telegraph-station, two dry-goods stores, three groceries, a harness-shop, two meat-markets, two livery-stables, a printing-office and a newspaper, a feed and grain store, a public library and reading-room, a large hotel, and not half enough boarding-houses to accommodate those who desired to board. His advertisements in Eastern and English newspapers had put him in touch with 2,500 families who were considering a move to the Far West, and he replied to their letters with such information as this: Colorado Springs has no excess of cold in winter or heat in summer, no fogs or vapors, and it is protected from storms by a high wall of mountains to the west. Its climate is such that all varieties of nervous diseases and diseases of debility are greatly relieved, and asthmatics and consumptives in the early stages are almost certain to get well. The country grows good crops of corn, barley, oats, potatoes, cabbages, beets, onions, melons, cucumbers, and tomatoes, and it is expected that profits can be made in growing peppermint, sugar-beets, seeds, sorghum, and broom-corn. In no country is there such a tendency for vegetables to go to flower and seed; and, acting upon this hint from Mother Nature, it is expected that the farmers will supply the Eastern markets with seeds for finer, sounder vegetables, fruits, and flowers than they can grow elsewhere. Irrigation is being carried on, but the General warns that it requires skill, expense, and time. Cattle, sheep, wool, butter, and cheese all offer opportunities for building up profitable business. There are inexhaustible mines of silver and gold lying to the west, and within 50 miles mountains of iron, inexhaustible beds of coal, and water-power.

The scenic delights of the region are painted in glowing colors. There is the Garden of the Gods, "fabled home and ruined castles of Jupiter before his historical residence in Asia and Greece," the ruined walls of which are still standing, reaching in some parts 317 feet, and are the wonder and admiration of all beholders. There are sparkling mineral springs so highly charged with carbonic-acid gas and so pleasant to drink as to make everyone who has once tasted them long to return to these parts. The first free school for children has been opened by "Mrs. General Palmer," churches are being built, and appropriate plans laid for making the city a center of culture. Those who fear the wild life in the West are reassured by the comforting news that the region has only friendly Indians; "the warlike ones are cut off from us by heavy lines of settlement." There are no animals that attack anyone, and no large yellow rattlesnakes. In fact, the native rattlers are made to seem almost like household pets—"there are only the little prairie rattlesnakes once so common in Indiana and Illinois."

In a circular of advice, those who make the trip west are advised to bring their family pictures and choice paintings, with good carpets, beds and bedding so as to have a few things looking like the old home. The well worn household goods will not generally pay freight. Many families sell their most valuable things and invest the money in land, living simply for a few years in their new homes. Don't come to farm without enough means to buy four cows, a stove and a few household goods, an ax and a few tools, and a few months' supplies, and own with others, if not alone, a team, a plow and a wagon. Families living on the cars should provide a good Lunch Basket to save expense. Be careful of confidence men, don't lend money on any security to strangers.

The opportunities are boundless. In the Far West labor brings a higher price than elsewhere, while the substantials such as beef, fuel, and shelter are much cheaper. And the General sounds the cheering note that "the social chasm between capital and labor is reduced here from a great gulf to a small stream. Fortunes are made so rapidly here that we have to respect all men, for how can we tell who is to be rich?" As to jobs, there are plenty of them in Colorado for people who really want to work. In Denver one can see any day orders at the employment offices for 300 men at $30 per month and board. "The fact is," says the new Colorado Springs newspaper, *The Out West,* "there is plenty of demand for laborers here at good wages; but the croakers are constitutionally opposed to heavy work and are only ready to accept light employment. They would take the presidency of a bank, the superintendency of a railroad, or the general management of some institution where brains and not muscle were required. We suggest that these fellows put on Dolly Varden shirts, part their hair in the middle and try servant-galism. That pays excellent wages and the demand is vastly in excess of the supply today." The newspaper is happy to note that there are at least a few newcomers who are willing to do heavy work, and calls attention to an advertisement reading, "Wanted—Two young men want situations on ranchos to do general work, take care of stock, or act as herders. Would like to raise cattle on shares." On this the editor comments, "This is as rare an announcement as it is commendable. It suggests the fact that these young men are on the broad road which leads to wealth and fortune. To the young men who every year crowd into this city to look for situations, we say go into the country, take up a farm, establish a dairy, raise pigs and poultry, put in fields of grain. Be industrious and independent and success is certain."

Within a year Colorado Springs had made much progress towards its goal of becoming a beautiful and prosperous city. Luxurious hotels were drawing tourists and health-seekers to the mineral springs at the rate of 1,500 a month, and the town was on the way to becoming what it was afterward called, "The Saratoga of the West." Broad streets shaded with trees had been laid out, parks and a sanatorium were planned, and a landscape-gardener had been engaged to beautify the town. "Now," said General Cameron, "we only need to solve the problem of colonization," and he estimates that from his correspondence with 3,726 heads of families, representing 18,630 persons, at least 2,500 individuals should be drawn to Colorado Springs within two years. A writer for the New York *Independent* stated that the

Colorado Springs post-office now delivered 11,000 letters a month, that 7,000 trees had been planted and not one died, and after expatiating on the climate, scenery, and growth of the community, concluded, "This looks, then, like an unqualified success."

With such a splendid array of achievement only the captious would utter any complaints whatever. But there are a few defects in the community that must be repaired. One correspondent complains that horses, cattle, and pigs roam at their own sweet will both day and night through the streets and gardens of the town, and something must be done about it. General Cameron promises drastic measures. Moreover, despite rigid prohibition, it seems that the bibulous are having no trouble in getting a drink. The front page of the newspaper carries an advertisement that "New Memphis is the best stopping place between Denver and Colorado Springs. Good liquor, cigars, Beer, Ale and Porter always on hand." And an indignant citizen inquires, "How comes it to pass that in a town where the sale of intoxicating liquors is prohibited, the citizens are liable to such a disgusting exhibition as took place the other evening when a drunken Irishman rolled along the streets? Rumor says that it is by no means difficult for a man to obtain a drink in Colorado Springs. When is something to be done about our whiskey holes, lager beer saloons, and gambling hells? All this back-building hole and corner business is disgraceful."

But the city continued to grow and to prosper. When General Palmer's Antlers Hotel was built, it was soon famous for its luxurious accommodations and service, and Colorado Springs became the most popular objective for vacation parties in the West. Of these early years Palmer wrote:

We had, of course, the inevitable fire, until which no Rocky Mountain town feels that it has really entered the lists for a permanent race in growth; the Jay Cooke panic in 1873, after which corn was 12½ cents per bushel in Kansas and Nebraska, and potatoes here were about as worthless as they now are on "the Divide"; a grasshopper invasion and an Indian alarm the same year, when the able-bodied men of the town were organized under Capt. Matt France, and on October 6, 1873, marched to Jimmy's Camp to meet 3,000 Cheyenne who were killing cattle, because, as they said, "The white man has been killing our buffalo." This was the last Indian alarm in this neighborhood.

Distinguished visitors came along. Among the first was Samuel Bowles, the able and spirited editor of the Springfield *Republican;* later on, Charles Kingsley, who helped to celebrate the third anniversary of the town, in the tent of Mrs. Giltner, who kept the shoe-shop; General Grant twice, Jefferson Davis, General Philip H. Sheridan, Henry Kingsley, Lord Dunraven, Asa Gray, Sir Joseph Hooker, the Duke of Northumberland, General Sherman, and many others. Some came to witness the operations of the colony and of the railroad of novel gage. Others were attracted by the budding fame of the locality for scenic interest and healthfulness.

Meanwhile, General Palmer was attending also to the development of his other properties in southern Colorado. Although there was no place for the Denver and Rio Grande Railway to go but Pueblo and there never was any intention of using any other route, the General had succeeded in creating an air of indecision about his plans which kept the Pueblo people on the anxious seat. A mass-meeting of citizens was held in the court-house "to inaugurate a campaign to secure a railroad for Pueblo," and the editor of the *Colorado Chieftain* had begun his effort to interest the road in Pueblo before the first rails were laid at Denver. Soon afterwards agents for the Rio Grande appeared in the town and intimated that the route of the road "would be changed to include Pueblo if the county would vote bonds and subscribe to a liberal amount of railroad stock." As a result the county voted to subscribe $100,000 provided the road were completed within a year and a depot established within a mile of the court-house. Later $50,000 additional was voted for a branch line to the coal-fields of Frémont County. As the road approached Pueblo, the excitement grew. In 1872 the newspaper editor wrote, "The track layers are crossing Sutherland's ranch, twelve miles north of town, and the rails are said to be arriving as fast as they can be spiked down. A large water tank is nearly completed at Sutherland's and on Monday next trains will come down to that point, leaving only twelve miles for the stage. Verily, the gap grows smaller and beautifully less."

But General Palmer had no intention of losing any of the possible financial advantages that should accrue from his entry into Pueblo. Directly south of the town was the 48,000 acres owned by his Central

Colorado Improvement Company, and in the new community of South Pueblo, but still within a mile of the court-house, he placed his railroad station. The entire tract was then put under irrigation, divided into acreage, and sold on easy terms to settlers. With characteristic energy Palmer's development of South Pueblo went forward, and the newspapers soon found it necessary to report:

Very quietly, almost imperceptibly, without any flourish at the hands of real estate owners or speculators, a new town has sprung into existence on the south side of the Arkansas, and unheralded and almost unthought of, is moving forward to commercial prosperity with the force and momentum of an avalanche. A few weeks ago the resident of Santa Fé Avenue found his vision obstructed only by one or two dwellings on the other side of the river. He now is surprised to behold roofs of dwellings and broad, well arranged streets, while his ears are assailed by the din and clatter of saws and hammers. . . . Due attention must now be given South Pueblo for it is not to be ignored by any mean, narrow, contracted spirit of jealousy. We are happy to say, however, that this spirit exists only in a few isolated cases. The majority of our citizens look upon South Pueblo as an integral part of old Pueblo, and accept the correct principle that the enterprise and industry which expands capital and improvements in one part of town tends to directly benefit the other portion, be it north, south, east, or west.

The General's next move at Pueblo, a few years later, was the establishment of the Colorado Coal and Iron Company, in which he merged the old Central Colorado Improvement Company, the Southern Colorado Coal and Iron Company, and the Colorado Coal and Steel Works Company. This merger was completed in 1880, and from it grew the great Colorado Fuel and Iron Company which was so important an industrial concern that its control was later contested for by such powerful forces as the interests of John T. Gates, Edward H. Harriman, John D. Rockefeller, Jr., and George J. Gould. After a few years General Palmer sold his interests and withdrew, but he had the satisfaction of seeing his original predictions justified, for the company he had fathered became one of the largest industrial organizations in the West, employing more than 6,000 men in its Pueblo plant and armies of workers in its coal- and iron-mines, selling steel rails, iron, and pipe throughout the West, and mining a million tons of coal a year.

The creation of South Pueblo was typical of Palmer's operations in town-building on the railroad. When he was extending his road to the coal-fields, he told the people of Cañon City that if they would vote $50,000 in bonds for the railroad and spend $3,000 in developing the hot springs near the town, he would build the line to a depot within three-quarters of a mile of McClure's Hotel, thus making Cañon City the coal center of Colorado. He did this, building to his own property. But a little later, finding the coal at El Moro of a superior quality, he built a line to that rival field, which so angered the people of Cañon City that they held a public meeting and invited the Santa Fe to build to their town, thus engendering the Royal Gorge war which was later to be a source of great anxiety and enormous expense to General Palmer. Another town from which Palmer reaped considerable profit was Durango. To carry out his purposes there he organized the Durango Company, which carried on real-estate and mining operations when the road was extended to that city in the mountains of southern Colorado. Dr. W. A. Bell, who had been an officer of the Colorado Coal and Iron Company and numerous other Palmer enterprises, presided over the destinies of the Durango Company and became the town's first citizen and one of the outstanding men in the State of Colorado.

Palmer's method of financing his railroad-building and community development is typified by the entry of the Denver and Rio Grande into Cañon City. Since the Colorado Coal and Iron Company had many coal- and ore-lands in the vicinity of Cañon City which it wished to develop, he induced the company to raise most of the money needed to build the road to Cañon City, taking in exchange therefor the stock of the railroad. In a similar fashion others of his companies bought up the coal- and iron-lands around Trinidad, Durango, Huerfano, and some other points; they then turned over one-half of their interests to the railroad, and from these properties the funds were raised with which the railroad was built. Palmer further tied all his interests together by reciprocal agreements which were beneficial to all the parties concerned. He got the men who were interested in the coal properties at Trinidad and Cañon City to see the advantages to them of building the iron and steel works at Pueblo and so raised most of the $2,500,000 needed to start that tremendous industrial enterprise. He then assured the railroad and the iron company a profitable business by arranging contracts between them which granted favors in the matter of freight-rates to the Colorado Coal and Iron Company and allowed no other concern to sell coal in the booming city of Leadville. Thus, even previous to 1880, his organization typified the same sort of combination of financial interests that was developed in later years on a larger scale by the heads of the great industrial trusts of the country. In the use of these methods for developing the resources of the new state, General Palmer had the people with him for the most part, for the opinion seemed to be general that Colorado needed more big monopolies to raise more money from outside the state to develop more industries. There was then no fear of big business in Colorado.

As fast as new coal-, iron-, silver-, and gold-mining areas were opened up in Colorado, General Palmer extended the Denver and Rio Grande Railway system, building additional branches every year until he had a network of lines running westward into the mountains from his base line on the eastern slope. In 1881 he began making his narrow-gage road standard-gage, and soon the two original rails were paralleled by a third on all the important sections of the road. In 1882 he began the construction of the Rio Grande Western from Denver to Salt Lake. In 1883 he resigned the presidency of the Denver and Rio Grande, and later he disposed of his stock to the Gould interests, which planned to extend the system to San Francisco by building the Western Pacific over a route which Palmer had already surveyed. Meanwhile, the developments he had expected to follow the building of his railroad in Colorado went steadily forward, his companies were successful, and his special pride, the town of Colorado Springs, prospered and waxed fat. As his private fortune increased, he gave generously but unostentatiously to a large variety of worthy enterprises, and it was said that his private charities were extraordinarily large although they remained forever a closed book. To the city of Colorado Springs he gave parks, and lakes, and 85 miles of boulevards, mountain roadways, and trails costing $700,000. He provided money and lands in the heart of the city for Colorado College, which the Congregational Church took under its auspices and to which it sent as first president a New Englander who bore the scholarly name of Jonathan Edwards. He gave the land for Cragmor Sanatorium for the treatment of tuberculosis at Austin Bluffs, on the outskirts of the city. And he left no stone unturned to make Colorado Springs one of the most attractive places for homes in the West. At his death, in 1909, it was conservatively estimated that he had given away $4,000,000, or nearly one-half of his entire estate.

But it was at "Glen Eyrie" that the General's taste and character found their fullest expression. When he first began his railroad explorations in Colorado, he had written in his diary, "I somehow fancy that an exploration of the dancing little tributaries of the Monument or the Fountain might disclose somewhere near where they come leaping with delight from the cavernous wall of the Rocky Mountains, some charming spot where one perhaps might make his future home." That spot was "Glen Eyrie," back of the Garden of the Gods in its own narrow, wooded cañon surrounded by strange red-sandstone formations. Here the General took up 160 acres of land under the Homestead Act, and here he built his castle, where he loved to receive his guests at garden fêtes, "tall and soldierly, clothed in immaculate linen, wearing a broad western hat, surrounded by his three pretty daughters." And the house was indeed a castle, with its greystone towers which might have graced the countryside of old England. It had great halls, paneled in beautiful woods, and a grand library housed in a separate wing; it was filled with rare paintings and furniture collected from all over the world; and it was surrounded by beautiful gardens which were likened to a poem in green, gold, and scarlet. Palmer entertained lavishly and constantly, both for his Colorado friends and for visitors from afar. One of the parties to which he must have keenly enjoyed playing host was that of the directors of the Kansas Pacific Railway, who came in 1874 and were shown how Palmer had developed the railroad and the territory which might have been theirs had they taken his advice a few years previously.

As to the General's princely habits of living, we need only refer to Hamlin Garland's description of one of his camping parties north of Sierra Blanca, where Palmer owned 700,000 acres of mountain and forest-land: *

In a lovely grove on the bank of a rushing glorious stream, we found the Lord of this Desmesne and his three daughters encamped, attended by a platoon of cooks, valets, maids and hostlers. . . .

Our luncheon, which contained five courses, came on with the plenitude

---

* Hamlin Garland, *A Daughter of the Middle Border.* Quoted by permission of the publishers, the Macmillan Company.

and precision of a meal at Glen Eyrie. The rusticity of the function was altogether confined to the benches on which we sat and the tables from which we ate—the butlering was for the most part urban. . . . For ten days we lived the most idyllic yet luxurious life beside that singing stream. We rode the trails, we gathered wild flowers, sometimes of an afternoon we visited the ranches or mining towns round about, feasting at night on turtle soup, and steak and mushrooms, drinking champagne out of tin cups with reckless disregard of camp traditions, utterly without care or responsibility—in truth we were all under military orders!

The General was a soldier even in his recreations. Each day's program was laid out in "orders" issued in due form by the head of the expedition —and these arrangements held! No one thought of changing them. Our duty was to obey—and to enjoy. . . .

For four weeks we lived this incredible life of mingled luxury and mountaineering, attended by troops of servants and squadrons of horses, threading the high forests, exploring deep mines, crossing Alpine passes, and feasting on the borders of icy lakes—always with the faithful "Nomad," the General's private Pullman car, waiting in the offing ready in case of accident.

The General on his horse was a familiar figure in Colorado Springs. At noon every day for years he rode into the town, and one of those who waited to see him was Jim, an old gray wolf who was chained to the hitching-bar in front of a livery-barn on Cascade Avenue. The General always brought him two lumps of sugar, and this treat was so welcome that Jim would sight the horseman blocks away and begin such wild antics that the tourists would scatter in fright. Even after he was injured by being thrown from his horse and had to be carried on his expeditions in a litter, General Palmer so well overcame his handicap that he continued to be the center of the large circle that enjoyed his hospitality, "gracious, full of fun, always fertile in thinking of diversions for the younger folk." When the men of the Fighting Fifteenth Cavalry came to Colorado Springs for their reunion as his guests, because he could not return to Pennsylvania, and he was carried up the marble stairs of his Antlers Hotel to greet them, his first concern was for their comfort. It had been raining, and he was afraid some of them might catch cold. "Get warm dry clothing for every man," he ordered. "Let none of them wear damp clothes or be cold." Even as an invalid he was still their commander, and they were still his men. As one of his friends said, "His dominant characteristic was courage which knew no defeat. Spare of figure, gentle of voice, the kindest of men, utterly unselfish, his face reflected the beauty of an indomitable spirit." And his career proves that he might have been speaking of himself when he wrote of Isaac Clothier that he had "a stout heart, inconquerable perseverance, a mind quick to expedients, and energy that scattered all opposition to the winds."

That he was not an unfeeling industrialist is shown by his generosity to his men at the time he sold the Rio Grande Western. On this occasion he and George Foster Peabody divided $1,000,000 among the railway employees, in a day when such a procedure was almost unheard of. President Heber J. Grant of the Mormon Church recounts the impression this story made on him:

When I heard it I laughed and said, "Oh, that is a fairy tale." I did not think much about it until ten years later, when I met Mr. Babcock, who was passenger agent here for the company at the time this was supposed to have happened. I met him in front of the Zion's Savings Bank, and I said, "Hold on, Mr. Babcock, I want to tell you a fairy tale that I heard about Mr. Palmer," and I told him this story. He laughed and said, "Grant, there is no fairy tale about that; I received a fraction over $25,000 of that $1,000,000 myself." I understand that there was many a section hand and many a man that had been with Mr. Palmer in the grading of the Road that got as much as $500.

Although General Palmer carried out his plans for giving Colorado a network of railroads that should tap its every resource, and gave his system a western outlet at Salt Lake, he was not able to complete his design for extending his line to the south. He originally intended to carry the Denver and Rio Grande through El Paso to Mexico City. The southern extension to Texas was never built, but General Palmer obtained concessions from President Porfirio Diaz of Mexico and built the Mexican National Railway from Laredo, Texas, to the City of Mexico. This accomplishment rounded out his railroad-building career, which had begun with the Kansas Pacific, had included the comprehensive surveys of the southern transcontinental routes to California, the completion of the Denver Pacific, and the building of the Denver and Rio Grande.

In appreciation of General Palmer's life and accomplishments George Foster Peabody, one of his closest associates, in 1929 caused to be struck a handsome bronze memorial bas-relief. It is characteristic of

General Palmer, showing him sitting with his riding-crop in his hands and his beloved mountains towering in the background. These plaques are now placed in the Union Stations at Denver and Salt Lake City, the Colonia Station in Mexico City, and in Colorado College at Colorado Springs and Hampton Institute in Virginia, educational institutions to which he made generous gifts. Fittingly memorializing one of the greatest railroad- and city-builders of the West, these beautiful tablets bear this inscription:

### WILLIAM JACKSON PALMER

#### 1836-1909

Union Cavalry General, pioneer railroad builder, prophet of Colorado's greatness. He mapped the routes of three transcontinental railways, supervised the building of the first road to Denver, organized and constructed the Denver and Rio Grande Railroad, stimulated the State's industries, cherished its beauties, founded Colorado Springs, fostered Colorado College, and served our Sister Republic of Mexico with sympathy and wisdom in developing its national railways.

PIKE'S PEAK AND COLORADO SPRINGS

The statue of General William Jackson Palmer was erected through public subscriptions of school-children and residents.
Courtesy of the Colorado Springs Chamber of Commerce.

"GLEN EYRIE"

Courtesy of the Colorado Springs Chamber of Commerce.

# CHAPTER VI

### RECLAIMING THE DESERT

GENERAL PALMER, the experienced man of the world, saw the scenic and industrial possibilities of his part of the West, and his vision took form in two outstanding community developments. He stamped the impress of his personality on his city of Colorado Springs, and it became, even as he predicted, a Mecca for tourists, a haven for health-seekers, and a favored center for the homes of the well-to-do. Few industries of any great importance have darkened its skies, for General Palmer never intended it to be a commercial center. Even to-day it retains something of that air of theatrical unreality and aloofness from the raw West which made it too refined for the taste of early Coloradoans; they dubbed it "little London," thus admitting, in a phrase, how completely it was the child of Palmer's imagination. Having paid his tribute to beauty and charm at Colorado Springs, the General, with characteristic versatility and with no less success, turned his attention to the virtues of smoke and grime, and to the south, at Pueblo, he brought to fruition his dreams of industry in a community which has since become the largest coal and steel center west of the Mississippi.

But the thoughts of other men of power and action, turning in different directions, left their impress on the West in other ways. As the railway pushed westward, many men who had grown up on Eastern farms began to dream vast schemes for peopling the farmlands and making the desert blossom as the rose. It took courage and imagination to make plans for such developments, for on all the maps in the days before the railroads came, the whole country between the Rockies and the Missouri was labeled with the forbidding caption, "Great American Desert." To the casual travelers it had always appeared that these immense areas of arid land, sage-brush-dotted or covered with bunch-grass, could never grow any crops of value, could at best furnish nothing more than a range for cattle. And it was not until the gold-mines were opened up around Denver in 1858, creating a heavy demand for farm-products, that men began to try to plant crops in the plains at the foot of the Rocky Mountains. Only when their pioneer efforts proved to be successful did people begin to think that perhaps it would not be impossible to reclaim the Great American Desert on a large scale. The chief agricultural experimenters had previously been the Mormons in Utah, who had turned their desert at Salt Lake into fruitful fields. So successful was this project of the Latter-Day Saints that Brigham Young pointed out to them in no uncertain terms the folly of migrating to California, seeking the uncertain profits of digging gold: "If you elders of Israel want to go to the gold mines, go and be damned. I would not give a picayune to keep you from damnation." As a result of this imprecation most of the Saints stayed at home and made sure of a safe and steady income from selling food and hay to those adventurous Gentiles who passed by Salt Lake in their wagon-trains on their way to the gold-fields.

Those first farming enterprises near Salt Lake City and Denver were the harbingers of a new day for the waste places of the West, when even the most forbidding-looking lands were to yield to the arts of the farmer—some of the valley lands by the ordinary methods used in the East, some of the more arid districts by the intensive cultivation of dry farming, and the most arid of all by the use of irrigation. In time, even the burning deserts of Arizona and southern California, where nothing could survive but the cactus, were to become as fertile as the valley of the Nile. But when the railroads first reached the Rockies, these developments were far in the future; little was known of irrigation; all Western farming was an experiment and an adventure. With the coming of the railroads, however, millions of acres of farm-lands were opened up, and the Eastern markets were made easily available to the remote districts of the West. And many hardy and imaginative spirits were willing to try their hands at turning the new country into an agricultural paradise.

The Union Pacific, the Kansas Pacific, and, finally, the Denver Pacific—the road which we shall see the people of Denver building to Cheyenne, Wyoming, when the Union Pacific left Denver off its main line—had been granted alternate sections of land for 20 miles on both sides of their rights of way. These railroads were naturally the most active agencies in developing the agricultural resources of the new country at the base of the Rockies. They advertised their land, told tall tales of its marvelous productivity, sold it cheap, and offered low rates for passengers who wished to come west to buy farms. As a result of these activities numerous groups were organized in the East with the purpose of emigrating to the West, buying large tracts of land, and establishing agricultural colonies. Among the colonizing enterprises that laid their plans to settle in Colorado were the Central Kentucky Emigration Society, the Illinois Colony, the Wyandotte Kansas Colony, the German Colonization Company of Chicago, the Tennessee Colony, the St. Louis Western Colony, and the Chicago-Colorado Colony, this last under the leadership of the famous Unitarian clergyman Robert Collyer. Most of these groups dealt with the National Land Company of New York, which was the selling agent for the lands of the Denver Pacific and Kansas Pacific railways, and whose agent, William N. Byers of Denver, fervently sang of the glories of Colorado farming in the promotional magazine *Star of Empire*.

Not all these hopeful groups of would-be emigrants actually reached the promised land, and some of those who did form colonies saw them perish from incompetent leadership. But at least one of these early ventures was built strongly enough to withstand the disintegrating effects of hardship, dissension, and a reluctant soil. This colony, which became a model for the development of farm communities and irrigation projects throughout the West, was the product of the leadership of Nathan Cook Meeker, agricultural editor of the New York *Tribune*, who named it after his famous editor-in-chief, Horace Greeley. And the story of Meeker and his colony of Greeley, Colorado, typifies the struggle, the disappointment, the refusal to bow before discouragement and seeming defeat, and the final success that have been the sequence followed by many a Western agricultural project through early difficulties to healthy maturity.

Nathan Cook Meeker was a curious combination of dreamer, enthusiastic theorist, social idealist, and practical, energetic builder. He had a clear vision of what he wanted to do in the new country; he went at his work with extraordinary zeal and dogged—even grim—determination; he carried out his plans painstakingly and consistently. But although he left a thriving town and a prosperous agricultural district as his monument, he never received during his lifetime the popular acclaim that his achievements might have been expected to bring. So wrapped up was he in his own ideas and his plans for putting them into effect that he had no time for cultivating the friendship of the crowd, no interest in idle conversation with his people on trifling topics of the day, no concern with anything but his project of making Greeley an ideal community. He was "too busy to dawdle, too serious to jest, too conscientious to flatter, too honest to deceive; he had also a blunt, direct way of approaching a subject or a man which tended, sadly enough, to repel strangers, to embitter foes, and too often to provoke the best of friends." This was the man whose able and determined leadership was responsible for the success of the farm community and pioneer irrigation project of Greeley, Colorado.

For many years before the Greeley project was actually undertaken, Meeker had cherished the idea of building such a community. His reading had brought him into contact with the ideas of François Fourier, the French socialist, who advocated the building of communities in coöperative phalanxes; and when Meeker heard that such a phalanx was being formed at Warren, Ohio, he and his young wife joined it. And there, in the three years before the community finally broke up because of bad management and ague, he says, "I learned how much coöperation people would bear."

Previous to this time Meeker had made his living entirely through writing, except for brief intervals of teaching school. As a boy he left Euclid, near Cleveland, Ohio, to journey to New Orleans, mostly on foot, where he got his first job as a cub reporter on the *Picayune*. Two years later he went to New York and attracted the attention of Nathaniel Parker Willis, of the New York *Mirror*, for whom he wrote poems and light verse. Although these were popular enough to be copied by other newspapers, they brought little money to Meeker's pocket; and, indeed, so meager were the financial returns that he gave up poetry in disgust, and in later years he always regarded with abhorrence those amateur practitioners of the art who hopefully brought their verse to be printed in his newspaper. He said that the only good turn his poetry ever did him was when he fell downstairs on a Mississippi steamboat and saved himself a broken neck by landing on his top-hat, which was stuffed with the manuscripts of his poetic master-pieces.

After the Warren phalanx broke up, even as did its famous counter-part at Brook Farm, Massachusetts, Meeker moved to Hiram, Ohio, where he was a neighbor of James A. Garfield, then leading the Campbellite sect in establishing Hiram College. Here he kept a store for a while and in his spare moments wrote a book describing the *Adventures of Captain Armstrong,* who was wrecked in the South Seas and taught the natives all the arts and sciences of civilization—even to the building of steam-engines—with none of its vices. There was a Mormon elder in the town who used to tell Garfield and Meeker and the others wonderful stories of the Rocky Mountains and of the ideal city built there by the Latter-Day Saints and presided over by Brigham Young. These stories took a powerful hold on Meeker's imagination, and he would take his little daughter Rozine on his knee, call her his "Rocky Mountain girl," and declare that he would some day establish an ideal community out there in the new country far removed from the noise and frivolities of society.

When the panic of 1857 nearly ruined him, Meeker abandoned his store at Hiram and opened up another at Dongola, Illinois, also operat-ing a small fruit-farm there. But, as usual, he devoted his spare mo-ments to writing—this time for the Cleveland *Plain Dealer,* through which he became a friend of Artemus Ward. When the Civil War broke out, he and his family suffered great indignities from their neighbors in this southern Illinois community, for most of them were secessionists, and Meeker was an ardent Union man. Some of his writings at this time attracted the attention of Horace Greeley, who telegraphed his representative at Cairo, "Meeker is the man we want"; and thus he became war correspondent for the New York *Tribune* at General Grant's headquarters.

At the close of the war, when he became agricultural editor of the *Tribune,* Meeker entered upon that phase of his career which was to culminate in the building of the town of Greeley. In this newspaper of nation-wide circulation his advice and comments on agriculture were read by farmers everywhere, and he became more or less of an authority on matters that concerned them. Meanwhile, he wrote another book, *Life in the West,* and a series of articles about the Oneida Community of northern New York which attracted much attention. In the autumn of 1869 he started on a tour of the Far West, writing his impressions as he went, intending to finish his journey in Utah, there to write about the Mormon colony in the same manner as he had treated the Oneida Community. A snow blockade on the Union Pacific held him up at Cheyenne, however, so he never reached the Mormon capital. But on the trip he joined a party containing Cyrus W. Field of New York, Colonel James Archer of St. Louis, and General William J. Palmer, and saw Pueblo, the Pike's Peak region, Denver, and the Gregory Diggings and mines at Central City.

Although Meeker had written about life in the West before, the West he knew was no farther toward the Pacific than Illinois. Now he had a chance to see the real thing. In a letter to the *Tribune* he described his impressions of the frontier town of Sheridan, Kansas:

Sheridan is at present the most remarkable place in America, or in the world; it's what Cheyenne was a few years ago, the terminus of the road where legitimate business centers, and where the most reckless men and women gather, in order that in the absence of law and in the unprotected state in which property is necessarily placed, they may reap a harvest of plunder. The town is composed of two half streets some 300 feet apart, the railroad being in the center. There are large commercial houses engaged in the Santa Fe trade, holding heavy stocks of staple goods representing capital ranging from $20,000 to $500,000. Some of the stores are as much as 150 feet long, and wide in proportion, and I saw one where many tons of Mexican wool were awaiting shipment. Besides these houses there are a few hotels and several buildings belonging to the railroad and the rest are saloons and gambling establishments, more than fifty in number, all open and apparently doing a good business. In almost every one are women; fiddles and accordeons are playing, glasses jingling; and there are billiard and roulette tables, and other gambling devices.

The men are able-bodied and strong; few are more than 35; the majority are less than 30 years old; their faces are flushed, their necks red and thick, and they speak as good English as any people in the states, using many common household expressions. But they have a restless, uncertain look and quickness of movement both strange and suspicious, and the more so because connected with much that is home-like and familiar. Of course they are well armed and ready in a moment for attack or defense; but I saw none who were either offensive or aggressive, though I have every reason to believe that they would commit murder on what we would call the slightest provocation, for they have been so audacious and bold that men of property have been obliged to resolve themselves into a vigilance committee and hang fifteen or twenty. Back of the town is a small graveyard where they have been buried, and only a few days before I arrived, one of them was hanged to the trestle-work a little out of town. For some time past the engineer has been in the habit of moving the morning train slowly over this spot in order that the passengers might see whether any one was hanging there by the neck. Among the aggressive acts of these men, it is related that, at a hotel, one asked a gentleman, sitting opposite, to pass the butter, and not being heard he immediately drew a small pistol and presented it at the head of the gentleman, with his finger on the trigger, saying, "Pass the butter."

Under General Palmer's guidance the party journeyed to Denver by way of southern Colorado in a buckboard. On this trip Meeker had opportunity to note the agricultural possibilities of the state, to see how the few farmers lived, and to feel the need for building in this wild new territory a model colony such as he had long had in mind. Here is his picture of one ranch in the valley of the Fontaine Qui Bouille, below what is now Colorado Springs:

Many of the houses were of adobe or sunburnt brick, occupied by Yankees, but no fences were to be seen. Having a lunch along, we stopped at an adobe house to warm and to eat. Two able bodied men, ragged and dirty, were the occupants, a smouldering fire was in the fire-place, a dirty table was covered with dirty dishes, and there were several large dogs. A good fire was built, and I swept up the hearth with a stump of a broom; one of the men sat on the bedside to grind us some coffee, and he hung a tea kettle over the fire; the other washed the dishes with a small dish cloth and, after squeezing it with one hand, wiped them with it. I have noticed that when men do housework their dish cloths are small, and that while cooking, they smoke a pipe. Three more men then appeared with dogs and guns, and sat on the beds while we ate our lunch. Some of these men were Irish and had served in the Confederate army, or more likely had deserted from it or the Union army; others were from the Northern States, but what they came for we did not learn. When asked why they did not marry they said they had wives in the states, that they were waiting till there was peace with the Indians, not to bring out their wives, but that they might get squaws.

At Denver, Meeker found a city of 7,000 which he compared with the first-class cities of Ohio and Illinois:

In many respects it resembles Chicago. The business men are as sober, as upright and as exemplary as in any other city, but they have a brusque rapid way. Everybody is busy, and the clerks look a good deal like boys that have just been washed and have neglected to comb their hair. As the city is out on the great plains, and below the divide, rain seldom falls, and cultivation would be without reward were it not for the introduction of water from the Platte, which, being taken out of this stream, twenty-four miles above the city, runs along the gutters of every street, and into gardens, and furnishes water for grist-mills. It is intended to extend ditches to higher grounds south of the town, where a vast extent of country can be watered, and besides, a water power can be obtained with one hundred feet fall.

This was Meeker's first view of a Western irrigation project, and though it was not on a very large scale, it offered him first-hand contact with irrigation such as he wished to use in his own farm community. He had seen enough on this trip to convince him that the formation of an agricultural colony somewhere on the plains east of the Rockies was the thing he most desired to do, and when he returned to New York, he broached the matter to his wife. Since she had already pioneered in two communities, she was not particularly enthusiastic over the prospect of enduring the privations of frontier life in a third, especially as the family was comfortably settled in a New York suburb. Nevertheless Meeker went forward with his plan.

It was in the luxurious setting of Delmonico's in New York City that Meeker first mentioned his pioneering project to Horace Greeley. He had already spoken of it to John Russell Young, editor of the New York *Standard,* who had in turn talked of it to Mr. Greeley. After a press dinner at the famous New York restaurant, when the crowd was breaking up and the air was thick with the smoke of cigars, Greeley called Meeker to him to discuss the plan. Since he himself had made a trip to Colorado several years previously, particularly to inspect and report on the state of affairs in the gold-mines at Denver and Central City, Greeley knew the country well, and the idea of an agricultural colony there appealed to him. "I understand you have a notion to start a colony to go to Colorado," he said to Meeker. "I wish you would take hold of it, for I think it will be a great success and if I could I would go myself."

Assured of this powerful backing, Meeker spent the whole of the next day writing an article on the subject. Greeley asked to see it set up in type, kept it a week making corrections, suggested that the town be divided into blocks of 10 acres each, and then wrote an editorial to accompany it. It was published on the 14th of December, 1869, in the daily *Tribune,* and later in the weekly and semi-weekly editions; and although Meeker thought Greeley overoptimistic when he predicted that there would be 1,000 replies, over 3,000 were actually received.

Two days before Christmas, Room 24 of the Cooper Institute was crowded with people who had responded to Meeker's call for founding a colony in the West. Preceding the meeting, the offices and stairs and hallways of the New York *Tribune* were thronged with those who wanted to discuss the project with Meeker. Among them was a large tall man with a broad-brimmed hat who buttonholed him as he went into his office and told him that he had been in the Army, and had had his sight impaired, and had had losses and troubles, and had published a paper in Indiana, and would like to go in the colony. This man was General Robert A. Cameron, who, with Meeker and H. T. West, later completed the triumvirate that ruled the destinies of Greeley, Colorado, and who also aided General Palmer in establishing the town of Colorado Springs.

At the Cooper Institute meeting, plans were discussed for a colony providing a central town with tracts of farm-land adjoining. The name of Union Colony was selected, but the probable location was not made public; Meeker was elected president, Cameron, vice-president, and Greeley, treasurer. Each member was to pay $5 for current expenses and $150 for the land to be bought. Fifty-five paid their first fee immediately, great enthusiasm prevailed, and shortly thereafter the locating committee, composed of Meeker, Cameron, a Mr. Fisk of Toledo, and H. T. West of Chicago, set out for the Rockies.

By the Union Pacific Railway the committee went to Cheyenne, and from there by the Denver Pacific to Evans, the point that railroad had reached on its way to connect the Union Pacific main line with Denver. Thence they went by stage to Denver and, with ex-Governor Alexander Cameron Hunt, to the Pike's Peak district which Meeker had already visited with General Palmer. Not finding any sufficient tract of irrigable land to the south, they investigated the country between Denver and Cheyenne, and also Evanston, Wyoming, and the Bear River country near Ogden, Utah, after which they returned to New York. No announcement was made of their decision, but on

April 6, 1870, William N. Byers of the National Land Company wrote General Palmer, who was then interested in building the Denver Pacific Railroad from Denver to Cheyenne, that he had secured the location of the Meeker colony on Denver Pacific land. On the 12th a circular was issued in New York, signed by Meeker's son, Ralph, as secretary, stating that "After many difficulties the Locating Committee has succeeded in purchasing 70,000 acres of railroad and government land on the Cache la Poudre, half way between Denver and Cheyenne." As a matter of fact, 9,324 acres were purchased from the railroad, 2,592 acres from private interests, including David H. Moffat, trustee of the Denver Land Company, and the remaining 60,000 acres was government land which was filed upon in the names of fictitious individuals with payment of the location fees. These homestead claims could have been "jumped" by outsiders at any time, but they never were, because they could have been of little value without irrigation and the colony controlled the water-supply, the use of which it granted only to its own members.

The cost of the land was $60,000, the money being furnished by the $155 subscriptions of the members of the colony, who were each permitted to select a town lot at from $25 to $50, 80 acres of government land by paying $75 for water-rights, and colony land varying from 5 to 40 acres according to the distance from the city. All lands were to be supplied with water and were subject to no assessment except to keep ditches in repair. The town was divided into business and residence lots, 277 lots being reserved for schools and churches, a 10-acre plaza was laid out at the center of the town, land was set aside for a park, and the construction of irrigation ditches was begun immediately. Final deeds to property were granted only when it had been improved by the purchaser, none but members were at first permitted to buy land, and each deed contained a clause prohibiting the sale of liquor, the prohibition feature being modeled on that of Evanston, Illinois, named after ex-Governor John Evans of Colorado, and that of Vineland, New Jersey.

In April, 1870, more than 400 would-be colonists had signed the rolls and paid the initiation fee, and about 200 were actually on the ground at Greeley, for the town had by that time been thus named, after Meeker had refused to have it named after himself. This group, who were mostly from New York, New England, Ohio, and Indiana, did not in all cases find Greeley as Elysian a community as they had expected. They had heard much about grand scenery, trout in mountain streams, cold pure water, healthful climate, and cattle grazing on a thousand hills, but little of the aridity, the difficulties of irrigation, and the hard work that would have to be done to make the country habitable.

On the 1st of June, 1870, the *Rocky Mountain News* reported the population as 460, but about fifty more had returned to their homes in disgust. And one colonist wrote to the Milwaukee *Sentinel*:

We have been at Greeley, and we speak that which we know, when we declare that although the climate is good, the air pure, and the stars very bright at night, there is nothing to induce a sane man to plant himself on that desert. No trees are within fifty miles, except a few stunted cotton-woods upon the banks of the stream. The soil is alkali, and poor enough. The thing is a humbug. If it shall serve the purpose of cooling the brains of a few hot-headed reformists by showing them the impracticability of their theories, it will serve a good purpose, but whoso reads this article and goes there, cannot say he was not duly warned of the humbug. Many have left it, and soon its last hovel will be deserted.

And another writer, in the *Missouri Republic,* declared that

Several stern wheel shanties and a few one horse tents comprise the population of Greeley, which is located—if there be such a thing as locating a baker's dozen of slab shanties, as many tool chests, a great ditch, and twenty acres of prickly pears—on a barren, sandy plain, part and parcel of the Great American Desert, midway between a poverty stricken ranch and a prairie-dog village on two sides; and a poverty-stricken ranch and a prairie village on t'other. It is bounded chiefly by prickly pears. The plucking of this choice plant from the part of their babies' corporeal frame to which in old times the punitive shoe was wont to be applied, gives the mothers of Greeley constant, if not pleasant, employment. (We would add par parenthesis that on that balmy May morning on which we regretfully bid adieu to Greeley, we left the men swearing, the women crying, and picking prickly pears out of parts indicated—a lively, if not a soothing, scene to snatch one's self away from on a bright morning in beautiful May.)

Because labor finds no employment; because there is no capital amongst the colonists; because no crops of any description (except prickly pears) can be produced at Greeley for the next three years—if indeed anything but prickly pears and prairie dogs' holes can ever be raised; because there is no wood, nor coal, nor lumber, nor anything else but disappointed men and weeping women and squalling young'uns, there, or anywhere about there—notwithstanding these things prove nothing against the future magnitude of the embryo capital of Colorado. But until this happy period arrives, the honest President Meeker tells his colonists that they must all go a keeping boarders (!) but suppose that they have all gone doing so, though we can't quite see where the boarders are to come from, we leave Greeley for the present, repeating the advice to the uneasy, restless readers of The Republic, that if they can't stay where they are, but must go somewhere else, don't ever dream of such a wild and foolish thing as striking out for the great colony of Greeley, Colorado Territory.

But despite the scoffing of the disappointed and the faint-hearted, the colonists who remained set cheerfully to work to build their new home. "The first night," said J. Max Clark, one of the early colonists, "I asked myself, who are all these people, gathered together under the leadership of one visionary old man, in the vain hope of building up a paradise in the sands of the desert? Evidently all of them cranks and fools, and myself pre-eminently the foolest fool in the lot." But the next morning the air was fresher and the soil did not look quite so sandy, "our spirits began to rise and we were not conscious of being quite the extraordinary fools we thought ourselves the day before; and then the first thing we knew, we were running frantically about looking for lots for ourselves, and quite disgusted, too, to think we had wasted so much time. We got some and that settled the business; we settled." *

Next day Clark had his first interview with Meeker, who replied very curtly to his doubts as to the fertility of the sandy soil and left him with the conviction that the leader was an honest man who had the success of the colony nearer to his heart than any other object in the world. Meeker's two coadjutors, however, did not always create so favorable an impression. H. T. West, who was the business man and accountant of the trio, "had the air of a sharper," and General Cameron "looked a good deal like a seedy, cast-off, played-out, third-rate politician." But together they formed a strong group—Meeker the ardent, idealistic, hard-working leader, Cameron the flowery, expansive promoter, and West the shrewd, careful business man.

Although Clark's wife, when she finally arrived, looked at the forbiddingly arid landscape and cried, "Oh, why did you bring me to this wretched country?" he was not discouraged. Like the other colonists,

* J. Max Clark, *Colonial Days* (Denver, Smith Brooks Printing Company).

he could conjure up in his mind's eye beautiful fields of waving grain, blossoming clover, and stately trees, although as yet not a furrow had been plowed or a tree set. But all the men who built the colony were living almost wholly in their imaginations; and they worked so vigorously that in a few months 400 houses had been built, real-estate prices had jumped from $50 to $1,000 for choice business locations, and the men on the street-corners were talking confidently of a city which would have 10,000 inhabitants in the near future.

But once the town was built, the colonists began to realize the overwhelming difficulties that confronted them in trying to improve the adjoining farm-lands by supplying them with water. Irrigation had seemed easy in theory, though no one in America knew much about it in practice; Meeker had remarked airily that "the cost of irrigation will be about the same as that of fencing," and had added, "A little water goes a great deal farther than people generally suppose. In California they use much more than is necessary." The colonists set the cost of the four ditches deemed necessary to bring the water several miles from the Cache la Poudre River to irrigate 60,000 acres at $20,000 and immediately began building the Big Ditch (officially known as Canal No. 2). This single canal cost $27,000 and was supposed to water 2,000 acres, but actually it carried so little water the first year that nearly all the crops died. There were some 40 miles of lateral canals to be "wet up" by the big canal, and since the ditch was new, the ground was so dry when the water was let in that it took nearly a week for any of it to get to the end of the canal. In New York Meeker had described to his audience of would-be emigrants how the water followed a man down the ditch like a little dog trotting at his heels, but the colonists found that it took a lot of coaxing to get the little dog to follow, and he frequently lay down in his tracks and refused to move.

Says J. Max Clark:

There are a number of the original Colonists left who will never forget the trials and tribulations of that first summer of agricultural experiment under canal No. 2. When we had sowed our wheat and killed our best horse in digging the lateral down to its margin through the desert, with anxious expectation we watched its feeble growth day by day, after it had pushed its way through the ground, and nursed its sickly vitality with the attenuated little stream of water that came creeping down through the mirage that hovered incessantly about the canal above us, until at last it withered, like a false hope, and died; then there came a hail storm that would have knocked seventeen vigorous lives out of that crop of wheat, if there had been any life there to destroy, and there wasn't a ghost of a chance for it if the hail storm had passed by on the other side; and, finally, barring the rich and useful experience gained that season, and employed to advantage in after years, that entire load of wheat might better have been sown in the road rather than with such profitless labor scattered upon our farms.

It was such experiences as these that caused one irrigator to post this wrathful notice at the flume headgate: "Whoever is found meddling with this headgate will catch hell and a great deal of it."

Yet even in this time of agricultural failure there were bold spirits in the town who were intent on grand schemes to make Greeley a great center of industry. Refusing to see that the success of the colony depended on the canals, they asked that the people turn their attention and the colony funds to the establishment of a woolen-mill. Toward this project Father Meeker preserved a mild neutrality, but General Cameron enthusiastically addressed a public meeting and declared that a woolen-mill would immediately advance the prosperity of the colony. The farmers who had watched their crops fail from lack of water were indignant at the idea of spending money on anything but enlarging the canals, and one of them brought to the meeting a bunch of wheat starved to death from want of water, measuring only a foot from tip to root. When the General had completed his persuasive speech in favor of building the mill to countervail the overproduction of the "gross products" of the farm, J. Max Clark gained the floor and told the assembly

that there was a number of us farmers out in the bluffs just then who felt very little concern as to what we would do with the gross product; that, on the other hand, we entertained serious fears that for some time to come the gross product might not make the bread to keep us alive. Then I pulled that bunch of wheat from under my coat tail, and, holding it up in full view of the audience, I asked if that looked like glutting the markets of the world. I couldn't talk much, but I had no need to talk; that bunch of drouth-withered wheat did the business; it was more eloquent than a host of tongues, and before the meeting closed it was a conceded point that the factory would have to wait.

Now the town was in a quandary. The colony funds had all been spent, but it was absolutely necessary that the Big Ditch be made bigger, or there would be an end of Greeley. The colonists were most of them poor when they first came, and they had by this time spent most of the money they brought with them. Meeker decided that the colony should sell its surplus lands to get the funds needed, and this was done; an assessment of 35 cents an acre was also levied, and $20,000 more was spent on the Big Ditch. In view of the original estimate that the total cost of all ditches would be $20,000, it is interesting to note that before this one ditch had sufficient capacity to meet the demands made on it, no less than $112,000 was spent on its construction. By the second year, the ditch was enlarged, excellent crops were grown, and the crisis in the history of this pioneer irrigation project was successfully passed. It is well that this was so, for what was learned about the theory and practice of irrigation at Greeley in those first years was of benefit to the entire West in its later agricultural development.

Irrigation was but imperfectly understood in the United States at that time. The Greeley Farmers' Club corresponded with others who had tried it in the West but could get little practical information; even the Mormons who had been successfully using it for years had not developed any system, collected any records, or contributed anything to the world's scanty knowledge of the subject. After searching everywhere for help the Greeleyites finally turned to Italy, and from the records of the 300-year-old irrigation projects in that country they formed estimates of what canals would be required for Greeley if all its lands were to be properly irrigated. At the Irrigation Convention in Denver in 1873 J. Max Clark of Greeley advanced views based on this research, but he was thought to be entirely too pessimistic. An English engineer, Frederick Stanton, declared that 25,000,000 acres of land could be reclaimed by irrigation in Colorado, and he suggested for the irrigation of 1,500,000 acres a canal 100 miles long, 12 feet wide and 3 feet deep. Then up rose Mr. Clark and addressed the convention with some feeling:

I am a farmer. I till the earth with my own hands. I am accustomed to carry the mud of the waters of irrigation on my boot heels, and the brown dust of the desert in my hair; and when I read in the report of the proceedings of the Farmers' convention of last June, what all the ex-governors, judges, lawyers and politicians had to say on the subject of irrigation, it occurred to me that if in this meeting there should mingle in with all that hopeful, enthusiastic, profound, professional thought upon so important a subject, a little more of the thinking of the practical, plodding, calculating element of the farm, it might not be inappropriate or amiss in a farmers' movement. . . . We have seen the area of our arable land estimated all the way from four to ten millions of acres, when we don't believe there are two millions; and we have read with fear and trembling how the Hon. Fred Stanton, enthusiastic upon the almighty resources of our common country and the agricultural resources of Colorado in particular, is proposing to cut a great gash in the earth, from South Platte cañon to Kansas City, and water all the land on both sides of the ridge.

Taking an average over the whole irrigated district of Italy, it requires a discharge of a cubic foot of water per second to irrigate sixty-six acres of land; and supposing Mr. Stanton should only propose to irrigate an insignificant strip of country two miles wide the whole length of his district, and in round numbers say 750,000 acres, he would require a discharge of 11,362 cubic feet of water per second during the whole irrigating season. The mean discharge of all our rivers north of the Divide for the irrigating season does not more than equal the eleven or twelve thousand cubic feet per second which Mr. Stanton would require for his one big ditch.

Clark pointed out that in Italy, after hundreds of years of experiment, there were only 1,600,000 acres under irrigation; that to irrigate the land suggested under Stanton's ditch would require the impossible current velocity of four miles per minute; that there was not sufficient water in the mountains even to fill it—and he would risk the government powder in time of war at its farther end.

Though such a dashing of cold water on the enthusiasm of theoretical irrigators was not popular, it was needed, for the professional promoters were already laying out vast areas of land which were covered with ditches but for which no adequate source of water was available. The Greeleyites were all against such activities, including "buncombe speeches filled with desert rose bushes, buncombe statistics of production that lie, and buncombe ditches on paper that can never be filled." The practical farmers of Greeley worked out practical methods of irrigation which were copied elsewhere, and they entered the hazy and highly controversial field of irrigation legislation, producing a law code which has been a landmark in the history of irrigation ever since. The Colorado irrigation laws developed by Greeleyites were studied and followed by the lawmakers of Wyoming, Nevada, and California; and a commission sent from Australia to examine American irrigation

NATHAN COOK MEEKER

Courtesy of the Meeker Memorial Museum.

THE MEEKER HOMESTEAD AT GREELEY

Now the Meeker Memorial Museum. From a photograph taken in 1889. Courtesy
of the Museum.

### THE FIRST SETTLEMENT AT GREELEY

From a photograph taken in 1870, looking west from the railroad tracks. Courtesy of the Meeker Memorial Museum.

### GREELEY TO-DAY

Practically the same view as the above, looking west on Eighth Street toward Lincoln Park. Courtesy of the Greeley *Daily Tribune*.

### A SUGAR-BEET FIELD UNDER IRRIGATION NEAR GREELEY

Courtesy of the Greeley *Daily Tribune*.

legislation reported, "As the laws of Colorado are by far the most successful, they may be fairly allotted first place."

While the practice of irrigation was being perfected and its code of laws hammered out by the more earnest spirits, the rest of the citizens were busily engaged in all the multifarious activities that made Greeley a full-fledged community. A dramatic club was formed which promptly obliged with "Ten Nights in a Bar-Room"; a billiard-saloon was denied a license; a school and several churches were built; a lottery to build a library was frowned upon; and when a whisky-saloon was opened by a German, the citizens one Sunday morning took the law into their own hands:

Before the benediction had been pronounced, a committee was appointed to interview the saloon keeper. About two hundred persons gathered around the liquor establishment, soon after the committee arrived. The proprietor said that he had paid $200 for the use of the building and he meant to stay until the lease expired. One of the committee got possession of the key and locked the door. The committee finally agreed to pay the whiskey dealer $200 for his lease, and to cart the liquor to a place of safety. Many were clamorous to burn the shanty and destroy the brandy casks. The den was soon after discovered to be on fire. Then the committee made a grand rush and succeeded in extinguishing the flames, besides saving the rum, with the card tables, decanters and dice-boxes. While the members of the committee were congratulating themselves on this feat, the building was discovered to be on fire again, but the flames were subdued only to break out again on the outside of the shanty, and this last conflagration entirely destroyed it.

The town records were enlivened with the names of several famous people. Phineas T. Barnum was one of the early members, and so was a Mr. Fisk, who was a cousin of the stock-plunger, Jim Fisk of Wall Street. Barnum wrote Fisk to hurry up with the building he was erecting and to make it as big as possible because Barnum intended to beat him with a bigger one when he got there—which he afterwards did. The Hotel de Comfort, a huge dormitory-like hall, divided into one sleeping-room for bachelors and one for families, was the center of the city's life and color, where they carried on heated discussions of topics of the day of so radical a nature as to bring upon it the opprobrious title of "the Jacobin Club." There were two lyceums "eternally in session," from which preachers urged their flocks to stay away if they would save their faith; an Army and Navy Club lured the less stable elements of the community, and in the conversation of the men gathered there "the Saints were roughly handled"; there were baseball teams and a hook-and-ladder company. A juvenile boot-black electrified the community by appearing on the streets and singing, "Black 'em up and make 'em shine. Less than a minute—only a dime." Soft-voiced hunters, dressed in buckskin with yards of fringe, brought in antelope and sometimes the carcasses of wolves and wildcats. Stocky teamsters, who slept outdoors on the ground under their wagons in coldest weather, drove in cattle from Atchison. There were herders and cattlemen with buckskin leggings, pistols and knives, jaunty Mexican hats, and long, jingling spurs; some were big cattle-owners who carried $50,000 in their belts and drafts on Denver for millions.

Two hundred couples joined in the Odd Fellows dance to the music of Smith's Quadrille Band, and of this social event "Sapho," the local correspondent for the Denver *Tribune,* somewhat tartly remarked: *

The supper (if I may be allowed to call it by that name) was furnished by Judge Childs, and if any one made themselves sick by eating too much, I should have been happy to have had a seat at the same table, and if ever another ball takes place at Greeley, if my advice is worth anything, I should say, let the job out to some hotel, which has accommodations and facilities for getting up a supper. Coffee and cake is pretty good, but something more substantial is better.... Among the many fair ladies present, was the beautiful and gentle blonde Miss Gussie N—ls, attired in a magnificent light silk, with point lace, sash and bow, "en pannier." Miss Belle S—ts was charmingly dressed in white, with black silk sash, and necklace of pearls. Miss G— was gotten up regardless of all expense, and was, beyond all doubt, the belle of the evening. Mrs. Harry L—e appeared, as she invariably does, par excellent, and was dressed in an elegant and costly manner. Miss Laura N—s was also very richly costumed in silks and diamonds. Miss Gussie P—s was neatly dressed in white muslin, with countless flounces and ruffles. And as white seemed to be the reigning color, Miss F. E. also chose it and with a profusion of cheap jewelry looked very well.

Finally, there was woman suffrage, and the Greeleyites learned that the ladies "can and will vote at a moment's notice." In the spirited campaign for postmaster there were

* James F. Willard, *The Union Colony at Greeley 1869-1871* (Boulder, 1918). Quoted by permission.

flags, bells, mottoes, posters and good-looking young men, and in a short time the hall was packed with women and girls, all crowding up to vote for Gipson. Then Mr. Flower sent for bells and a fast team, and gave orders for the driver to corral all the women who would vote, and bring them to the front. The news spread like new cider, and in the course of two hours the scene reminded one of a political camp-meeting. Courting a girl on the Lower Arkansas was nothing to the way in which Gipson and Flower seduced the loveliness and flower of Greeley from the undarned stockings of their domestic hearthstones. At five o'clock the perspiration fairly stood on the brows of the respective candidates. The excitement increased, and by sundown the sleighs were flying through the streets. The women were getting excited, and their enthusiasm glowed like pine knots. One of the leading merchants rushed up the street in a two-horse cutter, and soon returned sitting in the laps of three ladies, while the horses shot through the streets to the polls. At the polls, Mr. Gipson escorted the fair ones up stairs to vote, while the wholesale gentleman drove off for more. At dark fresh horses were procured and the excitement increased. At eight the polls were closed. Time was precious. Gipson knew of a dozen ladies up town, who must be brought at once. Marx rushed off for three girls on the east side, and so they came, young girls, servants, old ladies with silver hairs, brides, and women with young babes, until it seemed as though all the arguments that Brother Todd had ever made, were to be utterly swept away.*

The Greeley *Tribune,* owned and edited by Meeker, described the types of people who made up the community. There are, it said, educated mechanics who know quite well what a nice house should be and are anxious to build it; farmers who are handy with tools and close students of irrigation; well educated people who have learned to combine literary culture with everyday industry; ministers of good sense and with a knowledge of theology; and several politicians well schooled in all the arts, schemes, dodges, and devices of the fraternity. A majority of the married women have taught school, and

the disagreeable condition in which they have been placed for want of comfortable homes has given to many a sad cast of countenance, and some have scarcely appeared in public. Of late, and since houses have been plastered and conveniences have multiplied, a change for the better in the appearance of the women has been apparent, and the congregation at church is much more elegant and cheerful than it was two months ago. The truth is a woman is weak unless she can have a comfortable house; and a man is not only weak but untidy unless he has a housekeeper. As to

* *Ibid.*

intellect, the women are fully equal to the men and they only lack drill and wider means of obtaining information. Many of the females are remarkable for large perceptive and reflective powers, and these, often, are in excess of their vitality.

A company of young men equal to ours cannot be found in the world. Most of them are educated, all are well informed. There may be a few who, under other circumstances, would be irregular, but the influences surrounding them by reason of the good conduct and gentlemanly habits of the many, restrain them, and they are better than they could expect themselves to be. This general state of good morals among us does not arise from fanaticism, nor from any sort of uniformity in religious belief. Certain papers, and persons abroad have conveyed the idea that we are a set of straight backed Puritans, and that men are fined 10cts for taking a chew of tobacco. If any thing of this kind exists we have failed to see it, and it is uncertain whether a majority belong to any church; while it is certain that no one church predominates. As to the use of tobacco, some of our reformers frequently remark that they are astonished and grieved to see so many use it. For the most part, our young men neither chew nor smoke. How many of them have made the money they brought with them, or how many were supplied by their friends, cannot be known, but from the energy they display, and the careful use they make of money, it may be presumed that they acquired the most they have by their own efforts. Generally, a young man's grip on money is slight, it relaxes unawares, and his hand seldom closes firmly until a female hand, displaying a plain gold ring, is clasped over it. Then it shuts like a vice. It will be difficult to find so many young men elsewhere whose handwriting is so good, who are so well acquainted with ancient and modern literature.

Sometimes eight or ten can be found taking their meals in a back room from a table promiscuously spread with tin plates and odd pieces of crockery; some sit on chairs, others on benches, and not unfrequently they eat standing, holding a morsel of meat and bread in one hand and a cup of coffee in the other. You may be sure that the floor is not mopped every day, nor that the sheets, if sheets are used, show every night fresh folds made by the flat-iron. They have little cook stoves, and pots and pans and cupboards and dishes, and tumblers for visitors to drink out of, and looking-glasses, and there is always a shelf well filled with books. But the table is set in a haphazard way, and when they sit down to eat they so place themselves as to watch some article of food cooking on the stove, generally slap-jacks, that they may be eaten hot. As they are industrious and always have some kind of work on hand, the dishes are shoved away as soon as the meal is over, and when the next meal is to be prepared, these dishes are to be washed, or at least scraped. Some having been tossed much about the world, have learned to be good cooks, and they have imparted their knowledge to the rest, hence, their cooking is generally good; and with baking powder and our excellent Colorado flour, they make as nice biscuits as ever were eaten. They broil or fry steak nicely, and their stewed fruit is well sweetened. The art of making raised bread has not yet been acquired. Everywhere the tables are without covering, and it is doubtful whether a man running Bachelor's Hall ever provided a table cloth. They take a great many papers and magazines, and it would surprise a stranger to learn that a young man working by the day or month has kept files of the best magazines for years, and that there is no topic of general interest nor any important event of the day of which he is ignorant. Of course each one is the owner of a town lot, often of a business and of a residence lot, and also of outside farming land. In the progress and growth of the town and Colony he has an equal share, and the time cannot be distant when by the investment he has made of $155 he will have a property which will make him independent, while in the East he could have secured this only by years of persevering industry.*

As the people of Greeley struggled with the reluctant soil, they thought, no doubt, of the glowing descriptions of the delights of farming in Colorado printed by the National Land Company in its *Star of Empire*. According to this authority, it was easy to grow 26 to 28 bushels of wheat per acre, or, with extra care, 40 to 70; oats yielded 40 to 80 bushels; barley, 30 to 40; potatoes, 100 to 300. Actually, the first crops of wheat were 15 bushels, and later crops, 20; oats, 30 bushels; and barley, 20. The *Star of Empire* reported turnips 42 inches around and 20 tons of cabbages raised to the acre, and that cabbages weighing 50 pounds were too common to mention; a mother sending her child to the store for the smallest cabbage was surprised to have him haul back one weighing 40 pounds. Actually, it was said, in many a Greeley cabbage-patch in the early days three-quarters of the crop would be too small to harvest, and some would be not bigger than a man's fist.

Many were the difficulties faced by this pioneer irrigation colony. There was little market for vegetables, and the nursery business was a failure because of the cold winters. The colonists had expected to find plenty of timber, but it was impossible to bring it down from the mountains, for it could not be floated on the streams because of their irregular depth and the dams built for irrigation. They had heard that the whole country was underlain with coal which could be easily mined, but shafts 2,700 feet deep struck no coal. The colonists attempted to

* *Ibid.*

dam a stream for water-power to run a flour-mill, but it swamped the lots, the water rose in cellars, they paid the damages and abandoned the power project; all the water was needed for irrigation anyway. A coöperative stock and cattle company was formed which brought seventy-five head of cattle, but in the first winter hay rose to $40 a ton, and later the stock had to be sold at 50 cents on the dollar.

Since the country had previously been a cattle range, there was constant warfare between the stock-raisers and the colonists, a warfare which was repeated throughout the West wherever agriculture invaded the range. As soon as the grass of early summer was eaten, the cattle began to move into the cultivated areas; the colony had to employ herders to ward them off night and day, but these could not cope with the beasts from the range. In this emergency Meeker printed a proclamation declaring that since

cattle still roam through our streets and over our fields eating up the last vestige of our labors as a preliminary to an attack upon our shade trees and their total destruction, it is time that we meet and defend ourselves with the powers of the law. The protection of our strawberry grounds, containing as much as a quarter million of plants alone, demands our organization. This is not so much a question in regard to fences as in regard to order and decency, for our town and colony will be disgraced by cattle running at large through our streets; shade trees will be impossible, for even fences themselves will be comparatively useless since there are enough breachy cattle to demolish common fences, the same as in Denver, and in all the ranches of the territory where the vast herds will repeat this year their course of desolation. The law is right in compelling men to take care of their stock, and it is not possible to make stock profitable unless it is taken care of.

At this time Horace Greeley visited the colony, and in conference with Meeker they decided to fence the entire area. The fence was built along the ditches so that the vast hungry herds, driven by winter blizzards, would be checked by both the fence and the ditch. Barbed wire, which was later to solve the fencing problem in the West, was not yet manufactured; so the fencing was a very difficult and expensive enterprise, requiring a large post, costing 25 cents, every 16 feet and two smooth wires costing 8 cents per pound—an expense of $400 per mile (as compared to $100 for barbed wire), the entire outlay being $20,000. As soon as it was built, the legislature was petitioned to pass a law permitting communities to fence themselves in; but the law when enacted provided for inspection by a board which included cattle-men, and these made the situation as difficult as possible for the colonists, requiring the fence to be reconstructed to suit their whim. The war between cattlemen and farmers continued, and the colonists were called "Greeley saints who have fenced themselves in from the heathen round about." When they impounded the cattle found straying on their lands, three masked armed men rode in one Sunday when the guard was asleep and drove them away over the hills, after having had them fed all winter at the colonists' expense.

The last and most grievous of the afflictions suffered by the colonists was a plague of grasshoppers, which began in 1872 and continued with increasing intensity for four years. The farmers fought them with smudges, fire, and water; they gathered them into trenches and crushed them by the thousand with rollers. They plowed their eggs into the ground, turned hogs and poultry to feed upon them, but to no avail. The Greeley *Tribune* reported:

All gardens that were planted are destroyed, save peas and young corn. Currants and gooseberries have but a few leaves and their fruit buds are eaten out. Raspberries and blackberries that have been watered, and which are in a thrifty condition, are blossoming and will probably bear. Straw-berries that were watered promptly will bear perhaps half a crop, and the fruit is now a quarter grown. Grapes are not injured to any great extent. Pie-plant is all eaten down. Most kinds of quite young forest trees have suffered badly, but the box elder, though badly trimmed, is pulling through triumphantly. People are now planting cucumbers, melons and squashes, with the hope of having gardens. Tomato, cabbage, and other plants are yet kept within doors or under glass. Captain Boyd has fought the grass-hoppers successfully with his machine, but then he did not have the crowds others have had. Benjamin H. Eaton is fighting the enemy vigor-ously, and expects to save as much as two hundred acres of wheat. But as fast as the grasshoppers eat down a few acres, the plow is turned in, and corn is immediately planted. We must have as many as seven or eight inventors who have brought into use as many different kinds of machines for destroying the grasshoppers.*

At the height of the grasshopper plague,

* David Boyd, *Greeley and the Union Colony* (Greeley, Greeley Tribune Press, 1890).

A. Z. Salomon offered the best suit of clothes in his store to the man who would bring him a million grasshoppers. John Templeton, a canny Scotchman, using a trap, caught what he estimated to be a million or over. He counted an ounce and weighed the rest. When he brought them in, about a bran-sack full, Salomon refused to pay for them because they were dead. But nothing daunted, Templeton filled another sack with live ones, when the merchant insisted that he should count them. Templeton said that he would have to empty them out to do that, and as it was night, this would have to be done in the clothing store. Then Salomon gave in, and the canny Scot thereafter went around Sundays in a suit of the finest blue broadcloth.

During these troublous times Meeker was hopefully experimenting with the growing of trees and fruits. At first accepted as an agricultural oracle, it gradually became apparent that his knowledge was mostly theoretical. David Boyd, in his *History of Greeley,* says there never was a people who so set their hearts upon having orchards laden with fruit, and their efforts to grow trees were unceasing. It had never occurred to Meeker that Greeley was not a fruit country, and he had declared that they could grow apples, cherries, pears, peaches, apricots, and all kinds of grapes. But orchards did not thrive, and forest trees did little better. There is something pathetic in the letters that Horace Greeley wrote Meeker as to the planting of his own property. He wanted it

sowed with locusts, well scalded. At all events I wish I could find a bushel of hickory nuts, and two of white oak acorns that would germinate. I would like also to sow white pine seed, if they could be had in a fit condition. I do not want to plant trees that would cost too much; but mostly to sow seeds of the best varieties for your soil and climate. If we cannot find any that are just right but locust, let us sow that, and let a part of the land be sowed to grasses or roots till next fall, when we can get acorns and hickory nuts.

Of this experiment Meeker wrote:

Mr. Greeley's lot was planted in the spring with 1,000 small evergreens, 2,000 larches. Water was obtained with great difficulty. A few lived until next year; then all died. Then locusts and acorns were sowed, a few came up, fewer lived. The oaks grew only a few inches high. Then the whole was sowed to black walnuts which came up well, but winter killed. Mr. Greeley had no idea of the great difficulty that is presented in growing even hardy trees on this soil. The only trees now growing are cottonwoods and box elders, which are doing well.

Finally Meeker delivered himself frankly on the subject of tree- and fruit-culture:

When we located in this valley of Colorado, we had no kind of idea of the difficulties attending the culture of many kinds of vegetation. The great variety of forest trees which grew in the states without any trouble, many of them as spontaneously as weeds, can here scarcely be made to live when brought hither with the greatest care and cultivated with the utmost attention. Thousands upon thousands of evergreens and larches have been set in this town and vicinity, and now we know of one larch that is alive, and which perhaps grows an inch a year; and there are not more than a dozen evergreens. Perhaps twenty barrels of black walnuts, butternuts, and hickory nuts have been sown, and there can be found a few black walnut trees two and three feet high, which, during some winters, freeze to the ground. Chestnuts live about as well as bananas would. Of the vast number of apple trees obtained the first year, it is doubtful whether twenty are alive; and pears, cherries and plums have gone the same way. The hardiest sorts of apples, usually ironclads elsewhere, have been carefully nursed and watched, and they have grown into nice trees, but the fierce cold winds have struck them to the heart.

As the capacity of the irrigation canals was increased and the farmers learned more about the methods to be used, crops became more plentiful and prosperity more general. Hardy strains of trees were made to flourish. The ichneumon-fly finally destroyed the grasshoppers, and they never returned. The day came when J. Max Clark could write:

Hundreds of miles of lateral canals now link together the barren ridges and valleys of 1870 in one continuous cultivated garden. In their season, fields of emerald green of almost unlimited extent gladden the eye from every elevation. Great squares of wheat and oats and alfalfa delight the passerby on every thoroughfare, and fields of potatoes of astonishing size, with rows which fade from the vision in the distance, are seen on every hand. The horned toad, the prairie dog and the owl have retired to the sand hill and the plain beyond. The wolf only yelps at us from a distance as we pass him by, and the robin and the dove build nests in our groves.

On his last inspection of the colony, in 1879, Meeker wrote:

It seldom falls to the lot of mortal, short-seeing man in this uncertain world to have his hopes and views so completely realized—or, to tell the truth, carried out so far beyond what he had reason to expect, as is exhibited in the wide area of Greeley farms, and is actually beheld during the last week. I am sure I am a good judge of such things, for, in the way of duty and business, I have visited and critically examined the finest farm regions of our country, as in Central and Western New York, in Pennsylvania, Ohio, Michigan, and Illinois, and not excepting the fairest portions of the Southern States, and among all these I have nowhere beheld a more unexceptionable presentation—nowhere have seen wheat of greater average yield, corn of cleaner culture, potatoes of finer promise, clover of better stand; in short, I may say, that I have never seen the equal in clean and nice preparation, and in culture, wherever I went, and there was presented an unbroken and apparently boundless scene of the highest order— the result of intelligent rural industry. Let me not forget to add a few more things. That broad landscape is broken and enlivened by groves and lines of beautiful trees, many fruit trees now in bearing, imparting to the view such as one imagines is presented in the best parts of England, such as we have all seen in the old States, as the result of a hundred years' culture and growth. Everywhere beautiful streams of water skirt the fields and cross the roads. There are nice farm houses and cheerful homes. The schoolhouses are not absent, while from many a gentle swell of green or of gold one sees in the distant valley the town with its spires, as jewels set to adorn a gorgeous robe.

But with all the prosperity that came to his town of Greeley, little came to Nathan Meeker. When he began the Greeley project, he had saved some $15,000, but this was soon swallowed up in the expense of moving and settling in the new country. He built a large house, which cost him enormously because of the high charges for labor and building materials in the early days. He said later that he knew it was beyond his means, but he felt he ought to build it to show the rest of the people his faith in the community and to give them a sense of its stability. He did not take up any large tract of land, so he never profited from the rise in real-estate values. He felt that his legitimate part in the general scheme of things was to found a first-class newspaper and edit it, so he established the Greeley *Tribune*. The paper did not pay, and he was urged to sell out to the rival which had established itself, but he refused to do so. Later he borrowed $1,000 from Horace Greeley and put it into the paper on the understanding that it would be repaid only when Meeker was in good financial condition. Upon Greeley's death, however, his estate sued for the money; and after contributing 40 acres of land which the colony had deeded him in return for his many years of unpaid services, Meeker accepted the post of government agent at the White

River Indian Agency in northwestern Colorado in order to get cash to pay the balance and other debts.

Even in this time of seeming defeat, however, he took courage and satisfaction in the progress the colony had made and the fruition of his own ideas which it represented. "After all, Max," he said to J. M. Clark, "although the enterprise yielded me nothing in return, in a worldly sense, yet I am proud to have been the leader in such a movement; it will be counted an honor to every man who took part in the settlement of Greeley. I am more than compensated in the grand success of the undertaking itself and I have nothing to regret."

Just as he had approached the problem of farming and community building in a more or less doctrinaire spirit, so he approached the Indian problem. He felt that if the Indian could be induced to lead an industrial and agricultural life, all his difficulties would be solved. Meeker arrived at the Agency in May, 1878, and by November he had begun to institute his scheme for making the Indians self-supporting by putting twenty-five men to work digging an irrigation canal. He reported that they despised the work at first, but as time went by, he thought they were getting to like it better. A week later, however, they stopped and only agreed to go on when paid $15 a month and double rations; for work, they said, was beneath the dignity of Indians, and their treaty with the Government called for no such thing. While one group of Indians continued to work, another party sulked; but in the fall, when the water was turned into the ditch, Meeker thought that most of them were pleased and were anxious to begin farming. So sanguine of the outcome was he that he believed he now had the key to the solution of the Indian problem:

A great mistake was made at an early day, in supposing the Indians capable of civilization equally with the whites.... The proper course to pursue was to teach them to engage in common industries, and then a basis would have been laid for their education and improvement; for it is only upon rural life and its duties and cares that civilization and Christianity can rest, and if I were going to start a new religion I would make this the first article of the creed. Treated as if they were children, for they are little more, and entirely dropping the notion of their awful poetic character, and the sacredness of the land of their fathers; in short, coming down to the common sense of things, and in a few years they are bound to become as decent human beings as the average of us.

But Meeker was too optimistic. The sullen Indians were merely nursing their grievance in silence, which was broken by the announcement that they were going to leave the Agency and live by hunting; those who had had shoes given to them for working pulled them off and threw them in a heap on the floor of the Agency, withdrawing in savage grandeur. Meeker settled this strike after a week, extra rations were distributed, and joyful shouts rose from the red men's tents. But, although he tried to convince them that it was to their advantage to work on the land, they were still far from enthusiastic. Like all reformers, Meeker expected the change in their character and habits to be made overnight, and he blundered still further in a system of rewards for the workers which satisfied neither the industrious nor the idle.

All summer the Indians brooded over their wrongs. Finally a chief came to Meeker and said that the Utes did not want any more land plowed but wanted to live as they had always lived. When Meeker ordered the plowing to be continued, two Indians came with guns to stop it. After a big pow-wow it was agreed that the family who lived on the 80-acre tract being plowed would move away, Meeker would help them build a house and a well, and the land would be plowed. In celebration of this victory he wrote an article for the Greeley *Tribune* ending with this paragraph: "This stopping plows by bullets is by no means a new thing in America, for so to speak, the plow has plowed its way from the Atlantic to the heart of the Rocky Mountains, through showers of bullets, and the American plow is yet to turn furrows across China and the Steppes of Tartary, and even invert the soil around sacred Jerusalem—'Speed the Plow!'"

These words "Speed the Plow," appropriately enough, were the last that Nathan Meeker ever wrote for his paper. A short time later, when he was suffering from an injured shoulder, an Indian came into the Agency, seized him, and dragging him violently out of the house, threw him against a fence while other Indians placidly looked on. After this violence Meeker at last realized that the Indians were not as tractable as they appeared to be on the surface, and in September, 1879, he appealed to the military authorities for troops.

Major Thomas T. Thornburg was despatched to his aid from Fort Steele with 160 cavalry; but at the narrow cañon of Milk Creek, 25 miles from the Agency, the Indians ambushed the company, killed the commander and 12 soldiers and wounded 42, and killed 200 mules in the wagon-train. A scout having escaped and taken the news to the Army post, another small detachment of cavalry arrived on the third morning of the siege, and General Wesley Merritt also hurried from Cheyenne with 300 cavalry and 250 infantry. When they reached the White River Agency, the Indians offered no resistance; but General Merritt saw the wreck and carnage, the dead and wounded, and viewing the signs of the massacre on every hand, he turned aside and wept like a child.

On the afternoon of the battle at Milk Creek the Indians had advanced on the Agency, killed Meeker and the rest of the men, and taken the women captive. One of the survivors wrote, "It is not necessary to give here in detail the scenes of horror and desolation that met the eyes of the soldiers as they marched down to the silence of the ruined, sacked agency. One building was left standing and the ground was strewn with the murdered men. Father Meeker was horribly mutilated, the rest were lying where they were shot and were buried where they fell."

Thus was ended the life of one of the West's most faithful servants. Meeker's death was the tragic result of his attempt to lead the Indian, as he had led the white man, to "speed the plow." Memorials have been raised to him, but his true memorial is his beloved community of Greeley, reclaimed from the "Great American Desert," where now, in the surrounding County of Weld, there are 357,000 acres of land under irrigation, one-seventh of all the beet-sugar of the country is produced, and 3,000,000 bushels of wheat are grown every year. For although Meeker modestly said that he took no credit for the colony but gave it instead to the farmers who took hold and carried on the colony, Horace Greeley wisely declared, "In an important sense you *are* the colony. What would the Exodus have been without Moses, and Joshua, I fear, has not yet appeared." But it is not only the community of Greeley and the State of Colorado that owe him a debt of gratitude. Wherever men practise irrigation and live under its laws, they must pay tribute to the memory of that pioneer of irrigation, Nathan Cook Meeker. And all who travel through the beautiful countryside that he helped to create can unite with David Boyd, one of Greeley's early pioneers, in his final eulogy:

Every brick block, every church, every schoolhouse, every beautiful residence reared in Greeley is a monument to N. C. Meeker. Every tree planted, every lawn clothed in grass and bordered with flowers, every field waving with grain in and around Greeley is a monument to N. C. Meeker. Every bird that sings in the branches of our trees that border the fields and streets once covered with cactus, every bee that hums in our clover lawns or fields of alfalfa sings or hums a requiem to the ashes of N. C. Meeker.

# CHAPTER VII

TRANSPORTATION facilities, native resources, and pluck combined to determine the fates of the large cities that grew up in the West in the nineteenth century. Sometimes one of these factors predominated, sometimes another. In the case of Denver it was preëminently pluck. For this Rocky Mountain town had no particular advantage over her neighbors in the matter of near-by mining resources, and from the days of the earliest stage-coaches her citizens had to struggle constantly to put their town on the main routes of transportation. Always they worked whole-heartedly to get the railroads which meant life to Denver, but more than 70 years went by before their dream of a direct transcontinental outlet, east and west, was achieved.

Denver, the child of the gold-fields, was born on the 24th of June, 1858, when W. Green Russell and his party of 104 treasure-seekers, from Georgia, southern Kansas, and the Indian Territory, camped at the point where Cherry Creek runs into the River Platte and panned some minute particles of gold from the sands. It was not much color that they found, but it was enough to keep them interested; and some days later they had taken pay dirt to the value of $400 or $500 from one spot on Dry Creek. From Lawrence, Kansas, came another party of pioneer gold-diggers, who had been seized with the itch for adventure when an Indian, Fall Leaf by name, had showed John Easter, the village butcher, nuggets of glistening gold which he had picked up a year before in a stream "two sleeps from Pike's Peak." All pitched their tents in the vicinity of what is now Denver. Some began building log cabins, and two towns sprang up, Auraria, named after a town in Georgia, and Denver, named in honor of General James W. Denver, Governor of the Territory of Kansas, which in those days extended all the way to the summit of the Rocky

Mountains. In 1860 both towns were combined under the name of Denver.

Not more than $2,000 in gold was taken out that first summer. But two other Fifty-eighters continued the search. George Jackson of Missouri, on January 5, 1859, built a fire over a frozen gravel-bed on Clear Creek, 35 miles to the west of Denver, thawed out the ground, and panned coarse gold; he marked the spot, and in the spring he returned to take out $5,000 worth of placer gold from Jackson Bar, in what later became the mining town of Idaho Springs. John H. Gregory of Georgia, prospecting not many miles away, uncovered the bonanza placer ground of the Gregory Diggings, from which sprang Central City and Black Hawk, centers of one of the richest mining districts in the world. And the "Pike's Peak country" was made.

To the people of Denver, the beneficiary of all the golden treasure that was taken from the Rockies round about, it seemed certain that Fortune had marked their city as her own. By the irresistible law of gravity the gold flowed down the peaks and cañons of the Rockies to this Queen City of the Plains. Denver was the center of all the feverish activity and excitement that inevitably springs up around the mining of the precious metal. She was the goal of thousands of emigrants, who pushed forward in a never-ending stream in their covered wagons with "Pike's Peak or Bust," "Root, Hog, or Die," and other mottoes scrawled on their canvas sides, something after the manner of the decorations given their "tin lizzies" by the carefree youth of a later day. That she would be the commercial metropolis of the vast Western plain and mountain region and the principal city on the transcontinental route between Chicago, St. Louis, and San Francisco, none could doubt. It was only necessary for her to sit tight and wait for Fortune to make her great.

But despite the fact that Denver was the most lively center of population in the Rocky Mountain district, its citizens had to endure the ignominy of having their town left off the first main route of the transcontinental mail and passenger stage. It was generally considered that the remedying of this foolish oversight would be only a matter of a short time, but the fact remained that the transportation across the country passed the Rockies far to the north, and

Denver had to bear the unkind fate of getting its mails by a stub line coming down from Fort Laramie. To improve this unhappy situation it was proposed to lay out a stage-road from Denver directly east to Leavenworth, Kansas, and the commission to do this was given to B. D. Williams, who later became the first delegate to Congress chosen by the Territory of Jefferson. This new unit of government had been brought into being in June, 1859, when the people of the Pike's Peak district, with true, high-handed Western independence, held a constitutional convention, cut themselves off from the Territory of Kansas, and declared themselves to be the Territory of Jefferson. Although it was unrecognized by Congress for 21 months, when the Territory of Colorado was created, the people of the district lived under the rule of this hastily and questionably created provisional government. And the first Delegate had the additional honor of laying out the stage route to Leavenworth.

Now the citizens of Denver felt that they had indeed put their city permanently on the transcontinental traffic route, for the Central, Overland, California and Pike's Peak Express Company was soon running fifty-two fine Concord coaches over the line from Leavenworth, Kansas, making the trip in from 10 to 12 days. But although there was a good route directly east, there was none to the west. When traffic ran against that massive barrier of the Rocky Mountains at Denver's back door, it had to go either north or far south to find a way through. As yet there was no road east and west by way of Denver, cutting the center of the mountain-range, where the peaks were highest and most formidable.

The situation became serious when Congress, on March 2, 1861, two days after creating the Territory of Colorado, authorized the first daily overland mail to California, providing that mail should be carried to Salt Lake and Denver either by the main line or by branches. Clearly, this was Denver's opportunity to obtain recognition as the main stopping point on the road from the Missouri to the Pacific. Should she continue to be merely a branch-line station, should she fail to share fully in the benefits of this million-dollar mail contract, should her people permit their infant metropolis to be passed by in favor of the old emigrant road through the South Pass in Wyoming? No, a thousand times, no! Indignant at the thought, the citizens held a mass-meeting to initiate the construction of a great international highway through the heart of Colorado Territory. At this meeting Denver and the other Colorado towns affected subscribed men and money, and the Colorado civil engineer, Captain E. L. Berthoud, was entrusted with the task of finding a pass through the center of the Rockies over which a road might be built for the overland mail. Meanwhile, the mail company offered to run its main line through Denver and to the north by way of the Cherokee Trail provided the citizens would build the necessary relay stations from Denver north to Fort Bridger. But the people of Denver did not wish to be at the lower corner of the route; they were determined to place themselves once and for all on the main line of a direct east and west passageway over the mountains, and so they did not accept the offer but turned their attention to the exploration of the Continental Divide.

On May 6, 1861, Captain Berthoud, in company with the famous old scout Jim Bridger, who had been engaged by the coach company to lay out the route over the Cherokee Trail but was now diverted to this more important mission, set out to find a pass through the center of the Rockies. Several days later, after having climbed many peaks and ridges in fruitless efforts to discover a pass, the expedition broke up into three separate parties which scattered in different directions. Berthoud says he scrambled, jumped, and clambered over snowy cliffs all morning until he reached the summit of the divide, following the north branch of Clear Creek. Looking eastward, he saw another small creek, and after four miles of traveling he found that it started from a low, even, well-defined pass, which seemed to be lower than any other point in the Rockies north of the 36th parallel. Four days of reconnaissance followed, and on May 17, having satisfied themselves that this offered a desirable route over the divide, the men climbed a high peak adjoining the new trail and raised the American flag.

News of the discovery of Berthoud Pass as the route for a road directly west over the mountains electrified Denver. At last her manifest destiny was asserting itself; now she would be on the main line of America's march to the Pacific. Within 24 hours officers of the coach company hastened into the mountains to Empire City, where the Berthoud route began, examined it, and pronounced it feasible.

So impressed was the company's ex-president, W. H. Russell, that he invested heavily in lots and mining claims at Idaho Springs, the largest town on the route. He hurried back to Leavenworth by special coach, making a new record of 3 days and 21 hours, and held a special meeting of the board of directors, at which it was decided to send Berthoud and Bridger immediately to mark out the new route from Denver to Salt Lake. As a result of this survey Berthoud reported that beyond the shadow of a doubt a good wagon-road of easy, practicable grades could be built quickly over the 426 miles from Denver to Provo at a cost of $100,000.

While this survey was going on, the first day of July rolled around, when, in order to comply with the provisions of the act of Congress, the daily transcontinental stage-service had to be inaugurated. Since Denver had not built the relay stations required by the Cherokee Trail route, and as yet, of course, there was no road over the Berthoud Pass, she found herself once again left off the main line. The overland mail went west *via* Wyoming, and the Queen City of the Plains had to be content with a branch line.

Still the Denver people were undaunted. When the Colorado and Pacific Wagon, Telegraph, and Railroad Company was organized to build a road over the Berthoud Pass, Denver interests engineered a bill through the legislature by permitting the people of southern Colorado to locate the state capital at Colorado City in exchange for a right of way for the road company. No road, however, was built by the company backers, who were evidently interested only in selling their right of way at a high profit. The *Rocky Mountain News* insisted on action, declaring that it was only necessary to build and advertise the Berthoud Pass route and all western emigration, telegraph, and railroad lines would follow it as sure as the sun rises and sets. The editor and Governor John Evans personally examined the route and pronounced it practicable, and a subscription was started to make more detailed surveys. On the day the engineers left for this work, Congress passed the act authorizing the building of a railroad to the Pacific, and again Denver's anticipation of future greatness was aroused. Now there was no doubt that she would be the great half-way station on the railroad between New York and San Francisco.

But interest in the Berthoud Pass route lagged for two reasons.

In 1862 the new engineer's report showed the pass to be 11,495 feet high and the grade too steep for a railroad; for this reason, and because of snow in summer, a tunnel would have to be built at considerable expense. This bore out the opinion of old Jim Bridger, who, it was said, had long ago been called from St. Louis by the Union Pacific engineers to settle a debate as to the best route for the transcontinental railroad; with a look of disgust Jim seized a dead coal from the ashes of the fire, drew a rough outline map to Bridger Pass, and declared, "There's where you fellers can cross with your road and nowhere else without more diggin' and cuttin' than you can think of." While Denver was digesting the unfavorable report of the engineers, however, she received a word of cheer from Ben Holladay, "the Napoleon of the Plains." Holladay had bought the bankrupt overland-stage company, and he announced that, in return for a charter from the legislature of Colorado, he had instructed his agents to change the route, so that thereafter the overland mail would pass directly through Denver. Great was the rejoicing when, on September 12, the first through coach of the daily overland mail from the west reached Denver. With this glory achieved, the citizens felt that they could rest for a while upon their laurels, even though the direct route to the west over the Berthoud Pass was still a dream.

Denver had no doubt of her irresistible attraction for the transcontinental railroad. For from the first she had been a trading center and a magnet for all the mining and commercial interests of the mountains. In 1858 Uncle Dick Wooten had arrived among the cactus-plants, antelopes, and jack-rabbits and had astonished the town by the magnificence of the trading emporium he had opened; it was a mammoth store-room, 20 by 32 feet in size, one and a half stories high, with an actual board floor and a four-light window. Such lavish outlay presaged much for the future greatness of Denver; and when Uncle Dick opened some barrels of "Taos lightning"—so called because it was unnecessary for it to strike twice on the same person— and hung up a hospitable dipper for thirsty wayfarers, Denver celebrated its first Christmas with much good cheer and supreme confidence in a glorious to-morrow.

Other gold towns sprang up mushroom-like, ready to take away Denver's palm of preëminence, but none of them had that mysterious attraction which was steadily and surely making her the metropolis of the Rockies. The first years saw the arrival in this town of unhewn cottonwood-log houses and dirt roofs of William N. Byers, with his shirt-tail full of type, to found the *Rocky Mountain News*; of Professor O. J. Goldrich, graduate of Trinity College, Dublin, who drove up with an ox-team, faultlessly attired in a cutaway and top-hat, wearing a solitaire diamond as big as your thumb, and soon founded Denver's first grammar-school; and of Count Murat, the elegant barber, who gained fame by charging Horace Greeley a dollar for a shave. When snow began to fall, hundreds of miners came down from the mountains to winter in Denver. They dressed in buckskin trousers, woolen shirts, and slouch hats, and most of them were worn and ragged, for new store clothes were exorbitantly expensive in this frontier outpost. So was food: milk cost 25 cents a quart, eggs a dollar a dozen, watermelons three dollars apiece. But game was cheap, and on this luxury the pioneers thrived; antelope and deer-meat sold for only four cents a pound. In the summer of 1859 a man arrived with a sack of flour which he had wheeled all the way across the plains in a hand cart. There was a shortage of flour at the time, and he could have sold half of it for a corner lot, with two other lots added for the whole sack, which would have made him a profit of $10,000 within six months. But he refused, and six weeks later the market was glutted with flour, so he made nothing.

On the first overland stage from Leavenworth came Horace Greeley of the New York *Tribune*, who was to become famous for his widely advertised advice, "Go west, young man, go west"; Albert D. Richardson of the Boston *Journal*; and Henry Villard of the Cincinnati *Commercial*, a young man whom none then thought of as destined to be one of the nation's greatest railroad-builders. Their purpose was to investigate the mines, and their reports as to the quantities of gold being taken out were the most valuable advertisements early Colorado ever had. For they stimulated the coming of emigrants again, at a time when the stream lagged and many a covered wagon had returned in disgust to spread stories of played-out mining districts and to display a new wording of the old slogan, "Pike's Peak and Busted!"

Of his visit to Denver in 1859, Greeley wrote that every guest at the Denver House "is allowed as good a bed as his own blankets will make him. The charges are no higher than at the Astor or other first class hotels, except for liquor, twenty-five cents a drink for dubious whiskey, colored and nicknamed to suit the taste of customers. . . . Still, a few days of such luxury surfeited me, mainly because the drinking room was also occupied by several black-legs as a gambling hall and their incessant clamor, persisted in at all hours up to midnight, became at length a nuisance. Then the visitors of that drinking and gambling room had a careless way, when drunk, of firing revolvers, sometimes at each other, at other times quite miscellaneously, which struck me as inconvenient for a quiet guest." And he reported that there were "more brawls, more fights, more pistol shots with criminal intent in this log city of one hundred and fifty dwellings, not three-fourths of them completed nor two-thirds inhabited nor one-third fit to be, than in any community of equal numbers on earth."

Yet the miners listened attentively when Greeley rose to address them in the bar-room of this same hotel. Rotund, full-faced, with fringe of whiskers under his jaw from ear to ear, wearing large spectacles, a big, whitish, soft felt hat, a long frock-coat, and baggy trousers, he was a picturesque figure. On one side "the tipplers silently sipped their grog, on the other the gamblers respectfully suspended the shuffling of cards," while he stood in the middle and made a strong antidrinking, antigambling speech, which was politely received. Even if these frontier rounders were indifferent to his advice, they may have realized its fundamental soundness as a theory of action and agreed with him as heartily as did the Indian described by Albert Richardson: "The thousand Arapahoes encamped in the heart of Denver were ordinarily peaceful, but they were dangerous when intoxicated. One evening I saw a brawny brave, with a club, thwack two of his drunken brethren upon their heads, so lustily that the blows were heard a quarter of a mile away. Then, musing for some moments, he solemnly ejaculated, 'Whiskey bad! Make Indian bad!'"

The year after Greeley visited Denver, the city had a population of 4,000, supported three daily newspapers, and boasted a theater, the Apollo, seating 350, illuminated by candles, admission one dollar. Five thousand acres had been staked out into building-lots; strangers were plied with investments in real estate and mines. Blake Street was said to be as lively as Broadway in New York. Farming had reached sufficient proportions that in the grocery-stores one might see rich yellow pumpkins, potatoes, turnips, and cucumbers, sights which must have delighted the miners after their long summer in the mountains on the monotonous diet of dried beans and bacon. Adventurous young women had begun to be attracted to the frontier; some of them made the trip in male attire, and one advertisement asking for the services of a lad to fetch water and black boots stated that "no young woman in disguise need apply." New-comers were fascinated by the bustle and adventurous spirit of the two-year-old town; and always there was the additional fascination, the haunting lure, of the Rockies to the west—a dark, irregular, polychrome wall varying from deep, rich purple through mauve and pink to snowy white, endlessly changing in the changing light.

In these early times the arrival of the daily overland mail with its passengers from the East was one of the town's most colorful events. And many other vehicles added their rattle to the din, among them the stage from Santa Fe, carrying eight heavily armed guards and eleven passengers, two of whom rode outside. There was many a Conestoga wagon, with its curved body built water-tight like a boat so as to ford streams easily. But the heaviest part of the traffic was carried in "Concords," built in the New Hampshire town of that name and imitated, but never equaled, elsewhere. With no weight on the roof, they were less top-heavy than the stage-coaches; when empty, the Concord jolted and pitched like a ship in a heavy sea, but when full and nicely ballasted, its motion was easy and elastic; and its construction was so sturdy that it was said "Concords never break down; they just wear out." These vehicles with the supply wagons, pack-trains, and stages from the mines filled the Denver streets with dust all day long.

The stage-driver of the Sixties was a skilled expert who could drive six horses with a single hand and could sweep around mountain turns or pass another team with such ease and grace as to be the wonder of Eastern visitors. Dashing down steep mountain grades and over rough, circuitous roads (the stage-road to Central City crossed the Clear Creek bed fifty-eight times in eight miles), the driver never for a minute lost control; the horses responded to his every word, or if they failed to do so, they received the punishment of a lash from his curling whip which drew blood from their flanks. Ten miles an hour was not an uncommon speed over good roads, and the driver was a dignified, even majestic, and usually taciturn figure as he gathered up his reins and urged his horses forward. Indeed, some of the drivers were men of education, as were many of the other men who performed rough work in the West. It was not unusual, said a contemporary writer, "to find some graduate of Yale bullwhacking his own team from the river to the mines, looking as if he had seldom seen soap and water and had pitched his clothes on at some second hand shop."

For its letters and newspapers from the East, Denver was mainly dependent on Ben Holladay's Overland Mail, for that swiftest of messengers, The Pony Express, turned northwest at Julesburg. The ordinary mail, bringing a thousand letters a day, charged 25 cents for a letter, and, indeed, the 25 cent piece was the smallest coin in circulation; but the Pony Express, because of its speed, charged $5 for a half-ounce letter and would not take one at any price if it had reached its limit of carrying capacity, 20 pounds. Although it took 22 days to send mail from New York to San Francisco *via* Panama, the Pony Express carried it from the Missouri River to San Francisco in ten days.

But still Denver had no direct route to the west; the overland mail went out of its way to reach the city, and the Pony Express service was only a branch, coming down from the main line at Julesburg. To remedy this vexing situation various road-building companies were formed to build over the Berthoud Pass, but none achieved success. Finally, in 1865, the legislature dissolved the corporation to which it had granted the right of way over Berthoud Pass and gave it to Ben Holladay's Overland Wagon Road Company. But even with this powerful backing the road was not completed, and, indeed, no road was built over the pass until a decade later, in 1874. Now that the Pacific-railroad bill had been enacted by Congress, the Union Pacific was pushing on to the Rockies from the Missouri River, and the Central Pacific was rapidly laying its rails eastward from San Francisco. Of course they would pass through Denver—all the residents of the mile-high city were agreed on that, and the Queen of the Plains would soon occupy her rightful position as the great central metropolis on the new transcontinental railway.

The Union Pacific had already tried unsuccessfully to find a feasible route over Berthoud Pass. Its engineer, F. M. Case, had run several lines over the Pass, but all were considered too difficult; and in the course of his surveys Case reported the Pass to be 1,000 feet higher than Berthoud's elevation, a statement which caused him to be charged with misrepresentation. In 1866 General Grenville M. Dodge, chief engineer of the Union Pacific, had sent a surveying party under one of his best engineers, Percy Brown, to try to find a suitable route over the Rockies at their center, so that the road might be routed through Denver; and for several months they carried on their search. From his early writings it appears that Dodge had long since settled in his own mind the desirability of locating the road through the South, or Bridger, Pass, in Wyoming, and what is now Cheyenne; but Denver interests had brought pressure to bear on the board of directors, so he ordered a careful examination of the Denver route.

By November, however, no satisfactory progress having been made, Dodge himself joined the surveying party to see if he could be of assistance in finding a way through the center of the Rockies at the Hog Back. But whatever sympathetic feelings he may have had for Denver's interests received a serious setback when, on November 7, there came up a blizzard so terrific that even the mules would not face it. So severe was the snow-storm that Dodge saw that the only hope of saving his party lay in abandoning the pack-train and trying to get down from the mountains on foot. They cached the packs and turned the mules loose, and after a day and a night of hard struggle the party arrived safely in Boulder Valley. But the fact that such a blizzard could blow up so early in the season in that locality decided Dodge against any further attempt to push the Union Pacific through the Rockies at Denver's back door. He abandoned the survey and reported to the board of directors on November 15 that the Denver route was impracticable.

There were other reasons, too, for the Union Pacific's refusal to build through Denver, the early settlers said. Of course, construction over the Berthoud Pass would cost more than by the Bridger Pass; moreover the route through Denver was more than 100 miles shorter, and since the Union Pacific was getting $48,000 a mile in government subsidies for all track laid in the mountain section, it was no wonder that the directors wanted to send the road the long way around through Cheyenne and thus add half a million dollars to their payments. They also had opportunity to profit from real-estate speculation should they create a new city instead of building into an old one. Denver fought the matter to the bitter end; when the Union Pacific directors looked coldly on her aspirations, Colorado's two territorial Delegates in Washington, John Evans and Jerome B. Chaffee, waged a fierce battle to have the Union Pacific diverted to Denver, but to no avail. Again Denver found itself left off the main line.

So swift and incredible was the blow that the whole city was stunned. By this one act, it seemed, the future commercial leadership of the region had been snatched away from her and presented to the upstart railroad town of Cheyenne. So deep was the foreboding that many a resident sold out his interests and left the city, some to share in the bright future of the new town in Wyoming. By 1867 the Union Pacific had reached Cheyenne, the old Julesburg-Denver stage line had been abandoned, and the first coach had made the trip over the new stage route to Cheyenne in 24 hours. The future looked black indeed for Denver. The one ray of hope was the fact that in June, 1866, Congress had passed an act compelling the Kansas Pacific to become the Eastern Division of the Union Pacific, though remaining an independent corporation, and to connect with the main line at a point not more than 50 miles west of the longitude of Denver. However, the government subsidy in land extended over only a part of the proposed route, so the Kansas Pacific Company was not very strong financially.

Now began a nerve-racking time for Denver business men, while they were torn between the attractions of one scheme after another to secure rail connection with the Union Pacific. Dodge had recommended to his directors that a branch line be built to Denver, but it was soon apparent that this would not be done, for the directors declared they had no government authority to build such a line. W. A. H. Loveland, of the rival town of Golden, had organized the Colorado Central Railroad Company to build east and west through his town and over the Berthoud Pass, with the hope that the Union

Pacific would adopt this route and purchase his road. When the Union Pacific decided against the Berthoud Pass, however, Loveland turned his road into a project to build north and south and connect with the Union Pacific at Cheyenne; he asked the counties through which the road would pass to apportion among them the $600,000 required for construction, and Denver's Arapahoe County was assigned one-third of the cost. While Denver toyed with this idea, yet feared that if she accepted it, the promoters would, by some hook or crook, give Golden the favored position on their line, the Kansas Pacific declared that it would build immediately to Denver at no cost to the city. Loveland then started his survey from Cheyenne and declared his intention of building directly to Golden, giving Denver only a branch line. In this he was supported by all the northern mining towns, so Denver found the most powerful interests in the state arrayed against her. Although $200,000 in bonds had already been voted by Arapahoe County for Loveland's line, it was stipulated that the railway must be built directly to Denver; and when it was discovered that Denver was to be discriminated against, the irate citizens disgustedly broke off all relations with the Loveland project and pinned their faith on the Kansas Pacific.

The year 1867 was the crucial year in the city's history, for it was the decisions made and the action taken then that definitely determined where the future metropolis of the Rocky Mountain states was to be. Had her people bowed before the decrees of the great Pacific-railroad interests and surrendered the palm to Cheyenne, Denver might be a small town to-day. But the courage and energy and perseverance of the citizens of this frontier community of 7,000 people literally created a city from the ground up, and they acted like a magnet in drawing the railways and trade and population that made the pioneer town a cosmopolitan metropolis. In this year of 1867 many of the weaker-kneed and less imaginative were loudly declaring that Denver's day was over, and they were selling their property for what it would bring and moving to Cheyenne. Even the strong banks of Denver were establishing branches in the northern town, business was rushing there and deadly dull in Denver, and it looked as if the new town would be the future distributing point for the Rockies and Plains region.

Within the year a traveler was to write this requiem of Denver:

"The old mining excitement has ceased. The old overland stage has stopped and its business rushes past on a railroad one hundred miles to the north. Business is dull; the town is quiet; almost an eastern village. I see scarcely a new house going up, plenty of places to let." Agriculture was being carried on in only a small way in the territory tributary to Denver, and though mining was of some moment, it had died down considerably and was retarded by lack of railway transportation. Under these conditions the *Rocky Mountain News* was whistling to keep up its courage when it declared that "this Cheyenne excitement is *not* going to kill off Denver." Moreover, the arrogant railroad town now started a movement to form a new territory with itself as the capital, taking the land needed from Dakota and Colorado. The project was entrusted to General Jack Casement, the Union Pacific contractor, who promised to push it through Congress. At this high-handed proceeding the *Rocky Mountain News* exploded: "Colorado objects to submitting to the slicing up of its Territory for the mere convenience of a town on wheels which last fall was at North Platte, this spring at Julesburg, this fall at Cheyenne, and will be next fall at Rocky Mountain City or some other point on the Laramie Plains." But the gloom and humiliation were deep when it was learned that "back east" Vice-President Thomas Durant of the Union Pacific had said, "Denver is too dead to bury."

Even though left off the main Pacific railroad, Denver hopefully awaited the coming of the Kansas Pacific, which was now 310 miles to the east, in the comforting belief that half a loaf was better than none. But the cruelest blow of all fell when, on November 8, 1867, Colonel James Archer of the Kansas Pacific arrived in Denver for a conference with its citizens. At first he was hailed joyfully as the harbinger of good news, but when it was discovered that he came not to announce the day of the railroad's arrival but to ask financial aid, the city's leaders were sick with discouragement. For Archer demanded that Denver contribute the vast sum of $2,000,000 to enable his road to build into the city.

The repeated disappointments that Denver had suffered now hung a pall over the spirits of the people. They had been left off the Union Pacific, double-crossed by Loveland and his railroad, and now were asked for the impossible sum of $2,000,000 to get a branch line to

Kansas City. Morale was low, hope sick unto death; a new element, a new personality, was needed to bring courage and enthusiasm to the people. In this emergency Colonel D. C. Dodge of Denver wired his friend General Dodge, explaining the situation and asking for help and, if possible, a counter-proposition from the Union Pacific. In response to this request there hurried to the city none other than that effervescent and eccentric promoter, globe-trotter, and spell-binder, George Francis Train. In anticipation of his arrival, the business leaders of the city organized the Denver Board of Trade with the special purpose of looking after the city's transportation interests, and the stage was set for action.

On the evening of November 15, 1867, a mass-meeting was called which included the members of the new Board of Trade, and there that famous man of vision was presented to the assembled citizens of Denver. With utmost innocence he announced that he was willing to talk if they would only tell him what to talk about, but first they must come closer, closer to the platform, so that he could give them all a mental hand-shake. When this was done and the ice broken, this medicine man of the railroads declared that the audience might draw a sight draft on him for any kind of speech they wanted, and when some shouted "Railroads," he acquiesced with, "Railroads it shall be."

If General Dodge had not been particularly helpful to Denver in the matter of surveys, he did the Queen City a good turn now, for it was the speech of George Francis Train that put new heart into her people and set their feet on the road to riches. Train said that he wished it understood that he was not an orator, a linguist, a book-maker, or anything of the kind. He was also something else besides a lunatic and a damn fool, because, while he was making speeches, he was also making money. The public should know that the three great enterprises of the age were organized over his table. These were the Union Pacific, the Crédit Mobilier, and the Crédit Foncier. The first of these *crédits* owned the Union Pacific, the second the towns. He had also started the Atlantic and Great Western Railroad, connecting the Erie with the Mississippi road, forming a great broad-gage from New York to the West; and he had started the Eastern Division of the Union Pacific, formerly the Kansas Pacific, by loaning it money. He said that he, personally, had inaugurated the Union Pacific, breaking ground at Omaha, making it the initial point; and though the papers denounced and laughed at him on that occasion, the rails were now 517 miles west of Omaha, proving his prophetic vision. He had introduced the French system of finance to back the enterprise, and only by this beneficent device had the work been enabled to go forward. His Omaha lot speculation was appropriately referred to, and its success noted as a triumph of instinct over science. He had sold 6,000 lots there at $500 each, which was a fair beginning for a fortune, in his humble opinion.

Passing to Denver and her railway problem, the great man told his now spellbound audience that they had made a grand mistake. They had thrown their whole influence in favor of the Eastern Division (or Kansas Pacific) and opposed with their whole strength the northern line. How was it now? The Kansas Pacific was at Hays City, Kansas, and, judging from the past, it could not reach Denver for two whole years. Furthermore, the road really did not intend to come to Denver at all, but was proposing to shoot off through Arizona and New Mexico to California; it would do it and leave Denver out in the cold. Denver people had used their influence to help the Kansas Pacific get a land-grant through Colorado, and now Mr. Archer calmly informed them that they could have a road only by coming down with $2,000,000 in cash. The Union Pacific was only 100 miles north of Denver. What was the people's duty? To get to work and get that connection at once. They could have it in six months by energetic work. There was a natural route down the Platte, and this route he requested General Case to sketch on the blackboard. Picking up a pointer, Train showed his listeners how the road could be constructed; he said it could be done for $20,000 a mile, or $2,000,000, and he believed it might even be done for as low as $14,000 a mile. He declared that this road must be built or the town was gone. Everybody would move away. Denver could not afford to pay its present enormous freight charge of $1,000,-000 on 12,000,000 pounds. Such a charge would soon destroy any town. The railroad to the north must be built.

Train paused for breath, and the audience asked him how to proceed to bring this railway project to Denver. He replied that the people must force the Kansas Pacific to give up its lands, drop all thought of outside aid, and organize at once to build the railroad themselves.

He ended by crying dramatically, "Colorado is a great gold mine! Denver is a great fact! Make it a great railway center!" He then called for a vote. All those in favor of going to work would say "yes." (Loud responses of "yes.") The thing was already accomplished. The people would break ground to-morrow and build a mile of it. All in favor of this would say "yes." (Responses of "yes.") At this happy conclusion Mr. Train, who professed to speak on the spur of the moment and with no thought of what his subject might be, produced a list of names which happened fortuitously to be in his pocket, and declared that the meeting should organize to build the railway at once. And he suggested the membership of the provisional board of directors, including seventeen Denver men, Augustus Kountze of Omaha, Grenville M. Dodge of Council Bluffs, and John S. Casement of Omaha. After reading the list he asked all in favor of such a board to say "yes." Loud responses of "yes" left no doubt as to the wishes of the audience, and the board was declared to be organized. The meeting ended with three cheers for George Francis Train, those present later sending him a set of moss-agate jewelry as a token of their esteem.

Two days later, when the formal organization meeting was held, the citizens were told that the rising sun of Denver's greatness was at last to be seen on the horizon. They need only build the railroad to Cheyenne. Poverty would be no excuse either for the community or for any of its citizens. More money had been spent in the town on whisky and tobacco in the last three years than it would take to build the road. They were better off than if they had been put on the main line in the first place, because then they would have had only one railroad; now they would exert themselves and have at least two. In 50 years Denver would be not only the great railway center of the West, but the great bullion center of the nation. And it was declared that with the railroad built, property now worth two million dollars would be worth twenty million. "The time for talk is past," cried the chairman. "The time for action is come."

Stimulated by the bubbling enthusiasm that Train had inspired, the city took up its new task with high spirits. Railroad talk was in the air, railroad-building filled the newspapers, a railway map of Denver was printed on the envelopes used by every business man in the city;

and the Denver Pacific Railway, with a capital stock of $2,000,000, was organized, with Bela M. Hughes as president and David H. Moffat as treasurer, to build a direct line 107 miles long from Denver to Cheyenne. Now the people were called upon to save their city; innumerable meetings were held, and every man was reminded in the most solemn manner that he must decide what was the utmost he could invest in the railroad stock to ensure that his property would retain its value. As a result the people of Denver massed solidly behind the project with money and enthusiasm; many who could not give cash donated even cross-ties, labor, and other services; the community rose as a man to meet the crisis. Nearly $300,000 was subscribed to the railroad's stock; with hardly a dissenting vote the county passed a $500,000 bond-issue; work was begun, grading was pushed at the rate of two miles a day, and the Board of Trade confidently declared that a connection would be established with Chicago by November, 1868.

With the commitment to build a railroad connection, the town experienced a change of heart in regard to securing statehood for Colorado. Many had thought the territory was not yet strong enough to enter the Union, and the President of the United States had twice vetoed statehood bills. But now a government land-subsidy was needed for the Denver Pacific Railway, and since it could be obtained more easily with two Senators instead of two territorial Delegates in Congress, Denver was active in the movement to hasten the admission of Colorado as a state. In a letter to the daily paper J. H. Morrison pressed the matter:

The first bugbear, taxation, will be made up by increase of population and value of land. There is no community so oppressed as those whose prosperity is dried up by want of enterprise. Oregon runs her state government for $50,000 a year, and we can do it for less. As for a plan to get rid of Jerome Chaffee and John Evans as senators, I fear it will be more difficult. If they should resign, the people might reëlect them. We might, however, make it effective by hiring some one to kill them. This could be justified on the same principle as that of the gentleman who proposes to kill his children in order to reduce the size of his family to suit the servant girl who objects to enter his services because the family is too large. Seriously, is it not time that the twaddle about men should cease and all of us go to work together for the general interests?

DENVER, CITY OF THE PLAINS, AGAINST HER MOUNTAIN WALL

Lithograph after a drawing by A. E. Mathews, 1866.

THE MOFFAT ROAD IN GORE CAÑON

Photograph by McClure, Denver, Colorado.

GULCH MINING IN CLEAR CREEK CAÑON

*Frank Leslie's Illustrated Newspaper*, 1871.

The revivified spirit of coöperation and enterprise that was moving the people of Denver so impressed the Kansas Pacific, which had been playing with the idea of changing its route and building to southern Colorado, that it now repeated its offers to build direct to Denver and asked what aid the city would give. But the Kansas Pacific promoters were reminded, in a public meeting, of their broken promises; they were told that Denver was determined to build its own road, and that while it would welcome the Kansas Pacific, the railway would have to provide its own funds for the extension. Building south from Cheyenne, the Denver Pacific entered into an agreement with Thomas Durant and Sidney Dillon of the Union Pacific by which these worthies promised to provide the money to complete the road when the Denver company had expended $500,000 on construction, and it was further agreed that the road would be leased to the Union Pacific. Ironically enough, an effort was also made to get Cheyenne to issue bonds to help the project, but that city's Council referred the matter to a committee which promptly forgot it.

Colorado was not admitted to the Union until 1876, but her two territorial Delegates worked assiduously for her interests. They introduced a bill to grant the Denver Pacific the same land-subsidy as the Union Pacific; the Kansas Pacific fought it violently until it was apparent that the bill would pass, when it withdrew its objections and allied itself with the Denver interests, with the result that both roads were permitted to bond themselves at $32,000 per mile. Meanwhile, the Denver Pacific was encountering fresh difficulties; it was unable to sell its $500,000 worth of Arapahoe County bonds, and Durant and Dillon made no move to fulfill their obligation to help build the road. When they finally pleaded financial inability to meet the contract, it was canceled, and the Denver Pacific prepared to complete the road itself. It increased its capital to $4,000,000, made a deal with the Kansas Pacific whereby both roads were enabled to finance their construction, and, obtaining from the Kansas Pacific the assistance of General William J. Palmer, hastened the line into Denver.

For the moment Denver determined to take the matter into her own hands and build her railroad to the north without outside help, to the present day when she is still working to add to the spokes in the wheel of national transportation of which she has made herself the center, one figure stands out as representative of her purpose and her achievement—that of the late David H. Moffat. In 1867 Moffat was a slim stripling with a far-seeing eye, a practical mind, and boundless energy with which to carry his ideas into execution. Although never the president of the Denver Pacific, that position being ably filled by John Evans, one of the greatest of the early railroad-builders, who had succeeded Bela Hughes in that office, Moffat was from first to last one of its stanchest supporters; as its treasurer he grappled successfully with the difficult problem of its finance, and during his connection with it he acquired that grasp of Colorado's transportation problems which was to make him one of the country's outstanding railroad-builders. The story of Denver's rise to power and of her struggle to win a place on the direct east and west transcontinental railroad route is also the story of David H. Moffat.

Early in life the Western fever took possession of him, and while still a boy he longed to share in the bright fortune of the frontier. At 16 he had left his home in Washingtonville, Orange County, New York, journeyed as far west as Des Moines, Iowa, and become teller in the bank of the A. J. Stevens Company. A few years later he moved on to Omaha, became cashier of the Bank of Nebraska, and built up a paper fortune in real-estate speculation, a fortune which quickly vanished when the bottom fell out of the boom that George Francis Train started when the Union Pacific picked Omaha as its eastern terminus. With little formal education, Moffat nevertheless had a taste for reading, and this attracted him to the book business. When the gold excitement was at its beginning in the Pike's Peak country, he formed a partnership with C. C. Woolworth at St. Joseph, Missouri, to start a book and stationery store in Denver, Woolworth to stay east as buyer and Moffat to go west as storekeeper.

On St. Patrick's Day, 1860, a young man of 21, Moffat arrived in Denver with four wagonloads of supplies, one of which was driven by himself. And surely the town that greeted him was picturesque enough to satisfy the adventurous spirit of any young man. The clatter of wagons and the noise of drivers bawling at ox-teams and swearing at mules filled the congested streets; for so heavy was traffic to Denver that the overland express reported 1,200 wagons, Pike's Peak bound, passed in a single day and night. Miners and tenderfeet from the

East jostled each other in the stores and saloons, some busy buying outfits to go prospecting or arranging for the storage of their heavy luggage while they took reconnaissance trips into the mountains, others idly listening to the stories of gold-strikes which were everywhere the subject of lively conversation. Gold was the one matter of importance to Denver, and even the new-comer could believe the stories he heard when he saw that every man carried a buckskin pouch of the precious dust and every merchant had a gold-dust scale on his counter: the buyer passed his pouch to the vender, who dribbled out the dust on the scales to the proper amount; it was said that the waste by this method was 25 per cent, and the dealer had only himself to blame if he received too little dust to pay for his wares. During the week of Moffat's arrival the town was entertained by a duel between two officers of the Territory of Colorado, attended by 800 interested spectators, and the conviction and hanging of two murderers who were tried by a miners' court.

Moffat opened his stationery store on Eleventh Street below Larimer, later moving to Fifteenth and Blake, and shortly became assistant postmaster and agent for the telegraph company. Since every one in Denver expected or professed to expect letters with every pony express, his store soon became a center of activity, being surrounded daily by crowds of miners waiting for the mail to arrive. The telegraph business flourished also, although at first there was no direct line to Denver and messages came by horse from Julesburg, the rate for ten words from New York being $9.10, and from St. Louis, $7.50. Moffat took subscriptions for Eastern newspapers and delivered them in person for 25 cents per copy; and he often brought Editor Byers copies of St. Louis, St. Joseph, and Chicago newspapers that came ahead of the mail-coach on his own wagons. An example of his business acumen was his early recognition that the cabins of the town needed some more attractive decoration than newspapers pasted on the walls; he ordered 6,000 rolls of wall-paper and sold them like the proverbial hot cakes.

"Frank, engaging, willing to accommodate, and with an unlimited capacity for friendship," there was never any doubt as to Moffat's success as a storekeeper or his popularity as a member of the community. Although he remained a partner in the stationery business until 1870 and was for six years assistant postmaster and telegraph agent, he returned to his first profession of banking in 1867, when he was appointed cashier of the First National Bank. Founded by authorization of the Comptroller of the Currency in 1865, it had no success until Moffat took charge, after which it steadily increased in importance until it became the most powerful financial institution on the Plains.

As the Denver Pacific approached the city from the north, the people's enthusiasm grew; every one of them had a stake in the success of the enterprise, and most of them had contributed in cash. Every ear was waiting for the sound of the locomotive whistle, and one day in the spring of 1870 the newspaper announced that "the first locomotive ever heard in Denver was reported Tuesday evening. The wind was blowing in the right direction, and those who heard it were where no local noises interfered, so it is not a stretch of the imagination to believe they were not deceived." On June 22, 1870, the town went wild when the long-expected first locomotive, named the "David H. Moffat," steamed into Denver, and the eager crowds swarmed to greet "the first engine ever seen in these parts." The pioneers who had spent painful weeks crossing the prairies with ox-teams had seen no locomotives since they left the Missouri, and many of them had never expected to see another; they crowded around the marvel, examining every part with the pleased curiosity of children.

With the coming of the "David H. Moffat," 12 years after the first discoveries of gold, Denver definitely emerged from the village class and was on her way to becoming a city. People stopped moving to Cheyenne or elsewhere; they began building more costly houses, and the town took on an air of permanence; water flowed through the streets, trees were planted, the extraordinarily brilliant green lawns of Denver began to flourish; there was a feeling of solid confidence in the future and a new zest in living in the Mile-High City. In August, 1870, the Kansas Pacific was opened, giving Denver two connections with the East, the last 150 miles of track having been laid in four months—according to some authorities, in 92 working days. After this achievement General Palmer entertained the leading citizens at Chapiot's restaurant and provided a dinner for the workmen which included California fruits, champagne, and ice-cream. He was free then to turn his attention to the building of his own road, the Denver and Rio Grande. Even after his brilliant achievement in completing the Kansas Pacific and Denver Pacific and adjusting the business arrangements between the two, the Denver men who were his guests that day probably looked at the dashing young General a bit askance, for, as the Denver historian, Smiley, says,* "While the Denver people of that period believed almost anything within reason were possible, if guided by the indomitable captains of that time, most of them thought Palmer's enterprise was rather outside the borderline of reason, and not a few regarded it as a wild project that would bring financial ruin to every man who became an owner in it, and that if the road were built even no farther than the southern limits of Colorado, it would not be long operated before starvation would cause its abandonment."

At about this time a visitor to Denver, A. K. McClure, wrote of his impressions of the growing city in *Three Thousand Miles through the Rockies*:

Denver is a clever place, and has clever, substantial thrifty people. I have seen no place west of the Mississippi that equals it in the elements of positive prosperity. They have gone through the severest ordeal, and have come out purified in the crucible of sad experience. They have seen the day when gamblers, cut-throats, and thieves controlled everything—elected their municipal officers, possessed the wealth of the city, intimidated the officers of the law, and held high carnival in their work of robbery and death. But crime culminated, as it ever does, and gave birth to vigilance committees, which made a number of the most desperate outlaws dance jigs upon nothing on the hill hard by! ... Two years ago they had pretty well banished the characters dangerous to the peace and safety of the citizens; but the orderly gamblers still controlled the municipality, had vast wealth, and pursued their shameless vocations in open day. They had their gambling-houses in some of the best buildings and business localities of the city, conducted them in view of every passer-by, just like merchants and tradesmen, had bands of music playing in front of the doors to entice the stranger, and were most prosperous. Indeed, so powerful were they at one time, that they controlled the legislature—something after Pennsylvania fashion.... Last winter a year the growing morality of Denver rose up against the gamblers, and drove them out. They still doubtless remain in some numbers, but they dare not expose their business to the public gaze, and they are under as wholesome restraint as in our best-governed

* Jerome C. Smiley, *Semi-Centennial History of the State of Colorado* (Chicago, Lewis Publishing Company, 1913).

cities. To-day Denver is as free from open outrages upon public morals as any other Western place of the same size. Indeed, I regard it as far in advance of most of them. In Omaha the two most attractive and courted ladies at the most fashionable hotel in the place were, when I was there, known only as "Mrs. Faro" and "Mrs. Keno." Here they would not be tolerated in any circle outside of a church-pew or a horse-race. On Sunday the city was as quiet and orderly as Chambersburg, and the number of elegant churches, seminaries, schools, including a convent, reading-room, etc., leaves no room to doubt that Denver has a moral tone controlling its social life quite above the average of new cities. Upon the whole, I have found no place in the far West that appears to me so pleasant socially, and so substantial in its business as is Denver. True, it discounts its future development of the precious metals, but not more than is fully warranted.

It now numbers probably eight thousand inhabitants; has seminaries and schools, nearly half a score of churches, three daily newspapers, an excellent reading-room, the finest stores I have seen west of Chicago, and a class of business men unsurpassed in character and attainments in any of our Eastern towns of the same size. It has the common fault of all Western cities. While they grow at all, they grow with feverish, unhealthy pace. Instead of systematically laboring to cheapen homes, business places, and products, they all struggle to swell the tide of inflation. In a few instances, it may be sustained by fortuitous circumstances; but as a rule it results in financial disaster and in prostrating prices, business, and growth below their proper level. Denver was the creation of the mines. It now is floating on the waves of hope, and discounting all its prospects. If the mineral wealth of Colorado shall be mastered at an early day, then must Denver even surpass the expectations of its citizens; but if successive years of doubt and hope deferred should be the fate of Colorado, then must its decline be fearful and to very many fatal. I share fully the hope of the business men of Denver, that they have reached nearly or quite the depth of misfortune, and, while lots and rents are still at fabulous prices, I look for them to advance rather than decline. There is wealth enough to maintain the struggle until science shall pour into its lap the untold riches of the surrounding mountains, and the busy husbandman is yearly making the parched plains about the city to bloom and ripen with the golden fruits of the field.

The high cost of the necessaries of life makes the wages of labor very high, and the development of the country has thus been greatly retarded. Ordinary farm-hands command from forty-five to sixty dollars per month, with boarding, and in the mining regions five dollars per day is a moderate price. But the highest rates, comparatively, are paid to domestics, for the reason that female servants are exceedingly scarce. But few laboring women can afford to come to the Territories, and those who happen here get fabulous wages. The most ordinary female house-servants get fifty dollars per month, and board, and good female cooks command from seventy-five to one hundred dollars per month. One hundred ordinarily good female servants could now find permanent employment in pleasant homes in Denver, at an average of twelve dollars per week and boarding; and three months' wages would pay their fare from the East to this city. Besides the high wages they can get, they are in equal demand in the matrimonial market. The adult unmarried population of the Territories is probably ten males to one female, and here, as elsewhere, people continue to be given in marriage. The importation of several hundred virtuous, industrious, single females into Colorado would be a great benefaction both to the females themselves and to the people of the Territory.

It is true that I was not nearly so much crowded at church as I was at the race-course and at the theatre; but it is possible that most of the people were at the other churches. On Saturday a friend drove up to the hotel and invited Mrs. McClure and myself to accept a seat in his carriage for the races. His wife accompanied him, and on every side the youth and beauty of the city might have been seen driving in the same direction. Wishing to see Denver as it is, we concluded to go, and soon found ourselves on a splendid course belonging to the Agricultural Society, inclosed by a concrete wall, and cleverly filled with as fine turn-outs as could be displayed in any of the inland cities of Pennsylvania. Nor was the crowd confined to the elegant and fashionable. Here was a rude mountaineer on an Indian pony, with spurs something after the fashion of a cogged cartwheel; there was one on an obstinate mustang, with blanket and buffalo coat; and there were hundreds of others, from regular sports, boys and men, to the staidest the city can afford. Deacons and vestrymen act as judges, and elders time the horses and make clever side bets on their favorites. The ladies have their watches, time the horses, and are most enthusiastic over the result. This may seem odd enough far East; but they tell me out here that they don't raffle, as the churches do East, and they thank the Lord that they are not as other men.

Life in a city which combined the charms of the frontier West with a cosmopolitanism that earned it the title of "the American Paris" had a fascination that few could resist. When David H. Moffat first came to Denver, it was his intention to build up a fortune of $75,000 as soon as he could and return east to live on the income; he had no thought of staying in Colorado. But year by year he became more entangled in the enterprises of the new state and more enamored of her charms, and, like thousands of other Easterners who came west with the intention of staying only a few years, he found himself becoming a thoroughgoing Westerner who could never be satisfied to live elsewhere. His rise in power was rapid. In 1868 he was one of the backers of the United States and Mexico Telegraph Company, which built a line from Denver to Santa Fe; in 1876 he was appointed receiver for the Kansas Pacific Railway; in 1880 he became president of the First National Bank; in 1885 he was one of the organizers of the Denver Clearing House. In 1884 he became president of the Denver and Rio Grande Railway, and during his six years in this position he constructed 682 miles of standard-gage and 296 miles of three-rail track and built the road up until it was known throughout the country for its splendid roadbed and rolling-stock.

General Palmer may be called the railroad and promotional genius of Colorado during its early period, and David H. Moffat his legitimate successor in the following decades. To Palmer's plans for providing a network of rails reaching back into the mountains to the mines and his schemes for the exploitation of natural resources, Moffat added another idea, the determination to make the dreams of the pioneers a reality and put Denver on the main transcontinental traffic line. From the time he first entered the railroad business in 1867 to his death in 1911, this idea was in the back of his mind, and in his later years it became an obsession to which he sacrificed everything.

Throughout his life Moffat envisioned Denver as the hub of a wheel through which should pass lines of transportation from Texas, Puget Sound, San Francisco, Chicago, San Diego, and Canada. In 1881 he began one of these spokes which was to reach tide-water in Texas, the Denver and New Orleans Railroad, later the Colorado and Southern; and, with Grenville M. Dodge to help him, he built the line from Denver to Fort Worth. He built the Denver, South Park and Pacific to tap the rich mining resources of Leadville and bring them directly to Denver in competition with the Denver and Rio Grande. At the time of the Aspen mining boom he built the Aspen branch of the Denver and Rio Grande, and when there was a similar boom at Creede, he suggested that a branch be built to the town over the mountains from Wagon Wheel Gap. The directors laughed at the idea, and Moffat replied, "All right. I'll build it myself." When he did, it proved so profitable that the railroad was glad to take it off his hands.

The directors laughed again when he suggested building to the boom town of Cripple Creek, again he built the road himself, again it was a success, and the Denver and Rio Grande took it over. He also personally built the railroad from Boulder to the Marshall coal-banks. In all these new mining camps Moffat bought properties and became a leading mine-operator. He took fortunes out of such well-known mines as the Maid, Henriette, Resurrection, and Tabor's Little Pittsburgh at Leadville; the Caribou at Boulder; the Holy Moses at Creede; and the Victor, Anaconda, and Golden Cycle at Cripple Creek; and he was the first to use the cyanide process of gold-extraction invented by the Colorado engineer Philip Argall. Where he led, investors followed, and the First National Bank and the Moffat interests came to be synonymous with financial stability and success.

In the panic of 1893, preceding which the price of silver began its toboggan-slide and during which scores of Colorado banks failed, Moffat stood firm. He liquidated $2,000,000 worth of his own government bonds and put the money into his bank; when others were calling loans and foreclosing mortgages, he extended credit, with the result that not one of his customers failed. A story is told of the president of the First National Bank of Fort Collins, who came to him with a grip full of gilt-edged securities to borrow money, saying, "I have never done business with you but I need your help." Moffat swept the securities aside. "Put them away," he said. "I know your bank. Go back to Fort Collins, and if you need help, telegraph. I will send you a telegram stating that the First National Bank of Fort Collins will never go under until the First National Bank of Denver does. You can paste that notice on your front door."

Like E. H. Harriman, Moffat's idea of operating a railroad property was to spend money on it until it was in the best possible condition, to shorten routes and reduce grades and so cut operating expenses. By thus postponing dividends in the early years, he would prepare for vastly greater earning-power and increased value in the future. Acting on this principle, he completed the change of the Denver and Rio Grande from narrow gage to standard gage, and then made the startling proposal that the road spend from $8,000,000 to $16,000,000 to push the line straight through the Rockies from Denver. But again the directors laughed, and again it was left to Moffat to do it himself.

Years passed. The Moffat interests had become the most powerful in the state, and Moffat was truly an empire-builder; he controlled mines, railroads, power-projects, the Denver City Tramway, the Denver Water Works; he was one of the owners of the Fourth National and Western National banks of New York and a principal stockholder in the Equitable Life Insurance Company. He was a potent influence in politics and had several times refused to listen to suggestions that he be nominated for United States Senator. One day he showed a friend credits in New York banks for $7,000,000. "If I had that much," said his visitor, "I wouldn't do another thing for the rest of my life." And Moffat replied, with the spirit of the restless frontiersman who had come from New York to Iowa, to Nebraska, to Colorado, and had built an empire there, "I am not satisfied to do nothing. I want to be doing something new—building or developing. That is the way I get my pleasure out of life."

So, at 63, he startled Denver by announcing that at last the city was to have its direct route to the West, that he was going to build a railroad straight through the Rockies, tapping a vast undeveloped coal and mineral area in the northwestern part of the state that was without a railroad, and making Denver the great transcontinental transportation center of the Plains. Characteristically, he announced the name of the manager of this project without consulting him. When this man, Sylvester T. Smith, read the news in the paper, he hurried to Denver, and, thinking of the tremendous difficulties of the task, to master which some twenty railroad schemes had been launched, fourteen routes surveyed, and before the magnitude of which two national railways had recoiled in dismay, he said to Moffat, "I would not build that road now if I were in your place. It is going to be a very heavy, expensive piece of construction." But Moffat shook his head and replied, "I am going to build this road because I want to develop Colorado, and you are going to build it for me." So the Denver and Northwestern Pacific, later the Denver and Salt Lake, was organized with a capital of $20,000,000, and the project was commenced.

Now began the most complex, involved, heart-breaking series of discouragements that ever faced a railroad-builder. Estimating that the road to Salt Lake would cost $16,000,000, plus $4,000,000 for tunnels, and arranging with Senator William A. Clark that the line should join with his Los Angeles and Salt Lake Railway to reach the Pacific Coast, Moffat, in 1902, went to Providence and enlisted the aid of Marsden L. Perry and the Boissevain family of Holland. But he reckoned without those giants of the railroads, George J. Gould and E. H. Harriman, who now controlled the transcontinental routes and who wished no new line begun that would make the distance to the Pacific Coast shorter than by their own roads. Since Harriman owned land-filings on part of the route over which Senator Clark's line would pass, he soon persuaded him that he must not coöperate with Moffat, and this outlet to the coast was lost. Pressure was likewise brought to bear on the Providence and Holland interests, and they withdrew their support.

At this time the three railroad barons of the West were James J. Hill, Harriman, and Gould. Hill, who controlled the Great Northern, running from St. Paul to Puget Sound, was not unfriendly to Moffat, but he was engaged in a fight with Harriman of the Union Pacific, who had just bought the Southern Pacific. To checkmate Harriman in the north, Hill bought the Chicago, Burlington and Quincy. Harriman then bought heavily of Northern Pacific stock and formed a pool, the Northern Securities Company, to control both the Northern Pacific and the Great Northern. This corporation was later dissolved by decree of the United States Supreme Court; but in the preceding warfare Hill had no time for the Moffat road, and afterwards he could not be again interested in its development. The prospect of opening up enormous new coal-fields did not appeal to other capitalists who owned the established coal-producing properties; so half a dozen men who dictated the railroad affairs of the nation, and who were indignant that Moffat should plan to build a new national railway without their consent, passed the word to Wall Street, and he was everywhere met with closed doors. In this extremity he drew on his own fortune and pushed the road to Yarmony, high up in the Rockies, 146 miles from Denver.

Meanwhile, Harriman interests were active, inducing various individuals to file mining claims on the site of Moffat's proposed tunnel and holding up his progress at the narrow, red-stone gorge of Gore Cañon, a right of way absolutely necessary for him to own if he was to pierce the Rockies. There was an error in the railroad's filing which gave Moffat a route over the top of the mountains instead of through the Cañon, and this he maintained was due to an error in the government surveys. But suit was started by the newly organized New Century Light and Power Company, which had filed on the land for a reservoir site. Stormy legal battles followed, and when the New Century Company saw it was about to be worsted, it turned its rights over to the United States Reclamation Service and asked it to fight the case as a matter of public welfare. So strong and determined were the interests opposing Moffat that a succession of manufacturing interests in the East declared that the power was needed for great industrial enterprises, and they even induced the Los Angeles Chamber of Commerce to protest on the ground that the water was needed for Southern California. But borings showed that no dam could be constructed there, for there was no bed-rock for 110 feet, and the Government's case crumbled; meanwhile Moffat had bought the rights that the Burlington road had obtained through the Cañon long ago in the Eighties. Moffat was further embarrassed by a mysterious run on the First National Bank, which the newspapers said was engineered by Harriman and Gould. Finally, President Roosevelt sent his confidential agent, Carl Ewald Grunsky, who had represented him in the Panama Canal diplomacy, to investigate and hear both sides. At the hearing which followed, at the White House, when Moffat charged collusion between the rival railways and the Reclamation Service, Roosevelt showed that he understood the situation, for when the government engineers arose to testify, he remarked, "Oh yes, you represent the power companies and the opposing railroads, do you not?" After the hearing he ordered the Government to relinquish all claims on Gore Cañon, and Moffat was again free to go ahead.

In 1904 he reached Corona, altitude 11,660 feet, but, on account of the terrible snows, it was almost impossible to run trains there in winter. The construction of the Moffat road had taxed the engineering genius of the country; precipitous heights, narrow cañons, winter blizzards had all held back construction, but it had gone forward steadily, "piercing mountains of solid granite, crawling along the eyebrow of an abyss and gliding among summer flowers and perpetual snow along the summit of the continental divide, the highest standard gauge railroad in the world." It was draining away the Moffat fortune, and still it had not reached the rich coal-fields of Routt and Moffat counties, which government reports showed to be as great as those of Pennsylvania, with natural outcrops 80 feet thick, and the great areas of grazing- and farm-land as good as any in Wyoming, Montana, or Idaho. And so there was no income-producing traffic. But his lone fight must have excited the admiration of Harriman, even if it made him angry. It is said that he called Moffat to New York and told him, "Moffat, I will help you build the Denver and Northwestern. I will give you fifty per cent interest for the money you have put into the road and will raise all the funds to take it to Salt Lake. I will take all the bonds and give you fifty per cent of the stock." Whereupon Moffat replied, "Mr. Harriman, do you think I am a fool or a knave? I refuse your proposition. I know you better now than I have ever known you."

Construction went on, men were lowered into Gore Cañon by ropes, and the perilous job of laying the rails there was completed in 1907. A junketing party of Denver business men to the end of the track followed, but it was a forlorn gesture, for Moffat had reached the end of his money and could get no more. Failing to get business support, he was reduced to making pleas on personal grounds, and when his erstwhile friends, afraid to buck the powerful opposing financial interests, turned him down, he was hurt and came to hold himself aloof from his old associates.

But if most of the Denver business men could not see the Moffat road, there was one other old man who still had enough vision to share Moffat's dreams. Colonel D. C. Dodge, General Palmer's adjutant in all his railway-building and management, had never seen the rich country that the line was to tap, and when Moffat took him there, he became enthusiastic. An old war-horse of 70, he returned to Denver and began a campaign for funds, heading the list with $100,000, and so stirred the city that an additional $1,500,000 was raised and the line pushed on to Steamboat Springs.

Moffat still fought for Eastern aid, and in 1910 he thought that, with Harriman's death, the old opposition was passing, and also the opposition of Denver interests, as a result of which his home town had supplied him with less aid, he said, than had Colorado Springs and Arizona. The local opposition was jealousy, he claimed,

pin headed jealousy and nothing more. Here was I helping to build up the city and to increase the value of real estate in Denver, while the interests which could profit most were against me. It looked as if they feared I would be regarded as a great man, whereas I had no idea of greatness when I undertook the work. I wanted to do it for the good of the state and nothing more. As to the railroads, the Denver and Rio Grande opposed it because it would cut off 200 miles between Denver and Salt Lake, the Union Pacific didn't do it because of their government subsidies and the Burlington was scared by the construction cost. But the old opposition is disappearing. The interests in Wall Street see that I have built over the mountains, which they never thought I would be able to do, and I guess they have come to the conclusion that it will be of no avail to oppose me further. I have put my own money into the venture because I had confidence in it, and the results have demonstrated that I was right. I am going ahead with my plans for building the big tunnel. The Moffat Road today is a success and I expect to live to see it in operation between Denver and Salt Lake.

But alas for the hopes of the sturdy old lion! Moffat was not to live to see his road pushed through to Salt Lake, nor was it to be finished for many weary years. On a trip to New York, seeking funds, he died in the Hotel Belmont on March 18, 1911, just 51 years and a day after his first arrival in Denver; and almost his last words were, "If I succeed in putting Denver on a through transcontinental line, I will then think that I have done something for my state." All his fortune, estimated at $20,000,000, had gone, $9,000,000 of it directly into the road, the first 124 miles of which had eaten up $12,000,000. But his indomitable spirit had inspired others to pick up the work where he left it and to share the difficulties he had fought against; so, through an incredible maze of obstacles, the building of the Moffat road went forward.

Soon after Moffat's death, at Denver's behest the State of Colorado undertook to complete the project by building the great Moffat Tunnel north of the Berthoud Pass, thus eliminating the worst of the snow hazard and providing an open gateway through Colorado. This step had previously been held up because of lack of funds, but in 1911 bonds to the amount of $4,000,000 were authorized by the legislature. The opposition was so strong, however, that Governor John F. Shafroth failed to sign the bill within 30 days, thus returning it to the people for vote, and the measure was lost. In 1913 Newman Erb of the Père Marquette Railroad promised to advance half the funds necessary to push the road to Craig if Denver people would subscribe the rest, but he failed to carry out his agreement. Then the City and County of Denver voted bonds to build the tunnel; but an injunction was issued restraining the city, and the case was carried to the Supreme Court of Colorado, where the bonds were held invalid. Erb repeated his former promise, $1,500,000 was raised in Denver, and again Erb failed to produce his share and withdrew. The Moffat road went into receivership, investors lost heart, and the United States Railroads War Board was asked to take over the road. When snow blockades stopped the trains, the Board advised that operations be terminated, but it finally assigned the line to the Burlington system. A State Railroad Commission was appointed in 1919 by Governor Oliver H. Shoup, and Denver supplied it with $10,000 to survey in different sections of the state the routes for three possible tunnels through the mountains, one of which was the Moffat Tunnel. Speakers were sent through the state advocating the Tri-tunnel bonds, which the legislature authorized the people to vote upon, but Pueblo, which would be removed from the main line of the Denver and Rio Grande should the Moffat Tunnel be built, opposed the bonds so strongly that they were rejected by 10,000 votes. Governor Herbert S. Hadley then suggested the formation of an improvement district covering the territory to be benefited by the tunnel, but the opposing railroad interests knifed that.

A new figure now in the picture was William C. Evans, son of Governor Evans, who had succeeded Moffat as president of the Denver Tramway Company. Since his father and most of the other old-timers who had been associated with the Denver and Northwestern project had died, he determined to carry on the fight in their stead. A creditor's suit had been filed by the Bankers Trust Company of New York and others, and without Evans' assistance, it appeared that the road would be junked forever. In order to prevent a sale to any rival road which might stop construction work, the majority stockholders, headed by Evans, in 1917 organized a voting pool and pledged themselves not to sell for 10 years. This had to receive the approval of representatives of the bondholders, the Bankers Trust Company and the Seaboard National Bank of New York. At first they were skeptical, but finally, after Denver men had told them the whole tragic story of Moffat's fight with the other railroads and all the crises that had been weathered, the directors of these banks approved the plan, warning the Denver men, however, that they would give them no more financial or even moral support.

William R. Freeman, who had been appointed receiver jointly with Charles Boettcher, instituted economies in the operation of the Moffat road, invented an ice-machine to clear the tracks, and, since the territory served by the road was beginning to produce coal, oil, and mountain head-lettuce, he got considerable traffic and made a respectable financial showing. But the great Moffat Tunnel would still have had to wait had it not been for a disaster which stirred the whole country. When the Arkansas River overflowed its banks, June 3, 1921, spreading death and destruction, it completely inundated the city of Pueblo, and it was at once apparent that the state would have to step in and control the river. When Pueblo interests called for a special flood-conservation session of the legislature, Denver demanded that the Moffat Tunnel District be included, and this was done. It was soon apparent that no flood-conservation bill could be passed unless a bill creating the tunnel district were also passed; so Pueblo at last bowed to the inevitable, and the district was created, the bill being signed by the governor on May 12, 1922. A taxpayer's suit brought against the act was hurried to the United States Supreme Court, which sustained the measure in 1923. Bonds to the amount of $6,720,000 were issued and sold at a premium, and the driving of the tunnel commenced.

In the late summer of 1923 construction began on the 6.1-mile Moffat Tunnel, the longest on the American continent, which was to shorten the distance between the two coasts by 173 miles, or half a day's traveling time, and reduce the maximum transcontinental grade to two per cent instead of the prevailing three per cent. Paralleling the railroad tunnel and built simultaneously with it was a pioneer bore to provide the city of Denver with water from the western slope. The open cut at West Portal was started on August 25, 1923. The Water Tunnel was under ground on September 12 at West Portal, and at East Portal on October 13. Contractors actually started work on October 2, 1923. With the beginning of construction the physical difficulties encountered were fully equal to the financial difficulties that had preceded them. Solid granite had to be blasted away by the thousand tons, quaking mud was encountered, hot-water springs at 100 degrees F. boiled out and scalded the workmen, an entire lake drained through a

DENVER FROM THE AIR

The State Capitol, the City and County Building, and the Civic Center in the left foreground. Courtesy of the Denver Chamber of Commerce.

THE DENVER CIVIC CENTER
Courtesy of the Colorado Association.

THE EAST PORTAL OF THE MOFFAT TUNNEL

The Burlington stream-lined train "Zephyr" is entering the tunnel on its first transcontinental run over the Moffat route, June 16, 1934. Courtesy of the Chicago, Burlington and Quincy Railroad.

fissure of the mountain. At one time the tunnel workings were inundated with a flow of 3,100 gallons of water a minute, and when a blizzard broke the power-lines, and the pumps stopped working, the men worked for days in water up to their waists. Old and tried tunneling methods failed. Tough Douglas-fir timbers splintered like matches under the pressure, and timbermen and miners quit the job in fear. Among the labor recruited during the winter were the farmers of the mountain valleys who raised head-lettuce, and to the regular workers the derisive appellation "head-lettuce miner" became a fighting term. Finally, at the point of despair over the difficulties encountered in excavating, George Lewis, the engineer, regained hope when one night he suddenly remembered a house-moving operation he had seen and from it drew the idea of building a traveling cantilever girder which should advance into the tunnel and support the rock while operations went on. Although he was a poor man, he told the tunnel commission that if they would build this machine, they could take the cost of it out of his salary if it failed to work. Moving on tracks, overhanging 14 to 20 feet of the excavated tunnel, this invention was the first device they had found that was able to prevent cave-ins; it proved to be a complete success, and again the building went forward.

In 1925 funds ran out. Further powers of taxation were needed, but the tunnel commission feared to bring the matter before the Ku Klux Klan-controlled legislature; so they met in secret for months, exhausted legal counsel, and finally decided that they had a right to issue supplemental bonds. When this was done, taxpayers objected, and a state-wide uproar followed. Harassed by lawsuits, beset by engineering difficulties, and opposed by strong political factions, the commission nevertheless pushed the water tunnel on; and at last, nearly five years after it was legally authorized, and at a cost of $15,700,000, it was completed. On February 18, 1927, President Coolidge touched a button setting off 124 shots of dynamite, the last rock wall in the water tunnel fell away, and the construction gangs clambered through. "Who in hell built this tunnel?" yelled the West Portal gang. "We built the tunnel," shouted the East Portal gang. "We did, by gosh," yelled the West Portal. And they discovered that the two apertures were in perfect alignment, a tribute to the ability of the engineers who supervised the work. Even on this auspicious occasion the elements that had been conquered played a final hand by enveloping the special train in such a vortex of snow that the honor guests could hardly get into the tunnel they had come to dedicate. The blizzard shut down the power-lines and stopped the pumps, and water gushed into the tunnel. Rotary plows whirled the snow off the tracks only to have it close in just as heavily a moment later. The party of a hundred who had come up for the ceremonies were hauled through the worst drifts by horses, and they clambered into the tunnel cold and wet, dressed in slickers and rubber boots.

The worry and work, indeed, were far from over. The Water Tunnel had been completed, and a small bore for much of the railroad tunnel had been finished, but the excavation for the enlargement and completion of the railroad tunnel brought many problems. Among them was that of "swelling ground," where the tunnel floor arched upward and could be controlled only by steel girders; and it was July 7, 1927, before the railroad tunnel was holed through. The first train passed through the tunnel on February 27, 1928. Difficulties then developed in getting any railroad to lease the tunnel, and it was not until the depression year of 1932, when the Reconstruction Finance Corporation was created, that any road felt justified in building the line westward. In that year the Corporation loaned funds to the Denver and Rio Grande to build the Orestod-Dotsero cut-off, connecting the tunnel with its line on the western slope of the Rockies, substantially cutting the time and distance between Denver and Salt Lake, and giving Denver, at last, her place in the sun of transcontinental transportation. Up to the last the Moffat road lived up to its reputation as a trouble-maker; for as late as September, 1932, it was discovered that part of the right of way was still owned by an organization, headed by a Tammany politician, which had filed on the tunnel years before when Harriman was harassing Moffat.

Ultimately it was planned to build a direct independent line straight west from the Moffat Tunnel to Salt Lake City, but since the financing of this long line would be difficult, the 38-mile cut-off connecting with the Denver and Rio Grande on the western slope was decided upon as the most practical method of utilizing the tunnel. On June 16, 1934, the 38-mile gap between Dotsero and Orestod having been closed, the first regular passenger train moved through the Moffat Tunnel, and east and west service was inaugurated by the Denver and Rio Grande Western and the Chicago, Burlington and Quincy. On that day the graceful aluminum "Zephyr," the Burlington's new high-speed train, flashed over the track, part of which followed what had once been a Ute Indian trail, and slid smoothly through the mountains that generations of engineers had declared to be impassable. And Ralph Budd, president of the Burlington lines, declared that this was probably the last transcontinental railroad route that would ever be built across the Rockies.

As the people of Denver watch the trains roll over their direct east and west transcontinental highway, and as the passengers look out on the incomparable grandeur of the country it traverses, they must thank the indomitable spirit of David H. Moffat for the benefits they are enjoying. It was his work that subdued the Rockies at their most formidable point; it was his work, and that of others like him, that gave Denver the transportation and power and prestige that have made her a great city instead of a cross-roads hamlet. He gave the city an outlet which can never be controlled by any single railroad, a public gateway constructed by Denver capital, controlled by Denver men, supported by the taxation of thousands of humble property-owners who throughout the whole difficult operation kept a singularly strong faith in the project. It is indeed a tribute to Denver's spirit as well as to Moffat's vision.

Always generous, David Moffat remembered his boyhood home, and perhaps his own lack of formal education, when he gave a public library to his birthplace of Washingtonville, New York, and a pipe-organ to the church at Blooming Grove that he attended as a boy. During his lifetime he gave $100,000 to one of the faithful officers of his bank and $75,000 to another; and when a head waiter at the Hotel Belmont in New York expressed the wish that he could live on a Western farm, Moffat surprised him the next morning with a deed for a $15,000 ranch in Routt County. But his great generosity did not lie in individual benefactions or the support of institutions. It was his gift to the country he loved—Colorado. To further its development and the prosperity of its people all of his fortune went back into the soil of the state, so that he died a poor man. When a mining enginner once visited him in New York to interest him in the enormous profits to be made in West Virginia coal, he summed up his philosophy of giving thus: "When I was a young fellow, I went to Colorado, walking over the dusty plains, with very little cash in my possession. Denver was then a struggling village and I began in a very humble way to make my living. All I possess in the world to-day I made out there in those hills, and there is where it will all remain and be spent by me,—for the welfare of Colorado."

During his long career Moffat had managed or built nine railroads in Colorado, and he had held undisputed sway of tremendous public-utility interests affecting the welfare of the people of the state. Yet he hardly ever experienced public criticism, for the community held him in high regard as a man who, while advancing his own fortune, also advanced the common welfare. One who knew him well said of him, "His friendship is not so much the smiling as the helping turn. I speak not of what he gives away in charity. But in a straight business way, he has helped more men than any other man in Colorado. That would be little to say of him now, because he is the richest man in the state. But it could truly be said of him long before that came about and actually was said. To count David H. Moffat as a friend was not only an honor; it was an intense joy."

In the State Historical Museum there stands a silver cup almost as high as a man, its sides engraved with pictures of the tunnel project, Gore Cañon, and the mining camps and cities of Colorado, scenes and achievements that were connected with the life of David H. Moffat. Its handles are appropriately fashioned into the leaves and acorns of the sturdy oak, and it is further embellished with the state flower, the columbine. The inscription reads: "Presented to David H. Moffat by his business associates of Denver, as a tribute to his energy as an empire builder, his loyalty to every interest of his adopted city and state, and, above all, to that broad citizenship that will remain an inspiration for all the years to come in the upbuilding of Denver and Colorado."

The grit and determination of David Moffat and his willingness to devote everything he had to the completion of the one project dear to his heart is typical of the men who have made Denver. They wrested a city out of the dry prairies, built it strongly and beautifully, im-ported and planted every one of the towering trees that shade its streets, and by sheer force and magnetism made their city the center of the Rocky Mountains and the Plains. Their breezy recklessness and indifference to the quick turns of the wheel of fortune have given the golden city of the Rockies a dash and flavor which is as invigoratingly Western as the miner with his pan and the cowboy in his saddle. Fortunes have been made and lost there quickly; men have been out at elbows one year and rolling in wealth the next; life has always been mercurial, unconventional, bold.

And certainly, if the tourist wants to see the grand mountain country of the pulp magazines—the West "where men are men and God's good women grow"—he can find it by traveling from Denver westward and then along the western slope of the Rockies. For there is an exhilarating land as wild and beautiful and remote as any celebrated by the writers of Western thrillers—of whom, by the way, a large group live in Colorado. He will see the picturesque mining towns, their old brick buildings almost deserted—among them Central City, on the eastern slope, where Denver people reopen the old Opera House every summer to regale the public with such old-fashioned treats as *Camille*, with Lillian Gish as the phthisical heroine. And Ouray, that gem of a town in a Tiffany setting of rock, high in the mountains, in whose near-by mines Tom Walsh made his fortune. And the limpid, peaceful headwaters of the Colorado River, which glides through the mountains before it tears into the Grand Cañon and rushes on to Boulder Dam, where it is now being impounded for diversion to the silver taps of Hollywood.

From the heights of these mountains has poured the golden stream that has built the city of Denver, that has given her wealth and strength, that has erected her homes and caused her astonishingly vivid lawns to gleam in the sun, that has created the classic beauty of her symmetrical white Civic Center. It is to this wild, free Western country, with its bracing air, that Denver owes her greatest gift. For it has richly answered her plea, "Give me men to match my mountains," and the men have made her great.

# CHAPTER VIII

O F all the early Western cities, San Francisco was the one that had to fight least for its place in the sun. Always Lady Luck smiled upon her, and though her geographical position was not altogether favorable, she nevertheless became the beneficiary of all the rich commerce that flowed through the Golden Gate into one of the greatest natural harbors in the world. This vast harbor with its mile-wide gate curiously eluded the first five explorers who sailed along the coast of California, including Sir Francis Drake, who anchored at Drake's Bay a few miles to the north, a body of water which had previously been charted by the Spanish explorer Sebastian Rodrigues Cermeño and named Puerto de San Francisco. Probably the fogs obscured the narrow entrance to the real Bay of San Francisco when the explorers sailed by. At any rate, it was not discovered until 1769, when the Spanish *commandante,* Gaspar de Portolá, marched northward over the brown hills and, coming to the top of one of them, suddenly saw stretched out before him the polished silver sheet of that grand inland sea. But he did not recognize it as anything more than a body of water that inconveniently obstructed the approach to the Puerto de San Francisco a little farther north.

Even to come within hailing distance of the Puerto de San Francisco gave the Spaniards a thrill, however, and Father Junípero Serra considered the event little short of a miracle. For when he had suggested to Spain's Viceroy in Mexico, José de Gálvez, that one of the California missions be named in honor of St. Francis of Assisi, that dignitary had replied, "If St. Francis desires a mission, let him show us his harbor." And now the exploring party had miraculously approached the port of the Seraphic Father.

It was not until 1776 that the Spaniards decided that the shore of the large body of water was in reality the proper place for building the mission to St. Francis. In that year it was established on the Laguna de Nuestra Señora de los Dolores, the northernmost of a string of missions, a day's journey apart, extending along the King's Highway, *El Camino Real,* south to San Diego. And Father Serra exclaimed, "Thanks be to God that now our Father St. Francis with the Holy Cross of the procession of missions has reached the farthest boundary of the California continent. To go farther he must have boats." The Mission Dolores still stands, having survived fire and earthquake, and so does the Spanish military reservation, the Presidio, founded at the same time by order of Captain Juan Bautista de Anza, who was the first man to march over the desert from Mexico to California. Crossing the burning waste from below what is now Tucson, Arizona, he reached the Bay of San Francisco in 1776, explored it, and returned to Mexico, leaving his lieutenant, José Joaquin Moraga, to found the *presidio.* So the first settlement on the Bay of San Francisco was established when the Liberty Bell was ringing in far-away Philadelphia.

But the town of San Francisco finally grew up around neither of these landmarks. It was established, instead, to the east of the *presidio,* where foreigners began to erect their trading-houses on land which was covered with fragrant mint; and it bore the name Yerba Buena, which is to say, "the good mint." At this time California was closed to Americans and other foreigners, though the Spanish Government was willing to accept those who became Spanish citizens, and to one such, John Augustus Sutter, a Swiss, it had granted an enormous tract of land on the Sacramento River. This amounted to nothing less than an empire, which Sutter ruled from his fort at what is now Sacramento, issuing his own money, maintaining his own soldiers, welcoming American emigrants, and becoming as rich as a king. The other feudal overlord of the region was General Don Mariano Guadalupe Vallejo, who had a similar empire north of the bay around what is now Sonoma and the Valley of the Moon, the beautiful countryside where Jack London later lived and wrote.

As the fame of California spread eastward, the United States Government began to covet the Bay of San Francisco and to lay plans to possess it. With the revolution of 1821 California became Mexican territory, and a few years later the Mexican prefect, José Castro, was

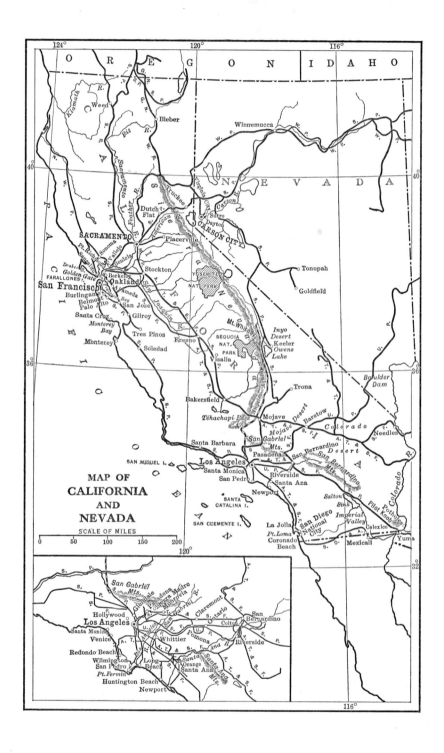

MAP OF
CALIFORNIA
AND
NEVADA

SCALE OF MILES

to write, not without reason, "These Americans are so contriving that some day they will build ladders to touch the sky and once in the heavens they will change the whole face of the universe and even the color of the stars." In 1843 seven thousand of them were at Independence, Missouri, ready to set out for the Pacific. In that year Captain John C. Frémont was sent to California on a supposedly peaceful scientific exploration, but he carried a 12-pound howitzer, and his men were armed. In September, 1845, the Mexican Government issued an order that no more American emigrants should enter California and that those already there must depart the following spring. But it was too late; the damage had been done, and nothing could stop the American flood. When spring came, a party of twenty-four Americans who did not want to leave California surrounded General Vallejo's house at Sonoma, took him prisoner, ran up their flag, which was adorned with the figure of a bear, on the Sonoma plaza, and declared a republic. On July 8, 1846, war having been declared between the United States and Mexico, Captain John B. Montgomery of the U. S. S. *Portsmouth* landed at Yerba Buena with seventy men and took possession. Three weeks later Elder Sam Brannan of the Mormon Church arrived with 200 Mormons who had sailed from New York with instructions from Brigham Young to found a city on the Bay, but, finding the Americans in possession, he abandoned the project. On August 26 Washington A. Bartlett was appointed *alcalde* of Yerba Buena, and on the 30th of January, 1847, he caused a notice to appear in Sam Brannan's new newspaper, the *California Star,* ordering the name changed to San Francisco.

This strategic move was made just in time to save the name for the city, for General Vallejo and his friends had already laid out on the north side of the Bay, on the Straits of Carquinez, what he considered to be the ideal city and port, and he proposed to capitalize all the advertising and prestige given the Bay of San Francisco by calling his town Santa Francisca, after his wife, and centering all the shipping and commerce of the Bay there. When Bartlett anticipated him, however, he called his port after his wife's second name, Benicia, and there it remains to this day, with the near-by town of Vallejo a memento of the fiery old general who used to rule the north country. In later years General William T. Sherman, who was then a lieutenant of artillery

stationed in Monterey, writing in his memoirs concerning the "impu-
dence" of Bartlett in seizing upon this name for the village of Yerba
Buena, added,

This little circumstance was big with consequences. That Benicia is the
best natural site for a city, I am satisfied; and had half the money and
half the labor bestowed on San Francisco been expended at Benicia we
should have at this day a city of palaces on the Carquinez Straits. The
name of "San Francisco," however, fixed the city where it now is; for
every ship in 1848-49 which cleared from any part of the world, knew the
name of San Francisco Bay, but not Yerba Buena or Benicia; and, accordingly, ships consigned to California came pouring in with their contents, and were anchored in front of "San Francisco!"

So, on the south side of the Golden Gate, the narrow opening between
the bay and the ocean, which Frémont said he named "Chrysophylæ,
or Golden Gate, for the same reason that the harbor of Constantinople
was called Chrysoceras, or Golden Horn," the city of San Francisco was
created. And Sam Brannan, the Mormon elder, became the first Yankee
town-booster. Before he fell from grace and was accused of mishandling
Mormon funds, he preached the first English sermon in the city and
solemnized the first wedding under the American flag. After he had
been tried by the first American jury, he set up the first flour-mill and
began to publish the first newspaper, the *California Star,* of which he
soon got out a special booster edition sent by Pony Express to the
Missouri River to attract emigrants. Indeed, so ardent a promoter did
Brannan become that he went into the desert to meet Brigham Young
and direct his entire colony to California. But Brigham, struck with
the beauty of Salt Lake and its geographical resemblance to the Promised Land of the Scriptures, refused to proceed further; and so Sam
returned to California alone and set up as a merchant at San Francisco
and at Sutter's Fort. A few months later, on January 24, 1848, just
nine days after Mexico had ceded California to the United States,
occurred the event that made Sam Brannan a rich man and San
Francisco a world-famous city.

When John Marshall looked into the mill-race of the uncompleted
sawmill he was building for Sutter at Coloma, 40 miles above Sutter's
Fort, and picked up a little piece of yellow gold, half the size of a pea,
he performed the initial act in a drama which drew into itself the whole
world. When his discovery was made known, it threw millions of men

the world over into a fever of excitement and started the greatest movement of people to a single goal that had taken place since the crusades of the Middle Ages. It destroyed the California that then existed, despoiling the empires of Sutter and Vallejo and turning their lands over to hordes of Yankee squatters with no legal right to them. It caused the currency markets of the world to tremble, raised the United States to new heights as a monetary power, and attracted to California the adventurous men who were to develop her resources and to center the financial power and transportation systems of the entire West in the new city of San Francisco.

Sutter dimly realized something of the sinister import in this discovery as he and Marshall tested the rough gold behind bolted doors at New Helvetia. They read all they could find on the subject in an old encyclopædia, and then they took an apothecary's scale with an equal weight of silver and the unknown metal in each pan and immersed it in water; whereupon the yellow metal outweighed the silver, and Sutter said, "I believe this is the finest kind of gold." As soon as Marshall got back to Coloma, he made the Indian and white workers promise that they would keep the discovery a secret for six weeks, until the Brighton flour-mill, on which Sutter had expended $25,000, could be completed. But such a promise was, of course, useless. Mrs. Wimmer, the cook, who had tried out some of the gold in a lye-kettle when making soap and found it untarnished, told the story. And soon Sam Brannan, who was still the publisher of the *Star* even while in Sacramento, had the news at first hand from one of his flock who was a workman at the mill. When he dashed through the streets of San Francisco on horseback, bearing a flask of the precious metal and crying, "Gold, gold from the American River," the 200 inhabitants were in a fury of excitement, and two days later not a man who could get to the diggings remained in the deserted village. Sutter tells of his experience during the gold-rush in a sort of diary which he prepared in 1856 and sent to a friend: *

*March 7, 1848*

The first party of Mormons employed by me left for working and digging Gold and very soon all followed, and left me only the sick and lame behind. And at this time I could say that every body left me from the

* *Diary of Johann August Sutter* (San Francisco, the Grabhorn Press, 1932).

Clerk to the Cook. What for great Damages I had to suffer in my tannery which was just doing a profitable and extensive business and the vats was left filled and a quantity of half finished leather was spoiled, likewise a large quantity of raw hides collected by the farmers and of my own killing: The same thing was in every branch of business which I carried on at the time. I began to harvest my wheat while others was digging and washing Gold, but even the Indians could not be keeped longer at Work. They was impatient to run to the mines, and other Indians had informed them of the Gold and its Value; and so I had to leave more as ⅔ of my harvest in the fields.

### *May 19, 1848*

The great Rush from San Francisco arrived at the fort, all my friends and acquaintances filled up the houses and the whole fort, I had only a little Indian boy to make them roasted Rips etc. as my Cooks left me like everybody else. The Merchants, Doctors, Lawyers, Sea Captains Merchants etc. all came up and did not know what to do, all was in a Confusion, all left their wives and families in San francisco, and those which had none locked their Doors, abandoned their houses, offered them for sale cheap, a few hundred Dollars House & Lot (Lots which are worth now $100,000 and more).... Some of the Merchants has been the most prudentest of the Whole, visited the Mines and returned immediately and began to do a very profitable business, and soon Vessels came from everywherse with all Kind of Merchandise, the whole old trash which was laying for Years unsold, on the Coasts of South & Central America, Mexico, Sandwich Islands etc. All found a good market here.

### *Some time in 1856*

People looked on my property as their own and in the winter of 1849 to 1850, a great Number of horses has been stolen from me.... Nearly my whole Stock of Cattle has been Killed.... I need not mention again that all Visitors has always been hospitably received and treated. That all sick and wounded found always Medical Assistance, Gratis, as I had nearly all the time a Physician in my employ.... I think now from all this you can form some facts and you can mention how thousands and thousands made their fortunes, from this Gold Discovery produced through my industry and energy, (some wise merchants and others in San Francisco called the building of this saw mill Sutter's folly) and this folly saved not only the Mercantile World from bankruptcy, but even our General Gov't. But for me it has turned out a folly, then without having discovered the Gold, I would have become the richest wealthiest man on the Pacific Shore.

It took seven months for the news to reach New York, and at first it was not believed there. But the Army officers, Lieutenants Sherman and Richard B. Mason, sent to Washington by way of Panama a special courier loaded with samples from the diggings, including a tea-caddy containing 230 ounces of gold. When this exhibit finally arrived, President Polk, on December 5, nearly a year after the discovery, confirmed the news in a message to Congress, and the country went wild with excitement. Meanwhile, gold had been sent to Honolulu, and the vessels in port there had carried the news to Portland, Callao, Valparaiso, and Mexican ports, so that by October the gold-seekers were pouring in, and by January, 1849, there were 6,000 men in the diggings around Sacramento, and San Francisco had become a city of 2,000 inhabitants.

To profit by the traffic from New York to the gold-fields the Pacific Mail Steamship Company, which was organized in April, 1848, to ply around the Horn to the Columbia River, now changed its plans and sent its ships to California instead. Its first ship arrived in the bay in February, 1849, and discharged 350 passengers at San Francisco. The crew promptly deserted, and it was with difficulty that the captain could pick up enough sailors to get out of the harbor. Desertion was popular with the soldiers too, and Sherman, with seven officers, pursued twenty-eight men of the Second Infantry who had decamped for the mines and brought back twenty-seven. The next Pacific Mail steamer to arrive anchored alongside a man-of-war in the harbor which guarded the vessel to prevent the crew from deserting.

By November there were 600 ships in the harbor, each of which had brought its full quota of passengers. No attention was paid to the normal capacity of a vessel; the travelers were packed in with an efficiency of action and an economy of space resembling the New York subway in the rush hours of a later day. Around the Horn the gold-seekers came, in overloaded and often unseaworthy ships; across the Isthmus of Panama, where many sickened of fever and died, and others, unable to get passage on any ship to San Francisco, returned to the States; over the deserts and plains and mountains of the interior of America in covered wagons, a terrible journey which killed many and sickened more and tried the hearts and bodies of the brave and the strong. From the villages of New England, from the frontier of the

Missouri, from the crowded cities of the East, and from the ports of the world, on they came in a never-ending procession—on to the mines, on to golden California.

Forty-two thousand came overland in the year of 1849, 9,000 from Mexico. They found in San Francisco a strange city, sandy, wind-swept, straggling, and unkempt, rising from low shore lands to near-by high hills. The harbor was crowded with deserted ships, several of which had been drawn up to the shore to serve as warehouses, and one as a hotel. And on the high hills, wherever there was room for foothold, the new-comers perched their houses, usually strips of canvas tacked around redwood posts, which, lighted up at night, made the town look as if hung with gigantic Chinese lanterns. The streets in the level part of the city alongside the bay were literally seas of mud, in which unwary pedestrians sometimes actually drowned at night. One corner bore a sign, "This Street Is Impassable—Not Even Jackassable." One of the new arrivals described a downtown sidewalk which

in any other portion of the earth would have been considered a very extravagant piece of work, hardly excelled by the golden pavements of the New Jerusalem. The first portion was constructed of Chilean flour in one hundred pound sacks, which, in some places, had been pushed down nearly out of sight in the soft mud. Then followed a long row of large cooking stoves over which it was necessary to pick your way carefully, as some of the covers had accidentally been thrown off. Beyond these was a double row of boxes of tobacco of large size. Although this style of walk may seem extravagant, yet, at the time, sacks of Chilean flour, cooking stoves, tobacco and pianos were the cheapest materials to be found, for lumber was in the greatest demand, selling for as much as $600 per thousand.

The powers that were still looked with disfavor on San Francisco as the site of the city that was to dominate the bay. General Persifer F. Smith, in command of the Pacific Division, established Army head-quarters across the bay at Benicia and reported to the Adjutant-General that the sea was too rough at San Francisco to load or unload ships three days out of seven, and that the town was on an extremely long point, cut off from the interior by an arm of the bay 30 miles long, with the only road impassable. The town, he said, was in no way fitted for military or commercial purposes; there was no harbor, a bad landing-place, bad water, few supplies, and an inclement climate. He hoped that the President would be given power to select the site for the port of entry and capital of California, and he suggested Benicia as a very favorable site for a town "larger than is likely to exist anywhere here for a century to come."

But the Forty-niners paid no heed to the General's sputtering, and even though his advice was sound, they applied themselves to building a city on the crazy sand-hills of San Francisco. The harbor then came up as far as Montgomery Street, and the huts of the squatters extended from the end of the business section around Portsmouth Square into the district now bounded by First, Second, Market, and Mission Streets, which was known as Happy Valley; south of this, as far as Howard Street, was Pleasant Valley; "lazy old, daisy old, Telegraph Hill" swarmed with ex-convicts, thieves, cutthroats, and ticket-of-leave men from Australia and bore the sinister name of Sidney Town; while at its foot was a crowded settlement of Chileans, as all South Americans were called by the Forty-niners. Huts and shacks were made of canvas or any other material that could be patched together, though the better class around Portsmouth Square had houses built in Boston and imported in sections; the foundations of small buildings were apt to be of such strange material as tons of wire sieves or barrels of beef. The salvation of this flimsy town was the keen, tonic salt wind that blew over it and kept it fresh and its people invigorated and healthy. An epidemic would have wiped out the population, for to be sick in the California of those days, with few doctors or medicines and unspeakably bad hospitals, was to die. But if it was spared epidemics, San Francisco was made to suffer trial by fire. Six times the flames swept over the old town, the total damage in less than 18 months being $24,000,000; six times it was rebuilt, and the city chose the phœnix for its crest.

The streets were a motley of crowding, jostling men, practically all of them young—to be 30 was be aged—who rejoiced in wearing the picturesque slouch-hats and sombreros, wool shirts, and top-boots of the mines and in letting their beards grow. There was a liberal sprinkling of foreign costumes, there were many Chinese with basket hats and hundreds of Mexican gamblers who wore high black beavers, white shirts, and diamond studs. France sent the new land "several thousand lying men and corrupt women," embarking them at the expense of the Government. Italy sent musicians, and also farmers who soon became rich, with eggs selling at from $6 to $12 a dozen. Germany sent dairymen, barbers, laundrymen, the last of whom inherited a profitable trade, for San Francisco had sent its laundry to Hawaii and China, the local price being $10 a dozen. From Chile came many laborers. All these combined in a riotous, cosmopolitan life which scorned all conventions and in which the main meeting-place was the saloon and the chief amusement the gambling-table.

Never did men become rich so quickly as in the California of '49. Although many never made more than day-laborer's wages, thousands struck it lucky. Nuggets worth thousands of dollars were found, and the miners, washing the gravel in creek-beds in their shallow circular pans and their large wooden rockers, discovered pay dirt which yielded fortunes. In the first five years nearly a billion and a quarter dollars' worth of gold was taken out of the soil of California, and much of it was spent in Sacramento and the mining-camps which rejoiced in such euphonious titles as Fleatown, Hangtown, Whiskey Gulch, You Bet, Poison Switch, You Be Dam, Delirium Tremens, Shirttail Cañon, and Lousy Level. But it was to San Francisco, known universally as "the City," and still referred to by that title in the West, that the miners repaired for their more exuberant and extravagant periods of relaxation, and the city became known throughout the world for its wildness, boisterousness, and extravagance. Gold-dust was the medium of exchange, a pinch taken from the miner's pouch being the price of a drink, and bartenders won or failed to win their jobs as a result of their demonstration in reply to the question, "How much can you raise in a pinch?" Prices were always high, but they fluctuated violently as the market was alternately skimped and glutted through the arrival of ships with various kinds of cargo. Flour would sell for $27 a barrel one week and less than half that price the next. Cargoes were often thrown into the bay because the cost of paying the excessively high wages required to land them would be more than they were worth. Rooms in the good hotels cost $250 a month; a large canvas tent used by gamblers rented for $40,000 a year. The best restaurants charged $5 a meal, and General Vallejo recounts that a man could sell a wagonload of fish caught in the bay for $5,000 at the mines.

Inevitably San Francisco became glutted with adventurers and criminals from all over the world. Indeed, so flagrant did the outrages of these men become and so impotent was the local government to cope with them that the citizens took the law into their own hands and organized the Vigilantes. At first under Sam Brannan, later under William Tell Coleman, this volunteer police force and court ruled the city from its headquarters at "Fort Gunnybags," gave a fair trial to criminals, and hanged or deported them if they were found guilty. Yankee rule dealt summarily with the owners of the old land-grants also. Although the treaty with Mexico provided that these claims should be held valid, the owners were required to defend their titles in courts set up by the Americans, and so costly, prolonged, and unfair were the suits that Vallejo and most of the others lost their lands and died poor men. Yankee squatters overran Sutter's land and destroyed his property, and although he spent the rest of his life trying to get recompense from Congress, he was never paid for his losses.

But however much of the wild and irresponsible riffraff of the earth the gold-rush brought to San Francisco, there was a handful of wheat in every bushel of chaff. The first shipload that came into the harbor included men who contributed much to the West, among them the Reverend S. W. Willey, one of the founders and first executive officer of the University of California; and every day saw the arrival of others who were to remain long after the gold-rush was over and to make California great. From New York State came the young lawyers Leland Stanford and Mark Hopkins, and also that native of Connecticut, the home of wooden nutmegs, Collis P. Huntington. There came also Charles Crocker, student in the university of hard knocks, peddler, miner, and trader in supplies. All these drifted to Sacramento, tried the mines for a while, and shrewdly deciding that money was to be made more safely and easily, if less spectacularly, by selling things to the miners than by swinging a pick or shaking a rocker, all of them went into business. These Yankees were to be known as "the Big Four" in Sacramento, and they were to become famous as the men who built the Central Pacific railroad.

At this same time the fates were bringing together another quartet of young men, all Irish, who were to write their names large in Western history. James Graham Fair came from Tyrone, Ireland, to Calaveras County and early showed his administrative talent by leading a large party of emigrants, most of whom were older than himself; John William Mackay came from Dublin, by way of New York, where he was employed in a ship-builder's office before embarking for Panama, and finally set to work with pick and shovel in Sierra County; James C. Flood, an Irish-born New Yorker of 23, landed on the muddy streets of San Francisco in 1849 and soon fell in with William S. O'Brien, another young Irishman, who proposed that they earn their fortunes with the towel and bottle instead of the shovel and pick by operating a saloon in San Francisco. There was also the keen-eyed young Jew, Adolph Sutro, who came from Aix-la-Chapelle, by way of New York and Panama, and who spent his evenings studying how to reclaim the treasures of gold that were lost in the crude rockers of the early miners; and the young lawyer William Sharon, shrewd, ruthless, daring, who was to make and lose a fortune in real estate and develop a great mining monopoly. Around the bar of Flood and O'Brien and in their lunch-room, where a particularly succulent fish stew was served, there gathered other men whose names were later to be famous: Darius Ogden Mills, financier; Elias Jackson ("Lucky") Baldwin, miner and landowner; John P. Jones, some day to be Senator from Nevada; and William C. Ralston, destined to become ruler of the largest banking monopoly in the West.

All these men were adventurers, all sought the gold, and when they later came to dominate the affairs of California, they gave the state that reputation for breezy recklessness, daring schemes, and bold operations which it has never lost. Not for them the soft ideas of public service and public trust which society in later years attempted to impose upon industrialists. They believed in the rule of tooth and claw. They saw what they wanted in the way of business monopoly, they gave their time and money to get it, they fought to hold it every inch of the way, and they considered whatever they gained to be their own private property, to do with as they chose.

In 1854 there came another man who was to have profound influence on the development of San Francisco, Theodore D. Judah, civil engineer, who conceived the idea of building the Pacific railroad and, after failing to interest San Francisco financiers, got the backing of the four Sacramento merchants, Hopkins, Huntington, Crocker, and Stanford, whom he started towards becoming the greatest railroad-builders in the country. This far-seeing engineer was born at Bridgeport, Connecticut, March 4, 1826, the son of an Episcopal clergyman. Educated at Rensselaer Polytechnic Institute, his first job was helping to build the Troy and Schenectady Railroad. When General William T. Sherman and others decided to build a California key-railroad from Sacramento east and north along the foothills to tap the rich placer-mining country, with extensions north, south, and east, they made Judah their engineer. But the problems of building a valley railroad were not sufficiently difficult to hold his interest, and he began to speculate on the possibility of building a railroad from the Pacific to the Atlantic, from San Francisco over the high Sierras. With a light one-horse wagon, a barometer, a compass, and an odometer, he crossed and recrossed the Sierras twenty-three times and located the line across the Dutch Flat route. He induced the state legislature to call a railroad convention, including delegates from Oregon, Arizona, and Nevada, in San Francisco in 1859, and on June 27, 1861, he was one of the incorporators of the Central Pacific Railroad.

Judah said that the reason no national railroad bill had been passed, in spite of all the grandiose schemes and flowery speeches in favor of it in Congress, was that no one had any facts; and he proposed definitely to answer such practical questions about a road to California as Congress might ask, giving data as to length, alignment, grades, number of tunnels, amount of excavation, masonry needed, and natural building materials available. In October, 1861, having obtained the support of Huntington and his group, he sailed for Washington, and there he turned the former Vice-President's room in the Capitol into a Pacific-railroad museum, where he showed Congressmen charts, maps, and reports. When his efforts were successful and President Lincoln signed the Pacific-railroad bill, he telegraphed, "We have drawn the elephant; now let us see if we can harness him." In spite of mutterings that "the Dutch Flat Swindle" never intended to cross the mountains and the refusal of Darius Ogden Mills and other San Francisco capitalists to give financial assistance, the work was begun and went speedily forward. But Judah was not always in accord with the partners on matters of policy, and they quarreled. He thought they had agreed that his services previous to the final organization would be taken as equivalent to the first 10 per cent payment on his stock, but Hopkins said he had no recollection of any such agreement, and the Big Four finally bought Judah out for $100,000. On his last trip to New York, where he intended to interest Eastern capitalists in the project, he contracted Panama fever crossing the Isthmus and died in the Astor House on November 2, 1863. So, at the age of 37, ended the career of the man who initiated the California railroad, an idealist and dreamer whose enthusiasm and vigor were equal to the practical demands of organization, promotion, and lobbying necessary to bring his ideas to reality.

Charles Crocker, the builder of the group, was born at Troy, New York, September 14, 1822. His father had been a merchant and a whole-sale liquor-dealer, but when Charles was young, he was very poor, and at the age of 12 he helped to support the family. When his father went to Indiana, Charles bought the right to carry the New York *Transcript* from a man who was in debt to the paper, earned all the living expenses of his mother and sister, paid the $200 debt on the route, and saved $500 additional. When the family followed the father to Indiana, Charles handed over his earnings to them, and when his mother died soon afterward, he set out for himself, all his property consisting of a pair of woolen socks, a cotton shirt, and a linen dickey tied up in a cotton handkerchief. On his first job he toiled from four in the morning until eight at night, cutting 200 oak rails a day and afterwards doing the chores. In the evening he worked by firelight making hickory brooms and ax-handles.

Crocker went to school three months and worked for a minister. Then he got a job in a sawmill, where he worked 16 hours a day for $11 a month; and when the owner inquired if he could take a raft of lumber down the river, Charles replied, "Yes, if I see you do it once." His next job was as apprentice in an iron forge, and he kept at this until he was 22 and had learned the trade of making bar iron as well as the book-keeping of the establishment. Desiring to set up as an ironmaster, he prospected for iron ore and, finding a bed of it, built a forge and stayed with it until 1849, when he sold out to his partner and started across the plains to California. With all this practical experience, coupled with his native powers, it is no wonder that he was made captain of his group.

At St. Joseph, Missouri, Crocker induced the owners of a river-

THE PRESIDIO OF SAN FRANCISCO

Louis Choris, *Voyage Pittoresque autour du Monde,* 1822. From the Stokes Collection, New York Public Library.

SUTTER'S MILL AT COLOMA

The scene of the first discovery of gold on January 24, 1848. *Gleason's Pictorial Drawing-Room Companion,* 1852.

SAN FRANCISCO IN 1849

Lithograph after a drawing by Henry Firks. From the Stokes Collection, New York Public Library.

steamer to supply passage to Council Bluffs provided he could furnish 250 tons of freight and fifteen first-class passengers. He more than fulfilled this agreement, but on the journey he learned that the captain proposed to put them all ashore at Sandusky. Whereupon Charles told his party to keep their shot-guns loaded and back him up in whatever he did. When all the freight was unloaded, the mate ordered the crew to take off the luggage of the passengers. "That box is not going ashore here," cried Crocker. "The first man who touches it is a dead man." "Shore that box," yelled the mate, but the crew made no response. Leaving the rest of the party to protect their property, Crocker went to confer with the captain, who told him there was not enough water in the river for the boat to go to Council Bluffs. Charles pointed out the driftwood floating down as evidence of high water, and when the captain said he had not enough wood to burn, Crocker said the passengers would cut all he needed. So the captain reluctantly ordered the boat to proceed, and when they at last reached Council Bluffs, he called Crocker into his cabin, opened a bottle of champagne, and said, "Well, by golly, old fellow, if anybody gets to California, you will!"

Arriving at Sacramento with $850, Crocker worked a claim at Placerville for a while and then decided there was more money to be made in selling supplies to the miners than in mining; so he opened a dry-goods store there in partnership with his brother, adding a branch in Negro Hill. He made money in mining properties and opened a large store in Sacramento, and when this was burned, he rebuilt it in brick, with the first iron front in town. By 1860 he owned valuable properties and was entirely out of debt. Always a Republican, he became acquainted with other members of the minority party in Sacramento, among them Mark Hopkins, who interested him in the Pacific-railroad project. In the spring of 1862 Crocker joined the others in the railroad work, selling his store to his clerks at a low price and giving them time to pay for it.

As a railroad-builder he was most successful. Of exuberant spirit, he could do more work than two ordinary men, and he never spared himself. While the other partners were dignified and conservative in bearing, he was the embodiment of push, vim, and energy. As supervisor of construction he combined economy and driving-power; he watched the spending of a sixpence as closely as $100,000, and he kept the men on their mettle. "When I took the first contract to build on this railroad, they wanted to know what experience I had," Crocker said. "I told them I had all the experience necessary. I knew how to manage men; I had worked them in the ore beds, in the coal pits, and worked them all sorts of ways, and had worked myself right along with them. I learned these valuable lessons in Marshall County, Indiana."

Just as Crocker started to do what he was best fitted for, so each of the others made his distinctive contribution. "We all came together and we were all anxious to succeed, all ambitious," he says, "and each one dropped into his place and filled it." Of his construction work Moses Hopkins says, "He was a man to go among the workmen and keep things alive. He had driving force, he was like an electric shock and always of good cheer, even if he had only a crust for breakfast." Crocker says he was very hard to live with while the road was building because he had to keep himself in a critical, fault-finding frame of mind which was contrary to his nature. "Why, I used to go up and down the road in my car like a mad bull," he said, "stopping along wherever there was anything going amiss and raising old Nick. The men were afraid because I was just looking for something to find fault with."

In his *History of the San Francisco Bay Region* Bailey Millard says that Crocker

was in the field at all hours and proved himself a master of expedition. At one time a bridge was washed out by a spring freshet. Unless another were in place in a few days the work at the end of the line would have to stop. The engineer having the rebuilding of the bridge in charge did not get busy fast enough to suit Crocker who demanded that trains be running over the canyon within five days.

"I don't believe it can be done," said the engineer, "but I'll try it."

"I don't want anybody to try it!" roared Crocker, testily. "I can get plenty of men to try it. What I want is a man who will go out and do it!"

"Well, I'll get the old plans and time sheets and study them out," was all the engineer would promise.

So Crocker went out and addressed a crowd of tracklayers who had been salvaging material from the wrecked bridge.

"Look here," he cried, "is there a man among you who can rebuild this bridge in five days?"

"I can," promptly spoke up a young man in a gray flannel shirt, coming forward.

"All right," asserted Crocker. "Go ahead and do it. You can have all the men you want."

The young man went ahead and threw up a bridge on corn crib piers and trains were running across in the specified time. In the course of time this man, William Hood, was made chief engineer of the whole system.

When it became evident that the Irish labor-supply would not be sufficient to build the road, Crocker started importing Chinese laborers, and these "Crocker's pets" soon totaled thousands. In *Beyond the Mississippi* Albert D. Richardson tells of a trip he took over the road and the 12 miles being graded over the summit, where he found 4,000 laborers at work—one-tenth Irish, the rest Chinese:

They were a great army laying siege to Nature in her strongest citadel. The rugged mountains looked like stupendous ant hills. They swarmed with Celestials shoveling, wheeling, carting, drilling, blasting rocks and earth, while their dull, moony eyes stared out from under immense basket hats like umbrellas. At several camps we saw hundreds sitting on the ground, eating soft boiled rice with chop sticks as fast as terrestrials could with soup ladles. Irish laborers receive thirty dollars per month, in gold, and board; Chinese thirty-one dollars, boarding themselves. After a little experience, the latter are quite as efficient and far less troublesome. The Hudson's Bay Company, in its palmy days, was compelled to import laborers from the Sandwich Islands; and without the Chinese the California end of the great national thoroughfares must have been delayed for years. Twelve thousand are now employed on it.

Crocker's pastor described him as a man of double character, one who was usually jolly, full of bonhomie, cheery, and affable, but who could instantly become the picture of negation, decisiveness, firmness, and reproof. Shrewd and full of guile, he kept his men from striking for more wages by suggesting to his superintendent that their pay be cut—this in the hearing of the committee who were calling on him to ask for a raise. When the Union Pacific sent a man out to see how much track could be laid in the last year of construction, Crocker and his superintendent carried on in his hearing a most lugubrious conversation, describing the difficulties encountered and the lack of supplies. As a consequence of this the Union Pacific man reassured his superiors by reporting that the Central Pacific could not lay 150 miles of track in a year, but it actually laid 501 miles in nine months and got the government subsidy that went with it. When the Sacramento *Union* declared the road to be unsafe over a 50-mile stretch, Crocker invited the United States commissioners to ride over it at 50 miles an hour, and he put a glass of water on the floor to show them that the track was so good that very little of it would spill.

It was Crocker, too, who helped move the Sierra Nevada Mountains 20 miles westward, thus increasing the amount of government subsidy by $640,000. He took Professor Josiah D. Whitney, state geologist, for a ride over the route, showing him a profile of the road from Sacramento to Truckee and asking him to designate the beginning of the Sierras, where the triple rate of pay from the Government began. The geologist decided that rising ground began at Arcade Creek, though the true base had generally been considered 20 miles east of this point, "but for the purpose of the bill Arcade Creek would be as fair a place as any." With this data as evidence Huntington was able to get Arcade Creek officially designated as the beginning of the mountains.

As a demonstration of what he could do as a builder, Crocker organized his men to lay 10 miles of track in a day. Although the superintendent said the number required to do this was so great that they would get in each other's way, Crocker organized the work as Ford later organized automobile building, so that each man tapped only one particular spike or made one motion in laying a rail. An Army general who watched the work said, "Mr. Crocker, I never saw such organization. It was just like an army marching over the ground and leaving a track built behind them—and all done about as fast as a horse could walk."

As to the Government's relation to the work, Crocker said that nothing could be done without money. "Not a clerk but wanted money to hurry things out of the pigeon hole—fifty or a hundred dollars. Things did not move until they were greased, then they would slide." Of the lobbying carried on by the road in Congress and state legislatures, he said, "We have always tried to prevent passage of those laws that were going to ruin us just as any man would throw a bucket of water on a fire that had attacked his house."

Decided, firm, and yet not obstinate, and as ready to handle fifteen thousand men as one thousand, Crocker did a work no ordinary man could have accomplished. He was not without generosity, building a home for the Boy's and Girl's Aid Society, making gifts to the University of California, and liberally supporting the Associated Charities of San Francisco, although he left no great philanthropy to bear his name. The Crocker Art Gallery in Sacramento is the gift of his brother, Judge Edwin B. Crocker, the legal adviser of the Central Pacific. On Charles' death in August, 1888, his high qualities were extolled in a lengthy memorial by "a Sacramento Pioneer," the first two stanzas of which read,

> The man of giant energies, the man of iron will,
> Where shall we find a man CHARLES CROCKER's place to fill?
> He that would scale the mountains to build a nation's way,
> Who tunnelled through the solid rock that seemed to bar his way.

> Then o'er the mountains, through the mountains he sped the iron horse
> Nothing that mortal could achieve could stay him in his course.
> Mountains he leveled, valleys he filled, through forest and o'er plain,
> And when he signal'd his iron horse, off sped his lightning train.

Mark Hopkins, the oldest of the group and the one who attended to the office work, was born September 1, 1813, at Henderson, New York. At 16 he was a clerk in a Niagara County store; then he ran a packet-boat on Lake Ontario, studied law in Lockport with his brother Henry, and moved to Michigan, where he opened a store at St. Clair. When the California fever was beginning, Hopkins went to New York and with a company of twenty-five others bought complicated mining machinery and a house in sections and took passage on a steamer bound around the Horn. Although their agreement read that they should have the same food as that at the captain's table, the associates were fed on beans, biscuit, and salt meat and treated like emigrants. Under the advice of Mark Hopkins they waited until they reached Rio de Janeiro, and there they put their case before the American consul, who assisted them in getting a new captain.

When they arrived at San Francisco, they abandoned their machinery, sold their house, and dissolved the company, finding, like many others, that such an organization was unsuited to the California mining situation. Hopkins and some others took a life-boat and went up the river to Sacramento, trading the boat there for an ox-team. He soon opened a general store at Hangtown, now Placerville, bringing his own goods by ox-team from Sacramento. Next year he went into the wholesale grocery business at Sacramento, making money fast and investing it in real estate. In 1856 he joined Huntington in the hardware and mining-supplies business, a venture which was most successful, although between 1870 and 1880 eight of the largest hardware firms in San Francisco failed. The firm was the symbol for all that was honest, progressive, and sagacious in mercantile affairs and was a training-school for young men. The association with Huntington continued until Hopkins' death in March, 1878.

From childhood, his brother Moses says, Hopkins was always a leader, whether playing soldier, hunting coons, or in business councils.

He had courage, nerve, prided himself on his judgment, decided each point at issue definitely, and stuck to his decision. He was independent and rebellious as a boy, particularly on attending church, and never seemed able to get ready when his parents wanted to take him to perform his religious duties. He was always pleasant, charitable and merciful to man and beast but his manner at the moment would lead one often to doubt there was much sympathy or respect for other people's ideas, if they did not agree with his own. He was not easily irritated and never exhibited intemperate passion. There was a stolid determination and ugliness in his action that did not tolerate argument or anything else.

Mark Hopkins was known as the mentor of the railroad associates, for whenever difficult problems arose, he was consulted as one who had a comprehensive grasp of the business situation and whose decisions were seldom at fault. The balance-wheel of the group, he was always the conservative, careful business man, seldom taking part in any discussion until there was a knotty problem to be solved, when he was ready to cut the knots. He took plenty of time to consider every question. The slowest of the four, he would analyze, combine, and render judgment, usually expressing himself last. Huntington called him "one of the truest and best men that ever lived. . . . Hopkins had one of those sharp analytical minds that could master anything he took hold of. He had general supervision of the books and the papers, and contracts. When he said they were right I never cared to look at them. . . . He was a very correct man in everything, a very able man. He never bought or sold anything the time he was with me." And again: "I do not know what we should do without him as he always seems to know just what is the best thing to do in all cases."

And again he said, "I never considered anything finished until Hopkins looked at it."

Distinctly an office man, Hopkins never left it to transact business. If a transaction could not be made from his desk, he never made it. He was willing to see employees, listen to grievances, and correct them when possible, but he never took part in the active affairs of the road. Crocker says he once went away leaving orders for Hopkins to stop the construction work at a certain time, but when he returned, the large force of men was still working, although it had long since finished the job. When he complained, Hopkins said, "Well, I knew you would return pretty soon and look after it." Crocker's estimate was, "Hopkins was a long headed man without much executive ability but was a wonderfully good man to counsel with, clear headed, understanding what he heard, and making up his mind on the state of fact very judiciously. He hated to give orders. He went out on the road only once a year. I knew every inch of the road, and traveling along it could wake up and tell where I was."

Carefully studying the situation, Hopkins and the others decided that the reason so many American railroads were not carried to completion by their original owners was that they were not economically managed, were built too largely on credit, and were drained by interest charges before earnings began. Hence they concentrated on economy, cheap loans, and postponed interest-payments. Hopkins was the financial and office man of the various building and railroad companies, and it was said that the last time the books of the Contract and Finance Company were seen, "Uncle Mark" was putting them into a box and screwing down the lid. Since an official of the company left for Paris shortly thereafter, the legend grew up in California that the books found a last resting-place at the bottom of the Seine. At any rate, no railroad investigating committee was ever able to find them or the books of Charles Crocker and Company, and consequently no Crédit Mobilier scandal was ever connected with the Central Pacific.

Hopkins, like all the other partners, was a Republican, a none too popular party affiliation in early California. He was described by a contemporary as a very thin man with long gray whiskers, who spoke with a slight lisp or impediment. He was the best letter-writer of the group and "could say more in a page of note paper than Crocker could say on six pages of foolscap." He was cautious and diplomatic and disliked political entanglements, as the following letter shows:

As a company our rule heretofore in political affairs has been to take no part except where an enemy endeavors to obtain position with intent to do us harm, then self interest induces us to oppose. I think our future course must be governed by the same rule. As business men and taxpayers in Nevada, we have a common interest with the people there—none have more at stake than we in her progress and good government. With your selections of U. S. Senators heretofore we have been content, and I naturally conclude we shall be in the future, because I think you cannot choose wisely for yourselves without doing equally well for the railroad interests which must continue to constitute an important element in the development, progress and prosperity of the state. What of company politics we have occasion for Stanford represents. The less I have to do with political matters, except to represent my native born personal Republicanism, the better I am pleased.

It was said of Hopkins that he liked to work more than the laziest man likes to loaf; his office window was often lighted until two o'clock in the morning, and he died of overwork. It was reported that he gave to charities and that he would rather hand out a check for $1,000 as a gift than waste a nickel. But he left no large gifts to philanthropy, and his estate was the subject of legal controversy by various claimants for many years. At the time of his death he was building a magnificent palace on Nob Hill in San Francisco; it was a gray-towered feudal castle set on top of steep, terraced gardens surrounded by a buttressed wall 40 feet high. One of its great rooms was modeled after a court of the Doge's Palace, the whole house was lined with carved Italian walnut, rare woods, and marbles, and it was said that the architect purchased the books for the library by the yard. On this house Hopkins spent nearly $1,000,000, and his brother Moses said of it, "Everything was perfect, solid, and very expensive. The completeness of whatever he had was the charm of it to him." At Hopkins' death one of the newspapers remarked that, though building a palace, he still lived in a $35 a month house, did his own gardening, took pleasure in picking up bits of old iron and odds and ends, and was "economical to a point of eccentricity in his apparel. No old clo' dealer ever saw any margin for speculation in his cast off garments." Later some of the Hopkins wealth went to the University of California, and the Nob

COLLIS P. HUNTINGTON       LELAND STANFORD
THEODORE D. JUDAH
CHARLES CROCKER       MARK HOPKINS

Huntington, Stanford, Crocker, and Hopkins, courtesy of the Society of California Pioneers; Judah, courtesy of the Southern Pacific Company.

SACRAMENTO IN 1849

Lithograph after a drawing by G. V. Cooper. From the Stokes Collection, New York Public Library.

Hill house was given to the California School of Fine Arts by Edwin F. Searles, an architect, who married Mrs. Hopkins after drawing the plans for a house she built at Great Barrington, Massachusetts.

Leland Stanford, the partner who handled the railroad's political affairs in California, was born at Watervliet, New York, in the Mohawk valley between Albany and Schenectady, on March 9, 1824. His father was a contractor, and the boy early showed his taste for business. His first venture in trade was to wash some horse-radish and send it to town by the gardener, who sold it for him for six shillings; a little later he gathered and sold $25 worth of chestnuts; and as a young man he cut 2,600 cords of wood from his father's land and sold it for a profit of $2,600. He attended Cazenovia Seminary, practiced law in Port Washington, near Milwaukee, Wisconsin, and came to California by way of Nicaragua in July, 1852. He opened his first store at Cold Springs, between Placerville and Coloma, and later another at Michigan Bluffs. During these early years his wife remained in New York, and Stanford lived in a corner of the store building. When his store was flooded, his great strength showed itself as he easily lifted barrels of sugar to the counter out of the water; his ingenuity was in evidence when he invented diluted whisky to sell the miners as a substitute for vinegar to flavor their beans. Finally, he and his brother took over the store at 56 and 58 K Street, Sacramento, and from this store and the grub-staking of miners he made in all about $400,000. Republican, antislavery in sympathies, he helped to organize the party in California, was its first nominee for treasurer, and twice its nominee for governor, being elected the second time. As Civil War governor, and the first Republican to hold the office, Stanford headed the state which contributed $178,000,000 gold to the Treasury, and he was a liberal supporter of the Sanitary Commission, predecessor of the Red Cross, of which he was state chairman. During his election campaign the Sacramento *Union* referred to him as a candidate who was not an orator but who was "a man of sound judgment, handsome talents, extensive business experience and a citizen without reproach."

From the beginning Stanford supported the idea of a Pacific railroad, and, like the other partners, he furnished fertile soil for Judah's appeal. He was described as a handsome man of impressive bearing, deep-chested, with large shoulders and arms, a large face with short whiskers and mustache; he was bland, unctuous, slow in movement, and inclined to procrastinate, in contrast with the fiery, energetic Crocker, who wanted everything done now. But it was said of him that "no she lion defending her whelps, or a bear her cubs, will make a more savage fight than Mr. Stanford in defense of his material interests." At his inaugural in 1862 he declared against the importation into California of more Chinese, but he later said little on this subject, for Crocker decided that he needed them to build the Central Pacific. One night Crocker took 500 Chinamen from a ship in the harbor, loaded them on trains, and dumped them at the head of the track; after that many thousands more were imported.

At the beginning of construction the Central Pacific was referred to as "Stanford's moonshine project," and the newspapers freely predicted that there would never be a railroad to Nevada by way of Dutch Flat, for the obstacles were too great. Stanford was one of the first to advocate an immediate direct connection with San Francisco, recommending building to Goat Island; but this terminal could not be obtained, and San Francisco offered no help, being, even then, "serene, indifferent to fate." So the western terminus remained for a while at Sacramento. While caring for his railroad interests Stanford became a political power in California, and from 1885 to 1891 he served as United States Senator. This widened a breach between him and Huntington, who, feeling that Stanford was using the Southern Pacific as an instrument for his own personal advancement, forced him from the presidency. Huntington assumed that position himself and declared that he intended to use the office to further the interests of the railroad and nothing else. He often made slighting remarks concerning Stanford, whose more lavish style of living and spending did not meet with his approval. To a representative of the historian H. H. Bancroft, who was seeking to gather material about the lives of the railroad-builders, he said: "I guess he will refer you to Curtis. I call Curtis Stanford's romancer. I think he helps him to write his biographies for him."

Stanford traveled much abroad; purchased a great farm at Palo Alto, down the peninsula from San Francisco, where he raised trotting horses; bought his wife collections of laces and rubies said to be unequaled; and entertained lavishly. When he was Senator, he gave a dinner for the Senate page boys, inviting them on engraved cards and presenting each with a $5 bill and a pair of gold cuff-links. He believed in spending money freely, and he also believed in sharing it with his employees, paying high wages as a matter of sound business. He has been described as a man of absolute justice, a man of long silences, and a gentle man in both senses of the words.

Yet he could be markedly intolerant. The story is told of a dinner at Stanford's house in San Francisco at which he complained bitterly of the ingratitude of the Government and the people toward the builders of the Central Pacific and dwelt on the many and enormous sacrifices that he and his partners had made, only to have the Government hound them as Shylock hounded Antonio for his pound of flesh. The room in which he spoke contained paintings, rugs, and statuary worth many thousands of dollars, and a vase on the sideboard was valued at $100,000. And Justice Stephen J. Field remarked to his dinner partner, "You need only look around the room to see how shamefully these gentlemen have been treated by an ungenerous and ungrateful Government."

At the time Stanford began breeding horses, it was thought that fast trotters were the result of accident rather than blood; the results Stanford obtained were instrumental in changing that belief. He was a good judge of horse-flesh, purchasing Electioneer, who sired many of his best trotters, although he was advised against this by experts. In Paris he criticized a painting by Meissonier, the "Cavalry Charge," on the ground that the horses were not rightly poised, and he convinced the artist so completely that he said he would never paint a horse again. To prove his belief that when a horse is trotting fast, all its feet are sometimes off the ground, and that in jumping it springs with its fore feet, Stanford spent $200,000 on electrically controlled cameras to take consecutive pictures. This resulted in the book *The Horse in Motion*, which was, in reality, the beginning of the motion-picture.

Something of a dreamer, Stanford took the large view of things. When asked about political affairs by a San Francisco *Chronicle* reporter on May 9, 1875, he said he was thinking of more important matters; he was looking forward to the time when the railroad system should be completed: "I shall see trains of cars loaded with merchandise and passengers ... from the line of the 32nd parallel ... from Mexico ... Washington ... Oregon ... ocean steamers bearing the trade of India, the commerce of Asia, the traffic of the islands of the ocean. ... I shall see our thronged and busy streets, our wharves laden with the commerce of the Orient, and I shall say to myself, 'I have aided to bring this prosperity to the state of my adoption and to the city in which I have chosen my home.' "

Grief-stricken when his only son died, Stanford turned his attention to the disposal of his great fortune as a memorial. To Dr. Beard, the rector of the American Church in Paris, he said, "I was thinking I might do something for other people's boys in Leland's name. When I was connected with the building of the railroad, I found many of those engaged in the engineering were inefficient and inexact and poorly prepared for their work. I was thinking I might start a school for civil and mechanical engineers on my grounds at Palo Alto." As this idea grew, he and his wife visited and inspected various universities, clarified their ideas, and sought advice, until they finally founded Leland Stanford Junior University, endowing it with $20,000,000. The establishment of this Far Western university with an endowment four times that of Columbia, five times that of Harvard, astonished the world, and it was doubted that California could ever furnish enough students to make proper use of it. As president Stanford selected David Starr Jordan, who added to the plans of the founder his own ideas on education, making Stanford one of the outstanding universities of the world, and who once remarked that the reason he was a good president was because he didn't want the job. As to the opinion the people of California held of Stanford, the Los Angeles *Times* remarked on January 21, 1885, "Amidst all the fierce antagonisms which the action of the colossal corporation of which he is head has aroused in California, but a small measure of it, comparatively, has descended upon the head of the chief himself, and there is to-day a not unkindly feeling towards him on the part of the whole people of the state." Stanford died on June 21, 1893.

Collis Potter Huntington, the railroad's financier and lobbyist, strongest of the Big Four and the last to survive, was born in Harwinton, Connecticut, October 22, 1821. From his Puritan father of

INTERIOR OF AN EARLY TRANSCONTINENTAL PALACE SLEEPING-CAR
Courtesy of the Union Pacific Railroad.

SNOW-SHEDS ON THE CENTRAL PACIFIC

Drawn and engraved by Joseph Becker. *Frank Leslie's Illustrated Newspaper,* 1870.

THE CLIFF HOUSE AND SEAL ROCKS

Engraved after a photograph. *Frank Leslie's Illustrated Newspaper,* 1870.

severe and miserly character he got much good advice, including this warning: "Do not be afraid to do business with a rascal—only watch him; but avoid a fool, for you can never make anything out of him." In his first year's work Collis earned $84 and saved every penny; when he had $175, at 16, he bought $3,000 worth of watch-findings on credit and peddled them for a profit. He then bought a lot of rather risky commercial notes owned by a man who had been selling clocks in the South, went down and collected them, and during the trip learned about the country and its commercial possibilities thoroughly, and, incidentally, came to think slavery a greater curse to the white man than to the Negro. He next opened a store in Oneonta, trading successfully with the shrewd farmers of up-state New York and developing the largest business in the county. "Those old farmers are sharp," Huntington once said. "They never keep their word. I always used to pay them something to make a contract with them. I was the only man who went eight years steady in the butter trade that did not fail."

He even pitted his wits against the wholesale butter-dealers in New York. When he took a large supply to the city and was dissatisfied with the price offered by one dealer, he went to others without obtaining any better price; and when he came back to the first dealer, this man lowered his offer a cent a pound. Again Huntington tried unsuccessfully to sell at a higher price elsewhere; again the dealer cut his offer a cent. So Huntington decided to sell the butter at retail himself. From a friend he got the use of an old building in West Street in return for paying the porter's wages, and he wheeled his butter to this building in a four-wheel truck, hoisting it up in slings with the help of the porter. He bought a smock and put it on and washed all the butter—every firkin of it, rested several days, and then set out to sell it. He got notes of introduction to hotels and boarding-houses and sold all his butter to them at retail prices. Then his brother sent more, and Huntington was on the way to becoming a power in the New York butter trade. But now the dealer who had tried to get his butter at a low price said, "I will buy you out if you will clear out. You are ruining my business." "Well," said Huntington, "I have sold my butter. I have not any good butter left but if you will give me 16 cents a pound for what I have got—it's all pretty poor—I will go home." The bargain was closed, and the country storekeeper, Collis

Huntington, thereafter commanded the respect of the big butter and egg men of New York.

Huntington was a fine physical specimen, never tiring no matter how hard he drove himself, so strong that he was known as "the best man in the county." When a boy he could whip any boy in school, and as a man he could take a barrel of flour by the chines and lift it to his shoulder. For recreation he cut wood, and when he left Oneonta, two of the citizens called on him and said, "We are willing to bet that you never sat down in a hotel or saloon in Oneonta." He always did everything he undertook thoroughly, for, as he said, "I used to have a theory when I was a boy; it was not a theory, it was a practice. I always took the work that was nearest to me. I always thought, now I will do this better than anybody's ever had this done. That will be a step nearer the next thing. I never troubled myself much about tomorrow and never made any complaint. . . . I have never failed to do anything I started to do."

He started for California, not much moved by the gold excitement, but simply because he thought there would be lots of money in circulation there. Detained at Panama, he says, "I rigged myself up for business and bought and sold anything there was money in. Many companies came down there and the captains and lieutenants quarreled and I bought them out." He hired boats to take passengers up the Chagres River; he purchased a little steamer, loaded it at ports on the South American coast with jerked beef, potatoes, rice, sugar, and syrup, sold them in Panama, and ran up the $1,200 he arrived with to $4,000. At San Francisco he did some more trading, added $1,000 to his capital, and then set out for Sacramento, where, he says, "I worked nearly a whole day in the mines and made up my mind it would not pay me." So he opened a store and became one of the city's most successful traders.

The surfeits of supply, coincident with the arrival of ships carrying huge cargoes, made various articles sometimes a drug on the market; then Huntington would buy. When there were plenty of shovels and no one wanted them, he bought the entire supply. He bought Ames steel shovels worth $12.60 a dozen at the factory for $2.50 a dozen. As the supply lessened, he bought all he could find at $25 and $35 a dozen; and finally he cornered the market by buying the supply a ship was bringing in at the unheard-of figure of $125 a dozen. And he told the captain, "You may put that in the paper if you want to." When this item appeared, it set the price, and then Huntington sold 2,000 dozen shovels at $120 a dozen, the last of the Ames shovels going at twice that figure. He spent much of his time in San Francisco trading, and there was never a clear morning while he was there that he did not look through his very fine field-glasses to see what ships had come into the bay. If there were new-comers, he would row out and board them. One day he went out and climbed aboard a ship and told the captain he wanted to buy cobbles. "I have no cobbles. Nothing but potatoes," said the cap-tain. Huntington said he might take a few if the price was right. The captain said he would sell at 10 cents a bushel, and Huntington took the whole cargo, binding the bargain with a thousand-dollar bag of gold-dust he always carried with him. He then went ashore and got orders for the supply at 18 cents, making a profit of $8,000.

Buying entire cargoes, Huntington filled his warehouses with a great variety of merchandise. At one time he bought a cargo containing 45 mattresses. He installed the mattresses in his store building and in-vited his customers from the mines to sleep there in the best beds in Sacramento, charging them nothing. For $29 he bought a library containing, he says, "Rollins Ancient History in true calf; Plutarch's lives was in it bound in very nice calf. . . . I made the book cases myself. . . . I gave the porter ten dollars to buy papers." Thus he equipped a comfortable, well-lighted library for his twenty clerks, and here he expected them to spend their evenings. He fed and housed them well, and it was part of their contract that they were to stay in his house from supper-time to breakfast, for he did not want them dissipating in the wild night-life of the mining-camp town. His scorn for the keepers of the city's bagnios was intense. He wrote, "Mrs. Caswell on 3rd and K had a fine brick house. Her man came in one day—I had the only preserved peaches in town. I asked $96 for them. They could afford such luxuries. Said he, 'Will you send it in?' Said I, 'Will you take it along? You tell Mrs. Caswell that if she pays $96 and takes the peaches along I have no objection, but my boys cannot go into her house.' " Of another, he said, "She came along with a silk dress trailing half way across the street and asked for corn meal. She said, 'What do you ask for a barrel?' Said I, 'Two ounces a barrel.' Said she, 'Do you think I am a damn fool?' 'No,' said I. 'I will be frank with you. I have not thought anything about you one way or the other.' She gathered her skirts up and went across the street."

With Hopkins, Huntington built up a great hardware business in Sacramento and San Francisco. In his relations with his partner he lived up to his motto of "Trust all in all or not at all." He said, "Not an unkind word ever passed between us. When our articles of co-partnership were drawn up, each took a copy and put it away and neither ever referred to it again." When "Pacific Railroad crazy" Theodore Judah asked him to subscribe to his project, Huntington gave nothing; but he asked Judah to come to his office the next night, and the small group he had gathered there gave all that was needed for the surveys. When Huntington entered the railroad project, he says, "People said I had a pretty good hardware store but I would leave it in the mountains if I started that road."

Shrewd financier, he was able to carry a loan of $7,000,000 at 7 per cent during the stress of the Civil War, while the Union Pacific struggled under much higher rates. When Flint, Peabody and Company of Boston said they could not sell the first issue of $1,500,000 Central Pacific bonds, Huntington went out on the street in Boston and sold them himself. He always got high prices for bonds, for, as he told the buyers, it was poor business for both parties to sell at $25,000 when the work to be covered by them would cost $40,000. In the panic of 1884 a banker in New York paid this tribute to him: "I consider Collis Potter Huntington was the key to the arch that held up the people here from May to the close of the year. It seemed to me as if all the imps at one time were trying to break him down but he met all calls made on him without wavering. Yet the shrinkage of his properties must have amounted to millions; still he never asked any special favors, and paid up whenever money was wanted."

When he wanted rails and Thomas C. Durant had advertised a blanket order for 60,000 tons, Huntington told the steel-makers that he knew the Union Pacific couldn't use that many and that he himself had plenty. The steel-makers decided not to raise the price; whereupon Huntington suddenly ordered from each mill the amount he thought it would supply without raising the price and then sent acceptances to all of them at once; thus he got a total of 60,000 tons at his own figure, while Durant's advertisements for bids were ignored. "Not a boy in the office knew I wanted those rails," he said gleefully.

When ships were hard to obtain, he succeeded in cornering the market in a deal which was typical of his crafty business methods. He went to a ship-broker, E. B. Sutton, in New York, and the following exchange took place:

I said, "Well, I want to get a good ship—a good steady ship—safe!" I said, "You go out and run around and give me a list of what you can find." He came in with three or four. He said, "You can have this one for so much and this one for so much." "Such a price," said I. "It is too high. I can't take one of these ships." "I am in no hurry," said I. "Ships are coming in all along." Well, he came back; he went out three times and he came back with twenty-three ships. ... I got them all down whilst talking. "Well," said I, suddenly, "I will take them." "Take them," said he, "take what?" Said I, "I will take these ships if they are A-1." "Well," he said, "I can't let you have them! I thought you wanted only one." He said, "I will have to have two or three of them myself." Well, those ships took about 45,000 tons of rails. Mr. Sutton told me afterwards, "Huntington, you would have had to pay $10 per ton at least, more, if I had known you wanted all those ships. That would have been $450,000."

In his relations with his workers Huntington always tried to get them to save their salaries and invest in homes, and he frequently made arrangements to help them buy property. He said, "There is one trouble in this country; employers don't go in among their men and consult with them. Everybody can find somebody below him. It don't cost anything to reach out and raise him up a little higher." To the people who traded in his store he was generous. He showed confidence in the worst dead beats and rarely lost money on them. He said, "I have sold goods for 51 years. I have trusted people others would not trust. I don't know when I remember suing a customer." Of labor he said, "I have always stood by the rights of inferiors as I understood their rights. Labor lies at the very foundations of society and our art, sciences and civilization. The aristocracy of labor is my aristocracy."

He showed his attention to detail when he started making gifts to Hampton Institute for Negroes in Virginia. Beginning with a gift of $50 in 1875, he soon added $1,000, the interest of which would pay the tuition of a colored student. Then, when the Institute began its industrial works with the gift of an 80 horse-power Corliss engine, Huntington sent his lawyers down to make a thorough investigation, after which he inquired the cost of the work to date and sent his check for $10,000 to cover it. During the two following years he made other gifts and then gave Corliss $4,000, the price of his engine; altogether his gifts totaled $31,000, covering the whole cost of the work. He said he wanted the blacks to have a fair chance, to learn thrift and economy; and on a visit to the works he stood by, watch in hand, at seven in the morning to see if they started on time. And he told General Samuel C. Armstrong, the founder of the Institute, that he would withdraw his help if they taught the higher branches of learning, advising him to "let them learn to read and cipher."

With all his practical shrewdness there was a certain trend towards mysticism in Huntington's nature which showed in his dealings with men, his trust of those whom others would not trust, and his understanding of character. He was fond of poetry, George Crabbe's being his favorite; he read Plutarch's *Lives, Paradise Lost,* and Virgil and never looked at a newspaper. He was not without an appreciation of nature. He said, "I used to go into the mountains and look around for myself; I would take my blanket and lay down and picket my horse. I used to enjoy it very much. There was a kind of vastness about it that was kind of enjoyable. I could see how the Indians liked that kind of a life." He had also something of that taste for collecting which marked his nephew Henry, though he would have been scandalized to see his own fortune poured out, as it was, for the paintings of the old masters. He said,

I like a good picture,—modern pictures; old masters you cannot get them —the prices are fabulous. I bought a picture the other day for $25,600; it is a story. There are seven figures in it—three cardinals of the different orders of their religion. There is an old missionary that has just returned; he is showing his scars, where his hands are cut all over; he is telling a story to these cardinals; they are dressed in luxury. One of them is playing with a dog; one is asleep; there is only one looking at him—looking at him with that kind of an expression saying what a fool you are that you should go out and suffer for the human race when we have such a good time at home. I lose the picture in the story when I look at it. I sometimes sit half an hour looking at that picture.

From the outset of the railroad project Huntington counseled moderation. "Now don't let's talk about a Pacific Road," he said. "Let's always keep in control what we build. Now don't spread yourself. We will meet somebody beyond. Let's go slow and steady and own what we build." As a result of this policy the Central Pacific built one section at a time and developed a paying traffic as it went, trusting to luck to meet the Union Pacific as far east as possible. When the latter road commenced to build, the Central Pacific had already reached Newcastle and enjoyed a profitable traffic. It was Huntington's generalship that successfully shouldered the finances for the first four years, when he borrowed from every bank where any of the partners had any credit, at one time owing William E. Dodge and Company $3,250,000. He believed in keeping money at work and said, "I would rather have an old sow and pigs than all the money in the world if I had to keep it locked up." In his *Reminiscences* his chief engineer, Henry Root, said of him, "He liked to talk of what he did when he was young and took great satisfaction in his financial success. He liked to have us think he was close in money matters, saying, 'Nobody can track me by the quarters I have dropped.' But when there were several along at lunch or dinner he always wanted to pay the bill for all."

The man who interviewed him for Bancroft said he was genial, sweet-tempered, polite, but added, "Mr. Huntington is a story teller and upon intimate acquaintance indulges in those which are outré in mixed society." He also recounted how Huntington left his private car in El Paso in order to go down and call at the house of an old friend, Mike Brannigan, who drove a hack. While he showed some sympathy with Chinese workmen, saying, "They know so much more than our people in many things," Huntington had no patience with those who would depreciate the accomplishments of Americans. In Paris he told newspaper reporters that the "United States can get up an international exhibition that will discount anything the world has ever seen. American engineers can, if they want to, build an Eiffel Tower a mile high which will last 1,000 years, this being simply a matter of enlarging your base."

Concerning railroads Huntington said, "My ideas don't agree— they don't coincide with anybody on the legislation of railroads. I think a railroad should be treated just like any other kind of property—handle it for the best of the community. Competition will regulate prices of fares and things and business interests. These things will regulate themselves. You cannot, in my opinion, legislate intelligently." And he always stoutly maintained that he never bought a vote in Congress, though he remarked sagely that "If you have to pay money to have the right thing done, it is only just and fair to do it." It was all a game to him, a game in which he played his hand with courage and finesse. "I like to do things," he said. "It has been a great pastime to me—in all my little dealings. I have got a good deal of sport out of it."

These were the men who built the Central Pacific, and whatever may be thought of the methods by which they obtained and held a monopoly of California's railroads, it must be conceded that they had courage, imagination, and tenacity of purpose. And without men of those qualities the railroads would not have been built. Those four men found in the project of railway-building a channel for the use of their fullest powers, and within their lifetimes they built up one of the world's largest corporations, a railway system operating 11,152 miles of track and earning in one year an operating revenue of $282,000,000. They put their mark on California, for better or for worse, and at least two of them left benefactions which will keep their memories pleasantly green when their hard practices have been obscured by time—the matchless library of rare books and art gallery at Pasadena, which was built by Collis Huntington's nephew who interited most of his fortune, and the great university built by Leland Stanford at Palo Alto.

# CHAPTER IX

## BUILDING THE CITY BY THE GOLDEN GATE

THE Central Pacific Railway Company was incorporated on June 28, 1861; the Federal Government passed the Pacific Railroad Act on July 1, 1862, and San Francisco disported itself with a celebration worthy of the event. Houses on the hills were lit up with candles in every window, hotels were hung with Chinese lanterns, and there was a grand parade with rockets, lamps, torches, Roman candles, and fifty illuminated transparencies bearing such sentiments as these:

Little Indian boy, step out of the way for the Big Ingine.

A union of lakes, a union of lands
A union of states none can sever
A union of hearts, a union of hands
And the Railroad Unites Us Forever.

San Francisco in 1862—100,000 inhabitants
San Francisco in 1872—1,000,000 inhabitants.

The Pacific Railroad—Uncle Sam's waistband.
He has grown so corpulent he would burst without it.

The Locomotive that makes the first through trip:—
We can't pay too much for its whistle!

Chesapeake Bay Oysters Six Days From The Water.

But the jubilation was succeeded by months of pessimism, when the railroad was considered an impractical dream, and money could not be raised. When the time came for driving the first spike at Sacramento, the canny Huntington remarked, "If you want to jubilate in driving the first spike here, go ahead and do it. I don't. These mountains look too ugly and I see too much work ahead. . . . We may fail and I want to have as few people know it as we can. . . .

Anybody can drive the first spike but there are many months of hard labor and unrest between the first and the last spike."

Yet the Big Four went forward with their gigantic task, bending all their energies and talents to pushing the railroad through the mountains. They drove the road rapidly through the lowlands and foothills, where the deserted mines had now been supplanted by flourishing vineyards, orchards, and fields of grain; they continued into the forests where sawmills cut the timber; they went on to the hydraulic mining claims and up into the clouds, where trestles spanned dizzy heights, tunnels bored the rocks, and snow lingered even in July, compelling the building of massive wooden corridors or snow-sheds to protect the line in winter. As the road went forward toward the rich traffic of the Comstock country in Nevada, it paid its way, which was more than the Union Pacific could do. And Huntington was able to get a bill through Congress permitting the Central Pacific to pass beyond the Nevada line and meet the Union Pacific tracks as far east as it could build, thus inaugurating the race between the two roads. He often said that if he could have had the support of San Francisco capital at this time, he could have built clear into Salt Lake and captured that trade for California. But Mills and the other capitalists gave him little besides moral support. Capital was always skeptical, and one London railroad man said the road could not be completed through the mountains in 20 years with all the money of the Bank of England back of it. Nevertheless, in 1869, seven years ahead of its time-limit, the tracks were joined, and the way was prepared for San Francisco to become the terminal point for rail and water transportation between the Orient and the Atlantic seaboard and the largest center of population on the Pacific coast.

While its connections with the East were being forged, the city had been steadily growing, preparing for the greater day that was to be hers as the commercial and transportation center of the western half of the continent. Samuel Bowles, editor of the Springfield *Republican*, visited the city during 1869 and described it in his book *Our New West*. From the days of '49 the metropolis on the Bay had held first place in the affections of the Pacific, all the people west of the Rockies feeling a peculiar personal pride in San Francisco, the city that had always been the one bright spot in the miner's desolate life. To Bowles its fascination was hard to define.

It is like the magnetism of an ugly or very improper person. The town sprawls over the coarse sand hills that have rolled and blown up, the business streets are chiefly on made land under the hills and by the bay. Many hills are so steep that it is impossible to drive upon them, and the houses are perched up in the air. Often one finds a suburban street blocked with fresh sand. There is sand and dust everywhere, such as would be the despair of a New England housewife, but the winds give health, and keep the town fresh and clean. No other American city holds in its midst such sweeping views or is more favorable to the growth of roses, evergreens, geraniums,—they blossom all the year around. The town is constantly in the draft, for the hills open at the Golden Gate to let in, like a tide of escape steam, the ocean breezes and mists. In winter, between showers, the sky is clear, and the air is balmier than in summer, which is so cold and windy that people leave town during July and August.

There is a sharp, full development of all material powers and excellencies, a wealth of practical quality and force; a recklessness and rioting with the elements of prosperity; much dash, a certain chivalric honor combined with carelessness of word, of integrity, or consequence; a sort of gambling, speculating, horse jockeying morality—born of the uncertainties of mining, its sudden heights, its equally surprising depths and the eager haste to be rich. . . . Wall Street can teach Montgomery Street nothing in the way of bulling and bearing, and the corners made here require both quick and long breath to turn without faltering. In consequence of the training in vicissitudes and frequent failures, and of the great interests and wide regions to be dealt with, the men we find at the head of enterprises of the Pacific Coast have great business power—a wide practical reach, a boldness, a sagacity, a vim which can hardly be matched anywhere in the world. This is evident in the Bank of California, the California and Oregon Steam Navigation companies, the great woolen mills and machine shops of San Francisco, the Wells-Fargo Express and Stage Company, in the mining companies, especially on the Comstock lode, in the Central Pacific Railroad Company, even in the large farms of the interior valleys and in the wheat dealing.

Society is audacious and original, and holds all sorts of elements in chaos. There are probably more bachelors, great lusty fellows, who ought to be ashamed of themselves, living in hotels or in lodgings in this town than in any other place of its size in the world. There is a want of femininity and of spirituality in the current tone of the town. . . . It is a town of men and taverns and boarding houses and billiard saloons.

The ladies dress in good taste but the styles are not so subdued as in our Eastern cities. Extravagance is lamented as a common weakness of San Francisco ladies. Perhaps in no other American city would the ladies invoice so high per head. Their point lace is deeper, their moire antique stiffer, their skirts a trifle longer, their corsage an inch lower, their diamonds more brilliant—and more of them—than the cosmopolite is likely to find elsewhere. The famous feature of feminine social life is the lunch party from high noon to two o'clock with attendant gossiping. Yet for high art in the delicate but industrious scandal-mongering and the virtuous plotting against masculine authority it seems that the New England conjunction of twilight and green hyson are much more favorable. How much more daintily and delicately the stiletto and the tongue, the knitting needle and the eye, can do their sweet work under a little softening of the shadows and the inspiration of hot tea on a stomach that has already done its duty for the day.

In many of the materialities of life—in excellence of hotels and restaurants, in facilities of inter-communication, in all ministrations to the sensuous wants of human nature,—San Francisco and California already set an example to older communities. The hotels are the equals of the very best of the Atlantic states; the restaurants are the superiors. The European habit of living in lodgings and taking meals at restaurants is very much in vogue and has stimulated the character and equalized the prices of the cafés. A dinner of several courses with wine is served in admirable style after the French form at the best of them for one dollar and a half, while a like meal in New York or Boston would cost four or five dollars. Food is certainly much cheaper in San Francisco than eastern cities, and wages and profits higher. The free and easy reckless extravagance of early California is not wholly outgrown; in luck today a man drinks champagne and flaunts his jewelry at the Occidental; while fortune frowning, tomorrow he is sponging his dinners and his drinks from his friends, and takes a fifty cent lodging at the What Cheer House. A drink at an aristocratic bar is two bits (25 cents), at a more democratic establishment one bit (10 cents). There is no coin in use less than a dime; one of these answers for a bit, two will pass for two bits, but the man who often offers two dimes for a quarter is voted a bummer.

One special pet dissipation, the very trump card of hospitality, is a drive to the Cliff House for breakfast and to look at the Seals on the rocks in the bay. A night among the Chinese houses and gambling holes is reserved for the curious, but the cliff and seals are for all ages and conditions of men and women. There is special life in the churches and the Sabbath is observed as well as in New York. The demand for ministers is for smart, effective orators as well as holy men, and we meet good Presbyterians at the opera and at balls as we should not do in the East.

Although San Francisco was founded on the profits from the gold-fields, it was also a city of silver, for 10 years later it benefited from the world's greatest silver-strike, which took place in its back yard, Nevada. In their effort to extend their empire from Salt Lake to California the Mormons had sent emigrants westward, and one group stopped in the Carson Valley of Nevada, where they panned gold in 1857. But their station at the foot of Mount Davidson and the others in cañons near-by never yielded any bonanzas, and the miners complained bitterly that as they advanced up the slope of the mountain, the gold became less fine, and the bankers in Placerville reduced the price from $18 to $13 an ounce because it was so mixed with silver. The significance of this fact was never understood by these early miners, who looked for gold on the surface only and knew nothing about great underground veins of silver. In fact, when he had worked over the surface of the Gould and Curry Mine, later to produce millions, Alvah Gould sold his half-interest to George Hearst, father of William Randolph Hearst, and others for $450, and he congratulated himself that he had "done the Californians." But, as usual, Hearst, who had come west in 1850 as a laborer, had made a good bargain, just as he continued to do in buying claims in California, Montana, Arizona, Colorado, Idaho, and Mexico, and as a partner in the San Francisco firm of Haggin and Tevis. In later years, when Hearst was enjoying the profits from his Gould and Curry venture, Gould was running a peanut-stand in Reno. In this he was typical of many another old-time miner, for almost without exception in the history of Western mining the original discoverers of rich strikes died in poverty, while fortunes were enjoyed by those who succeeded them in ownership.

Among the picturesque old miners of the Carson district was Henry Thomas Paige Comstock, known as "Old Pancake." From Allen and Hosea Grosch, two young New Englanders who had discovered the secret of enormous silver-deposits in Gold Cañon, Comstock learned that the place was rich in treasure. But they died in 1858 before he learned that the riches were silver. Nevertheless, he located on claims and on farm-land in Gold Cañon and found diggings rich in gold. When he rode out one day in 1859 and discovered that Peter O'Riley and Patrick McLoughlin had made another rich strike of gold, he declared, "You've struck it, boys, and on my land." Claiming to have located there the year before with another man, he was so vehement and wild-eyed that the Irishmen, rather than have a dispute, added his name to their location notices. So, even though his claim was doubtful, Comstock shared in the ownership of the property that became the famous Ophir Mine. But none of these miners knew what they had discovered; they dug the gold and threw away the troublesome blue-black deposit that was mixed with it—the black silver-sulphide ore which was later to make this same Comstock Lode the richest bonanza in the world. All the half-dozen men connected with this first strike, including Comstock, died penniless, but to others it brought great fortunes, some of which still endure.

When a California miner brought some of the discarded black ore to Judge Thomas Walsh of Grass Valley, California, to be analyzed, and it ran several thousand dollars to the ton, the rush to the silver-fields began. During the first winter California miners poured in, who, ignorant of how to work a silver-mine, spent most of their time in locating claims and trading them in the saloons of Virginia City. But bars of silver appeared in San Francisco, and by March of 1860 the adventurous men from that city began to push through the snow-covered passes of the Sierras. The first arrival put up a tent, sold $200 worth of drinks the first evening, and rented blankets and a place to roll them on the floor for a dollar apiece a night. In the spring, men from San Francisco swarmed up the river to Sacramento by boat and then traveled from four to six days by stage and mule-back over the terrible roads of the Sierras, in bitter cold and with only flimsy shacks for night-shelters. But the Californians, who knew the overland trail in the days of '49, laughed at these hardships and continued to fill Virginia City and the camps round about. The first mine to sink a shaft on the Comstock was the Ophir, and it soon ran into a vein of silver which widened to 50 feet. This was of such extraordinary size and so overladen with loose country rock that the miners did not know how to timber it, since the pressure splintered the heaviest logs to bits. In this emergency the owners got the German engineer Philip Dudesheimer to come up from San Francisco, and he designed portable "square sets" of timbering, built up in cribs, which solved the problem so successfully that the method is still used.

The next problem was the reduction of the ore by chemical processes, and among those who skilfully solved this was Adolph Sutro, who set up an ore-reduction plant at Dayton. One of those who had come across the Isthmus of Panama to San Francisco in 1850, Sutro now began a career which was to have great influence on Virginia City and on San Francisco. Indeed, these two communities, though separated by 300 miles and the Sierras, may almost be considered as one; for San Francisco furnished the men and supplies for the Comstock, its citizens became the leaders of the silver camp, the Comstock mining stocks were speculated in on the San Francisco mining exchange, the city's money financed the development of the mines, and the profits of the silver-strike flowed into San Francisco, just as had the profits from the gold of '49.

Within a few years the bonanza town of Virginia City enjoyed easy access to San Francisco over perfectly built toll-roads which would be a credit to highway-builders of this day. Over this highway traveled a steady procession of wagons, drawn by twenty-mule teams, carrying a miscellany of mine machinery, building materials, and staple foods, as well as champagne, lobsters, oysters, and caviar; for Virginia City had developed into a miniature San Francisco so far as its expensive tastes were concerned. It boasted a luxurious hotel, the International House; its love of the drama, burlesque, and professional fights was served by McGuire's Opera House; and its newspaper, the *Enterprise,* had on its staff no less distinguished a literary light than Samuel L. Clemens, who here adopted his *nom de plume* of "Mark Twain." The service of this silver metropolis created a freight traffic totaling millions a year in charges, a circumstance which forcefully presented itself to Messrs. Huntington, Stanford, Hopkins, and Crocker and caused them to build over Judah's route to Dutch Flat as quickly as possible, extending wagon-trains from that point to Virginia City, so as to capture this lucrative business for the Central Pacific. With enormous fortunes being made on the Comstock the mining exchange in San Francisco assumed such importance that a telegraph line was hastily built to Nevada, and the financing of the Virginia City enterprises began to attract the major attention of some of the leading San Francisco capitalists.

Indeed, the king-pin of finance, William C. Ralston, cashier and leading director of the Bank of California, now entered the Virginia City arena. Coming from Ohio to California during the gold-rush by way of the Isthmus, he had been offered a position as agent for a steamship company at Panama; he had remained there for a time but later was sent to represent the firm at San Francisco. He had gone into the banking business, and in 1864 he induced Darius Ogden Mills and others to form the Bank of California, which soon became the most powerful financial institution of the West, agent of the Rothschilds and internationally famous. The man Ralston sent to Virginia City as the bank's representative, destined to become King of the Comstock, was William Sharon, St. Louis lawyer, who had come overland to the California gold-fields in '49, started a store in Sacramento and later a real-estate office in San Francisco, and earned a small fortune. It was said that the appointment was objected to on the ground that Sharon was an inveterate poker-player. "What kind of a game does he play?" asked Ralston. "Oh, he always wins," replied the director. "He's the best player on the coast." "Then," said Ralston decisively, "he's the very man we want for our agent."

When Sharon arrived as manager of the Virginia City branch, local banks were lending money at from 3 to 5 per cent a month; he promptly offered it at 2 per cent, and the Bank of California soon became the chief financier of the Comstock Lode. During 1863-64 there was a slump in mining, many of the mines having run out of rich bonanza ore; but they continued work by levying assessments on their stockholders, and Sharon, who had made himself thoroughly familiar with the Comstock and had confidence in its possibilities, freely lent them money. He also lent money to the owners of the mills for reducing ore, for these were idle and had no stockholders to assess. Although practically no ore was being produced, millions of dollars were invested in reducing equipment which could not be sold because the freight-rates back to California were prohibitive. At 2 per cent a month it did not take long for the interest to pile up so high that the Bank of California foreclosed on many of the best milling properties on the Comstock. So heavy did the loans become that the main business of the bank now seemed to be the financing of the Comstock, and it was so deeply involved that it could not afford to quit; if the Lode behaved according to the hopes of the

JAMES G. FAIR          JAMES C. FLOOD
WILLIAM S. O'BRIEN
GEORGE HEARST          JOHN W. MACKAY

Fair, Flood, O'Brien, and Mackay, courtesy of the Society of California Pioneers; Hearst, from Alonzo Phelps, *Contemporary Biography of California's Representative Men.*

VIRGINIA CITY

Lithograph after a drawing by Grafton T. Brown, 1861. From the Stokes Collection, New York Public Library.

optimistic, the district would become the world's richest producer of silver; if it did not, the bank would fail.

When Mills and Ralston visited Virginia City, Sharon proved to them that it was the bank's duty to step in and reorganize the mining industry and systematize wasteful methods; if they withdrew, he said, the whole of Virginia City would be in jeopardy, and San Francisco capital as well. So the bankers fearfully continued, and when the Bank of California had lent $3,500,000 on Comstock properties, the depression lifted, and the Chollar-Potosi and other mines began to strike it rich again. Now that the crisis was passed, Sharon formed a scheme to organize a new company to take over all the foreclosed properties from the bank, a company which would reap the profits from the future development of the Comstock and control its destiny. Accordingly, with Ralston, Mills, and a few other San Franciscans, Sharon organized the Union Mill and Mining Company, which was to monopolize the district and exploit its riches to the utmost, and under whose shrewd and efficient methods no time was to be lost in developing the Comstock into a bonanza.

Certainly, it was already a bonanza for the Union Mill and Mining Company, for it promptly served notice on the mines that they could either send their ore to the company mills for reduction or get no more loans from the Bank of California. As a result, independent mill-owners were frozen out, their properties fell into the hands of the syndicate, and Sharon, Mills, and Ralston made money, even though production of ore on the Lode was steadily falling. But money continued to pour into Virginia City as the result of assessments on the stock. Some mines took out millions in silver, distributed dividends, and then levied an almost equal amount in assessments. The only communications many investors ever received from their mines were requests for assessments; the dividends were never forthcoming. The insiders worked the mines on the money furnished by a gullible public; and whenever a rich strike was discovered, they would buy up all the stock on the San Francisco exchange and reap the profit, as Sharon did when he bought all available Belcher stock at $6 and saw it rise to $1,500 within three months. But if he squeezed the investors, he also cut down the costs of operation. When the Union Mill and Mining Company entered the field, it cost $50 a ton to reduce the ore; the company was able shortly to effect economies in operation which reduced the cost to $14, thus enabling the working of much ore that was previously too poor to pay for reduction.

Having reduced costs, Sharon's next move was to reduce freight-charges, especially on timber used in the mines from the Carson River sawmills, and to put transportation control in the hands of the syndicate. Various railroad schemes had been projected, but Sharon suddenly started surveys, bought the charters of the old lines, secured a new charter from the legislature and gifts of $500,000 from two counties, and in eight months had completed a line from Virginia City to Carson City, making the public furnish most of the money for construction and keeping control in the hands of the syndicate. Now the reduction in freight-charges made it possible to work low-grade ore at a profit, and Sharon declared that it would increase the production of the district $5,000,000 a year. Controlling ore-reduction and transportation from the sawmills, the syndicate now reached out for the forests that supplied the tremendous quantities of wood that went into the mines for timbering; widespread fore-closures on forest-lands, flumes, and sawmills of men who had bor-rowed from the Bank of California followed, and Mills, Ralston, and Sharon soon had a new monopoly and still higher profits. And Sharon turned his attention to the project of extending the railroad to Reno to connect with the Central Pacific, thus to do away with all freighting by wagon and give the syndicate absolute control of transportation.

While the Union Mill and Mining Company became the symbol of ruthless, grasping monopoly to the mine-owners and merchants and citizens of the Comstock Lode, its power was already being threatened by two new elements, of whose existence it was hardly aware. These were Adolph Sutro and that Irish quartet, Mackay, Fair, Flood, and O'Brien.

In his laboratory in San Francisco Sutro had worked out a process of ore-reduction which was most efficient, and in his plant at Dayton he had made a profit of $10,000 a month reducing ore from the Gould and Curry Mine; but his contract had expired and his mill had burned, and he was speculating on other and more far-reaching projects. As the mines on the Comstock Lode went deeper and deeper into the side of Mount Davidson, they encountered trouble: no longer could the ore be raised to the surface by bucket, but steam hoists had to be used; in the lower levels floods of water developed, which had to be pumped to the surface at great trouble and expense; the problem of ventilation became constantly more serious, and the dangers of fire increased. Meditating on these conditions, Sutro decided that if a tunnel could be driven four miles into the side of the mountain, 2,000 feet below the surface of the mines, it would be possible to drain them easily, to run the ore out by gravity, to save the water for irrigation, to ventilate the mines so that men could work at any level, to reduce the fire-hazard, to insure the profitable working of lower-grade ores, and to save millions of dollars for the owners. This extraordinary scheme became an obsession with him, and in 1865 he obtained from the Nevada legislature a charter for a mining and drainage tunnel to be finished in eight years. Since the project seemed desirable, Sutro was able to get the endorsement not only of the leading miners of the district, but also of Ralston and of Sharon, who had then just arrived in Virginia City. Armed with this endorsement, he obtained contracts from nineteen leading mines to pay him $2 a ton on all the ore they produced after his tunnel had drained and ventilated their properties. For this support he agreed to start work in 1867, with $3,000,000 subscribed, and to spend $400,000 a year on driving the tunnel. Because of the depression in mining, it was hard to raise money; but Sutro got the support of all Western newspapers, and at Washington he presented a petition asking government aid for the tunnel as a stimulus to mining. He secured the passage through Congress of a bill confirming his right to build the tunnel and making the validity of the titles of all the mining companies with whom he had contracted for service dependent on their fulfilment of the agreement. He then induced the Nevada legislature to send a memorial to Congress stating that the tunnel would so stimulate mining as to pay the costs of the Civil War, and thus the House Committee on Mines was persuaded to recommend a loan of $5,000,000.

But now Sharon, seeing that the scheme would cut the cost of treating ore at the tunnel-mouth below that of the syndicate's mills, put the whole power of the Bank of California against Sutro's project.

Banks refused loans, mines tried to cancel contracts, and Sutro was forced to go to Europe for funds. Meanwhile, conditions in the mines were getting worse: ventilation was almost impossible, floods were frequent, and the ore could be got out only with great difficulty and expense. The climax was reached in 1869, when fire broke out in the Yellow Jacket, Kentuck, and Crown Point mines; scores were killed, and since the flames could not be stopped, it was necessary to seal these mines up. Production was low, prices of mining stock were depressed, and the miners were still stricken with the memory of the awful fire when Sutro held a public meeting for his tunnel. He showed the miners how they could easily escape from burning mines when the tunnel was finished, how they would always work in pure, cool air, and how the scheme would revive the mining industry. From this group he got $50,000 to go ahead with the project even though the Bank of California fought it, and on October 19, 1869, with banners flying and a brass band blaring, he broke ground for his tunnel.

While the prices of mining stocks were low, two mine superintendents who well knew all the underground passages of the Comstock Lode took the opportunity of getting control of what they considered the most desirable properties. These men were John W. Mackay, who had begun work in the mines as a mucker at a few dollars a day and risen to be superintendent of the Caledonia Mine, and James G. Fair, superintendent of the Ophir. Both had accumulated some money through mine investments. They bought the Bullion and an interest in the Kentuck and then turned to the Hale and Norcross, whose shares had dropped from $2,100 to $42 on the San Francisco Exchange. In buying into these last two properties they met two other Irishmen who were also heavily interested, James C. Flood and William S. O'Brien, the proprietors of one of the most popular bars in the San Francisco financial district. These two men had profited from their acquaintance with the mining operators and bankers who were their patrons by trading in stocks on the basis of the information they received, and they had succeeded in accumulating considerable money. Shrewd business men, they joined forces with the young engineers to form what became an unbeatable combination, Mackay and Fair furnishing the engineering and mining knowledge,

Flood and O'Brien the financing. They added the Savage to their holdings; the Hale and Norcross struck it rich: they added the Consolidated Virginia, and in this last property, in March, 1873, they opened up the big bonanza of the Comstock, a vein 54 feet wide which was estimated to contain $116,000,000 worth of ore. Indeed, Philip Dudesheimer announced that in this mine and the adjoining California, in which the partners were also interested, there was a billion and a half worth of silver in sight. Stock in the two mines rose to $600 and $700 a share, they produced $2,000,000 a month, other mines were booming, and San Francisco entered upon a period of mining speculation such as had never before been seen. Cooks, waiters, bankers, clergymen—every one joined in the buying of stocks. The Exchange was a frenzy of excitement—brokers actually fainting from exhaustion, and the curb was lined with stock-selling women who were called "mudhens."

And now William Ralston, of the Bank of California and the Union Mill and Mining Company, began to spend vast sums of money on the development of San Francisco, the city that he expected to make one of the world's greatest. He projected the $6,000,000 Palace Hotel, the Mission Woolen Mills, the Kimball Carriage Factory, the Cornell Watch Factory, the West Coast Furniture Factory, the San Francisco Sugar Refinery, and the California Theater; he started ferry lines to cross the bay, a dry-dock, an irrigation project in the San Joaquín Valley, the Rincon Hill cut, and the extension of Montgomery Street. His magnificent home at Belmont, down the peninsula, had guest-rooms enough for a hotel, a beautiful oval ball-room lined with mirrors and lighted by a great crystal chandelier, and a stable where the horses luxuriated in stalls of polished inlaid wood. The Ralston house was a center of California's social life, and there the master entertained noted men and women from all over the world, driving them out from San Francisco at furious speed in his four-horse char-à-bancs. Gertrude Atherton tells of the time Anson Burlingame, on his way to the Orient to negotiate a treaty for the United States, was a guest. A large company gathered in his honor were all seated in the library, when suddenly one wall of the room gave a slight shiver and went up like a curtain, revealing an immense banquet-hall with a gorgeously decked table and a regiment of Chinese servants in white starched uniforms. Next morning Ralston asked Mr. Burlingame to select the site for a town he was about to build; it was named in his honor and became the most select suburb of San Francisco.

In 1875 the boom reached its height, and when San Franciscans were feverishly speculating on margin and the finances of the whole coast were tied up in silver stocks, there came rumors that the mines were played out. Immediately stocks crashed on the Exchange, losing $60,000,000 in value. The Bank of California failed, Ralston resigned at the request of Darius O. Mills, and a few hours later his body was found in the bay—suicide, according to his enemies; an accident during his daily swim, in the opinion of his friends and his physician.

While Sharon and Mills were reorganizing the Bank of California, Mackay, Fair, Flood, and O'Brien stepped in and bought up all its Comstock properties, which they forced the bank to relinquish, put millions into the organization of the Nevada Bank of San Francisco, and when the dust cleared away, they ruled the Comstock. Despite a $10,000,000 fire which all but destroyed Virginia City, they prospered: Fair was building an ornate mansion on San Francisco's fashionable Nob Hill; Mackay had become a world citizen with town houses in Paris and New York; Flood had built a grand house down the peninsula; and O'Brien was disporting himself with his cronies in San Francisco bars, giving away silver dollars to all comers. For several years profits continued to roll in for these men, even if the great mass of speculators had been ruined in the mining boom. But in 1877 Squire P. Dewey, an investor in their mines, accused them of fraud at the annual meeting of the stockholders of the Consolidated Virginia. He declared that their syndicate, the Pacific Mill and Mining Company, which had succeeded the Union Mill and Mining Company, had worked over the tailings from the mills, after the ore had been reduced, and gained from them more than $16,000,000 which the Bonanza Four had put into their own pockets; that they had also gouged all the other mines of the district; and that they had privately prospected the company's properties with diamond drills, boring out a long core and analyzing it secretly so as to secure advance information as to the value of the ore.

As the public raged, production in the mines fell off, and dividends were passed. Meanwhile, Adolph Sutro, in spite of the opposition of the Bonanza Kings, had gone on with his tunnel. He had got the House Committee on Mines to report favorably on a loan of $2,-000,000, in spite of expert testimony against it by scores of witnesses who had been assembled by the old Bank of California. He obtained loans from English bankers and kept hundreds of men at work on the excavation. To circumvent him in Washington, Sharon had got himself elected Senator, his enemies said at a cost of $500,000, and Sutro's bill in Congress had been defeated. Even when the head of the London banking house of McCalmont, which was financing him, was stricken with paralysis, Sutro raised enough money from other sources to go on, and on July 8, 1878, stripped to the waist, he fired the shot that broke the 20,000-foot tunnel through into the Savage Mine. The inrush of the outer air was so strong that it almost knocked the men off their feet, as it swept out the smoke, gas, and dust that had accumulated for years and had made work in the lower levels of the mine a misery. Very soon after this event a mine was flooded, and a profitable agreement was made by the Sutro Tunnel Company to drain it. The Hale and Norcross and the Belcher also shortly got into difficulties with floods and made terms with Sutro, and soon all the mines fell into line. But the new ruler of the Comstock, having triumphed, did not long remain; he sold out within a few years, took his profits, and turned his attention to developing San Francisco.

Although the mines furnished San Francisco with plenty of money and excitement, it was to the railroads that she owed her more permanent prosperity. Having completed the Central Pacific and tasted the rich profits that came from it, Messrs. Stanford, Huntington, Hopkins, and Crocker began to have larger visions of railroad-building. To the southeast of California they saw other railroad promoters making plans to build into the state; from the north they were threatened with an extension of the Union Pacific to Portland and with the building of the Northern Pacific by Henry Villard. Either project endangered the Central Pacific, for either would drain off transcontinental traffic. Meditating on these dangers, the erstwhile merchants determined to dominate the State of California, to keep out all other railroads, and to obtain such complete control as to be able to dictate freight-charges—in a phrase, to charge all the traffic would bear. To carry out this policy meant a continuation of railroad-building on so large a scale as to make the great Central Pacific project, which once seemed of such staggering importance, only one incident in a program of gigantic scope. It meant, too, the centering of all the transportation, and, incidentally, the financial system, of the Pacific Coast in San Francisco, whither the partners had moved the headquarters of their road. And however much San Francisco, in the darker moments of later days, may have maligned the Southern Pacific, which was to be the chief instrument of the partners' dominance, and declared it to be a monopolistic incubus, hanging on the neck of the state like the Old Man of the Sea, it has nevertheless been one of the main factors in building up California and in making San Francisco a great city.

The partners began to carry out their bold design by bottling up the Bay of San Francisco. As General Smith had long since pointed out, the city occupies a narrow peninsula of land, 30 miles long, on the southwest side of the bay, and the dimensions of the harbor are so large as to make it difficult of access from the mainland. To this day passengers from the north and east leave their trains across the bay and enter the city by ferry, which is a quicker and more convenient approach. So the Big Four determined first to control all the avenues of entrance at the north and east, then those at the south, and having thus blocked the access of rival railroads to San Francisco, to extend their lines north to Portland and southeast across the continent to establish direct connection with the Atlantic Coast. Since they did not broadcast this scheme, it was only as they executed it, piece by piece, that the public began to be aware that San Francisco was to be the focal point of a nation-wide railroad system to be built by four of her own citizens, and that the state was to come into their absolute control—commercially, industrially, politically.

In September, 1869, the Pacific railroad was open for traffic from Omaha to Sacramento, but not as yet to San Francisco. Travel conditions were far from ideal: the speed was only 19 miles an hour, cars were heated with smoky stoves, sleeping-car accommodations were scanty, and the trains lurched around curves and labored up steep grades that had to be eliminated later. But, even though imperfect, transcontinental travel was at last a fact, and freight and passengers had begun to enter and leave California by rail. Obviously, the Central Pacific could not be considered completed until it reached the Bay, and the Big Four made their first step in this direction by obtaining control of a short railroad running from Sacramento to San José, which had been built in 1860 by local capitalists. Next they built a branch to Oakland and acquired a virtual monopoly in the Oakland water-front, from which ferry connections could quickly be made with San Francisco. They then turned their attention to San Francisco itself and almost succeeded in tying up its water-front through grants from the state legislature, but the newspapers made such an outcry that the grants were reduced, although the railroad still received 60 acres of valuable water-front and terminal property. Through Congress the company tried to get control of Goat Island, now Yerba Buena, lying part way between Oakland and San Francisco, which was later to be the first stopping-place of the great bridge commenced in 1933 with aid granted by the Reconstruction Finance Corporation; but there was another outcry from the people of the city, and the railroad did not get this terminal. The company then purchased two small railroads connecting San Francisco with Alameda and Oakland, and thus by 1870 its entry into San Francisco was completed.

The Big Four next took over another short railroad running from Sacramento to Vallejo, extended it to Benicia, and put in a ferry service to Port Costa, thus throwing an arm of defense clear across the north side of the bay. They then bought the line from San José to San Francisco, which had been built by citizens of the two towns, completing their net around the harbor north, south, and east. To the southeast of San Francisco extended the rich San Joaquín Valley, and the partners began their domination of this prosperous farming section by absorbing short lines and adding to them until they had a through track to Goshen, in the northwest corner of Tulare County. Meanwhile, on December 2, 1865, they had organized the Southern Pacific Railroad Company, ostensibly a rival of the Central Pacific, to build down the edge of the coast to San Diego; but the real nature of this road, as a subsidiary of the Central Pacific, appeared when it changed its route from the coast to the center of the state, securing permission and grants of land from Congress to build through the

Tehachapi Pass to Los Angeles and on to Yuma and Needles, Arizona, there to connect with transcontinental roads. To keep rivals from coming up the coast the partners extended two short branches from their line at Gilroy to Soledad, Monterey County, and Tres Pinos, San Benito County, completing the spinning of the web that cut off all approaches to the Bay of San Francisco.

The immediate effect of the transcontinental railroad connection was not all that had been anticipated; for instead of ushering in a period of prosperity for California, it permitted some of the San Francisco business to be cared for by Chicago, the cessation of construction threw many out of work, and the arrival of hordes of emigrants still further depressed wages. Moreover, real-estate values had more than discounted the effect of the arrival of the railroad, and they dropped; there were droughts in the south; the Nevada silver-mine production was slowing down; and the country as a whole was feeling financial stringency. Consequently there was considerable dissatisfaction with conditions, and all the discontent was focused on the Central Pacific Railroad. While admitting the temporary disadvantages of having California's isolation destroyed, however, the San Francisco *Bulletin* remarked that the railroad "has nevertheless done more to create a back country for the city than all other things combined: ore now pours in from the mines, merchants are afforded better opportunity to buy in San Francisco—even if Chicago shares the advantage, and merchants will visit San Francisco in the next ten years from a hundred towns whose names are not yet on a map. The railroad has furnished the backing for a great city and the need now is for a thousand miles of local railroads in California."

There was, however, considerable agitation against the Central Pacific: each town thought rates were too high and that it was being discriminated against; the state began efforts at regulation, and the railroad began a carefully planned publicity and political campaign to protect its interests. Stanford appealed to the public through letters to private organizations, newspaper articles, and testimony before legislative bodies, setting forth the idea that agitation against the railroads was based on misunderstanding of facts. Railroad rates, he said, were cheaper in California than in other states; if the people wanted them lower, they must not put added burdens on the roads;

if the state wanted to control them, it must buy the roads and pay the owners their full value. As president of the Central Pacific, Stanford attended to local political and business matters, with the assistance of Crocker, Hopkins, and, later, of General David D. Colton. Huntington, in Washington, New York, and Boston, looking after the tremendous problem of financing and of lobbying in Congress. Thus the influence of the Big Four in both state and national politics became formidable. In California their interests were involved in almost every department of state and local government; among their special concerns in Washington was the postponement of repayment or the cancellation of the Central Pacific loan by the Federal Government, and the defeat of the plans of Thomas A. Scott, president of the Pennsylvania, who sought to build a railroad from Texas to the Pacific.

The Texas and Pacific Railway Company was chartered on March 3, 1871. The eastern section of the road consisted of two branches: The Northern, starting from Texarkana, a point on the Red River opposite the terminus in Arkansas of the Cairo and Fulton Railroad which gave direct connections with the north and east; and the southern, starting from Marshall, 50 miles west of Shreveport, the principal shipping-point on the Red River, with rail connections with New Orleans, Vicksburg, and the railroad and water transportation centers of the southern and Atlantic states. The two branches were to converge at Fort Worth, where they were to unite, forming a main line near the 32d parallel to San Diego, California.

Having conceived the idea that the Big Four must monopolize the railroad business of California, Huntington was determined that no rival line from the east should reach San Francisco Bay or any other California harbor. While Scott secured government subsidies to build his Texas and Pacific to the harbor of San Diego, Huntington did the same for building from San Francisco to Yuma, Arizona, there to meet Scott's road from the east. But Huntington sought to persuade Congress to forbid the Texas road from building west of Yuma, because, he said, it would compete with his road and there was not enough business for two, and also to permit the Southern Pacific to build eastward until it met the Texas and Pacific, just as the Central Pacific had met the Union Pacific years before.

In his letters to General Colton, Huntington gives an interesting picture of his activities at the national capital, of the fight between the two railroad-builders, and of the general tactics of lobbying in that day. Extracts from these letters follow, all dated from New York:

### Nov. 20, 1874

Scott is prepared to pay or promises to pay a large amount of money to pass his bill but I do not think he can pass it, although I think that this coming session of Congress will be composed of the hungriest set of men that ever got together, and the d—— only knows what they will do. ...Would it not be well for you to send some party down to Arizona to get a bill to build in the Territorial legislature granting the right to build a R.R. east from the Colorado River (leaving the river near Fort Mojave), have the franchise free from taxation on its property and so that the rates of fare and freight cannot be interfered with until the dividends of the common stock shall exceed ten per cent? I think that would be as good as a land grant, It would not do to have it known that we had any interest in it, for the reason that it would cost us much more money to get such a bill through if it was known that it was for us. And then Scott would fight it if he thought we had anything to do with it. If such a bill was passed I think there could at least be got from Congress a wide strip for right of way, machine shops, etc.

### Sept. 27, 1875

Scott is making the strongest possible effort to pass his bill the coming session of Congress. If we had a franchise to build a road or two roads through Arizona (we contracting, but having it in the name of another party) then have some party in Washington to make a local fight and asking for the guarantee of their bonds by the United States, and if that could not be obtained, offering to build the road without any, and it could be used against Scott in such a way that I do not believe any politician would dare to vote for it. Could you have [Governor] Safford call the [Arizona] legislature together and grant such charters as we want at a cost of say $25,000? If we could get such a charter as I spoke of to you it would be worth much money to us.

### Dec. 22, 1875

The committee is not necessarily a Texas Pacific but it is a commercial com. and I have not much fear that they can be convinced that ours is the right bill for the country. If things could have been left as we fixed them last winter there would have been little difficulty in defeating Scott's bill, but their argument is it is controlled by the Central. That does not amount to much beyond this: It allows a member to vote for Scott's bill for one reason, and give the other, that it was to break up a great monopoly, etc. If these damn interviewers would keep out of the way it would be much easier traveling.

### Jan. 17, 1876

I have received several letters and telegrams from Washington today, all calling me there, as Scott will certainly pass his Texas Pacific bill if I do not come over.... It costs money to fix things so that I would know that his bill would not pass. I believe with $200,000 I can pass our bill, but I take it that it is not worth that much to us.

### April 27, 1876

Scott has several parties here that I think do nothing else except write against the Central Pacific and its managers and get them published in such papers as he can get to publish them at small cost, then sends the papers everywhere, and there is no doubt that he has done much to turn public sentiment against us.... If he wants some committeeman away he gets some fellow (his next friend) to ask him to take a ride to New York or anywhere else, of course on a free pass, and away they go together.... Scott has had a large number of that drunken, worthless dog Piper's speeches printed and sent them broadcast over the country.

### March 7, 1877

I stayed on in Washington two days to fix up the R. R. Committee in the Senate. Scott was there working for the same thing, but I beat him for once, certain.

### March 14, 1877

After the Senate R. R. Committee was made up Scott went to Washington in a special train, and got one of our men off and one of his on, but they did not give him the com.

### Oct. 5, 1877

Sec. of War in Washington when the first order went out to stop work on the bridge.... Sec. of the Interior had his war paint on and was to attack us in his message, etc., etc.

### Nov. 9, 1877

Some parties are making great effort to pass a bill through Congress that will compel the U. P. and C. P. to pay large sums into a sinking fund, and

I have some fears that such a bill may pass. . . . Jay Gould's enemies are in it and will pay money to pass.

### Dec. 17, 1877

The Texas and Pacific Company have been fighting us for years but have had but little money, but have used passes and promises largely; but the latter, as they say, is about played out, and some little time ago they joined teams, as I am told, with the N. P. They had a little money to use as they had no mortgages or floating debt. . . . Jay Gould went to Washington. . . . Since which time much money has been used very freely . . . and some parties have been hard at work at the T. & P.-N. P. that never work except for ready cash.

### May 3, 1878

The Texas and Pacific folks are working hard on their bill, and say they are sure to pass it, but I do not believe it. They offered one M. C. one thousand dollars cash, five thousand when the bill was passed, and ten thousand of the bonds, when they got them, if he would vote for the bill.

Before a Committee of the House in 1875 Huntington introduced General Colton as the representative of the Southern Pacific, saying modestly that he himself had "a small interest" in the railroad and that the Central Pacific owned only a bare two-sevenths of the stock. Scott declared that his road must get to tide-water at San Diego and that there was no good route directly east from San Diego, or even east through Mexico, so the Texas and Pacific must build to Yuma and parallel the Southern Pacific for some miles. Huntington objected to this, said he would be delighted to pro-rate the freight business to tide-water with the Texas and Pacific and meet the road farther east, and added, "Whatever time you give to complete the road in, we will agree to cut it in half." And General Colton mildly reprimanded Mr. Scott by saying, "I am afraid you are trying to take business away from the Southern Pacific!"

Huntington brought up Scott's past record of railroad construction and monopoly in an unfavorable light, and he even offered to build the Southern Pacific through to the East without any subsidy whatever. When Scott appeared before the Senate Committee, he took three or four hours; Huntington took ten minutes. When Scott said, "We are beating you," Huntington replied, "Yes, that is the way I should state it because you are beating me out of nine things and

I shall only beat you in one. You will beat me in demoralizing the press; you will beat me in sending colporteurs over the United States to get petitions to your bill; you will beat me in getting Boards of Trade; you will beat me in this and that, but in building the road, that is one thing I shall beat you." While the controversy was going on, the Southern Pacific was steadily building, first to Yuma, then beyond. Huntington said if he had dealt with Scott alone, they could have reached an agreement. He first offered to meet him at Yuma, but Scott's friends urged him to keep up the fight to get the full government subsidy of $68,000,000 to build to San Diego. Within a year the Southern Pacific had reached Yuma, and Huntington said, "I will meet you at Tucson"; but Scott would not accept. Next year Huntington said, "We will meet you at El Paso—that will make you build 600 miles, we 200 miles." But Scott refused to say definitely; he had to consult his friends first. Huntington said he would get his final reply at seven next morning, and when he sent a man to Scott's hotel, he found him not yet dressed and with no definite reply. So Huntington went before a Committee of the House that morning and obtained a vote of eight to five in favor of permitting the Southern Pacific to build to the East.

Scott said Huntington was the hardest block he had ever stumbled against. And Huntington said of his rival, "Tom Scott was as clever a man as ever lived but he died from turning night into day and day into night. No man can live and do hard work transposing night into day. He started from an office boy—swept out the office; he grew up and died ... worth six or seven millions." And Stanford said of Scott's project, in the San Francisco *Chronicle* of May 19, 1875:

The people of San Francisco will never appreciate how great a danger menaced them, nor how great a peril they escaped. Had Tom Scott built his road to the Pacific, he would have taken from us our best prospective traffic and carried it east. . . . He would have given San Francisco a blow from which she never would have recovered. We are quietly but resolutely expending our every exertion to build the Southern Pacific Railroad. We are toiling for the greatest prize this continent affords. . . . Magnificent destiny awaits this city when we shall have brought to its doors the vast trade of Arizona, New Mexico, Sonora, Chihuahua, for it is nothing less than this we are striving for.

Just as the partners had raced the Union Pacific in getting to Salt Lake, they raced the Texas and Pacific and every other road that might intend to reach California over the desert from the southeast. Despite government orders forbidding it, they had laid rails across the Yuma Indian Reservation and built a bridge over the Colorado River; they had hurried through Arizona, New Mexico, and Texas almost to Louisiana, where they purchased a short line to New Orleans from the Morgan interests, giving the Southern Pacific an outlet from San Francisco to the Atlantic. In 1887 they had completed a line north to Portland, Oregon, and as a culmination of their building efforts the partners consolidated all sections of their railroad network in the Southern Pacific Company, organized under the beneficent laws of Kentucky, which, from its office in Anchorage, Kentucky, has since been the legal holding company for the vast Southern Pacific system.

But all this was accomplished only through the most strenuous lobbying efforts on the part of Huntington. "I have thought I could stand anything," he wrote, "but I am fearful this damnation Congress will kill me. I returned from Washington last night and I am as near used up as I ever was in my life before. I am spending my last winter at Washington. As I feel to-day I would not agree to spend another there for all the property we have." In later years it was claimed that millions were spent influencing votes in Congress, but Huntington always denied this. He said it was "bad policy" to buy votes. Huge sums of money, however, were paid out by the Big Four without vouchers, or merely as "expense" or "legal expense." One of Huntington's agents at Washington was General Richard Franchot, and when the National Pacific Railroad Commission of 1887 tried to find out why he drew $30,000 to $40,000 a year without vouchers, Huntington said, "We had to get men to explain a thousand things. A man who has not had the experience would hardly imagine the number of people that you have to explain these matters to." In reply to the query as to why $60,000 was used by Franchot in 1873, Huntington said, "He was of strictest integrity and as pure a man as ever lived, and when he said to us 'I want $10,000,' I knew it was proper to let him have it. . . . He had to get lots of attorneys to help him." When the Commission inquired who these were, he said, "I never asked him." The Commission wanted to know how Huntington knew the attorneys were employed, and he deposed, "Because he told me so. He said, 'For these explanations I have to pay out a little here and a little there and that aggregates a great deal.'" When asked what were the nature of General Franchot's services, Huntington replied, "He was a very honorable man whom I had known since I was a boy, and he had my entire confidence." And he sagely concluded that "most of the money was expended, no doubt, to prevent Congress and the Departments from robbing us of our property."

Meanwhile, affairs in California had reached such a state that hostile newspapers were accusing the Southern Pacific of all the crimes on the calendar, and public feeling was further inflamed by controversy between the company and farmers who had settled on railroad lands and claimed that the company did not live up to its agreements concerning these. In one attempt at ejectment of settlers at Mussel Slough, Tulare County, several were killed, and the people of the state were aroused to bitter indignation. Frank Norris later used this incident dramatically in his novel about the Southern Pacific, *The Octopus*. It began to be said that wise people who wanted anything from the State went to the railroad offices in San Francisco rather than to the Capitol at Sacramento, and it was a current jest that of every three drops of rain that fell in the San Joaquín Valley, two belonged to Collis P. Huntington. The fact that the railroad had been one of the original importers of Chinese labor was not forgotten, and in 1877 a labor-leader, Denis Kearney, began agitation against the Chinese, the Pacific Mail Steamship Line, and the Big Four. Meeting in a sand-lot on Market Street across from the City Hall and shouting the slogan "The Chinese Must Go," Kearney's followers terrorized the capitalists of the city and threatened to burn the homes of the millionaires on Nob Hill, particularly that of the man who had brought so many Chinese into California, Charles Crocker, who called them "sandlotters who seek to play the social reformer under the mask of bandit." It was partly as a result of the sand-lot agitation that the state formed a new constitution and set up a board of commissioners to control the railroads, a board which, curiously enough, never returned a single majority report against the Southern Pacific in 16 years.

All these things were unpleasant enough for Huntington, but most unpleasant of all was the fact that the day of reckoning with the Government was drawing near—the day when the $27,500,000 borrowed to build the Central Pacific must be repaid with accrued interest, a total of from $60,000,000 to $80,000,000. Huntington first asked for cancellation of this debt. Then he suggested that the Government refer the question of the amount of indebtedness to a committee which should take into account the saving to the Government through the road's completion before the specified time, the fact that the bonds had to be sold at a large discount, the fact that the Government had created and subsidized rival transcontinental roads which competed with the Central Pacific, and the fact that the railroad had saved the Government much money on transportation; these allowances having been made on the sum due, the balance was to be divided into semi-annual payments with interest at 2 per cent to extend over 125 years. The opposition pointed out that this refunding scheme was unfair to the Government, and Huntington's lobbying met heavy opposition, the man who successfully led the fight being none other than the erstwhile King of the Comstock, Adolph Sutro.

Having sold out his tunnel interests for about $5,000,000, Sutro had returned to San Francisco, and finding the city in the throes of depression and under the domination of Denis Kearney and the sand-lot politicians, he had begun to purchase all the land he could lay his hands on. Owners who thought the city was going to the dogs were only too glad to get rid of their holdings; so Sutro bought until he had 2,200 acres, finally being said to own one-tenth of San Francisco. Among these properties were large areas of sand-hills in the north-western part of the city, some of which were on the seashore, and Sutro turned his attention to reclaiming and beautifying this unpromising land with the same enthusiasm he had given to his even more quixotic scheme of tunnel-building. On the inland sand-hills he planted millions of seedlings, being the first importer of the Australian gum-tree, the eucalyptus, and he introduced Bermuda and bent-grass to hold down the sand, turning the barren waste into what is now Sutro Forest. On the high ramparts of his seashore property at Point Lobos he planted trees and flowers, laid out lawns and gardens, cut stairways, blasted rocks, to produce Sutro Heights. Here was a lovely park, plentifully sprinkled with a Teutonic miscellany of statuary of assorted sizes, Greek and Victorian, stone deer, gnomes, dogs, Venuses, bacchantes, cupids, mountain-goats, and characters from Dickens. To these Elysian heights all San Franciscans might freely come to rest and play, to gaze across the Golden Gate to Mount Tamalpais, to view the misty Faralone Islands out at sea, and from his famous Cliff House to look at the Seal Rocks below, a view which had charmed people from all over the world.

As the crowning achievement of this development the master had built along the side of the cliff the amazing Sutro Baths, airy and graceful, roofed with colored glass, surrounded by terraced galleries seating 2,500 people, with six swimming-tanks, one of which looked large enough for a boat-race. In this extraordinary structure Sutro brought his engineering genius into play by blasting the swimming-tanks out of solid rock and harnessing the tides to bring in the sea water, both hot and cold. Moreover, he included as museum exhibits a bewildering display of statuary, paintings, stuffed animals, fish, the arts of Alaska Indians, Roman lamps, tarantulas, needlework, and 2,500 medallions, and he declared Sutro Heights to be his rarest jewel, which he would not sell for a million dollars.

The immediate cause of Sutro's rancor against Huntington, Stanford, *et al.*, was their refusal to grant a five-cent fare to Sutro Heights. The Big Four now controlled the street-railways, had built cable lines to their homes on Nob Hill, and had extended the system throughout the city, charging a five-cent fare; but to Sutro Heights they operated a steam line charging two five-cent fares. For 10 years the railroad had charged this 10-cent fare to Sutro Heights, and Sutro now demanded the same fare as the rest of the city and the construction of a cable line which could take on passengers at every block instead of only at the city railroad station. In an interview in the San Francisco *Examiner* of May 14, 1894, he declared that the Southern Pacific had enslaved California and absorbed the street-railways of San Francisco and that now its desire was to absorb the Cliff House and the Ocean Beach. Having maintained Sutro Heights at an expense of $25,000 a year, free to the public, Sutro thought the railroad should coöperate with him by reducing the fare. He said that if it would put in a proper cable line with good service and a five-cent fare, he would deed Sutro

Heights to the city as a gift; if not, he would build the cable himself. Then he boarded up the entrance to the park and required a 25-cent admission until such time as the railroad should come to terms.

When he invited Collis P. Huntington and his friends out to see the baths, that gentleman said that he was astonished at their splendor. Sutro made his request to Huntington for the cable service and told him, "I will not deal with Fred Crocker because he has no sense"; and when Huntington definitely refused a five-cent fare, Sutro said, "I do not want to frighten you because I know you are not a man who is easily frightened, but I simply want to tell you what I am going to do. I will make you do this before you get through with it." Better far for Collis Huntington had he gracefully acceded to Sutro's request, but the greatest railroad magnate in the country was not going to be dictated to by an insignificant little San Francisco promoter of baths and real estate. So he said "No." And the battle royal began.

From 1894 to 1897 Sutro fought Huntington, who was making the effort of his life to get the Government to modify or remit the railroad debt. In championing the cause of the people against the railroad monopoly Sutro occupied the limelight, and as a result he was elected Mayor of San Francisco, receiving more votes than all his four opponents combined. In 1894, when he opened the campaign, he declared, "I can stand abuse. I got twenty-four scrap books full of it when I built the Sutro Tunnel, and they are big ones." In 1895 he entered a solemn protest to Congress against the passage of any funding bill whatever and called upon all men and women to telegraph and write protests to all members of both houses. He said he believed the railroad was willing to spend $3,000,000, or $20,000 apiece, for the number of votes necessary to pass its bill, and he called on the people to "ring the alarm bells every day until Congress adjourns." The matter being held over until the next session, Sutro continued his efforts, and in 1896 he declared,

Any funding bill which Congress will be asked to pass will more seriously affect the welfare of the Pacific Coast than any measure which has come before the people since California became a state. It means practically the gift of eighty millions of dollars to C. P. Huntington, and the three estates of his partners, and that means the enslavement of our

WILLIAM SHARON       WILLIAM C. RALSTON
ADOLPH SUTRO
JOHN P. JONES       DARIUS O. MILLS

Sharon, from H. H. Bancroft, *Chronicles of the Builders of the Commonwealth;* Ralston and Sutro, courtesy of the Society of California Pioneers; Jones and Mills, from Alonzo Phelps, *Contemporary Biography of California's Representative Men.*

STAGE-COACHES FOR THE NEVADA MINES

Coaches of the Concord type operated by Wells, Fargo and Company from the Central Pacific railhead at Colfax, California, in the Sierra Nevada. From a photograph taken in 1865. Courtesy of the Southern Pacific Company.

ENTRANCE TO THE SUTRO TUNNEL AT SUTRO, NEVADA

Courtesy of the California State Library.

people. The Central Pacific and the Southern Pacific of Kentucky, which consist of the same men, have domineered over the people of this coast during the existence of these corporations; they are the cause of the existence of bossism and corruption in nearly all the branches of our state and municipal government.

These are the men who owe the Government $80,000,000, and after having robbed the properties which they held in trust for the United States of everything of value, they have the effrontery to ask Congress to make them practically a gift of what they owe. If there is any manhood or any justice left in the land this measure will be defeated again, as it has been already at the two last sessions of Congress. I declare here and now that if we don't win this fight I shall be ashamed to live here.

While Sutro continuously lambasted the Southern Pacific and its iniquities at home, Huntington improved each shining hour in Washington. The New York *Evening Post* of April 22, 1896, paid its respects to his efforts: "The most pitiable and at the same time the most disgusting spectacle that now offends the national capital is the Huntington lobby. The list of paid lobbyists and attorneys now numbers twenty-eight, and their brazen attempts to influence Congress to pass the Pacific Railroad Refunding Bill have become the disgrace of the session." When previously interviewed on the matter in New York on February 1, Huntington had said, "I am paying very little attention to the refunding bill. I have such absolute confidence in Congress that I am not worrying at all. I believe they will do what is right and fair and that is all we want. We will of course do what they command us if we can. If we can't we can't and that is all there is to it. If they had taken the offer and advice I gave them in 1871, there would have been no trouble like this now. I hardly remember what the details were. They were something that would have arrested all this though."

But the onslaught waged by Sutro continued with vigor, the Mayor declaring that "if you want to fight a rhinoceros you don't go after him with kid gloves; you take a big club and knock him down." His program included mass-meetings, petitions, a request to Kentucky to repeal the railroad charter, and the flooding of Congress with sensational pamphlets, one of which bore the title, "How Congressmen are Bribed. The Colton Letters. Declaration of Huntington that Congressmen are For Sale." All these things received full publicity in the

Hearst papers, as well as in the New York *World*; and, indeed, William Randolph Hearst made the matter a major issue in his press. He sent that master of satirical invective, Ambrose Bierce, to Washington and published his daily despatches on the front page of the San Francisco *Examiner*; accompanying him was the most gifted cartoonist of the day, Homer Davenport, and between them they made poor Huntington's life miserable. Each morning San Francisco woke up to laugh at a devastating picture of Uncle Collis, portrayed as pilfering the Government in various guises, usually with a sign in the background, "Beware of Pickpockets." One cartoon showed a burlesque statue of Huntington with the caption,

> He left his grateful country little pelf
> So kindly reared this monument himself.

And every day Ambrose Bierce lashed out in an article full of biting sarcasm, describing what was going on in Washington, liberally besprinkled with such remarks as, "Of our modern forty thieves, Mr. Huntington is the surviving thirty-six." When Charles Crocker explained the loss of the Contract and Finance Company's books by saying that the late Mark Hopkins used to destroy things that he called "trumpery," Bierce remarked in the *Examiner*, "Unfortunately there is too much reason to believe that both Mr. Hopkins and the books have been burned."

Uncle Collis, meanwhile, called his opponents "as uncanny a crowd as ever farmer found lurking around his hen roost." And he plaintively declared that "If the Government of the United States, after all I have done for it, should decide to give me no consideration and sell me out I should make no attempt to prevent it. The Government has done nothing for me." If by "selling him out" he meant requiring the payment of the Central Pacific debt, that is exactly what the Government did. For the Huntington power, strong as it was, could not resist the steady barrage of telling shots laid down under the generalship of Messrs. Sutro, Hearst, Bierce, and Davenport. In July, 1897, Congress passed an act providing for a debt commission to accept nothing less than the full principal and interest due. And to the surprise of everyone, the banking firm of James Speyer and Company of New York, which had issued Central Pacific securities, was able to make arrangements satisfactory to the Government and Mr. Huntington whereby the whole debt was covered by issuing new securities and getting the Southern Pacific to guarantee the interest.

In these years Huntington had joined the other partners on Nob Hill, moving into the white Italian palace built by his late colleague Colton, not far from where Crocker, Stanford, and Hopkins had built their homes. And here they were neighbors to Jim Flood, who surrounded his brownstone mansion with a $30,000 fence of pure brass which required the constant attention of one servant to keep it polished. Near-by was the house of Flood's partner, Fair, who had been made Senator. Fair had quarreled with Mackay, who is said to have sworn that "Jim Fair shan't sit in the Senate another term," developed San Francisco real estate, built the railroad from San Francisco to Santa Cruz, and seen his two daughters marry Herman Oehlrichs and William K. Vanderbilt, Jr., in a blaze of social glory. John W. Mackay, the Beau Brummel of the Bonanza Kings, having quarreled with Jay Gould, joined with James Gordon Bennett, who had attacked Gould and the Erie Railway scandals in the New York *Herald,* to form the Postal Telegraph system as a rival to the Western Union. He almost wrecked the Nevada Bank when he and Flood tried to corner the wheat-market to aid the French Minister of War, General Georges Boulanger, in his plan for a war on Prussia; the institution was only saved from failure by Fair and I. W. Hellman of Los Angeles, who took it over and reorganized it. Mrs. Mackay became the leader of American society in Paris and was made a character in Ludovic Halévy's novel *L'Abbé Constantin.* Mackay's other claim to fame was his endowment of the Mackay School of Mines at the University of Nevada—and, perhaps, the stir created in later years when his granddaughter married the Jewish song-writer Irving Berlin. Senator William Sharon was not long in recovering from the collapse of the Comstock. As an old miner said of him, "He was like a cat thrown out of a window—always landed on his feet." He was said to have made a fortune of $25,000,000, and he succeeded Ralston as host at his great Belmont estate and also as promoter of the Palace Hotel and the Spring Valley water-works, becoming the largest taxpayer in San Francisco. Darius Ogden Mills built up one of the greatest fortunes on the Pacific Coast, investing heavily in all sorts of promotion schemes. His son, Ogden Mills, became Secretary of the Treasury under President Hoover.

Adolph Sutro, always a public benefactor, had given the city a statue, "The Triumph of Light," which had been placed atop one of its hills and had earned a fervid eulogy from California's favorite orator, the Honorable Samuel M. Shortridge, which may be quoted in very small part:

Happy man, you stand to-day upon an eminence which a king might envy. Thrice happy man: for after a life spent in works of philanthropy and patriotism, a life full rounded and complete, you can seek the eternal rest of the grave with the consoling assurance that your name will not perish with your bones; for so long as the incoming sailor from the islands of the sea shall joyfully catch the light flaming from yonder uplifted torch . . . so long as this solid granite rests upon the spot made hallowed by this day's work . . . the name of Adolph Sutro, citizen, philanthropist, patriot, will be uttered with emotion, and the example of your life be cherished as a rich legacy to the sons and daughters of freedom.

Sutro had also been collecting fine and rare books and manuscripts, including the Sunderland library of the Duke of Marlborough, spending half a million dollars in building up a splendid library which he presented to the City of San Francisco. At his death in 1898 he left a trust fund which was to be available in 40 years, when it should have totaled $5,000,000 to $10,000,000, to be applied to charities and institutions of learning or science and to be used as premiums for distinguished scholarship and scientific discovery. But some of his heirs protested, and the courts held that the bequest was invalid because the terms were too vague. In recent years a movement was begun to build a heroic statue of Sutro on the heights overlooking Point Lobos, so as to be visible far inland and out at sea, but this memorial died a-borning. And in 1933 the State of California even proposed to deprive San Francisco of the Sutro Library on the ground of saving the $4,000 a year paid its librarians.

Huntington's death in 1900 ended the California railroad monopoly created by the Big Four. During the settlement of the debt negotiations, civic interests, headed by the Spreckels family, had organized a rival road, the San Joaquín Valley Railway Company, to build southward to serve the valley for which it was named. In December,

1898, this was purchased by the Santa Fe, giving it an entrance to San Francisco shortly before Huntington's death. This road had been begun in 1895, and by July, 1898, it had a line from Stockton to Bakersfield, including a loop through Visalia, a total distance of 278.91 miles, and work was being actively pushed from Stockton to Point Richmond, across the Bay from San Francisco, at the time of the line's purchase by the Santa Fe. The work between Stockton and Point Richmond proved somewhat more difficult than anticipated, owing to peculiarities of soil encountered and to a prolonged rainy season; but it was completed in the year 1900, and connection from Point Richmond into San Francisco was provided by ferry, as is the case up to the present time. The entire line from Mojave to San Francisco was open for freight purposes on May 1, 1900, and for passenger service on July 1, 1900.

Meanwhile, the Southern Pacific had gone out of politics, so it announced, and Huntington aptly summed up his opinion of the prevailing statesmanship by saying, "There is very little now that divides the two parties except the seven great reasons—the five loaves and the two fishes." Until the end of his life Huntington kept a firm grasp on the railroads he had built. It seemed that the old Titan would never give up. When he was over 70 he outlined such a vast program of railroad expansion to his friend Sir Rivers Wilson that that gentleman said in amazement, "But you will have to live fifty years to complete such a program!" and Huntington grimly replied, "I intend to." After his death his widow and his nephew, Henry E. Huntington, sold their stock to the new giant of the railroads, E. H. Harriman, who combined the Southern Pacific and Union Pacific in an immense system, until the Government dissolved the merger in 1913.

When Harriman purchased the Oregon Short Line, he closed it to the traffic of the Denver and Rio Grande, the old road built by General Palmer, who had sold it to George Gould. Then, when Harriman bought the Southern Pacific, cutting the Rocky Mountain road out of an outlet to the coast, Gould built the Western Pacific from Salt Lake to San Francisco, as originally planned by Palmer. W. J. Bartlett, attorney for a San Francisco bank which owned a small railroad running from the Stockton water-front to interior coal-mines at Tesla, sold this line to Gould together with location for a road along the Feather River, and the Western Pacific was built on this route. Its completion took six years, the cost was $60,000,000, and the expense and interest charges threw the Denver and Rio Grande into bankruptcy; but on July 1, 1911, the Western Pacific was completed, giving San Francisco another outlet to the East.

A fourth outlet came years later, as a result of the war between James J. Hill, the empire-builder, and E. H. Harriman. Hill bought the tracks of his Great Northern from St. Paul to Puget Sound and then threw a branch line from Spokane to Portland along the north bank of the Columbia River. When Hill completed this road, both he and his rival, Harriman, sent engineers into central Oregon to occupy the Deschutes River cañon with the idea of building a line to penetrate California from the north. Hill won and pushed his line rapidly down from Columbia to Bend; but then the World War came on, and the unsettled finances of that time prevented further building. On November 10, 1931, however, Arthur Curtiss James, the largest holder of railroad securities in the country, boarded the same private car that Jim Hill used to ride to Bend in 1911 and traveled to Bieber, California, where he drove the golden spike that marked the entry of the Great Northern system into San Francisco territory. Following the route for connecting the Sacramento Valley with the Columbia that Lieutenant Philip H. Sheridan surveyed for Secretary of War Jefferson Davis in 1853, this extension of the Great Northern opened a market of 6,000,000 inhabitants to San Francisco.

Long before this, San Francisco had passed through the ordeal of earthquake and fire and had won the admiration of the world by her courage and speed in rebuilding. On April 18, 1906, four square miles, including nearly all the business district, was swept clean; 28,000 buildings were destroyed, and the stricken people lived in tents in Golden Gate Park—tents labeled "Camp Thankful," "Camp Glory," "Camp Hell"—and ate in bread lines. Six days later the first contract for rebuilding was signed, and while the débris was still warm, work began on clearing the ground, a labor that would have baffled Hercules. Thousands of horses were imported, wagons, tools, and supplies were sent in by the trainload, and 40,000 men in the building trades went to work. Theaters were the first buildings to rise, for the nerve-racked people needed relaxation; then came other buildings uptown on Fillmore Street; and finally downtown Market Street, which had been the most heavily affected, and which it was predicted would never come back, was rebuilt. Within a few years, and with the aid of $750,000,000 in insurance payments, the city had risen from its ashes more strongly and more beautifully built than before.

In the rebuilding of San Francisco two men were outstanding: one was Hugh S. Johnson, who directed the work of the United States Army in the stricken city and who was later to become famous as the head of President Franklin D. Roosevelt's National Recovery Administration; the other was E. H. Harriman. As soon as he heard of the earthquake and fire, Harriman hastened to San Francisco and put all the resources of the Southern Pacific at the disposal of the city. He bought vast quantities of food in Los Angeles and rushed it to San Francisco; the day after the fire started he moved 1,073 carloads of refugees out of the city; he gave gasoline and explosives, put the railroad hospital at the service of the sick and injured, opened nine information bureaus to supply the city with news bulletins, and for five weeks lent the railroad telegraph wires to the Western Union. No charge was ever made for these services or for Harriman's own work. He gave himself and his railroad freely and completely to the city, and it was in large part due to his organizing genius and energy that San Francisco was able so quickly to rally from the disaster.

During this time of rebuilding the iniquities of the Rueff-Schmitz city government were dramatically unearthed by Frémont Older, who was kidnapped during the furore, James D. Phelan, who became mayor, and Prosecutor Francis J. Heney, sent to the city by President Roosevelt. From this reform movement grew the Lincoln-Roosevelt League, which elected Hiram W. Johnson governor and was later merged in the Progressive Party. In 1915 San Francisco celebrated its rebuilding and the opening of the Panama Canal with the Panama-Pacific International Exposition, in buildings of fairylike beauty. And every night soft bluish lights bathed their rosy walls and marble copings, revealing for the first time on a large scale the possibilities of indirect electric lighting. Fortunately, one of the masterpieces of this exposition, the Palace of Art, still stands, its lovely columns rising above blue lagoons as a reminder of the surpassing beauty of that world's fair.

To-day San Francisco remembers her kings of the last century chiefly on Nob Hill. The Crocker property was given to the Episcopal diocese as the site of Grace Cathedral; the Flood house is now the Pacific Union Club; across the street are the massive Fairmont Hotel, built by the Fair family, and the skyscraping Mark Hopkins Hotel, around the back of which the feudal stone wall still stands; the site of the adjoining Stanford house is occupied by the Stanford Court Apartments; and the Huntington property is now Huntington Park. Downtown there is a Flood Building on Market Street, and a great bank bears the name of Crocker; and down the peninsula the brown-stone quadrangles of Stanford University spread over the Palo Alto "farm"—all mementos of

> The good old rule, the simple plan,
> That they should take who have the power
> And they should keep who can.

They played their part, those ruthless barons of rails and gold and land, in making San Francisco great. They helped to swell her wealth, to establish her as a world port and a center of Western trade, to crown her Queen of the Pacific. Their cunning added power to the magnet that drew the bold, the hardy, the restless, the romantic, the adventurous across the plains and mountains and the seven seas to build the well-beloved city of San Francisco.

It was these men and their kind who gave San Francisco her unique flavor and that dash of devil-may-care naughtiness which has always made her interesting, even to the censorious. For generations that roaring bit of hell, the Barbary Coast, was famous for iniquity wherever sailors sailed. And the reputation of San Francisco as the home of crime, dissipation, and excitement moved that choleric satirist Ambrose Bierce to remark, "It is the paradise of ignorance, anarchy and general yellowness. It needs another quake, another whiff of fire, and more than all else a steady trade wind of grape-shot. It is a moral penal colony. It is the worst of all our Sodom and Gomorrahs in the modern world." The Barbary Coast has long since sunk into innocuous desuetude, and the garishly ornamented fronts of the dance-

THE SKY-LINE OF SAN FRANCISCO FROM THE BAY

Courtesy of Californians, Inc.

SAN FRANCISCO'S CIVIC CENTER

In the background, the City Hall; behind it, the Municipal Opera House and the Veterans' War Memorial; left, the Civic Auditorium; right, the State Building; in the foreground, the Public Library. Courtesy of Californians, Inc.

THE SAN FRANCISCO OAKLAND BAY BRIDGE

The world's longest bridge, 8¼ miles long, 5 miles over water, as it will look when completed in 1937. The San Francisco Civic Center in the center foreground. Courtesy of the California Toll Bridge Authority.

halls on Pacific Street for years stared vacantly on empty sidewalks until a weak replica of its old life was revived for tourists. San Francisco is not so wicked as she used to be, and she has been thoroughly cleansed politically, so that if Ambrose Bierce were to write his descriptive tirade to-day, it would be attributed to nothing worse than a morning-after headache. But an aromatic flavor of naughtiness still permeates the city, and San Franciscans are rather proud of that fact. They feel more metropolitan and sophisticated than their neighbors, and they rejoice when Will Rogers remarks, "A Los Angeles man coming to San Francisco is just like a country boy going to town."

Climbing over its steep Telegraph and Russian hills, reaching around the blue waters of the bay and out to the whitecapped ocean at the west, San Francisco is a city bathed in beauty. On the lower side of the Golden Gate the military reservation of the Presidio guarantees that streets and houses shall never encroach on that great tree-covered park by the sea. Across the Gate are Mount Tamalpais and the green hills of Marin County, and over the bay to the east far-spreading cities glisten in the sun. From the Cliff House, or from any tall office building or any hillside house, or along the shore at the old Fair Grounds, or at Fisherman's Wharf—its bay filled with brown-sailed skiffs and its beach lined with drying nets—one looks on vistas of surpassing beauty. And always the city's electric atmosphere is a tonic; winds blow over it, fogs swathe it, and its sun glows white above.

This San Francisco sunlight typifies the difference between San Francisco and Los Angeles. The sun over the southern city is hot, bright, effulgent, and relaxing; the sun over San Francisco is pale-gold, having in it something of the quality of an electric arc-lamp, and never hot enough to enervate. And the cities are the same. Los Angeles is full of blazing color, brightness, exotic beauty, and shine; San Francisco is gray, subdued, delicately pastel, dignified, even venerable. Her magnificent Civic Center might be a group of ancient palace and government buildings of an Imperial dynasty. The Los Angeles Civic Center gleams white and bright in the sun, its clean, angular lines carrying no message from the past, expressing instead the spirit of the day—yes, of the hour and the minute—in terms typically modern, typically American. Slow and substantial of growth, sophisticated, serene, indifferent to fate, cosmopolitan San Francisco is poised, sure of herself, a stately dowager in a stomacher, who taps her beautiful and exuberant southern flapper sister disapprovingly with her fan.

But, however dignified, San Francisco has never outlived, will never outlive, her youth. She likes to play and frolic; she loves a good time; she is to-day the best show town for the speaking stage outside of New York and Chicago. Always she has the joy of living and the energy of youth. And if it can be said that California's women are beautiful, it can also be said that San Francisco's women are *chic*. As to their poise, one need only observe the nonchalance with which a shopper stops dead still in the middle of Market Street to permit two clanging street-cars to rush past each other while she stands tightly imprisoned in a narrow slot—a terrifying experience which leaves her apparently unperturbed.

Above all, San Francisco loves good victuals and good drink. Even though times have changed, she has never outgrown those days so touchingly described by Will Irwin in *The City That Was*:*

Listen! O ye starved amidst plenty, to the tale of the Hotel de France. This restaurant stood on California Street, just east of old St. Mary's Church. One could throw a biscuit from its back window into Chinatown. It occupied a big ramshackle house, which had been a mansion of the gold days. Louis, the proprietor, was a Frenchman of the Bas Pyrénées; and his accent was as thick as his peasant soups. The patrons were Frenchmen of the poorer class, or young and poor clerks and journalists who had discovered the delights of this hostelry. The place exuded a genial gaiety, of which Louis, throwing out familiar jokes to right and left as he mixed salads and carried dishes, was the head and front.

First on the bill of fare was the soup—thick and clean and good. Next, one of Louis' three cherubic little sons brought on a course of fish—sole, rock cod, flounders, or smelt—with a good French sauce. The third course was meat. This came on *en bloc;* the waiter dropped in the center of each table a big roast or boiled joint together with a mustard pot and two big dishes of vegetables. Each guest manned the carving knife in turn and helped himself to his satisfaction. After that, Louis, with an air of ceremony, brought on a big bowl of excellent salad he had mixed himself. For beverage there stood by each plate a perfectly cylindrical pint glass filled with new, watered claret. The meal closed with fruit in season—all that the guest cared to eat. I have saved a startling fact to close the paragraph —the price was fifteen cents!

* Will Irwin, *The City That Was* (New York, B. W. Huebsch, 1906; now published by the Viking Press).

To-day this city of gaiety and laughter and good living looks back longingly on the days when one could get the best table d'hôte dinner in the world with a bottle of red wine for a dollar. And such names as The Poodle Dog, Bergez Frank's, Tait's, Techau Tavern, Papa Coppa's, Negro and O'Brien's, Solari's linger lovingly in the memory of good San Franciscans.

Now scores of millions of dollars are being spent on two of the largest bridges in the world, which are to cross San Francisco Bay, drawing the communities around it together, after a lifetime of disunion. The beautiful undulating hills of Marin County, over which the live-oaks and cypresses spread in lovely patterns of irregular design, are being joined with the Presidio by a bridge across the Golden Gate; and the people of the east Bay cities of Oakland, Berkeley, Richmond, and Alameda will soon be able to dash quickly in their cars over another bridge from Oakland to the San Francisco Embarcadero. This welding of the Bay cities into one community must inevitably lead to a greater and faster-growing metropolis. But San Francisco is not avid for mere numbers. For this "pearl on a peninsula" already is laden with other and more precious gifts of the gods: she has distinction, beauty, charm, and many lovers. One must envy the good fortune of those who are yet to come under her spell. When such a one comes for the first time to this glamorous city, he will learn to love her cool, gray beauty; he will delight in seeing her rise ghostlike on her high hills—an uneven, sawtoothed Whistler silhouette, dimly outlined against an indefinable sky. And sometime he will watch from a ferry at sunset those startling color-changes which turn the sky from flaming apricot to blue and then to that cool, compassionate, all-encompassing gray which lays its mask over the city like a visible hush. At the Golden Gate he will see the sun lie low in a bed of cherry coals, flaming between black headlands. And then, suddenly, the city will be swallowed up in darkness, and all will vanish save the flashing jewel of Alcatraz, fantastic island castle of a pastry-cook's dream.

# CHAPTER X

WHILE San Francisco graciously, indifferently, permitted the gods to drop the fruits of fortune into her lap, her sister city to the south had to climb the tree and pick the prizes with her own fair fingers. Whatever good things Los Angeles has obtained—and they are many—she has herself alone to thank for nearly all of them. Her railroads, her harbor, even that basic necessity, her water, have been brought to the City of the Angels by sheer force. She has attracted, seduced, bullied, and overpowered every one of her adversaries, brought them captive into camp, and made them like it. Originating in a few dry brown hills 30 miles from a harbor that was not a harbor, starting without a railroad, Los Angeles has shown the power of mind over matter by promoting herself into the great metropolis of the Southwest and one of the most beautiful cities in America.

It was altogether fitting that the first voice crying in the wilderness to proclaim the delights and virtues of "Los Angeles, the beautiful, with roses in her hair," should be the seductive voice of the realtor. The precursor of those modern sirens who lean from the windows of buses parked on Hill Street and lure the unwary pedestrian on all-day expeditions to remote subdivisions, with the bait of smiles, an automobile-ride, and a free lunch, was none other than Captain Fernando de Rivera y Moncada, *Commandante* of the Spanish province of California. And he deserves the proud title of First Realtor of Los Angeles.

In 1781 the Spanish Governor, Felipe de Neve, having decided that the fertile soil in this favored spot demanded settlement and desiring to grow grain for the army in upper California instead of importing it from Mexico, founded *El Pueblo Nuestra Señora la Reina de los Angeles,* making Los Angeles the first legally ordained city in California. He platted the city six miles square, with a plaza at the center around which he laid out building-lots, and a short distance away from the town he added a district of seven-acre tracts for planting. Like all good realtors, having mapped out the metropolis of the future and its suburbs and envisioned it teeming with the annual increase in population which was sure to come, de Neve found it necessary to begin a little promotion work. So, for the task of letting future inhabitants in on the ground floor, he despatched to Mexico Captain Rivera, a resident of California for eight years (in fact, the first white man to enter California by land) charging him with the task of describing the beauties of landscape and perfection of climate so as to secure at least twenty-four settlers, healthy, strong, and of good character, including a mason, a blacksmith, a carpenter, and their female relatives, if any. The fact that this early realtor was shortly thereafter murdered by the inhabitants may or may not be regarded as having a sinister significance.

At any rate, the settlers came, lured by the offer of free land, which they could not sell but which they could bequeath to their children, a gift of $116.50 a year for the first two years, $60 for the next three, two horses, two cows and a calf, two sheep, two goats, a mule, a yoke of oxen, a plow-point, a spade, a hoe, an ax, a sickle, a musket, and a leathern shield. Even if more spectacular, the rewards promised by the enthusiastic realtors of later years were less practical and immediate in nature, and doubtless the Mexican emigrants thought a dollar in the hand worth ten in the bush. So, on the 4th of September, 1781, an expedition from the Mission San Gabriel set out to the new real-estate enterprise of Los Angeles. The Governor led, followed by soldiers carrying the gorgeous silken blue banner of Spain; then came the priests of San Gabriel, with their Indian acolytes, and forty-four settlers—eleven men, eleven women, and twenty-two children. Around the plaza this impressive procession marched, while the Indians of the original settlement of Yang-na looked on in awe and bewilderment; the priests asked a blessing on the new city, the children elevated the banner of the Virgin Mary, and Governor de Neve made an address describing the future of Los Angeles, dwelling, doubtless, on its matchless climate, its commercial possibilities, and its inevitable and extraordinary growth.

Although the founding of the *pueblo* of Los Angeles occurred nearly 250 years after the Spanish *conquistador* Hernando Cortes had discovered California, the site was by no means a new discovery. In 1542 Juan Cabrillo had sailed from San Diego to San Pedro, now the port of Los Angeles, and had named Santa Monica harbor the "Bay of Smokes," probably because the Indians of Yang-na were engaged in hunting rabbits by setting fire to the prairies, as was their custom; he proceeded up the coast as far as San Francisco but did not enter the bay; returning, he died on the Island San Miguel, off Santa Barbara, of an infection from a surgery on a broken arm. In October, 1767, soon after the first Spanish governor of the Californias, Gaspar de Portolá, had reached San Diego, he set out on a trip in search of the harbor of Monterey, going north by land. As his party neared what is now Los Angeles, they crossed the Santa Ana River, naming it *El Rio del Dulcissimo Nombre de Jesús*, but, a slight earthquake occurring, they supplemented this to read, "The River of the Sweetest Name of Jesus of the Earthquakes." They arrived at the Indian village of Yang-na on the 2d of August, which was the feast-day, beloved of the Franciscans, of the Virgin patroness of their founder's chapel, "St. Mary of the Angels," the hallowed *Porziuncula*; thus they named the place in her honor, *Nuestra Señora la Reina de los Angeles de Porciúnculo,* "Our Lady the Queen of the Angels."

By 1800 there were three *pueblos,* or towns, in California—San José, Santa Cruz, and Los Angeles, and three *presidios,* or military posts—San Diego, Santa Barbara, and San Francisco. Los Angeles consisted of thirty small adobe houses, thatched and covered with *brea,* or tar, taken from pits discovered near-by, pits which afterwards were to yield extraordinary specimens of the bones of prehistoric animals. A small dam had been made in the river to provide the *pueblo* with water; wheat, maize, and vegetables had been planted, and a wall erected to keep out the Indians. Three members of the community had been expelled on the ground that they were "useless to the *pueblo* and to themselves." One of these migrated to San Francisco, which the *Angeleños* no doubt thought an appropriate place for him.

These were days of the great land-grants, made to favored Spanish citizens on application to the governor. In 1785 Juan José Domínguez received the San Pedro Ranch, three leagues square; to José Maña Verdugo went the San Rafael Ranch of the same size; to Manuel Nieto all the land between the Santa Ana and San Gabriel rivers, the mountains, and the sea. On these princely domains thousands of cattle were soon running, the rambling, low, white ranch-houses of adobe bricks with red-tile roofs were the centers of a leisurely, opulent, and beautiful social life. Hospitality was bountiful: guests were always welcome to come and stay as long as they liked; they were given entertainment, welcomed to the inner *patio*, where fountains played and flowers grew, and under whose cool arches were always set tables furnished with wine and chocolate for the family and guests. Mission and ranch vied with each other in caring for the traveler: at each stop a *caponero* of ten or twelve fresh horses would be provided, and a *vaquero* to guide the next day's journey; and the traveler was always permitted to lasso and kill a fat steer for meat if he would leave the hide and tallow for the owner's use. Money was not much in evidence, for the *padres* and *rancheros* supplied their needs by bartering hides and tallow with the ships that anchored at San Pedro; but in each guest-room it was customary to place a little pile of coins under a napkin, from which the guest was expected to help himself as needed. It is recorded that once when an Englishwoman, a stranger, attempted to pay for her entertainment, the owner of the ranch knelt on the floor and cried in anguish, "Give no money, no money at all. Everything is free in a gentleman's house."

Commerce began in the region around San Pedro, the port of Los Angeles, with the hunting of the sea-otter, which had first been discovered in the Aleutian Islands by Bering's men in 1741. So beautiful was the fur that the Russians were able to sell single pelts to Chinese mandarins, who appreciated it as royalty did ermine, for as much as $2,000. In the later Mexican period the whaling industry also discovered the possibilities of the waters around San Pedro, and men from Yankee ships were soon keeping the fires hot under their blubber-pots and laboring at the presses for extracting the precious oil. Finally the cattle ranches became the attraction that drew ships to the coast; the hides went to Boston, as did the horns to make combs, and the tallow went to Peru. But commerce was always difficult, for

Spain had laid down the most stringent restrictions on trading. In order to stifle competition the Government had decreed that the colonists could trade only in Spanish vessels and through a single port, Seville. The times of arrival and departure and the methods of trading were carefully specified, and the colonists were prohibited from growing any crops that would compete with Spain, including olives, tobacco, hemp, and grapes. As a consequence of these prohibitions the Los Angeles district became a community of smugglers; contraband trade was carried on with Hawaii, and Yankee clipper ships found a warm welcome. A captain would anchor his vessel on the lee side of Catalina Island, make a quick dash into San Pedro, exchange his goods, and sail away; and so flagrant did the smuggling become that the Government was forced to relax its restrictions. When the Mexican rule succeeded the Spanish, foreign vessels were admitted to the port of Monterey, where they supposedly paid full duties on their goods; but it was customary for ships to enter the harbor, get their clearance papers, and then lie along the coast while other vessels transferred cargo to them which they, in turn, sold to the inhabitants. Indeed, smuggling became so common that smugglers were regarded as just as respectable as anyone else in the community.

The Yankee ships were veritable department stores from which the ranch-owners could buy everything they desired from decorated crystal goblets and carved ivory fans to plows and horseshoes. They carried, as Dana remarked, "spirits of all kinds (sold by the cask), teas, coffee, sugars, spices, raisins, molasses, hard-ware, crockery-ware, tin-ware, cutlery, clothing of all kinds, boots and shoes from Lynn, calicoes and cottons from Lowell, crapes, silks; also, shawls, scarfs, necklaces, jewelry, and combs for the ladies; furniture; and in fact, everything that can be imagined from Chinese fire-works to English cart-wheels—of which we had a dozen pairs with their iron rims on." Luxury, idleness, and ease marked the life of the upper-class Spanish in the pastoral age of California. The Californians thrived under the blue skies and bracing air of the north and the warm sunshine of the south; the men were tall and strong, the women remarkably beautiful, graceful, and charming. As a people they were happy and contented. Incivility, robbery, fraudulent creditors, and other banes of civilization were unknown. Indeed, life was so idyllic that Ban-

LOS ANGELES IN THE FIFTIES

Lithograph after a drawing by Charles Koppel in *Reports of Explorations and Surveys to Ascertain the Most Practicable and Economical Route for a Railroad from the Missouri River to the Pacific Ocean,* 1853.

THE STATION OF THE LOS ANGELES AND SAN PEDRO RAILROAD

Courtesy of the Southern Pacific Company.

PHINEAS T. BANNING        ELIAS J. BALDWIN
WILLIAM B. STRONG
WILLIAM A. CLARK        HENRY S. HUNTINGTON

Banning, from J. M. Guinn, *A History of California and an Extended History of Los Angeles;* Baldwin, from Alonzo Phelps, *Contemporary Biography of California's Representative Men;* Strong, courtesy of the Atchison, Topeka and Santa Fe Railway; Clark, from Helen F. Sanders, *History of Montana;* Huntington, courtesy of the Henry E. Huntington Library and Art Gallery.

croft says, "It would be difficult to find in any age or place a community that got more out of life with less trouble, wear, and wickedness than the inhabitants of pastoral California." But the calm of ranch and mission was disturbed at the beginning of the nineteenth century, when, after the Napoleonic wars, Mexico and the South American provinces rebelled against Spain. In this revolt the Californians sided with the mother-country against Mexico; but the Mexican Empire was soon established, and Spain was left with nothing of her possessions in the vicinity of America except Cuba and a few other islands. On the 11th of April, 1822, California became a Mexican province.

Spain probably shed few tears over the loss of California, for the province had always been on the wrong side of the ledger. The Government spent $100,000 a year there and sometimes got back only a small fraction of that sum in customs. During the revolution the Government had borrowed money for the army from the *padres* to the amount of $400,000, and the drafts were never paid. Under Mexican rule the *padres* continued to supply funds to the Government, for the continual revolutions depleted the Mexican treasury, and the deficit in providing for government in California, amounting to from $30,000 to $50,000 a year, was made up by the missions. The Mexican rule lasted for 25 years, during which eight governors ruled California. When the Mexican Empire fell, it was succeeded by the Mexican Republic, with frequent changes of government; and during all this time the *pueblo* of Los Angeles was a storm-center of revolution. It had grown somewhat, adding population from the shipfuls of criminals sent from Mexico, transportation to the Californias being a form of punishment; and once it was presented by Mexico with a boat-load of orphans. The vineyards had started to grow, and the priests complained to the Governor that the citizens were being demoralized through an excess of enthusiasm in promoting home industry by drinking up the product in the form of brandy. In addition to its good citizens, the *pueblo* harbored a worthless and vicious lot of loafers who were such a source of trouble that the prefect of the southern district was wont to begin his reports to the Governor with the heading "Los Diablos" instead of "Los Angeles."

Now things were happening in far-away Texas which were to have repercussions in California. Americans had settled this Mexican territory and, in 1836, had declared themselves an independent state and applied for admission to the Union. For years Congress dallied with the question, but finally statehood was granted Texas in 1845, on the eve of the war that Manifest Destiny declared on Mexico in April, 1846. Commodore John D. Sloat seized the northern part of California in July, and in August Captain John C. Frémont and Commodore Robert F. Stockton, with sailors and marines, took Los Angeles without a struggle and sent the report back to Washington by Kit Carson. Yerba Buena, as San Francisco was then called, never rebelled again, but the *pueblo* of Los Angeles was full of citizens to whom revolution was as much a matter of course as breakfast, and 500 of these drove out Captain Gillespie and his men, who had been left to guard the post.

Meanwhile, General Stephen W. Kearny, advancing overland from Santa Fe with 1,600 troops, having had the report that all was well, distributed his force along the route and was advancing with only 121 men when, at San Pascual, December 5, 1846, he met an attack by Governor Pío Pico with 80 lancers and suffered the loss of 18 men. Then he joined forces with the sailors and marines of Commodore Stockton at San Diego, and all advanced on Los Angeles, the sailors having some difficulty in riding horseback gracefully without hanging on to the animals' necks. On January 10, 1847, they entered the town, and the band played them to the plaza, much to the delight of the inhabitants, whose revolutionary ardor was somewhat overcome by the grand music. Captain Frémont, in the meantime, had privately met the revolutionary leaders outside the city to the north and arranged peace-terms, while Commodore Stockton and General Kearny carried on a spirited argument as to which was in command. To the south, General Winfield Scott marched on Mexico City, the Mexicans surrendered, and the Treaty of Guadelupe Hidalgo was signed, giving to the United States Texas and New Mexico, Utah, Nevada, and California. Thus the old *pueblo* of Los Angeles became an American town. In 1850 California was admitted to the Union as a free state, permanently upsetting the equilibrium between the slave and free states which had been carefully preserved up to that time so as to prevent conflict between the North and the South. For his unauthorized independent activities during the siege of Los Angeles, Frémont was court-martialed and resigned from the Army; later he was made governor of the Territory of Arizona and was a candidate for the presidency of the United States.

Before the middle of the nineteenth century Los Angeles began to experience some of the growing pains which the other frontier towns of America had felt. Its dreamy, romantic combination of *pueblo* and *misión* and *rancho* was slowly slipping away, and in its stead was appearing the rough and ready life that characterized all the towns along the American frontier. By 1850 Los Angeles was said to be the toughest town in the country. In 1853, when there were more murders in California than in any other state in the Union, Los Angeles headed the list, and during the first twenty years of American occupation there were thirty-five lynchings in the city, four times as many as were credited to the famous Vigilance Committee of San Francisco. At one time the mayor himself resigned office to head a lynching party, and after the shooting of Sheriff Banton fifty bandits were put in jail and eleven were hanged. In one attack on Chinatown the mob took $40,000 in cash and killed nineteen Chinese. And the *Southern Californian* for March 7, 1855, laconically remarked: "Last Sunday night was a brisk night for killing. Four men were shot and killed and seven wounded."

But, with all its wildness, Los Angeles was becoming something of a commercial center. The Forty-niners on their way to the goldfields of the Sacramento passed through the city from the south and west; it was the central market for cattle, and its population was slowly increasing. Perhaps the largest item in its growth was the demobilization of a force of 1,000 Mormon soldiers from Salt Lake City, who had enlisted with the stipulation that they should settle in California; some of these afterwards purchased the site of San Bernardino from one of the Spanish ranch-owners for $16,000 in fifty-dollar gold slugs. It was about this time that the American residents of Los Angeles began to consider that the future interests of the city demanded the development of the harbor at San Pedro, 30 miles away, and this may be taken as the beginning of the building of the metropolis. From the time of Cabrillo sailors had dreaded this shallow, open harbor, for although Point Fermin protected the anchorage on the west and Catalina Island, 20 miles away, gave some protection on the southwest, there was no protection at all in the southeast, whence came fierce storms which lashed the harbor to a foam and made it a dangerous haven, feared by navigators and disliked by sailors. In his *Two Years before the Mast* Richard Henry Dana tells of his first trip to San Pedro in 1836, when he was a Harvard undergraduate of 19:

Leaving Santa Barbara, we coasted along down, the country appearing level or moderately uneven, and, for the most part, sandy and treeless; until, doubling a high, sandy point, we let go our anchor at a distance of three or three and a half miles from shore. It was like a vessel, bound to Halifax, coming to anchor on the Grand Banks; for the shore being low, appeared to be at a greater distance than it actually was, and we thought we might as well have staid at Santa Barbara, and sent our boat down for the hides. The land was of a clayey consistency, and, as far as the eye could reach, entirely bare of trees and even shrubs; and there was no sign of a town,—not even a house to be seen. . . .

I also learned, to my surprise, that the desolate-looking place we were in was the best place on the whole coast for hides. It was the only port for a distance of eighty miles, and about thirty miles in the interior was a fine plane country, filled with herds of cattle, in the centre of which was the Pueblo de Los Angeles—the largest town in California—and several of the wealthiest missions; to all of which San Pedro was the seaport. . . . Two days more (to our no small joy) gave us our last view of that place, which was universally called the hell of California, and seemed designed, in every way, for the wear and tear of sailors. Not even the last view could bring out one feeling of regret. No thanks, thought I, as we left the sandy shores in the distance, for the hours I have walked over your stones, barefooted, with hides on my head;—for the burdens I have carried up your steep, muddy hill;—for the duckings in your surf; and for the long days and longer nights passed on your desolate hill, watching piles of hides, hearing the sharp bark of your eternal coati, and the dismal hooting of your owls.

The first step toward making Los Angeles a center of trade was to secure recognition of its harbor; so, on May 30, 1850, a memorial to Congress was sent to Senator Thomas H. Benton of Missouri, always a staunch friend of development in the West, begging that San Pedro be made a port of entry. "So numerous and aggravated are the evils which your memorialists suffer for want of a Port of Entry," read the petition, "that they can but feel some little delicacy in bringing them to the notice of your Honorable body. For it is fully believed that in no section of the United States has there ever existed obstructions so serious in character to the prosperity of trade and commerce, and which have been so long and patiently endured by the same number of people as that to which your memorialists are and have been subjected." The petition then went on to recount that the gold-mines were taking the men away from Los Angeles, so that no cultivation of the soil was possible and the city was dependent for bread, peas, beans, oats, and barley on foreign supply. These were brought to San Francisco and reshipped to Los Angeles at enormous cost, the freight-rate for the short distance between San Francisco and San Pedro being twice that from New York to San Francisco, with the rate on flour $10.25 a barrel. It was pointed out that the "people of this region are to a large extent of Spanish descent and race, and whole cargoes of goods would be imported from Mexico and sold at a large advance that are never found at all in the markets of San Francisco in consequence of the population there being so essentially American in character." The petitioners declared that the port would receive "cargoes of rice and coffee from Central America, panocha [brown sugar] from Mexico, flour from Chile, and sugar from Peru." Moreover, the Masters could run their vessels better to San Pedro for there was not the same temptation to desert there as in San Francisco. And they ended in a burst of characteristic optimism: "This region is infinitely superior to any other part of California to sustain a dense population. There is more arable and irrigable land, and the climate, it is fully believed, will compare favorably for salubrity and evenness of temperature with the finest regions of Europe."

When San Pedro was declared a port of entry, by act of Congress, August 3, 1854, the citizens made a beginning at cleaning out the shallow waters to form a harbor at the mouth of Wilmington Creek or Estuary. And Richard Henry Dana, returning in 1859, after 24 years, was able to revise his opinion of Southern California:

The next morning we found ourselves at anchor in the Bay of San Pedro. Here was this hated, this thoroughly detested spot. Although we lay near, I could scarce recognize the hill up which we rolled and dragged and pushed and carried our heavy loads, and down which we pitched the hides, to carry them barefooted over the rocks to the floating long-boat. It was no longer the landing place. One had been made at the head of the Creek, and boats discharged and took off cargoes from a mole or wharf, in a quiet place safe from southeasters. A tug ran to take off passengers from the steamer to the wharf for the trade of Los Angeles is sufficient to support such a vessel. . . . The Pueblo of Los Angeles I found a large and flourishing town with brick sidewalks and blocks of stone or brick houses. . . . The wife of Don Juan, who was a beautiful young girl when we were on the coast, daughter of the Commandant of San Diego, was with him and still handsome. This is one of several instances I have noticed of the preserving quality of the California climate. The vintage of last year was estimated at half a million of gallons. Every year new square miles are laid down to vineyards and the Pueblo promises to be the center of one of the largest wine producing regions in the world. Grapes are a drug here and I found a great abundance of figs, olives, peaches, pears and melons.

Now that the old *pueblo* and its port had shaken off the restrictions of the Spanish and Mexican governments, which had throttled its trade and had kept the settlers from planting the fruits and crops that could also be grown in the mother countries, new ventures were being started which promised prosperity and importance for Los Angeles. Wise men began to see that the future of the city rested on the cultivation of its soil and the development of its makeshift harbor into a deep-water port. Among these was Don Francisco Supelveda, owner of a vast Spanish land-grant at the harbor, the Palos Verdes Ranch, who, with the coming of the Americans, had adapted himself to the new order of things so well that he served in important elective and appointive offices under the new régime, as he had under the old, until the end of his life. A shrewd business man, he saw the possibilities of the port as the only harbor between San Diego and San Francisco, and in 1865 he organized a company to build a wharf at San Pedro. But his activities were insignificant compared with those of the energetic Yankee promoter Colonel Phineas T. Banning, a gentleman of impressive portliness and persuasive oratorical powers, who seems to have been one of the first to develop the rich imaginative faculty peculiar to the Southern Californian. He saw the boundless opportunity of the *pueblo* and its harbor and visualized, as had some of the *padres* before him, one city from the mountains to the sea.

By 1852 the good ship *Sea Bird* was making three round trips a month to San Francisco, "steamer-day" furnished the natives a new mark for measuring the passage of time, and Banning profited from the steamship service by conducting the stage-line that carried the passengers and freight from the harbor to the city. By 1864 he was recognized as the first citizen of the harbor district, and he owned his own newspaper at Wilmington, adjoining San Pedro, through which he sang the praises of Southern California and its port and the necessity for its development. In his fertile brain was born the scheme of building a 30-mile railroad from the harbor to the city, a project so enormous and unprecedented as to stagger the more conservative citizens. But Banning overrode objections and moved ahead with his plans until, in 1863, he secured the passage of an act through the state legislature permitting the city of Los Angeles, which had been chartered in 1850, and the County of Los Angeles, which had been organized in the same year, to bond themselves for $150,000 to build this road. So unprepared was the populace for such a project that he agitated it five years before bringing it to a vote, and then he did so only over the opposition of some of the wealthiest and most substantial citizens, who declared the proposed line to be a madcap scheme which would bankrupt the county, and who conservatively estimated that two trains a month would carry all the freight the railroad would ever obtain. But Banning created enough sentiment in favor of the road so that the bond issue was approved at the election of 1868; the road was opened in November, 1869, and within a few years it was running fifty cars of freight a day. As his share of the resultant prosperity, the Colonel derived a profit from the lighterage business that carried freight and passengers from wharf to ocean-going vessel by tug, charging $1.50 a passenger from ship to shore and sharing in the railroad freight-charge of $6 a ton from Los Angeles to the vessel.

So successful was the Los Angeles and San Pedro enterprise that the old *pueblo* began to long for more railroads, and it looked hopefully towards San Francisco, where the Central Pacific was now running trains from the Golden Gate to the East. A branch line was being pushed southward by the railroad's newly formed subsidiary, the Southern Pacific, but the canny owners made no secret of the fact that they did not anticipate making Los Angeles even a tank town on their new road. They proposed, instead, to shoot off over the desert from Mojave to San Bernardino, many miles away from Los Angeles. However, Messrs. Crocker and Huntington opined that they might change their plans provided certain inducements were offered, these inducements being a subsidy amounting to five per cent of the assessed valuation of the county, or $600,000, a free right of way, and 60 acres in the heart of the city for a depot.

This was quite a large sum for a city of 7,000 population, but when the people looked out into the San Fernando Valley and observed that the towns that had not acceded to the Southern Pacific's suggestion had been ignored by the railroad and left to shrivel and die, they decided to pay what was asked. Amid cries of pain from taxpayers and a flood of letters by Pro Bono Publico declaring that the county was heading straight for ruin by accepting such an enormous obligation, the bond-issue was passed on November 5, 1872; the county paid the road $377,000 in 20-year 7 per cent bonds and donated its stock in the San Pedro railroad to cover the remainder of the subsidy, thereby virtually presenting the Southern Pacific with a monopoly of the rail entry to the harbor of Los Angeles. By the time the Southern Pacific had tunneled the San Fernando Mountains and built over the Tehachapi Pass, which divides southern and northern California, the amount paid by the county was generally considered to be not exorbitant. And when the bonds were finally due, the assessed valuation of the county had increased to $100,000,000, partly by reason of the arrival of the railroad, and the $600,000 seemed a trifle.

To San Francisco and her railroad kings the arrival of the Southern Pacific in Los Angeles was an insignificant incident. To the people of Los Angeles, however, it was a breath-taking event which they had struggled and sacrificed to bring about, and they rightly regarded it as the beginning of a new era. Up to this time the *Angeleños* had had no rail outlet for their products and had been forced to make the long journey to San Francisco by stage in order to take the train for the East. And the metropolis of San Francisco had remained indifferent to the needs of the city or even to its existence. One of the early versifiers has touchingly described the growth of Los Angeles

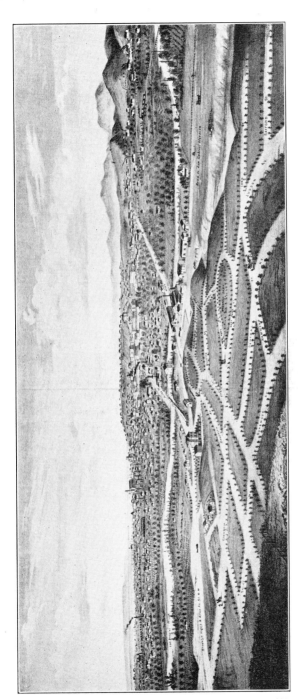

AN EARLY REAL-ESTATE PROMOTION

Los Angeles in 1877, from the east; the Brooklyn Heights subdivision and the Los Angeles River in the foreground; in the background the ocean and the Santa Monica Mountains. Lithograph after a drawing by E. S. Glover, issued by the Brooklyn Land and Building Company. From the Stokes Collection, New York Public Library.

A PALM-LINED STREET IN A MODERN SUBURB

Beverly Hills. Courtesy of the Los Angeles Chamber of Commerce.

A WINTER VISTA IN LOS ANGELES COUNTY

Palms and snow-capped mountains. Courtesy of the Los Angeles Chamber of Commerce.

as aided and abetted by her friends, the cities named for the saints, that cluster around her:

> Francisco the Friar of Grey Orders
> His benison sends from afar,
> And the saints that dwell over the borders
> Most faithful of servitors are.

But he was overly optimistic, for it has not been recorded that San Francisco ever showed any excess of generosity or helpfulness to the city in the south, which she later derisively referred to as "Spring Street and the surrounding lemon orchards." On this gala occasion, however, some fifty San Franciscans joined three hundred and fifty *Angeleños* to celebrate the linking of north and south with rails of steel. On September 6, 1876, at the station of Lang, on the sandy desert dotted with sage-brush, greasewood and pancake cactuses, while the fine sand and black dust of the region blew along in clouds under a high wind, the golden spike was driven. As the visitors looked on, hordes of Chinamen, wearing huge basket hats, swarmed into the open space where 1,000 feet of track was to be laid and completed the job in 8½ minutes, the track-layers from the south beating those from the north by a single rail, much to the delight of the *Angeleños*. Then up stepped Charles Crocker, builder of the Central Pacific and the Southern Pacific, swinging an orange-wood and silver sledge-hammer, and, holding up the golden spike, declared that it was made of this precious metal because it symbolized the vast wealth that would flow into the coffers of San Francisco and Los Angeles—and, he might well have added, the Southern Pacific—when this road should be finished. He dwelt on the beautiful valleys full of prosperous, happy people that would replace the barren desert, and concluded, "I am not a speech maker but I can drive a spike." Six blows of the hammer and the job was done. The portly form of Colonel Phineas T. Banning, known as "the Pathfinder," being seen in the crowd, he was called on for a speech; he told his audience that "If a man is a benefactor who causes two blades of grass to grow where only one grew before, how much more is he who causes grass to grow where none grew before!" after which he flowed smoothly into poetry of his own composition. Perhaps Crocker remembered these noble lines some years later, when, after being kept waiting in an anteroom for several hours by the Los Angeles City Council, he declared in an outburst of rage that he would make the grass grow in the Los Angeles streets.

But this was only the prelude to a banquet which the *Angeleños* had planned with their tenderest care and adorned with their most gorgeous arts and crafts. When the party returned to the city, they entered a hall which was a riot of decoration, worked out in fruits, cornucopias, evergreens, pomegranates, grapes, wines, and roses, with a 58-pound watermelon as the *pièce de résistance*. Floral pieces declared San Francisco and Los Angeles to be sister cities, canaries sang in their cages, vast cakes of ice showed imprisoned fruits and flowers, and the ladies had prepared an illumination which was a fitting precursor of the electric street signs that were to blossom forth so abundantly in the Los Angeles of future years. This was a gorgeously decorated fountain surmounted by a large glass globe, illuminated with copious jets of gas which produced a rich ruby-colored light. From the fountain sixteen separate streams of water were released, falling in drops lighted by the rich ruby reflection "shining with all the hues of the kaleidoscope," much to the astonishment and delight of the spectators.

After having dined sumptuously in this exotic setting, Charles Crocker arose in response to a toast. He said that he was not the orator of his company; he was the worker, and when work was to be done, he took his station at the front; but they had some good speakers who were also entitled to credit, Governor Stanford for instance. With this left-handed compliment he introduced the Governor, who told his listeners that the object of the partners was not to make money alone; certainly not; they all had a roof over their heads and enough to eat, but their wish was to develop an empire, and this could be done only if all the people of California would help them in their great work. Whether the *Angeleños* knew it or not, they were already enlisted in this beneficent project and were mightily to sweat and strain to help the great work of Stanford, Crocker, Huntington, and Hopkins for the rest of their lives.

Perhaps the party had now reached the stage when all could heartily join in the lines of a local poet who had composed some stirring stanzas of song for the occasion:

Let men boast as they will of the wines of Castile,
    Oporto or Isles of Canary,
But since I've been here my opinion is clear,
And from it I never shall vary,
That of all to be proud of with which we're endowed,
And for which we're to thank nature's bounty,
There are none anywhere that are found to compare
With the wines of Los Angeles County.
If you drink the pure wines of Los Angeles vines
You'll ever keep cool, bright and steady
Be rugged in health, have plenty of wealth
As many I know have already.

The visitors from San Francisco were told that in time Los Angeles County would rival some of the most famous nations of Europe in the extent of her wine interests, would equal the interior counties of New York in her cheese-production, and the best Mississippi Valley sections in the growth of corn, wheat, barley, bacon, beef, and mutton. But the editor of the *News* reassured them by saying that they saw in Los Angeles "a young city which is destined to become great but which can never aspire to rival your own superb metropolis."

And, certainly, the Los Angeles of that day never dreamed of approaching the power and prestige of imperial San Francisco. For it was still a small community of a definite Mexican flavor, centered around its historic plaza, producing no crops of much value other than wine grapes—a sleepy, sunny old town, its streets lined with adobe houses, overhung with pepper-trees dropping their red berries in the dust. Gaily clad Mexican *caballeros* rode through the streets, their horses adorned with silver-studded saddles; mule-team freighters dragged their heavy cargoes into the city, and horse-cars jogged pleasantly along under palm and eucalyptus. In the American section huge, ornate white houses of the gingerbread-Mississippi-steamboat style of architecture were set back from the street in verdant lawns, on which disported themselves the iron deer, surrounded by spear-pointed century-plants and hedges of blazing crimson geraniums as high as a man. Up to the time of the arrival of the iron horse the prevailing temper of Los Angeles was the soft and comfortable spirit of *mañana*. But the railroad changed all this overnight.

Assuredly the transportation princes from San Francisco had no thought of Los Angeles as a rival for their metropolis; and, indeed, if the city had resigned itself to the ministrations of Crocker, Stanford, and Huntington, its progress would have been slow. For these gentlemen now began a series of rate-makings which caused Los Angeles to pay heavily for the privilege of being on their railroad line, discriminations which continued even when the road was extended to the east through Yuma. When this line was finally put into operation, Los Angeles merchants thought they would be able to buy cheaper in the East, since the road ran directly into their city; but even then the Southern Pacific arranged the tariff so that they had to pay the equivalent of the rate to San Francisco and back, 974 miles of additional hauling, which was added on paper but not done in fact. The wholesale trade of the state was thus centered at San Francisco, and the Southern Pacific discriminated further by charging so much for freight that Los Angeles could not profitably ship into her own contiguous territory. An example of the railroad's rate-making which grew famous was that given the farmers of San Joaquín, who wanted to ship and sell the castor-beans which grew wild in their county. They harvested and sacked them and piled them along the railroad track waiting shipment. But when they asked the railroad to put a freight-rate on this innocent commodity, it was listed under the extra maximum tariff, along with dangerous blasting-powder and combustibles of the most hazardous kind. Shipment was thus so expensive as to be impossible, the beans were left to rot, and another black mark was chalked up against the Southern Pacific.

Spalding tells of a year when Southern California growers produced a surplus of hay and wished to ship it into Arizona.* The printed schedules did not include this item, and, following a request for the quotation of a rate, the following conversation took place between the hay-dealer and C. F. Smurr, the traffic manager of the Southern Pacific Railway Company:

"What are you paying for hay here?" Smurr asked.

"Twelve dollars a ton," replied the dealer.

"What can you sell it for in Tucson?"

"Twenty dollars."

* William A. Spalding, *History of Los Angeles* (Los Angeles, J. R. Finnell and Company).

"Then," said Smurr, "the rate will be eight dollars a ton."

This was certainly living up to the Southern Pacific policy of charging all the traffic would bear. And discrimination continued, so that in 1885 the *Times* complained that Los Angeles was paying on freight to Yuma nearly twice as much per ton-mile as San Francisco, and to El Paso and Tucson about 50 per cent more; and it remarked, when the fruit-growers petitioned the Southern Pacific to lower the carload rate to New York from $600 to $300, that it appeared to be a mere question of time when the railroad would discover that its true interest lay in the direction of encouraging the fruit industry and making rates as low as possible. About this time the Southern Pacific began to adopt a more conciliatory attitude, for its monopoly of California trade was fast disappearing. It successfully fought Thomas Scott's threatened advance with his Texas and Pacific, but it met a new rival in the Atchison, Topeka and Santa Fe, which was steadily creeping over the plains from the Middle West to California.

This now powerful and prosperous railroad had set out to the Far West over the old Santa Fe Trail, along which pack-mules, ox-wagons, and stage-coaches had successively traveled from the Missouri River to New Mexico. Begun by Cyrus K. Holliday, the man who founded Topeka and made it the capital of Kansas, it was chartered in January, 1859, and was given a grant of 3,000,000 acres of land. This was relatively modest in comparison with the other roads, for the Union Pacific and Central Pacific each got 27,000,000 acres, the Northern Pacific 43,000,000, the Texas and Pacific 23,000,000, and the Southern Pacific 14,000,000. So scanty were the resources of the Santa Fe promoters that when they journeyed to Atchison to organize their company, they took cold lunches and traveled in a hack donated by a Topeka livery-stable. When ground was broken at Topeka in 1868, laughter greeted Holliday's prediction that those present would live to see the road reach Santa Fe. But by 1872 it had built clear across the State of Kansas, one of its division points being the town of Dodge City, with its cattle, buffaloes, Indians, gamblers, murder and sudden death, and it was making large earnings.

The Santa Fe sold its lands profitably through newspaper advertising, by running excursions in June when the fields were full of grain and the corn waist-high, and by importing 15,000 Mennonites who were about to be driven from Russia by Imperial decree. In 1877 William B. Strong became general manager, in 1881 president, and under his direction the road expanded until it was one of the major transportation systems of the country. It purchased the government franchise of the proposed Atlantic and Pacific road, thus gaining access to California, and then the program of expansion began. Its lines reached El Paso, Texas, on May 31, 1881, and were extended to tide-water on the Pacific at the port of Guyamas, Mexico, by October 25, 1882. Building straight west, the Santa Fe reached Needles, a station just across the Arizona line in California, in August, 1883. Alarmed by the aggression of this road and the fact that it already had access to a seaport at Guyamas, from which President Strong threatened to operate a steamship line to San Francisco and San Diego, the Southern Pacific was disposed to be conciliatory. It therefore leased the Santa Fe 140 miles of its track extending westward from Needles to Mojave. At about the center of this stretch of road was Barstow, and from that point the Santa Fe began to build south toward Los Angeles, reaching San Bernardino, 60 miles from Los Angeles, on November 9, 1885.

Meanwhile the Southern Pacific had granted the Santa Fe running rights over its track from Mojave to San Francisco. But the Santa Fe had no intention of depending on this agreement to reach a California harbor. It therefore made arrangements to purchase the California Southern, which had been built by San Diego capitalists northward from their city with the hope of getting a transcontinental railroad connection. Hence, with the completion of the line from Barstow to San Bernardino, the Santa Fe gained its own Pacific outlet at San Diego. Shortly preceding this, on September 24, 1885, the Santa Fe had leased a free and equal use of the Southern Pacific's tracks between Colton and Los Angeles, so that its access to California's three large ports was now complete. In 1887 it extended its own tracks from San Bernardino to Azusa, 25 miles from Los Angeles, connecting these with the Los Angeles and San Gabriel Railroad, which it purchased, thus completing its own tracks into Los Angeles.

As the Santa Fe built westward, the Los Angeles *Times* commented on the fact that the city had grown from 11,300 to 30,000 in five years and added:

Railroad competition is now the one thing required to place the trade of our city on a metropolitan basis and give us all the advantages of an entrepot for the great southwest. ... Our fruit and wine trade will extend throughout the United States. As yet we have only been sending out samples. ... We must have such railroad freights as will justify eastern shipments. The transportation companies must be content with a fair share of the profits, leaving margins for the producer, the shipper and the seller as well. We have seen freights on fruit reduced from $400 per car to $250 and $225. There may be a further reduction to $150 or even $100 per car load without any danger of placing the railroad in the hands of the receiver.

Now for the first time the Southern Pacific felt transcontinental competition. When the Santa Fe asked for 50 per cent of the southern California business and 27 per cent of the northern, the Southern Pacific refused, and the Santa Fe declared war. Freight that had been $5 a ton was cut to 30 cents, passenger fares that were $55 fell to $8. A ticket from Chicago to Los Angeles cost $10; from Kansas City, $5; from New York, $23; and at one time the rate was cut to $1 between Los Angeles and St. Louis. People began to pour into the city; personally conducted "popular Pullman palace parties" arrived from the East, many of whose members decided to stay and gave away their return tickets or even burned them. The Santa Fe advertised California everywhere, and the Southern Pacific was forced to follow suit.

Never willing to hide her light under a bushel, Los Angeles had set up a tremendous flare wherever it might be seen in the East and Middle West, with such dazzling effect that the San José *Times Mercury* declared on April 4, 1885:

Our brethren of the city and would-be state of the Angels understand how to advertise. The average eastern mind conceives of California as a small tract of country situated in and about Los Angeles. The mines, parks, vineyards, and redwood forests are all there or thereabouts. ... Circulars, posters, pamphlets, all singing the praises of Los Angeles were distributed by millions; and all our ultramontane brethren whose lives have been spared through the recent awful winter are vowing that as soon as they can sell out they will emigrate to Los Angeles. The result shows the pecuniary value of cheek. Suburban lots at Los Angeles are worth a prince's ransom, and the appalling waste of alkali and sage brush in which the angels have built their city is almost as valuable to sell as our rich willow lands.

The advertising of the city and the competitive railroads combined with cheap fares to produce the great boom, a boom which made previous land speculations in the Middle West look like very small potatoes indeed, which even surpassed in extravagant grandeur that early financial fantasy, the Mississippi Bubble. For John Law amazed Europe by selling his colony in Louisiana at $5,500 a square league, whereas Los Angeles land sold at $2,500 an acre or $14,400,000 a square league; and the $15,000,000 capital stock of John Law's bank was equaled by the sales of Los Angeles real estate in a single month. Low railroad fares brought tourists and settlers in such numbers that the hotels were flooded and it was not uncommon for guests to sleep in bathtubs; promoters from Kansas and other former boom states flocked in; and the increase in land values and sales, which started in an orderly and conservative way when the Santa Fe arrived, began to leap in geometrical progression. The rich verbiage of the professional promoter and the beauty of the lithographer's art combined to portray the glories of Southern California in brochures and broadsides marked by all the shrinking reticence and modest understatement of the publicity for a circus.

In the spring of 1887, as the Santa Fe approached Los Angeles, towns were laid out along the route until there were twenty-five between the city to the county line, an average of one to each mile and a half. Eight more towns were platted on the parallel line of the Southern Pacific, and three others between the roads. Nor were the promoters niggardly in their use of the raw land: Monrovia was eight square miles in extent, Pasadena the same; Chicago Park occupied 3,000 choice lots in the rocky wash of the San Gabriel River. "Picturesque Carlton, Nature's Rendezvous," was precariously perched on the Santa Ana Mountains, so far removed from civilization that water had to be hauled in by wagons; yet its promoters declared that a sumptuous tourist hotel was already rising, along with a massive bank and safety-deposit vault. The promoters of Gladstone presented England's prime minister with a building site and gave the impression that his arrival to build a winter home on his property was imminent. An exceptionally gifted promoter named Homberg laid out Border City and Manchester on the mountains at the edge of the Mojave Desert, easily accessible by balloon and field-glass, and sold lots by mail to eager purchasers, who, it is to be hoped, were spared the pain of attempting to visit their property. Customers who bought during the boom were not unduly particular about the details of their purchases. The fact that most of the lots, even in the remote subdivisions, were only 25 by 100 feet did not bother them; and Mr. Homberg even went so far as to carve 2,304 lots out of 160 acres— the cost of the land being 10 cents a lot, the sale price as high as $200.

On came the new Californians—rich Eastern emigrants in palace-cars instead of the traditional prairie-schooners; Iowa farmers who had tired of getting up early to thaw out the pump on chilly mornings and who longed to settle down to a life of ease, untroubled by rheumatism, amid the orange-groves; and invalids in search of life-giving sun and balmy air. Most of them had money to invest, and they eagerly read the real-estate news in the daily papers, which also contained complete lists of the names and addresses of every excursion party, much to the delight of the visitors and the refreshment of realtors engaged in making out sucker-lists. These newspapers were interlaced with full-page advertisements declaring Garvanza to be the loveliest spot in Pasadena, a five-minute walk from the street-car line (soon to be built), and stating that Boyle Heights was free from malaria, fanned by ocean breezes from San Pedro untainted by being blown over the city, and served by a cable line (to be built in a short time), the advertisement closing with the pointed remark that "During the rainy season you do not require boats to travel in the streets at Boyle Heights." Advertisements set forth in bold-face such undoubted facts as, "You will get Fat at Rosecranz," "Buy land in Los Angeles and Wear Diamonds"; and one well-named city, Ballona, located in a swamp, boasted of its "harbor." When the sale of lots at the town of Azusa opened, buyers stood in line all night; the second man in the queue sold his place for $1,000, the third man his for $500, and fifty-four others theirs for $100 or more, while number one, deaf to all offers, clung stubbornly to the door-handle. In this development $280,000 worth of lots were sold the first day to frenzied speculators, of whom "not one in ten had ever seen the place and not one in a hundred intended to live there."

In his *Millionaires For a Day* T. S. Van Dyke describes how lots were sold at Elysian Heights, where prospective purchasers were entertained by a brass band attired in purple and gold, led by a drum-major with a gilded staff, and were fed by a caterer in a dress-suit with a white necktie and a diamond pin.

Hundreds of people were already on the ground, and barouches and broughams drawn by sleek horses in silver plated harness, driven by combinations of silk hats, white neckties and dog-skin gloves, were steadily unloading fat old bankers with their wives and daughters, retired merchants and stock brokers, grain dealers, liquor dealers, lawyers and doctors out for a picnic at the expense of a stranger.... The auctioneer, arrayed in costly garb, was an ex-minister of the Gospel, who had been lured from the path of duty by the superior attractions of the rising real estate market.... The owner knew by long experience that the race of real estate buyers are the silliest of sheep, and need leading even to their own good. And the auctioneer had been so often impressed with the sheeplike nature of man, while trying to lead another kind of sheep to another kind of welfare, that he had no scruples about enveigling the crowd into what his conscience told him was really a fine bargain. So he had a dozen assistants distributed judiciously about the audience, none of whom were supposed to know one another or the auctioneer. Some were provided with gold coin to jingle on the table when they made their payments, while others, who looked like business men, had check books. All asked numerous questions about the country, its resources and prospects before the sale began.

After the band had nearly raised the roof off an immense live oak, under which it was stationed, the auctioneer mounted the stand, announced the terms of sale, and pointing to a large cloth map on which a boy had located a lot with a long fishing-pole, said, "Now ladies and gentlemen, here is one of the finest lots in the whole tract, with the privilege of taking the next two at the same price. Give me a bid now, quick."

"A hundred dollars," called out a middle aged man in gold spectacles, silk hat and toothpick shoes.

All eyes were turned upon him, but he withstood their gaze without flinching. None suspected that he was an assistant. But he was, and had been in such haste to bid, for fear the owner of some rival addition would offer five or ten dollars so as to spoil the sale that he forgot his instructions and bid fifty dollars less than he had been told.

"I am not selling you the map," said the auctioneer in a withering tone. "It is a fifty-foot lot I am offering you!"

"One hundred and fifty," said another man, quietly and with the solemn dignity becoming a genuine buyer of wealth and standing.

"One hundred and fifty only! Why, gentlemen, this is positively ridiculous. These lots will bring a thousand dollars apiece in less than six months. Still, they have to go. This sale is positively without reserve," said the auctioneer with an air of despondency. "One fifty-fifty, fifty; give us two hundred, now quick."

Under such methods the sale proceeded to arouse the enthusiasm of even the most tepid of the visitors, and by the time of sundown the owner had sold one-fifth of the property for more than he had contracted to pay for the whole of it, while the buyers were eagerly looking for other buyers on whom to unload at a profit.

By 1887 the boom had reached its height. Speculation was rampant, thousands of new-comers kept flooding in; there was no longer any need for guarantees of railroads, waterworks, colleges, or hotels, no necessity for abstracts, or even the showing of lots. All that was needed was a map with some plots marked "sold" and a notice: "Prices raised twenty per cent to-morrow," a collection of 25-foot lots, and clerks to fill out bills of sale. The realtor simply bought, for $10 or $20 an acre, waterless tracts, and sold them, divided into lots, for from $1,000 to $10,000 an acre. An advertisement designed to lure the tired business man is typical of the times:

Rowena is the loveliest of spots for the rest of man after the busy toil of daily labor. Each under his own fig tree was the sum total of the ancients' happiness, and now is offered to the weary and the rest-seeker a land which will enable him to be where the wicked cease from troubling and the weary can rest in the eventide. There is no drawback to Rowena! You need not till the soil. You can look on while the earth sends forth her plenty. Flowers, the first luxury that nature knew, in Eden's pure and guiltless garden grew, at Rowena!

After looking somewhat longingly at the amazing flood of dollars pouring into Los Angeles County, the editor of the Oakland *Tribune* laid down this formula for producing a local boom:

Begin digging a duck pond at Mowry's landing, call it a harbor for the white winged argosies of commerce, big enough to float the combined commercial fleets of the world. Organize three competing railroads to run their lines into the duck pond. Lay out a town, all corner lots, at the Fish ranch, and have a line of eager buyers camp all night outside the auctioneer's office waiting to buy themselves rich. Season liberally with brass bands, free lunches and windy speeches. That is the way they do it down south and it pays. The man who discovered that it costs nothing to own an incorporated company with a name a yard long was a great inventor. Los Angeles rises up and calls him blest.

The ridiculous aspect of some of the suburban promotion was apparent even in Los Angeles itself, where a dealer in metropolitan real estate satirized it in the following circular:

BOOM! BOOM! BOOM!

*The newest town out! Balderdash! Watch for it! Wait for it! Catch on to it!*

To meet the great demand for another new townsite we have secured 10,000 acres of that beautiful land lying on the top of Old Baldy, and will lay out an elegant town with the above very significant and appropriate name. The land is away up and has attracted more attention than any other spot in Southern California. Nine thousand acres will be at once divided into fine business lots 14x33 feet. All lots will front on grand avenues 17 feet wide and run back to 18 inch alleys. For the present one-tenth of the entire tract will be reserved for residences in case anyone should want to build, but judging from the success of other similar schemes none of it will be needed for this purpose. To accommodate the inquisitive who are afraid to invest without inspecting the property a fast balloon line will be started in the near future. Parties will be permitted to return on the superb toboggan slide to be built in the sweet bye and bye. All lots will be sold at a uniform price of $1100 each. This is considered a very low price for such high lands but the projectors of the scheme are philanthropists and are willing to sell at very close figures and give purchasers the benefit of the rise. All offers for lots will be refused previous to day of sale, and in order that all may have a chance no person will be permitted to buy more than 500 lots. Free lunches and cots will be offered to those who want to camp in front of the office a few days previous to the opening of the sale.

It was during these years that E. J. ("Lucky") Baldwin was developing his enormous Santa Anita Ranch and stables at Lamanda Park. Baldwin had owned a livery-stable in San Francisco and had made his first big strike at fortune when he bought 1,000 shares of stock in the Crown Point Mine on the Comstock Lode at $3 a share. When the price declined, he told his broker to sell when it again touched $3, but he sailed for China without leaving power of attorney; the stock could not be sold, and when he returned, it had multiplied in value to make him a millionaire. His brokers then decided to make some money for themselves by selling him $500,000 worth of the Ophir Mine at $10 a share, and in a short time the big bonanza came in. When the Bank of California tried to get his broker to vote Baldwin's stock in its favor, he was angered and sold out at the top price of $300, after which the bubble burst. He built a hotel and a gorgeous theater in San Francisco, and when no others would lend to the Temple and Workman bank in Los Angeles, Baldwin did. In return, when the bank failed, he got its large holdings of Southern California property, then considered worthless but later to be of great value, including the Santa Anita Ranch which he so developed as to make it famous.

Many other strange geniuses were attracted to Los Angeles in the Eighties. Charles F. Lummis, the writer, who was to turn out numerous books on the Southwest, arrived on foot, after traveling 3,507 miles from Cincinnati in 143 days, to be city editor of the Los Angeles *Times*. There came also Helen Hunt Jackson, who told the world of the wonders of California and began to write her novel *Ramona*. With her, as another United States commissioner to examine Indian affairs, came Abbott Kinney, world traveler, relative of Holmes and Emerson, and, at the time, health-seeker, who settled in Sierra Madre. Twenty years later he developed the seaside city of Venice, modeled after its ancient namesake, utilizing its worthless tide-lands to construct winding canals on which floated imported gondolas manned by imported gondoliers. He spanned the canals with graceful bridges and lined them with exotic buildings, among which were an auditorium with a pipe-organ, a glassed-in plunge, and a ship café. He planned to make this resort the home of the wealthy, cultured, and romantic; but his dreams of playgrounds, fine music, opera, and lectures for the masses faded away, and in later years Venice became, instead, a successful amusement park, where the shrieks of the roller-coaster addicts mingled with the odor of the succulent hot dog and the raucous cry of the side-show barker.

In the Eighties, too, came General Frémont, appointed Governor of Arizona, to marvel at the changes of 30 years, and before the boom was over so many other celebrities that the town could not keep track of them. The *Times* undertook to classify those who should not come to Los Angeles: "dudes, loafers, paupers, those who expect to astonish the natives, those who are afraid to pull off their coats, cheap politicians, business scrubs, impecunious clerks, lawyers, and doctors." But the flood continued, and late in 1887 the *Times* sounded a mild warning to the buyers of real estate in boom towns outside the metropolis: "Beware of being the last man in the line of speculators. Beware of being caught in a speculator's town"; and Eastern papers were freely predicting the end of the Southern California boom. Most of the speculators drove blindly on, however, in full confidence that prices would continue rising to the point they desired and then give them due notice of their intention to stop. It was not a boom at all, they said, but only a sudden recognition of what the world had long been looking for and had just found. Van Dyke records some of the conversations typical of the times:

"This is now the central point of a thousand converging lines from every town, city, and hamlet in the United States," said General Theophilius Turkeytail, who had made three millions on the boom, looking down with the air of a St. Bernard, examining a little whiffet of a man who had made only half a million out of nothing. "She is going by her own momentum, sir. We have 60 million people on this side of the Atlantic, sir, and when the supply is exhausted there are lots more on the other side." And the smaller millionaire looked gratefully up into the great wise countenance, drew a long breath of satisfaction, and went off to buy something more on credit, to increase his load when the day of reckoning came.

"I always knew it would be so," said General Spraddlebuck, who for several years before the boom had been vainly trying to sell his town lots for one-fourth what they cost him ten years before, so as to be able to go to another town, but who was now, according to the newspapers, "a great enterprising and progressive citizen, whose undying faith in our beautiful city has made him rich."

"We have thought at times that we were going too fast, but we have been merely trembling at the shadow of our own greatness," said the Rev. Solomon Sunrise, who, on week days had been more successful in getting a cheap option on a piece of valuable property than in beating the devil out of an immortal soul on Sundays. "We have but girded our loins for the race, and are now running like a strong man rejoicing in his strength, knowing no fear."

"What! Can that lot on Banana Street be bought for $20,000? It seems incredible!"

"What do you think of the situation? How long is it going to last?"

"Well," said the banker with the ponderous gravity of utterance becoming the wisdom of wealth, "I can't fully agree with those who think it is going to last forever. But I am satisfied that the top is still a long way off. I am holding on to every thing I have, and I see no special cause for doing otherwise. Of course I would not advise any one to buy what he cannot pay for; but I see no reason for sacrificing anything, and to sell now before winter is certainly to sacrifice."

As 1888 approached, there were many who felt that they would like to see some of the money and energy being spent on laying out towns diverted into the more productive channels of developing natural resources, establishing factories, and seeking out and securing water-supplies for the dry, unproductive lands. In January there was a slight slump; people were not quite so eager to buy. Soon there seemed to be more private holdings appearing in the market than usual. Suddenly the market was full of sellers with no one offering to buy. Then the panic began, and the boom was over. To a less favored territory the slump might well have been fatal, but when the casualties were all counted, it was found that Los Angeles had gained much in the period of inflation. She had thousands of new and moneyed citizens as permanent residents; she had thousands of acres of outlying agricultural lands planted to fruit-trees; she had made comprehensive plans for the development of a great city. Because of the slump in real estate many of the remote "cities" of Los Angeles County, an area as large as some Eastern states, were sold for taxes and put under the plow to be a productive source of income for Southern California; and when materials and labor dropped to low prices, people began building substantial houses. Not a single bank failed, and the Security Trust and Savings Bank, which was destined to become one of the great banks of the nation, was founded at this time. Capital believed that it was a good time to start things, for values had at last reached rock bottom. Street improvements, cable roads, irrigation works, long needed, were developed, and the town took fresh courage when a new group of Chicago capitalists came in and built a large office-building on Spring Street. Nothing could stop the growth of Southern California!

# CHAPTER XI

ALTHOUGH the Franciscan fathers planted oranges as well as figs, grapes, and olives, the growing of citrus fruits did not soon become an industry of importance, and before 1875 "nothing worthy of the name of orange had been produced in California." The orange was thick-skinned, sour, puffy, dry, and the dry, spongy lemons had skin half an inch thick. The farmers did not yet understand how to use the California soil. Their work was "a combination of laziness, imitation of Mexican methods and general shiftlessness and ignorance of the peculiarities of California." Before the penetration of the railroads there was no market for oranges except San Francisco, and hence no encouragement for growing the fruit. Furthermore, the Californians had not yet discovered that apparently worthless, barren, dry upland regions could be made amazingly fertile by irrigation and were actually far superior to the valley land in productivity. But after the collapse of the real-estate boom Southern California found the slowly, surely developing citrus industry to be one of her most valuable assets.

After the secularization of the missions in 1834, their orange-groves deteriorated, and 12 years later Frémont wrote that little remained of them. A few seeds from Central America and Hawaii were planted at various places, but it was not until 1873 that the growing of oranges had its real beginning through the introduction of the Washington navel orange from Bahia, Brazil, by the United States Department of Agriculture. Having received from Bahia a letter mentioning a seedless orange of large size and fine flavor, the Department asked for cuttings and received a small box of orange twigs, utterly dry and useless. The Department then offered to pay for grafting a few buds on young stocks, and ultimately a box arrived from Rev. F. I. C. Schneider, the first Presbyterian missionary to Bahia, containing twelve newly-budded trees. There was a supply of young orange stocks in the Department, and as fast as buds were secured, they were grafted on these stocks. The first two young plants were sent to Mrs. L. C. Tibbetts of Riverside, California, who had called at the office in Washington and asked for them. They prospered with her, and when they bore fruit of large size and fine appearance, it was called the Riverside Navel, a name which was afterwards changed to the Washington Navel by other Californians who did not wish to advertise the town of Riverside. Planted in the dooryard of her home, the trees attracted attention on account of the size, quality, and seedlessness of the fruit, and their superiority led to the rapid propagation of this variety in and near Riverside. So profitable was the sale of buds that the trees were surrounded by high barbed-wire fences to prevent the thieving of budwood from them. And the fruit from the pioneer orchards propagated from these trees laid the foundation for the subsequent development and commercial success of the entire citrus industry of California. An orange-tree from the original parent trees was planted in the courtyard of the Mission Inn at Riverside by President Theodore Roosevelt on May 8, 1903.

In 1884 the California orange created consternation in the hearts of Florida fruit-growers exhibiting at the New Orleans exposition. When the Los Angeles contingent saw that Florida was about to capture the premiums, they induced the judges to wait for their exhibit, meanwhile paying the expenses of the Florida exhibitors in order to induce them to remain. And when the luscious, golden California fruit arrived, the Floridans had to wrap their pale oranges in green and crimson tissue-paper to prevent an unfavorable contrast, and California took practically all the first prizes. The rivalry that started then continued, and Los Angeles newspapers never lost an opportunity of playing up storms, hurricanes, and disasters in "Frosted Florida." In 1885, with the coming to California of the Santa Fe and its promotion work, there began a period of wholesale planting of orange-groves. T. S. Van Dyke describes the contrast between conditions in the Seventies and the Eighties on one ranch. On his first visit there was 60 acres of land on a little creek, indifferently cultivated with what the owner called "irritating ditches," because he said they were the most irritating things on earth; there were a few hives of bees, and there was a poor house of rough lumber mounted on stilts, set full in the sun. In 1885, ten years later, the new owner of this same property had built above the valley on a broad knoll, once cactus-covered, a handsome house surrounded by hedges of lime, cypress, and pomegranate and India-rubber, camphor, and other tropical trees. The garden was a profusion of geranium, fuchsias, heliotrope, roses, and honeysuckles; the orchard showed long, regular lines of orange-, lemon-, and olive-trees; while in the vineyard there were thirty varieties of grapes. The stream had been diverted with a concrete tunnel and cement-lined ditches, the barren hillside bloomed, and the sad gray land had been turned into a maze of green, while the plow had turned up rich chocolate-colored loam under the sand.

This was the story of thousands of Southern California fruit-ranches. Returns were large, as much as $3,000 having been made in one year from a single acre. Land prices shot up, irrigation projects flourished, and in 1886 2,250 carloads of oranges and lemons were sold. In the Nineties, however, the California orange-growers began to experience financial trouble. To the country at large, oranges were a luxury to be indulged in only at Thanksgiving and Christmas or on some gala occasion, and not a staple article of diet; commission-merchants were more interested in their own profits than in those of the farmers; the railroads had no fast fruit-express service, and refrigerator cars were not developed, so the crop was often sold at small profit or a loss. To obviate these conditions the growers started the coöperative association that became the California Fruit Growers Exchange. Branch sales-offices were established in all large cities, members delivered their entire crops to the association, and the industry was financially stabilized. In 1905 the president, Francis Q. Story, initiated an advertising campaign in Iowa; the Southern Pacific coöperated by sending the fruit in trains adorned with banners, accompanied by much newspaper publicity; bill-boards carried the slogan, "Oranges For Health—California For Wealth"; and as a result the consumption of oranges in Iowa was greatly increased. Indeed, so successful was this state campaign that it was expanded to cover the whole country, and the trade-name "Sunkist" was adopted.

Meanwhile, Mr. Story was busily engaged in improving growing and packing conditions in California; he led the growers in devising better methods of handling, in fumigating trees, substituting sharp clippers for hand-picking, installing rotary brushes to clean the fruit, adopting grading by machinery and wrapping in tissue-paper. In order to keep the identifying wrappers and name on the fruit until it was sold, the association offered consumers a silver orange-spoon in return for twelve wrappers and twelve cents. When the orange-growing industry had become an outstanding commercial success, an interviewer seeking to discover the reasons asked Mr. Story what the "Q" in his name stood for; he replied, "Quality," a word which summed up all that he had put into the industry. The association now ships 150,000 carloads of fruit a year, owns plants for utilizing surplus fruit in making various chemical and flavoring products, and operates a factory for making the electric juice-extractors which have done much to increase the use of citrus fruits in soda-fountains and homes. The California Fruit Growers Exchange has been a major factor in the prosperity of Southern California, and one of the most successful co-operative enterprises in the world.

But the activities of Los Angeles civic leaders were many-sided. Not only did they include the building up of the citrus industry and the encouragement of other crops which made Los Angeles County the richest agricultural county in the United States. The coming of factories and industries was always actively encouraged; the need for ample rail connections with the outside world was never overlooked; and the opening of Los Angeles to the commerce of the sea through the development of a harbor was a project long uppermost in the minds of her citizens.

It was the indefatigable Phineas T. Banning and a few others who, in 1869, induced Major Robert S. Williamson of the Army Corps of Engineers to make a survey of the shallow harbor of San Pedro to see what could be done towards bettering it. As result of his report Congress the next year appropriated $200,000 to straighten and deepen Wilmington Creek and to remove the shoal at its entrance so as to accommodate small coastwise vessels. Even if a few far-sighted pioneers guessed that this modest undertaking meant the beginning of a great ocean commerce for Los Angeles, the community as a whole was but tepidly interested, and many of the old settlers "figured that the Government must have a great deal of money to waste if it could spend so many thousands of dollars on a useless mudhole like the Wilmington Lagoon."

Nevertheless, the backers of the project persisted at each session of Congress; and by 1892 the inner harbor had received twelve small appropriations totaling something over $500,000, the Wilmington Estuary had been improved so that four-masted schooners drawing more than 18 feet could be accommodated, and the government customs collections at the port almost equaled the cost of construction. In 1881 Stanford, then president of the Southern Pacific, inquired if the harbor could care for vessels of 20,000 tons, such as he proposed to put in service to the Orient, and was told that, although the inner harbor on the Wilmington Estuary could not, it would easily be possible to construct an ocean breakwater to make the outer harbor of San Pedro capable of caring for vessels of any size.

But the prospect of making a really great port for Los Angeles was not bright, and certainly at this time no one in the harbor cities of San Francisco or San Diego would have considered it seriously. The sea-going aspiration of Los Angeles, Queen of the Cow Counties, was a joke. But the people of the community were in earnest, and in 1881 they formed a Chamber of Commerce, which Secretary Frank Wiggins later made one of the most potent in the United States, with the avowed purpose of developing a deep-water harbor at San Pedro. Whenever a Representative or Senator arrived within hailing distance of Los Angeles, this organization would seize him and transport him to the harbor, while the boosters bombarded him with propaganda concerning the future greatness of the city and its foreign trade. One such visitor was Senator William P. Frye of Maine, of the Committee on Commerce, and as he stood on the barren San Pedro headlands after the 30-mile ride from Los Angeles, his reaction was not much more favorable than that of young Dana on his first trip.

"Why, where are all the ships?" inquired the Senator from Maine. "As near as I can make out, you propose to ask the Government to create a harbor for you almost out of whole cloth. The Lord has not given you much to start with, that is certain. It will cost four or five millions to build, you say; well, is your whole country worth that much?" At this harsh speech the boosters' committee sought to explain how Southern California was destined to become great and to assume

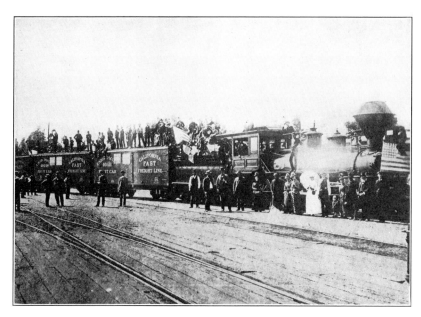

THE FIRST SPECIAL FAST FRUIT TRAIN FROM SOUTHERN CALIFORNIA
June 24, 1886. Courtesy of the Union Pacific Railroad.

AN ORANGE GROVE IN LOS ANGELES COUNTY
Courtesy of the Los Angeles Chamber of Commerce.

LOS ANGELES HARBOR

Courtesy of the Los Angeles Chamber of Commerce.

THE LOS ANGELES AQUEDUCT

Courtesy of the Los Angeles Chamber of Commerce.

major importance as a center for Oriental trade. But the Senator replied with awful jocularity, "Well, it seems you have made a great
mistake in the location of your city. If you Los Angeles people want
a harbor, why not move the city down to San Diego? There is a good
harbor there."

Despite the unfavorable opinion of the Senator from Maine, however, in 1890 Congress was induced to grant $5,000 for a survey of a
deep-water harbor project for Los Angeles, and a commission came
west to examine the possible sites and to hold public hearings. Although there is no natural deep-water harbor along the coast near
Los Angeles, there are several points where artificial harbors might be
constructed. One of these is Santa Monica, developed by Senator
John P. Jones of Nevada, who, having made a fortune in the Comstock
Lode, where he started as a mine superintendent, had some years
previously formed a scheme to develop silver-mines in the Panamint
Mountains. So confident was he that these mines on the edge of Death
Valley would rival the Comstock that he looked around for a seaport
in Southern California from which to ship his ore. Santa Monica was
his choice, and there he laid out a town and built a wharf and a railroad to Los Angeles. But the mines never produced, the road was sold
to the Southern Pacific, and Senator Jones recouped his depleted
fortune by booming Santa Monica as a seaside resort. Another possibility was Redondo, near-by, where the Portland capitalist Captain
John C. Ainsworth had built a wharf, connected by a narrow-gage railway with Los Angeles. The third was the old port of San Pedro, served
by the Southern Pacific, where the Terminal Railroad Company also
had acquired trackage rights with the purpose of permitting other
railroads to use its tracks to get access to the harbor. The Congressional commission, having considered the various sites, decided San
Pedro to be the most desirable, estimating that a favorable deep-
water harbor could be made there by spending about $4,000,000 for
a breakwater.

Now the people of Los Angeles were ready to go forward with the
project so near to their hearts. They would have their harbor at San
Pedro, and that speedily, just as the government engineers had recommended. But they reckoned without Collis P. Huntington, who had
become interested in getting a port for Los Angeles when the Southern

Pacific began to fear competition from the northern railroads reaching the coast at Portland, Tacoma, and Seattle. At this juncture he contrasted the advantages of having a harbor that all railroads might enter with one controlled exclusively by the Southern Pacific; and in 1892 he informed the Senate that the San Pedro harbor was not suitable because the ground was so rocky that piles could not be driven into it, and that the railroad was therefore abandoning its wharf there and building at Santa Monica. A board of five Army officers was appointed to examine the proposed sites, and again the decision was in favor of San Pedro. But Huntington went on building his million-dollar pier at Santa Monica, and his representative, addressing a Los Angeles Chamber of Commerce banquet, suavely remarked, "Somewhere on your border there is to be a harbor, and I am asked a question regarding Santa Monica, and the intentions of our people. To be frank with you, I will say that their intentions seem entirely apparent. They are making a wharf there for deep-water vessels. They must intend to land at the wharf with deep-water vessels."

At this point, Harrison Gray Otis, owner of the Los Angeles *Times*, entered the controversy, putting his newspaper actively behind the San Pedro project and declaring that Congress should not appropriate money, against the advice of its experts, for a harbor that would benefit only one corporation. Huntington added to the general unrest at a Chamber of Commerce conference by declaring,

You people are making a big mistake in supporting this San Pedro appropriation. The Rivers and Harbors Committee of the House will never report in favor of that place—not in a thousand years. I know them all and I have talked to them about the matter. Now, I propose to be frank with you people. I do not find it to my advantage to have the harbor built at San Pedro and I shall be compelled to oppose all efforts to secure appropriations for that site; on the other hand, the Santa Monica location will suit me perfectly, and if you folks will get in and work for that, you will find me on your side—and I think I have some little influence at Washington—as much as some other people, perhaps.

And he concluded his talk by banging on the table and saying, "Well, I don't know for sure that I can get this money for Santa Monica; I think I can. But I know damned well that you shall never get a cent for that other place."

Although faced with this powerful opposition, the Chamber of Commerce voted on the two sites and again decided in favor of San Pedro; but Huntington succeeded in getting the House Committee to consider his plea for a $4,000,000 breakwater at Santa Monica. The Chamber of Commerce objected, the Santa Fe protested that it would not have free access to Huntington's harbor, the Senate voted to postpone action for a year, and the New York *World* inquired, "Is this a government for the people, or a government by Mr. Huntington, for Mr. Huntington? The question may as well be settled in the Santa Monica-San Pedro controversy as anywhere."

In Los Angeles the Free Harbor League was organized, and there was a campaign to get citizens to write their old Congressmen "back east," inquiring how long a crafty corporation could defraud the people of their right to a free harbor. Public finances were so low in 1896 that it was held impossible to get a large appropriation for San Pedro, so California contented itself with asking for $390,000 to continue work on the inner harbor. But again they reckoned without Huntington and the magic his name worked in Congressional committee-rooms. When the Rivers and Harbors bill was reported to the House, the people were astounded to find an item of $2,900,000 for a breakwater at Santa Monica; moreover, the House Committee said that if Southern California would not accept this, the San Pedro item would be stricken out also. The fight was carried to the Senate by Senator Stephen M. White, where, over Huntington's opposition, another commission was appointed which was to decide where the $2,900,000 appropriation was to be spent. Again the decision was in favor of San Pedro. So, ironically enough, the money wangled out of an economy Congress by the powerful Huntington was appropriated for the benefit of the rival harbor.

Far from being licked, however, Uncle Collis persisted in his obstruction, hoping to throw the matter back into Congress where he could defeat it. Secretary of War Russell A. Alger declared that the bill of 1896 was not clear and that it had not taken account of sunken rocks at the entrance of the harbor; and when the Senate ordered him to proceed to call for bids, he refused, saying that the request should have come also from the House. When he said he had no money to advertise for bids, Los Angeles newspapers offered to pay the costs; but this the Secretary thought would be undignified. Alger twice appealed to the Attorney-General for an opinion, and he succeeded in delaying matters two years before President McKinley ordered him to proceed immediately. Finally, in 1898, when the item making an initial appropriation of $400,000 for the construction of San Pedro harbor was reached in the appropriation bill in the House, Charles H. Grosvenor of Ohio rose to say that private enterprise—meaning Mr. Huntington—would build a harbor free of charge in the immediate vicinity—meaning Santa Monica,—and he suggested that the appropriation be postponed. Whereupon Harry A. Cooper of Wisconsin rose and said,

This matter of San Pedro harbor is to me in many respects the most astonishing I have ever encountered since I have had a seat in this House. I do not believe it ever had its counterpart in the legislative history of the country.... Is it not strange that after two boards of Engineers had said that San Pedro was the only place to improve, nevertheless, the provision was inserted in the bill of the last session for the improvement of Santa Monica? ... It is time that people who propose to fight as these have, violating every precedent, should be taught a lesson that the patience of the American people on this subject has been exhausted.

Thus ended the free-harbor fight, a fight which called out the courage and perseverance of the people in strongest measure and gave them a schooling in what could be done by determined coöperation which was to bear fruit for a generation in the building of a greater Los Angeles. In April, 1899, President McKinley touched a button which was to set in motion the machinery that should dump the first bargeload of rock for the breakwater; but the mechanism failed to work, and the stone had to be laboriously pushed off by hand—an episode which Charles D. Willard said was symbolic of the entire undertaking: "Nothing about it had come easily; it was all hard work, and but for the most tremendous individual and community exertion, it could never have been accomplished." For his efforts on behalf of the project, as secretary of the Chamber of Commerce, Mr. Willard received a loving-cup, and the people erected a tablet on the building of the Los Angeles *Times* in appreciation of its effective service in the contest for a free harbor.

The port of Los Angeles, wrested from an unfavorable coastline by an ambitious people, is now one of the nation's greatest. A maze of wharves and terminals lines its shores, and it is open to every railroad that enters the city. From the day when Wilmington Estuary had a bar over which the water was only 18 inches deep at low tide, the shallow mud-flats have been dredged and developed and the harbor protected until ships of any size and draft can be accommodated. And the people of Los Angeles County, having added $30,000,000 worth of improvements to the Government's $11,000,000, are now spending $7,000,000 more to extend the breakwater to protect the combined harbor of San Pedro and Long Beach.

With the building of her harbor Los Angeles was on the way to becoming a great metropolis. The Southern Pacific and the Santa Fe took her products to all parts of the country, her steamship lines began to reach out to the Orient. Her hinterland was developing into one of the richest agricultural districts in the world. Her climate attracted and her industries supported a growing population. But there was one portentous bar to her future progress. Not much was said about it, but to some of her wise men it was a nightmare—the thought that the city was permanently limited and forever endangered by lack of water.

By 1900 Los Angeles was reaching the limit of her water-supply; every apparent source was being tapped, and there was no more in sight. Already the underground water of the region was being overdrawn by the irrigated districts of Southern California, and for Los Angeles to make further inroads on that source would interfere with agriculture and the city's own prosperity. But one man, Fred Eaton, former mayor and former city engineer, was quietly working out a solution, and in 1905 he confided it to William Mulholland, city engineer. It was no less than a spectacular plan to pierce the Sierras and build across desert and mountains an aqueduct 250 miles long to bring water to Los Angeles from Owens Lake, a dead sea in the Inyo Desert.

On various trips to this district Eaton had noticed the bed of a prehistoric river that had once run out of Owens Lake to the Mojave Desert before Owens Valley was cut off by a lava-flow, and he proposed to utilize this to transport the water for a large part of the way to the city. After examining the project, Mulholland, who had been baffled by the water-supply problem, agreed that it was the right and apparently the only solution. Eaton had secured options on the lands and was prepared to go ahead with the project as a private enterprise if the city would not take it over; but Mulholland seized it enthusiastically, realizing that the very existence of the city depended on it, and declared that "If Los Angeles doesn't get this water now, it will never need it." Fortunately the Los Angeles Water Board was an organization of strong, able, and aggressive men, for quick action and secrecy were necessary. Mulholland estimated the cost of the project at $25,000,000, the Board told him to go ahead at once, and before land-speculators knew anything about it, the city had acquired the site and all the land needed and the announcement of the *coup d'état* was made in the Los Angeles *Times*.

Mulholland was a self-made engineer. While still a boy he had come to Los Angeles, from his home in Ireland, as a sailor. Having got a job as *zanjero*—keeper of the irrigating ditches—in the old *pueblo,* he studied engineering in his cabin at night until he became an expert; and many years later he was given the difficult post of chief engineer of the Water Department. When his plans were approved by a board of nationally known engineers, Mulholland pushed the scheme with energy, and in six years' time he brought the Owens River water into Los Angeles on schedule and within his original estimate. But not without many a struggle. Aside from its engineering difficulties, the project was fought so violently by private interests that it was finally necessary to get a bill through Congress granting free right of way for the aqueduct over public lands. And so strong were the opposing forces that without the personal insistence of President Theodore Roosevelt it would have been lost.

From the foot of Mt. Whitney in the snow-covered Sierras the water was brought through Sequoia National Park, across the Mojave Desert, across the San Gabriel and San Fernando mountains, in the course of which hundreds of miles of highways and railroads were built, 53 miles of tunnels, and a strange steel "jawbone" syphon to carry it down a precipitous mountainside. On a brilliant day in November, 1913, while thousands looked on, the water was turned into the great spillway, and William Mulholland said, "There it is; take it." This water has been used for irrigation schemes, it has enabled Los Angeles to take in other towns near-by—Hollywood, San Pedro, Wilmington, and it has provided electric power which the city has been able to sell at a low price. In the process the people of Owens Valley suffered, for the value of their property was ruined even when the property itself was not actually destroyed. President Roosevelt had realized that this would be so, and his willingness to have the city proceed was based only on the ground that the project would benefit a tremendous number of people, even if it should hurt a few. The people of Los Angeles have always maintained that they would pay in full for all damages suffered by the residents of Owens Valley, a start in this direction has been made, and an investigating committee has reported that the points at issue between the land-owners and the city can be satisfactorily adjusted.

In the early part of the twentieth century another dream of Los Angeles began to take shape. For years there had been hopes of giving the city a direct connection with the country around Salt Lake City, Utah, and a shorter route to the East. With this end in view a company had been organized which obtained a franchise for a railroad along the east bank of the Los Angeles River. It built to Glendale, Whittier, and Pasadena, and was then taken over by interests which extended the road to Long Beach and San Pedro and called it the Terminal Railroad. It was still purely a local road with a harbor connection, however, when Senator William Andrews Clark of Montana took it over and laid out a line to the northeast, crossing the desert and mountain country, to give Los Angeles direct access to Salt Lake and to bring the city nearer to Denver, Omaha, and Eastern cities than was San Francisco.

A picturesque figure, Senator Clark, who conceived and built the Los Angeles, San Pedro and Salt Lake Railroad. Born at Connellsville, Pennsylvania, in 1839, he had come west as a young man, after being a student of law and a school-teacher in Missouri. He drove his own ox-team to Colorado and worked in the mines there until 1863, when he went on to the bonanza mining district of Bannack, Montana. Fifteen-hundred dollars' worth of gold washed out in Horse Prairie Creek provided him with capital to buy and bring in a load of provisions from Salt Lake, the beginning of a prosperous commercial venture. Finding a shortage of that most necessary commodity, tobacco, in the Helena, Montana, mines, he went to Boise, Idaho, and bought several thousand pounds, all he could find in the city, hauling it back to Last Chance Gulch, where he sold it to the eager miners at his own price. In 1866 he rode on horseback clear to the Pacific Coast and brought back goods for his Elk City store; he took a contract to haul the mails from Missoula, Montana, to Walla Walla, Washington; and he built up a banking and wholesale business in Deer Lodge and Butte, Montana. Feeling that he needed more technical knowledge to help him in buying and developing mining properties, he went back to New York and studied at Columbia University, after which he built the first stamp-mill in Butte. He followed this with the first smelter, and gradually he became owner of some of the richest mines in Montana. In Arizona he bought the great United Verde copper-mine, built a model town for workmen at Clarksdale, expanded his interests to include refrigerating warehouses, grain-elevators, and a sugar-mill. Montana elected him to the United States Senate, and finally, to crown his achievements, he decided to build a railroad.

So Los Angeles profited by the opening in her back yard, in 1905, of a line which tapped vast deposits of lead, iron, copper, and gold ores, districts producing marble, sandstone, coal, silica, borax, and salt—seven barrels of the waters of the Great Salt Lake making one barrel of that commodity. There were timber-lands and farming valleys too, rich in wheat, alfalfa, vegetables, and fruit. Passing through the Meadow Valley Wash for 100 miles in southern Nevada, the line had to be lifted high above it to avoid floods, and it used the old gorge where the Mormons first blazed the trail on their overland journey, opening up new scenic glories which were later to become Zion National Park. In entering the Meadow Wash Cañon Clark found himself at war with E. H. Harriman. The great railroad magnate had decided that Clark might effect a combination with the Denver and Rio Grande and the other Gould lines to form a transcontinental system, and he resolved to check this. At this time Harriman controlled the Union Pacific and the Southern Pacific, and Gould controlled about one-half of the total mileage of railroads in the Southwest. The Gould holdings included the Missouri Pacific, the Texas Pacific, the St. Louis and South Western, the International and Great

Northern, a total of 21,000 miles. Practically all the Southwestern freight traffic was routed *via* St. Louis or Kansas City over his lines. Just before the depression of 1893 an old subsidiary of the Union Pacific, the Oregon and Utah Northern, had graded 290 miles from Salt Lake into the narrow Meadow Wash Cañon, and Harriman now revived this abandoned project. He occupied the cañon; Clark did likewise. There were battles between gangs of workmen, and the courts decided that both roads had a right to build there. So a compromise was effected whereby each acquired a half-interest in the other's right, and Harriman made sure that Clark would not enter a combination with Gould.

Aside from his satisfaction in developing Southern California, in which, he said, "my faith has never wavered," the Senator received $29,000,000 for his railroad, in 1921, from the Union Pacific. Meanwhile, he had spent 12 years building a palace at Fifth Avenue and Seventy-seventh Street in New York and filling it with Persian rugs, Spanish tapestries, paintings, and statuary. The bequest of this collection, worth $3,000,000, was refused by the Metropolitan Museum after the Senator's death because he had stipulated that it must be housed intact, and the Museum officials felt that the *objets d'art* were so varied that they would quarrel like Kilkenny cats. Los Angeles later benefited culturally from the benefactions of his son, William A. Clark, Jr., who long supported its Symphony Orchestra with a gift of $200,000 a year and opened to the public his library, containing one of the finest collections of English classics in the world.

With the coming of Senator Clark's road the transportation needs of Los Angeles were amply provided for. Some competition for advantageous locations in the Southwest still continued, however, between the Santa Fe and the Southern Pacific. In 1904, Harriman wanted to change the location of the Southern Pacific between Lordsburg, New Mexico, and Yuma, Arizona, in order to avoid heavy grades. He chose the Gila River route; so did the Santa Fe. A contest accordingly developed, with the rival companies organized to occupy Gila Cañon. In filing its route Harriman's road was 20 minutes ahead of President Edward P. Ripley's, but both began construction. When the case was taken into court, the Santa Fe, fearing defeat, capitulated by selling Harriman its line. Harriman's policy in dealing with competing roads was to smooth out their difficulties by coöperating on matters of mutual interest. To this end he offered to give the Santa Fe people two seats on the Southern Pacific Board of Directors in exchange for two on theirs. When this offer was not accepted, he purchased $30,000,000 worth of Santa Fe stock and placed H. H. Rogers and Henry C. Frick as his representatives on the Santa Fe board, after which there was peace between the two roads.

But, beneficial to the city as were the transcontinental railroad-builders, the most potent single factor in the upbuilding of Los Angeles as a world city was undoubtedly Henry Edwards Huntington, who abandoned transcontinental railway-building to concentrate his attention on local electric lines. This favorite nephew of Collis P. Huntington set his organizing genius to work to develop Los Angeles as a center of interurban transportation, and he built up a traction system such as had never been seen before.

The fourth of seven children of Solon and Harriet Huntington, Henry was born at Oneonta, New York, on February 27, 1850. As a boy he worked in his father's general store, and in later life he often spoke of how he used to get up before six in the morning to sprinkle the floor, sweep it out, and tidy up. So industrious was he and so shrewd that the villagers generally agreed, "You can't get ahead of Ed Huntington"—an opinion which his later life amply supported. When a young man he went to New York City, applied for a job at a hardware-store whose proprietor he knew, and when he was told that there was nothing available except a place as porter, he took that. On the small pay he earned he lived frugally in a New York hall bedroom, refusing to ask his rich Uncle Collis for money, a mode of conduct which greatly appealed to the elder Huntington. Recognizing the boy's ability, Collis Huntington soon took Henry to West Virginia to inspect a railroad property he had just bought, and he left him in charge of a sawmill cutting ties at West Albans, West Virginia. Under the young man's management the production of the plant was increased and costs lowered, and he soon bought a small interest in it, later borrowing money and buying the entire plant.

At the age of 36 Henry Huntington became manager of the Kentucky Central Railroad and was given a free hand in reorganizing it, which he did with such success that he made a name for himself among railroad men. In 1892, on his way to San Francisco to work for the Southern Pacific, he stopped at Los Angeles and was entertained at the San Marino Ranch near Pasadena, which so impressed him with its beauty that in later years he bought it for his home. As he traveled all over the state, he became convinced that Southern California was to have a remarkable growth, and in 1898 he began to sell his San Francisco holdings and to invest in Los Angeles. In 1900 he was made first vice-president of the Southern Pacific Railway, president of the road in Arizona and New Mexico, and president of the Market Street Cable Company. In his management of the street-railway of San Francisco he had become convinced that cable- and steam-cars would be entirely supplanted by electric traction, an idea which he later developed on a vast scale in Los Angeles County. In 1902 he moved to Los Angeles and began the construction of the intricate network of electric street-car lines and interurban railways which made that city the nerve-center of Southern California. Street-car service was poor when he arrived and bought into the Pacific Electric traction system, and Huntington, working as E. H. Harriman did in the national railway field, rapidly improved it, connecting and consolidating lines and extending trackage throughout the suburban area. So large was his view of the possibilities and so prodigious his construction projects that the local capitalists who were originally interested in the property with him could not agree with his plans for expansion, and they withdrew, leaving him to carry on the enterprise alone.

Having begun the Pacific Electric system in 1902 with the Pasadena short line, Huntington rapidly added lines to Monrovia, Whittier, Glendale, Newport, San Pedro, Huntington Beach, Santa Ana, Sierra Madre, and Redondo. In 1911 the system was sold to the Southern Pacific, but Huntington remained in charge and retained complete control of the Los Angeles street-railways, continuing to absorb and extend lines until in 1916 the total interurban trackage was 1,063 miles. In 1903 Huntington started the building of downtown skyscrapers with his Pacific Electric Building, and the stimulus furnished by the building of his electric lines started real estate moving in quantity for the first time since the Eighties. In later years the system was enlarged to include a subway which brought all the Hollywood and San Fernando Valley street-cars into the heart of the city underground.

As he knitted the whole of the Orange Empire into a unit with Los Angeles as its center, Huntington turned his attention to the development of real estate in the suburbs served by his lines, buying immense tracts of land, laying them out with beautifully landscaped winding roads and parkings, and planting them with trees. He built the magnificent Huntington Hotel at Pasadena and organized numerous public-utility companies to serve the southland. And Los Angeles did not disappoint him. Indeed, it grew faster than its most ardent boosters predicted. After announcing that $64,000,000 was to be spent to enlarge the Pacific Light and Power Company and reorganize the Los Angeles Railway Corporation, Huntington said in 1914, "I have found this region has grown so rapidly that we will have to develop power that we calculated would not be needed until 1917. Los Angeles has developed three years ahead of our mathematics. I have always had the utmost faith in its growth but the rate beats my most sanguine expectations. It is a problem to handle the people who wish to ride."

In 1900 Collis P. Huntington had died, leaving his nephew several millions and the bulk of his fortune to his widow with the request that Henry should supervise the estate. In 1913 the widow and Henry were married, and he retired from business in order to develop his magnificent estate at San Marino and to put into the collecting of books and paintings the same energy and genius for organization that he had given to his railways. "I retired from business before business retired me," he said. "That is the reason why I have a docile liver, an appreciative stomach and muscles which are joyfully responsive of demands." On his ranch he began an extensive botanic garden, sending his superintendent on a tour of the United States and Mexico to collect plants and obtaining others from every continent; he built up a comprehensive collection of tropical and subtropical plants, including an eight-acre cactus garden of 20,000 specimens, with the idea of discovering every plant of beauty or utility that would grow in Southern California. His purchases of private libraries, single volumes, and rare manuscripts continued until he had assembled one of the choicest collections in the world.

Concentrating on the literature and history of English-speaking peoples, Huntington's library included a Gutenberg Bible, more Shakespeare folios than are owned by the British Museum, Beverley Chew's library of early English literature, the Kemble-Devonshire collection of English plays, the Church, Hoe, and Halsey collections, the Chatsworth library of the Duke of Devonshire, the Britwell Court collection of Americana, and 40 per cent of the known editions of books published in England in English before 1641. In 1920 all these books, worth some $20,000,000, were brought from the Metropolitan Club in New York and elsewhere to San Marino. Later Huntington added Lincoln manuscripts and mementos, the manuscripts of various American authors, and a million manuscripts owned by the Buckingham family. His collection of paintings included canvases by Velásquez, Gainsborough, Reynolds, Romney, and various other English, American, and modern Spanish painters. To house these treasures a building was erected on the estate, and Huntington presented the whole to the public, creating in the Henry E. Huntington Library and Art-Gallery a foundation modeled after that of Leland Stanford Junior University. To build up the library so as to make it useful to scholars Dr. Max Farrand was made director of research in 1926. The value of the benefaction was estimated at $40,000,000. Mrs. Henry Huntington also presented the family place at Oneonta, New York, to the city for a park and gave Harvard University $250,000 for the Collis P. Huntington Laboratory of Bacteriology at the Medical School and $100,000 for the Collis P. Huntington Memorial (Cancer) Hospital. Henry Huntington adopted his wife's son by her first marriage, Archer M. Huntington, who became founder of the Hispanic Society of America. Mrs. Huntington died in 1926, and a year later Henry Huntington died while on a trip to Philadelphia.

It was said that Collis Huntington could ride across the country on railroads he owned, and Henry could do the same on railroads of which he was a director. He once said that although Darius Ogden Mills had declared in 1888 that he was afraid of the Central Pacific, thinking it a poor investment, he was proud to say that the financier's son and daughter, Ogden Mills and Mrs. Whitelaw Reid, had become the two largest stockholders of the Southern Pacific. One of his largest enterprises was the Newport News Shipbuilding Company. His relations with his employees in this concern and others were pleasant, and he said he gave the resident employees full responsibility for the promotion of the shipbuilding enterprise, spending scarcely more than an hour a day on its affairs although it was an enterprise employing 6,000 men. He often entertained his electric-railway employees, and at one picnic held at Redondo the families of his 5,000 workers brought the total of his guests to 25,000. He was popular with his men, and one of his engineers expressed the prevalent feeling of his employees when he said that he was proud to have worked for him, and that while he had worked hard, he had never worked half as hard as Henry Huntington.

Like his Uncle Collis, who said there was never a day that did not give him a chance to work 18 or 20 hours, Henry always worked long hours and assumed arduous duties. In later years he watched the easy, pleasure-filled lives of the sons of his friends and complained that it was hard to find young men who would knuckle down to concentrated hard work. He long had an aversion for college-trained men, although he finally outgrew it. He also disliked to see women in business and never hired them if he could help it.

Huntington advised young men to save if possible, and if not, to go into debt to invest: and he once said, in an interview on his return to Los Angeles from a long trip,

I am always averse to saying anything that may influence people in investing for I would not want to be the means of causing any one to lose money; but, by and large, I will say that whatever real estate has been sold of my holdings since I went away will double the money of the buyers. I always have done business on the principle of not trying to get all that I thought a piece of property was really worth; the best way to do is to sell when you can get at a fair profit, reinvest the money and sell again and keep your money rolling. The way the city has grown in all directions has astonished me and I'm rather difficult to astonish, for I know from years of experience how Los Angeles does extend.

Of street-car finances he said,

For some years past the street car company has returned me red ink balances running yearly up in the many hundreds of thousands of dollars; now the tide seems to have turned; if the street railway had been in other hands it would have been in a receiver's possession long ago and we would have had six or ten cent fares, as they have in many other cities. I am determined to fight it out on a basis of a five cent fare.

From his experience in Los Angeles he came to be an advocate of the consolidation of the Bay cities of San Francisco, Berkeley, Alameda, and Oakland, of which he said,

A metropolitan area so likeable, in fact loveable, cannot fail to grow in those graces with which nature and the initiative of her people have endowed her so richly; and to that growth municipal unity would be likely to contribute. These cities are practically one now, just as there are cities around Los Angeles which are practically one with that city. There is a general feeling in the south that consolidation, wherever affected, has benefited alike Los Angeles and the communities which have come in.

It is largely due to the imagination and practical ability of Henry E. Huntington that Los Angeles has expanded to absorb so many of its suburbs and that its retail market has come to include eighteen suburban cities and a total population of 2,500,000. And his system of quick transportation extending in all directions from Los Angeles is responsible for the extraordinarily extensive and prosperous suburban growth of the city and the consequent absence of slums. For this made it possible for workers to go out into the country and buy homes of their own, and it developed one of the richest districts of small fruit-ranches and gardens in the world. When it was suggested that Henry Huntington should have a biography written, he said, "No; never. I have been approached regarding a biography, but I do not want that. This Library will tell the story. It represents the reward of all the work I have ever done and the realization of much happiness." He was in favor of everything being done to beautify Pasadena and enrich its cultural life, including the Little Theater, and added that there is also "beauty in going to the mountains 500 miles away, and freeing power from its bond of rock, and bringing it here to do its work of making this wonderful region more wonderful, more comfortable."

Along with all the benefits derived from the work of powerful individual builders, Los Angeles was constantly profiting from the remarkable spirit of coöperation of her own business men. Consistently and persistently they have sought to develop not only the city, but also the adjoining towns in Los Angeles County and the whole of Southern California, for they have realized that all were interdependent. The civic spirit made its appearance early. In 1845 Regidor Don Leonardo

Cota prayed that an order be given to make the inhabitants white-wash their houses and said, "If I succeed in this I shall be satisfied to have coöperated somewhat to the glory of my country." And as early as October 24, 1874, the editor of the San Bernardino *Guardian* publicly recognized this abiding spirit in Los Angeles and recorded his convictions:

The progress made by the city in three years is almost incredible. New and magnificent buildings are being built, new industries have been created, and new lines of commerce opened. The entire community seems imbued with progressive enterprise. There is none of the happy-go-lucky free and easy element among the business men. They understand the value of coöperation for the public good. They are not afraid to spend ten dollars to make twenty; the merchants extend their ramifications throughout the neighboring counties with true metropolitan confidence. Los Angeles looks upon itself as the present and future commercial center of Southern California, and all her energies are put forth to maintain that proud preëminence. Every project tending to concentrate commerce in Los Angeles is liberally supported. Its moneyed men have their eyes constantly fixed on the future of their beautiful city. No cost is spared to divert the trade of the surrounding counties to Los Angeles. The people really seem in love with their city. . . . If Wilmington can be engineered into a port—and we believe it can—then Los Angeles must become a great commercial city. . . . Its people deserve it as they are the most public spirited and coöperative people on the Pacific coast.

Successively proving the truth of this estimate in their efforts to build the harbor and to bring in water from the Owens Valley, Los Angeles was to display yet another and more astonishing achievement in coöperation and energetic driving power—the building of the Boulder Dam in Nevada, 200 miles away. When the Owens River water system was completed, Los Angeles had a population of 300,000, and it was estimated that her new supply would permit the city to grow to a million, a size which her most optimistic inhabitants thought of, at the time, as the limit of expansion. But the million soon came, and again the city was forced to take thought of increasing her water-supply. Extensive surveys showed that all the water of the high Sierras adjoining Southern California was being used, and that if an adequate supply was to be obtained, it must come from outside the state. However, the Los Angeles Chamber of Commerce, which had once objected to the building of the Moffat road near far-away Denver on the

THE VENICE OIL FIELD
Courtesy of the Los Angeles Chamber of Commerce.

AN IRRIGATED VINEYARD IN SOUTHERN CALIFORNIA
Courtesy of the Los Angeles Chamber of Commerce.

BOULDER DAM

May 1, 1934. Height, 360 feet above foundation, with 370 feet still to go. Courtesy of the U. S. Bureau of Reclamation.

ground that California needed the water-power, was not to be balked by mere distance. So the *Angeleños* looked over into the state of Nevada and began to figure on a plan to dam the Colorado River and bring a large part of its power and water to the City of the Angels. Securing the coöperation of the Imperial Valley, which needed the dam to protect it from threatened floods and to increase its productive acreage, the Southern Californians set out on what may be described as the battle of the century. Private electric and water-power interests, irrigation enterprises, those opposed to government ownership, and all the states entitled to Colorado River water-rights entered the grand mêlée, with the result that only the most prodigious driving effort was able to push the project through Congress. But the Los Angeles people never wavered in their fight, for they knew that without this additional source of water the city and its neighbors would face a disastrous shortage within a few years.

The project was nothing less than the damming and harnessing of the Colorado River, the third largest in the country, near Las Vegas, Nevada, to provide hydro-electric power and water for Southern California, to prevent floods, and to bring additional irrigation to the Imperial and Coachella Valleys, 200 miles away. Rising in snows of the Rockies 1,700 miles distant, the Colorado was one of the most terrifying forces for destruction in the United States, for it carried the silt torn away from the backbone of the continent down to the Gulf of California and had built up its delta until it flowed along land higher than the surrounding valleys. At the Mexican border it was 100 feet higher than the Imperial Valley canal, and the lower part of the valley was 300 feet below the river. Obviously, dikes and levees could not do much to hold back the river that had hollowed out the Grand Canyon, and to the people who lived in the Imperial Valley it was a constant menace. So its 60,000 inhabitants gladly joined with the *Angeleños*, who looked covetously upon the possibility of getting a billion gallons of water daily for drinking, bathing, and watering lawns, along with the energy of a million horses to do their work.

Authorizing the expenditure of $165,000,000, the Swing-Johnson bill finally passed Congress and was signed by President Coolidge on December 14, 1928, the three pens used in making his signature going to three who had fought most heartily for the project—Senator Hiram

Johnson, Representative Philip D. Swing, and George G. Young, publisher of the *Examiner*, the Hearst paper in Los Angeles. There followed seemingly endless quarreling among the states involved, including a conference at Santa Fe where Secretary Hoover represented the Federal Government, until it was finally agreed that the water should be divided equally between the lower-basin states of Arizona, California, and Nevada and the upper-basin states of Colorado, New Mexico, Utah, and Wyoming. The Metropolitan Water District was organized to contract for the use of the water in Southern California, and the Secretary of the Interior was empowered to proceed to work as soon as he had valid contracts sufficient to pay off the cost within 50 years. When these contracts were forthcoming from Los Angeles, Pasadena, Glendale, Burbank, the Southern Sierra Power Company, the Los Angeles Gas and Electric Corporation, and the California Edison Company, and when the belligerent state of Arizona and its bulldog Governor George W. P. Hunt were finally satisfied with the allocation of water, the Southern Californians rejoiced.

And now engineers and workmen are hurrying to completion the great Boulder Dam, "set in the path of the turbulent Colorado in a sheer-walled narrow gorge at the bottom of an inaccessible cañon in the remotest region of the United States,—a work ranking with the greatest ever attempted by human hands." And Los Angeles and thirteen neighboring communities have combined to build the Colorado Aqueduct across the State of California, a costly construction project which will provide the greatest water system the world has ever known. To build it will require the employment of 10,000 men for six years, with a pay-roll of over $100,000,000; an equal amount will be spent for materials, equipment, and supplies; and its completion will add two or three billion dollars annually to the production of industry, mining, oil, and agriculture and will enable Los Angeles to provide water for a city the size of New York.

The same powerful force of coöperation has been turned upon every civic problem confronting Los Angeles. Coöperation resulted in the building of the $8,000,000 Biltmore Hotel; the Los Angeles Coliseum, seating 80,000 people; the raising of a million-dollar fund to advertise Southern California; the formation of a plan for a civic center near the old plaza; the building on a sage-brush-covered hillside of the beautiful Hollywood Bowl, where Mrs. Artie Mason Carter inaugurated the Symphony Concerts and Mrs. Christine Stephenson the Pilgrimage Play; and the staging of the Olympic Games in 1932. But, potent as have been the effects of whole-hearted coöperation, Los Angeles was also the recipient of two golden showers of fortune either one of which would be sufficent to build a city—oil and the movies.

The city had long been a center for the financing of petroleum production in the West and in Mexico, for it was the home of Edward L. Doheny and also of his less known partner, Dr. Norman Bridge, who had come west from Chicago when he was a young professor in Rush Medical College. Settling in Sierra Madre on account of his health, Dr. Bridge invested his small capital in his friend Doheny's projects, and these investments grew to such dimensions as to enable him to make princely gifts to the California Institute of Technology at Pasadena and the University of Southern California. Doheny's oil developments began in the Nineties, when the demand was only for kerosene and axle-grease, and continued through the period of fuel oil, locomotive oil, and automobile gasoline. And Doheny financed archæological explorations, built the beautiful St. Vincent's Church (dubbed by the facetious "Doheny's fire-escape"—this after the Teapot Dome unpleasantness in which many Los Angeles business men believed that he was unjustly assailed), and gave the University of Southern California its magnificent library. In the early nineteen hundreds scattering deposits of oil were found literally as well as figuratively in the backyard of Los Angeles, and in the front yard as well. Beautiful lawns in the best residence districts, gardens, beach-resort properties, and tide-lands, all were tapped by the ubiquitous oil-derricks, bringing æsthetic ruin but financial profit which permitted the owners fittingly to express their æsthetic ideals in other localities. Prospecting continued, and in later years whole forests of derricks sprang up at Huntington Beach and in numerous other outlying districts, and California's production of oil rose to more than $300,-000,000 a year, with a large part of the profits pouring into Los Angeles.

Most amazing of all the gifts of the gods to Los Angeles, however, if Aimee Semple McPherson Hutton and her mother be excepted, was the movies. To the suburb of Hollywood, founded by Kansas prohibitionists, came from New Jersey, soon after 1900, David and William

Horsley, who rented a barn and turned it into the first motion-picture studio, though they refused to buy the five-acre property for $4,000 because they had been warned against California real-estate salesmen. With only $2,500 capital the Nestor Film Company began shooting a western "horse opera" next day, frightening the natives as their troop of hard-riding armed cowboys pursued the fleeing villain up Beachwood Drive into the hills where now is Hollywoodland. Before this, Colonel William N. Selig had rented an old mansion downtown in Los Angeles and produced against its ornate backgrounds the first full-length film, "In the Sultan's Power," and the old Bison Company had turned out a "Western" every day and a half at Edendale. Lured by the almost constant sunshine and the variety of mountain, ocean, rural, and desert scenery, which made it an ideal locality for shooting the ever-popular "Westerns" as well as other pictures, Eastern film men continued to flock to Hollywood. In 1910 the old Biograph Company arrived, with David Wark Griffith as director, Mack Sennett, Owen Moore, and Mary Pickford. Essanay and Kalem followed, and in 1913 came Jesse L. Lasky, bringing Cecil B. De Mille and Dustin Farnum. He promptly bought property around his stables for a few thousand dollars, established a permanent studio, and, as Hollywood grew, saw the value of his real estate mount to millions.

The first big "wow" of the movies that knocked them out of their seats from Key West to Tacoma was the "Birth of a Nation," a super-spectacle produced by Griffith with great skill from the novel *The Clansman*, using thousands of extras, making stars of Henry Walthall, Mae Marsh, and Lillian Gish, and bringing in $15,000,000 to the box-office. Griffith, who had originated the cut-back, the fade-out, and sustained suspense, to say nothing of improving the final clinch, had already startled the world by paying Mary Pickford $1,000 a week to appear in "Tess of the Storm Country," and his successes helped to make Hollywood secure as the capital of the motion-picture industry. In 1913 Charlie Chaplin came to the coast as the star of Karno's troupe of English vaudevillians, producing a "Night in an English Music-Hall." In this act, which went the rounds of the old Sullivan and Considine circuit, he portrayed an inebriated gentleman in evening clothes sitting in a box observing a performance on a miniature stage, and his amusing pantomime, expressing approval and disgust as the various acts appeared, was such as to prove that words were not necessary to excite an audience to violent laughter—those hearty "belly laughs" that the movies so yearned for. He went to work on the Keystone lot for $150 a week, his first appearance being as an interpolated feature in an automobile-race picture, in which he would stroll unconcernedly out on the course with his ridiculous hat, shoes, cane, and mustache just as the racing cars shot by, appearing constantly in danger of sudden death and making hair-breadth escapes such as only Chaplin could negotiate. Within a few years he was getting $10,000 a week, and so was William Farnum; Theda Bara had created the verb "to vamp"; William S. Hart had begun to make "westerns" for a coffee-and-doughnuts salary; and a San Diego high-school girl, Anita Loos, had been paid $15 for a scenario. Mary Pickford had signed a million-dollar contract; Douglas Fairbanks had been advised by Griffith to take his athletic prowess into Keystone comedies; Rudolph Valentino had become a matinee idol of the country through "The Four Horsemen of the Apocalypse"; Betty Compson, Thomas Meighan, and Lon Chaney had been brought to stardom by "The Miracle Man"; and Charlie Chaplin had brought Jackie Coogan, "a small boy who had winked at him in a Los Angeles Railway Station," to fame in "The Kid." In 1921 came the Arbuckle trouble, the death of Wallace Reid, and the Taylor murder, all arousing such attention and criticism in every village of the country that the producers sought to placate public opinion and avoid state censorship by the appointment of a dictator who should know how to put on the soft pedal. The man who got the job was the Indiana Presbyterian and arch-Republican Will H. Hays, who resigned as President Harding's Postmaster-General to act as the film industry's public-relations expert.

By this time the motion-picture companies constituted a major industry, operating on great "lots" where they built up city streets, Moorish palaces, and English cathedrals as suited their fancy; their expenditures ran as high as $1,000,000 for a single picture; the rise of their stars was meteoric and their lives an Arabian Nights' dream. And now, for better or for worse, for blessing or for curse, the flickering films had penetrated every cross-roads village of America, carried strange new ideas of the white man and his civilization to the remote corners of the world, and made a visit to Hollywood the goal of young and old the country over. No such aura of romance was ever before spread over an American community; the talk of oranges and climate that drew the hordes of tourists in the Eighties was as nothing compared with this new magnet; the lure of seeing the stars and, better yet, actually getting a chance to work in the movies drew to Los Angeles a steady stream of ambitious and stage-struck youth. To a few near-Venuses and Adonises who happened to have luck and to screen well, it brought fortune; to many, intermittent work as "extras"; to most, disappointment and a job as a clerk or beauty-parlor operator or soda-jerker. But those who stayed in Los Angeles, and there were many, made their distinctive contribution to the make-up of this strangest, most amazing, and, in some respects, most American of cities.

Never before had such a conglomeration of elements been gathered into one mixing-bowl and in a few swift years fused into a city. There was to begin with the old Spanish and Mexican population, which fell more and more into the background as the city grew; there were the wealthy Easterners and Mid-Westerners who came in the first boom, and a tremendous influx of well-to-do people from Iowa, Nebraska, Kansas, Missouri, and other predominantly rural states, who came steadily, year by year, and helped to create the second boom of 1923, when the city was making an annual population gain of 100,000 with clocklike regularity. Some of the older people sought a comfortable place in which to retire from active life, in a climate where it was no longer necessary to get up on a winter morning and thaw out the pump. Many of these retired farmers bought suburban property where they could raise gardens and fruit, while the younger members of the family entered into whatever occupations were open to them. There came also thousands of health-seekers to find in the balmy air relief from tuberculosis and other maladies that were benefited by a mild climate. There came people who had grown rich in other parts of the country, seeking a pleasant place in which to spend their money; and there were swarms of promoters, real-estate men, and ballyhoo artists of all kinds to help them spend it. There were hordes of winter and summer tourists living in luxurious hotels and in tiny cottages. And to this collection were added those who had suddenly become millionaires in Los Angeles from ventures in oil and real estate, and those glamorous darlings of fortune, the movie queens and kings, who had been miraculously transported from lives of humdrum mediocrity to imperial splendor at the touch of the new Aladdin's Lamp. Finally, there was an army of happy, ne'er-do-well "tin-can tourists," who cranked up their old Fords, gathered together enough money to pay for gas, and joyfully rolled their creaking and exhausted motor-cars across the desert into Los Angeles to settle down and spend the rest of their days by the lazy sunset sea.

With such elements superimposed upon and fused into the core of the city's population—a substanital core, whose cross-section would show much the same sort of business men, working-men, and housewives as the ordinary American city—Los Angeles came to scintillate, in many aspects of its life, with a tinsel brilliance which was unlike anything else on land or sea. Where else could one find such an assortment of ice-cream stands built in gigantic freezers with the handles slowly turning, windmill bakeries, refreshment stands hollowed out of an orange or a hot dog—even a restaurant in a building modeled to suit its name, the Brown Derby? Where could one see such vast areas of pink- and yellow-stucco cottages, their sides decorated in jazz patterns, their walls as thin as tar-paper? Where else could one discover such an assortment of fortune-tellers, faith-healers, "psychologists," swamis, strange religions, raw-food enthusiasts, nature doctors, health homes, bungalow courts, "shoppes" of all kinds, that iniquitous Los Angeles invention, the cafeteria, and Aimee Semple McPherson?

The vogue of the incredible Sister Aimee typified much that was bizarre, romantic, cheap, sensational, thrilling, aspiring, and naïve in the life of Los Angeles. This evangelist was plentifully endowed with magnetism, beauty, sex-appeal, and that subtle, indefinable something which gives a few chosen souls, like Sophie Tucker, Texas Guinan, and William Jennings Bryan, the power to reach out and pick an audience up and hold it in the hollow of the hand. With her mother she began evangelistic meetings in a tent, and within a few years she had so attracted people and money that she owned an enormous white tabernacle overlooking Echo Lake Park and turned thousands away from her meetings every week. This tabernacle itself was a symbol of Los Angeles; it was, in its way, gorgeous, and it was like no other church in the world. It was, in fact, a gospel plant rather than a church, for it included a training-school for missionaries, innumerable offices and meeting-rooms, a prayer-room where the faithful constantly sent up their supplications, a commissary for food to be given to the poor, a publishing house, sewing-rooms where the women made garments, a luxurious home for Sister Aimee, and a radio station. Aimee also improved on the ordinary church service by adding a stage on which she appeared with elaborate scenery and light-effects to illustrate each sermon. There was a brass band playing secular music, to some of which she had written sacred words. There was a veritable vaudeville show with each service, and to get in at all one had to go several hours ahead and, if lucky enough to get a seat, patiently wait for the performance to begin. Moreover, concealed under all the blare and ballyhoo there was undoubtedly considerable sincerity, even if it was overlaid with artifice and trickery; the woman had a hold on a powerful force whether or not she was entirely worthy of it or completely understood it, and many could testify to the fact that she had lifted their lives out of the slough of despond and given them "that old-time religion."

These things were the froth and foam on the life of Los Angeles, the strange spectacles that impressed first, along with the electric name-sign on the lawn of one of the movie stars and the startling fact that 100,000 people attend the Iowa Picnic. But there were always much more powerful influences at work underneath, civilizing influences which have made Los Angeles truly great. There was, first of all, a very high plane of physical living: food, including fresh fruits and vegetables, was abundant and cheap; the city was clean, well paved, and well provided with sanitary facilities; swimming-pools and playgrounds were plentiful; there were practically no slums; the average income was high; and the people could live easily and simply, spending much of their time, winter and summer, out-of-doors. In their teachers and in their plants the city schools were unsurpassed; there were several colleges, as well as the University of Southern California and, later, a branch of the University of California; the churches were numerous and vigorous; there was a city-wide library system; clubs flourished, some, such as the Friday Morning Club for women, occupying costly buildings of their own. And, added to all these advantages, the people of Los Angeles were constantly surrounded by beauty, sunshine, flowers, green grass, palm-trees, towering mountains, and the sea.

Inevitably this natural beauty impressed itself upon that part of Los Angeles fashioned by man. The gleaming white sky-scraper tower of the City Hall, the bright murals in the Public Library are evidence enough, but the pattern of clean-lined simplicity coupled with brilliance of color can be traced everywhere. Everywhere there has been added to the beauty and opulence and graciousnss of nature the products of the art and skill of man. No longer is there any feeling of architectural bad taste in Los Angeles; on the contrary, there is no other city in the world that possesses such numbers of magnificent houses set in beautiful gardens, not in one district of the city alone, but in scores of districts—miles upon miles of palm-lined drives bordered with beautiful and costly homes. And there are seemingly endless sections of unpretentious but attractive small houses, each with its own pocket handkerchief of lawn and flower-bed, and, incidentally, its garage.

From this favored city which has had the energy and driving force to build itself to greatness from unfavorable beginnings, which has come to maintain an extraordinarily high standard of living, which benefits the year around from fresh air and sunshine and the outdoor life, is it too much to expect the emergence of a new race? Not if the bronzed athletes of the University of Southern California, who have carried away so many championships from the older institutions of the country, are to be accepted as a sign and a portent of its possible physical development. Not if the robust, sun-tanned thousands who play winter and summer on its ocean beaches are an indication of its future health and beauty. Not if the vision of its builders make it the center of culture of which they dream. If, in generations to come, such a new people does develop, it will be Greek in its physical perfection and love of simple beauty and the out-of-doors; it will inhabit a region as fertile and well tilled as the valley of the Nile; and it will have the rugged strength of that sturdy Nordic stock which has peopled our plains and prairies, which first drove the plow into the wheat- and corn-lands of America.

# CHAPTER XII

SAN DIEGO, the city of the perfect bay and the perfect climate—so perfect and so frequently mentioned by the inhabitants that Los Angeles long ago dubbed the town "Baynclimate"—is the favored spot where European civilization had its beginning on the Pacific Coast. The "landlocked and very good harbor" was described by the Portuguese Juan Roderiguez Cabrillo, who visited it in 1542 and then returned to Spain to tell of his adventures. He found a good audience, for the Spanish had long had a romantic interest in California "whose foam is amber and whose sands are gold." Her novelist, Montalvo, had described it as an island very near this side of the Terrestial Paradise, peopled by courageous and beautiful black women, without a man among them, who made their weapons, and the harnesses of their beasts, of gold. This musical-comedy setting must have intrigued the imagination of every good Spaniard, but it was 166 years before any attempt was made to colonize this fabulous land. And then it was discovered that the inhabitants were not beautiful Amazons at all, but fat and ungainly Indians with protruding abdomens and shrunken legs, who must have looked like the creations of a comic-strip artist and who lived on bugs, lizards, and raw fish. Alas, for the romantic dreams of Spanish conquest!

The Spanish colonization began when Spain, which had occupied Baja (Lower) California, in what is now Mexico, decided to move northward and include Alta (Upper) California as well. The Catholic Order of Jesuits had been given permission to colonize and Christianize California, and they had raised the "Pious Fund" for this purpose; but their political activities brought them into disfavor in Spain, and they were expelled. The Church's work in Baja California was given to the Dominicans, and the extension of it to Alta California was assigned to the Franciscans. So Father Junípero Serra came north from Mexico to join with the newly appointed Governor, Gaspar de Portolá, in colonizing and Christianizing Alta California. Reaching this "country of joyous aspect," where the good *padre* found vines loaded with grapes and roses like those of Castile, they established themselves on the lovely bay named for the Spanish saint San Diego de Alcala. On July 16, 1769, the cross was raised, the royal standard unfurled, and Father Serra celebrated mass at the open-air altar, praying that they might "put to flight all the hosts of hell, and subject to the mild yoke of our holy faith the barbarity of the gentile *Diegueños.*" On this summer day, as the mission bell rang out from the branches of a near-by tree, the community of San Diego was born, and the civilization of the Pacific Coast had its beginning.

But no converts were made for a year, and since no supply ships came to replenish the company's larder, the Governor set a day for departure from Alta California. This was a cruel blow to the hopes of Father Serra. Because he could not bear to see the expedition fail, he prayed fervently for nine days that help might come to them. On what was to be their last day in San Diego, March 19, 1770, he went to the top of Presidio hill, overlooking the harbor, and prayed all day long— prayed that the country might not be abandoned, that the savages might be saved, that his plans for Christianizing California might not fail. And at sunset there miraculously appeared a sail. Captain Pérez, on his way to meet Portolá at Monterey, had lost his anchor and put into the harbor for safety. So, with supplies and reinforcements at hand, all thought of leaving San Diego was abandoned, and the *padres* joyfully continued their attempt to Christianize the natives. By 1773 seventy-three converts had been made, and a new San Diego mission was built farther inland where the soil was more fertile. Although the Indians, both converts and non-converts, were treated most gently, a party came down from the mountains on November 4, 1775, robbed the mission, and burned it. On that dreadful night, Father Luis Jaume rose from his bed, advanced to the howling savages, and, as they seized him, said, "Children, love God." He was cruelly murdered and mutilated; and when Father Serra heard of his noble death, he said, "Now the soil is watered; the reduction of the *Diegueños* will be completed." And again it was proved that the blood of the martyrs is the seed of the Church.

Within a few years there was a line of sixteen missions, a day's journey apart, extending up the California coast from San Diego along *El Camino Real,* and in these the Franciscan fathers taught the Indians the Christian religion and attempted to reclaim them from savagery. From mission to mission, with untiring zeal, Father Serra walked— after the custom of the Franciscans, scorning the use of horses despite an infected leg which was sore all the rest of his life. His enthusiasm was such, it is recorded, that when he founded the mission of Los Robles, he ordered the bells hung in the branches of a tree and, as he rang them, shouted, "O, Gentiles! Come, come to the holy church. Come, come, come to the faith of Jesus Christ!" "Why do you tire yourself?" his followers asked. "There are no Indians to hear. It is useless to ring the bells." And Father Serra replied, "Let me satisfy the longings of my heart, which desires that this bell might be heard over all the world, or at least that the Gentiles who dwell about these mountains may hear it." With such zeal and hope was the Christian religion planted in California.

The *padres* provided a place for the neophytes or converts to live in the buildings of each mission, taught them to plant the fields and harvest the crops, instructed them in the arts of carpentry, leatherwork, blacksmithing, milling; taught the women cooking, sewing, and weaving; and built up a prosperous, industrious civilization along 600 miles of frontier. Each mission excelled in the production of some commodity—wine, brandy, soap, leather, hides, wool, oil, cotton, linen, hemp, tobacco, salt, or soda, and their total products sold for about $2,000,000 a year. Since the Franciscan fathers were cultivated men, many having been scholars, engineers, soldiers, artists, lawyers, and physicians before they joined the Order, they were able to transform thousands of the ignorant, low-grade Indians of California into skilled artisans. As to their ability to teach the Indians, one need only look for proof at such an object of craftsmanship as the simple, graceful copper baptismal basin on its square stone pedestal in the San Gabriel Mission, beautifully fashioned by Indian workmen trained by the *padres.*

There were finally twenty-one missions in California, with 30,000 Indian converts, nearly 500,000 cattle, and 60,000 horses and mules, raising 40,000 bushels of grain a year. Then came the debacle. Mexico ousted Spanish rule and secularized the missions, reducing them to parish churches, and divided their lands among the settlers and the Indians. Within a few years the whole system had fallen into ruins, and the Indians had reverted to savagery and gone back to the mountains. So ended a system of community life which had taken half a century to build and which had given the Indian at least a modicum of civilization, even if it treated him more or less as a child and in some cases probably inflicted on him the restrictions and cruel treatment accorded to a serf. California remembers this colorful epoch of her past in the Mission Play by John Steven McGroarty, produced every year at San Gabriel.

Through all the mission period the old town of San Diego slept peacefully in its warm sunshine. It had been a Spanish town, it had lived under the rule of Mexican Empire and Mexican Republic, and on January 19, 1847, it awoke to find itself in the possession of the United States. Politics and war disturbed it little, and, as William E. Smythe says in his *History of San Diego*, "It was taken, lost, and taken again by the American forces before the new flag went up to stay. In the midst of it all, the stream of social gaiety flowed on with only slight interruptions, and the joy of it was actually increased, at times, by the presence of gallant soldiers from abroad." Two years later San Diego, whose population was then 500, began to feel the effects of being under Yankee rule. It took its first step toward becoming a city when it was made a port of call by the Panama Steamship Line, and next year a steamship line to San Francisco was begun. But the town remained a village and would have long continued so had it not been for the arrival, on April 15, 1867, of Alonzo Erastus Horton, the man who woke the sleeping community to life, the father of modern San Diego.

Born in Union, Connecticut, on October 24, 1813, Horton had grown up near Oswego, New York, clerking in a grocery, learning the cooperage trade, working as a sailor, owning and commanding a schooner carrying grain to Canada. Advised to go west on account of tuberculosis, he went as far as Milwaukee, where he engaged in buying and selling land and warrants and founded the village of Hortonville, which he sold for a profit of $8,000. In 1851 he came to California, and after trying work in the gold-mines he decided there was more money to be made in trading in gold-dust, which he did with profits as high as $1,000 a month. He also located some ice-fields in the mountains, cut the ice, and hauled it to the mining camps, making a profit of $8,000. Returning east *via* Panama in 1856, he was dining in a hotel with 200 other passengers when one of the riots broke out in which the natives periodically robbed and killed foreigners. Horton assumed command of the party, held off the mob with pistols, shooting several, and got the Americans back to the ship, losing his baggage and $10,000 in gold-dust in the process. When the ship reached New York, Horton went to Washington, as representative of the passengers, to try to get recompense for the losses they had incurred. By the time a settlement was reached, in 1861, Horton had made so many trips to Washington and had become "so obnoxious to the commissioner from New Granada that his own name was stricken from the list of creditors."

Soon after the outbreak of the Civil War he returned to the Pacific Coast and spent some time in mining and trading in the Cariboo district in Canada. In 1866 he returned to San Francisco and opened a furniture-store at Sixth and Market Streets. One night a friend invited him to a meeting where a lecturer discussed the ports of the Pacific Coast and their future. Commencing with Seattle, the speaker pointed out the sites of the big cities of the future, ending with San Diego, which he said was one of the most healthful spots in the world and possessed an unsurpassed harbor. Horton was so interested he could not sleep that night, and at two o'clock he got up and looked at the map to see exactly where San Diego was. Next morning he told his wife he was going to sell out and go there, and within three days he had sold all his stock and taken passage. When he got off at the wharf, he thought the sage-brush-covered site the finest he had ever seen for a city, but no one lived there; the old town was miles away at the foot of Presidio Hill. When he arrived at this point, after a long jogging wagon-ride, he said to one of the merchants, "I would not give you five dollars for a deed to the whole of this. Never in the world can you make a city here. It doesn't lie right. The city ought to be down by the wharf. I have been nearly all over the United States and that is the prettiest place for a city I ever saw."

Thinking that he might buy 40 acres, Horton asked if there was any land for sale and was told that any quantity could be bought if put up for auction by the city trustees. But he found the trustees were holding office illegally after their regular term had expired because the town did not wish to spend money for an election. The county clerk refused to call an election because he said it would cost too much. "How much?" asked Horton.

"As much as five dollars," replied the clerk.

"Here is ten," said Horton. "Call the election."

He went to a service at the Catholic Church, dropped five dollars among the dimes in the plate, and after the service told Father Ubach of his plans. "Who do you want elected for trustees?" asked the priest. Horton told him, and he said, "You can have them." They were elected, and the auction took place under trustees legally entitled to sell the land.

At the auction Horton bought 1,000 acres at an average of 26 cents an acre. On a fractional section near what is now the center of the city, he says, "Judge Hollister bid $5 over me. I told him he could have it and then he begged me to bid again. I finally raised him 25 cents and he said, 'You can have it. I wouldn't give a mill an acre for all you've bought. That land has lain there for a million years and nobody has built a city on it yet.' 'Yes,' I said, 'and it would lay there a million years longer if it depended on you to do it.'"

Under Horton's management New San Diego thrived. He built a wharf costing $45,000, gave away many lots free on condition that the owners would build on them, and sold many more. Every time a steamer from San Francisco arrived, he would sell $15,000 or $20,000 worth of real estate. He never missed an opportunity to improve the appearance and desirability of his town. Down near the water-front were new-built houses which Horton thought would make a better showing if they were whitewashed; he offered a free supply of lime and brushes for this purpose, but the owners said they had no time to do the work. Then Horton offered to hire men to whitewash the seaward sides of the houses, and after this was done, the people liked the result so well that they decided to whitewash them all over and finished the job themselves. "These houses," he says, "made a fine show, and people coming in on the steamers thought the town was growing very fast."

In later life Horton said he had given away a million dollars' worth of property and sold an equal amount. He sold the plaza to the city for $10,000, though offered $50,000 by private interests. He subscribed $5,000 to secure a telegraph line from Los Angeles; he started an independent line of steamers to San Francisco, forcing the fare down from $60 to $30 round trip and freight from $15 to $9 a ton; he built a fine hotel, the Horton House, and spent $8,000 lobbying in Washington to get a railroad to San Diego.

As early as 1854 the first railroad, the San Diego and Gila, was organized to build to Yuma, Arizona, there to meet whatever line might arrive from the East and connect it with tide-water at San Diego's harbor. Although 8,500 acres of land was granted, it remained a railroad on paper only, for the Civil War destroyed the influence of the South and consequently the Southern railroad route, with the result that the first transcontinental railroad went to San Francisco instead. But the far-sighted leaders of San Diego realized that the future of their city depended on getting a rail outlet from the East to their harbor, and they never ceased trying to bring this about.

Numerous schemes for building railroads to San Diego along the 32d parallel tantalized the citizens, and finally, in 1871, the great Thomas A. Scott of the Pennsylvania Railroad obtained a charter for his Texas and Pacific, to extend from the Mississippi River to the Pacific Ocean. Whereupon Horton went to Washington to induce the company to build simultaneously from both ends of the line. In August, 1872, Scott came to San Diego by steamer with General Grenville M. Dodge, the builder of the Union Pacific, who was to have charge of construction, and "all San Diego drew a breath of relief and hope." Scott's demands were moderate: he wanted the old San Diego and Gila land-grant, a right of way from the ocean to the Colorado River, and terminal lands. On April 27, 1873, "Father" Horton threw the first shovelful of dirt for building the new road and said he felt more honored than if he had been elected governor. But the town's triumph was soon turned to defeat. Ten miles of road were graded when Scott went to Paris to sell his bonds. As "railroad king" of America he was enthusiastically received, and Paris bankers agreed to finance the road; but Scott left the city to dine with the King of the Belgians, and in the intervening 36 hours there occurred Wall Street's Black Friday, when the great financial house of Jay Cooke and Com-

SAN DIEGO IN 1846

W. H. Emory, *Notes of a Military Reconnaissance from Fort Leavenworth, Missouri, to San Diego, California,* 1848.

THE MISSION OF SAN DIEGO DE ALCALA

Lithograph after a drawing by Charles Koppel in *Reports of Explorations and Surveys to Ascertain the Most Practicable and Economical Route for a Railroad from the Missouri River to the Pacific Ocean,* 1853.

ALONZO E. HORTON       GEORGE CHAFFEY
THOMAS A. SCOTT
FRANK A. KIMBALL      JOHN D. SPRECKELS

Horton, from the Herbert R. Fitch Collection, courtesy of the San Diego-California Club; Chaffey, from J. A. Alexander, *Life of George Chaffey;* Scott, courtesy of the Pennsylvania Railroad; Kimball, courtesy of the California State Library; Spreckels, courtesy of Frye and Smith, Los Angeles.

pany failed. Consequently, when he returned to Paris, the bankers refused to sign their agreements. In San Diego Horton was left with an empty building which he had built for the railroad offices, and swarms of real-estate buyers besieged him asking to be released from their contracts, to whom he returned all the money they had paid.

Huntington and Crocker, building their Southern Pacific south from San Francisco, dallied between San Diego and Los Angeles; but the former town still clung to Scott, and the latter provided a subsidy, so the city at the Silver Gate lost out again. Scott appealed to Congress for a subsidy to build his road, but he was opposed and defeated by Huntington, and in 1876 he offered to relinquish his San Diego lands to any other railroad that the people could induce to build to their city. As a result of Scott's failure the town's population fell from 4,000 to 2,500, and the people were despondent; but there was at least one man who never lost faith in the ability of the town to become a railroad terminal and who made this attainment his main object in life. Frank A. Kimball, with his brother, had purchased the National Rancho south of San Diego in 1868 and had laid out the town of National City, built a wharf, and developed a small community. In 1869 he tried to interest General John C. Frémont in building his Memphis and El Paso to San Diego Bay; in 1878 he wrote Cornelius Vanderbilt, who replied that he "never built a mile of railroad any faster than pushed to it by competition." A little later Jay Gould told him, in response to his plea for a road, "I don't build railroads; I buy them."

Failure to interest these railroad men only spurred Kimball on. In the spring of 1879 he called a secret meeting of business men at which $450 was subscribed to send him east, and he raised the remainder needed by mortgaging his house. At Philadelphia he found there was no hope of reviving the Texas and Pacific; in New York he learned that no help could be expected from Huntington; so he went on to Boston and began a three months' campaign to attract the Atchison, Topeka and Santa Fe. This road was building west and would have to have an outlet on the Pacific, although its directors had no thought of building to San Diego. But Kimball talked with President Thomas Nickerson and with the board, and he talked so successfully that the railroad acted favorably. For this enterprising San Diegan offered not only 10,000 acres of his own land at National City for a terminal, but

$10,000 in cash to pay for the right of way and further assistance in pushing the matter through Congress. The railroad engineers reported favorably, and all went well until the Santa Fe decided to join hands with another railroad project which already had a land subsidy, the Atlantic and Pacific. This affiliation required the roads to enter California far north of San Diego, at Needles, and they hoped to make their terminus San Francisco. Again Kimball went east and raised the ante, this time offering 6,000 more acres on which to build a railroad town. Thomas Scott was induced to release his old Texas and Pacific lands to the city, a local group built the California Southern Railroad from San Diego to San Bernardino to connect with the Santa Fe, and on November 18, 1885, the first through train from the East arrived.

Now San Diego felt that its future preëminence was assured, for its people believed that Providence had designed their harbor to be the ocean outlet for Los Angeles and all of Southern California. As the San Diego *Californian* remarked, "The fact is that for years the Los Angeles papers have found their greatest delight in willfully misrepresenting our harbor and city, well knowing that it is far superior to the puddle at San Pedro as the Pacific Ocean is to the Sacramento River." The Los Angeles *Times*, however, continued to label its dispatches from San Diego with the derisive head-line, "Baynclimate"; said that the San Diegans awaited the arrival of the railroad as the Pueblo Indians awaited the coming of Montezuma; and when the first trains arrived, carried an article under the supercilious head-line, "Happy San Diego! Ambitious Little City Wild with Joy." And later the *Times* gave her southern neighbor a little sound advice:

It seemed to many of our people for some years a question whether the coming of the railroad was a blessing or a curse. People had suffered themselves to expect too much; their hopes were not always grounded in reason, and in many cases were doomed to disappointment or to be long deferred. It will be so in the case of San Diego. The new connection will be a great benefit and will be the means of bringing to her a measure of prosperity otherwise impossible for her to attain, but her citizens will find out very soon that the railroad alone will not make them rich, prosperous and happy: they will have to put their own shoulders to the wheel and push with might and main to win. The prosperity of a city depends largely upon the energy and enterprise of its business men. Given the resources and advantages necessary to make a flourishing city, and there is still needed the brain power, brawn power, will power and money power of strong, daring, and yet level headed and conservative men in order to make the combination of successful elements complete. Success follows intelligent and persistent effort: God helps those who help themselves. Let our San Diego friends, whose success we shall gladly record, remember this prime truth.

The Santa Fe, however, did not do all that San Diego expected; it established no steamship lines to the Orient, its grand terminal melted into air, and four years later it transferred its general offices to Los Angeles. But the railroad had given San Diego a new impetus, and it began to grow. With the finest summer and winter climate in California, beautiful scenery, and a spacious harbor, San Diego became a Mecca for Easterners, real-estate prices shot up overnight, and by 1887 the population was 30,000. It was a time of lush enthusiasm, grandiose predictions of future greatness, and inflated prices, and real-estate advertisements reached rare heights of literary display, as the following sample shows:

Here upon block 42, Middletown Addition, we are surrounded by a grander view than can be seen anywhere else, even in this favored land. Loma, to our right, with brow of purple and feet of foam outlined against a sky of crimson. Far down the southern horizon towers Table Mountain outlined against the gathering dusk. The electric lights glint across the bay to sleeping Coronado and San Diego buzzes and hums at our feet.... Buy these four lots on one of which we stand, pay us five hundred dollars for them—it will be an enchanting site for a home and an investment that will repay you thousands.

One day when the San Diego boom had just about spent itself, a gleaming white yacht sailed into the harbor, and its skipper came ashore to buy supplies and look at the city of "Baynclimate"—an occurrence which caused some excitement among the town's business men for the visitor was none other than the wealthy and aggressive young San Franciscan, John Diedrich Spreckels. If they could only interest this powerful financier in their city, they thought, he could do much for San Diego. So they called upon him, banqueted him, and even offered him franchises for any project he might be interested in starting. And Spreckels was deeply impressed with the possibilities of this town which as yet had no outstanding capitalist to boost and exploit it, for it offered him the opportunity to play at development on a big scale without competition. He was 34. He was able and ambitious. He had plenty of money. So he adopted the town.

John D. Spreckels was the son of Claus Spreckels, the California sugar king, who had arrived in San Francisco in '49 and had become a successful brewer. Having noticed the waste in the manufacture of sugar, in 1863 he returned to New York to master the technique of sugar-refining, after which he went to Hawaii. There he bought plantations and built mills and became such a power that King Kalakana, to whom he loaned $1,000,000, was said to take all his orders from him. At 14 his son John went to Europe alone to study at Hanover Polytechnic, where he mastered chemistry, mathematics, and music; but when he accepted a challenge for a duel, he was peremptorily ordered home by his father. At 22 John was superintendent of one of his father's sugar refineries, having begun at an ordinary workman's job at $50 a month, and shortly he went to Hawaii to train other superintendents. Always interested in the sea, he soon built a 500-ton schooner there, named it the *Claus Spreckels,* and applied to his father for freight, underbidding all competitors. Then he organized the shipping and trading firm of John D. Spreckels and Brothers, returning to San Francisco and buying a fleet of nine tugs. He joined the Vigilantes; shot a San Francisco newspaper editor who printed disparaging remarks about the elder Spreckels' management of his companies; established the Oceanic Steamship Company to link California with Australia and New Zealand; became a duly qualified deepwater shipmaster, and became a power in California journalism by buying the San Francisco *Call.*

This was his story when he chanced to drop into the city of "Baynclimate," and the rest of his life is the story of San Diego. For he became the greatest single factor in its growth and development. His first enterprise was the building of a wharf, and having watched the wasteful methods of handling coal at San Pedro, he designed model bunkers for the efficient coaling of ships. At about the time he completed this, the boom burst, and the Santa Fe announced that it would be compelled to abandon its San Diego branch because it could not pay expenses. In this emergency John Spreckels offered to provide the railroad with coal on credit in order to keep the trains running. When the account reached $500,000, the railroad offered to give him the branch line to settle it, but he told them he had so much confidence in the future of San Diego that he would wait for his money.

Not only was the railroad in difficulties, but every other enterprise was suffering from the collapse in values. Among these was the Coronado Beach development begun by E. S. Babcock on the long, narrow "silver strand" across the bay. This scheme, including the palatial tourist hotel and a town and summer camp, had resulted in the sale of $2,000,000 worth of lots, but it was now bankrupt. So John D. Spreckels added Coronado to his holdings, completed the beautiful and luxurious hotel, provided the peninsula with water, railroad, and ferry service, and built a tent city which attracted thousands of tourists. During the boom T. S. Van Dyke had brought water down from the mountains to San Diego, and Babcock had organized the Otay and Tecate water companies; but in the early Nineties there was so severe a water famine that baths were prohibited and drinking-water was peddled in the streets. Again John D. Spreckels came to the rescue and built an adequate water-supply system, the Southern California Mountain Water Company, laying down the sound principle, "Get your water first, for without water you get your population under false pretenses and they quit you when the water runs dry."

Meanwhile, San Diego had added another illustrious visitor to her population. This was the king of the penny press, Edward Wyllis Scripps—"Lusty" Scripps his biographer calls him—who came to San Diego in December, 1890, as a tourist, hired a horse and buggy, and drove out over the mesa toward the mountains. Fascinated by the flowering shrubs, the blue sky, and the dry air—as dry as his favorite Algiers or Egypt, where he had been sent to recover from lung trouble, he decided to make this place his winter home; and that afternoon he purchased 400 acres on a little rise overlooking mesa and mountain. Later this was increased to 2,100 acres, and here he built "Miramar," a 60-room one-story house of whitewashed brick and glass with a court and fountain in the center, the first large modern Spanish-type house to be built in Southern California by an American. In seven years Scripps completed the house, planted trees and gardens, and put in a water-supply system; and he built roads radiating from it so successfully that the people of the county called upon him to head their road-building commission.

Originally attracted to the place because it would isolate him from his business interests, which included the Cleveland *Penny Press*, Cincinnati *Post*, and other newspapers, he soon found himself lured into the local newspaper game; he bought the San Diego *Sun*, and when it lost money, turned it over to a $15 a week reporter named Porterfield. When it finally climbed out of the red, he gradually added others to the Western group, including papers in Los Angeles, San Francisco, Fresno, Berkeley, Oakland, Portland, Seattle, Tacoma, and Spokane, and from his San Diego home he ruled these and his other newspapers throughout the country. All were purchased at bargain prices, and most of them became valuable properties.

In 1900 Scripps bought a quarter-interest in the town-site of La Jolla, a subdivision left over from the boom, obtaining 500 lots for $3,200, and from the development of this lovely seaside resort his brother, Fred, made a fortune. When the city of San Diego asked him to purchase from a San Francisco bank a ranch it needed for water supply, he did so, spending $35,000; but the bond election failed, John D. Spreckels accused him of speculating in public utilities, and when he was left holding the bag, he swore off all real-estate operations forever. While in San Diego he expanded his chain of newspapers, organized the Newspaper Enterprise Association, bought and built up the United Press, and to initiate the public into the discoveries of scientists he organized Science Service, of which Edwin E. Slosson became editor. During those years he built his newspapers into such a power that Postmaster-General Albert S. Burleson wired him, after President Wilson's second election, "I want you to know that I know it was the Scripps papers that determined the election." In many of his enterprises his sister Ellen was a close associate, and she contributed one of his first newspaper features, the "Miscellany." Edward gave the University of California the Scripps Institute for Biological Research at La Jolla, and Ellen endowed Scripps College for Women, on the Pomona College campus at Claremont, between San Diego and Los Angeles. In addition the Scripps name lives in San Diego in the roads he built and the thousands of eucalyptus trees he planted on the barren mesa.

But Scripps and Spreckels were ever enemies. Each owned a newspaper in which he belabored the other, Scripps championing the cause of the workingman and the common people against a grasping monopolistic capitalist, and Spreckels accusing Scripps of radicalism and unfair and libelous statements concerning his aims and interests. Spreckels felt, and rightly, that he had contributed much to the up-building of San Diego, for, as he said, when he came to the city, "I was not a capitalist seeking new investments; I was a young man seeking opportunities for doing things on a big scale." So he went on with his developments. He bought the entire south side of Broadway, building hotels, a newspaper plant, an office-building, and a magnificent theater. He gave a public library and a city hall to Coronado. He tried to attract capital for factories. He bought banks and in one instance saved one such institution from failure through his own generosity. He built a city-wide traction system, and since the city charter permitted only 25-year franchises, which were insufficient to attract capital, he used the new initiative and referendum to get the people to vote 50-year franchises, after which he vigorously extended his railways.

The work of John D. Spreckels had been a strong antidote for the general debilitation and headache that followed San Diego's boom. And others made valuable contributions to the city's permanent well-being. Among the more picturesque examples of these was the U. S. Grant Hotel, built by Ulysses S. Grant, Jr., as a memorial to his father, and the beautiful development at Point Loma where Katherine Tingley established the international schools and headquarters of the Theosophists. Most valuable of all was the work of the many land-owners and farmers who developed San Diego's fertile country, planted orange and lemon groves, and laid the beginning of a prosperous agriculture. But away to the east still stretched that vast sea of burning sand, the Colorado Desert, which was considered a total loss so far as economic value or practical use was concerned. This great desert was formed in past ages by the rushing Colorado River pouring into the Gulf of California, carrying the silt torn away from the soil of the Rockies and the Grand Cañon and depositing it in a vast delta. This gradually filled the upper end of the Gulf and built up a wide barrier of desert sand which cut off the waters at the northern end to form the Salton Sink, 250 feet below sea level. Always this desert had been a horror to all who had to cross it, but one man at least had looked upon its arid, useless waste with the eye of a dreamer and had seen a way to make it friendly to man. As early as 1853 Dr. O. M. Wozencraft of San Bernardino formed the idea of using the water of the Colorado to irrigate this waterless, treeless, lifeless million acres and make of it a fertile valley. He induced the state legislature to grant him California's interest in the desert and to help him push a bill through Congress to give him 1,600 square miles of the worthless land in return for its irrigation, but the Civil War made it impossible to pass the bill, and the project lapsed.

Others occasionally considered the scheme, but Wozencraft was the only enthusiast, and nothing practical was done until 1892, when John C. Beatty commissioned C. R. Rockwood to make surveys for irrigating the desert by diverting the waters of the Colorado at Pot Holes, 11 miles north of Yuma. A cousin, James H. Beatty of Canada, contributed $30,000, and a total of $175,000 was raised in a stock-selling campaign, but when it was all spent, nothing had been accomplished, and Rockwood sued for his $3,500 salary, receiving the instruments and camp supplies for his claim. Colonel S. W. Ferguson of San Francisco secured an option on 20,000 acres of land adjoining the international boundary and a contract to buy 350,000 acres for 60 cents an acre across the line in Mexico. With Rockwood and Beatty he organized the California Development Company, a New Jersey corporation with a capital of $1,250,000 and $350,000 in land scrip. They divided the stock, sold the land scrip at 10 cents on the dollar, and spent the money. Not a spade had been turned, and there were no assets when Ferguson and his friend L. M. Holt asked an engineer of standing to construct the necessary canal in return for one-quarter of the stock.

This man was George Chaffey, Canadian-born, an engineer of genius, an organizer and a financier. Self-educated in his profession, he had learned shipbuilding as a boy in his father's plant at Kingston, Ontario, and was early given a navigator's license for the Great Lakes. He had built ships of his own before he came to California in 1882 and took up the study of irrigation at Riverside. Seventeen years before, when Chaffey was new in California, Dr. Wozencraft had tried to interest him in the Colorado Desert irrigation project, but after he had visited the desert, Chaffey decided it was a visionary and impractical scheme, one of his chief objections being that settlers would not live in a district where the temperature rose to 120 degrees. But this cold-blooded Canadian was to learn differently within a few years, and in the meantime he turned his attention to other projects for irrigating the more favored valleys of California. With his brother, William Benjamin Chaffey, he laid out and developed an irrigated tract near San Bernardino, known as Etiwanda, and he distinguished himself by being the first engineer in the West to file on a mountain stream for electrical energy as well as for water. With power from this first hydro-electric project, he wired his ancient ranch-house, built of bricks brought on donkeys from San Francisco, to make it the first electrically lighted house west of the Rockies. On the peak of the roof he put up an arc-light as an advertisement for his colony, precursor of the ubiquitous electric sign; he built the first long-distance telephone in California, then the longest in the world, from his house to San Bernardino; and he organized the Los Angeles Electric Company to take power to the city, making Los Angeles the first electrically lighted town in the country.

When Etiwanda was sold and payments for the land were trickling in, Chaffey organized a second colonization scheme, Ontario, at the foot of Old Baldy of the Sierra Madre Mountains, and he soon brought water to this parched tract of sage-brush, jack-rabbits, and coyotes. He shared the water-rights from mountain streams with the near-by town of Pomona, a place which was so dry that Barnum said he would not stop there with his circus because there was not enough water to give the elephant a drink. If dry, Pomona scorned the rival Ontario as even dryer and declared that nothing could ever be grown there. But Chaffey, not content with rights to half the surface water and all the electric power, followed out his theory that the rivers of California run bottom-side up and drove a tunnel 3,000 feet long into a near-by cañon bed, tapping a copious supply of underground water for his colony. And to confound his enemies at Pomona he built a fountain close by the railroad track, and every time a train went by, he had it cast a profligate jet of water high into the air as a symbol of the abundance of moisture his colony enjoyed. At Ontario he platted the land so that every 10-acre tract had a street-frontage, and he developed the idea of mutual water companies in which each acre of land carried with it a share of stock in the water company, thus providing for irrigation without troublesome litigation over water-rights. He laid out magnificent tree-lined Euclid Avenue, built Chaffey Agricultural College, which afterwards became the state-supported Chaffey Union High School and Junior College, and brought an excursion of special trains from Los Angeles to advertise his land.

In 1886, just before the Southern California boom began, Chaffey sold out his interests and went to Australia, where he laid out two great irrigation projects, Mildura and Renmark. Although various political and financial difficulties beset him, he lived to see these colonies most successful, but he did not profit from them as he deserved. When he returned to California 12 years later, almost penniless and discredited, he found Ontario suffering from drouth, and with his uncanny gift for discovering water, he brought in enough underground springs and seepages to give the town an ample supply. He also purchased a tract of dry land for $1,600, sank artesian wells, and sold the abundant water which gushed forth for $75,000 a year.

It was with this money that he thought of joining the California Development Company, but his first inspection of Rockwood's survey discouraged him, and he declined to enter the project. Chaffey's fear that people would not live in a hot country was gone forever, however, for the Murray Valley, scene of his work in Australia, was one of the hottest regions in the world inhabited by white men, yet the colonies planted there throve. But even after he had rejected Rockwood's scheme, the fascination of the vast project of irrigating the desert still lured him, and he finally decided to see if he could not make a better irrigation plan. With an Indian guide he plunged into the desert at Yuma, braving for three weeks the heat and wind and sand along the border, incidentally becoming deaf through the hardships he suffered, and discovered on the Mexican side ancient dry water-courses which could be utilized for bringing the Colorado River water to irrigate the dry lands of Southern California.

Enthusiastic over his discovery of the new channel, in April, 1900, Chaffey contracted with the California Development Company to construct a canal to divert 400,000 acre-feet of water a year. Rockwood's original estimate of the cost had been $1,000,000. Chaffey offered to do it at a cost not to exceed $150,000 and to raise the money himself, in return for which he was to have one-quarter of the stock, control for four years, and $60,000 to be paid later out of revenue. Unfortunately, he did not discover that the company was bankrupt and was about to lose its charter because of non-payment of taxes, that it did not control the land along the Mexican border necessary for the construction, and that it had sold all its land scrip, which would have to be redeemed at face value for water-rights just at the time when cash would be needed. He should have made sure of these things, but he was told the books were in New Jersey, and he assumed all was well. Since he was the only person who could handle the project, he might well have withdrawn when he discovered the true state of affairs and organized his own company. His son, Andrew M. Chaffey, frankly advised him not to undertake the scheme, but he said, "Let me do one more big thing before I die," and went ahead. Adhering to his original agreement, he personally made the negotiations necessary to get new options on the land, organized, financed, and engineered the whole project, and 12 months later he had completed the 70-mile canal, extending from Pilot Knob through Mexico and reëntering California at the twin cities of Mexicali and Calexico, at one-tenth of the original estimate and one-third less than his contract price.

Meanwhile, the magnitude of the project of reclaiming the desert had attracted national attention, and by the time the water was turned in, the Imperial Valley was alive with settlers, who came to take up the government land. In 1901 there was not a white resident in the Valley; by 1905 there were 14,000, distributed among seven towns, farming 120,000 acres irrigated by 780 miles of canals. George Chaffey had named the valley Imperial, had founded the twin border towns of Calexico and Mexicali, and had devised a variation of his mutual water-company scheme to provide the settlers with equitable water-rights. As the water entered Mexico, it was sold to a Mexican corporation, and as it came back into the United States, it was resold to the mutual water companies; being the property of a foreign corporation, it was thus not subject to interference by state rate-making bodies. The Imperial Valley was a bonanza for the settlers, who bought the land from the Government for $1.25 an acre and paid from 75 cents to $20 an acre for the water-rights, thus coming into ownership of property worth $150 an acre. But it was not a bonanza for George Chaffey, who, facing loss of control of the company, in 1905 sold out his interest for securities which later netted him only $100,000.

But the Imperial Valley, which had defied man for generations, was not yet entirely conquered. Three years after George Chaffey had severed his connection with the project, other engineers constructed an exceedingly risky canal around the diversion head-gate, and soon the whole Colorado River burst into the Valley. Within nine months the river had cut two channels 50 feet deep, 1,000 feet wide, and 43 miles long, and had carried into the Valley four times as much earth as was excavated for the Panama Canal. The dry Salton Sink became the Salton Sea, 40 miles of Southern Pacific track were covered with water, and it was only a question of time before the whole district would be flooded and all the great development irretrievably lost. How to dam a rushing river that was now 2,500 feet wide and 30 feet deep was a problem which baffled the engineers; every attempt was a failure.

In its extremity the California Development Company turned to E. H. Harriman, who now controlled the Southern Pacific, and he agreed to spend $200,000 to dam the river if the company should be put in his hands. This was done on June 20, 1905, and during July and August Harriman made two attempts to stop the river, but without result. Only one-third of the Colorado was now following its old channel; the remainder flooded into the Imperial Valley to the Salton Sea. The next sum of $250,000 was advanced by Harriman as he sat in his office directing railroad relief work amid the smoldering ruins of San Francisco after the earthquake and fire, and the dam constructed with this money was carried away like a match. President Roosevelt, petitioned for help, said the Reclamation Service could not act as the cut was in Mexico; and he asked Harriman to take the full responsibility, although that gentleman wired him that the Southern Pacific Company had already spent $2,000,000. Congress was adjourned, however, and no authority for the Government to act could be obtained, so Harriman gave the order to stop the river "at all costs." Harry T. Cory was put in charge and in 52 days spent $1,600,000 dumping in nearly 6,000 carloads of rock and gravel and driving 1,200 piles; and on February 10, 1907, the break was closed, the river was flowing back in its old channel, and the Imperial Valley was saved.

Meanwhile, George Chaffey had turned his attention to another irrigation project, the East Whittier–La Habra Valley near Los Angeles. Here, by drilling wells in the dry bed of the San Gabriel River, he turned 12,000 arid acres into valuable citrus lands, completing this last of his great irrigation projects with the help of his son, Andrew M. Chaffey, who had become a financial power as president of the California Bank in Los Angeles, where he introduced the Australian system of branch banking. Surely, George Chaffey had built himself imperishably into the civilization of Southern California. Four times he had made the desert blossom as the rose, once on the largest scale ever known to man. He had pioneered in irrigation, town-building, development of hydro-electric power. His Ontario project had been reproduced by the Government as a model at the St. Louis Louisiana Purchase Exposition. He had solved every problem of engineering, building, and financing an irrigated colony and had paved the way for the extensive work to be undertaken by the United States Reclamation Service. Ontario and Whittier are to-day beautiful and prosperous towns of 15,000 people; the Imperial Valley tills half a million acres of land and sends out freight-cars by the tens of thousands loaded with cantaloups, lettuce, grape-fruit, oranges, grapes, alfalfa, dairy products, all produced in vast quantities in the districts that George Chaffey reclaimed from the desert.

The completion of Boulder Dam will add several hundred thousand acres to the irrigated area of the Imperial Valley; and the residents in 1933 voted to contract with the Government to spend $33,500,000 to build the all-American Canal, keeping the waters of the Colorado entirely within the United States on their way to the Imperial Valley—a project which the great wealth of the district now makes economically feasible. Incidentally, when Los Angeles was completing its project to bring water from the Owens Valley, George Chaffey found himself opposed to the city, for in 1905 he had filed on streams there with the idea of developing hydro-electric power, an irrigation project, and an electric railroad from the Valley to Los Angeles. When the city took the matter to Washington, inducing Gifford Pinchot to extend the forest-reserve to cover the property, it tried to make capital of Chaffey's alleged failure in Australia; whereupon the Prime Minister, Alfred Deakin, wrote, "Mildura to-day has 4,000 people irrigating 11,000 acres. I am convinced you would have made a great success if you had

been permitted to carry out your plans without the senseless inter-
necine strife which compelled you to cease your control. Your courage,
ability, resource and energy merited very different treatment than that
which you received from the short-sighted people who proved to be
their own worst enemies when they assailed you."

Another irrigation scheme, on a tiny scale compared with the Imperial project but of considerable value, was that of William Ellsworth
Smythe, who had been an editorial writer on the Omaha *Bee,* founder
of the *Irrigation Age,* and leader of national irrigation congresses at
Los Angeles and Denver. After trying out his theories at New Plym-
outh, Payette Valley, Idaho, he came to San Diego and organized
"the Little Landers" at San Ysidro, propagating the doctrine that a
family could live comfortably in San Diego County with true independence on one acre, or at most two or three.

But the development of the Imperial Valley at San Diego's back
door was not as great an immediate advantage to the city as it should
have been. For throughout its history the city had been virtually on a
branch line of the railroad, and now it had no direct rail connection
with the rich Imperial Valley. In 1906, however, John Diedrich Spreckels, resting after an illness and the shock of the San Francisco earthquake at his Coronado Beach Hotel, determined to give San Diego this
vitally necessary railroad connection as well as its long dreamed-of
direct railroad route to the East. After conferences with E. H. Harriman, who shared the wish for a direct line to the East, he announced
the incorporation of the San Diego and Arizona Railroad Company to
build east through Mexico and the Imperial Valley to Yuma. On November 15, 1919, after numerous financial and engineering difficulties
had been overcome, the golden spike was driven on the summit of
Carriso Gorge, in a setting of unsurpassed scenic grandeur, and John
D. Spreckels said,

I was very much gratified to have the evidence of your approval of my
efforts in the building of this road. Some of the speakers have given me
credit which I don't think belongs to me. I was not the originator of
this road, but it was the biggest railroad man in this country and that
man was Mr. E. H. Harriman. He projected the road and selected me
to carry out the work and to act as his agent and trustee. Things went
along very nicely until the year of his death. He was furnishing the money
and I was spending it. But the time came shortly thereafter when there

was a change in the administration of the affairs of the Southern Pacific and I was informed that no more money was to be advanced for the building of the road. This was a staggering blow to me. It was tantamount to a knockout, but, gentlemen, let me tell you that before the count of ten arrived I realized what it meant and I said to the president of the road, "Why do you wish to discontinue or to withdraw?" And he said, "For financial reasons; money is tight and we have great expense to make up for the roads through Nevada." "Well," I said, "then let me do it." And from that moment on I did it, and continued the building with such funds as I could spare from my business and such funds as my brother aided me with.*

Well might John Spreckels take pride in his accomplishment. The road had cost no less than $18,000,000, and construction had been marked by continuous reports of fresh engineering difficulties which resulted in enormous building costs. Spreckels had personally obtained from President Diaz the concession to build through Mexico, and for 12 years he had fought for the road and kept faith with San Diego when many a less courageous man would have withdrawn. When the first train rolled into the Union Station and San Diego became at last the real terminus of a Pacific railroad, the name of John D. Spreckels was lifted high in the hearts of the people. At the celebration given in honor of the arrival of the railroad, Spreckels said,

The San Diego and Arizona railway is now an accomplished fact. It is finished. It is behind us. Most of the difficulties that lay in our path are overcome. They are merely memories and I certainly need not tell you that I am mighty glad of it. What is to be done now rests more with you people here this evening than it does with me and the gentlemen associated with me in this railroad enterprise. The road is built. It is at your service. If it is to fulfill the purpose for which it was built—the upbuilding of San Diego into one of the leading cities of the coast, with prosperity for the city and its people—the completion of that purpose lies in the hands of the men and women who are here tonight and the rest of the people who have their homes in San Diego.... It has been my principal aim in life for a number of years past to make of San Diego a city of the first class—populous, prosperous and popular—and I think I may reasonably claim that I have done my bit.... I have always had a profound belief in the future of San Diego, ever since the day I first came here many, many years ago. I have never lost faith in its future and my

* H. Austen Adams, *The Man John D. Spreckels* (San Diego, Frye and Smith, 1924).

judgment has been backed by my brother for we have both believed that San Diego was a city of opportunity. Our climate, our harbor, and our back country, supported by Imperial Valley, one of the most remarkable and prolific producers of nearly everything that can be grown on land with the aid of sunshine and water, must mean prosperity for San Diego. This new railroad opens up a wide field for enterprise in Imperial Valley, Arizona, New Mexico, and through the Middle West to the Atlantic coast. Its benefits cannot be estimated at the present time, but those benefits will grow and year by year they will become greater and greater and San Diego will fulfill her destiny.*

On many aspects of the city's life John D. Spreckels set his imprint. He reproduced an old Spanish mansion in Old Town, calling it "Ramona's Marriage Place," where visitors might visualize the sort of life described in Dana's *Two Years Before the Mast,* and he gave an outdoor pipe-organ costing $100,000 to Balboa Park. On this occasion California's premier orator, the Honorable Sam Shortridge, later to be Senator, indulged in an ornate tribute to San Diego's first citizen, striking a high note in his opening words, "Within hearing of yonder ocean whose billows break on Coronado's sands, we come—age with its memories and youth with its hopes—to receive a precious and splendid gift." Spreckels permanently engaged an eminent organist to give free concerts, and when his brother Adolph erected in Lincoln Park, San Francisco, overlooking the Golden Gate, a magnificent replica of the Palace of the Legion of Honor in Paris, he gave it another pipe-organ, also valued at $100,000. His crowning contribution to San Diego was to make possible the Panama-California Exposition, giving it his hearty support along with the great outdoor organ, a check for $100,000, and another check for a like amount to help keep it open a second year.

But, despite his benefactions, there were many who strenuously objected to the size and variety of his holdings and blamed all San Diego's troubles on the fact that it was a "one-man town." So strong did this feeling become that in 1923 John Spreckels gave a dinner at Coronado to which he invited 600 of the city's leaders for a heart-to-heart talk. On that memorable evening, which marked the beginning of a new civic spirit for San Diego, he said,

* *Ibid.*

SAN DIEGO IN 1870
Courtesy of the San Diego-California Club.

SAN DIEGO HARBOR AND BUSINESS SKY-LINE

In the foreground the aircraft-carrier *Saratoga*. Courtesy of the San Diego-
California Club.

ROCKWOOD HEAD-GATE OF THE ALAMO CANAL

Colorado River on the left. The Alamo Canal passes into Mexico about one mile downstream and reënters Imperial Valley about 60 miles to the west, serving 500,000 acres in Imperial Valley and 200,000 acres in Mexico. Courtesy of the El Centro Chamber of Commerce.

A CANTALOUPE RANCH IN THE IMPERIAL VALLEY

This early sweet variety reaches Eastern markets in early May. A normal season's shipments reach 18,000 carloads. Courtesy of the El Centro Chamber of Commerce.

I had faith in San Diego. I still have. That is why I am still here. Faith! It may be able to move mountains, but, gentlemen, no amount of mere faith ever built a city. Only one thing can build a city—coöperation. It is team-play alone that can put a city on the map and keep it there. Big cities require big men—men big enough to forget personal differences and pull together without jealousies or suspicions or factional bickering. In other words, before you can turn a small town into a real city, you have got to shed the small town skin.

Now, gentlemen, between ourselves, what is the matter with San Diego? Why is it not the metropolis and seaport that its geographical and other unique advantages entitle it to be? Why does San Diego always just miss the train somehow? I will tell you. In three words: Lack of coöperation. We have no team-play. The moment anybody appears with any proposition of a big constructive nature the small town undertakers get busy digging its grave. And if anyone dares to invest too heavily he is warned that San Diego objects to being a one-man town. Well, gentlemen, if being a one-man town is bad for the town, it's hell for the one man.... A one-man town! My God! If you only knew how often I have turned heaven and earth to induce men of large means to come to San Diego. For thirty years I have hoped and worked for men with big ideas, big ability and big capital to come and get into our big game down here. God knows we need them! Just see what brains and capital have done for Los Angeles. Why? Well, simply because Los Angeles business men see the need for whole-hearted coöperation; and San Diego business men do not. That is the story in a nutshell. They pull together; we indulge in a tug of war. ... I have had my say. I have spoken frankly in the hope that from now on a larger and more genuine spirit of coöperation may prevail. I ask no favors. I ask only for coöperation. If the young, red-blooded, progressive business men of the city will only get together and stick together nothing will be too big to expect for San Diego.*

That this meeting did result in a better coöperative spirit was soon evident: within a week the leaders of the city joined in a huge appreciation dinner for John D. Spreckels, and the spirit that was born there has continued to animate San Diego.

So to-day San Diego stands proudly on its heights above the Silver Gate, its sunlit bay protected by the headlands of Point Loma and the Coronado peninsula, the Mexican mountains blue in the distance —a beautiful city and the most venerable on the Pacific Coast. Its downtown garden, Balboa Park, is lovely with the buildings remaining from the Exposition of 1915, buildings in the Spanish Colonial

* *Ibid.*

style which combine simplicity of line with gorgeousness of carving and ornamentation, striking examples of "the most glorious temperamental architectural expression to be found on the American continent." And this architecture and its ancient Spanish heritage give San Diego a charm which cannot be effaced by any number of go-getter business men or marred by any amount of industrial development. However much it may grow, San Diego will never be just another busy American town; the soft, balmy air will fortunately prevent it, keep the spirit of *mañana* alive, and make lotos-eaters of even the luncheon-club addicts.

# CHAPTER XIII

## PORTLAND, THE CITY GRAVITY BUILT

IN the motion-picture, "The Covered Wagon," there is a scene in which the emigrants on the Oregon Trail are told of the gold that has just been discovered in California. When they hear this story of unlimited wealth to be had for the taking, many of the travelers change their plans and head for the Sacramento. But a certain pig-headed contingent from Missouri refuses to be diverted by any such glittering lure of easy fortune. Their reply to the tempters is that they set out to drive their plows into Oregon soil and to Oregon they will go. Such stubborn citizens as these Missourians settled the Willamette (pronounced with the accent on the second syllable) Valley, and their dogged determination, industry, thrift, and conservatism go far to explain the temper and substance of Oregon and of its chief city, Portland.

From Missouri and the Middle West came many a farmer to make the black soil of Willamette and Tualatin valleys yield up their riches. And from New England came men of equal vigor and determination whose outlook was the sea rather than the plains—shrewd Yankees, keen business men, sharp traders, endowed with the calm tenacity of the barnacle—to found the city of Portland. Among the first seamen to enter the Oregon trade was Captain John H. Couch, who came from Newburyport, Massachusetts, in 1840, at the behest of the old New England firm of Cushing and Company, to establish a salmon fishery on the Columbia. Encouraged to the enterprise by the advice of the Methodist missionary Jason Lee, the Cushings hoped to establish a profitable business, but the Indians proved to be such unreliable workers that the venture was abandoned. Captain Couch left his assistant at Oregon City, went to the Sandwich Islands, sold his vessel, and returned to Newburyport. But on his trip he had learned the needs and seen the possibilities of the Oregon trade, and in 1842 he

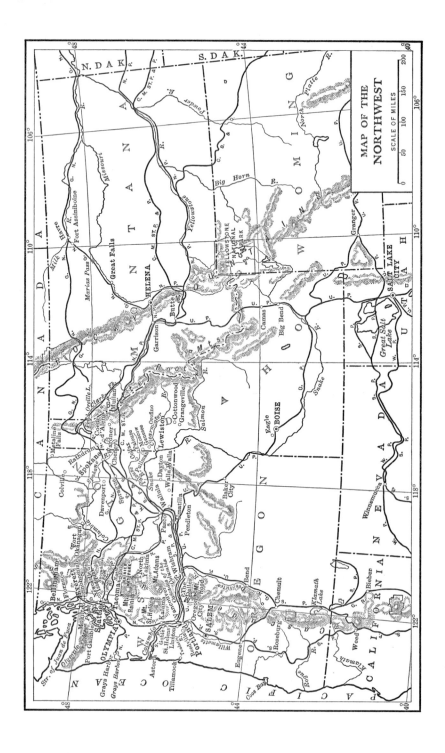

MAP OF THE
NORTHWEST

SCALE OF MILES

0    50    100    150    200

returned to the Northwest with a stock of goods to open a store in Oregon City.

By this time there was no question that somewhere near the mouth of the Columbia a port would be established to serve the empire drained by the river and its tributaries. The force of gravity determined this, and the Columbia, Snake, and Willamette rivers were its visible signs. For the waters that fell in the far-distant Rockies found their way to the sea on the Oregon coast, and the traveler who wanted an easy route to the Pacific followed the Oregon Trail to the Willamette Valley. It was the easiest route for water and men, and some day it would be the easiest route for rails. The only question that puzzled the pioneers was the exact spot where the metropolis that was to benefit by this force of gravity was to be located. Astoria, founded by John Jacob Astor at the mouth of the river, was the first possibility, and there were numerous other available sites all along both sides of the Columbia for a hundred miles to the mouth of the Willamette. Near this point, on the north side of the Columbia, the Hudson's Bay Company had built its trading-post, Fort Vancouver; and a few miles up the Willamette, at the falls, was the pioneer settlement of Oregon City, which had the double advantage of being the seat of the provisional government of Oregon Territory and of having an ample supply of water-power—already being used to operate a grist- and a sawmill.

A great port might be established at literally dozens of points along the river system, but Captain Couch determined that the best place was Portland, for he easily drove his sailing-vessel as far as what is now the foot of Washington Street, tied it up, and gave it as his opinion that any vessel that could pass over the bar at the mouth of the Columbia could reach that spot. This was perhaps the most important single act in the founding of the city, for it persuaded the hundreds of sea-captains who knew Couch that Portland was the place to drop anchor and discharge cargo, that this was the site of the future metropolis of the Columbia River basin. Captain Couch himself brought a cargo of goods from New York in a ship commanded by Captain George H. Flanders, and the two captains then went into business together and remained in Portland for the rest of their lives.

The actual founding of the city occurred in 1843, when a young

Tennesseean, William Overton of Oregon City, stepped out of an Indian canoe on the west bank of the Willamette ten miles from where it joins the Columbia and determined to make the place his home. A few days later he invited a fellow-passenger in his canoe to step ashore and look at the site. The passenger was impressed; he noted the deep water and the fertile soil; and when the penniless Overton offered to give him a half-interest in a square-mile town-site if he would pay the costs of surveying and filing on the land, the deal was quickly closed. Overton's newly acquired partner was Asa Lawrence Lovejoy, native of Groton, Massachusetts, graduate of Amherst College, recent companion of the Congregational missionary Marcus Whitman on a long return journey to the Missouri by way of Santa Fe, a bold, hardy soul who had three times braved the dangers of the overland trail in less than two years.

Before the two men could get their cabin built, however, Overton sold his interest for $50 to Francis W. Pettygrove and departed for Texas, where it was said he was hanged. Pettygrove was a New Englander, a native of Calais, Maine, who had first come to Oregon by way of Honolulu to bring a stock of merchandise to Fort Vancouver for an Eastern firm. He had settled and engaged in the fur business at Oregon City, where he was the first American to build a warehouse and enter the grain trade. He and Lovejoy now owned the site of the new city, although there was only a provisional government to grant them a doubtful title, while Great Britain and the United States were still quarreling over the ownership of the Oregon country. But they blithely went ahead staking out lots and preparing for an early boom in real estate. Each wanted to name the town after the principal city of his home state, so they flipped a penny for the honor; it came up once "heads" for Boston and twice "tails" for Portland.

While the Tualatin and Willamette valleys were slowly filling with farmers and before the infant city had made much progress, Lovejoy sold out his interest to Benjamin Stark, and Pettygrove sold his to Daniel H. Lownsdale for $5,000 worth of leather, a small enough price to pay for a city, even if a somewhat better deal than the Indians made for the island of Manhattan. Lownsdale had also an adjoining land claim of his own, so he became the virtual proprietor of Portland, Oregon. Born in Kentucky and having lived in Indiana, Georgia, and

Europe, Lownsdale had seen enough of the world to realize the advantages of the site and also to know how to promote it. He gave away land in order to get it improved, sold lots at a nominal price to attract settlers, and offered inducements for the opening of business enterprises. To help him he enlisted another born realtor, that optimistic and energetic native of Maine, Stephen Coffin of Oregon City. As their legal adviser they retained William W. Chapman, who had come west on the first ship bringing gold-seekers to San Francisco. A Virginian by birth, Chapman had been the first Delegate to Congress from Iowa; he had been United States district attorney for Iowa and had furthered legislation out of which grew the Homestead Act. These three men owned the Portland Townsite Company and set Portland on the way to being a city.

Portland's principal rivals were Oregon City, where John McLoughlin, the former chief factor of the Hudson's Bay Company, had settled; Milwaukie, a few miles below; Linnton, farther down the Willamette towards the Columbia; and St. Helens on the Columbia. Lot Whitcomb at Milwaukie carried on the most vigorous warfare, operating a sawmill, selling the product to San Francisco, and making plenty of money. He added to Portland's discomfort by buying a ship's engine at San Francisco, hiring the nautical engineer Jacob Kamm to build a ship, and launching it on Christmas Day, 1850. When this vessel was put in service between Oregon City and Astoria, the citizens of the embryo metropolis were filled with dismay. And even worse opposition developed when the Pacific Mail Steamship Company abandoned its terminal at Astoria and built its docks up the river at St. Helens, almost at Portland's door.

Now occurred one of those crucial events such as have determined the fate of many cities. Lownsdale and the rest of the Portlanders determined to fight. Although they were few in numbers and light in purse, they decided to compete with the powerful Pacific Mail by operating their own steamer to California. At their request the side-wheeler *Gold Hunter* came up from San Francisco—the first ocean steamer to anchor at Portland. The owners wanted $60,000 for a controlling interest in the vessel, and although this was a large figure for the struggling city to consider, the citizens decided to buy it. So the necessary money was raised in Portland's first community campaign, and the town forcibly established itself as the northern terminus of the California steamship route. The Pacific Mail, however, had no intention of permitting such high-handed domination of the maritime trade; it secretly bought out some of the stockholders, took the *Gold Hunter* off the run, mortgaged the vessel, sent her to South America, and sold her for a trifle. But even if the Portlanders lost their money, they established their city, for they had made it plain that Portland was the logical place for a terminal port; farmers were bringing their produce to the city and refusing to go to St. Helens, and in 1851 the Pacific Mail capitulated and made Portland its terminus. Once the battle with the steamship company was won, the enterprising owners of Portland made sure of their victory by building dirt and plank roads and establishing ferry and river-steamboat services. And these radiating lines of transportation settled once and for all the site of the metropolis of the Columbia.

From the many private interests operating steamships and sailing-vessels on the Oregon rivers there soon emerged three powerful figures who were to do more than any others in centering Western transportation in Portland and contributing to the growth and importance of the city. These men, known as "the Triumvirate," were Captain John C. Ainsworth, Simeon G. Reed, and Robert R. Thompson. The doughty Captain Ainsworth was a native of Ohio, having been born at Springboro on June 6, 1822. At seven he lost his father, and in his early teens he began to make his own living on Mississippi River steamboats. He learned the art of navigation and the geography of the river so as to become a pilot, and finally he was made master of a steamer plying from St. Louis to the north. On this boat Samuel L. Clemens was his pilot at the time he conceived his *nom de plume* of "Mark Twain," and in later years he presented the Captain with a massive gold watch as a memento of their early association. When news of the gold-rush to California reached him, Captain Ainsworth went west with William C. Ralston, who was to become the leading banker of San Francisco, and their friendship persisted to the end of their lives. Indeed, it may be said to have been responsible for the starting of the Bank of California. After Ainsworth went on to Oregon and became captain of the steamer *Lot Whitcomb* in 1850, he asked Ralston for a loan of $50,000 which was quickly granted. When the latter's partner, Kelly, returned from a trip to New York and looked over the books, he observed the unsecured loan and demanded that it be immediately recalled. Much against Ralston's wishes, a letter to this effect was sent to Ainsworth; but as he had already cleaned up $100,000 on his deal, the money was returned before the letter reached him. The incident so disgusted Ralston, however, that he quit his partner and organized the Bank of California.

When Ainsworth first arrived in Oregon, he was satisfied for a time with command of the *Lot Whitcomb;* but later he added to his steamboat interests until he and his associates controlled the system that was the key to Northwest transportation. His first lieutenant, Simeon G. Reed, was born at East Abingdon, Massachusetts, on April 23, 1830, and there he worked in a shoe-factory for $12 a week. He later went to Quincy, where he failed in the grain business but succeeded in marrying the wealthiest and most beautiful girl of the town, Amanda Wood. In 1851 he came to San Francisco by way of Panama, and the next fall he pushed on to Portland, where he became a clerk in the mercantile house of W. S. Ladd and Company. In 1859 he became a partner of William Sargent Ladd's brother, John Wesley Ladd, under the style of "Ladd, Reed and Company, wholesale dealers in liquor and groceries," and a few years later he formed a partnership with W. S. Ladd to buy land and operate farm-property. In 1858 Reed bought an interest in the river-steamers *Belle, Señorita,* and *Multnomah,* and this marked his entry into the field of transportation which was afterwards his major interest.

But transportation on the Columbia was a complicated business in which many conflicting interests were engaged. Up the river 160 miles from the mouth the five-mile stretch of the Cascades stopped the steamers, and freight and passengers had to be unloaded and transported around the obstruction on a portage. Boats could then proceed to the Dalles, 60 miles farther, where they were again stopped by 12 miles of rapids and Celilo Falls, necessitating another portage. While the lower part of the river was gradually coming into the control of Ainsworth and Reed, the part above the Dalles was completely monopolized by R. R. Thompson. A native of Ohio, he had come west as a government Indian agent; later he had built sailing-vessels to carry freight and passengers above the Dalles, using Indians for much of the labor. From Celilo to Fort Walla Walla he carried freight in bateaux operated by Indians for $100 a ton, but when the commandant of the Fort suggested that he build a steamboat, he followed the advice. With this steamer he made three round trips a week, loaded with freight at $80 a ton, and enabled passengers to go from Walla Walla to Portland in 30 hours. As Captain Ainsworth clearly saw, the control of river transportation required an alliance with Thompson and also the ownership of the portages; so he began dickering with the various interests controlling rival river-steamers and resolved to obtain the right of way through the narrow pass of the Cascades and the portage there on the Oregon side, a horse railway owned by D. F. Bradford and his brother. These gentlemen cheerfully charged $20 a ton for carrying freight over their six-mile portage while the steamers received the same amount for carrying it all the rest of the way between Portland and the Dalles. The portage above the Dalles, leading to that part of the river where Thompson operated, was owned by Orlando Humason and J. S. Ruckle, who hauled the freight by team and likewise exacted a heavy charge. Thus by the time any goods reached points on the upper river, they had been handled by three steamers and two portages, each of which exacted its toll. To combine all these in one unified system of transportation was the purpose of John C. Ainsworth.

After much negotiation the owners of the various boats operating below the Cascades, between the Cascades and the Dalles, and above the Dalles were drawn into one group in which Ainsworth, Reed, and Thompson were the leading figures, and this was organized in Washington Territory in 1862 as the Oregon Steam Navigation Company. It was modestly capitalized at $172,500, and certainly this was conservative enough, for the company in later years spent $2,000,000 on improving its property, distributed $2,500,000 in dividends, and never levied a stock assessment.

From the outset good luck followed Ainsworth and his associates. At about the time the company was organized, rich placer gold-mines were discovered in Idaho, eastern Washington Territory, and Montana, and there was a rush of prospectors up the Columbia River to these points. All the steamers were crowded, people vied with each other to get passage, and at times the whole length of the portages was lined with freight that could not be handled. At this time the company strengthened its position by buying the portage above the Dalles and spending $100,000 on wagons and teams in an effort to expedite the forwarding of freight to the mines. Ainsworth then went to San Francisco and purchased at a bargain a lot of 20 miles of railroad iron, and work was at once begun on a railroad to supplant the portage wagon-road. At the Cascades the Bradfords, who owned the portage on the Washington side, had become alarmed at the greater proportion of business that was going to the owners of the portage on the Oregon side, Messrs. Ruckle and Humason. Ainsworth therefore was able to induce them to permit him to build a railroad on the Washington side, and once this project was begun, the owners on the Oregon side succumbed and sold their portage to the company for $155,000.

The monopoly was now complete. From Portland to the far-inland points reached by the Columbia and the Snake the Oregon Steam Navigation Company was in control. The company was reorganized in the State of Oregon with a capital of $2,000,000, October 18, 1862, and Ainsworth, Reed, Thompson, and the Ladds secretly organized a pool to acquire the stock of the other interests. It was rumored that the control was going to California men, panicky stockholders threw their shares on the market, and soon the pool owned all the stock. The capital was then increased to $5,000,000, and the stock was listed on the New York Stock Exchange.

Now began such an era of prosperity as few water-transportation concerns have ever enjoyed. The interior mines were developing so rapidly and settlers were coming to the agricultural lands in such numbers that the company was unable to handle the business offered. Although night and day crews were operated on the portages, the freight piled up there, and in Portland drays stood in line for days and nights at a time to get a chance to deliver cargo to the steamers. Drivers sometimes paid a $20 gold-piece in exchange for a place at the head of the line. And the company was said to have paid for a new boat from the receipts of a single trip. The triumvirate increased their profits by completely throttling competition and charging all the traffic would bear. A set of stringent regulations, signed by Vice-President Reed, proclaimed that if a shipper shipped goods to any

point on the river and transferred them to the boats of any other company for further shipment, the Oregon Steam Navigation Company
should be entitled to the full freight-rate to the final destination.
Furthermore, if goods were delivered to the company at any point by
steamers owned by others, the company should be entitled to payment
for carriage from the original shipping-point. This was monopoly with
a vengeance, and to it was added the further burden of an ingenious
scheme of charges which assumed 40 cubic feet to be a ton, no matter
what the actual weight might be. To calculate the weight of a wagon,
its length was measured from the rear wheel to the end of the tongue;
then the tongue was turned up at right angles, and the height was
measured from wheel-base to tip of tongue. These dimensions served
to determine the freight-charges; no scales were needed, and after the
measurements were made, the tongue was detached and put under the
wagon-bed to save space. At the rate of $40 for each 40 cubic feet,
or so-called ton, from Portland to Lewiston, Idaho, the cost to shippers
was 10 cents per ton per mile, about ten times the rate charged on
the Missouri. And often the article measuring a ton would weigh only
200 pounds, so that the rate was sometimes really a dollar per mile.
It is recorded that once when an employee was puzzled as to how to
measure a cannon—small in bulk but heavy in weight—so as to get
the usual high price per ton, the problem was solved by hitching a
mule to it and measuring the ensemble. Stories were told of a con-
signment of shovels on which the river freight to Lewiston was a
dollar apiece, of a dozen brooms on which the charge to Hood River
was a dollar; and old-timers recall the merchant who, when he was
asked why a single darning-needle cost the large sum of 25 cents,
replied, "But, madam, you forget the freight!"

In all transactions of the Navigation Company the responsibility
of thinking through the details and of making final decisions lay with
Captain Ainsworth. Reed was a sportsman who spent most of his
time with his horses and in travel. Thompson paid no attention to
detail, but his counsel was wise and far-sighted. At a meeting he would
say nothing, but after thinking things over a few days, during which
he might spend most of his time playing pool, a game at which he
was an adept, he would tell Captain Ainsworth his opinion of what
was to be done and offer his advice; and Ainsworth said that advice

was never wrong. The triumvirate worked so smoothly and built up such a complete monopoly of transportation on the Columbia that it began to attract the attention of the railroads building to the Pacific Coast; and the insiders, in turn, began to wonder how they could continue to enjoy such enormous profits in the face of possible rail competition.

In 1871 the Northern Pacific, which was rapidly building westward, began to negotiate for an interest in the Oregon Steam Navigation Company, and Ainsworth and Thompson went to New York to confer with the railroad officials. They finally sold a three-quarter interest for $1,500,000, one-half in Northern Pacific bonds, with the provision that the old owners continue in the management. But with the failure of Jay Cooke and Company the railroad bonds dropped to 10 cents on the dollar, and it looked as if the Oregonians had sold their company for nothing. Luck was with them again, however, for when Jay Cooke's assets were thrown on the market, Eastern investors were not familiar with the value of the Oregon company's stock, and so Ainsworth, Reed, and Thompson bought it all back at about half the price they had sold for.

By this time Portland was a flourishing city of about 10,000 people, who, as Samuel Bowles of the Springfield *Republican* observed in his *Our New West,*

keep Sunday with as much strictness almost as Puritanic New England does, which can be said of no other population this side of the Rocky Mountains at least. Whether this fact has anything to do with it or not, real estate we found to be very high in Portland—four hundred dollars a front foot for best lots one hundred feet deep on the main business street, without the buildings. . . . The Oregonians lack many advantages of their neighbors below; their agriculture is less varied and rampant, but it is more sure; mining has not poured such intoxicating wealth into their laps; they need, as well, a more thorough farming and a more varied industry; they need, also, as well, intelligent patient labor and larger capital; but they have builded what they have got more slowly and more wisely than the Californians; they have less severe reaction from hot and unhealthy growth to encounter,—less to unlearn; and they seem sure, not of organizing the first state on the Pacific coast, indeed, but of a steadily prosperous, healthy and moral one,—they are in the way to be the New England of the Pacific Coast.

Already a New England aristocracy had grown up, the leaders of which were the Ladds, the Corbetts, and a few other families which are still names to conjure with in Portland. Henry W. Corbett, born in Westboro, Massachusetts, in 1827, started his career with a total fortune of $21 as a clerk in a wholesale dry-goods house in New York. When the California gold-rush started, he saw that there would be a demand for Oregon products and that Portland would be a good trading-point, so he determined to go there. After seven years of faithful work his employers had such confidence in him that they sold him a large stock of goods which he brought to Portland around Cape Horn. He opened a store in 1851, acting as proprietor, clerk, and bookkeeper, and in one year cleared $20,000 in this town of 400 people. He went into the hardware business and with Henry Failing, of New York, built the firm of Corbett, Failing and Company into the largest of its kind on the Coast. Later these two partners bought the First National Bank and made it one of the great financial powers of the West. William S. Ladd was another who came to Portland to make his fortune selling merchandise. Born in Holland, Vermont, in 1826, he early became railroad freight-agent in his home town, but the success of his friend Charles Elliott Tilton in San Francisco drew him to the West. Arriving in Portland in 1852, he conducted a small store until he sold his stock, and then he traveled through the country buying chickens, eggs, and farm produce. At Portland again, he worked for a Mr. Godkin, who had opened a store, and within a year had made $1,000. He then went back to San Francisco, formed a partnership with Tilton to buy out Godkin, and brought back $60,000 in gold coin in his stateroom. The mercantile business was most prosperous, and he made his brother, John Wesley Ladd, his partner. In 1859 Ladd and Tilton opened the first bank in Portland and became the financial bulwark of the Oregon country.

Certainly, Portland in those days had a Yankee outlook on life. The annual New England Dinner was the leading social event of the year, and the Unitarian and Congregational churches early came into prominence, along with the Episcopal church, where the young men vied with each other to see which could furnish the most magnificent upholstery for his pew. Amusements were simple, but they included many dances, some of which were enlivened by the music of the military band from

Fort Vancouver. After the dance it was customary to eat ice-cream made by a confectioner who cut ice from the river and stored it and sold his product at 25 cents a dish. Church fairs and sociables were among the most popular events, and everyone turned out to attend them. There were boating parties up the river with picnics at Milwaukie. The ladies of the town gave afternoon luncheons with such substantial fare as oysters, chops, chicken, and hot biscuits, and the bachelors, a group of whom lived in the old gas-works, entertained with chafing-dish suppers. It was all very gay, especially when some social leader set the town agog with an evening of daring originality, as did Mrs. Corbett when she gave a "wishbone party."

It was all very like a small edition of Boston, and even at this day one can reconstruct the life of the time by strolling among the deserted old buildings with their ornate fronts that still stand in the river district. All the observers of the time commented on the New England flavor of the town, somewhat in the spirit of a writer for the Boston *Journal* who said, "To New England folks, Oregon has peculiar attractions. It is more New England than any of the states on the coast. The scenery is like that along the Penobscot.... The people are mainly from New England. The social status is Eastern. The industry, the thrift, the briskness of business all remind one of Maine."

The owners of the Oregon Steam Navigation Company had gobbled up the river traffic of the Northwest, but other men were looking longingly at the railroad routes and hoping to monopolize the approach to Oregon from California and the southeast, for Oregon products found a profitable market in California, apples having been known to sell for as much as $4 apiece at the mines. The traffic between Portland and San Francisco was handled by steamers, except for such hardy souls as responded to the advertisements of Henry W. Corbett's stage line, a handbill for which read,

> Overland mail route to Oregon
> Through in Six Days to Portland
> Avoid risk of ocean travel
> Most beautiful and attractive as well
> As bold grand and picturesque scenery
> Stages stop one night at

Ureka and Jacksonville for passengers to rest
Lay over at any point and continue journey within one month

July 20, 1866                          H. W. CORBETT & CO.
      $50                    PROPRIETORS, OREGON STAGE LINES.

In 1863 the California legislature granted privileges to a group of seventy men who proposed to make surveys for a railroad to Oregon. Among them was an engineer, Simon G. Elliott, who had become interested in railroads while listening to Theodore Judah expounding his plans for a line over the high Sierras. Elliott began the survey to connect southern Oregon with San Francisco, and on June 29, 1865, the California and Oregon Railroad Company was chartered at Sacramento to build along the route surveyed and obtain grants of land. In the same year a sister company, the Oregon and California Railroad, was organized in Oregon to carry the road to Portland and obtain land-grants. Through the influence of these companies a bill was passed in Congress granting twenty sections of land per mile along the track of the railroad that should be designated to receive it by the Oregon legislature.

Meanwhile, to combat the Californians Oregon interests had organized the Oregon Central Railroad. This also was to connect Portland with southern Oregon and California. Before the incorporation papers were finally completed, Joseph Gaston, the secretary, took them to the secretary of state, who penciled on them the date, October 6, 1866. Four days later the Oregon legislature designated the Oregon Central as the road that was to receive the land-grant. Final papers of incorporation, however, were not filed by Gaston until November 21, and meanwhile Elliott and his California group had filed papers incorporating another Oregon Central Railroad in order to beat Gaston. This second company was known as the "East Side Company" because it proposed to enter Portland on that side of the river and follow the Elliott route through the Willamette Valley, while Gaston's company was known as the "West Side Company" since its route went south closer to the coast and entered Portland west of the Willamette. Both companies broke ground in Portland in the spring of 1868, and the East Side Company wrote to the Secretary of the Interior to obtain the land granted to the Oregon Central Railroad, only to learn that Gaston had already filed acceptance of it for his Oregon Central. Immediately

EARLY PORTLAND

Lithograph after a drawing by Kuchel and Dresel, 1858. From the Stokes Collection, New York Public Library.

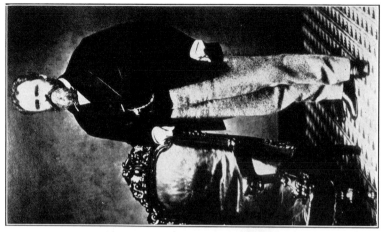

BEN HOLLADAY

SIMEON G. REED, JOHN C. AINSWORTH AND ROBERT R. THOMPSON

Courtesy of the Oregon Historical Society.

an extraordinary legal battle began to determine which of the two companies of the same name was the actual Oregon Central Railroad at the time the legislature of Oregon assigned the land.

The Gaston West Side Company had as incorporators Ainsworth, Reed, Thompson, and other prominent Portlanders, a much more imposing array of names than those of the East Side Company. But the East Side Company had some shrewd financial wanglers, and it proceeded to get work started while the West Siders were still marking time. Elliott presented to his board a contract on behalf of "A. J. Cook" to build 150 miles of road for $5,200,000 in 7 per cent mortgage bonds plus $2,000,000 in preferred stock, and when it was accepted, "A. J. Cook" obligingly assigned the contract to Elliott for $1. Another contract for 210 miles more was made and assigned to Elliott. Parts of these contracts were assigned to others for about $20,000. Some stock was disposed of for about $8,000, bonds were issued, and with the cash received Elliott managed to create the appearance of great activity, although he actually had no substantial financial support. At this critical period he succeeded in interesting a new-comer in the building of the railroad, and from that time forward the East Side Oregon Central became the gorgeous, scintillating sky-rocket of Oregon finance. The new-comer was none other than the powerful and glamorous "Little Napoleon" of the stage-coach business, Ben Holladay, who, in September, 1868, took over the contracts, receiving twenty-four fortieths for himself, ten fortieths for his partner, C. Temple Emmett, and allowing Elliott the six fortieths remaining.

It was appropriate that Holladay should take over the East Side road, for immediately upon his arrival in the city he had bought a large plot of land east of the river and declared that the city of the future would be on that side, that the grass would soon be growing on Front Street, and that he would make a rat-hole out of west-side Portland. He thus antagonized in a single breath the rich men of the city, all of whom owned west-side property, and their antagonism never abated. But Holladay did not care. He had the dash and bravado of the Plains. He deferred to no man. He was forceful, bold, unscrupulous, domineering, pompous, lavish, scheming, and, his enemies said, dishonest and immoral. He drove his Oregon railway project with all the breakneck speed, dust, and thunder of a runaway stage-coach, while staid Portland clasped her mittened hands and looked on in horrified fascination.

The man who threw consternation into Oregon business and society was born in Kentucky in 1819, soon after which his parents moved to Weston, Missouri. As a boy he clerked in a small drug-store where the officers of Fort Leavenworth congregated and exchanged stories of life on the Western plains. Fascinated by their accounts, Ben left his pills and bottles to work for Sublette and Bogy on their St. Louis–Santa Fe wagon-train. On his first trip the young drug-clerk noted what articles made the largest profit, and on his return he made up a train of his own—fourteen wagons, sixty mules, and twenty saddle horses—carrying bacon and farm-produce bought from the Weston farmers on credit. On his second venture, with a train nearly twice as long, he carried 270 chests of tea, which he had bought in New York for 28 cents a pound and shipped by sea and river to Fort Leavenworth. He sold this for $1.50 a pound in New Mexico, and all his other transactions were on a similar scale of profit. In order to get over the bad roads quickly he had his tires widened from four inches to ten, and this enabled him to make three trips to Santa Fe in one season, thus breaking all records. When the California gold-rush began, Ben showed his shrewdness by making up two wagon-trains loaded with chests of tea and coffee. He rode ahead to Salt Lake City and sold the tea and coffee at high prices, for the Mormon Saints had difficulty in obtaining these cheering stimulants. Then he bought all the butter and bacon he could get, and when the train arrived, he emptied the lead-lined tea-chests, filled them with butter, carried them to Sacramento, and sold his cargo for a dollar a pound. He also brought out wagonloads of whisky which he sold for $5 a gallon. He charged Indians a beaver skin for two drinks, and the driver would measure out the liquor in a half-pint cup coated a quarter of an inch deep with buffalo grease. He would hold two fingers of his left hand in the cup while the Indian drank, and by this saving device of fingers and tallow undoubtedly did high service for the cause of temperance and the purse of Ben Holladay.

In Sacramento, Ben met Pratt Harbin, who had 700 tons of wild oats, and to him Holladay entrusted a herd of cattle he had purchased en route and driven out to be fattened. Then he went on to San Francisco and contracted with the Pacific Mail Steamship Company to furnish their ships with American beef at an enormous price. Since

Spanish beef was as tough as leather, the company was glad to buy, for it charged passengers the high rate of $500 from San Francisco to New York *via* Panama. With plenty of money in his pocket Ben paid $75,000 for the Confidence Mine in Tuolumne County, and it produced large sums for him for 12 years.

In 1862 Holladay advanced money to the Leavenworth stage-coach owners, Russell, Majors and Waddell, at a time when they were in financial difficulties; thus he came into possession of their overland stage lines between Leavenworth, Denver and Salt Lake City. His enemies said that the firm had advanced him $600,000 worth of securities to hold for the partners while it went into bankruptcy, and that when the proceedings were over, he refused to return the property. By 1864 Holladay was operating lines to Salt Lake, Idaho, Montana, and the mining regions around Denver. He had a monopoly on the overland business from the Missouri River to Salt Lake, charging Wells, Fargo and the other express agencies what he wished because he controlled the only route between Denver and Atchison. But this was threatened when D. A. Butterfield opened his competing Overland Despatch to Denver. Now that there was only a 600-mile gap between Denver and Salt Lake, the express companies sent Holladay a letter threatening to put in a line between these points if he would not lower his rates. But Holladay had anticipated this and already had a careful inventory of the rival stage line. On the day the express companies issued their ultimatum threatening to "stock the gap," Holladay had dinner with the president of the Park Bank of New York, who owned the competing stage line, and completed a deal to buy his interests. Then he said to his secretary, "Answer those express companies and tell them to stock and be damned."

By 1866 Holladay controlled nearly 5,000 miles of stage line, with as complex an organization as a modern railroad. His line was divided into three divisions: from Atchison to Denver, from Denver to Salt Lake City, and from Salt Lake City to Placerville, California. In his *Overland Mail* Leroy Hafen has this to say of him: *

In 1866 a contemporary described him as "a man apparently about forty-five, tall and thin, of large grasp and quick perception, of indiffer-

* Reprinted by permission of the publishers, the Arthur H. Clark Company, from their *Overland Mail*.

ent health but indomitable will, fiery and irascible when crossed and a Westerner all through. Apparently he carried his vast business very jauntily, without much thought or care, but he crossed the continent twice each year, from end to end of his stage routes and saw for himself how matters were getting on."

Henry Villard described him as "a genuine specimen of the successful Western pioneer of former days, illiterate, coarse, pretentious, boastful, false, and cunning." Mark Twain tells a story with reference to Holladay. A youth who had crossed to California in the overland stage was subsequently traveling in the Holy Land with an elderly pilgrim who thus tried to impress upon the young man the greatness of Moses, the guide, soldier, poet, lawyer of Ancient Israel.

"Jack, from this spot where we stand, to Egypt, stretches a fearful desert three hundred miles in extent—and across that desert that wonderful man brought the children of Israel!—guiding them with unfailing sagacity for forty years over the sandy desolation and among the obstructing rocks and hills, and landed them at last, safe and sound, within sight of this very spot. It was a wonderful, wonderful thing to do, Jack. Think of it!"

"Forty years? Only three hundred miles? Hump! Ben Holladay would have fetched them through in thirty-six hours."

In 1866, anticipating the coming of the Pacific railroad, he sold out his lines advantageously to Wells, Fargo and Company. And very shortly thereafter the golden profits stopped. For the Union Pacific reached Cheyenne, the Kansas Pacific reached Hays City, 571 miles west of St. Louis, and the Central Pacific had reached Cisco, 94 miles east of Sacramento. Meanwhile, Holladay had bought four old ships which the Pacific Mail had tied up in the harbor of Benicia near his meat-butchering establishment. Fortunately for Holladay the gold excitement on the Fraser River in Canada broke out almost immediately; the result was the making of another fortune from his steamers. When the Fraser River rush died down, Holladay plied his ships between San Francisco, Portland, and San Diego. His luck continued strong when he mortgaged his ships to buy an interest in the Ophir Mine in Nevada, which came to be the greatest silver-producer of the Comstock Lode. He built an estate, "Ophir Farm," in Westchester County, New York, paid Frederick Law Olmstead $10,000 to landscape the grounds, and there his wife and daughters lived in lavish style, spending, it is said, $7,000 a month on entertaining. Such was the career of the man who burst into Portland with the grand scheme of buying the East Side railroad and extending it to California.

In the legal battle between the two contesting roads, Gaston's West Side Company gained a victory when the courts ruled that it was organized prior to the East Side Company and had sole right to the name, Oregon Central Railroad. Simeon S. Reed and Company was organized to build the Gaston railroad, and work began with a rush. But Holladay decided that the legislature of 1868 should be prevailed upon to give his company a chance of getting the rich prize of the Oregon land-grant upon which Gaston had already filed, and he set out to bring this about in characteristic fashion. Royal entertainment was provided for the legislators, and it was said that money was freely used otherwise to influence their decision. Holladay and a band of his henchmen kept open house in Salem, entertaining in such grandeur as the Oregon legislators had never seen and seeking to influence the press of the state as well as the lawmakers. He also entertained certain chosen spirits on one of his river-boats turned into a yacht, on which, it was said, the decks were damp with champagne.

Torn between the claims of the two rival roads and the advantages offered by each to different counties, and overwhelmed by the personality and blandishments of Ben Holladay, the legislature was in a turmoil. The Senate decided that the West Side Company was not in existence when it was granted the land. The House said that if the West Side Company did not own it, no other company could own it. And they finally agreed to redesignate the road to receive the grant and to give it to the first company completing 20 miles of road by July 1, 1880. Under Holladay's influence Congress passed a bill extending time for filing acceptance of the land-grant act and provided that the grant should go to the line that first completed 20 miles of road by December 25, 1869. Holladay completed the 20 miles from Portland to Parrott Creek on December 24, 1869, and thus became the recipient of the grant. Holladay then told the East-Side directors he would stop construction unless they turned over all the stock to him, and they gave him every share but one. In 1870 he offered to return this stock if the directors would pay him the $1,000,000 due him on his building contract. This, of course, they could not do. So he made another proposition, in the name of the Oregon and California Railroad, a company newly organized by him, to purchase the entire property and pay for it by assuming the debt of $1,000,000 owing to Ben Holladay. This proposition being accepted, Ben was in complete control of the Oregon Central through his legally organized company. He immediately issued $10,500,000 worth of bonds and sold them at 70 per cent, mostly in Germany.

Meanwhile, another scheme to give Oregon a transcontinental railroad connection had been fostered by B. J. Pengra, surveyor-general of the state, who proposed a line from Portland south through the Klamath Lake country to Winnemucca, Nevada, there to connect with the Central Pacific. This plan had the support of Collis P. Huntington, who saw in it an opportunity to make the Oregon line one branch of his system. In December, 1867, he wrote Colton from New York, "C. E. Tilton here tonight. He is of the firm of Ladd and Tilton, Portland, Or. He is a good man and I have told him we would like to have him and a few of his friends come in and build the Pengra line.... [Gould] feels that he is being menaced by the extension of the S. P. although I tell him that it is in the U. P. as well as the C. P. interest that we take care of that line." When the bill giving this road a land-grant was brought up in Congress in 1869, Washington was a beehive of lobbyists representing conflicting interests: Huntington had his Central Pacific, the Northern Pacific was strongly represented, Simeon G. Reed was there for the Oregon Central, and John H. Mitchell pulled all the wires he could for the East Side road. In the turmoil the Pengra bill was amended so as to require that his road connect with Holladay's in the Rogue River valley. Since this would give Holladay complete control of the Portland business, Huntington promptly withdrew, and the project was lost.

Pengra still clung to his hope of a Winnemucca connection, however, and in 1875 the newly organized Portland Board of Trade obtained a promise from Huntington to investigate the proposed route again, in return for which favor the Board promised to use its influence to obtain whatever grants and subsidies he might require. Judge of their feelings when he replied that he thought a $25,000,000 subsidy from the State of Oregon would be justified by the advantages to be gained from the project. His specific terms later provided that the company be exempt from all taxes until such time as its net earnings should exceed 10 per cent per annum on the capital stock—surely a joke to anyone familiar with the financial wizardry of Huntington; Portland was to provide $1,000,000 outright and the State of Oregon $210,000 a year; freight-rates were not to be subject to state control, but they were not to be in excess of those charged between San Francisco and the East plus the charge for rail or steamship carriage between Portland and San Francisco. In other words, Portland was to be sold down the river to San Francisco with Huntington in the rôle of Simon Legree. The Portlanders tried to prune down Huntington's demands and insisted on equality of rates with San Francisco. Various conferences were held, but they came to naught, and in 1876 the Board of Trade withdrew.

When it appeared that the land-grant was slipping from the grasp of the West Side railroad, Simeon G. Reed and Company stopped work on construction and had its contract canceled. Since Huntington had lost interest in any connection of the West Side road with his Winnemucca project, and there was no question that Holladay had the funds to complete his line ahead of the other and thus secure the land-grant, the West Siders decided to capitulate. When Holladay first offered to buy the West Side road, Ainsworth opposed the sale, saying that once he had obtained access to Portland from the south on both sides of the Willamette, Holladay's next move would be to build a line up the Columbia River and compete with the Oregon Steam Navigation Company. But William S. Ladd was in favor of selling out to Holladay. "Holladay will find this a very different proposition from building his road from Oregon City to Salem across prairies where the grading is purely nominal," he said. "The only way to break such a man is to let him do just what he wants in the present instance and to load him down with more unproductive property than he has capital enough to carry." The sale was concluded next day at two, and at five the triumphant Holladay and his family sailed for San Francisco.

The sale of the bonds for the Oregon Central and the Oregon and California railroads had been negotiated in Germany and England by Holladay's friend Milton S. Latham, president of the London and San Francisco Bank. Fearing that he would lose his job when there was a partial default on the bonds, Latham paid the interest as due to the English investors but paid the Germans nothing. When the Germans sent a representative to San Francisco, Latham pacified him; but when the second default occurred, after the panic of 1873, they sent a shrewder man to discover what was the matter, and this step marked the entry into American railroad affairs of Henry Villard, born Heinrich Gustav Hilgard, who became the king-pin of transportation in the Northwest and whose meteoric flight across the financial skies was the sensation of two continents.

Henry Villard was born in Speyer, Germany, in 1835. After he had graduated from the *Gymnasium* in 1853, he came to America and stayed with an uncle on a farm at Belleville, Illinois. There he amused himself by writing for the local German paper, and he continued writing when he studied law at Peoria and in Chicago. Becoming proficient in English, he reported the political debates between Lincoln and Douglas in 1858; then he covered the Indiana and Illinois legislatures for the Cincinnati *Commercial,* and in 1859, with Horace Greeley and Albert D. Richardson, he investigated the gold excitement in the Pike's Peak region. After attending the Republican National Convention that nominated Lincoln for President in 1860, he was sent to Springfield to write despatches concerning Lincoln until the President-elect left for Washington. Lincoln invited Villard to accompany the Presidential party to New York, and this led to his establishment in Washington as political correspondent. At the outbreak of the Civil War he went into the field as correspondent for the New York *Herald* and covered various important campaigns, being on the flagship *Ironsides* at the attack on Charleston. Having given up active field service because of illness, Villard in 1864 organized the first news-agency to compete with the Associated Press. Then he joined Grant's Army of the Potomac, and his despatches were printed in six newspapers, including the Springfield *Republican.* In 1865 he became Washington correspondent for the Chicago *Tribune,* and early the following year he married the only daughter of William Lloyd Garrison. Going abroad for the *Tribune,* Villard visited Paris and his native Germany, and on his return he became secretary of the American Social Science Association. It was this connection that caused him to become interested in the study of public finance and railroad securities, and he formed a plan to induce German bankers to join him in trying to establish a mortgage bank in America.

Convalescing in Germany from an apoplectic stroke, he was visited by a gentleman who had bought the 7 per cent bonds of the Oregon and California Railroad Company and wanted his advice. When the data from the Frankfort Protective Committee were obtained, Villard gave an unfavorable opinion. Nearly $11,000,000 worth of the bonds had been sold abroad at 70, and the holders had discovered that instead of 375 miles of road being built south of Portland, there was only 200 miles. Since only one-third of the interest was being earned, the bondholders decided to assert their rights, and in 1874 Villard was given the task of negotiating with Ben Holladay.

Villard met Holladay in New York and was not favorably impressed. He described him as a genuine specimen of the more uncouth of the old-time Western pioneers—illiterate, coarse, pretentious, boastful, false, and cunning. What a contrast there must have been between the calm, highly cultured German-American newspaper man and the blustering Western master of the Plains! After their interview Villard went west and was soon investigating Latham's delinquencies, although that gentleman never knew he was in San Francisco. He then went on to Roseburg, Oregon, and secreted himself there, getting information from his friend Paul Shulze of Portland, while Holladay's agents looked for him in vain. By the time he reached Portland, Villard had enough information to make Holladay decidedly uncomfortable. Latham was lavishing the investors' money on an unproductive narrow-gage road from Sausalito to Bolinas, across the Golden Gate from San Francisco, and Holladay had spent $300,000 of unaccounted funds in politics and the most riotous kind of living.

But as to the Oregon railroad prospects Villard was enthusiastic. He recommended that a bureau of immigration be founded to encourage settlers to come to the fertile Willamette Valley and the substantial city of Portland, and the bond-owners approved his plan and made him the head of the organization. He made a contract with Holladay under which it was agreed that all receipts of the railroad companies should be turned over to a financial agent who should pay the bills, and that Holladay should have no part in the sale of railroad lands so long as any part of the principal or interest on the bonds remained unpaid. But it was soon evident that Holladay had no intention of abiding by this agreement. His management was so indifferent and incompetent that

Villard decided he must be finally removed. He accordingly retained the powerful law firm of Mitchell and Dolph to prosecute Holladay, and these moves so frightened Ben that he entered into an agreement whereby he surrendered control of both the East Side and West Side railroads to the German bondholders and also gave them the only paying properties he owned—the five steamships of the Oregon Steamship Company, some of whose ships plied to Sitka, Honolulu, and Mexico.

So pleased were the German bondholders with Villard's conduct of their affairs that they made him president of both the East Side and West Side railroads and the Oregon Steamship Company, and he set up a temporary residence in Portland. In addition to his Oregon duties at this time he was called into the reorganization of another railroad property in which the Germans had invested. This was the Kansas Pacific, and the business involved took Villard back to Denver for the first time since he had investigated the Pike's Peak mining excitement 17 years before. What a transformation he saw in the plain and mountain country! Civilization had come with the railroad. Denver had changed from a mining village to a busy city. The great herds of buffalo had vanished, even their whitened bones having been gathered off the prairies and shipped east to be used in manufacturing. This view of what a railroad could do in promoting the prosperity of a frontier territory must have encouraged Villard as to the prospects of his Oregon venture. His connection with the Kansas Pacific also involved him in a financial duel with the most crafty of railroad promoters, and the result added to his experience as a financier.

At this time the celebrated railroad manipulator Jay Gould had a large interest in the Union Pacific, and with its president, Sidney Dillon, he began to try to get control of the Kansas Pacific in order to consolidate the two competing roads. Gould dickered with the representatives of the stockholders and with Villard as representative of the bondholders. There were three issues of mortgage bonds, and Villard insisted that they should be redeemed at par, although they were then selling at around 50 and 30. The stockholders listened to Gould and seemed willing to accept his terms, but Villard refused. To break down his resistance Gould abused him in the press and tried to get him removed as receiver of the Kansas Pacific. Although under the terms of the act founding the Kansas Pacific it was to have a share of the transcontinental freight, which was to be routed over its subsidiary the Denver Pacific between Cheyenne and Denver, the Union Pacific had never permitted traffic to be prorated. This depressed the Kansas Pacific earnings and the price of its securities. Now Gould threatened to reduce its income further by building a line paralleling the Denver Pacific from Denver to Cheyenne and taking away the mainstay of the Kansas Pacific traffic, the Denver business. Villard refused to be bluffed, however, and in the end Gould accepted his terms, taking the bonds at par, the only concession being the reduction on the accrued interest of the third-mortgage bonds from 7 per cent to 6 per cent. Gould had bought Kansas Pacific at 12 when Union Pacific was selling at 60 and 70. After the consolidation of the two roads, with the Kansas Pacific as the Eastern Division of the Union Pacific, the stock of both roads went above par, and the bonds followed, one issue with six years' accrued interest going to 140. Gould cleaned up more than $10,000,000 on the deal. The negotiations carried on by Villard, who successfully protected his interests against the most unscrupulous manipulator of the day, greatly enhanced his reputation.

Villard now began to lay his plans for making Portland not only the focus of local lines, but a great western terminal-point for the railroads of the country. For he saw that the force of gravity made the Columbia River the easiest and cheapest route to tide-water. In planning to connect the properties of which he was president with a transcontinental outlet, his first thought was a line from Portland to Salt Lake along the route originally surveyed by General Dodge to form a part of the Union Pacific. The advantages of this route had been consistently touted in recent years by W. W. Chapman of Portland, who organized the Portland, Salt Lake and South Pass Railroad and once almost succeeded in getting Congress to deprive the Northern Pacific of much of its land-grant and give it to his company. In 1879 Villard interested Jay Gould in the project and entered into an agreement whereby he and Gould were to form a construction company to build the road from Ogden to Portland. But control of entry to Portland from the east would not be possible without control of that grand monopoly of the Columbia, the Oregon Steam Navigation Company; and so they decided that, as the first step in the

plan, Villard must try to buy it. Imagine with what licking of chops
Captain Ainsworth welcomed into his office this callow young East-
erner who had the temerity to aspire to the control of Oregon's perfect
monopoly! With Reed and Thompson he made a careful inventory of
the property, which, it is said, totaled $2,500,000. Whereupon Thomp-
son, who was known as one of the best poker-players in the United
States, said, "Double it! It's just as easy to get five million as two
and a half!" So the price was set at $5,000,000, they all took a
trip over the line, and Villard accepted the valuation as fair. Five
million dollars was a bagatelle in the schemes of national transportation that were taking shape in his mind.

By this time the German bondholders of the steamship line to California had become disgusted at their lack of profits and desired to
sell the property. Villard had quietly organized a New York syndicate
to buy it. He now proposed to Ainsworth and Reed that they should
all combine to form a new company which should take over both the
river and ocean lines and build a railroad from the Cascades on the
Columbia to Walla Walla, Washington, so as to control completely
the Columbia River valley. This sounded well, but Ainsworth and
Reed undoubtedly thought that the $100,000 they had exacted from
Villard for an option would be forfeited and that he would be unable
to redeem his pledge. Their agreement provided that they would sell
40,320 shares of their Oregon Steam Navigation Company stock, which
was to be purchased at par, half in cash, 20 per cent in the bonds
of the new company, and 30 per cent in its stock. The new corporation, to be known as the Oregon Railway and Navigation Company,
was to have capital stock of $6,000,000 and 6 per cent bonds of the
same amount. Villard was to be allotted $1,000,000 stock and $1,200,000
bonds to buy the old Holladay Oregon Steamship Company, which
owned the line to San Francisco, and to build an additional ocean
steamer; he was to have $1,800,000 in stock and $1,500,000 in bonds
to build the railroad to Walla Walla, and $2,000,000 in stock and
$2,500,000 in bonds to raise the cash to pay the Ainsworth group.

Thinking that he would never be able to raise the large sum required, Ainsworth and Reed bade Villard good-by at the end of May,
1879. In New York he presented the proposition to the Union Pacific,
as represented by Gould, and was surprised to receive a cool note

saying that he declined to participate. This withdrawal of Gould has been variously interpreted, but it was probably due to Huntington, who wanted no new transcontinental road built to parallel the Central Pacific and who probably threatened to make reprisals on the Union Pacific should Gould further this scheme. Villard then turned to his own financial friends, asking them to subscribe for the bonds at 90 with a bonus of 70 per cent in stock, and within ten days he was able to telegraph Ainsworth to deliver the Oregon Steam Navigation Company stock in New York and receive cash. After paying for this stock there was enough money left to build in 1880 the new ocean steamer *Columbia,* which was the first to be equipped with electric lights, and the railroad to Walla Walla. Villard then went to Europe for a vacation, and when he returned in November, the stock he had given as a bonus was selling at 95. This brilliant coup added to his reputation at home and abroad.

As Villard pushed the construction of the Oregon Railway and Navigation Company tracks eastward to meet the Oregon Short Line, with which it connected in 1880 at Huntington, he began to fear that the Northern Pacific would menace his concern by building down the opposite bank of the Columbia. And he saw that his Oregon lines must fight the northern road as a competitor on the vast checkerboard of farm and mining and timber country of the Northwest. After much maneuvering he concluded in 1880 a traffic agreement by which the Northern Pacific was to occupy and develop the country north of the Snake River while the Oregon Railway and Navigation Company was to have the territory to the south. The Northern Pacific was to run its trains into Portland over the Oregon company's tracks, and the Oregon Improvement Company, a subsidiary organized by Villard to go into the land, coal, and transportation business and to hold the Oregon-California railroad, was to buy 300,000 acres of Northern Pacific lands in the Palouse country. Villard also offered to form a syndicate to provide funds to complete the Northern Pacific, but this was refused.

Villard had always regarded the Northern Pacific as a weak rival which would some day fall into his hands, but he changed his opinion when the road negotiated a loan of $40,000,000 and proceeded to build rapidly westward. He must now do one of three things, buy control of the Northern Pacific, sell out to the Northern Pacific, or sell out to the Union Pacific. Sidney Dillon was urging the latter course and showing the advantage of a through line from Portland to Ogden. One of Villard's directors, William Endicott, Jr., of Boston, wrote him:

Our true policy, as I look at it, is, instead of gobbling up the Northern Pacific, to be in a good condition to be gobbled up. When we are at Baker City our road will be a very attractive object to either of two suitors, and I am persuaded we can sell out to one of them on very satisfactory terms. The Union Pacific being much the stronger, I should prefer to cultivate an intimacy with it. As the Central Pacific has control of the Southern, it will be important for the Union Pacific to have another outlet on the Pacific and the Oregon business will enable them to pay us a good price.

But despite the opportunity to make money by selling his road, Villard determined on the more fascinating and dangerous scheme of acquiring control of the Northern Pacific. He secretly bought all the stock he could on his own account and then sent out a circular to fifty men asking for subscriptions to an investment fund of $8,000,000, the purpose of which was not disclosed. The mystery of the request coupled with Villard's reputation as a financier brought instantaneous response; bankers vied with one another in making subscriptions, and despite the stringency of the times the money for his "blind pool" was immediately forthcoming. A month later, having purchased all the Northern Pacific stock needed, he announced the incorporation of the Oregon and Transcontinental Company, whose purpose was to control both the Northern Pacific and the Oregon Railway and Navigation Company. It was one of the first of the holding companies which in later years became so numerous. Twelve millions additional was subscribed to the new concern, President Frederick Billings of the Northern Pacific resigned to permit Villard to assume control, and the new company aided the Northern Pacific in completing its transcontinental line. This triumph of Villard meant that Portland would be the main beneficiary of the Northern Pacific, since he had no intention of ruining his Oregon properties by permitting the railroad to build over the Cascade Range and carry its traffic directly to Puget Sound.

At this development Portland rejoiced, for despite her control of the only water-grade route from the Inland Empire to the sea, she needed help to overcome some of her natural disadvantages. A hundred miles inland from the ocean, the port of Portland suffered by comparison with the broad, deep inlet of Puget Sound. There was a wild, tempestuous bar at the mouth of the Columbia with a natural depth of only 20 feet; the channel to Portland was only 10 feet deep and was obstructed by several islands and a particularly dangerous bar below Portland called "the Hog's Back"; and the seasonal variation in the height of the Willamette at Portland was as much as 30 feet, making dock construction difficult. The route was so dangerous and the cost of loading and unloading so much greater than at Puget Sound that six English shipmasters wrote to the Liverpool *Mercury* in 1881 stating that "the exorbitant prices charged at this port surpass any that have ever come before our notice. The danger connected with the bay, the pilotage and the steam expense on the river are such that they literally swallow all the profits." And sometimes shipping was completely interrupted when the river was frozen over, as on the occasion in December, 1880, when Villard's lieutenant, Thomas Oakes, wrote to him: *

The weather here has been very cold during the past three or four days. Navigation of the Columbia above the Willamette was suspended on Thursday and on the Willamette yesterday. This embargo on the commerce of Portland is not flattering to the enterprise of her people. . . . If the Northern Pacific people were smart they would build a line from East Portland to Kalama [the point to which the Northern Pacific had extended southward from Tacoma] and take the grain trade during the winter to Puget Sound, and this, in my opinion, would be followed by the diversion of a considerable part of that trade in other seasons of the year. . . . There has been a lamentable lack of enterprise here. A large number of persons have made a great deal of money and live in fine houses, but they have shown so little public spirit, it is not difficult to guess their money has been made almost exclusively in trade without competition, and that with the infusion of new blood they will give way to another class.

As yet, Oregon was not noted for civic improvement. And even as late as 1890 Rudyard Kipling in his *American Notes* described his

* James Blaine Hedges, *Henry Villard and the Railways of the Northwest* (New Haven, Yale University Press, 1905).

entry into Portland, then a city of 50,000 souls, over a plank road that
would have been a disgrace to an Irish village. He wrote of the
pleasant countryside of the Willamette Valley dotted with small townships, and roads full of farmers in their town wagons, with "bunches
of tow-haired boggle-eyed urchins sitting in the hay behind," and said
that the Oregon men generally looked like loafers although the women
were well dressed.

Villard was now building the Oregon Railway and Navigation Company line from Portland up the Columbia, extending the Oregon and
California from Portland to California, and completing the transcontinental Northern Pacific. He next organized a $3,000,000 terminal
company to build a depot in Portland, a bridge across the Willamette,
and docks and machine-shops. And since Portland had no good hotel,
he purchased a site and had plans prepared for what afterwards became the Portland. He had caused the Union Pacific to build from
Ogden to Baker when he started to extend the Oregon Railroad and
Navigation Company to that point, and so he was able to promise
Portland not only one transcontinental railroad but two. The road
also connected with General Palmer's Denver and Rio Grande Western,
which was completed in 1884. In 1883 Villard crowned his largesse
to Oregon by giving $50,000 to the State University at Eugene, which
promptly named a hall in his honor.

But all this expansion was not without its risks, and Villard was
beginning to get beyond his depth. Faced with financial difficulties by
reason of the surpassed estimates of the cost of the Northern Pacific,
he hurried the work forward so that the main line could be completed as quickly as possible. To the driving of the last spike, near
Garrison, Montana, he invited the entire diplomatic corps, prominent
German and English bankers, governors of states, and members of
Congress. And in the late afternoon of September 8, 1883, the job
was done. It has been said that the spike was driven home by Villard
after his baby daughter had touched it with her fingers, but it was
actually driven by H. C. Davis, general utility man in the traffic
department, in a scene of general disorder, and instead of being of
gold it was of ordinary steel. The road had actually been completed
for traffic on August 22, and a locomotive puffed across the spot
where the gap had been, while citizens of Missoula and Helena looked

PORTLAND IN 1867

From a photograph. Courtesy of the Southern Pacific Company.

"WOODING-UP" A COLUMBIA RIVER STEAMER

*The West Shore,* 1886.

THE FIRST TRANSCONTINENTAL TRAIN ON THE NORTHERN PACIFIC

This gala train, bearing Henry Villard and his guest notables to the driving of the last spike at Gold Creek, Montana, in 1883, proceeded after the ceremony to Portland. Courtesy of the Northern Pacific Railway.

on. But the track over which the trains moved was a detour, and a space of 2,737 feet was left in the main-line track so that the guests —four trainloads from the East and one from the West—could see the last rails laid. Among those watching were General Grant, James Bryce, the British Ambassador, Sitting Bull, and two thousand Crow Indians in war-paint and feathers.

Villard had also completed the extension of the Northern Pacific Tacoma line from Kalama to Portland; he had bought out the "Oregonian," a Scotch narrow-gage railroad which threatened to complete a rival line from Portland to California; he had fought the Utah and Northern extensions of the Union Pacific in Montana and made favorable trackage agreements with this line; and he had faced the unpleasant situation of a $14,000,000 rise over the engineers' estimates in the cost of building the Northern Pacific. He had also paid high dividends on the Northern Pacific securities, the first being a cumulative dividend of $11\frac{1}{10}$ per cent on the preferred stock, although the road's earnings did not justify this, and it was said that every department of the railroad was extravagantly, if not dishonestly, run by the employees.

Under such conditions it is not surprising that the financial structure of Villard's enterprises became top-heavy. Moreover, the driving of the last spike did not bring the prosperity to the Northern Pacific that he had anticipated. Instead, revenues fell off when materials for construction were no longer being freighted. The spike-driving excursion had served to dampen the spirits of the American bankers, who were frightened by the road's vast expanse of uninhabited and seemingly worthless land, and they refused to make further investments. Nevertheless, the German bankers who had been Villard's guests at the spike-driving had been sufficiently impressed so that $20,000,000 of second-mortgage bonds were sold to the Deutsche Bank. The issuance of these bonds, however, depressed the price of Northern Pacific stock, and to add to Villard's difficulties the Oregon and Transcontinental Company was staggering under a load of stocks that it had purchased in his other companies. It expected to pay for these with another issue of its own stock, but the value of the securities it had issued fell so far that this was impossible. As the financial condition of his companies became steadily worse, Villard saw that he could not save his fortune, and in December, 1883, he asked a group of his friends to advise with him on his financial plight. After examining the books they declared him to be insolvent. They then formed a syndicate to take over his Oregon companies, and he turned over to them all his cash and securities. The Boston *Transcript* said that the reason for his downfall was that he had a blind following and did his work in the dark, that he had paid from $5,000,000 to $10,-000,000 in commissions on his loans, that the $300,000,000 capital of the Oregon and Transcontinental was too large for the meager territories served, and that he had unnecessarily increased the indebtedness of that company and the Oregon Improvement Company, his real-estate holding company, organized in 1879. After the crash Villard resigned from all his companies except the Oregon and California Railroad and went to Europe to recover from the shock.

Villard's schemes lapsed for a while, and the stone foundation-walls of his Portland Hotel stood untouched for years before anyone had courage enough to finish the building. But Portland and Oregon had gained much from his control of Northwestern transportation. He had established the city as the hub of railway and steamboat traffic, he had made large investments and improvements, and he had brought thousands of settlers to the state and to the vast Inland Empire drained by the Columbia. In New York his agents met the European immigrants and converted their attention to the Northwest; in Boston they encouraged the owners of worn-out New England farms to emigrate to Oregon; at Topeka and Omaha they directed the faint-hearted on to the Northwest and diverted those who had started for California. In Liverpool, in Germany, Scotland, Wales, and Scandinavian countries glowing literature about the Northwest was distributed, and in the Portland offices there were European employees who could speak to the new-comers in their own tongue. It was this indefatigable industry and widespread organization that explained what the San Francisco *Chronicle* called the "strange fondness of immigrants for the wet slopes of the Cascade Mountains and the solitary banks of the great Columbia."

By this time Portland was the acknowledged center of transportation, business, and banking in the Northwest, although there were not lacking vivacious spirits in rival towns who might have added an adjective and called it "the dead center." For the conservatism of Portland bankers and business men was so pronounced that they earned the unappreciative sobriquet of "mossbacks." Even that journalistic rock of ages the *Oregonian* was shaken from its accustomed aplomb on April 21, 1887, when it declared editorially that Portland's leading citizens were afraid of the advent of new wealth or new energy that might injure their business and displace them from their thrones. Said the *Oregonian*,

There are men of wealth in Portland who not only refuse to take the lead themselves in undertakings that would push on the industrial and commercial development of this city and the country that surrounds it, but, what is far more culpable, they systematically discourage every proposition of men from abroad to do so.... Men come from the east to Portland looking for opportunity to make investments. They would establish cable roads in the city or construct suburban railways or build bridges or erect lumber or flour mills.... Or, they would place here reserves of capital, to be used in the development of the resources and industries of the country.... When the inquirer asks about this thing he is told that "it will not pay" or about that thing that "there is nothing in it." He is assured that there is money enough here now for all legitimate investments; that the banks of Portland are in fact full of money, and that if there was anything in these matters ... they would have undertaken them long ago....

The class of larger merchants ... discourage investments in productive industry here because they are handling at a profit the products of the industry of the Eastern States or California. So they join the banker ... and run through the old gamut of all that chronic pessimism can suggest till the newcomer, almost believing he has reached the place over whose portals Dante's terrible line is written—"Who enters here leaves hope behind,"—starts for his hotel, pays his bill and sets off to find a place where the people have some faith in their country and in themselves, and don't talk habitually in sepulchral and hopeless tones....

It is an unfortunate thing for a city when, before it has really made itself master of its situation, it acquires a feeling of serene confidence and security, taking its character from a congeries of wealthy and conservative citizens whose faces are towards the past rather than towards the future. Portland herein demonstrates how wealth becomes obstructive rather than helpful.

One of the most distressing features of the Portland scene was the Columbia River bar, and Portlanders tried to reassure themselves about this by repeating over and over that it did not exist, or at most was greatly exaggerated. But those who calmly considered the matter admitted that something must be done. From the outset Villard had seen the necessity of improving the bar and deepening the channel to Portland; and Huntington too had remarked that if the Winnemucca road was built, he would spend a million dollars on river-improvement. In 1881 a sea-captain told the newly appointed committee on river improvement of the Portland Board of Trade that they had to consider whether it was cheaper to pay freight to Puget Sound or maintain dredging operations on the Columbia, and the *Oregonian* began a campaign to improve the bar and open the river, declaring that "the loss which the people of Portland have suffered with patience not above reproach aggregates many millions of dollars.... This matter is not more important to Portland than to other sections of the state. The farmer who produces wheat is the loser by increased cost of shipping, not the Portland shipper, who trims his sails to suit the breeze."

Roused by all these warnings, the Oregonians began a consistent effort to deepen the bar and the channel, and as a result millions of dollars were subsequently spent on this work by the United States Government. Consequently, by the time the Northern Pacific had built its line directly to Tacoma over the Cascades, shipping conditions were so much better at Portland that the city did not feel the new competition so disastrously as had been expected. Now more than ever, however, Oregon needed its own railroad connection with the East which would fight the Puget Sound route above and the California route below. And this was achieved in 1887, when the Union Pacific leased the Oregon Railway and Navigation Company's connection through its Oregon Short Line to Ogden, guaranteeing the 6 per cent interest on the bonds for 99 years.

In order to protect the Oregon Railway and Navigation Company and keep the Northern Pacific from infringing on it, the Oregon and Transcontinental Company now tried to increase its holdings of Northern Pacific stock. Under the presidency of Elijah Smith this holding company of Villard's purchased 60,000 more shares, and in 1887, faced with difficulty in renewing its loans, the burden of this purchase was so heavy that it appeared to be on the verge of collapse. In its emergency the company turned to Henry Villard, who by this time had recovered his poise if not his fortune and had returned to

America as agent of the Deutsche Bank. He had acquired some capital through the sale to Whitelaw Reid of his house on Madison Avenue in New York and was ready to recoup his fortune. To help the Oregon and Transcontinental Company and its bankers, Chase and Higginson, out of a tight place, he purchased $5,000,000 worth of the company's bonds. In return for this assistance he received the management of this company, as well as of the Oregon Railway and Navigation Company, and sufficient proxies to elect his own board of directors on the Northern Pacific. Thus, in a few years after the loss of his fortune Villard was unexpectedly returned to control of his former properties.

But his interests were not now wholly with Portland. The Northern Pacific had completed its line over the Cascades to tide-water at Tacoma, both the Northern Pacific and the Oregon Railway and Navigation Company were building extensions into the Inland Empire, and the business of this vast territory, once exclusively the tributary of Portland, was being divided between that city and Puget Sound. In order to keep the rival roads from wasting funds in competitive building and to protect the interests of both, Villard sought to arrange a new agreement for a division of territory and business. Villard, Billings, and August Belmont considered the matter for the Northern Pacific and arranged the terms of a joint lease whereby the Northern Pacific would bear equally with the Union Pacific the guarantee of the 6 per cent dividend which the Union Pacific had made on the Oregon Railway and Navigation Company stock. The Northern Pacific was to build branches north of Snake River, the Oregon Company south, and the Oregon Company was to have the right to purchase the independent Hunt lines which were gridironing the wheat district around the Snake River in Washington. And tariffs were to be arranged so as to permit freight from points in the Inland Empire north of the Snake River to reach the sea at either Portland or Tacoma.

Opposition to this lease immediately developed. The Walla Walla–Pendleton region wanted no longer to be the sole property of the Oregon Railway and Navigation Company, which had continuously exploited it. As an example of its extortionary rates it was pointed out that 500 fire-brick from England to Walla Walla incurred a greater freight-charge on the 245 miles from Portland to Walla Walla than from Liverpool to Portland, the Oregon Company charging 6½ cents per brick. And Portland, instead of rejoicing to have the Northern Pacific and its Tacoma line confined to the north of the Snake River, now objected to giving up the business from the Cœur d'Alene, Idaho, mines. Moreover, if the rates were to be the same to Portland and Puget Sound, Portland demanded that the Oregon Railway and Navigation Company be required to conduct lighterage and pilot service between the mouth of the Columbia and the city at a cost no greater than the charges for similar service from the entrance of Puget Sound to Tacoma. Portland also demanded that a railroad be built to tap the country north of the Snake and insisted that the Northern Pacific be kept out of the south. In order to satisfy all parties endless negotiations developed between Villard and President Charles Francis Adams of the Union Pacific. The situation was further complicated in that the Oregon Railway and Navigation Company was under the presidency of Elijah Smith, who was hostile to the Northern Pacific, its president, Charles B. Wright, and its port, Tacoma.

Believing that Portland's demands should be considered, the Union Pacific withdrew from the lease and allied itself with Elijah Smith against the Northern Pacific. Ruinous duplication of branch lines followed, extensive litigation developed, and a further threat to the Northern Pacific came when James J. Hill pushed his St. Paul, Minneapolis and Manitoba on to the coast, with the intention of forming a connection with the Oregon Railway and Navigation Company at Spokane and getting a through route to the sea. To protect the Northern Pacific interests and check Hill, Villard began an effort to secure complete control of the Oregon and Transcontinental Company, which in turn controlled the Oregon Railway and Navigation Company and owned one-quarter of the Northern Pacific. In this he was opposed by the Union Pacific, which also desired to control the Oregon and Transcontinental Company in order to weaken the Northern Pacific. The contest that developed threw all Wall Street into one or other of the two camps, but in the end Villard defeated the other interests and assumed control. After he had won, he found that the exclusive lease of the Oregon Railway and Navigation Company tracks to the Union Pacific could not be abrogated, so his victory did not permit him to carry out his purpose of granting their use to the Northern Pacific.

He therefore caused the holding company to sell its Oregon Railway and Navigation Company stock to the Union Pacific, and that was the last of the Northern Pacific's entry to Portland along the lower bank of the Columbia River and also of Villard's connection with the Oregon railroad lines. While Villard had been trying to maintain the *status quo* of the Northwestern roads, Portland had experienced a change of heart toward him. Since he was no longer fighting exclusively for her, she conceived him to be her enemy. And the *Oregonian* even went so far as to demand that the nefarious Oregon and Transcontinental Company, which had been created by Villard for Portland's protection, be disincorporated.

While he had been occupied with the larger aspects of transcontinental railroad-building, the project that had originally brought Villard to Oregon had lapsed. The Oregon and California Railroad had reached Roseburg, and the Oregon and Transcontinental Company had agreed to extend it to California, but financial difficulties had prevented this. The road was not making the interest on its bonds, and it finally went into the hands of a receiver. In 1885 Collis P. Huntington took it over for the Central Pacific, and two years later it was absorbed in the Southern Pacific system, giving Portland a direct connection with San Francisco. One of the first things the new management did was to revalue the lands received from the Government under the Oregon and California grant, and this opened the way for future trouble because the lands were given the railroad on the express condition that none be sold for more than $2.50 an acre and that all be sold in small lots to actual settlers.

Until the panic of 1893 there was little change in the transportation situation at Portland. The Union Pacific gave her an unobstructed outlet to the east, and the Southern Pacific to the south. But in this financial storm railroads were shaken to bed-rock, the Union Pacific and Northern Pacific and fifty other roads went into bankruptcy, and when the débris was cleared away, there emerged a new figure destined to become the most powerful force in American railroading. This man, who was profoundly to affect the fortunes of Portland, was E. H. Harriman.

Edward Henry Harriman was born in the Episcopal rectory at Hempstead, Long Island, on February 20, 1848. Two years later his father set sail for California, where he founded Episcopal churches in Stockton and Sacramento, to return broken in health to a parish in Jersey City. At 14 Edward decided to quit school and go to work. He started as office-boy at $5 a week in a brokerage firm. There was no ticker in those days, and he became a "pad-shover," carrying a pad on which the current prices of securities were penciled. Before he was 20, he became managing clerk of the office, and at 22 he borrowed $3,000, bought a seat on the New York Stock Exchange, and opened an office of his own. He attracted many important customers, among them August Belmont, who said Harriman might draw on him at any time up to $1,000,000. In these years he spent much time at Paul Smith's camp in the Adirondacks with his friend Dr. Edward Trudeau, who had begun the country's first tuberculosis sanatorium, and he founded the Tompkins Square Boy's Club in New York City, the first organization of its kind in the country.

At 33 Harriman entered the railroad field by purchasing a run-down short road operating between Canandaigua and Sodus Bay on Lake Ontario. Believing that if this property were improved, it would be valuable as an outlet to either the Pennsylvania or the New York Central, Harriman reorganized it as the Sodus Bay and Southern. He improved the line, built a grain-elevator at the harbor, and then offered it to both the larger railroads, with the result that he sold it to the Pennsylvania at a large profit. This transaction made him a firm believer in the desirability of continuously improving a railroad's physical condition.

His friend Stuyvesant Fish having been made president of the Illinois Central, Harriman became interested in the possibilities of this road, bought its stock, and was made a director. At once he became a powerful influence on the board, urging expansion and influencing the road to add a thousand miles to its trackage in the five years of his service. Since its credit was high, the directors of the road were able to carry on its financing on excellent terms. Its 4 per cent bonds to pay for the new properties were sold at par while other roads were paying 7 and 8 per cent and selling at a discount. It was during these years that Harriman, as chairman of the finance committee, learned the value of borrowing cheaply, a principle he carried out in all his later financing. When the road needed to buy one of its feeders, the

Dubuque and Sioux City, Harriman and Fish were opposed by Drexel, Morgan and Company, the agents of the stockholders, who refused to sell their stock for less than par. Since the opposition had the majority of the stock, Harriman knew that he must apply the strictest care to every detail of his campaign; and he was resolved to win. At the meeting the proxies of Drexel, Morgan and Company were carefully examined and refused because they were signed by the firm personally and not as trustees. Having elected his own board of directors, Harriman later offered to pay 80 for the stock, and the Morgan firm reluctantly accepted his offer. This little skirmish earned Harriman the respect of Wall Street and the enmity of J. Pierpont Morgan—an enmity which deepened when, in later years, he opposed Morgan's plan for reorganizing the Erie and lived to see his predictions of disaster for that plan fulfilled.

Feeling a presentiment of approaching depression, in 1889 Harriman suddenly changed his advice to the directors of the Illinois Central and urged retrenchment instead of expansion, with the result that the road was able to weather the panic of 1893 which threw into bankruptcy the Union Pacific, Santa Fe, Northern Pacific, and many others. As chairman of the finance committee, Harriman's uncanny ability to judge the trend of the times was of great benefit to his road. As Otto H. Kahn said, "The Illinois Central never had bonds for sale except when bonds were in great demand; it never borrowed money except when money was cheap and abundant; periods of storm and stress found it amply prepared and fortified; its credit was of the highest. The few acquainted with the facts conceded that Mr. Harriman was a shrewd financial manager." Under Harriman's influence the road added trackage, improved its roadbed and rolling-stock, and more than doubled its earnings; and during these years he learned the art and science of successfully operating a railroad property.

During the panic of 1893 the Union Pacific paid heavily for its previous overexpansion and bad financing. When Jay Gould incorporated in it the unprofitable Kansas Pacific and the Denver Pacific, he severely weakened its financial structure; and during the administration of Charles Francis Adams many branch lines had been added while the road was forced to meet additional competition and its business was reduced. It also had to prepare to meet in 1895 the payment

of the $53,000,000 borrowed from the Government. When the road went
into receivership, J. P. Morgan and others struggled with reorganization plans to no effect; Jacob H. Schiff and Chauncey M. Depew then
tried the job, but they soon found that they were running against
hidden obstacles in everything they attempted to do. They thought it
must be Morgan, but he denied any animosity, and then suspicion
settled on "that little fellow Harriman."

George Kennan, in his biography of Harriman, tells the story of the
interview with Schiff:

"Mr. Harriman, my associates and I, as you doubtless know, are trying
to reorganize the Union Pacific. For a long time we have been making
good progress but now we are meeting everywhere with opposition and
I understand that this opposition is being directed by you. What have you
to say about it?"

"I am the man," replied Mr. Harriman.

"But, why are you doing it?" asked Mr. Schiff.

"Because I intend to reorganize the Union Pacific myself."

This was somewhat surprising, but Mr. Schiff merely smiled and said,
"How do you propose to do it, Mr. Harriman? Most of the securities
of the company are in our possession. What means have you of reorganizing the Union Pacific?"

"The Illinois Central ought to have that road," replied Mr. Harriman,
"and we are going to take charge of the reorganization; we have the best
credit in the country. I am going to issue $10,000,000 in three per cent
bonds of the Illinois Central Railroad Company and am going to get
close to par for them. You, at the best, can't get money for less than
four-and-a-half per cent. In that respect I am stronger than you are."

Mr. Schiff was amazed at the confident boldness of these assertions,
but he merely replied, "You'll have a good time doing it, Mr. Harriman,
but, meanwhile, what is your price?"

"There is no price," replied Harriman. "I am determined to get possession of the road." *

Rather than face the opposition of such a fighter, Schiff finally
decided to make Harriman a director of the Union Pacific and a member of the executive committee, and he told him that if he proved to
be the strongest man on the committee, he would probably get the
chairmanship in the end. Reorganization went forward, Kuhn, Loeb
and Company bought the road for $81,000,000, and Harriman began

* George Kennan, *E. H. Harriman* (Boston, Houghton Mifflin Company, 1922).

to study the property. After the road had gone into bankruptcy in 1893, the receivers had sold various of the subsidiaries. Among the branch lines that had been lost was the Oregon Short Line from Granger, Wyoming, to Snake River, connecting with the Oregon Railway and Navigation Company line to Portland, and Harriman determined to get this back. In 1898 the company reacquired the Kansas Pacific and the Denver Pacific, which it had also lost after the panic of 1893, and Harriman made plans for a trip over the entire property. He had a special train made up with an observation car in front and the engine in the rear, and he made the whole trip from Omaha to Portland in daylight, sitting on the observation platform and taking notes on every aspect of equipment, grades, and ballast—and, as one division superintendent said, every poor tie, blistered rail, and loose bolt on the road; and this was almost literally true, for he later made suggestions about shortening the length of bolts and the width of track-ballast which saved the road hundreds of thousands of dollars. From Portland Harriman continued the trip to San Francisco and back to Ogden, Butte, and Omaha. As a result of what he saw, he determined to build the road up by straightening the track, laying heavy rails, and buying heavier locomotives and larger freight cars, so that more freight could be hauled in fewer trains at less expense. He wired the board for authority to start works totaling $25,000,000 and personally invested $330,000 in the stock of the road, stock which was to form the basis of his great fortune.

Although Schiff was so discouraged over the prospects of the road that he paced the floor in his hotel in Omaha all night, Harriman was enthusiastic. He believed that prosperity was about to return, and he saw the enormous possibilities of the territory served by the Union Pacific. His directors came to share his optimism, and in less than a year his genius as a railroad man had caused them to make him chairman of the board and of the executive committee, with complete control of the Union Pacific. Under the Harriman régime thousands of new oversize cars were bought, doubling the freight capacity; powerful engines were ordered; and the road was straightened, relocated, ballasted, and made what was later called the most magnificent railroad property in America. In 1899 Harriman reacquired the Oregon Short Line, spent $6,000,000 on it, and obtained control of the Oregon

Railway and Navigation Company, giving the system its outlet to the sea at Portland. Within two years after Harriman took control, the earnings of the Union Pacific had been doubled, and the road was in prime financial condition. And the common stock continued to rise from the 1898 price of $25 until it was $195 in 1906. During his control freight-rates were decreased 15 per cent and service rendered increased 140 per cent.

Seeing that he must also build up the Central Pacific, which connected San Francisco with the Union Pacific at Ogden, if he was to maintain the efficiency of his system, Harriman began to reach out for control of this road, and when Collis P. Huntington died in August, 1900, he had his opportunity. He floated a Union Pacific loan of $100,-000,000 in 4 per cent convertible bonds and acquired control of the Southern Pacific system. It was the greatest railroad property in the country, stretching from New Orleans to San Francisco, and of it Harriman said, "We have bought not only a railroad but an empire." Efficiently to carry the freight delivered to it by the Union Pacific at Ogden, the Central Pacific was virtually reconstructed; its length was cut by 50 miles, and a bridge was built directly across Salt Lake, a scheme first visioned by Huntington, the total cost of improvements within eight years being $242,000,000. The consolidation of the two roads resulted in economies and efficiency of operation, and it also stopped competition for freight at common points, where, it was said, "the shippers played poker with the railroad agent in a near-by hotel for rebates while the cars were being loaded."

In 1895 another man entered Oregon who is entitled to be remembered among the railroad-builders, although his enterprises ran the gamut of commercial and industrial development. This was Andrew B. Hammond. Born in St. Leonard's, New Brunswick, July 22, 1848, he had gone to Missoula, Montana, at 19, and there he had opened a store, organized a bank, and built two railroad lines which were later absorbed by the Northern Pacific. In the later Nineties he conceived the idea of building a railroad a hundred miles down the Columbia from Portland to the seaport of Astoria, there to establish ocean terminals and to tap the rich coast timber belt. This was in line with Huntington's early ideas of extending the Central Pacific to Astoria, and Hammond interested him in the scheme. To help finance the road he was also joined by the Mark Hopkins estate and John Claflin of New York.

Work was begun in August, 1895, and the road was completed in April, 1898. With this rail connection Astoria confidently looked forward to becoming the great ocean terminal of Oregon, since she was just inside the mouth of the Columbia while Portland was one hundred miles up the river. But Portland had no intention of surrendering the business to this rival. Her financial interests fought the development of the port of Astoria from the outset, and again it was proved that geographical advantage is only a small part of the battle in building a city. Portland had the concentration of jobbing houses and was the converging point of railroads, so that cargoes could be easily assembled as well as discharged there. And though Astoria valiantly fought for precedence, building a model municipal port in later years, she was never able to obtain any large share of the ocean commerce.

Hammond, through the Hammond Lumber Company, built mills at Astoria and elsewhere and acquired extensive timber holdings in western Oregon and northern California. In time he became the leading figure in the California redwood-lumber business, being the first to use large steel ships to carry lumber instead of small wooden vessels, and the first to manufacture finished products, such as doors, at the mills instead of shipping the lumber to be manufactured elsewhere. After he was eighty years old, he brought about a consolidation of the redwood interests of northern California, combining properties worth some $60,000,000. The Astoria road was sold to the Hill interests in 1907 and later became a part of the Spokane, Portland and Seattle Railway.

At the time Hammond began his operations, Portland was the northwestern terminus of the country's most powerful transcontinental system, and it had the support of Harriman and his protection against James J. Hill, who was centering his Great Northern system at the rival port of Seattle. Moreover, the Columbia and the Willamette had been so much improved that Portland no longer feared that her shipping business would disappear in favor of Tacoma and Seattle. The city was, of course, firmly established as the metropolis of the Oregon country, and any development of that territory automatically benefited her. The towns that were the erstwhile rivals of Portland declared, however, that Portland "had never lent a helping hand to the interior" and that the city and its commercial bodies were against all progressive measures that would directly benefit any other part of the state.

One of the barriers to the development of Oregon was the fact that the vast areas of land granted to the Oregon and California Railroad had never been opened for settlement to any extent; this acreage was therefore unproductive and unpeopled. When Harriman took control of the Southern Pacific in 1901, he immediately withdrew all this land from sale, in order, he said, that the books of the company might be examined and put in shape. During the San Francisco fire the company lost many records, and this served as a further reason for temporarily closing the Oregon lands to settlement. But when it developed that this was to be Harriman's permanent policy, the legislature of Oregon in 1907 asked Congress to investigate the matter and force the company to live up to its agreement, which was to sell the land in small lots to actual settlers at not more than $2.50 an acre. Investigation showed that the company had flagrantly violated this agreement: in order to save taxes much of the land had never been patented; certain lands had been sold at high prices and in immense tracts. Nine years of controversy followed, seventeen volumes of testimony were presented to the Supreme Court in 1915, and in 1916 Congress gave effect to the Supreme Court's decision of forfeiture by an act which reverted 2,300,000 acres of the company's lands into the public domain, the company receiving $2.50 an acre for them. These government lands were then thrown open to settlement, adding much to the productivity of Oregon.

But Harriman was not to be permitted to rule Oregon alone. There was another Titan in the offing, looking covetously into the Columbia basin and to the undeveloped territory of the central part of the state, and canny observers felt sure that James J. Hill was getting ready to strike. He threw down the gauntlet, appropriately enough, at a banquet given at Portland's world's fair, the Lewis and Clark Exposition, in 1905. Hill then publicly announced his intention of entering and developing Oregon, and from that day forward his every move was opposed by Harriman. Already Hill had quietly completed surveys down the north bank of the Columbia to Portland, to occupy the water-level entry that the Northern Pacific had long ago intended to use before Villard diverted it to his railroad tracks on the south side. Various conjectures as to the identity of the interests backing the survey were made, the most popular being the Great Northern or the Northern Pacific, although Hill, as was his custom, had the business carried on by a locally organized company. The public announcement of the identity of the North-Bank builders surprised every one, however, for it then appeared that Hill had commissioned Howard Elliott, president of the Northern Pacific, to build the road for the joint use of both railroads, and thus both the northern systems would have an entry into Portland.

Alarmed by this concerted attack on his territory, Harriman immediately began obstructionist tactics. He organized the Columbia Valley Railroad Company and the Cascade Railroad Company to oppose the Hill interests and made paper surveys of a line from the Washington town of Wallula to Vancouver to conflict with the Hill locations. Wherever Harriman's surveys crossed the Hill line, he applied to the United States land-office, under the right of eminent domain, for certificates to build. When these were granted, they furnished ample excuse for legal warfare, even if Harriman never intended actually to build over the route he surveyed. At the towering rock promontory of Cape Horn Harriman started to build a tunnel with half a dozen men wielding picks and trundling wheelbarrows at the west approach; but this was such a pitiful display in contrast to the $30,000 equipment Hill was using at the east approach that when the matter was taken into court, it was decided that Harriman had no actual intent to build, and Hill won the case. Harriman also occupied the old narrow-gage portage railroad that Captain Ainsworth had long ago acquired on the Washington side of the river at Cascade Locks, which was then being used to transport fish; but the North Bank engineer, A. J. Witchel, outwitted him by running his line underground for four miles and then getting through the narrow gorge on a 27-foot right of way purchased from private owners. Most of the Hill–Harriman contest was fought in the courts, but their workmen took it as a personal matter; they indulged in fist fights and in several instances tried to dynamite each other. It was said that during the battle Harriman had to be operated on for appendicitis, and that as soon as his doctor said he could use the telephone, he called Hill and told him that the operation was over and that he was feeling fine and ready to go on with the fight. The last suit was tried in 1906 and resulted in a victory for Hill. Meanwhile, Harriman had carried his warfare into the enemy's country by buying a right of way for an extension of the Union Pacific to Puget Sound, purchasing terminals at Tacoma, and starting to dig a tunnel into that city and one under the Portland suburb of St. Johns. The upshot of the matter was that a compromise was effected whereby Hill double-tracked his line to Puget Sound and permitted Harriman to run his trains into Tacoma and Seattle over the Hill rails, while Harriman stopped his obstruction of the Spokane, Portland and Seattle Railroad, as the North Bank line was afterward known.

So Hill won his first entry into Oregon, and he jubilantly announced to its citizens that his line

will be the best new road that was ever built in the United States. It will be a road of low grades and few curves. Low grades are equivalent to deep water in the harbor. Portland can overcome the lack of deep water by easy grades. The Columbia River offers great opportunities in low grades, but construction is frightfully expensive. There are miles where the cost of building the road will run over $100,000 to the mile. And this is exclusive of the cost of tunnels of which there are several to the mile in many places.

When more than $35,000,000 had been spent, the last spike was driven on March 11, 1908, and trains began to roll into Portland over the water-level route. Citizens of Vancouver, across the Columbia, congratulated themselves that since every car of freight had to pass through their town, Vancouver would be the coming metropolis and front door, while Portland would soon have to content itself with being the back.

But Hill was ever an aggressor, and once he had an inch in Oregon, he proceeded to take a mile. One spring a certain John F. Sampson went fishing in the Oregon interior, in the Bend country. He fished for trout, carried an elaborate collection of flies, seemed to have plenty of time and plenty of money—so much money, in fact, and such a liking for this sportsman's paradise, as the guide-books will have it,

OCEAN SHIPPING AT PORTLAND DOCKS

Courtesy of the Portland Chamber of Commerce.

MOUNT HOOD AND PORTLAND TO-DAY

Courtesy of the Portland Chamber of Commerce.

that he bought land-grants, ranches, options, and when he had all he needed, he disappeared. Young Billy Nelson of Portland owned the controlling stock in the Oregon Trunk Railroad, which had been surveyed down the east bank of the Deschutes River but never built, and he was astonished when this same mysterious stranger made an appointment to meet him in City Park and there paid him $150,000 for his interest in this moribund road. When these strange transactions had been completed, the sportsman stopped playing his game and gave his right name—John F. Stevens, formerly chief engineer of the Panama Canal, now agent of James J. Hill. With the Stevens right of way in his possession, Hill began action. Running across the Columbia from the Washington side of the river near the Dalles, he projected a line straight to Bend, 165 miles south, where the smoke of a railroad engine had never been seen. That move was dangerous enough to alarm Harriman, but anyone could see that Bend was only a half-way house for Hill. He had his eye on San Francisco, and if Harriman permitted him to occupy central Oregon unmolested, he would next press on to the Golden Gate and there contest the rule of the Southern Pacific.

So Harriman fought Hill every inch of the way. On the west side of the Deschutes River he laid out the Deschutes Railroad, parallel to Hill's Oregon Trunk, and rushed construction at equal speed. Harriman's engineer was George W. Boschke, who had built the sea-wall at Galveston, an intrepid and resourceful field general. The Hill construction was under the charge of Porter Brothers, who had built the North Bank road for him. Under such capable leadership the two giants of railroading raced to reach the central-Oregon goal, building along both sides of the narrow Deschutes Cañon with its 2,000-foot wall of rock, while their construction gangs carried on a relentless and sanguinary war. Dynamite was planted and exploded so as to interfere with the work, men were killed by strangely falling boulders and slides, officers of the law galore were unable to bring about even a semblance of order. Harriman spent $100,000 on zigzag wagon-roads cut down into the cañon, roads which were so rough that nitroglycerine could not be trucked down them. All supplies, even hay, had to be packed in by 2,600 men building for Harriman and 2,600 building for Hill. As soon as the dirt roads were built, the procession of four-horse teams using them was almost continuous. In their wild race the two outfits bought farms, closed public roads, and fought each other in the courts. The crisis in the battle came at mile 75, when an attempt was made to entice Boschke away by sending him a fake wire, "The Galveston sea-wall has broken." But he calmly replied, "It's a lie. I built that wall to stand. Double the force on mile 75." Mile 75 was the place where the Oregon Trunk crossed to the west side of the Deschutes River. Here the Oregon Trunk surveys antedated those of the Deschutes Railroad and had been approved at Washington. But a homesteader, Smith by name, had previously filed on the land; later he proved his claim and sold it to Harriman, thus giving him the advantage over Hill. As there was no other route to get into the country except by way of a narrow defile at the Smith ranch, Hill decided to arbitrate, and the opposing parties stopped fighting. A truce was arranged by which Hill agreed to build only as far south as Bend and to permit Harriman to run his trains to that point over his 42-mile track from the town of Metolius. From the town of Bend, 4,500 feet in altitude, a train could practically roll downhill to Portland, and when a road south should be built, it could do the same to San Francisco.

On October 1, 1911, central Oregon bade the stage-coach good-by and greeted the new purveyor of transportation, James Jerome Hill. He drove the golden spike that marked completion of his road to Bend, while 7,000 citizens cheered and the Indians marveled at "the white man's cow-pony," the locomotive. The remarks of the Empire Builder on this momentous occasion were in his usual ingratiatingly ingenuous homespun style:

When the Southern Pacific railroad drove its lines into this country, they had a hard time and now the country is growing to a point where it is easier for them, and in order to help them out and in order to make it still easier, we have come over to extend them a helping hand and help them open up this country; and if they are not ready to go ahead, we will try to take the load ourselves, but I hope they have got breath and life in them strong enough to keep them well up to the front.

We have spent between Spokane and Portland and in Oregon between eighty and ninety millions and we have not received any returns on it. But we have faith. We will if you will help us, because every dollar that we ever get, you have got to win it first, and if you are poor we are going to be poor, and if you are prosperous we ought to have a little share of your prosperity, and we hope to get it.

We are like Daniel in the lion's den. Now we mean to get along with our neighbor the Union Pacific. When they get in a tight place we are going to extend the helping hand of fellowship and if we get into a tight place we will call on them. We won't make faces across the fence. We found that there was room for two railroads down there on the Deschutes and we hope both of them will have all they can carry.

Although it was expected that Hill would soon build south to California, he turned his attention to other matters, and this was the end of his railroad construction in central Oregon. He bought electric lines to compete with Harriman in the Willamette Valley as far south as Eugene, however; and he bought ocean terminals near Astoria at the mouth of the Columbia, put two immense steamers on the run to San Francisco, and, by sending passengers from Portland to the docks on a boat train, made such fast time that he could compete with the Harriman rail lines. Harriman built extensions to Tillamook and Coos Bay and planned a new Southern Pacific main line from Weed, California, to Portland by way of Klamath Falls, east of the old line, but he died before this was completed. Hill was deterred by the financial condition of the country and the war, so that the Great Northern extension to San Francisco was temporarily dropped. And when it finally was completed in 1931, it was the project of a successor of the Empire Builder, Arthur Curtiss James, the then dominant figure in Western railroads.

Of the Oregon transportation kings, Ben Holladay was the first to suffer eclipse. After he gave up his interests to Villard, he went to Washington to press his claims against the Government for the losses his stage properties had suffered from Indian raids, and it appeared that he might get half a million out of them. But Congress failed to pass his bill, and he returned to Portland, still swaggering, wearing a top-hat, smoking a big cigar, and interlarding his conversation with his favorite phrase, "Don't you understand?" His only friend among the first families of Portland was Captain John H. Couch, who visited him until the end. All the rest of the city's leaders gave Ben the cold-shoulder, and he spent most of his time conferring with lawyers and attempting to borrow $20 gold-pieces from acquaintances. When he had gone into bankruptcy, he had deeded his real estate to his brother Joe, who had made, and penuriously saved, a fortune. This fortune had its beginning in the bar-concession on Ben's California boats, where Joe sold liquor at 25 cents a drink. When Ben reminded Joe of his agreement to return the property on demand, Joe had forgotten it; not only that, but he also claimed that Ben owed him $160,000. The property, originally valued at $400,000, was now worth from three to five times that much, and Ben's creditors all started suits, claiming that the agreement between the two brothers was a conspiracy to defraud them. Ben now had no property left except the Hot Springs of Virginia, on which he received a rental of $5,000 a year, but this was nothing for a man of his extravagant tastes and inordinate expenses for legal counsel. As his financial troubles increased, so did his addiction to morphine. For years he had carried a syringe in his pocket, and he finally succumbed to the effects of illness and the use of the drug, in Portland, July 8, 1887. His brother Joe later received $500,000 of the disputed property, and Ben's creditors got the rest. There is no monument in Portland to mark his fame, and it is doubtful if many people know why a residence street, a grade school, and a small park bear the name of Holladay. Yet in his day he was undoubtedly the leading figure of Oregon, if not of the Pacific Coast.

Henry Villard, whom Holladay's ventures were responsible for bringing to Oregon, continued to struggle with the Northwest transportation problem for many years. As chairman of the board of the Northern Pacific he evolved a scheme for refinancing the three existing mortgages on the road and providing funds for extensions. This was no less than the floating of the largest general mortgage ever created for an American railroad, amounting to $160,000,000. He also tried to mitigate the threat of the extension of the Great Northern to the Pacific Coast by buying a majority interest in the St. Paul, Minneapolis and Manitoba, which controlled the Great Northern. He thought he had induced the wily Hill to sell this stock at 120, and he made arrangements for a loan of $20,000,000 to buy it. But at the hour when the papers were to be signed, Hill failed to appear, and the deal, which would have meant continuous prosperity for the Northern Pacific, fell through. Evidently Hill never had the slightest intention of parting with his rich property, although Villard thought otherwise. In order to inconvenience Hill as much as possible, however, Villard's company bought the Seattle, Lake Shore and Eastern Railroad so that Hill could not acquire this western outlet to the sea.

In 1890 the North American Company, which Villard had evolved to take over the Oregon and Transcontinental Company, was in difficulties. In Germany he raised several million dollars to help it, but its New York bankers failed, and the company lost most of its assets. At this time he began to predict that the country was headed for disaster unless the Sherman Silver Act were repealed and the gold standard maintained. To broadcast his ideas he bought the New York *Evening Post* and worked for the election of Grover Cleveland. But the financial panic arrived in 1893, and the Northern Pacific, which had spent $30,000,000 in building unprofitable extensions, went into the hands of a receiver. Villard resigned from this company and the North American Company in the summer of that year. From that time on he had little contact with the Western railroads until 1899, when he went over the Northern Pacific again. On this trip, his first in eight years, he found Portland a city of 90,000, Tacoma, 45,000, Seattle, 65,000, and Spokane, 40,000. It proved to be his last inspection of the great railroad he had developed, for he died in New York on November 12, 1900.

But Villard's memory still lives in Oregon. For he started the practice of making large gifts for public uses in the state, and Villard Hall still stands as a memorial of this philanthropy at the State University at Eugene. Realizing the significance of Villard's benefaction, Judge Mathew P. Deady said, on the occasion of receiving this gift,

This $50,000 given to the University of Oregon is the only considerable gift of private capital to public uses ever made in the state. For a third of a century wealth has been accumulating in the hands of the enterprising and fortunate but no town can yet boast a building, monument, arch, fountain, hospital, asylum, gallery, school or church, the gift of one of its citizens. Let us hope that this auspicious beginning will prove to be the stone loosed from the side of the mountain that shall fill the whole valley.

At the time of Villard's death, the pioneer William Reid, who had built the old Oregonian narrow-gage railway and was the last survivor of the old railway men, proposed that the city erect a statue of Villard in the plaza in front of the Court House,

just as he appeared, September 8, 1883, on the day when he gave Portland her first transcontinental railway connection with New York. He was the first who saw and utilized for Portland the advantage she has long since permanently acquired for using the line down the Columbia which, coupled with the 25-foot channel to Astoria, is the sole key to Portland's prosperity. If he had delayed the building of the Oregon Railroad and Navigation Company and made the first rail connection to Puget Sound, where would Portland be to-day?

Captain John C. Ainsworth, the leader of the river-transportation monopolists, in his later years spread his financial interests all over the Pacific Coast. He bought much real estate at Tacoma, spent $3,000,000 developing Redondo Beach, near Los Angeles, and ran a steamship line from that point to Portland. He organized the Ainsworth National Bank of Portland and the Central Bank of Oakland, California, and finally moved to Oakland, where he died in 1893. His name is remembered in Portland, and his influence as a banker survives through the connection of his family with the United States National Bank. And the old Captain's son, John Churchill Ainsworth, who controls the great bank, commemorates the beginnings of the family fortune in a room devoted to housing models of all the old river-steamers owned by the Oregon Steam Navigation Company. There, among the gaily colored models of boats with such luscious names as *Harvest Queen* and *Wide West,* one can reconstruct in imagination the life on the river when the Triumvirate ruled and built up the fortunes which are still a potent influence in Portland.

R. R. Thompson, who, like Reed, was something of a stock-breeder and introduced the Merino ram into Oregon, moved to California in later life and joined Ainsworth in the development of Redondo Beach, of which the young Captain George Ainsworth was made manager. His name is not familiarly connected with anything in Portland to-day, unless it be the Multnomah Hotel, which was built by his estate on some of the property he owned near the old center of the business district.

E. H. Harriman's railroad interests were so large that he cannot be said to have represented Portland chiefly, but his pet, the Union

Pacific, headed up in that city, and whatever plans he might have made for improving his system would have ministered to Portland's greatness. In the last decades of his life he was concerned with a round-the-world transportation system which involved control of the Trans-Siberian Railway, and he conducted diplomatic negotiations in the Far East with this end in view, but these negotiations were never successfully completed. Had he controlled the Siberian Railway, he would, of course, have modernized the property and enlarged its carrying capacity, and this, as his biographer, George Kennan, has pointed out, would have enabled Russia to carry huge quantities of supplies over it, with the result that the trend of the World War might have been changed. Among his schemes in the later years of his life was the acquisition of the Grand Trunk Railway, now the Canadian National, but nothing came of this. He spent the summer of 1907 at his Pelican Bay lodge on Klamath Lake in southern Oregon, and with him was his friend John Muir, the naturalist. Muir describes in his book on Harriman how, on the way back to Portland, the crowds turned out to meet the train and cheer the railroad-builder who had done so much for the West even if he had been reviled as a malefactor of great wealth. Roosevelt had called him an undesirable citizen, and when a friend, Moreton Frewey, rallied him on this title, he said, "I may be undesirable at the White House, but have I not shaved down my railroad grades? The West will always remember me for those grades."

Harriman's conviction was that the only way to make a good property valuable is to put it in the best possible condition to do business. When there was a question between increased returns to the stockholders and increased efficiency of the railroad, the railroad always came first. Although the successful prosecution of this policy brought him a great fortune, he said, "I never cared for money except as a power for work. I was always lucky and my friends and neighbors, observing my luck, brought their money to me to invest, and in this way I have come to handle large sums. What I most enjoy is the power of creation, getting into partnership with Nature in doing good, helping to feed man and beast, and making everybody and everything a little better and happier."

He spent most of his time on his country estate and at his house on Madison Avenue in New York City, next door to Whitelaw Reid, a house built, curiously enough, by his distinguished predecessor in the Northwestern railroad field, Henry Villard. In Los Angeles in March, 1909, he told reporters, "Physicians have warned me that I must step out; they say I have done enough. I am 61 years old and have led a very active life." Like Huntington and Hill he could not lay down his work; he was unhappy in idleness, took no pleasure in leisure. It was not long after he gave this interview that he died, on September 9, 1909. There might well be a monument to Harriman in Portland, but there is none, and he left no personal benefactions to the Northwest.

Evidently the prowess of Portland's transportation kings is to be remembered in the future chiefly because of the benefactions of Simeon G. Reed. He was the bon vivant, the man of the world, the amusing conversationalist of the Oregon Steam Navigation triumvirate, and when legislators were to be interviewed or new capital interested, Ainsworth and Thompson gave Reed the job of doing the talking. His wine-cellars were noted for their choice vintages, and his faculty for entertaining was called upon in Portland, in the national capital, and in New York, where his headquarters were at the old Fifth Avenue Hotel. He was fond of hunting and had accidentally shot off two fingers while on a hunting trip in Idaho. He also loved travel and made many trips abroad.

As time went on, Reed enlarged the scope of his interests, making bold and shrewd business deals and gaining a reputation for luck as well as wisdom. With William S. Ladd and Henry W. Corbett he had built the telegraph line to California, and when the first service came over it, on March 5, 1864, the *Oregonian* printed a special edition with news from the East only 20 hours old. Later he built the telegraph from Portland to the Dalles and purchased the Walla Walla and Columbia Railroad. He paid $1,250,000 for the Bunker Hill and Sullivan Mine, the richest silver-producer in the Cœur d'Alene, Idaho, district, and he also owned a number of gold-mines. In 1879, with Darius Ogden Mills and A. Onderdonk, he built the first section of the Canadian Pacific Railway from Port Moody to Kamloops, British Columbia. He developed his Broadmead Farm property until it sold for $200,000 after his death. At the Reedville farm he kept a stable of thoroughbred trotting horses and maintained a private half-mile track on which to test their speed before entering them at public race-tracks. He not only bred fine horses, but also laid the foundations of a pure-blooded live-stock industry for Oregon. The Reed stock included Cotswold and Leicester sheep and Berkshire swine, Shorthorn and Ayrshire cattle, Clydesdale and trotting horses. They were selected from prize-winners in Eastern state fairs, many of which were imported by William Watson, whose father was the founder of the Aberdeen-Angus breed of cattle, and they were brought to Oregon on two especially chartered steamers, the *Ajax* and the *Oriflamme*. The stock was in charge of Thomas Withycombe and his young son James, who later became governor of the state. The great Broadmead Farm of 3,000 acres in the most productive part of Yamhill and Polk counties contained orchards, gardens, walnut-groves, and the crops were so diversified that the farm products included all the food necessary for its employees, the superintendent buying only such articles as sugar and salt.

One of Reed's most ambitious schemes was the Oregon Steel and Iron Company, in which he and his associates invested several million dollars. Their plan was to mine the low-grade iron ore along the Willamette near Lake Oswego and reduce it at their smelter there. But when their operations had just begun, the Mesabi Range was discovered in Minnesota, and they could not meet the competition of mines where the ore could be scooped out with steam-shovels; so the project lapsed, and the lands acquired by the company now form the beautiful riverside residence district of Dunthorpe. It was near this point, on the Whitehouse road, that Reed and other sportsmen used to try out their trotting horses.

For the most part Reed was both sagacious and lucky in his business deals. He early saw that business was about to move away from the river-front, and he headed the advance by building a large office-building on Third Street and installing in it the first elevator in the city. The *Oregonian* thus characterized his business career:

Temporary disarrangements of his plans by unforeseen mishaps disturb him but little; he simply commences anew, tries other expedients and is very apt to succeed where a majority of men would have succumbed at the first failure. He is naturally hopeful, is full of resources and is strongly self-reliant; and when his judgment approves a course he is not afraid to stand alone. More than once in his career have these elements in his character been conspicuously shown and almost uniformly have results indicated the correctness of his judgment.

In later years Reed came to think of his fortune as a trust, and on his death in Pasadena in 1895 he left it all to his wife with the request that she, in turn, leave it to found an educational or cultural institution of some sort for the people of Oregon. After the heirs had tested the will, under the California law that provides that only one-third of an estate may be left to philanthropy, and it was decided that the Reeds were residents of Oregon, the Reed Institute was founded. It at once made a survey of the needs of the state and decided that the institution most needed by Portland was a liberal-arts college; and the General Education Board supported it with the opinion that Portland was the best unoccupied spot in the United States for such a college.

Reed College was the result, and its first president, William Trufant Foster, startled Portland by proposing a college such as her citizens had never heard of—and incidentally by printing the college announcements in simplified spelling. There were to be no intercollegiate athletics, no fraternities, no honor societies; there was to be complete student self-government and credit for quality rather than quantity of work. Graduation was to occur only after the passage of a final oral examination given partly by examiners from outside the college; students were not to be told what their grades were in the various courses; no attendance records were to be kept, the burden of interesting the classes being on the instructor. There were to be few examinations, and these, in accordance with the honor principle, could be written whenever the student wished. Emphasis was to be focused resolutely on the intellectual life. This was the beginning of widely copied educational reforms which culminated in the system of independent study under tutors during the last two years inaugurated by the second president, Richard F. Scholz.

But these strange educational practices were only a beginning. President Foster assembled a unique faculty of brilliant young teachers, and Reed College became known throughout the country as an institution of unusual character and promise. The faculty not only stimulated the students, but carried new ideas to Portland by means of extension lectures. Indeed, so new were some of these ideas to the conservative that a reputation for radicalism was developed which would have startled capitalist Simeon Reed. But he would have enjoyed the leadership that the college named for him came to exercise in education, its eagerness to blaze new trails, and its willingness to be daringly original. And he would have approved its beautiful dwelling-halls, reminiscent of Oxford, its lovely lawns, and the forthrightness and vigor of its teachers. Of the first faculty one is now president of Massachusetts Institute of Technology, another headed President Hoover's Research Committee on Social Trends, two others are college presidents, and others are similarly distinguished in their various fields. So Simeon Reed's money produced thoroughbreds in education as well as in horse-flesh.

At the time of its founding, in 1910, Dr. Wallace Buttrick of the General Education Board pointed out that Reed College had $500,000 more endowment than Williams and $150,000 more than Amherst, and he called upon the Portland people to add to this by donating buildings and funds. William S. Ladd gave the campus and Eric Hauser, years later, the library; but for the most part Portland has neglected Reed College, which is better known in the rest of the world than at home. The city has always regarded it with something of the bewildered uncertainty of a hen who inexplicably discovers among her brood a duckling. For Portland is by nature conservative and subscribes to the Petrine doctrine, "Let there be no innovations except those which are handed down."

In temper, like Philadelphia, Portland is solid, strong, venerable, dignified, and self-sufficient. Freeman Tilden once wrote that in order to know how Portland, Oregon, would react in any given situation, it was only necessary to know how Calvin Coolidge would react. But with all her dignity and conservatism and respectable calm, Portland is beautiful. Her prophet and priest, Frank Branch Riley, calls her the Cinderella of the Pacific Coast, the loveliest of the sisters and the least appreciated. And perhaps this lack of appreciation explains what has been called the Oregon inferiority complex. A former president of the State University described it as a state-wide feeling of complaint to the Creator that he put Mount Hood and Crater Lake so far apart. Portlanders are pleased to have Mount Hood overlooking the city, but they do not "boost" the mountain as Tacomans and Seattleites do theirs. There is a great tourist hotel on Mount Rainier where you can arrive in dinner clothes and be completely outfitted for roughing it in half an hour. You will be given clothes for mountain-climbing, including "tin pants" for nature sliding, and you will find numerous exploring parties organized under licensed guides leaving for distant points every hour on the hour; illustrated lectures are given nightly for your education; entertainment is provided; everything is done to make the tourist comfortable and to lure him to the mountain. But at Portland one can find out how to climb Mount Hood only with difficulty. The hotels in the city do not seem to know much about it and are indifferent; the mountain resorts are comfortable but unpretentious. Their equipment for climbing is relatively meager, and there is little organized exploitation of the peak as a vacation place. Probably Portland is proud of that. Exploitation has an ugly sound, even if it is sometimes a welcome convenience. And Portland prefers to treat her mountain as a primrose by a river's brim rather than a chrysanthemum in a hothouse.

But if she will not exploit her scenic beauties, Portland is not averse to exploiting everything possible that will be to her commercial advantage, and in this she has been peculiarly successful. When President Franklin Roosevelt first proposed to build a great irrigation and power dam on the Grand Coulée on the upper Columbia River, in the State of Washington, Portland objected, although any improvement on the Columbia would benefit her trade territory. She used her influence against the project in order to center government appropriations on the Columbia River hydro-electric dam at Bonneville, close at hand, only 50 miles from Portland. The Grand Coulée project, nevertheless, was approved, as was also the Bonneville project, and the Tacoma *Daily Ledger* remarked editorially:

Selfishness is not a fault confined to an individual. The doctor, the baker or candlestick maker may be a perfectly estimable business man, giving to the needy and treating his fellow man fairly. But let the city or state be concerned and he becomes insatiable in his grasping demands. Civic consciousness becomes civic selfishness. And nothing can be done about it. In fact such a citizen is praised by his chamber of commerce if he is instrumental in putting over a deal to the advantage of city or state. Civic consciousness, or selfishness, if you will, is particularly strong in Portland. They are against everything that will not benefit Portland directly—bridges, dams or what you will.

It is a case of grab, grab with most cities and states and no odium attaches to that community or commonwealth which grabs the most. So perhaps we should take Portland as an example and learn her methods. Learn for instance, how she gets that way in the matter of appointments and appropriations with only two of her representatives in Congress belonging to the ruling party, while Washington's entire delegation is Democratic.

But much can be excused Portland because of her beauty; and her neighbors who visit her to complain must remain to admire, their harsh criticism dead on their lips. The city nestles on a green plain, with the snow-capped peaks of Mount Hood, Mount St. Helens, and Mount Adams gleaming to the north and east, while on the west abruptly rises a green crown of fir-clad hills which offers rest for the eye even from the center of the business district. From Portland Heights the city appears spread out far below like a carpet of intricate design, with the lazy Willamette meandering through its center in a graceful, sweeping curve. And these same heights provide the sites for homes of a distinctive type of hillside architecture, which cling to every declivity and are neatly tucked into every cranny. Indeed, there is no place in America where the homes are more uniformly beautiful, of better architecture, or so attractively surrounded with green lawns, flowers, and, above all, the gorgeous roses for which the city is famous. And everywhere there is a profusion of luxuriant trees, shrubs, and greenery which make the whole community a park. Certainly there is no prettier city in America. The narrow downtown streets and the buildings limited in height make Portland snug and cozy, a veritable right little, tight little town. And, withal, the city has an air and atmosphere pleasantly distinctive and one which its people love. In answer to the visitor's remark, "Portland hasn't changed much," your true Portlander will reply with energy, "No, and I hope it never does."

Unharried by mushroom booms and undeterred by depressions, Portland has gone steadily ahead, gravely, serenely building a beautiful and substantial city. The force of gravity works for her to-day as always, rolling down to her door the wheat and fruit and cattle from the far-away Inland Empire, while the northern ports must battle against the barricade of a mountain-range. She has the best jobbing area of any Northwestern city—all of Oregon, the southern half of Washington, and the country tributary to the Columbia. She has preferential freight-rates south of the Columbia in Washington, and she is steadily working for the canalization of the Columbia and the Snake, so as to improve her inland water-transportation system. Her 29-mile fresh-water harbor has been improved with the most modern terminals, to which sixty steamship lines send their ships. The channel to the sea has been deepened to 30 feet and is soon to be 35. She has built a beautiful and conveniently located island airport. She is one of the leading manufacturing centers of the West. And she has made herself one of the country's most attractive places in which to live, with unusually fine libraries, schools, public buildings, clubs, parks, golf-courses, an art museum, and a notable symphony orchestra. A magnificent scenic highway built by Samuel Lancaster, an engineer who was also an artist, leads from the city far up the Columbia, and at its lower end the waters of the Pacific dash their spray against long white sand beaches. This Columbia River Highway represents in part a benefaction to the state at the hands of Simon Benson, wealthy timber-owner, who also gave the city the many bronze drinking fountains that bubble on its downtown street-corners.

But life is not all a bed of roses for Portland. For her dignity has frequently been upset by the unseemly jesting and hectoring of her boisterous neighbor Seattle. The boosters up the Sound have unfeelingly taunted her with being "the world's largest dry land seaport"; they have called her "the biggest country town in America"; they have delighted in picturing her as a middle-class New England spinster in a pair of goloshes and carrying an umbrella; and her $60,000 cow-pasture has long been an object of derision. This cow-pasture was maintained for many years in the very center of the business district, as an adjunct of the Corbett residence which occupied a square block of green lawn across from the old post-office. The Failings occupied a similar plot in the next block, and that family eventually gave way before the onward march of business and sold the plot for an office-building. The Corbetts, however, with the well-considered dignity of a first family which has kept its cow for a generation in a $60,000 pasture, refused to succumb completely to this modern invasion. They sold the front part of their block for an office-building, but they retained the back half, and there they continued to live. So to-day, if you walk a block from the Portland Hotel, with its fine open court and its polished brass sign, "Park Bicycles Here," you will find yourself in front of this luscious example of Victorian architecture. Hemmed in by business buildings and surrounded by a picket fence, the chocolate-brown mansion sits back majestically in the shade of its towering trees. Through its high windows, hung with white and gold shutters, show glimpses of lace curtains and elaborate jardinières on ornate pedestals. Its Corinthian columns, the pot-bellied pillars of its balconies, and its cast-iron fountain are reminiscent of the days of Grant and Arthur. And although the family cow is no longer parked in the enclosure, there still remains the family stable, with its Gothic windows and its ornamental turret rising just behind the porte-cochère. And, appropriately enough, across the street from this relic of the gay Nineties stands the symbol of Portland's civic spirit. It is the austerely plain brick building, two stories in height with a flagpole on one corner, almost completely overgrown with luxuriant Virginia creeper, behind whose discreet Venetian blinds are carried on the city-boosting activities of the Portland Chamber of Commerce.

# CHAPTER XIV

## TACOMA, A RAILROAD CREATION

IT has been said that Tacoma was born when George Francis Train, that eccentric railroad- and town-promoter of Union Pacific fame, put his finger on the map and said to the directors of the Northern Pacific, "There is the place for your terminus." It would be pleasant to believe this, for such a rubbing of Aladdin's lamp would fit in admirably with the grandiose career and character of Mr. Train, but it is not true. The actual choosing of the terminal site was dramatic enough, however, even though Train was not in the picture. For in an instant this arbitrary choice converted a raw sawmill village on the frontier of civilization into a potential city of importance.

The deep waters of Commencement Bay, so deep that the old settlers boasted that ships could come up to the bank and tie their hawsers to the tree-trunks, early attracted homesteaders and sawmills. It had been a part of the Puget Sound Agricultural Company's claims, and this subsidiary of the Hudson's Bay Company carefully guarded it from overpopulation by selling goods to settlers at high prices and buying from them as little as possible. The Company's only purchases from the settlers were shingles, which it bought for $3 a thousand and sold in San Francisco for $13. In 1853 Nicholas De Lin, a Swede who had come round the Horn to the California gold-fields and pushed on to Portland, continued north to the head of Commencement Bay, so named by Charles Wilkes of the United States Exploring Expedition in 1841 because he began there his surveys of the waters of Puget Sound. De Lin dammed two creeks to operate a wooden turbine and opened a little sawmill, a mill whose mysteries so attracted the Indians that they would gather around and sit watching it as if hypnotized for hours at a time.

Next, a Prussian, Peter Judson, took up a 320-acre claim on the bluffs above, land which later became the center of Tacoma's business

FREDERICK BILLINGS      HENRY VILLARD
JAY COOKE
JAMES J. HILL      EDWARD H. HARRIMAN

Billings and Villard, courtesy of the Northern Pacific Railway; Cooke, from the collection of Frederick H. Meserve, New York; Hill, courtesy of the Great Northern Railway; Harriman, courtesy of the Union Pacific Railroad.

TACOMA, TERMINUS OF THE NORTHERN PACIFIC

Lithograph after a drawing by E. S. Glover, 1878. From the Stokes Collection, New York Public Library.

district; then, from California, seeking to find what might become the western terminus of the northern transcontinental railways, came the Hoosier Job Carr and his clairvoyant wife. After sounding the bay and discovering its great depth, Carr paddled along the shore in a canoe, and when he reached what is now Tacoma, he cried, "Eureka! Eureka! There is my claim."

Following Carr came the adventurous Morton Mathew McCarver, who had been one of the first land speculators in Burlington, Iowa, and who had left Sacramento in disgust after failing to complete an agreement to promote that town for Captain Sutter. In Portland, De Lin told him of the fine town-site at the head of Commencement Bay, and McCarver arranged with the First National Bank there to help him promote the new city. In 1868 he was 61 years old. He had been a delegate to the California Constitutional Convention at Monterey and a member of its first legislature, where he was known as "the old brass cannon." He had made $30,000 in Sacramento and had been the owner of an Oregon City farm, where he had introduced horse-radish west of the Rockies and developed the McCarver apple. He had been commissary-general of the Oregon millitary forces in the Indian wars and had gone to Washington to press Indian-war claims. He had journeyed to the Fraser River during the mining excitement and to New York to finance quartz-mining schemes. And now he became the father of Tacoma.

McCarver bought the Carr claim, settled in Old Woman's Gulch, where the stadium was afterwards built, and wrote his Portland partners that there were so many fish in the bay he could throw out with his bare hands enough smelt to supply a camp of fifty men. The bankers, Lewis M. Starr and James Steel, fearing they would be accused of promoting a rival town, did not want their connection with the enterprise known in Portland; neither did Governor Moore of Washington Territory, who bought 40 acres of land and asked that it be kept quiet. From the beginning McCarver believed that the bay would be the terminus of a railroad, and he rejoiced when Philip Ritz, who had influence in railroad circles, visited the site and was favorably impressed. His enthusiasm grew when he investigated the discovery in the hills near-by of the first bituminous coal-fields on the Pacific Coast and found the product good. He sold land for the first large sawmill, built by Charles Hanson and John W. Ackerson, and wrote his backers in Portland, "I think more of our place since seeing Seattle. The railroad engineer who would give it preference, taking everything into consideration, would recommend his employers to take counterfeit instead of gold and silver. Inspection is all we need in order to secure selection of our town as the railroad terminus."

At this time railroad projects were numerous. Two companies were formed to build from Portland to Puget Sound, among the backers of one being Simeon G. Reed of Portland, and the other enlisting A. A. Denny of Seattle. Still a third project was sponsored by Ben Holladay. And it was believed that an extension of the Union Pacific would soon be made to Puget Sound. To all projectors of railroads McCarver unceasingly sang the praises of Commencement Bay as a terminus, while the older and larger communities of Olympia, Steilacoom, and Seattle looked on in amused contempt, each expecting that the terminus would come to it as a matter of course. Meeting at the First National Bank in Portland in October, 1868, Starr and McCarver determined to add to the attractions of their town by giving it a more euphonious name; so they changed it from Commencement City to Tacoma, after the Indian name of Mount Rainier, the great white peak that rose over the bay. And so certain was McCarver that the railroad would come to his sawmill village that he sold no lots outright, but issued only "bonds" calling for deeds at a later date and providing that the price should be tripled if the road arrived within five years. And the possibility of this happy event increased as the company organized to build over the northern transcontinental route, the Northern Pacific, perfected its plans.

The idea of this northern railroad to the Pacific was the child of Asa Whitney of New York, who first popularized it, although it had been suggested as early as 1834 by Dr. Samuel Barlow of Massachusetts. Having lived in China, Whitney understood the needs of Oriental trade, and he calculated that goods could be shipped from the Far East to Liverpool by way of a railroad across the United States from Puget Sound more quickly and, of course, with less mileage than by sea around the Cape of Good Hope. In 1845, with a company of young gentlemen, he ascended the Missouri River for

1,500 miles, and on his return he launched a scheme to build a railroad to the Pacific Coast on the proceeds of a grant of government land 30 miles wide on either side of the track. At first greeted with derision by Congress, he went through the country speaking, writing, and organizing to bring public opinion to bear on the Government; and so successful was he that in 1847 and 1848 he obtained favorable resolutions from the legislatures of fifteen states as well as from many public meetings in the large cities. He proposed to send annual emigrations to the farm-lands along the route, to employ the emigrants to build the road, paying them partly in land, and to detail groups of them to cultivate a portion of each tract so that those who worked on construction one year could begin farming the next. In 1848 the Senate reported favorably, but Senator Benton attacked the bill "in a boisterous and unparliamentary manner," and it was tabled. Whitney continued to spend his time and money on the fight for several years; but nothing came of it, and he died penniless and discredited, driving a milk-wagon. But so ardently had he preached the advantages of the Puget Sound route, which offered the possibility of a continuous band of settlement and escaped both the heavy snows of the Sierras and the burning deserts of the Southwest, that he created a widespread sentiment in its favor and paved the way for its final success.

The next advocate of a northern Pacific railway was a Vermonter, Edwin F. Johnson, an engineer of ability who was engaged in building the road that afterward became the Chicago and North-Western. When the line was being built to Fond du Lac, Wisconsin, he used to discuss the possibilities of extending it to the Pacific with another Vermonter, Thomas H. Canfield, who was one of its financial backers. Johnson wrote letters on the subject for Poor's *Railroad Journal,* and Canfield induced him to print these as a pamphlet. This brochure, calling attention to the low altitude of the passes from the Missouri to the Columbia and the light snowfall, was given to Secretary of War Jefferson Davis; and it was instrumental in causing him to obtain authority for surveying all the transcontinental routes, with the evident intention of making a report favoring the most southern as opposed to any northern line. His choice of the engineer to make the northern survey was Isaac I. Stevens, later to be the first governor of Washington Territory. Under him Davis placed Captain George B. McClellan, who was to be commander-in-chief of the Army of the Potomac during the Civil War and afterward Democratic candidate for President. Stevens operated from St. Paul, while McClellan went around by way of Panama and reported to him from Puget Sound that the passes over the Cascade Mountains would be less favorable than the route along the Columbia River to Portland. Stevens, however, preferred the direct route to Puget Sound, declared the climate to be milder than that of Virginia, showed the transcontinental distances to be far shorter than over the route to San Francisco Bay, and so forcefully presented the case for the northern Pacific route in pamphlets, letters, and speeches as to weaken the effect of the opposition of Secretary Davis. With A. A. Denny and William S. Ladd he was one of the incorporators of the first Northern Pacific Railroad Company, chartered by the legislature of Washington Territory in 1857, which, however, remained a paper organization.

Meanwhile, another New Englander, Josiah Perham of Maine, had become infected with the Pacific-railroad virus. Country storekeeper, woolen manufacturer, Boston wool commission-merchant, he had made and lost several fortunes and had embarked on replenishing his finances by exhibiting an immense panoramic painting of the Great Lakes, Niagara, and the St. Lawrence River. To view this spectacle, known as "The Seven Mile Mirror," he brought excursion parties to Boston from all over New England. So successful was this venture in attracting tourists that he began selling excursion tickets from Boston to New York and Washington—in fact, Perham initiated the business of conducting tours and selling low-rate round-trip tickets in America. Rich and well-known and enjoying the confidence of the railroads, he launched his scheme to build a railroad to the Pacific under the erroneous impression that he could finance it by selling a million shares to as many individuals at $100 apiece. "I want the whole people of the country to subscribe to the stock," he said. "I want twenty thousand people of Massachusetts to subscribe for one share each, within two weeks after the books are open, which will give it such force as to sweep the whole country like a whirlwind." To those who objected that he could not raise the money required in small subscriptions, he crushingly replied, "By a reported list of the open drinking saloons in New York City, it appears from a careful examination and calculation, that the receipts of those places, on Sundays only, in a single year reaches the large total of one million dollars. This total is made up of five and ten cent pieces."

The People's Pacific Railroad Company was chartered in Maine originally to build to San Francisco, but when Congress refused to give it a franchise, Perham changed it to the northern route from Lake Superior to Puget Sound and joined forces with Governor Stevens. Through friendship with the most powerful man in Congress, Thaddeus Stevens of Pennsylvania, a bill providing for a large land-grant, but no bonds or financial aid, was finally passed and was signed by President Lincoln on July 2, 1864. But no million citizens rushed forth to hand Perham their $100, and no support could be obtained from New York bankers; so the promoters tried to interest Boston men in making the line tributary to New England, and an arrangement was entered into looking toward the use of the Grand Trunk Railway through eastern Canada and the Vermont Central into Boston. In 1866 John Gregory Smith, who controlled the latter road, was named president of the new board, enough money was paid Perham to discharge his debts, and two years later he died, like Asa Whitney, in poverty. A change of ministry in Canada ended the possibility of the international railroad consolidation that the Boston men wanted, the United States Congress refused to give any more aid, and an extension of the charter was only secured when Thaddeus Stevens tacked it on as a rider to the Kansas Pacific Railroad land-grant bill fostered by Thomas A. Scott, the doughty president of the Pennsylvania Railroad.

Convinced that nothing further could be expected from the Government and faced with the powerful opposition of Ames of the Union Pacific, Huntington of the Central Pacific, and all the other transcontinental-railroad promoters, President Smith decided to secure the support of the large Eastern railroads, and to this end he enlisted Thomas H. Canfield of Burlington, Vermont, long an ardent advocate of the northern Pacific route. Canfield's first step was to print the Northern Pacific Charter Act in a pamphlet, and with this he approached one of the most powerful railroad men in the country, William B. Ogden, president of the Chicago and North-Western.

Herbert Hunt in his *History of Tacoma* gives Canfield's report of his conversation with Ogden at his home in New York: *

"Long after midnight," said Canfield, "I felt that he was won for the cause. I can see him now as he paced the room, completely absorbed in the subject."

"How much money will it take to put this enterprise on its feet and begin the work of construction," he asked.

"It will take a great deal of preliminary work and your experience teaches you that it will take a great deal of money," I replied.

"And what are the chances of getting our money back?"

"About one in fifty."

"And what is your excuse for asking me to place money at such a risk?"

"This enterprise is one of the greatest ever undertaken in the world," I answered. "It is equal to that of the East India Company; it is the only continuous charter ever granted across this continent from water to water, and with the prevailing sentiment of hostility to railroad grants which is increasing in this country, if this charter is allowed to lapse another year, one will never be granted. The road will open an empire now occupied by savages, and withal it will be the great highway for the trade of China, Japan, and the East Indies across the continent. It is due to the people of this country and to this nation that you gentlemen whom Providence has placed at the head of the great transportation interests of this country should step in at this crisis and use your influence and advance money to save this magnificent enterprise from destruction."

"And suppose I put my money in for such a laudable purpose, what have you to give me or to others to show for it? You have no company. This charter is not the Northern Pacific Railroad Company's. You have not organized and cannot organize under it." This was true and I simply answered:

"I have nothing to give. I have suggested the names of twelve men, including ourselves, whom I believe to be honorable men, and whose word once given will serve every purpose. If you go in on that basis, I believe we can secure these men, if they seem to you suitable, and we can pull together until we are in a position to organize."

"It is simply a matter of honor among gentlemen?"

"Exactly," I replied.

"Well, that is certainly a high position on a high and noble purpose. I will take hold with you. The charter must be saved. Meet me at my

* Herbert Hunt, *Tacoma, Its History and Its Builders* (Chicago, S. J. Clarke Publishing Company).

office to-morrow and we will lay siege to the directors of the Chicago and North-Western."

The Original Interests Agreement worked out next day, covering less than two sheets of note-paper, was the basis for a revival of activity in the affairs of the Northern Pacific It divided the enterprise into twelve shares at $8,500 apiece and provided that each owner should elect one director, a thirteenth to be named from the Pacific Coast. When it was completed, night had fallen, and as there was no gas in the office, candles were sent for. As Ogden and the others, walking up Broadway, passed Trinity Church, Smith said, "Now the turning point in the affairs of the Northern Pacific has come."

The twelve partners included Robert Berdell, president of the Erie Railroad; William G. Fargo, vice-president of the New York Central Railroad; D. N. Barney, A. H. Barney, B. P. Cheney, who had large express interests with Fargo; Edward Reilly, a friend of Thaddeus Stevens of Pennsylvania; J. Edgar Thompson, president of the Pennsylvania Railroad; and G. W. Cass, president of the Pittsburgh, Fort Wayne and Chicago Railroad. Edwin F. Johnson was appointed chief engineer, systematic surveys at both ends of the route were begun in 1867, and it was recommended that work start at once on the line between Portland and Puget Sound in order to accommodate the business of the region and to facilitate settlement. Canfield represented the railroad in Washington, where he worked for the passage of bills permitting the road to issue bonds, extending the time for completion to July 4, 1877, and allowing the line to Portland to be designated as the main line, so that the mileage to tide-water might be increased, if desired, with consequent increase in subsidies.

Having made this much progress, the directors were anxious to get powerful financial agents to sell the bonds of the company, and they turned to Jay Cooke, Philadelphia and New York financier, who had sold the government bonds issued to pay for the Civil War. He had a talent for what the French call *"grande finance"*; he was optimistic, bold, contagiously enthusiastic; and Eugene V. Smalley, in his *History of the Northern Pacific*, says of him, "His great defect was a want of caution and foresight. He failed to understand that alternate expansion and contraction is the law of finance, and that the business of the world progresses like the frog in the well of the old arithmetic problem, which leaped up three feet and fell back two. Mr. Cooke's schemes were based on the delusive idea that the pendulum of trade and finance always swings upward. He did not make provision for the inevitable downward swing."

Jay Cooke was cautious enough, however, about entering the Northern Pacific Railroad arena. For over a year he kept the directors on the anxious seat while he sent special engineering expeditions to the Coast to investigate. When the reports as to the value of the lands and the feasibility of the road were favorable, he insisted that legislation should be passed making the railroad's mortgage cover the land-grant, and in 1869 he drove a hard bargain with the directors in his contract to sell $100,000,000 of the company's bonds. He chose to pay $7\frac{3}{10}$ per cent on these bonds, as this was the rate the Government had paid on the war bonds he had sold, and it permitted him to make the alluring statement that a $50 bond would return the holder one cent a day. His own remuneration was to be 12 cents on each dollar's worth of bonds sold, $200 worth of stock for every $1,000 in bonds sold, and one-half the remainder of the $100,000,000 of stock authorized by the charter. The twelve proprietary interests were increased to twenty-four, of which Cooke was given twelve, which included a half-interest in the company formed to promote town-sites. He held power of attorney on all stock given away with bonds. His agreement to raise $5,000,000 within 30 days was fulfilled by forming a pool in Philadelphia, and on this he immediately made a profit of $1,200,000.

Cooke had hoped to sell most of the bonds abroad, and he sent his partner, Morehead, to interview the Rothschilds. But Morehead was not enthusiastic, and he made such a poor presentation that they were not interested; he then advised Cooke by cable to drop the whole business and went off to Egypt to spend the winter. In Washington Cooke met two young German bankers at dinner at the house of the Prussian Minister, and this led to the formation of a syndicate of foreign bankers to take half the bonds; but when Napoleon III began his attack on the Rhine, the negotiations were broken off. Thus Cooke was forced to fall back on the American market, and the cultivation of the small investor.

Now began one of the most comprehensive publicity campaigns in the history of the country, when Cooke set out to popularize the Northern Pacific Railroad and its bonds. Advertisements were printed in city dailies and country weeklies, favorable editorials were widespread, and letters, telegrams, and pamphlets, and magazine articles flooded the country. Of this effort Smalley says,

For many months it was almost impossible to take up a newspaper in any part of the Northern States without finding something in it concerning the Northern Pacific. Prominent statesmen and army officers wrote letters describing the merits of the country the road was to traverse. Generals, members of Congress, Governors of States, and the Vice-President of the United States gave the weight of their endorsement to the project. Their opinions, together with extracts from the reports of engineers and others sent out to survey the line and reconnoiter the country, were printed in pamphlets and spread broadcast. An effective circular was compiled from the arguments of the men in Congress who had opposed the grant to the company because of its great extent and of its fertility and value for settlement.

As a result of this campaign the ownership of the bonds was distributed over nearly every state in the Union; moreover, the pamphlets were translated into French and German, and the people of those countries also became investors in the great enterprise.

Bubbling with enthusiasm, the publicity presented the Northern Pacific country as a land of plenty where the world's largest yields of wheat, oats, and barley could be obtained, where fruit-trees flourished more vigorously than anywhere else on earth and were not infected with insects; and it stated that "nowhere in the world is there grass to compare with that combination of timothy and oats, the 'bunch grass,' which covers most of this land grant." The literature declared that the forests of Washington Territory surpassed "the woods of all the rest of the globe in the size, quality and quantity of the timber. . . . The paradox of firs too large to be profitably cut into lumber is to be seen all over western Washington. . . . So prodigal is Nature in this region, and so wastefully fastidious is man, that lands yielding only 30,000 feet of lumber to the acre are considered to be hardly worth cutting over." Rich deposits of gold, silver, copper, iron, platinum, great coal-beds were described; and, as a crowning attraction, the pamphlets pointed out that the warm winter winds from the South

Pacific gave Washington Territory the climate of Virginia and Montana the mildness of southern Ohio, adding, "The Mexican horses, stolen by the Sioux, Cheyennes and Assiniboines, are turned out to shift for themselves on the fall of snow, from latitude 45 up to 53, and come in in the spring, fat, sleek, and strong. Unsheltered, unfed, they thrive in the open air on grass reached by pawing off with their hoofs the occasional covers of snow."

In response to these glowing descriptions of the new land of heart's desire, a steady stream of money poured in to buy bonds; and although "Jay Cooke's banana belt" was held up to derision in some quarters, most of the things he said about it were true, even if it was difficult for Easterners to imagine a country so far north as Puget Sound enjoying mild winters or to believe the astonishing stories of forest-, farm- and grazing-lands. As proof of the mildness of the climate Ezra Meeker in 1870 took east from his farm near Tacoma, fifty-two varieties of flowers found blooming in the open in the first week of December. These were presented to Horace Greeley, who commented on them in the New York *Tribune*. When Cooke saw this item, he invited Meeker to visit him and purchased from him 5,000 eighty-page pamphlets describing the attractions of the Puget Sound country. He hired Meeker to distribute these to a selected list of possible customers in New England and to give talks on the West, and he kept him for months in the Cooke offices to answer the questions of prospective investors. Meeker says that a day when less than $100,000 worth of Northern Pacific bonds was sold was considered poor.

In 1870, with the proceeds of the first $5,000,000 of bonds sold by Jay Cooke, construction was begun in Minnesota, a short railroad was bought in that state, and the eastern terminus was established at St. Paul; the line from Kalama on the Columbia River to Puget Sound was started; and a controlling interest was bought in the Oregon Steam Navigation Company, which operated steamboats on the Columbia, Snake, and Willamette rivers and Puget Sound. Thirty million dollars was expended in two years, and 600 miles of road was built when, in 1872, President Smith retired. It was felt that he had to give too much time to the affairs of the Vermont Central, of which he was receiver, and also that he had spent the money too lavishly, taking too hopeful a view of the future and acting as if the treasury were "a widow's cruse of oil which would never run dry."

General George W. Cass, the next president, was elected while he was a member of a committee of the board cruising around Puget Sound to select the western terminus of the road. For a week they inspected possible sites: the capital city of Olympia was rejected "because the receding tide left its port a wide expanse of mud and mussel shells for half of every twenty-four hours"; the old pioneer town of Steilacoom, which boasted that it would be chosen because no railroad could go northward without passing through it, was discovered to be upon a strait rather than a good harbor; the little lumbering town of Seattle was found to have hills which were too steep and no room for extensive railroad tracks on level ground. As Smalley says,

> Considerations of economy had already begun to press upon the board. They wanted to start building to the nearest point on the Sound where they could find a good harbor, good shore facilities for wharves, and plenty of cheap land to acquire for the future city. So they pitched upon Tacoma, on Commencement Bay, as the place best fulfilling all these conditions. There were a sawmill and a few houses called by the name, with a background of primitive forest, facing upon a beautiful broad bay, on which the gleaming summit of magnificent Mount Rainier looked down like a pyramid of ivory from the blue heavens.

Final decision was left to the board in New York. Mukilteo, Tacoma, and Seattle were being considered, and a commission was sent to examine these three sites and report. This consisted of Captain John C. Ainsworth of Portland, who was made managing director for the Pacific Coast, and Judge R. D. Rice, vice-president for the Pacific Coast. At Steilacoom they were waited on by many interested landowners desirous of influencing the choice of the terminus, among them a delegation from Seattle, concerning which the Steilacoom *Express* remarked:

> Seven of the Seattle delegation came up on the A-1, fast sailing, big pressure steamer "Zephyr" on Friday last, with their hats full of blanks to make their "last and final" bid for the terminus. The delegation comprised the "big" men of Seattle, and as they marched in double file arm in arm through the streets of Steilacoom to Hotel de Rhinehart to meet

the locating commissioners, their lofty beavers glistened in the noontide sun like an African's phiz in a field of cane. They came, they saw and— that was all; for the heads of the locating commissioners were too well balanced to lose their equilibrium on meeting this august delegation of great men from the town of sawdust and fleas.

On June 30, 1873, the commissioners telegraphed New York:

The situation is substantially this: At Tacoma the Puget Sound Company have about 1,100 acres by purchase; bonded donations to Puget Sound Company and our company about 1,500 acres; bonded to purchase 60 acres mill property for $100,000 gold. This whole territory in solid body amounts to about 2,700 acres, with unbroken waterfront of over two miles, and riparian rights to tide flats of, say 600 acres, to which can be added company lands in vicinity, including natural parks with beautiful lakes, enough to swell the amount to, say, 10,000 acres.

Seattle offers about 2,500 acres and 450 lots in city limits, some 6,500 acres in vicinity, $60,000 cash, 4,800 feet front on navigable water and release of riparian rights of tide flats near city, title to pass on completion of road to that point. City limits very large. To carry out plan of a city company on $2,000,000 basis with any prospect of success, as now advised, shall unhesitatingly decide in favor of Tacoma. The mill property to be purchased cost them more than is asked for it, but it is vital to success of enterprise as it covers half a mile of best waterfront.

On July 3 General Cass telegraphed in cipher that the executive committee agreed on Tacoma, and July 14, from the railroad town of Kalama on the Columbia, the commissioners wired General Mc-Carver of Tacoma, "We have located terminus on Commencement Bay." It was said that Thomas A. Scott of the Pennsylvania Railroad also believed the head of Commencement Bay to be the logical place for the railroad to reach tide-water.

McCarver did not make a fortune from his lands, however, because the committee decided to put the town on the bluffs at the head of the bay, whereas his property was some miles away, on the peninsula below. The lands purchased by the railroad were turned over to the Lake Superior and Puget Sound Land Company, later the Tacoma Land Company, and the building of the town began. The Northern Pacific in the east was by this time nearing the town of Bismarck, North Dakota, and in the west was building from Portland to Puget Sound. It was a time of great prosperity, though the first rumblings of disaster to come could be faintly heard. Jay Cooke was not selling bonds quite as fast as previously; the railroad owed him $1,500,000, and, in keeping with the expansive spirit of the day, he had invested funds in the promotion of many other enterprises from which no immediate return could be expected. The burden of pushing a railroad through an utterly unproductive and unsettled country and at the same time paying 12 per cent of cash received for promotion and between 7 and 8 per cent interest on the bonds was beginning to show its impracticability. The first intimation that all was not well came in June, 1873, in a telegram to Captain Ainsworth saying, "$30,000 and no more will be supplied to carry the line to tide-water." In August the Tacoma Land Company was hurried into organization, spurred on by another wire saying, "Delay will be fatal to plans for procuring money," and additional funds to aid construction were obtained from the sale of this stock. But in September, when the financial crash came and the house of Jay Cooke and Company was swept away, the railroad was still 22 miles from Tacoma, although Captain Ainsworth had advanced money necessary for construction from his personal fortune.

As the country was gripped by panic and one bank after another failed, the men building the Northern Pacific threw down their tools and struck for their back pay. They built an armed barricade around their camp and refused to allow trains to go over the track. To reason with these hard-boiled laboring-men, most of whom had learned to be tough in the Fraser River mines, came the governor and the chief justice of the Territory with officials of the railroad. Held up by pickets 200 yards from the barricade, the officials parleyed with the strike-leaders until Captain Ainsworth personally paid part of the wages and gave the men due-bills on the store at Hanson and Ackerson's mill for the remainder. Thereupon "Skookum" Smith, the contractor, put on a high-pressure drive to carry the rails into Tacoma, and the line was completed just 24 hours before the charter expired. The first train came through in the middle of December, the Indians gathering to watch the strange spectacle of the "hiu chick-chick" as it roared over the steel rails, belching smoke and showering the countryside with sparks from its wood fire. The formal ceremony of driving the last spike was observed on December 16, 1873.

Now that the terminus was definitely fixed and one mixed train of passengers and freight bumped its way to the Columbia River every day, the Tacoma Land Company began its plans for the building of a great city. Charles B. Wright of Philadelphia, millionaire and one of the investigating committee that had chosen the terminus, was its guiding genius. The town plat was drawn by Frederick Law Olmstead, the landscape architect who laid out Central Park in New York, and it was received with consternation in Tacoma. For it created a city of curving streets (bearing such exotic names as Orinoco and Monoca), terraced drives, and seven parks, which the pioneers voted "the most fantastic plat of a town that was ever seen. There wasn't a straight line, a right angle or a corner lot. The blocks were shaped like melons, pears and sweet potatoes. One block, shaped like a banana, was 3,000 feet in length and had 250 lots. It was a pretty fair park plan but condemned itself for a town." It was doomed never to become a reality, however, for the town-builders submitted another and less spectacular plan modeled after that of Melbourne, Australia.

As if to ridicule Olmstead's artistic dream, the raw little town straggled over its muddy streets among the fir stumps and wild berry-vines, the center of its life and color being Whiskey Row on Pacific Avenue, famous for its fist fights and boggy mud. Harry and Pitt Cooke, nephews of Jay Cooke, opened the town's first bank, and everywhere there was a tremendous cutting of trees, burning of stumps, and building of houses. But the town really began to become a city when, down on the wharf, a first-class hotel was opened by Mr. and Mrs. W. B. Blackwell, who had arrived on the first Northern Pacific train. Blackwell, who had been chief clerk at the Sherman House in Chicago, had come west for his health and had been induced by General John W. Sprague, manager of the railway, to come to the Northwest. He had already opened a hotel in Portland for Ben Holladay and one in Kalama for the railway. Later he became president of one of Tacoma's large banks, a builder of the Tacoma Theater and various other enterprises, and an owner of the Tacoma Hotel. In 1873 St. Peter's Episcopal Church was built, with a bell, given by its namesake in Philadephia, hung in "the oldest church tower in America," a giant fir-tree close to the side of the church, cut off 48 feet above the ground. And the Steilacoom *Express* was well justified in declaring, "Tacoma is a fixed fact. Rings cannot submerge her, whether composed of disappointed speculators or interested editors. Tacoma is the star of the West and center from which all luminaries radiate."

With western emigration checked by the panic, no money in the treasury, and a road that ended at Bismarck, North Dakota, in a veritable no-man's land, things looked black for the Northern Pacific in 1873. Moreover, the investors who had lost money in Northern Pacific stock set up a dismal chant of disillusionment which was enough to cause even the stout of heart to abandon everything connected with the railroad. A poet of the day paraphrased Tennyson by writing,

> Broke, broke, broke
> By railway loans, J. C.
> And I would that my heart could utter
> The thoughts that arise in me.

In order to save something for the investors and to protect all the parties interested, the road went into receivership, and the $100,000,000 of stock was divided so that the holder of each $1,000 in bonds got $1,400 in preferred stock. The remainder of the preferred stock, $9,-000,000, was left in the treasury for general purposes; those who owned the original capital stock received a new issue share for share; and all the remaining stock was divided among the owners of the proprietary interests. By this brilliant achievement in reorganization, which was completed in record time, the road found itself free of bonded debt, the owner of 600 miles of road and 10,000,000 acres of land, with the prospect of 30,000,000 acres more to come as soon as the line should be completed. President Cass resigned to act as receiver, and Charles B. Wright became president.

Wright, who was to do so much for Tacoma, had been a merchant and banker in Erie, Pennsylvania, had been active in building the Philadelphia and Erie Railroad, and had been general manager of the United Railways which served the oil-fields of Pennsylvania. He had been active in the financial management of the Northern Pacific, coming to its rescue at crucial times with his own private funds and credit. His was now the heavy task of refunding the $5,500,000 the road had borrowed, of placating the creditors, and of operating a 600-mile road through the wilderness. The only bright spots in the

picture were the fact that General Cass was attracting settlers to
the lands in Minnesota by demonstrating on his enormous Red River
farm that wheat-growing there was profitable, and the returns from
the Portland–Tacoma line, which in 1876 had netted a surplus of
$300,000.

Meanwhile, coal had been discovered in quantities along the route
of the proposed direct line east from Tacoma over the Cascade Mountains, and other railroad enterprises were preparing to build into this
territory. For it was thought that the Northern Pacific did not intend to build directly over the Cascades as originally planned, but
instead would permanently use its entry to Tacoma by way of Portland. In order to show that the company was determined to occupy
the Cascades route, Wright started building, and when no loan could
be negotiated, he bought a cargo of iron for the line on his own
credit and shipped it to Tacoma around Cape Horn.

Now Tacoma began to move forward: Wright built the first brick
building at Ninth and Pacific Avenues, the sawmill made 15,000 bed-
slats for a California concern, and Wilson's Grand Parisian Circus
and Menagerie played to a full tent at a dollar a head. At the eastern
end of the Northern Pacific, President Wright was adding trackage
in Minnesota, and in 1878 a bond-issue of $2,500,000 was made to
extend the road from the Missouri to the Yellowstone, with the avowed
intention of building on over the Cascades directly to Tacoma. This
news was received with joy on Commencement Bay, for at that time
Northern Pacific passengers from the East traveled a long way by
stage and then were carried to Portland, whence they were relayed
by boat to Kalama where they took the train to Tacoma. The city
of Portland, however, lost no opportunity of using her influence against
the building of a direct Eastern connection.

In 1879 Wright resigned the presidency and was warmly commended
by the directors, who declared,

To have successfully brought the company to its present position has
been a task which required talents of no common order; to rebuild the
fallen edifice of credit which, when once shaken, is the most difficult of
all things to restore; to combine, as he has done, a thorough and searching economy with the full maintenance of efficiency; to have preserved
friendship where it existed, and to have conciliated almost every hostile

WINDJAMMERS LOADING AT TACOMA'S WHEAT DOCKS

From a photograph taken in 1899. Courtesy of the Tacoma Chamber of Commerce.

NORTHERN PACIFIC WESTERN HEADQUARTERS

The "Half Moon" freight storage yard, the wheat piers, and the old headquarters building on the right at the top of the inclined street. Courtesy of the Tacoma Chamber of Commerce.

element that was to be encountered—these are indeed laurels to any administrator.

Wright was succeeded by Frederick Billings, a Vermonter who had come to San Francisco in 1849 and successfully practised law there, after which he returned to New York. He was one of the promoters of the Overland Stage Company and the Atlantic and Pacific Railroad, whose franchise was in later years taken over by the Santa Fe. He was one of the original owners of a proprietary interest in the Northern Pacific and had been managing director of the road's land department. Under his presidency was financed the Pend Oreille division, which was built by General Sprague of Tacoma, the company's general manager on the Pacific Coast. In 1881 Billings negotiated a loan of $40,000,000 from Winslow, Lanier and Company, Drexel, Morgan and Company, and A. Belmont and Company to provide funds for completing the road to tide-water at Tacoma, and for this financial coup he was congratulated by President Hayes. He entered into an agreement with Henry Villard for the temporary use of the tracks of the Oregon Railway and Navigation Company down the Columbia from Wallula to Portland; and at his retirement, in 1881, Northern Pacific preferred stock, which once sold for $8, had risen to $80, and the common stock, which had been as low as $1.50, was quoted at nearly $50.

Now that most amazing manipulator of money and railroads, Henry Villard, was about to take over the management of the Northern Pacific, but in the interim A. H. Barney, who had been executive manager of the United States Express Company and an owner of the Western Union Telegraph Company, assumed the presidency. In order to protect his Oregon Railway and Navigation Company, Villard had obtained control of the Northern Pacific, and Portland was cheering him on in the hope that the building of the line over the Cascades, a project heartily ridiculed by the *Oregonian,* might be abandoned. Seattle, too, hoped he might be induced to take away from Tacoma the advantages it had gained, and its citizens had begun a movement in Congress to have the railroad's land-grant abrogated. Assailed from both north and south, Tacoma was being crushed between the upper and the nether millstones. New and enlarged terminals of the Northern Pacific were planned at Portland, and under the Villard régime

Tacoma became merely an afterthought in the railroad's plans. Building projects languished, work stopped, new-comers passed by to settle in Portland or Seattle.

Villard seemingly promised much when he spoke in the city in 1884, and Tacomans revived their flagging hopes until it was found that he had made the same diplomatic speech in every town he had visited. He added to the anger of the disappointed citizens when he built a small, unattractive, wooden railway station in a remote location, which was referred to derisively as "Villard's depot." Hope was born again, however, in 1884, when Villard resigned as his financial schemes crashed to earth, and Tacoma's friend, Charles B. Wright, returned to the board. During his presidency Villard had obtained for the Northern Pacific about $2,000,000 in Portland, and he had also received large sums from Seattle on the promise of building a branch to that town.

Villard had pushed the railroad construction at both ends of the line, building from Duluth westward to join the Oregon Railway and Navigation tracks which were being laid eastward from Portland. In 1883 he put an end to the carrying of passengers from Portland to Kalama by boat by laying tracks from Portland to Goble, and the following year a ferry, the *Tacoma*, was put into operation which carried the whole train across the Columbia River, providing direct train connection between Portland and Tacoma. Thomas F. Oakes, who succeeded Villard as president, made one of his main objectives the completion of the Cascades line to Tacoma, the project opposed by Villard and his Portland friends. He also began to make cuts in operating expenses and to curb the extravagance that had been characteristic of the Villard régime.

In 1884, spurred by the promise of the completion of the direct line to the East and profiting from the improved financial condition of the country, Tacoma began to grow rapidly. Interest in the West was general, and Henry Ward Beecher added to it by declaring, "If I were young I'd settle in Washington Territory. It is going to be the Italy of America." The departure of ships laden with wheat was no longer a novelty, despite the fact that Harvey Scott of the *Oregonian* had recently said, "Tacoma has shipped one cargo of wheat and it might possibly, before the end of the century, ship another."

Moreover, shipping men declared that the trip up the Columbia and Willamette to Portland cost $3,500, whereas they could come into Tacoma for less than a tenth of that sum. The first cargo of tea arrived from China in 1885 and was sent east in a train adorned with banners advertising Tacoma. A steamer was brought around the Horn to be put in the Tacoma–Victoria service. General Sprague was active in the promotion of all sorts of business enterprises, including a gas company, and he arranged with Editor R. F. Radebaugh of the Tacoma *Ledger* to send to California farmers special editions of his paper telling of the agricultural possibilities of Washington Territory. The benefactions of Charles B. Wright permitted the building of the beautiful St. Luke's Episcopal Church as a memorial to his wife, the Annie Wright Seminary for girls, the Fannie Paddock Memorial Hospital, named after the wife of Bishop John A. Paddock, and Wright Park. The Tacoma Hotel, planned by Stanford White of McKim, Mead and White, the New York architects, was completed, and guests were amazed at its beauty. It had been furnished by Wanamaker's at a cost of $40,000, and it contained such novelties as an oven large enough for 250 pies and a machine which would peel a barrel of potatoes in 20 minutes.

When Nelson Bennett was awarded the contract for building the Northern Pacific east and driving a tunnel through the Cascade Mountains, real estate began to move rapidly. Bennett, Canadian-born, had gone to New York State as a youth and later been successful as a driller of oil-wells in Pennsylvania. He became a school-teacher in Missouri, going thence to Montana, where he ran stage-coach and freighting lines with Senator William A. Clark. There he met Washington Dunn, Jay Gould's representative, and began building under him as a subcontractor. When Dunn died, Bennett took over his contracts. He built the first street-railways in Butte and developed a similar system in Tacoma. In later years he founded the town of Fairhaven, now Bellingham; built mills, factories, and a hotel there; operated a steamship line to Tacoma; and built railroads in the north of the state which were later bought by the Great Northern. He bought the Tacoma *Ledger*; built the great irrigation project at Twin Falls, Idaho; spanned the Chilkoot Pass in Alaska with a tramway; and built various lines for the Northern Pacific, including the Nelson

Bennett Tunnel under Point Defiance along the shore-line into Tacoma.

In 1887 the Northern Pacific determined to wait no longer for the completion of the Stampede Tunnel through the Cascades in order to reach Tacoma, but to climb over the mountains on a switchback track. More than 2,000 men were employed on this, and within four months a bottle of champagne was broken over the last spike. Although Villard had celebrated the driving of the last spike in Montana four years before, this later event, June 1, 1887, really represented the completion of the Northern Pacific to tide-water over its own line. Special crews and special engines were used to bring the trains over the pass, an hour and a quarter being required to haul five cars over the hazardous eight miles. On the Fourth of July, to celebrate the completion of the railroad, there was a grand parade and other festivities which were attended by officers of H. M. S. *Caroline,* the commander of which, Sir William Wiseman, had given Gilbert and Sullivan the inspiration for "Pinafore."

When the Stampede Tunnel was bored through, May 3, 1888, Tacoma was in the midst of its great boom. Nearly two miles long, the second largest tunnel in the United States, it had been pushed through in about two years at a cost of $1,000,000, and Bennett had made $250,000 on the contract. The tunnel was named "Stampede" because the engineer, Virgil G. Bogue, put a foreman in charge of the trail-cutters who pushed the work faster than the men wanted to go. When they threw down their tools one afternoon, the foreman informed the cook that the food in the kitchen was for men who were working for the Northern Pacific Railroad and that these men had struck and could therefore not be fed. Whereupon the men rolled their blankets and "stampeded" down the trail. Bogue told W. P. Bonney, secretary of the Washington Historical Society, that he was sorry he had insisted that the pass be named Stampede when the railroad officials wanted to name it Bogue Pass, because he considered it the best piece of engineering he ever did. In the building of the Stampede Tunnel thirteen lives were known to have been lost, and the captious said that many more men, mostly Chinese, had been killed in the blasting, buried under the rocks and never reported. Nelson Bennett provided a hospital with doctors and nurses in attendance; he gave his men comfortable quarters, and it was his custom to regale them with frequent feasts at which he would serve a hundred turkeys and distribute five thousand cigars after dinner. The whole country had watched the progress of the tunnel through the Cascades, and George Francis Train's wire to Nelson Bennett, "Bore, Bennett, Bore; Bore, Bennett, Bore," was widely quoted. The celebration of the completion of the tunnel was held on May 5, and a telegram was received at this meeting reporting the successful completion of the first two spans of the Northern Pacific bridge across the Columbia at Pasco, which was to supplant the old ferry service in bringing trains westward.

Boom psychology was now in the saddle: the million-dollar Tacoma Smelter, to be used by the mines of Alaska and South America, was begun; million-bushel grain-elevators, flour-mills, iron-works, furniture factories, wharves, and warehouses lined the bay for miles; the mails were so heavy that the postmaster was hiring assistants at his own expense; excursions arrived from the East daily; and real-estate operations grew so fast that a group of business men, among them Hugh C. Wallace, who was one day to be Ambassador to France, organized the Tacoma Real Estate and Stock Exchange.

Chief among the realtors was Allen Chase Mason, who had been an Illinois school-teacher, writing texts on arithmetic and pedagogy, when he read about Tacoma in the Chicago *Times*. He wrote to the city to verify the facts and then came west, arriving with so little money that after paying a month's house-rent he had only $2.85 left. His first commission was $2 for renting a house; he made $10,000 the first year and was soon spending $5,000 a month advertising Tacoma in Eastern newspapers. To open up the north end of the town he built a bridge and presented it to the city, after which he platted thirteen additions all overlooking Puget Sound, in accordance with his motto, "Keep in View of the Water." He built waterworks, railways, a gas-works at Olympia; irrigated 6,000 acres of farm-land at North Yakima; owned another house and a bank there, and others in Tacoma and Bellingham. With Nelson Bennett, then of Butte, he obtained a Tacoma street-railway franchise. He saw the possibilities of wheat-growing in the Palouse country and financed farming there. His investments in the Northwest were said to amount to $10,000,000, and his advertising was the most powerful magnet drawing people to Puget Sound.

Twenty-six steamers and more than a hundred sailing-vessels were operating from Tacoma to Alaska and foreign ports, numerous large hotels were being built, John D. Rockefeller had visited the town and been favorably impressed. Everybody was busy, everybody was making money in real estate. Herbert Hunt tells of a clerk who put his week's pay in an option on lots, sold the next day at a profit greater than his salary for the year, quit his position, and in four months had made $28,000; and of a newly arrived farmer from Illinois who was separated from his savings by a real-estate man in return for acreage he had never seen, sold it in a week for a profit of $8,000, and continued his speculations so successfully that 18 months later he arrived back in Illinois by way of the Orient and Europe, traveling in a private car. In all his dealings he had never had a deed to anything.

It was about this time that the young English writer Rudyard Kipling arrived in Tacoma and found the town staggering under "a boom of the boomiest." In *From Sea to Sea* he described the new planked streets; the new brick business-blocks sandwiched in between board shanties; the horse-car line over the steep hills; the ornate hotels and homes of the rich; the conversation, which was all of money-making, and the occupation, which was mainly drinking. Kipling concluded his description by declaring that a man nearly pulled a gun on his traveling companion because he would not immediately agree that Tacoma would outstrip San Francisco, and he departed for Canada endorsing his observation that "they are all mad here, all mad."

But if Kipling was not impressed by Tacoma's boom, many experienced American business men were. Even Henry Villard, who had never been particularly friendly to the city, succumbed. So bright did Tacoma's future seem to him that as soon as his fortune had been resuscitated, he began to invest heavily in real estate and bought the street-railway system from Nelson Bennett. There was, moreover, a steady flow of money from Wright's associates in Philadelphia, and it was rumored that the Union Pacific would make Tacoma its western terminus, agents of Jay Gould confirming this report. The town was jubilant when the beautiful Tacoma Theater, with one of the largest stages in the country, was opened, and the Duff Opera Company played for a week to standing-room only every night. Real estate became a mania: brass bands advertised new subdivisions, fortunes were made in a few days, and $100,000 companies were organized every hour on the hour. One grandiose scheme was to transport ice to the city from the mountain by means of a wooden chute, and when it was objected that this was impractical because the friction would set the boards on fire, the promoter replied that the moisture from the ice would put it out.

The boom period saw the organization of what later became the largest lumber-mill in the world, the St. Paul and Tacoma Lumber Company. This concern had its beginning when two groups of lumbermen who happened to be in the city were introduced to each other by President Oakes of the Northern Pacific. These men, who became outstanding figures in the Northwest, included Chauncey W. Griggs, Charles Hebard Jones, Addison G. Foster, George Browne, and Henry Hewitt, Jr. Colonel Griggs, who was Connecticut-born, had been principal of a school at Tolland, and at Willimantic part owner of a store, which he sold when the year's profits were only $100. He had been a bookkeeper and banker in Detroit, owner of a livery-stable in Ohio, and of small stores in Iowa. He had built up a large wholesale furniture business in Detroit, and in St. Paul, where he had been associated with James J. Hill, he had been a successful contractor and dealer in fuel, merchandise, and real estate. Charles H. Jones was a Vermonter whose family had moved to Wisconsin when he was a boy. There he worked in his father's mill and spoke-factory, taught school, owned a sawmill. He lost his mill in the panic of 1873, and it took him five years as manager of a stave-factory to accumulate $2,500 for a new start. With Henry Hewitt he went into the milling and timber business in Wisconsin, and together they were visiting Tacoma when they met Colonel Griggs. When the Northern Pacific agreed to sell the group all the timber it needed at a low price, the company was organized, and Jones, as the practical mill man of the party, decided that the tide-flats at the head of the bay offered the best site. Although he was told that the piling would not stand, that the place would be flooded, that no foundations would be safe, he insisted on trying, and his judgment was sustained, for this choice property is now the center of the manufacturing district of Tacoma. When the mill was built, Jones introduced the first band-saw for cutting fir and other newfangled machinery, all of which was looked on with suspicion by older mill men but which proved its worth.

George Browne, a third partner, was a Boston and New York man who had made a fortune in Wall Street. In addition to the lumber enterprise he interested himself in real-estate, coal, and dry-dock projects; his son Belmore later became famous as artist, explorer, and member of the first party to ascend Mount McKinley. Henry Hewitt, Jr., of English descent, who became treasurer of the company, began his career at 16 in Wisconsin, as a timekeeper and team-driver for his father. He early learned to cruise timber, became a contractor, and built a $100,000 lock and dam at Portage, Wisconsin, for which he took his payment in timber-land. He was cashier of a small bank in Wisconsin, built a smelter at Nogales, Arizona, inspected the redwood forests of California, and finally reached Tacoma, to enter the partnership with Griggs and the others. During his lifetime his timber-holdings became the largest in the Northwest; he founded the town of Everett, developed coal, coke, and copper properties, owned gold-mines in British Columbia and 30,000 acres of land in Arkansas. It is said that he based his business success on two axioms: "See what the people are going to need; see it first; then get it and the market will follow," and "Admit nothing; make them prove everything." Like his partners, he was a pillar of the First Congregational Church in Tacoma, and the story is told that when an Eastern visitor asked him to explain the significance of the four small towers on this edifice, he succinctly replied, "Father, Son, and Holy Ghost, and the St. Paul and Tacoma Lumber Company."

During the boom and in the years following, Tacoma was the home of a number of noted journalists. Among them were Franklin K. Lane, editor of the *News,* one day to be Secretary of the Interior; and Colonel William Lightfoot Vischer, editor of the *Union* and author of poetry which was widely copied, who had left the *Oregonian* editorial office "because he hadn't heard one hearty laugh in Portland and never had seen a smile in the *Oregonian* office." There was also a man named Frederickson, editor of the *Globe,* whose chief claim to fame was the head-line he had written for the Chicago *Times* to put over the story of the hanging of a criminal—"Jerked to Jesus." The *Globe* was owned by Harry Morgan, proprietor of a palatial gambling-house where there flourished faro, roulette, keno, craps, poker, and chuck-a-luck. His game was nationally known, it was said to be honestly conducted, the sky was the limit, and gamblers came to Tacoma from all over the country to play in Morgan's place. Adjoining the gambling-rooms was his Comique Theater, a Bowery music-hall type of place, where variety shows continued till early morning, champagne corks popped, and loggers were often drugged and relieved of their money.

But perhaps the most picturesque figure ever to walk the city's streets was George Francis Train. Having profited from the founding of Omaha, spurred Denver on to building her railroad to Cheyenne, and shared in the money made by the Crédit Foncier, Train, now living in Boston, had turned his attention to journalism. His "Van der Billion Psychos" were a feature of the Tacoma *Ledger,* and he had so loudly touted Tacoma as the coming metropolis of the West that an Eastern editor had inquired, "Who the devil is paying this man Train for boosting Tacoma?" No one was paying him; he had simply adopted Tacoma, named it the "City of Destiny," and proceeded to wax eloquent about it in his own peculiar manner. After having been jailed by the British for building the first tram-car line in London, Train had returned to America. He signalized his repatriation by fasting 60 days in order to beat the record of 40; refused to shake hands with any adult because each contact robbed him of electrodynamic energy; introduced a fruit and chocolate diet; and imposed silence on himself for years, so far as grown people were concerned, while he renewed his youth among little children and the birds in Madison Square in New York. He invented the word "crank," which he applied to himself, and called himself "citizen," because he said he was neither Republican, Democrat, Catholic, Presbyterian, or representative of any other organized sect or belief. The editor of the Louisville *Journal* called him the "apotheosis of talk—the incarnation of gab. Handsome, vivacious, muscular, as neat as a cat, clean to the marrow, a judge of the effect of clothes, frugal in food and irregular only in habits, with the brains of twenty men in his head, all pulling in different directions."

When Nellie Bly had completed her 72-day trip around the globe in 1890, Train suggested that he could better her record, starting from

Tacoma, and prove the city to be on the shortest route around the world and 600 to 800 miles nearer the Orient than San Francisco. R. F. Radebaugh, editor of the *Ledger,* accepted the offer, a lecture was arranged at the Tacoma Theater which subsequently netted Train nearly $5,000, and he set off for Tacoma, getting yards of newspaper publicity on the way. In explaining the advertising that would accrue from the trip, Train wrote the following colloquy, dropping articles and personal pronouns and following his own strange scheme of thought and punctuation:

Reporter—"Why do you round world from Tacoma, Citizen Train?"

Citizen Train—"Because Tacoma is New York of Pacific! City of Destiny! overlooking Portland! rival of San Francisco! beat Boston in Decade! rival Chicago 1910! Because on shortest line world around!"

Reporter—"I see Portland newspapers disposed to smile at pretensions of Tacoma."

Citizen Train—"No honor bright in smile? If Portland were growing five times as fast as Tacoma (reverse being true)! If Great Republic's ribs stared City of Destiny in face at harbor entrance as they do Portland! If Tacoma wheat ships and tea ships and lumber and coal ships were seeking cargoes at Portland (again reverse true)! If Congress were being urged to appropriate $5,000,000 to improve Puget Sound which has open sea depth all way to dock? If it cost $3,500 pilotage, towage, and lighterage to get vessel in and out of Tacoma as in case with Portland? If there were room in Commencement Bay for only ten or twelve ships? If Puget Sound were frozen up several months in year? If Lloyd's had entered name of Tacoma in black list and proclaimed to four quarters of globe that Tacoma harbor and its approaches were extremely dangerous, we should not be able to smile a very honest smile? Let them have their bar? Their $5,000,000. Oregon is one gate of Puget Sound! Nature made Tacoma, not Congress!

"Twenty-one years ago on the O. R. and N. steamer, *Willson G. Hunt,* supplied me by Captain Ainsworth, Portland, I launched this magic town of nation's great inland sea. Guests were Samuel Wilkeson, Engineer Roberts and Jay Cooke's son. Olympia and Seattle made big bid for historical point and paid me their silver dollars for lectures, but there where we found shanty of old Carr at the old sawmill keeping company with a grizzly bald headed eagle and a polecat, I planted the future."

As a matter of fact Train had been invited by Canfield to accompany the party from Portland as a sort of entertainer, and if he made any recommendations to the officials, they were not received seriously.

One day in March, 1891, the white-haired, white-suited Citizen, gripsack and umbrella in hand, stepped off the polished brass plate in front of the *Ledger* office and started round the world, taking a special steamer to Victoria. San Francisco papers scoffed at this effort to advertise a rival route to the Orient, and Seattle burlesqued the trip by proposing to send the stolid Siwash Indian Princess Angeline, daughter of Chief Seattle, on a similar jaunt around the world. After numerous vicissitudes and much advertising of Tacoma, Train arrived back at his starting-point in 67 days, 13 hours, 3 minutes, and 3 seconds. Through unfortunate accidents and the machinations of enemies of Tacoma, the Northern Pacific did not provide the special train across the country he expected, and Train was forced to come back by way of Portland and to stay in the depot five hours. He wired Radebaugh for a special train, with the plea, "Don't let me lie five hours in a town that has been calling me names for twenty years"; but Radebaugh had broken his leg, and Train had lost his wallet, so no special could be obtained. When he reached Tacoma, where he was greeted with the firing of cannon, Train said, "The actual time round world has been 65 days, beating Nelly Bly by five days and reducing the world to crabapple pie."

The year of Train's trip was a great year for Tacoma. Real-estate transactions amounted to $16,000,000, the town had grown to 35,000 in a few years, and its harbor was constantly becoming more prominent as a shipping center. The Tacoma Smelter had come into the control of W. R. Rust, who brought $30,000 from the Colorado mines to invest in the property, and he was developing it to the point where he was to sell it to the Guggenheims for $5,500,000. The Tacoma Railway and Power Company had been organized and was under the direction of a bright young man, Sidney Z. Mitchell, who was in later years to be heard from in the formation of the Electric Bond and Share Company in New York. The *Oregonian* had pointed out that it cost a ship $6,075 for bar and river towage and pilotage to Portland and for expenses of loading and unloading there, whereas it cost the same vessel only $2,059 at Tacoma; and the *Ledger* called attention to the fact that ships "don't have to sneak into our harbor like a chicken thief, and it is so deep that they might as well try to anchor in the middle of the ocean." One of the expenses of using Portland's harbor was that of hauling away ballast; in Tacoma it was simply dumped over the side into the capacious bay.

In 1892 George W. Vanderbilt of New York brought his investments in Tacoma up to $300,000, and the city seemed to have hit its stride as the future metropolis of the Pacific Coast. But the fall of Baring Brothers, the London bankers, upset the whole world, and with it Tacoma took a body blow which for the moment appeared to be fatal. In 1893 one after another of its twenty-one banks closed their doors until only seven remained solvent. Herbert Hunt tells in his *History of Tacoma* how the financial débâcle affected the town that was then riding on the crest of the wave:

Crash followed crash. The commercial universe seemed to be but a house of cards. The country was in the throes of hysteria. . . . Yet there had to be a cleansing. The fabric was shot through with fictitious values and a form of fraud with which periods of speculative enthusiasm usually are poisoned. The gigantic liquidation was in progress and it paralyzed every sinew. The Northwest suffered most. Rich men sawed wood, picked blackberries and dug clams for a livelihood. Women with diamonds and valuable deeds resorted to kitchen labor to keep the larder replenished. "Remittance men," who had been despised by their fellows, now were followed about—they might have a few nickels to lend. Men who had ridden in carriages walked, though the empty street-cars, rattling in their own poverty, would carry them for five cents. . . . At the sheriff's auction block, judgments for $75,000 against a well known Tacoman were bought by his friends for $75. . . . There was want in high places and the laborer who had a steady job at $1.50 a day could pity many of his fellows who, a few months before, had been spending incomes of several thousand a year. . . . Some of the men who owned good buildings became the janitors of them, struggling to retain possession.

One man became elevator operator in his own building. Congressman Edward E. Cushman said that during the depression people ate so many clams that their stomachs rose and fell with the tides.

At the height of the boom Henry Villard had backed a scheme for building an immense tourist hotel on the bluffs overlooking the Sound. Of the French château style of architecture, with buff-colored brick towers and turrets, it was planned to dominate the heights above the harbor as does the Château Frontenac at Quebec. When the panic stopped construction, about $500,000 had been spent on it; years later it was burned, and the shell was finally taken over by the city and reconstructed, on a smaller scale than originally planned, into a high school. A concrete stadium seating 30,000, its open end fronting the bay, was built at its side, making Stadium High School one of the most striking and beautiful public-school properties in the country. This development was typical of much that grew out of the boom and panic: there was a period of quiet for a while, a reëxamination of values and a readjustment of plans, followed by a slow, steady development along more conservative lines.

Villard had given Seattle a branch of the Northern Pacific, much to Tacoma's disgust, and it was known as "the orphan road." But Tacoma was firmly established as western headquarters of the line and its steamship connections, and it seemed that the destinies of the city and its railroad were inseparable. The Union Pacific, too, had shown its intention of entering Tacoma. In 1891 it had built a short line in the suburbs and announced that this was the beginning of what was scheduled to become its western terminus. But in 1896 the Union Pacific suddenly stopped work on the extension it was building to Commencement Bay.

Allen C. Mason tells of the interview of its engineer, Virgil C. Bogue, with Jay Gould and Sidney Dillon, who controlled the railroad. As soon as he had paid off the laborers, Bogue hurried to New York to attempt to dissuade them from abandoning their advantageous Tacoma terminus.

Mr. Gould came into the office first and walked up and down the room while Mr. Bogue, with all the magnetism and vigor he possessed, pleaded for orders to resume the construction. When Mr. Dillon came in, Mr. Gould said, "Mr. Dillon, I am convinced that we have made a mistake in abandoning the line from Portland to Tacoma. What say you that we instruct Mr. Bogue to go back and resume work?" To which Mr. Dillon replied, "But how can we raise the money?" Facing him, Mr. Gould said slowly, "Give me the use of your name with mine and I'll raise it in 24 hours." Mr. Dillon slouched down in his arm chair, put both hands to the back of his head and said, "I am too old. I am too old." Whereat Mr. Gould snapped his fingers, turned sharply and went out, causing Tacoma to drag along with bumps and in the dumps until the revival came like a clap of thunder out of a clear sky by the unheralded building of the Milwaukee.

In 1905 the Union Pacific again entered the field, buying terminal property and right of way and starting construction from Portland to Puget Sound as part of Harriman's fight against Hill. Millions were spent for terminals and deep-water docks and warehouse sites, and Tacoma raised $100,000 in 48 hours to purchase freight yards for the road. This period saw an influx of real-estate promoters to the city, among whom was William J. Bowes. He gave the city two heroic sphinxes to be erected in Wright Park, but they were made of plaster, and they soon disintegrated under the gentle Puget Sound rains. Major Bowes later became manager of the Capitol Theatre in New York and a familiar voice on the radio, but he never replaced the sphinxes. In the Union Pacific boom, however, Tacoma was destined to be disappointed; for, after half a mile of its tunnel into the city had been constructed, the project was abandoned, and E. H. Harriman entered into an agreement with James J. Hill for trackage rights into Tacoma and Seattle over the Northern Pacific. It is reported that when this arrangement was completed, Harriman said, "To-day the Union Pacific has closed the biggest deal it has ever made and Tacoma has got the blackest eye she will ever get."

Meanwhile, Jim Hill had pushed his Great Northern on to Puget Sound and had decided that he could fight the Northern Pacific better if he did not choose Tacoma as its terminus. Because Tacoma was the child of the Northern Pacific, he had no desire to promote its welfare, and it was said that he once vowed that he would make the grass grow in its streets. This enmity was softened somewhat by his friend Robert Laird MacCormack of Tacoma, head of the Weyerhauser Timber Company, who induced Hill to invest in a Tacoma bank. But his railroad was distinctly an appanage of Seattle, and Tacoma always counted him, along with Villard, not among her special friends. Another railroad official whom Tacoma did not love was Charles S. Mellen, president of the Northern Pacific at the time of the Klondike gold-rush. He took the company's steamship lines away from Tacoma and gave them to Seattle, leaving Tacoma with only one steamship line to Alaska, operated by Hugh C. Wallace, and cutting her out of the major part of the Alaskan trade.

Until the Great Northern ran its first trains into the city over the Northern Pacific tracks in May, 1909, Tacoma suffered under the inconvenience of being a one-railroad town. This happy event was followed by the entry of the Union Pacific over the Northern Pacific tracks from Portland in January, 1910, and on May 31, 1911, the Chicago, Milwaukee, and St. Paul arrived, making the city its Pacific Coast terminus. A water level route to the city, extending southward along the shores of Puget Sound with a tunnel under Point Defiance, was built in 1912 by the Northern Pacific at a cost of $10,000,000.

During the years when Tacoma was a one-railroad town, it at least felt that its destinies were inseparably bound up with that railroad and that each would fight for the other. But in 1920 it began to appear that Seattle was succeeding in her efforts to lure away the Northern Pacific and to capture its western headquarters. In that year the traffic department left the old Northern Pacific headquarters building in Tacoma and moved to Seattle. And in 1921 it became evident that the whole headquarters staff was to follow. Tacomans protested valiantly to President Howard Elliott, and Paul Johns, president of the Lumbermen's Club, telegraphed, "Removal of your coast head-quarters from Tacoma without more reason than apparent will be generally looked upon as throwing over an old love for a new." Whereupon Mr. Elliott smoothly replied,

Your telegram was received and considered at a meeting of the board of directors Wednesday. The decision of the board was arrived at only after very mature study of the situation since government control ceased. We are in no way throwing over an old love for a new, but we believe Tacoma, with its wonderful facilities, can and should participate even in a greater degree in the future than it has in the past in the benefits to be derived from the railroad. Our terminals remain in Tacoma and our trains will continue to run in and out and we will work just as hard to help Tacoma to get its share of business to, from and through the Puget Sound country. A small number of men are leaving Tacoma but there will be nearly 2,400 employes of the Northern Pacific remain-ing in Tacoma, which means a very large payroll.

Despite this reassuring message, the impressive old headquarters build-ing which had housed the Northern Pacific since 1886 was soon drearily vacant, a visible sign that the railroad had more or less abandoned the city it had brought into being. And it was finally sold to the city and converted into a police station.

Meanwhile, Tacoma had become the terminus of another trans-continental road, the Chicago, Milwaukee, and St. Paul. In 1904 this Mid-Western railroad began to work toward the Pacific Coast for an outlet for its system. This move was brought about because the Milwaukee was feeling strongly the competition of the through trunk lines to the West—the Northern Pacific, Great Northern, and Burlington in one group; the North-Western, which had abandoned its plan of extending from Lander, Wyoming, to Marshfield, Oregon, and the Union Pacific in another; the Canadian Pacific and the Soo Line in a third. Faced with this competition for overland and trans-Pacific traffic, the Milwaukee was being strangled, and extension westward was imperative. From the time he became president in 1899, Albert J. Earling had urged the road's financial backers, among whom was William Rockefeller, to support his plan to meet the growing encirclement of competing roads by building to the Pacific Coast. After the line was extended to Rapid City, South Dakota, in 1907, a severe financial depression ensued, and Earling urged the advantage of pushing on while costs were low.*

In 1906 the Milwaukee had floated bonds to begin the Pacific Coast extension, and the work was pushed forward in 1907. Of the funds raised, $2,500,000 was allotted for the road's ocean terminals on the Tacoma tide-flats, where it would connect with the Osaka Shoshen Kaisha steamship lines to the Orient. The Milwaukee purchased its first property in Tacoma in May, 1904, surveys for the Pacific extension were begun in October, 1905, construction started early in 1907, and the first train passed over the main line in June, 1909. Through freight service began in July, 1909, and regular passenger service one year later. During these few years, the Bitterroots had been tunneled, the Columbia bridged, and the Milwaukee had passed over three mountain-ranges and one panic. The road crossed the Cascades by way of the Snoqualmie Pass, which had been the choice of the pioneer road-builders of Washington Territory, whence it dropped easily down to Tacoma and Seattle. Fighting Jim Hill every inch of the way, "the Rockefeller road," as the Milwaukee was called, had

* The material on the history of the Chicago, Milwaukee and St. Paul Railroad is from *The St. Paul—Yesterday and Tomorrow*, an unpublished manuscript by John Leeds Kerr.

EAST PORTAL OF THE STAMPEDE TUNNEL THROUGH THE CASCADES
Courtesy of the Northern Pacific Railway.

THE PORT OF TACOMA PIERS
Courtesy of the Tacoma Chamber of Commerce.

TACOMA'S BUSINESS SKY-LINE AND MOUNT RAINIER

Courtesy of the Tacoma Chamber of Commerce.

TACOMA FROM THE AIR

Looking northeast over the business district to the tide-flat industrial area in front of the city. Courtesy of the Tacoma Chamber of Commerce.

gained entrance into his strongholds of Montana, Dakota, and Manitoba. The road expected to make rich profits from carrying lumber, fruit, agricultural and dairy products, and Oriental imports to the Mid-West and bringing back manufactured products from the East. It built extensive ocean terminals at Tacoma, along with a large plant for converting and handling Oriental vegetable oils. Its tea and silk imports were soon very large, and its orange-colored trains became a familiar feature of the Northwestern landscape. It purchased the Tacoma Eastern road to Rainier National Park to get terminal facilities in Tacoma, and it constructed branch lines to Grays Harbor and to the Olympic peninsula as feeders for its system. In 1914 the Milwaukee began its great project of electrification, which by 1920 resulted in the running of its trains by electric power for 400 miles in the Montana Rocky Mountains and 215 miles in the Cascades. By 1924 this had resulted in savings of $12,400,000, or one-half the original cost.

But for all its well worked out plans, the Milwaukee was not destined to become rich from its Pacific Coast business. It was, instead, crushed between the long established competing systems to its north and south, and on March 18, 1925, the road went into bankruptcy. This was an ironic situation, for the Milwaukee had been so conservatively financed that it had weathered the storm of 1893, when the Santa Fe, the Union Pacific, and the Northern Pacific failed as a result of their transcontinental expansion. It failed chiefly because of its inability to meet some $17,000,000 of Pacific Coast extension bonds which were to mature in June, 1925. Volume of traffic had not come up to expectations; freight-rates were low, and James J. Hill was interested in keeping them low; the opening of the Panama Canal caused a heavy decrease in all Western railroad tonnage; and the depression following the World War was the final blow that shattered the Milwaukee. The system was sold at auction on November 22, 1927, in front of the railway station at Butte, Montana, drawing one bid of $140,000,000 from Kuhn, Loeb and Company and the National City Bank. This bid did not represent the value of the road, but was simply $15,000,000 more than the sum fixed by the courts to cover indebtedness and refinancing. The receivership was terminated after it had passed through a storm of criticism, chiefly from those who felt that the junior bondholders had been made to bear the major portion of all the losses.

As western terminus of the Chicago, Milwaukee, and St. Paul, Tacoma anticipated much benefit from the activities of the road, of which her native son A. M. Ingersoll was vice-president. It started out grandly enough with plans for an imposing railway station and with the actual construction of a commodious ocean terminal. But Tacoma's satisfaction was short-lived. For several years she was indeed the point of transfer between the railroad and the steamships to the Orient, and the Milwaukee silk trains leaving the City of Destiny broke all freight speed-records in reaching the Chicago end of the line. But in 1926 the Osaka Shoshen Kaisha moved its headquarters to Seattle, and the Milwaukee did likewise. So the great ocean terminals were abandoned by the railroad and were turned over to lesser fry, and the company's western headquarters are still at the northern port.

It was about this time also that the controversy over the name of the mountain was brought to at least a temporary conclusion. For years Tacoma had insisted that the snow-capped mountain in her dooryard be called by its Indian name, Tacoma, and Seattle, whose dooryard it somewhat more remotely graced, had been just as insistent that the name Rainier, given it by Admiral George Vancouver, be retained. On this controversy was focused all the pent-up feeling that existed between the rival cities.

Ordinarily peaceful citizens grew fierce when the subject was mentioned, and visitors to the region were at a loss to know which name to use. Most of them avoided trouble by naming no names but enthusiastically referring to the glories of "the mountain," thus half-satisfying everybody. Under the aggressive leadership of Sam Wall, who had accompanied Train around the world, a militant offensive was begun to restore the Indian name to the mountain. A Justice to the Mountain Committee was organized, literature was published, and political log-rolling was begun to settle the name of the mountain once and for all as Tacoma. And Tacomans were not alone in their desire to perpetuate the Indian name. James Bryce, the British Ambassador, had long ago written of "the mountain which the people of Seattle insist on calling Mount Rainier—no doubt the name originally given by Vancouver but which used, when I wandered through its forests and traversed its glaciers thirty years ago, to be called by the more sonorous Indian name, Tacoma." And Theodore Roosevelt had inquired, "Why should we Americans abandon the splendid Indian name Tacoma in order to call our noblest landmark after an obscure foreigner whose only connection with our history is that he fought against us when we were an infant nation?"

The mayor of Boston and the governor of Massachusetts added their influence in support of the Indian name because it had been authenticated by Theodore Winthrop of that state in his *Canoe and Saddle,* a circumstance which afterward caused Tacomans to name a community-built hotel in his honor. While the Seattle delegation to the state legislature was peacefully unaware of the threatened danger, Tacoma secured the passage of a memorial to Congress urging that the name of the mountain be changed from Rainier to Tacoma, and then the battle began in earnest. Rival lobbies were maintained in Washington, it was said that Seattle sought to undermine national integrity by titillating Congressional palates with rare foods and drinks, while back on Puget Sound activity was fierce and unremitting. Pastors railed in their pulpits, school-children poured in letters to Congress, newspaper editors pointed with pride and viewed with alarm, and a personable young-lady vaudeville artist perched on a grand piano at a meeting of the Tacoma Chamber of Commerce while she sang to admiring applause a song of her own composition:

> Call it Mount Tacoma. Let the whole world know
> That you love every inch of its cedared breast
> With the flowers peeping through the snow.
> It's part of your heart and it's really a shame
> That this mighty mount should be known by any other name,
> So call it Mount Tacoma—Mount Tacoma belongs to you.

A national convention of Indians went on record for Tacoma, and their magazine, *The Indian Tepee,* the organ of the red race of North and South America, bore on its cover a picture of the mountain with the legend, "We pray the Great Spirit Kitchemanitou to restore to the Indians Tacoma, meaning Nourishing Breast." Madame Amelita Galli-Curci was all for removing from the so glorious mountain the name of the cruel butcher of American sailors. And Mary Roberts Rinehart declared that she knew Seattle would be angry but she had to record her conviction that "the Government that permits that wonderful Peak to retain the name Rainier when the old Indian name is available is committing an unspeakable crime against good taste." On the other hand, a facetious resolution was introduced in the legislature to change the name of Puget Sound to its old Indian name of Whulge; and as it was said that the Indians also called Mount Rainier Stiquak, Tiswauk, Chebollyp, and Yalemite, it was suggested that one of these names be restored.

In order to show that its campaign for the Indian name was entirely disinterested and that it did not wish to cash in on the advertising value of the mountain but merely to label it with a patriotic American name, Tacoma had offered to accept a new designation. Whereupon the G. A. R. suggested Lincoln, and other organizations offered Roosevelt, Chantilly, Hart, after the governor of the state, and Harding. Seattle-ites suggested Deception, and that distinguished explorer Dr. Walter Traprock obliged with a hybrid which he thought would solve the difficulty—Tanier. Officers at Camp Lewis suggested Rainiertacoma, and other helpful observers advised that the difficulty be solved by having Mahomet go to the mountain and changing the name of the city to Rainier. In British Columbia the Victoria *Colonist* declared that "as a matter of fact there never was such a word as Tacoma until one of the boosters of the Northen Pacific terminus invented it by mispronouncing an Indian term. There is a word variously pronounced Tahomah, accent on the first syllable, and Yakima, accented the same way, and probably pronounced quite differently by the Indians, which means a snow peak." And George Himes of the Oregon Historical Society said that his investigations had revealed only two replies as to the original Indian name of the mountain: "Hiu cole snass," meaning "Lots of frozen rain," and "Halo kumtux," meaning "Don't know."

Despite the decision of the United States Geographic Board to retain Rainier, the United States Senate on April 21, 1924, passed a bill to change the name to Tacoma. Through Seattle influence, however, the bill was held up in the Public Lands Committee of the House, and so the name of the mountain remains Rainier. But Tacomans say the case is not closed yet, and maybe some day, who knows . . . ?

Throughout her history Tacoma had depended on the natural depth and security of her harbor as an attraction to shipping, but in 1917 Chester Thorne aroused the citizens to the necessity of making large improvements if Tacoma was to retain her place in ocean commerce. He told Tacomans that "ships and shipping men are no more satisfied with docks and water-front facilities equipped in the style of twenty years ago than you would be with an automobile of the same date," and as a result the Port of Tacoma was organized, several millions in bonds issued, and extensive modern shipping facilities installed. It was about this time, too, that the people of Pierce County determined to put one of the Army training-camps at the door of Tacoma, on the beautiful, tree-covered, gravel-grounded prairies to the south of the city. A tremendous tract of land was purchased and presented to the Government, with the result that one of the largest concentration camps in the country, Camp Lewis, was located there. It is now being improved with brick and stone buildings as a permanent Army post, Fort Lewis.

Always self-conscious and on the defensive about her size, her future, her rivals, and her mountain, Tacoma has aggressively carried her banner before the world with two slogans. The first was "Watch Tacoma Grow," a legend which greeted visitors to the Lewis and Clark Exposition in Portland in 1903; the second was "You'll Like Tacoma," a prediction which blossomed forth in the "world's longest shore line electric sign" at the Alaska-Yukon Pacific Exposition in Seattle in 1909. The first slogan was dropped when it became evident that those who watched Seattle and Portland would see even faster growth; the second brought many visitors to the city, even though some confused observers thought that the much advertised Tacoma was a breakfast food. Now the city has adopted a third advertising phrase: "Tacoma, the Lumber Capital of America." And so it is. Her lumber and timber concerns, mills, door-factories, veneer and plywood plants, and furniture factories easily make the city the center of the production of lumber and allied products on the Coast. Tacoma is also the city with a snow-capped mountain in its dooryard—even if that mountain is officially named Rainier, a fact which draws a steady stream of tourists, who can drive from the city to the alpine glaciers and snow-fields of the mountain—Mount Tacoma, if you please, though located in Rainier National Park—in four hours. And to the flapper and the radio-fan let Tacoma's claim to fame be that she produced Bing Crosby.

Books have been written to show that Tacoma is to be the New York of the Pacific Coast, and perhaps she will be at some far-distant day, though it is more likely that she will be its Philadelphia. She has all the natural advantages for the making of a great metropolis— one of the best natural harbors in the world, plenty of room for rail-road tracks, an ample expanse of tide-flats for the location of factories, and cheap hydro-electric power developed by the municipality. Her smelter and lumber industries are among the largest producers of freight in the West to-day, and it is reasonable to suppose that other large industries will make use of her facilities in the future. Until that day of greatness comes, however, she can rest content—a city of pleasant homes, of thrifty, satisfied people, and of beauty. No rivals can take away the calm, blue waters of Puget Sound, or the surpassing grandeur of the mountain in her dooryard, or the graceful shore-line of her harbor, which Hugh Walpole selected as one of the most beautiful things in America and celebrated as "the lovely curve of Tacoma."

# CHAPTER XV

## SEATTLE, BORN OF THE SPIRIT

LEGEND has it that two visitors to Seattle once argued as to which could make the better definition of the Seattle Spirit. Each laid a dollar on the table, and each attempted to explain the nature of this strange, invisible ectoplasm. When the judge had made his decision, the lucky man turned to pick up the two dollars, but, alas, they were nowhere to be found. They had been seized, absorbed, and, as the magicians say, "vanished" by that all-pervading force they had defined.

Some say that this legend was invented by jealous rivals of the Queen City of Puget Sound. But none deny that the Seattle Spirit exists, that it animates all good Seattleites, and that it has accomplished more baffling feats of legerdemain than the simple sleight-of-hand performance that cost the argumentative visitors two dollars. Nor is it a modern bottle-imp invoked by Chamber of Commerce ballyhoo and Rotary pep-meetings. It is as venerable as Seattle itself, having made its first inspiring descent upon the citizenry in 1857, when the captain of a passing sailing-vessel shouted to Lee Terry, standing in front of a little row of cabins near the water, "What town is this?"

Perhaps there was derision in his tone. At any rate, Terry was inspired to seize upon the proud name of his former home in the East, and he replied, "New York."

"Yes, sure," roared the skipper, as his ship disappeared round the point. "New York Alki, I reckon,"—Alki, pronounced by the pioneers with a short *i*, meaning, in the Chinook Indian jargon, "by and by." So New York–Alki it became. And thus baptized by the fire of civic aspiration, the city that was by and by to become the New York of the Northwest had its auspicious beginning.

The names of the first settlers of Seattle are inscribed on a stone monument at Alki Point, now a bathing-beach. There were twelve adults and as many children, and when they landed in a ship's row-boat in the dense forest on the shores of Puget Sound on a dismal day in November, 1851, it is no wonder that the women sat down on a water-soaked log, gathered their children about them, and wept. There were no houses, no shelter, no inhabitants but half-naked savages; and the insistent, monotonous, continuous winter rain of Puget Sound dampened and made limp the spirits as well as the sunbonnets of the pioneer mothers.

The Denny and Boren families had started out for Oregon from Cherry Grove, Illinois, that same year. In four wagons, loaded, according to emigrant rule, with articles worth not less than a dollar a pound, they made the long, dangerous journey over the overland trail, embarked on the Columbia at the Dalles, Oregon, and reached Portland after 108 days of travel. On the way they met the wagons of John Low and proceeded to Portland with him. At Portland they discovered that the rich lands of the Willamette Valley had all been taken up, and having heard favorable reports of the Puget Sound country, they decided to continue northward. While most of the party remained in Portland suffering from ague, John Low and David Denny went on afoot, carrying their blankets on their backs over the 200-mile trail to Olympia. Here, where they hired Captain Fay to take them north by boat over Puget Sound, they were joined by Lee Terry, who was to name their future home. On the shores of Elliott Bay they met the native Indians, among them Chief Sealth, and next day they moved on to a near-by point of land with a gravelly beach, which became New York–Alki. Low returned to Portland carrying a letter from David Denny to his brother Arthur, telling him to hurry on to this land of the Duwamish Valley, where there was plenty of room for a thousand settlers. And so the whole party left Portland by water in a 60-ton sailing-vessel, which, proceeding down the Columbia, up the Pacific Coast, and into Puget Sound, put its seasick passengers ashore at Alki eight days later.

In a few weeks, when four log cabins had been built, the brig *Leonesa* from San Francisco fortuitously arrived, and the captain asked the new settlers if they could sell him some piling to build wharves in California. Could they? Just give them a chance! This was their heaven-sent opportunity to establish trade relations with the outside world, to bring money and supplies into this far-northern outpost, to lay the foundations of a city. All hands turned to, and, not even stopping work on Christmas Day except to eat a wild-duck dinner, they cut over 13,000 feet of timber in less than three weeks. And when the captain of the *Leonesa* left, he carried not only the first timber cut on Elliott Bay, but also orders for pork, flour, molasses, boots, mustard, pepper sauce, cloth, windows, tools, sugar, soap, hickory shirts, whisky, and a kitchen stove. Few pioneers have established themselves in a profitable business as quickly as did these settlers in New York–Alki. Perhaps it was the first coöperative manifestation of the Seattle Spirit.

The Seattle Spirit stirred again when W. N. Bell, Carson D. Boren, and the Dennys, dissatisfied with Alki Point, decided to discover the exact spot best fitted for the building of a city. They felt they must have deep water for shipping their timber, so one morning at dawn they set out to find it, paddling along the shore in a canoe and taking soundings with a bunch of horseshoes tied on the end of a clothesline. Before the day was over, it appeared that the deepest water in the vicinity was on the east side of the bay, and there, in a dense forest, where there were springs of water and fertile soil, they decided to stake their claims. Boren took the most southerly plat, beginning at what is now First Avenue and King Street. Arthur Denny and W. N. Bell each took 320 acres along the shore to the north. David Denny took up his claim north of Bell's, fronting on Lake Union as well as Puget Sound. Together, these four occupied what became the choicest and most valuable land in the city.

A little later Dr. David S. Maynard closed up his store in Olympia, put his goods on a barge, and set out for New York–Alki. With the others he crossed the bay, took up a claim south of Bell's, and opened a log-cabin store at what is now First Avenue and Main Street. He had come north at the suggestion of his Indian friend, the big Chief Sealth or Seattle, and probably it was he who suggested that the community be named in honor of the Indian brave. In her *Story of Seattle* Roberta Frye Watt recounts that "the old chief was not favorably impressed by the honor conferred upon him. He was very angry at first that such liberties should be taken with his name, fearing, according to an Indian superstition, that harm might come to his spirit—that after death, every time his name was spoken on earth, he would turn over in his grave. Then after a time, he bore the affront in dignified silence. Later he became very proud of his namesake."

The Indians around Seattle were for the most part easy to deal with and peaceable, but as the white settlers increased, encroaching on the land formerly used by the red men, hostilities developed. In 1854 a settler was killed by an Indian two miles from Olympia, and in retaliation Commander Swartout of the United States Navy, on duty in Puget Sound, attacked the Indians' village at Port Gamble on November 20, killing twenty-seven, wounding twenty-one, and destroying their huts and canoes. Colonel William Farrand Prosser in his *History of the Puget Sound Country* says there were at that time 1,500 warriors west of the Cascades and that these warriors had begun to plan to draw in other Indians from east of the Cascades to carry on a warfare that would exterminate the whites. In 1855 Governor Charles H. Mason called for United States troops to be ready for an anticipated uprising of the Yakima Indians, and in that year volunteer companies were organized to capture Leshi, chief of the Nesquallies, who had been preparing for hostilities in the Puget Sound country. On October 28, 1855, Lieutenant McCallister was killed by Indians near Olympia, and on the same day many settlers were massacred in the White River Valley near Seattle. The Puget Sound tribes of Indians now planned a general uprising against white settlers, and they drew in Indian tribes from east of the Cascades to make an attack on Seattle.

The United States sloop of war *Decatur* had been ordered from Honolulu to the Northwestern waters, and fortunately her commander, I. S. Starrett, chose to enter Puget Sound rather than the Columbia River. He anchored near Seattle on October 4, 1855, when settlers were fleeing to the town because of rumored Indian uprisings, and the presence of his ship kept the Indians at bay for a time. On January 26 Seattle was attacked, and after an all-day fight the Indians were finally routed by cannon-fire from the *Decatur*. They were so thoroughly defeated that they never again attacked the whites west of the Cascades, but during their attack they had ruined crops, burned houses, and murdered settlers. So devastating had been their warfare that the white settlers were kept in fear for years, and there was continual unrest until peace treaties with the Indians were negotiated and ratified by the United States Senate in 1859.

In those early days the Denny family was already conspicuously showing those qualities of thrift and industry and community service which made them then and later the leading citizens of Seattle. David Thomas Denny, the first of the name to set foot on Puget Sound, was born on March 17, 1832, in Putnam County, Indiana, of Scotch-Irish-English ancestry. He had some elementary schooling and then became a clerk in a village store at Knoxville, Illinois. At 19 he drove a four-horse team to Oregon in his father's train of 1851. At Seattle he began cutting timber at what is now Third Avenue and Republican Street. The Civic Auditorium is on his original farm site. David's brother, Arthur Armstrong Denny, was born at Salem, Indiana, on June 20, 1822. Crossing the plains to Portland in 1851 and coming by boat to Seattle, he built a big log cabin on the bluff and engaged in cutting timber. Shortly thereafter he became the first postmaster, custodian of the letters that were brought to the colony *via* Portland at the cost of 25 cents apiece.

Another early arrival who later became an outstanding leader of the community was Dexter Horton. Born in De Kalb County, Illinois, his early life was spent on the farm, a little schooling occupying his spare hours. At 16 he could cut 200 black-walnut rails a day, but his arithmetic did not extend beyond the rule of three. He married young, and in 1852, with his wife and daughter, he set out for the Pacific Coast, traveling with five other families who took along sixty horses. After a year in Salem, Oregon, Horton walked to Olympia, the capital of the new Territory of Washington, and thence to Seattle, where he worked chopping piles for W. N. Bell at $2.50 a day. Returning to Salem and finding no work in the harvest, he took a team and set out for Seattle. On September 15, 1853, Horton arrived in Seattle, with no money and $50 in debt. He and his wife took a job cooking for a logging-camp at Port Gamble at $130 a month, and in this humble capacity began the careers which were to culminate in their becoming a leading family of the Northwest.

In those days the Seattle Spirit, though dormant, was far from moribund. Its next and most surprising manifestation occurred when Henry L. Yesler of Portland arrived on the Sound looking for a site for a sawmill. No committee of go-getter business men wangling for the location of a factory in later years could have improved on the technique of the Dennys and the other first settlers. Quickly recognizing the advantage the mill would be to them, they determined it should be planted nowhere but in Seattle. They entertained their visitor with the best banquet their women folks could provide and then took him on a tour of the city, showing him all the sites available for his mill; and despite the fact that all the land had been allotted, though not yet officially filed on at the Land Office, they offered him his choice. He decided on a central strip of land and water-front at what is now Pioneer Place, and Maynard and Boren, whose property it was, obligingly moved their claims over to accommodate his wishes. Thus did the city boosters lure the first infant industry to the budding metropolis.

Richly rewarding this early display of community coöperation, the whine of Yesler's steam-saw soon played sweet music for pioneer ears; there was work for everybody, farmers began to settle the Duwamish Valley, more ships came in for lumber, and Seattle had earned its right to a place on the map if not in the sun. Seattle's first industrialist, who was thus encouraged to start the wheels of progress moving, was born in Washington County, Maryland, in 1810. His education was scanty and mostly self-acquired. In 1830 he went to Massillon, Ohio, and entered the sawmill business. In 1851 he journeyed to Portland, where he continued in lumber. Then came a trip to California and the operation of a mine at Marysville. Here a sea-captain told him of the great harbors on the Puget Sound and the vast stands of timber, and he came to Seattle.

Frederick James Grant's *History of Seattle* says that Yesler's sawmill was the life of the place.

Here most of the men in town earned their money, here the ships came for cargoes and discharged their groceries. Its puffing, buzzing, and blowing of steam made the music of the bay, and the hum of its saws was the undertone of every household. By its whistle all the clocks were regulated and the whole business of the village was carried on. The cook and mess house served as town hall, court room, meeting house, and hotel. All the legal business was transacted here and here nearly all social gatherings were held. It was the lounging place where the men collected and heard the news and told stories. A long low rambling affair without architectural pretensions, it possessed a certain homely attractiveness and was the last of the log buildings to be taken down.

The sawdust from the mill was used to fill in the low lands at Washington Street, and that district which is now called the Skidroad, home of the itinerant lumberjack, was in the early days known as "down on the sawdust." The sawdust pile served the town as the field for games and athletic contests during the early days.

Even when Seattle was only a little collection of shacks around a sawmill, her people looked gravely into the long-distant future and saw themselves great. Always the Seattle Spirit animated its chosen people and made its young men dream dreams and its old men see visions. By 1853 they were already talking of Seattle as the terminus of the transcontinental railroad that was soon to push its rails westward—and, of course, to Seattle. The first preacher, David Blaine, wrote that Governor Isaac I. Stevens had arrived to explore the passes over the Cascades with a view to locating the railroad, and Mrs. Blaine clearly showed the intoxicating effects of the Seattle Spirit when she added this postscript: "The governor's home is at Olympia *at present.*" Evidently Seattleites considered it only a matter of time until the capital of the newly formed Washington Territory would be snatched away from ancient Olympia.

Even at this early date they had decided that lumber and shipping alone would not build a metropolis. They already had what Ezra Meeker called "a mania for roads." They looked ahead and saw Seattle as the center of shipping on Puget Sound and the center of a network of wagon-roads radiating into the interior. And, further, they saw a road over the Cascades through the Naches Pass bringing the farm-products of eastern Washington to tide-water at their docks, as the logical prelude to the railroads of which they dreamed. After they had built a road from Seattle to Fort Steilacoom, where the United States troops were stationed, they braved the towering, snow-covered Cascades, requiring every resident to give his labor and levying a $14 fine on each of those who refused. When the rough road and crude bridges were built as far as the summit, the builders turned back, as winter was coming on. And very soon thereafter the first party of emigrants to cross Naches Pass came over the mountains.

What a trip that was! They killed oxen to make rawhide for ropes to lower the wagons over the precipices and endured such hardships as to make those of the Oregon Trail seem a picnic. As one survivor of the party said later, "If I hadn't done it myself, I wouldn't believe that anyone ever got over that terrible road."

Indeed, the road was so dangerous that no more covered wagons came; the rank undergrowth of the Puget Sound country soon overran it, and giant trees fell across and barricaded it so as to make it useless. Since this Naches Pass road was not a success, the pioneers turned to another route over the Cascades, the Snoqualmie Pass, which had been explored by Governor Stevens. They hoped to obtain government aid for opening this route for a wagon-road, thus preparing the way for the coming of the railroad. In 1859 a mass-meeting was held in Seattle and $1,050 was subscribed for surveying the road over Snoqualmie Pass. The territorial legislature petitioned Congress for help, and the House appropriated $75,000, but the bill never reached the Senate. By 1864 it was evident that Washington was losing thousands of settlers to Oregon because there was no road over the mountains; so another mass-meeting raised $2,500, and the King County commissioners began to aid the project.

During the succeeding years a good many thousands of dollars were raised locally and like sums appropriated by the legislature, and by 1869 the road was sufficiently opened that there was some traffic over it in summer, although heavy rains, snows, and falling trees made its upkeep expensive. In 1870 the Northern Pacific Railroad put two men in the Pass to make temperature readings; they stayed until the next May, finding that the snow reached 17 feet and the lowest temperature was 3 degrees above zero. The railroad then made surveys for a mile-long tunnel to shorten the line over the summit. And Seattle rejoiced, for this activity made it seem certain that the town would be the western terminus of the railroad.

But the Snoqualmie Pass road was entirely closed in winter, and during the rest of the year it was hardly more than a trail. Evidently even more heroic efforts must be made to open it. Having tried public subscriptions, aid from the King County commissioners, and petitions to the legislature, and still having built no proper highway, the citizenry took counsel of the Seattle Spirit and decided to raise the money needed by lotteries. H. L. Yesler and others organized the First Grand Lottery of Washington Territory, with 60,000 tickets at $5 apiece (or eleven for $50) and 5,575 prizes. The first prize was Henry Yesler's mill property, valued at $100,000, which brought in rents of $700 a month; second prize, Hovey and Barker's downtown corner, valued at $41,000; and third prize, the Pacific Brewing Company's property, valued at $5,000. But before the grand distribution took place or all the tickets had been sold, the scheme fell into disrepute and was declared illegal. Before it was dropped, however, some of the money was turned over to the King County commissioners and used on the road that is now the Sunset Highway.

Meanwhile, Seattle had been waiting in pleased anticipation for the announcement that she was to be the terminus of the Northern Pacific Railroad. One by one the other competing towns on Puget Sound had been eliminated until only Mukilteo, Tacoma, and Seattle remained. Since both the others were insignificant hamlets, Seattle felt it was all over but the shouting. Imagine Arthur Denny's chagrin, therefore, when the telegram from Captain John C. Ainsworth arrived, announcing that Tacoma had won the prize. If the Seattle Spirit had not been of high potency, that might have been the end of the aspirations of the town on Elliott Bay. But the defeat merely aroused her citizens to fresh exertions. If the short-sighted, ignorant Northern Pacific did not have sense enough to build to Seattle, then Seattle would build her own railroad to the East and run it herself. Thus counseled the Seattle Spirit. And thereupon the little sawmill town with the big ideas actually embarked on the gigantic project of pushing a railroad over the Cascades. The Seattle and Walla Walla Railroad and Transportation Company was organized; a committee including Arthur Denny, H. L. Yesler, Dexter Horton, and James M. Colman visited Walla Walla, where it was received with enthusiasm if not with cash; and Seattle began the project which, it was estimated, would cost $4,000,000. Where the money was coming from, nobody knew, but they went ahead with as much assurance as if it was already in the bank.

Since no one came forward with $4,000,000 or any part of that sum and since the state legislature was indifferent, the Seattleites resolved to give a practical demonstration of what muscle and determination plus the Seattle Spirit could do. And so, on May Day, 1874, the whole community set out to the old mill east of town, took off its collective coat, rolled up its sleeves, and proceeded to build its railroad. In the early morning every church-bell and mill-whistle summoned the people to assemble, and they were joined by well-wishers from the other near-by communities. A brass band enlivened the faint-hearted, and to its music everyone in town embarked in boats to go up the Duwamish River or clambered into carriages or wagons. Arrived at the appointed spot, three hundred men threw off their coats and immediately set to work, while the women prepared a dinner of chicken and hot biscuits and fixings which was served at noon in a half-completed grist-mill. Speeches followed food, the last of them made by Henry Yesler, who stopped his incessant whittling long enough to sound the key-note of the day by shouting, "Quit your fooling and go to work." That day's activity resulted in the completion of a lot of grading, but, more important, it crystallized Seattle's determination to have a railroad over the mountains at any cost; when they left, the citizens pledged themselves to give one day's work a week until the project should be completed. By October, 12 miles had been graded, and the fame of that May Day picnic had spread to the East, advertising the pluck and energy of the Seattleites and attracting many promising young Easterners to settle in the enterprising community.

By 1875 the road was completed to the Renton coal-mines, where a profitable freight business began. Appeals to Congress for aid being effectively blocked by the Northern Pacific, the infant railroad was taken under the wing of James M. Colman, who himself subscribed $20,000, while other business men added $40,000, and the road was extended to the mines at Newcastle. But if the Seattleites were defeated in Congress, they scored one point against the Northern Pacific, for they urged that its land-grant be reopened to settlement, and the fight they made was sufficiently irritating to cause the railroad to consider giving Seattle a branch line. Certainly, the growing town needed one, for there was no way to go from Seattle to Portland without staying overnight in Tacoma, since the Northern Pacific arranged its steamer schedules so as to make this a necessity. One could not buy a railroad ticket from an eastern point to Seattle, and

THE BATTLE OF SEATTLE

January 26, 1856, five years after the first settlement. The *Decatur* shelling the Indians, who are standing on the present site of the Chamber of Commerce Building. From a contemporary painting. Courtesy of the Seattle Chamber of Commerce.

SEATTLE IN 1870

From a contemporary painting. Courtesy of the Seattle Chamber of Commerce.

the railroad's agents met all inquiries concerning the town with bland indifference.

In 1881, however, hope was revived in Seattle when Henry Villard became president of the Northern Pacific. At this time Seattle offered to contribute $150,000 towards a direct connection with the main line; and although Villard did not accept the offer, he caused his Oregon Improvement Company to purchase the Seattle and Walla Walla Railroad, paying $250,000 for the road and $760,000 for the coal-mines and the vessels used to carry coal to California. Finally, in 1883 an extension was built to Stuck Junction, where a spur had been constructed from Tacoma, and Seattle at last had a rail connection with the Northern Pacific. But Villard retired from the presidency in 1884, when his schemes crashed to earth; and Tacoma interests succeeded in stopping the running of trains on the Seattle branch, leaving "the orphan road," as it was called, securely stuck at the appropriately named junction.

But the Seattle Spirit refused to be downed. Mass-meetings of farmers in the valley traversed by the railroad were held, and it was decided that if the Northern Pacific would not operate the branch, the farmers would have it condemned, because it was built on public land, and operate it themselves. The railroad resumed half-hearted operation of its line, but Seattle merchants could get goods only in carload lots, rates were exorbitant, and passenger service execrable. And the proud city of Seattle refused to tolerate such conditions. Since it was evident that the Northern Pacific intended to continue its discriminations in favor of Tacoma, Seattle business men determined on another bold move. They would build a railroad northward to connect with the Canadian Pacific and thus forever shake off their dependence on the Northern Pacific. Under the leadership of Judge Thomas Burke and David Hunt Gilman the Seattle, Lake Shore and Eastern was organized.

It was to the organizing genius and zeal for public service of Judge Burke that Seattle owed not only this early railroad but her second transcontinental connection. What the history of Seattle would have been without him is hard to picture. Thomas Burke was born in Clinton, New York, on December 22, 1849. He worked on the farm as a boy and moved to Iowa while still a child. He was soon earning his own living carrying water to a gang of railroad laborers—surely a sign and portent of what his later connection with railroads was to be. He worked in a store in Ypsilanti, Michigan, to earn money to go to the academy there, and after a year in school he became a teacher. Burke then went to the University of Michigan, and during part of his college years he studied law in an office in Marshall, Michigan, becoming city attorney there in 1875. Here he read in the newspapers about Seattle and decided to migrate to that pioneering city. Soon after his arrival he was elected probate judge of King County. He entered a law partnership which was engaged chiefly in collecting wages for working-men, but his services were soon called for by larger enterprises. He bought real estate, built a large concrete office-building twelve stories high on Second Avenue, and although it was freely predicted he would fail in his grand enterprise, he succeeded.

When the Northern Pacific construction ceased in 1883, with the fall of Henry Villard, the Northwest found itself with a great many Chinese railroad laborers on its hands. Since they were competing with white men, there was intense feeling against them, and at Tacoma on November 3, 1885, every Chinese was driven from the city, and their buildings were burned. Seattle would have followed this example had it not been for Judge Burke, who denounced the lawless expulsion and urged Seattleites to remain calm. Anti-Chinese attacked the Home Guard, of which Judge Burke was a member, several of the aggressors were killed, and he was charged with murder. The city was put under martial law, and a grand jury finally decided that the charge against Burke was false. But by his courageous stand he had earned the gratitude of the city and become perhaps its leading citizen. He was one of those good citizens who, on the day when the whole business district was laid in ashes, voted not to use the money just collected for the sufferers of the Johnstown flood for the relief of Seattle which sorely needed it, but to send it on to Johnstown as originally planned. Although he defended individuals at law, often without pay, Judge Burke's practice came to be largely with corporations and business firms. He served on the school board of Seattle and was a member of the territorial board of education.

In 1881 it was well for Seattle that Judge Burke and David Gilman put all their force behind another railroad project, the building of a railroad eastward over the Cascades. They went east to raise money and succeeded in getting the promise of $500,000 provided Seattle would raise $50,000. This was done, a building company was organized, and the road proceeded to the Issaquah coal-fields, where a profitable freight traffic could be expected. The Northern Pacific interests countered this move through a friendly company that was building a line south from Bellingham and had secured from Congress the right to build across rivers—a right which it held was exclusive and prohibited any other road from building a bridge on its route.

In his *History of Seattle* Clarence B. Bagley tells how Judge Burke outwitted the adversaries of his railroad who were trying to stop the company's work on a bridge over the Snohomish River. In Seattle, Burke was pursued by a process-server of this hostile road who carried a writ in his hand, so he hurried to the train that was waiting to carry passengers to Snohomish, climbed into the engine cab, and told the engineer to carry him up the line.

"But it is just about time for this train to leave for Snohomish and there are a lot of passengers waiting," protested the engineer.

"I'll take care of you," said Burke. "All I want you to do is to let her out and travel as fast as possible. And never mind stopping at Ballard; shoot right through to Snohomish."

As soon as they got to Snohomish, the Judge hunted up the sheriff, William Whitfield.

"Billy, how many deputies have you?" asked Burke.

"Two," replied the sheriff.

"Don't you think there are some desperadoes somewhere on the outskirts of the county that would require the attention of yourself and your force for the next day or two?"

"I am quite sure there are," said the sheriff. "What's up?"

"Canfield and his crowd are trying to give us trouble in getting our bridge to this side of the river. They have a writ and I don't wish it to be served. If you will keep after those desperadoes until I send for you, I think you will be showing commendable enthusiasm in discharge of your sworn duty to stamp out lawlessness." *

* Clarence B. Bagley, *History of Seattle* (Chicago, S. J. Clarke Publishing Company, 1916).

When the sheriff and his men departed, Burke put every available man to work on the bridge, and before any officers could be found to serve the writ, the bridge was completed and the writ useless.

Now the Seattle men showed the Northern Pacific that they meant business—business of the biggest kind. In New York they raised a fund of $1,000,000, and in far-away eastern Washington they started to build a section of railroad from Spokane westward toward Seattle. Added to the threat of this cross-state railroad, the Northern Pacific officials had also to face the powerful opposition of James J. Hill, who was pushing his rails across the country from Minnesota to Puget Sound; consequently, they made the only move open to them by buying the Seattle, Lake Shore and Eastern, at a fat profit to its owners, in order to keep it out of Hill's hands and to make it harder for him to reach tide-water. But the city had now grown to 40,000 without the help of the Northern Pacific, and that road had to begin to scramble for a share of its business. Henry Villard, who had shown his friendliness for Seattle by his investments there, as well as by the fact that when he first visited the city, he had contributed money to keep the almost defunct State University alive for two years, was still assiduously cultivated by Seattle. On September 14, 1887, the mayor wired him, "Four years ago today the citizens of Seattle had the pleasure of receiving you and your friends. Our confidence and faith in you have never faltered and to-night with illuminations, cannon and universal rejoicing we are celebrating your return to the directorate of the Northern Pacific."

It was about this time that a certain famous pink-whiskered statesman got his start in Seattle. James Hamilton Lewis had lately come to town from Georgia and was engaged in working as a longshoreman on a dock. When a fellow-workman said he needed a lawyer to help him establish a claim, Lewis admitted that he was an attorney, and in his blue dungarees he went to court and successfully represented his client. His entry into politics was as Congressman-at-large from the State of Washington, and he was later the state's candidate for Democratic nominee for Vice-President.

But James Jerome Hill now occupied the center of the picture. The master railroad-builder was approaching the Pacific Coast with the Great Northern, and he kept the people of all the Puget Sound ports on tenter-hooks as they wondered which he would select as his terminus. Hill was a canny Scotch-Irishman, who knew every detail of transportation from soliciting freight to laying rails and operating at a profit. He was born at Rockwood, Ontario, on September 16, 1838. After attending Rockwood Academy he left his Canadian home for New York and Philadelphia with the intention of shipping as a sailor to the Orient; but no ship offering him a job, he decided to travel overland and go to the Far East from the Pacific Coast. His idea was to go into business of some sort in the Orient, and even at this early age he had dreamed of an elaborate scheme of building steamers to open transportation on the Ganges, Hoogly, and Brahmaputra rivers in India. His journey ended at St. Paul, Minnesota, however, and at this river outpost on the edge of the wilderness he began his career.

Hill got work as a clerk for the agents of a Mississippi River steamboat line, and he continued in such positions for nine years, reading intensively, meanwhile, on a wide variety of subjects. He learned all about fuels and steamboat building and operation; he read history, chemistry, geology, engineering, law. And all the time he was learning how to carry on a business and to get trade. His versatility was such that he sold one of the first threshing-machines in St. Paul and set it up himself, and he became sufficiently skilled in navigation to act as pilot of a river-steamer. The first shipment of wheat grown in Minnesota passed through his hands, and he cut the stencil for the first label on the first flour made in the state. Since Minnesota flour was then unknown, it was branded, "Muskingum Mills, Troy, Ohio— The Genuine."

He helped to raise a company of volunteer cavalry for the Civil War, but his lack of sight in one eye prevented his acceptance by the Army; so he stayed at home and joined in the ruthless competition of the Mississippi packet lines. No maneuvers, tricks, or dodges of transportation were unknown to these river-freighting companies: they fought for business, slashed rates, even bought cargoes outright and took their chances on selling at a profit rather than allow a rival to carry the freight. In this warfare James J. Hill was so successful that in 1865 he went into the business on his own account. He became agent in St. Paul for the Northwestern Packet Company, which connected with the Chicago, Milwaukee and St. Paul Railroad and the Illinois Central. From this time on he became the leading handler of freight in St. Paul. To stimulate his business he gave shippers the lowest rates from the East, and he permitted anyone having freight sent in his care to have it transferred from cars to boats free of charge. He formed a partnership with a firm in Dubuque for conducting a transportation, storage, and commission business, and he made a contract with the First Division of the St. Paul and Pacific Railroad Company to care for its freight in St. Paul, making no charge to shippers for transferring river freight that was to be shipped on the railroad.

Realizing the dependence of the cold north country on adequate fuel supplies, Hill entered this business. He formed a partnership with Chauncey W. Griggs, who was later to become a leading citizen of Tacoma, for a freighting, merchandising, fuel, and warehouse business, wherein his special province was transportation, while his partner specialized in fuel. Hill, Griggs and Company bought wood-land from the railroad, cut the wood, sold it to the road for fuel, and brought the surplus into St. Paul to sell on its own account. During these years Hill studied coal and its production so thoroughly that he knew every deposit in the West, and he was later able to buy advantageously thousands of acres of choice coal-lands in Iowa, Montana, and elsewhere.

Soon Hill was shipping flour for all the seventeen mills of Minneapolis, and he began carrying freight and passengers from Winnipeg by way of steamboats on the Red River and wagons to St. Paul. In this scheme he rivaled the powerful Hudson's Bay Company, and he monopolized the business by inducing the Government to enforce a dormant law requiring that all goods going to Canada be bonded in the United States customs. Hill had posted his bond, his rivals had not, and for a time he kept them from doing business. But the Hudson's Bay Company assigned its steamers to its St. Paul agent, Norman W. Kittson, who was an American citizen, and as soon as he had posted the required bond, traffic was resumed. A little later Hill took Kittson into a partnership to form the Red River Transportation Company.

In 1870 Hill set out up the Red River to investigate Louis Riel's rebellion, an insurrection of a group of trappers who resented the surrender of the territorial rights of the Hudson's Bay Company to the newly formed Dominion of Canada. On this trip he first met the Scotchman Donald A. Smith, who had risen from clerk to chief factor of the Hudson's Bay Company in Labrador and had then become governor for the company in Montreal. They met on the snow-covered prairie in dog-sleds, 140 miles from a house, and there began a life-long friendship between the governor of the great British company and the man who had successfully opposed his transportation interests on the Red River. Smith settled the rebellion satisfactorily, and Hill investigated the future possibilities of the country as a tributary to St. Paul.

On frequent trips into Canada he collected information until he was convinced that the Red River country extending north to Winnipeg was destined to be the richest prize in the development of transportation in the Northwest. He was aided in his scheme of exploiting this territory by the Jay Cooke panic of 1873, which threw many of the railroads of the country into bankruptcy. Among them was the St. Paul and Pacific, a collection of short lines running out of St. Paul into the Red River country. This concern, largely financed by Dutch capital, had fought with the Northern Pacific for supremacy in the region and had erected a devious and complicated financial structure to pay for its building operations. Despite the fact that the road was a scrap-heap of unrelated lines, badly managed, Hill saw that it had immense possibilities for future profit if properly operated. The tottering Northern Pacific held stock in the road and in ordinary times would not have permitted it to escape from its hands. But when the Chicago, Milwaukee and St. Paul defaulted on its bonds and was foreclosed, the Northern Pacific was itself in such a plight that it could not acquire the Red River lines.

To own this road became an obsession with Hill, and he confided his plans to Norman W. Kittson, the general forwarding agent of the Hudson's Bay Company at St. Paul who was also Hill's partner in the Red River Transportation Company, formed in 1872 by Kittson and Hill, Griggs and Company. They next interested their friend Donald A. Smith, later to be Lord Strathcona, chief commissioner of the Hudson's Bay Company, who saw in the road a southern outlet for the proposed transcontinental Canadian Pacific. Unable to raise the necessary funds, the three sought a fourth partner in George Stephen, later to be Lord Mount Stephen, president of the Bank of Montreal. Working fast so as to save the land-grants of the road and to prevent the North-Western and the Milwaukee railroad systems from competing for the property, the four made an offer to the Dutch owners for their bonds. This offer, drawn up by Hill, was so hard on the sellers that it could not possibly be accepted; but it gave opportunity for him to report pessimistically concerning the prospects of the railroad and resulted in his discovering from the agent some idea of the figure at which the Dutch committee would sell. The next proposition made various offers for the different issues of bonds totaling $4,330,180, and it was so cleverly drawn that the Dutchmen construed it as an offer to buy outright, whereas it was only an option, permitting the associates to try to raise the money required. In his investigations Hill had made the discovery that $188,250 expended on additions and improvements during 1877 had been charged to operating expenses, thus making the earnings seem much smaller than they actually were; and he also saw a source of profit in the large influx of settlers to the Red River Valley that he felt to be imminent. He set the figure of $5,540,180 as the total amount needed to buy the bonds, complete the lines, and care for the other costs of the transaction. And he conservatively judged the property to be worth $20,000,000 as it stood.

Meanwhile, the Northern Pacific was negotiating with the Canadian Government for an exclusive connection of a Canadian railroad with its line at the border, a project whose success would ruin the chances of the St. Paul and Pacific. Using all his influence against this, Stephen hurried to England to get cash to finance the St. Paul purchase. But he could not interest British capital, so the disappointed partners made a third offer to the bondholders. They agreed to buy the bonds at the prices previously suggested and to pay 7 per cent interest on the money until the mortgages were foreclosed, whereupon the whole was to be paid in 6 per cent gold bonds of the new company, with a bonus of $250 in 6 per cent preferred stock for each $1,000 bond; and they further agreed to extend the line as needed to save the land-grants. The appetite of the Dutch bondholders had now been sufficiently whetted for a sale, and they agreed to these terms on March 13, 1878.

Fighting court delays set up because of the receivership, the partners hastened the completion of the road, straining every effort to raise money and to hurry construction. At the same time Hill was encouraging emigration and helping farmers to finance their crops. He told President Charles B. Wright of the Northern Pacific that his company must stop its agitation against the St. Paul and Pacific, and if they could not arbitrate their differences, the new road would draw in other railroad interests to build a parallel line to the Coast. Seeing in this statement a threat of getting Jay Gould, who now owned the Union Pacific, as a rival, the Northern Pacific quickly joined in a schedule of freight tariffs and trackage rights into St. Paul agreeable to Hill and promised not to build any competing lines. Although the partners were beset by all sorts of vexations and hindrances, they completed their lines in time to hold the land-grants, and during the first year under their management the net earnings increased by nearly $500,000 over those of the previous year.

In 1879 a new company, the St. Paul, Minneapolis and Manitoba, was organized; the president, George Stephen, was authorized to buy in the St. Paul and Pacific properties at foreclosure; and a few months later, when this had been done, the first melon was cut, and $15,000,000 in stock and $16,000,000 in bonds were turned over to the partners in payment for the properties and the money they had advanced the new road. It was Hill's long vision and canny shrewdness that had brought about this enormous profit. He had been sure of the prosperity of the Red River Valley from the day he first noted how rank the grass grew where the wagon-wheels displaced its rich black soil, and he had yearned for years to control its badly managed railroad; when the time was right, he had struck swiftly and gathered in the prize, and now he reaped the profit. Rapidly he added other lines and terminal properties, and within 12 years the road was carrying, instead of 2,000,000 bushels of wheat, 67,000,000 bushels, with corresponding profits.

Meanwhile, the idea of extending his road to the Pacific had already formed in Hill's mind. He watched Henry Villard's building of the Northern Pacific and smiled enigmatically when that gentleman asked at what price he would sell the Manitoba. He added to its tracks, developed its strength, encouraged emigration, made a blanket bond-issue of $50,000,000 on his system, and was ready to extend his lines westward. But in the meantime his powerful Canadian partners had begun the project of building the Canadian Pacific from ocean to ocean in order to bind together the warring interests of the provinces of Canada. And they turned to him for help. At their request Hill laid out the line over the best available passes and through the most productive country from Winnipeg to Vancouver; and incidentally he saw to it that the Government provided that no competing lines were to be surveyed between the Canadian Pacific and the United States border for 20 years. After giving generously of his time he withdrew, since a great hue and cry was set up over the connection of this rival American railroad power with the Canadian Pacific, and Smith and Stephen also withdrew from the management of the Manitoba.

But all these activities were merely preliminaries to the crowning achievement of James J. Hill—the building of the transcontinental Great Northern from St. Paul to the Pacific Coast. In the Red River lines were the roots of this system, roots which furnished him with a steady flow of funds for the extensions that he now rapidly pushed westward. For years the plans had been slowly maturing in his mind, and all his experience in constructing his other lines and in laying out the Canadian Pacific was drawn upon in maturing the transcontinental project. But he did not make his plans known, for he did not wish to inform his rivals. The Union Pacific had already pushed a line up into Montana from Ogden, and the Canadian Pacific had been invited by the people of Helena to send a branch down to their city. Nor did he wish to alarm his own stockholders, who might be expected to view his extension to the Coast as another "Jim Hill's Folly." He did need to obtain favorable legislation from the Minnesota legislature, however, and after this was enacted, a committee was appointed to see what methods had been used. No bribery was ever proved, but it was shown that railroad interest was very influential in the state legislative halls. Hill was a strong Democrat and high in the party councils; but he also helped Mark Hanna raise $5,000,000 for McKinley's campaign because he feared Bryan and his greenback policies.

Since there were only a few routes of easy access to Montana, Hill moved secretly and fast to occupy the most favorable location. Here was another opportunity for pioneering, and just as he had peopled and developed the Red River Valley, so now he looked forward to building up Montana. Quietly the Montana Central Railroad was organized in 1886 as a local project to build from Great Falls to Helena. In 1887 the Manitoba road, though strongly opposed by Gould in Congress, was given right of way to build westward from Minot, North Dakota, through the Indian reservations in North Dakota and Montana, provided it paid for the land used. The work was rushed with utmost speed, 500 miles of roadbed being graded in about four months. Shortly previous to this, the Manitoba board of directors officially noticed for the first time, strangely enough, that the Montana Central had occupied the only available route between Helena and the Missouri River, and they voted to buy it "if it could be obtained." It was obtained, and in 1888 it began to pay a profit as soon as Montana coal found a market in St. Paul. Through passenger trains were soon running from St. Paul to Butte, with connections to Oregon and California over the Union Pacific, and the road was making money. "Another piece of Jim Hill's luck," said the observers, little realizing that every detail of the scheme had been worked out in Jim Hill's mind for years.

Hill now began making surveys to the Coast. By 1890 the entire line had been laid out from Fort Assiniboine, Montana, to Spokane, and it was rumored that he had acquired the Seattle, Lake Shore and Eastern for an entry to Puget Sound. But this rumor was not true, for the Northern Pacific had assumed control of this road with the express purpose of keeping Hill out. The real nature of Hill's plans were now made public when he organized his transcontinental railway company. In February, 1890, the Minneapolis and St. Cloud Railway, which had been operating under a more liberal charter than that of the Manitoba Company, changed its name to the Great Northern Railway Company and leased the properties of the St. Paul, Minneapolis and Manitoba for a period of 999 years. The legal organization of the great railway system that Hill planned was now complete.

Each harbor on Puget Sound now began to press its claim as the best possible terminus for this new road, and Hill sent his representative, Colonel William P. Clough, to make an investigation that would supplement his already considerable knowledge of the situation. Tacoma was soon eliminated, since it was the headquarters and port of a rival road; and it appeared that Bellingham was to be the favored city, since the first survey was made over Skagit Pass to Bellingham Bay. This location for a terminus had often figured in the plans of transportation experts, for it had been said that the harbor farthest north and closest to the ocean would be the great harbor of Puget Sound. With similar logic Hill later thought that Astoria would be the great harbor of Oregon, and he built a steamship terminal near-by; but he later abandoned it, and Portland, a hundred miles inland, remains the shipping center of the Columbia basin.

But Judge Burke determined that Seattle should be the terminus if anything he could do would bring that about. He interviewed Colonel Clough and promised him that he would personally see to it that the Great Northern obtained all the franchises necessary for a right of way into the city, and that he would obtain terminal lands from private owners at low cost. Nothing was heard from Hill for some months; then his attorney suddenly appeared and told Judge Burke that Seattle had been selected as the terminus, and he asked the man who had been so successful in building local railroads to represent the Hill interests. It was said that one of the strongest factors in drawing Hill to Seattle was the town's aggressive spirit and the quality of its leading citizens.

It looked as if the water-front entry to the city was tied up by the Seattle and Walla Walla franchise, but Burke surmounted this obstacle by organizing a new railroad, under the laws of Washington, the Seattle and Montana, and petitioning the city council to lay out a new street, Railroad Avenue, on the tide-flats under water and have it built as an earth fill. On this street, 120 feet wide, the Hill line was given 60 feet, with the provision that other roads could use the tracks by paying rent; the Seattle, Lake Shore and Eastern was given 30 feet; and 30 feet was left for other roads. When this was proposed, the Northern Pacific set up a great moan over the fact that such action meant bottling up the city against all future railroads, and a bitter controversy raged for months. But Judge Burke carried his fight to the city Council, and within one week a special meeting was held at which the Hill plan won by unanimous vote. Burke then began to secure right of way over the tide-flats, and soon he was able to present Hill with a strip two blocks wide and a mile long for his entry into Seattle. Grading on the Seattle and Montana began on August 1, 1890, and on November 27, 1891, it was opened from Seattle to New Westminster, British Columbia, the northern part being built by and acquired from a Canadian corporation. The completed line included the tracks of the Fairhaven and Southern and the Seattle and Northern, two short roads purchased by Colonel Clough.

Seattle had entertained the hope of being a transcontinental terminus for so long and had been so frequently disappointed that she refused to believe completely in her present luck. The Council, doubting the reality of its good fortune, was anxious to anchor the Great Northern in Seattle by requiring it to build a costly depot, and Judge Burke appeared in person to reassure its members. The company had already expended $30,000,000 to reach Seattle, he said, and $325,000 more for a depot site, and he hoped that the Council would not insist on a time limit or a specified amount of money, but would trust Mr. Hill to erect a suitable building. But the councilmen called to mind Tacoma, where the Northern Pacific had even yet only a shed for a railroad station, and demanded a guarantee even if the Great Northern had already done more for Puget Sound than fourteen Northern Pacifics. "If the demand for this depot would cause them to go to Everett or Podunk, they are not the city's friend," said one member, "and if they do so, Seattle would like to have the depot as a souvenir of their visit."

But Seattle was reassured as to Hill's intentions as he made it more and more plain that the city was to be the center of his transportation system. "I intend to have a road like a rake," he told Judge Burke in New York, "with Seattle as the focal point and prongs that reach all the principal cities of the Northwest. The handle will be the trunk line extending east." Work on the prongs and the handle went on steadily. The 828-mile Pacific extension, from Havre, Montana, to Everett, Washington, was completed in 38 months from the time grading began, and it had been pushed through more than 400 miles of unexplored country. Heavy snows in the mountains and the almost tropical luxuriance of undergrowth in the tall-timber country had been among the obstacles overcome. In reaching the Pacific Coast the Great Northern was able to cut its line 70 miles shorter than the Northern Pacific between St. Paul and Spokane through the discovery of the Marias Pass, 200 miles north of Butte. This pass had been described to Isaac I. Stevens, who made the first government surveys for a road to the Pacific, by Chief Little Dog of the Blackfeet in 1853, but his engineers failed to find it. In 1889 the Pass was discovered by Hill's engineer in charge of Rocky Mountain reconnaissance, John F. Stevens.

The work was carried forward so expeditiously that trains were running into Seattle from the East in July, 1893. It was planned to commemorate this event with a great celebration, to which Hill promised to bring men representing "a thousand million dollars"—all eager for investment opportunities. But the unsettled financial conditions of the day balked this plan, and the only large celebration was held at the St. Paul end of the line, to whose parade Seattle sent a giant log hauled by twenty horses as a sample of Northwestern timber. The ceremonies in Seattle were combined with the usual Fourth of July celebration.

At about this time Hill came into possession of government lands in Washington, Idaho, and Montana worth many millions. In 1891 he had claimed thousands of acres of homesteaded lands in the Red River Valley, on the ground that they had been granted by Congress in 1857 to the railroad that should traverse the valley. The original railroad was defunct, and the General Land Office had opened the land to entry. When Hill won this case, the settlers set up such an outcry at the confiscation of their lands that Congress permitted Hill to choose an equal amount of government land elsewhere. With his canny knowledge of the country he chose thousands of acres of the most valuable Far Western fir timber-lands, from which he further profited when it was discovered that much of them contained valuable mineral deposits.

When completed, the Great Northern was shorter than the other transcontinental roads and had flatter curves and lower grades. Hill had insisted on this, even though the cost was made heavier, so that he could haul his trains more cheaply and offer lower freight-rates. The heavy grades were concentrated so that the use of extra engines could be economically confined to short stretches. The distance to St. Paul was 1,816 miles on the Great Northern, 1,931 on the Northern Pacific. Hill immediately began to cut both freight and passenger rates, and after examining the standing timber in the State of Washington he declared that he would offer such a low rate on lumber that he would haul east no more empty cars. He felt this would be an economical policy for the railroad, and he also believed that until the timber was cut off, the agricultural development of western Washington would be retarded. When it was suggested that a profitable lumber business might be built up with the Middle West if the rate were cut from 90 cents to 60 cents a hundred, Hill laughed at the idea, saying that Western lumber could not compete with Southern at this rate. He therefore cut it to 40. It was the lowest rate ever granted, and railroad men declared that it would bankrupt the Great Northern; but, on the contrary, it created a profitable lumber-hauling business for the railroad, and it initiated great prosperity for the Puget Sound country, which, in turn, meant larger railroad earnings.

Meanwhile, Seattle had acquired an Oriental steamship connection. About the time the Great Northern first came to Seattle in 1893, Captain James Griffiths, who was then living at Port Townsend, read in some trade journal that the officials of the Nippon Yusen Kaisha line had their eyes on a service to the United States and that they contemplated using San Diego, California, as their port of entry. Captain Griffiths suggested to James J. Hill that he try to get this line to come to Seattle. As a result Hill sent Captain Griffiths to the Orient on this mission, and he accomplished it so successfully that Seattle became the port of entry for this great steamship line, which had been developed by Baron Kondo, a pioneer of Japanese trade expansion.

The Nippon Yusen Kaisha's first ship to arrive in Seattle was the *Miike Maru*, which steamed into the harbor on August 31, 1896. For three preceding days the city had been in a fever of excitement, and practically all the people in the town were crowded at every vantage-point on buildings, wharves, and far up on the hillside to catch the first glimpse of the ship. The oncoming vessel was announced by fire signal and curfew from Magnolia Bluff immediately after she was sighted. A public holiday was declared, the waters of Elliott Bay were filled with gaily decorated boats, and the city was in a festive mood.

"It is an epoch-making event in Seattle's history," declared John Leary, civic leader of the day. And from the instant that the Associated Press flashed out the news of the compact by which, for the first time in the history of America, Japanese trans-Pacific steamers undertook to carry cargoes to and from the United States, Seattle became a center of international interest. Eastern economists, transportation leaders, and manufacturers began investigating the potentialities of the Japan trade by way of Seattle. The service begun that day has never been interrupted.

Railroad connections were also established with Canada, the line between Bellingham and Sumas being built by D. O. Mills and others of the Northern Commercial Company. They platted New Whatcom, now a part of Bellingham, when they built the railroad. The first locomotive had come around Cape Horn in an American sailing-ship and had been used by Mills to grade sand lots in San Francisco. It was said that he considered this locomotive the foundation of his fortune and would never consent to scrap it.

In 1897 Hill visited Seattle with Frederic W. Weyerhaeuser, the man who owned the most standing timber in the world; this was the preliminary move in interesting him in the lumber industry of the Northwest, where he later acquired the largest holdings of any individual, much of them purchased from the Hill interests. At this time the reporters were anxious to know how much power Hill had in the management of the Northern Pacific, and they asked him, "What do you know about the Northern Pacific?" to which he cryptically replied, "It is a long railroad and a very good one."

The president of this long and very good railroad, Charles S. Mellen, soon made an announcement which caused Hill considerable concern. In the summer of 1898 Mellen saw the necessity of enlarging the Northern Pacific terminals at Seattle in order to capture some of the Alaska trade. This was a sharp change from the former policy which had slighted Seattle and worked to the advantage of what the *Post-Intelligencer* succinctly calls "a then rival city, Tacoma." Mellen originally proposed to buy the entire water-front holdings of the Pacific Coast Company, successor of the old Oregon Improvement

BIRD'S-EYE VIEW OF SEATTLE IN 1884

In the distance, Lakes Union and Washington. Lithograph after a drawing by H. Wellge. From the Stokes Collection, New York Public Library.

THE TERMINUS OF THE PUGET SOUND AND WALLA WALLA RAILROAD

The circular trestle carried the railroad out to the ships. From a photograph taken from Beacon Hill in 1880. Courtesy of the Seattle Chamber of Commerce.

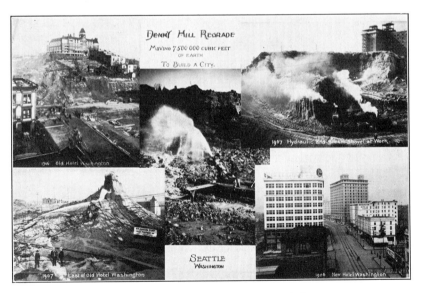

THE REDUCTION OF DENNY HILL

Courtesy of the Seattle Chamber of Commerce.

Company, but here the Hill interests checked him by obtaining a strong foothold in the company's affairs. Both Hill and Mellen then tried for control of the Seattle and International Railroad, which was partly owned by the Canadian Pacific and through which it had an entry into Seattle. Mellen won this contest, after which he bought all the water-front property from Yesler Way to University Street, with the exception of J. M. Colman's dock, and he proposed to use this important part of Seattle's water-front for railroad tracks.

In August Mellen declared that he wanted to build a $500,000 Union Station and take in the Hill lines. But Hill's interests were far south of Mellen's, and he had no desire to see a Union Station planted where it might suit the Northern Pacific. In September, therefore, Hill arrived in a special train in order to take personal charge of the fight. He declared that he had made a proposal to Mellen for a Union Station, but since hundreds of miles of track were required, the terminal must be away from the water-front; and he added this pointed statement: "I am strongly in favor of a terminal arrangement in Seattle whereby both lines will be on the same footing, but if this cannot be done, the Great Northern will conduct its operations from some point 25 or 30 miles from Seattle. This would mean a stub train from Snohomish, and Seattle off the main line of the road."

Mellen laughed at Hill's offer to sell half of his King Street holdings to the Northern Pacific at cost, for, he said, Hill had no holdings of a size suitable for terminals there; and he declared that Seattle was giving up nothing in vacating its streets for the Northern Pacific but would be getting a greatly improved water-front. In the controversy that followed, the whole city was lined up on one side or the other. Judge Burke made a most telling summary of the case, in which he said that to close the water-front streets desired by the Northern Pacific would be a calamity, for

the entire fleet of Sound steamers lands there; it would drive away commission houses, depreciate First Avenue property, be dangerous to traffic and drive other railways away. And a passenger station at the foot of Madison Street would be a public nuisance. If the city should give to the Northern Pacific Railway Company the streets and approaches which it asks, it would be investing that company with an absolute uncontrollable monopoly over the commerce of the city within those limits. The road has made no pretense that it intends to do its trans-Pacific shipping from this point. Naturally it would not. Tacoma has been made its shipping port. There it has, at large expense, provided its shipping facilities. And when, not very long since, the shippers of this place appealed to the Northern Pacific Railway Company to land even one of its Oriental steamers here, the answer came back that it would allow one of its steamers to call here upon condition that the city would pay a subsidy of $10,000 a year.

In the end Burke's arguments prevailed. In 1900 the city Council voted twelve to one in favor of the Hill plan, and the one came in to make it unanimous. In 1902 Hill showed Burke his plan for bringing trains into King Street through a tunnel, and in 1905 this was completed and the King Street Station used by both the Great Northern and the Northern Pacific.

By this time the original group of pioneers who settled Seattle had developed into first citizens of an important metropolis. David T. Denny, who had worked at drawing in the logs in Yesler's sawmill, had soon begun to acquire land everywhere, and he had platted seven additions to Seattle. He built the electric line to Ravenna Park and became president of the Consolidated Electric and Cable Company system. He built the narrow canal from Lake Union to Lake Washington. He was a large stockholder in several banks and president of the water company and other corporations. He was a member and a generous supporter of the Methodist Episcopal Church. He had been one of the fighters who defended Seattle against the Indian uprising of 1856, using firearms with skill in hunting men as well as beasts. Known as one of the town's best hunters, it is said he killed the last antlered elk shot near Seattle. Denny had married Miss Louisa Boren, another pioneer, and they were the first couple to be married in Seattle. He always had faith in the town, and the growth of the city found him ready to meet it with appropriate plans for its commercial and intellectual growth. He was so dependable that he was known everywhere as "Honest Dave," and this pleased him more than the wealth he accumulated or the position of influence he held. At various times he was town councilman, county treasurer, county commissioner, probate judge, school director, and regent of the Territorial University.

Arthur A. Denny, risen from the position of screw-tender at Yesler's mill, had likewise been active in nearly every project for the good of

Seattle. He was to be largely responsible for bringing the city the University of Washington. He headed a group of eighteen men who guaranteed $1,800 in tolls to save the telegraph line from San Francisco for Seattle in 1873. He was an incorporator of early railroads and industries. He served as a delegate to the first territorial legislature, was a Delegate to Congress in the early days of the territory, and Lincoln appointed him register of the Land Office at Olympia. He invested heavily in Seattle real estate and acquired a substantial fortune through its sale. He became a partner with Dexter Horton in the first bank of Seattle, and his interests included mining, milling, merchandising, and everything that he thought was to the best advantage of the city. He was a member of the Congregational Church and gave liberally to philanthropies.

Henry Yesler also prospered and served the community well. In his sawmill in the early days he employed many Indians, and he became very friendly with the various tribes, learning their languages and acting as interpreter. He carried messages from Governor Stevens to their chiefs during the negotiation of the Indian treaties. Yesler was twice mayor of Seattle and a county commissioner several times. Before Seattle had good hotels Mr. and Mrs. Yesler were the official hosts of the town, entertaining all distinguished visitors in their house, the finest on Puget Sound, where the City and County Building now stands. After the great fire of June 6, 1889, which destroyed Seattle, Yesler started immediately to build substantial and imposing buildings on his property, and he surrounded Pioneer Place with brick and stone structures of which the city was proud. He was public-spirited, putting much time and energy into the promotion of the Seattle and Walla Walla Railroad, the waterworks, the first street-railway company, and he could always be counted on to advance money for projects that he felt were for the good of the community. He endowed a home for young women in memory of his first wife.

When he first came to Seattle, Dexter Horton was one of the early workers in Yesler's mill, and his wife was a cook for the Yesler crew. In those days Horton worked from one in the afternoon until midnight, and in the mornings he cleared some lots he had bought to get them ready for sale. He later went into partnership with David Phillips in a store. Here the milling and logging men used to bring him their pay, which he would put in bags bearing their names, and these he would keep in meal sacks and coffee barrels. The men got in the habit of depositing their money-bags with him, taking out cash as they wanted it and leaving a receipt, and sometimes a year would elapse before they claimed possession of their property. So great was the demand for this service that at the close of the Indian wars Horton sold his store and opened the first private bank in the territory. During the time he was building up his own business, he was also helping Seattle. He was one of the builders of the first wagon-road over the Cascades and a promoter of railroads to serve Seattle. He sold his bank to William S. Ladd of Portland in 1889. After the disastrous fire of that year he began to rebuild his property and erected some of the finest buildings in the city. Always generous in contributing to philanthropies and business development, he became one of the outstanding figures in the Northwest and one of its wealthiest men.

Another colorful and important figure in the history of Seattle was Jacob Furth. Born in Bohemia, November 15, 1840, as a lad he learned the confectioner's trade. He came to San Francisco with adventurous gold-seekers in 1856, and from there he went to Nevada City, where he worked in a clothing-store mornings and evenings and attended school in the daytime until he had learned English. Beginning at $40 a month, he was soon earning $300, and by 1862 had saved enough to open a dry-goods store. In 1870 he established a store in Colusa, California, and in 1882 he came north to Seattle. He organized the Puget Sound National Bank with a capital of $50,000 and became cashier. From 1893 he was president until the bank consolidated with the Seattle National Bank, when he became chairman of the board. He organized banks in Snohomish, bought land and stock in eastern Washington, and was largely responsible for the building of an electric-railway system in Seattle and its expansion to own the street-car lines of Tacoma and most of the other towns on Puget Sound. He constantly bought and sold Seattle real estate and timber-lands, acquiring a large fortune. At the time of the San Francisco earthquake Massachusetts raised $1,000,000 for relief and looked about for a trustworthy agent to handle its expenditure. Jacob Furth was the man selected. On his death J. E. Chilberg of the Chamber of Commerce described him as "essentially a product of that early history of Seattle which necessitated coöperation and banded business men together for the common good."

Until 1897 there had been fierce and unremitting rivalry between Seattle and Tacoma, with the advantage first on one side and then on the other—the only cessation of hostilities occurring at the time of the Seattle fire, when Tacoma at once generously contributed $100,-000 for relief; but an event of that year gave Seattle an impetus which carried her forward in seven-league strides until she became the principal city of the Northwest. This was the discovery of gold in the Klondike district of Alaska and Canada. Seattle was nearer the region than any other large city, President Mellen of the Northern Pacific had removed the Alaska steamers from Tacoma to Seattle, and Seattle set out systematically to capitalize her advantages and make herself the acknowledged center of the Alaska trade.

On July 14 the steamer *Excelsior* landed at San Francisco, bringing the first results of the Klondike gold-strike—$750,000 in dust and nuggets, and three days later the *Portland* reached Seattle with sixty miners and $800,000 in gold. A list of the returning citizens and the amounts they brought out was enough to raise the temperature of Seattle people to a fever: T. S. Lippy, former secretary of the Y. M. C. A., $50,000; J. O. Hestwood, theatrical scene-painter, $5,000; Fred Price, who used to work for the White Star Laundry, $5,000. All these Seattleites had landed at San Francisco, driven to the Palace Hotel, and been besieged by reporters and mobbed by the curious. Lippy, with the true Seattle spirit, immediately wired, "I hope the Seattle idea still prevails and that the banks there will club together so as to take care of the dust brought in with ready cash; if the banks do not do so, the men will be compelled out of force of circumstance to go to San Francisco."

When the *Portland* arrived, Seattle was prepared. Joseph Mayer and Company cast gold bricks twenty-four hours a day, banks bought dust, and advertisements at once began to appear in the papers offering for sale "Klondike stoves" and other supplies suitable for the Alaska trade. The *Post-Intelligencer* reported that

the excitement is indescribable and the output of the New Klondike district almost beyond belief. Men who had nothing last fall are now worth a fortune. One man has worked forty square feet of his claim and is going out with $40,000 in dust. One-quarter of claims are now selling at from $15,000 to $50,000—some valued as high as $1,000,000. At Dawson sacks of dust are thrown under the counters in the stores for safe keeping. Labor is $15 a day and board with 100 days' work guaranteed.

At the time of the first discovery, in August, 1896, the gold taken out of the creek-beds averaged $1.60 per pan, and one of the first miners made $1,400 in three weeks with three sluice-boxes. So plentiful was the dust that it was stored in old syrup cans and five-gallon oil cans. These and other stories grew ever brighter as they were bandied about the streets of Seattle, where the crowds surged back and forth, intoxicated with the news of gold. The mine-outfitting places were busy, but all other business stagnated while the employees talked of clubbing together to raise a thousand dollars to grub-stake one of their number, after which they would all live the rest of their lives on their golden profits. So strong was the excitement that a delivery wagon full of tents marked for the gold-fields was mobbed by the curious. Everywhere old-timers babbled of the glories of California in the Fifties, of Virginia City and the Comstock, even of the Transvaal, and declared that the new strike made all these insignificant.

Best of all, the depression which had clouded the atmosphere since 1893 was over so far as Seattle was concerned. She began to feel the effects of that ready flow of gold which enabled Klondike saloons to clear $3,000 a day and which prompted the miners in one camp to pour $400 into a bottle as a thank-offering for the privilege of reading a few stray copies of a Seattle newspaper. Wholesale grocers and outfitters worked double shifts, and steamship lines and railroads were overloaded with freight and passengers. The excitement soon became a fury, and it extended clear to New York, the city which had furnished the greatest number of Forty-niners and which seemed about to duplicate that record for the Klondike. Would-be miners came to Seattle from every walk of life and every part of the country. The mayor of Seattle resigned to go to the Klondike, and the commonest expression heard on the streets was, "I would leave for Alaska by the next steamer if I could make some provision for my family."

All the Pacific Coast cities were now trying to get the lion's share of the Alaska business. Tacoma organized a committee, and the Seattle papers contemptuously quoted an interview given out by

Colonel S. Albert Perkins of that city, assistant secretary of the National Republican Committee and private secretary to Mark Hanna. In New York Colonel Sammy described the boom and declared Tacoma to be the greatest outfitting point, and the New York *World,* using, Seattle said, "an antiquated map," showed Tacoma as the terminus of the Northern Pacific Railroad and its steamship lines to Alaska. San Francisco and the Southern Pacific sought to get the Alaska trade, the Canadian Pacific worked for Victoria and Vancouver, and the *Oregonian* rightly predicted that Portland would get only the crumbs unless the city acted.

But Seattle had no intention of letting the prize slip. No sooner had the discovery of gold been made than she began to clamor for a government assay office, and she showed her flair for occupying the limelight by sending out the following newspaper despatch:

The news that the telegraph is bringing the past few days of the wonderful things of Klondike in the land of the midnight sun has opened the flood gates, and a stream of humanity is pouring through Seattle and on to the golden Mecca of the North. It is a crowd at once strange, weird, and picturesque. Some say it eclipses anything in the days of '49. The good ship *Portland,* which recently brought a million and a half of treasure to this port, sails for Alaska to-morrow at noon. She will carry every passenger and every pound of cargo that she has the ability to transport. The *Portland* has booked for this passage fifty first class and ninety-eight second class passengers. The names of an ex-governor and a general are on the list. Fifteen hundred passengers are booked for Alaska on the overland passage. Every available steamer is full. The steamers *Queen, City of Mexico, City of Topeka,* and *Al-ki* in rotation will sail by August 5th, to be followed by the *Willamette, City of Kingston,* and *City of Seattle* pressed from service elsewhere.

This good beginning was shortly followed by a meeting of business men called for the purpose of considering the advertising of Seattle as the principal outfitting point and to counteract the efforts of other cities. Four days later a committee reported in favor of a heavy schedule of paid advertising and propaganda, to be under the direction of its chairman, Erastus Brainerd. Three-quarters of a page were taken in the New York Sunday *Journal* to dwarf the modest advertisements of Portland and Victoria; generous appropriation was made for the *Review of Reviews,* which had carried Canadian matter; and other advertisements were placed in *Munsey's, McClure's, Cosmopolitan, Century,* and *Scribner's.* Brainerd soon proved his genius as a ballyhoo artist by laying down such a barrage of magazine and newspaper articles and advertisements that no other city had a chance to be heard, as a result of which it was soon reported that Seattle was getting five times as much publicity as any other outfitting point. Brainerd then sent out the following crafty telegraphic news despatch: "As a result of the Klondike excitement, which has overwhelmed the city with inquiries from all parts of the world as to routes of transportation and costs of outfitting, there has been established under the auspices of the Chamber of Commerce a public Bureau of Information."

Inquiries were now rolling into Seattle by the thousand, and to further increase the flood a Klondike edition of the *Post-Intelligencer* was published, of which Brainerd sent a copy to each of the country's 70,000 postmasters, to each of its 600 public libraries, to its 4,000 mayors of cities, together with 10,000 copies for distribution by the Great Northern and 5,000 by the Northern Pacific. Advertisements were placed in rural papers with a circulation of 9,940,000, and Brainerd held confidential meetings at factories and business houses to obtain the names of Seattleites who had recently come from the East. These were then provided with letters to their home-town papers describing the Klondike excitement and advertising the city as the point of departure. The letters were stamped and addressed and needed only a signature.

Even greater heights of press-agentry were scaled, so dizzy in fact that Brainerd might well have called himself even in those simple times a public-relations counsel. He concentrated on a campaign of articles in newspapers the country over, stressing the point that Seattle was *the* port of departure for the Klondike. He sent a helpful communication to all governors of states and mayors of cities, seeking to be of assistance to those who were interested in the Klondike. From these officers he sought information concerning the possible influx of prospectors, in order that the conservative business men of Seattle might avoid the pitfalls of a stampede and might have the opportunity of informing inquirers as to the true facts; he expressed solicitude for the good of the public and inquired the names of prospective emigrants and their place of outfitting. The governors and mayors obligingly gave this letter to their newspapers, and another flood of inquiries resulted.

Brainerd next induced the secretary of state of the State of Washington to issue and sign a bulletin of information, containing advice on such varied matters as canned goods, underwear, and how to ford rapids, and calling attention to the purchase of supplies and steamer tickets and the securing of more information in Seattle. This document was duly forwarded by the diplomatic representatives in Washington as an official communication to the governments of France, Belgium, Italy, Switzerland, and other countries and was gratefully printed in their newspapers. He then started a campaign of patriotic intent, urging prospectors to get their gold on the American Yukon in Alaska—embarking from Seattle—and calling attention to the 30 per cent duty levied on supplies at Canadian Klondike ports; and he urged Congress to establish Army posts in Alaska and make the district into two territories instead of one. In this campaign he quoted "a correspondent of *Harper's Weekly*" upon the advantages of Seattle. The correspondent was himself. And as a crowning decoration for his elaborately frosted publicity-cake, he sent collections of photographs of the Klondike, Alaska, and Seattle as Christmas gifts to all the crowned heads of Europe. This thoughtful attention was gratefully acknowledged by all of them except the Kaiser, who refused to open his package for fear it might contain dynamite.

So Seattle and the Klondike became inseparable in the public mind, the bulk of the Alaska trade was permanently secured for the port, and it has ever since been recognized as the connecting link between the States and Alaska. This publicity campaign is typical of all that Seattle has done to build herself into a city. The Seattle Spirit has always been boldly aggressive, shrewd, and powerful in obtaining whatever it set out to get. One of the first and most picturesque of the city's successful onslaughts was its effort to plant the Territorial University in Seattle. This institution had been allotted two townships of land by the Act of Congress establishing the territory. At each session of the legislature the University and all the other public institutions were parceled out to various competing communities, but since there was usually no money appropriated, the possession of one of these state agencies was an empty honor. So it caused little concern to any one that, in 1861, Arthur Denny succeeded in having the University relocated in Seattle. It had had various sites before, but this time the Seattleites were determined to pin it down permanently. To bring this about, Denny, Charles Terry, and Edward Lander gave for a site the land now occupied by the Metropolitan office-buildings and theater and the Olympic Hotel in the heart of the city. The three University commissioners paid their own money for the first clearing of the site and then opened the two townships of land granted them, selling the 20,000 acres for $1.50 an acre. And from the $30,000 proceeds they built the University, set high on a hill, adorned with stately white entrance columns and surmounted by a belfry covered with tin to make it shine.

But at the next meeting of the legislature a storm of criticism broke. It was declared that the commissioners had no right to sell the land, that Seattle was the worst possible location for a university. An investigating committee was appointed to visit and report. But the Seattle people well knew that a soft answer turneth away wrath. They met the belligerent committee with a brass band, the ladies served an open-air luncheon on the campus, and they made the visit of the investigators the occasion for the dedication of the University with the committee as the guests of honor. With such blandishments and attentions what could the poor men do? They examined Daniel Bagley's books and reported that the affairs of the University had been handled "with commendable economy, prudence and energy." And Seattle kept its University.

Another equally striking example of the potency of the Seattle Spirit came many years later when the city library of 30,000 volumes was burned. Clarence Bagley tells the story in his *History of Seattle.**

In the fall of 1900, just prior to the destruction of the library building by fire, Librarian Smith and Charles E. Shepard had made a trip to the East to visit other libraries and to ask Mr. Carnegie to help Seattle in the way that was then making him famous. They received a cool reception from Mr. Carnegie's secretary. He advised them that Seattle was a hot air, boom city and that he had been so advised by S. A. Perkins,

* Clarence B. Bagley, *History of Seattle* (Chicago, S. J. Clarke Publishing Company, 1916).

of Tacoma, and that he did not consider it worth while to suggest to Mr. Carnegie the donation of any amount for library purposes. So the two Seattle men came back empty handed. And when the fire laid low the Yesler residence, Seattle was not only without a library but saw no way to procure one. In spite of the rebuff the city's representatives had met in the outskirts of Carnegie's office, the members of the board who wished to restore the library after the fire could think of nothing but the Scotchman's gold when their minds grappled with the question of ways and means. It was a natural mental condition, for at that time to think of a library builder was to think of Carnegie. Seattle took a chance.

So the committee wired Carnegie offering to provide $50,000 annually for maintenance if Carnegie would give the library, and he replied:

Sorry indeed to hear of library being destroyed. Seattle should build fireproof next time. Am disposed to give Seattle suitable building if site and maintenance provided by city. Your wire says city would expend $50,000 a year in maintenance which may be an error in transmission.
ANDREW CARNEGIE.

A further interchange took place, and then Carnegie wired:

There is only one point about which I am not clear. What does a city of 80,000 inhabitants need of $50,000 annually to maintain a library? Seems to me that is somewhat more than is necessary for the city to tax itself. Atlanta has more population, and I have allowed that city $125,000 for the building. Presume this would give you a building suitable for present needs, but site should have vacant grounds for additions.

Whereupon the *Post-Intelligencer* wired back:

Increase in population from 1890 to 1900 Atlanta 37 per cent; Seattle 88 per cent. Seattle's population all white and all readers. Actual revenue for 1900 is $30,000. We would like to build fireproof for the future as well as for the present. In less than five years a building costing $250,000 and maintenance of $50,000 will be none too large for our real needs.

And Carnegie replied:

I like your pluck offering $50,000 yearly for library purposes. You may build up to cost $200,000 which I shall provide as needed. We remember our visit to Seattle and kind reception with great pleasure and are delighted to shake hands as it were over this matter. Be sure to have spare grounds about building for additions which Seattle's brilliant future will surely require. Happy New Year to all her people. CARNEGIE.

But when the building neared completion, $20,000 more was needed for equipment, and there was nowhere to get it. So the Seattle Spirit prompted Reverend J. P. D. Llwyd of the board to undertake the delicate mission of going to Scotland, where the Laird of Skibo was shooting golf, and ask him for more money. When Mr. Llwyd alighted at the station, he was surprised to find Carnegie pacing the platform. As Bagley says:

He fell in with the Laird and while he walked he introduced himself and explained his mission. Mr. Carnegie was visibly and volubly agitated. "Why do you follow me to the ends of the earth?" he fairly yelled. "I just came here for the purpose of getting away from such things as libraries." But Dr. Llwyd persisted and continued to pace by his side until he stopped walking and listened to the story of Seattle's predicament, after which he said, "All right. I'll give you the twenty thousand dollars."

And the Seattle Spirit had won again.

Even the barriers of nature have proved to be evanescent under the attack of the Seattle Spirit. Rival cities had always contentedly pointed out the fact that Seattle had no room in which to grow. The city was confined on a narrow neck of land between Lake Washington and Elliott Bay, 26 miles long and a few miles wide. The high hills began almost at the water's edge, leaving only a few level places for business streets, and there was hardly any land along the water-front available for railroad tracks or factories. That these inconvenient barriers would securely bottle up Seattle forever was the confident opinion and hope of Portland and Tacoma. But Seattle thought otherwise. And so did Reginald H. Thomson, an engineer who had come from the East looking for a city in which to establish himself. After examining all the Northwestern ports Thomson came to the conclusion that Seattle offered the best opportunities for growth but that it needed extensive changes. So he settled in the city, studied its topography, and made plans for its remodeling.

Reginald Heber Thomson was born in Hanover, Indiana, March 20, 1856, of Scotch-Irish parentage. His father was professor of mechanical philosophy and mathematics in Hanover College, and later he went to Healdsburg, California, and conducted the Healdsburg Institute. After graduation from Hanover, Reginald also went to Healdsburg and became a teacher of mathematics in his father's school. He followed the profession of civil engineering in California, migrating to Seattle in 1881. He was assistant city surveyor for two years, when he built bridges and sewers. Then he became the locating engineer of the Seattle, Lake Shore and Eastern Railroad, later absorbed by the Northern Pacific, and in March, 1888, he went to Spokane, where he made the locations and built the eastern terminals of the road. After 1889 he did some mining engineering and in 1892 began his long service to Seattle as city engineer. He laid the first vitrified-brick pavement on the Pacific Coast, pushed the gravity water system for seven years until it was adopted and the city spent $3,500,000 to bring its water from Cedar Lake, 26 miles away. He built a municipal electric plant, using power derived from the water project, and planned an elaborate system of lake boulevards in Seattle, unmatched in the world, beginning its development as a modest series of cindered bicycle-paths so as to disarm criticism of his extravagant scheme.

But Thomson's most extraordinary service to Seattle was in performing the Herculean labor of remaking the city's topography. He saw that the city needed easy access at the south to the White and Duwamish river valleys, from which it was cut off by hills. To the north he saw the center of the business district filled with the great bulk of Denny Hill, and he determined to remove this. He saw other areas that must be leveled, and he desired to widen the 60-foot business arteries to 90 feet and to reduce the 35 per cent grades to 3 per cent. To accomplish all these changes he formed a comprehensive plan to tear down the hills, use the dirt to help fill in the tide-lands, and regrade the entire business district.

So vast a scheme, involving a third as much excavation as the Panama Canal, certainly could never have been embarked on by any timid city. It took courage and gusto and the Seattle Spirit to grasp the scope of such a plan and to permit it to be carried through. Although Thomson was often assailed by interests on whose toes he trod, the city as a whole gave him the necessary backing, and he went triumphantly forward to carve out of the hills a new Seattle. A method of financing was devised whereby the owners of property were to pay half the cost and the city the remainder, the work to start when a petition was signed by three-quarters of the owners. Ten years was given to pay assessments, and bonds were issued for the work.

Real-estate values, which had already risen high, were expected to increase sufficiently to pay for the expenditure.

Such a digging and hauling and cutting as began in 1906 was never before seen in any American city. Old methods soon were discarded and hitherto unheard-of ones devised. The hills were sluiced down by hydraulics, powerful jets of salt and fresh water tearing down the clay and hard-pan as easily as it had washed gold from gravel in the mining operations of the past. In the regrade of First Avenue, streets were lowered 17 feet, and 111,000 cubic yards of dirt were used to fill in the tide-lands below. In the Denny Hill regrade 5,000,000 cubic yards of earth were removed. Numerous streets were lowered 100 feet and much property reclaimed for business purposes that had hitherto been of small value. At the south, to get easy access to Rainier Valley, fifty city blocks were cut down, and at Dearborn Street 1,250,000 cubic yards was sluiced into the tide-flats below Beacon Hill.

As a result of these operations Seattle looked for years as if an earthquake had struck it. Buildings perched aloft at uncanny angles; householders came home at night to find that a cañon had been cut in front of their yards which deprived them of access to their homes; and the streets were cluttered with ditches, flumes, machinery, red lanterns, and houses and buildings being moved to more favorable locations. When the Seattle Athletic Club had the hill taken from under it, it merely added two additional stories underneath in the hole that was left; and the owners of the five-story New York block on Third Avenue calmly took out the middle section of the building, moved it to the back, and pushed the front into the remaining space in order to adapt their property to changes in topography. The old Washington Hotel on top of Denny Hill was replaced by the new building on level land at the same site but a very different altitude after the hill had been washed away, and all around it modern buildings sprang up as soon as the contractors finished their work. One iron-works owned a parcel of land under water on the tide-flats which it had purchased for a few thousand dollars; when the filling in was completed, the value had risen to $250,000 a lot.

As if these gigantic operations were not enough to keep him busy, Thomson had built a new and adequate mountain water-supply system, developed a sewage system, and realigned all the piers at an angle so that steamers could move into their berths in a straight line from the mouth of Elliott Bay. And his activities also resulted in increasing the tide-land area, of which considerable had already been filled in by a company building a canal to Lake Washington.

This building of a canal to connect the 25,000 acres of fresh water with Puget Sound had long been a dream of Seattle. In 1853 Captain McClellan reported to Jefferson Davis that such a connection would make this port "the finest naval resort in the world." At the Fourth of July picnic next year Thomas Mercer broached the idea of linking the two bodies of water and of connecting Lake Union with Lake Washington as the first step toward the Sound. In 1860 Harvey L. Pike, drunk with the Seattle Spirit, started to build the big ditch, himself, with a pick, shovel, and wheelbarrow. Seven years later Army engineers reported favorably on the project, and soon afterward Pike platted Union City and reserved a strip of land 200 feet wide for the canal. In 1883 David T. Denny, Judge Burke, and others organized the Lake Washington Improvement Company to connect the two lakes, but the contractor engaged soon struck hard-pan and quit. The concern promised to connect the Lake with salt water by 1884, and sixty-seven Seattle firms subscribed $25,000 toward the project.

When Henry Villard came to Seattle, he ordered a belt line to be built by the Northern Pacific connecting Salmon Bay and the two lakes. And Captain Henry H. Gorringe, who had transported Cleopatra's Needle from Alexandria to Central Park, New York, reported to Villard that the cost of the canal would be $3,000,000. Had not all his energies been absorbed in building the Northern Pacific, Villard might have constructed the canal as a private venture. In 1884 Frank H. Osgood arrived and built an interlake canal suitable for logs and small boats. Six routes for the big ditch were now proposed, and when Washington was admitted to the Union, in 1889, a memorial was presented asking the Government to build the canal. At this time it was decided that all tide-lands belonged to the State, and the State Harbor Line Commission was formed with Colonel William Farrand Prosser and Eugene Semple of Seattle as its moving spirits. The Commission provided that waterways could be cut and the dirt used to fill tide-lands, the party doing the work having first lien on the land to the amount of the expenses plus 15 per cent. Under this regulation a company was started to undertake construction, and the State entered into a contract with it to build a canal from the south end of the Lake to the Sound. The Mississippi Valley Trust Company of St. Louis backed the project with the provision that the city must promise a subsidy of $500,000 on completion, and this amount was quickly subscribed. The Seattle and Lake Washington Waterways Company reclaimed 1,400 acres of tide-land, formerly as much as 16 feet under tide-water, at no cost to the city except for streets and sewers; but after 2,000 feet of the canal had been excavated, opinion favoring the project changed, legal obstructions were made, and the St. Louis financing stopped.

Meanwhile, Judge Thomas Burke was supporting a plan to build the canal at the north end of the Lake, for, he said, "The south canal will create a private monopoly, will charge tolls, will cut a great ditch across the center of the city obstructing traffic and weakening its heart beat; it will expose vessels to dangers of collision and overcrowding and it involves too much excavation." The Chamber of Commerce began to back the northern scheme, and King County secured the canal right of way for $250,000. The Government was again petitioned, and the legislature passed a bill exempting the United States from damage claims for lowering the waters of the lake. Army engineers reported the south canal feasible but the cost prohibitive, the north canal "not advisable at this time," and added, "There seems to be no immediate necessity for any canal at all."

Undaunted by the apathy of the Army, Seattle redoubled her efforts to get the Government to build. The south route was completely abandoned except as a tide-land-filling scheme, and the warring factions joined on the north. After much prodding, Congress in 1901 was induced to appropriate $150,000, and this was the beginning of the end. In 1909 King County promised to do the excavating if Congress would provide the locks and the upkeep. Next year the State platted and sold shore lands to provide some permanent buildings for the University as part of the Alaska-Yukon-Pacific Exposition, which was built around the campus, and when $250,000 was found remaining, it was turned into the canal fund. In 1910, despite objections from other communities, all Seattle factions got together and induced the state legislature to appropriate $1,350,000, and on June 25 the building of the canal was authorized by Congress with an initial appropriation of $2,275,000.

Again the Seattle Spirit had won, and the city soon found itself the possessor of a canal next in size to the one at Panama, with a fresh-water harbor of a hundred miles of shore-line able to accommodate all the fleets of the world. In Lake Union and Lake Washington, ships could load and unload lumber without interference from tides; there were no marine borers to undermine the piling of wharfs and mills; and vessels could easily enter the fresh water to rid themselves of barnacles and other salt-water growths. Since that time there has been some concern over the fact that Puget Sound seems to be slightly infiltrating into the fresh water and destroying its effectiveness as a re-mover of marine growths. But there is no immediate danger, and although it is not likely that the capacity of Lake Washington will soon be taxed by incoming ships, Seattle has the canal, and the Government pays the bills. Banzai!

If Seattle has earned the criticism of her rivals by her cajoling of the State and the Nation into spending money on her harbor, she is entitled to their respect for spending plenty of it herself. She has always had a large mosquito fleet plying to ports on the Sound; she has had extensive coastwise and Alaska trade, a trans-Pacific service initiated by the Great Northern, a lumber trade with South America and Australia, and a grain trade with the United Kingdom and Europe. Before 1910 the capacity of her docks was taxed to care for this commerce, and she began to feel the need of building more modern terminals if she were not to be left in the race for trade. So the formation of the Port of Seattle was authorized by the State of Washington, with credit up to 3 per cent of the assessed valuation of the district, and a splendid development of the port was made, providing docks and equipment as fine as any in the country. Seattle was building for the future, and it is well that she did so, for since that time her population has doubled and her commerce increased eightfold. Moreover, just when the port development was completed, the commerce of the world was temporarily diverted to new routes on account of the World War. The trade of the East Indies and India was forced to abandon the Suez route because of submarines in the Mediterranean and South Atlantic and come through the Pacific, so that the commerce of Seattle swelled until it was second only to that of the Port of New York. By this fortunate circumstance the Port not only repaid its entire investment, but also created a surplus of $1,000,000, and it has since been able to carry on without levying any assessments on the taxpayers.

During the years of Seattle's rapid growth her railroad facilities were constantly being increased, and James J. Hill remained the most important factor in her transportation system. So well had Hill built his road that it was in a position to haul freight at lower costs than either of its adversaries, the Northern Pacific or the Union Pacific; and it was so conservatively financed that its fixed charges and operating expenses were very low. Consequently, it was in a position to control the Northwestern railroad situation and ruinously to compete with the Northern Pacific. Six months after Great Northern trains were put in operation, however, the Northern Pacific went into bankruptcy, in August, 1893, and observers declared that now Hill would be unable to compete with a road which was insolvent and therefore had no longer to meet its ordinary interest-charges.

No such fear was in Hill's mind, however. He went ahead with his schemes to cut down the costs of operation and to build up the country he served to produce more profitable business, and he saw in the bankruptcy of the Northern Pacific a chance to step in and control both roads to the profit of each. It was clear that the only hope for the owners of the Northern Pacific lay in making some arrangement whereby Hill's great genius for railroad operation would be used at least partially in favor of the competing road instead of entirely against it. By recognizing a community of interest and controlling the whole Northwestern empire, both roads could make money; but if they carried on cutthroat competition, each would be the loser, and the Northern Pacific would lose the most. These considerations moved J. P. Morgan and the others who were working out the plan of reorganization to look to Hill for both advice and participation.

After having carefully examined the financial situation of the Northern Pacific and its operating expenses, Hill, in 1895, wrote that by reducing all unnecessary mileage on the road, a very large saving could be made; and he added that if the Northern Pacific could be managed so as to reduce its costs per ton-mile to that of the Great Northern, its profits would be $3,000,000 more a year. Both these statements pointed to the advantages of coöperation. In conferring with Edward D. Adams of the Deutsche Bank, which owned a large block of Northern Pacific stock, Hill said that he saw in Adams' mind "a remote desire for unification of the two properties." And this remote desire shortly was crystallized in the London Agreement of May 10, 1895, whereby the Great Northern guaranteed the payment of the $100,000,000 of Northern Pacific bonds and the interest not to exceed $6,200,000 a year, and received in return half the common stock of the Northern Pacific and a majority of one in the board of directors of nine. But this scheme was stopped by the courts, because joint ownership of competing lines was forbidden by law. To carry out its intent Morgan and his associates then formed a syndicate to reorganize the Northern Pacific and buy its stock, and it was agreed in London that Hill and his friends were to have the right to subscribe for $16,000,000 worth of stock. This gave them a large voice in the management and made possible informal coöperation in the running of the two roads, which was the one thing both interests desired. After this arrangement was completed, Morgan and Hill worked shoulder to shoulder, and the earnings of Northern Pacific began to increase and its operating expenses to fall.

Hill now began to try to get possession of a through line into Chicago and St. Louis, and he and Morgan were in agreement that this should be done so as to open up the markets of the Mid-West and South to the products of the Northwest and the traffic of the Great Northern and Northern Pacific railways. They considered the purchase of the Chicago and North-Western, with its network of lines in Illinois, Iowa, and the Dakotas; the Chicago, Milwaukee, and St. Paul, which was strong in Wisconsin, Minnesota, Iowa, and Illinois; and the Chicago, Burlington and Quincy, which operated in Iowa, Missouri, Nebraska, and Colorado. Morgan was in favor of buying the Milwaukee, and he attempted to do so; but the officers of this road would not sell, and he turned to the Burlington, which was Hill's first choice. Their great rival, Harriman, made a low offer for this property, in consequence of which Hill hurriedly raised his offer to $200 a share, after which the deal was quickly completed. The new roads purchased 1,075,772 shares of capital stock, issuing joint collateral-trust bonds and scrip to the amount of $215,154,000 to pay for it. With this purchase the Hill roads were able to add to their territory and to diversify their freight so that a failure of the wheat or corn crop would not be so devastating to them, and they could compete in rates with ships going from New Orleans or Galveston through the Panama Canal. As a result, business increased so fast that the Great Northern was able to reduce rates from St. Paul to Puget Sound from 10 to 15 per cent, and the Northern Pacific was also able to reduce rates without cutting dividends. And Seattle felt the effects in increasing population and prosperity.

During the fight for control of the Burlington, Harriman purchased as much Burlington stock as possible in the open market and then tried to reach an agreement with Hill to purchase a one-third interest in the road. When Hill refused and bought the road himself, Harriman determined on the bold plan of snatching the Northern Pacific away from Hill and Morgan and thus becoming master of the whole Northwest railroad situation with one brilliant coup. So buying for Harriman began, and before Morgan and Hill knew what had happened, the Union Pacific people owned a majority of all stock of the Northern Pacific. But they did not have an actual majority of the common stock, and Harriman was afraid that the Northern Pacific directors would meet the situation by voting to retire the preferred stock, thus outwitting him, so he ordered 40,000 more common, although the price was very high. Unfortunately for Harriman, this order was not executed, for his brokers thought that since he had a majority of the total shares, the purchase would not be needed. Meanwhile, Morgan cabled from Europe to purchase 150,000 Northern Pacific common, and the stock advanced forty points in two days. The failure of Jacob H. Schiff to execute Harriman's order caused him to lose the control of the Northern Pacific which was within his grasp. But the contest precipitated the panic of 1901, when a large bear group sold Northern Pacific short and was unable to cover after the price advanced fifty points. Then Northern Pacific sold up to $1,000 a share, and other securities were dumped on the market at a fraction of their value.

The question now rose whether the Northern Pacific directors had the right to retire the preferred stock, and in the legal wrangling which followed, Hill and Morgan made peace with Harriman by admitting a number of his friends to the Northern Pacific board. After this there was a general cessation of hostilities, and a trackage agreement was made permitting the Union Pacific to use the Northern Pacific tracks from Portland to Puget Sound.

It was this fear that Harriman or someone else might again disturb the Great Northern interests that led Morgan and Hill to form the Northern Securities Company as a holding company for both Northern roads. This corporation was organized to purchase a majority of the stock of both roads. It was capitalized at $400,000,000, and its directorate included six representatives of the Great Northern, four of the Northern Pacific, and three of the Union Pacific, with two additional members representing nobody in particular. Hill always maintained that it was not intended as an operating concern, but the cry of monopoly was raised, and suits to dissolve the corporation were commenced under the direction of President Roosevelt, who held that it violated the Sherman Antitrust Act of 1890. Finally, on March 14, 1904, the United States Supreme Court ordered the Northern Securities Company dissolved.

Incidentally, Harriman made an unexpected profit from the deal. He had turned in more than a majority of the capital stock of the Northern Pacific to the Northern Securities Company in exchange for its stock, but when it was dissolved, Hill refused to return the Northern Pacific stock. Instead, he made a pro-rata distribution of the assets so that Harriman got for each share of Northern Securities 39.27 shares of Northern Pacific and 30.17 shares of Great Northern. He objected to this, for had he received his Northern Pacific shares, they would have been worth $78,108,000 and produced an annual income of $5,467,560; instead, he received stock valued at $56,709,300, producing an income of $3,969,667. But there came a boom in stocks in 1905 and 1906, and Harriman sold these securities for a gain of $58,000,000. So he profited royally from the transaction in the end and often boasted about the money he made on it.

During these years Hill had been active in many projects of expansion. He had organized a steamship line on the Great Lakes, built

grain-elevators at Buffalo, built a great transfer freight-yard between
St. Paul and Minneapolis, developed the Duluth and Superior terminals, and quietly built and absorbed various short lines necessary
to his system. In all his operations he had made it his business to
know about every detail of the country to be served and its future
possibilities; he had occupied every advantageous position; he had
spent money lavishly on construction to keep grades and curvatures
low. So well did he build that his lines traversed the richest portions
of the country, and his operating expenses were kept so low that no
other road could compete with him.

While carrying on these operations Hill was also importing the
finest cattle in the world—animals which combined high qualities of
both beef and milk production—and giving them away to farmers along
his lines so as to improve the strains of cattle in the Northwest;
and he was advocating diversified farming and planting scientifically
on his own farm to show what could be done. He was backing his
belief that a railroad profits most when the people who live along
its tracks are prosperous, and all his life he labored to prove this
theory, to develop the territory he served, to send people "back to
the land," and to become in fact what he was called, "the Empire-
Builder."

From his boyhood Hill had been fascinated by the Orient, and in
later years he formed a plan to link his railroads with the Far East
by a great steamship line. He sent agents to China and India, and
their investigation showed him that he could build up a profitable
grain and flour trade with Japan and China. He said that if the people of a single province of China could be induced to eat an ounce
of flour a day, it would require 70,000,000 bushels of wheat a year
and would raise the price in the Middle West 20 cents a bushel.
So he tried to obtain a steamship connection with the Orient, and
in 1896 he made a contract with the Nippon Yusen Kaisha which
enabled the combined rail and steamship service to ship freight profitably from as far east as Pittsburgh. Through this arrangement Hill
was able to lay down steel rails in China and Japan cheaper than
they could be obtained from Belgium or Great Britain and to ship
cotton in competition with India. In 1900 the Great Northern Steamship Company was formed, and the *Minnesota* and *Dakota,* the two

greatest freight-carriers in the world, were built to sail from Seattle to the Orient.

Judge Burke summed up Hill's contribution to the Northwest in a speech at the launching of the steamship *Minnesota,* April 19, 1905:

The important event of the launching of the *Minnesota* impresses me like the fulfillment of a prophecy, or the realization of a wonderful dream. It is now something more than twelve years since, in the course of an evening's conversation at St. Paul, Mr. James J. Hill outlined to me a plan, a system of transportation by land and by water which would reach from New York to Yokohama and Hongkong. As the details of the project were laid before me, the boldness of the conception and the colossal character of the undertaking made me think that the author was dreaming or giving me a chapter out of some new Arabian Nights; but, as events soon showed, it proved to be no idle dream, for with unexampled energy and rapidity the new railroad line was pushed forward in its course across the continent, over two great ranges of mountains, across to the shores of Puget Sound. Never before had so stupendous an enterprise been successfully carried through without government aid.

The reputed wise men of the day characterized the enterprise as fool-hardy and predicted disaster as the result. Under the kind of railway management that formerly prevailed, the prediction might have been verified; but a new and original force had arisen in the world of trans-portation and of commerce, one who united in himself the imagination to conceive, the power and energy to execute and the power and wisdom successfully to manage and direct great enterprises, a combination rarely found united in the same person. Long before the last spike was driven on Puget Sound, wise and energetic measures were taken to secure the early and rapid settlement of the country. The best class of settlers from the eastern states and from among the most thrifty and industrious populations of Europe were encouraged to seek homes in the new land by unusually low rates, by timely advice and aid in the selection of the place for the future settlement and by the thousand and one little at-tentions which go so far to smooth the way for the unfamiliar stranger. And now, in less than a decade, what was practically a wild and unin-habited country has been transformed as if by magic into cultivated and productive farms, supporting in comfort and independence hundreds of thousands of people, with houses and villages and cities springing up all along the line of the railway and with the little schoolhouse and the church in sight of almost every farm. . . .

Temporary disarrangements of his plans by unforeseen mishaps dis-turb him but little; he simply commences anew, tries other expedients and is very apt to suceed where a majority of men would have succumbed at the first failure. He is naturally hopeful, is full of resources and is strongly self-reliant; and when his judgment approves a course he is not afraid to stand alone. More than once in his career have these elements in his character been conspicuously shown and almost uniformly have results indicated the correctness of his judgment.

Twenty-five years ago, he found the Northwest, between Minnesota and Puget Sound, practically a wild, uninhabited and inaccessible country. A considerable section of it used to be set down in the old geographies as a part of the Great American Desert. Yet, largely owing to his superior knowledge of the real character and capabilities of this new land, and through his wonderful energy and ability in providing for it, even in advance of population, the most judiciously planned, the most economically constructed and the most wisely managed line that has ever served a new country, that region has, in less than fifteen years, given four new states to the Union with an aggregate population of more than one million five hundred thousand people.

In 1907 James J. Hill resigned as president of the Great Northern, the position in which he high-mindedly refused to take any salary but by means of which he gathered in tens of millions of dollars, and his son, Louis W., succeeded him. He had grown tired of those endless columns of figures and vast masses of statistical detail that he had carried around in his head for years. And it is small wonder, for so insatiable was he for this type of information and so retentive his memory that his mind was a veritable encyclopedia of railroad economics. It is related that he talked so exhaustively to a British railroad magnate on an overland trip that the man excused himself and retired to his state-room completely done in; an hour later a secretary knocked at the weary man's door with a handful of papers covered with figures which Hill said "would continue their conversation." In later years Hill grew increasingly irritable; he threw a telephone through a window, stormed up and down his office, and once fired an inoffensive clerk because his name happened to be Spittles.

In 1906 Hill sold 7,000,000 tons of iron ore in the Mesabi Range of Minnesota to the United States Steel Corporation, and the Great Northern reaped a profit of many millions. He filled his house in St. Paul with art treasures, developing a rare taste in paintings, particularly of the modern French school. Yale gave him an LL.D.; Harvard named a chair of railway economics in his honor. He made many speeches, cultivated his model farms, watched over his pedigreed

THE WEST PORTAL OF THE CASCADE TUNNEL
Courtesy of the Great Northern Railway.

ELECTRIC FREIGHT HAULAGE IN THE CASCADES
A giant locomotive pulling a string of 107 cars. Courtesy of the Great Northern
Railway.

PANORAMA OF SEATTLE'S HARBOR AND BUSINESS DISTRICT

Courtesy of the Seattle Chamber of Commerce.

live stock, continued to attempt to educate the farmers of the Hill domain in crop diversification and stock-raising. He always held that the uplift of American life and standards must come from the great open spaces—the prairies, and he said, "Population without the Prairie is a mob, and the Prairie without Population is a desert." He gave liberally to religious colleges because he thought they would bolster the existing order; gave to the Catholic Church, of which his wife was a member, for the same reason. And on May 29, 1916, he died, with a Roman Catholic prelate at his bedside, although he himself was not a Catholic.

Hill had succeeded in almost all he set out to do, and his motto was still, "Work, hard work, intelligent work, and then some more work." His only failure was his scheme for operating steamship lines from Seattle to the Orient, and this was made impossible by unfavorable legislation governing the American merchant marine and the laws prohibiting railroads from owning steamship lines and making competitive export rates. So his dream of American domination of world shipping and a James J. Hill transportation system encircling the globe was abandoned. On his death his friend Clarence W. Barron, owner-editor of the *Wall Street Journal,* wrote of him:

With a big mind went also a lion heart that never could contemplate either surrender or compromise. Hence, since two stars keep not their motion in one sphere, the inevitableness of the clash with Harriman over the fate of the Burlington. The only adversary that Hill could not down was the shackling influence of restrictive legislation. The narrowness of that put a quietus upon at least two of his largest conceptions—the full scope of Northwestern railroad development through the Northern Securities Company, and the ambition to link up Northwestern railroads with the Orient through the medium of magnificent marine carriers.

If he had only lived to use that keen, crafty brain of his to formulate new schemes of transportation, what might not it have meant to the story of Seattle?

When the fight between Hill and Harriman was settled, the trains of the Union Pacific—or Oregon–Washington Railroad and Navigation Company, as the local subsidiary was called—began to run into Seattle, and a beautiful depot for the road was built near Hill's King Street Station. By this arrangement Hill's Great Northern also had access to Portland over the same tracks. The Chicago, Milwaukee, and St. Paul arrived on March 29, 1909, using the old Snoqualmie Pass and a portion of the right of way of the ancient Seattle and Walla Walla Railroad project, and it made Seattle its Pacific Coast steamship terminal in May, 1909. Thus, the transportation supremacy of the Queen City was assured, and it became the northern center for steamship lines to the Orient, California, and Alaska.

To celebrate the purchase of Alaska from Russia and the discovery of gold in the Klondike, Seattle set out to entertain the world at an exposition which should make Portland's Lewis and Clark celebration look like a poor relation. The work of organizing the Alaska-Yukon-Pacific Exposition was only well begun when the panic of 1907 hit the country, but Seattle went ahead with her project, raised the money, turned hundreds of acres of raw land on Lake Washington into beautiful lawns and gardens, and despite financial difficulties opened on time in 1909. The lovely exposition grounds and some of the buildings were given to the University of Washington.

Panics and depressions may dampen but they do not quench Seattle's imagination. The "Biggest Town of its Age in the World" can always be depended upon to do the surprising thing, to think in terms different from her neighbors, to be more daring and original than her rivals. She delights in upsetting the apple-cart of conventionality and, at critical moments, in releasing that devilish bottle-imp, the Seattle Spirit, to spread consternation and excitement and add to the gaiety of nations. Consider her first university president, Asa Mercer. Surely the leader of higher education in the Northwest, securely ensconced in an administration building of classic dignity—so classic, indeed, that its pillars are still preserved as an architectural inspiration— could be depended upon to uphold the conservatism and ponderosity of the Commonwealth. Elsewhere, yes; but not in Seattle. Asa conceived the scintillating idea that there were not enough likely young women in Washington Territory to supply a proper choice of wives, and that it would be a good thing to import a few boatloads of marriageable ladies from New England and New York so as to give the bachelors a break. Since he was not only a thinker but a man of action, he himself engineered two expeditions, obtaining the help of President Grant and experiencing the double-dealing of the steamship magnate Ben Holladay in the process. After many vicissitudes the ships actually came around the Horn and disembarked their first "Pinafore" chorus at Seattle on May 16, 1864, with the result that to-day many leading families of the city proudly trace their ancestry back to the Mercer girls.

Come forward a few generations, passing by Ole Hanson, that firebrand of one hundred per cent Americanism and death to the I. W. W., and enter the reign of another extraordinary Seattle phenomenon, "Big Bertha," Seattle's woman mayor. The wife of Dean Henry Landes, of the School of Science in the State University, and the sister-in-law of David Starr Jordan, this lady undertook to show the world what a woman could do in municipal house-cleaning. When Mayor Edwin J. Brown, the painless dentist, went to the National Democratic Convention in New York in 1925, Mrs. Landes, as president of the Council, became acting mayor. Everyone was pleased. Bouquets of roses were sent to her desk. Women's clubs rejoiced over their tea. It was assumed that Mrs. Landes would gracefully carry on the routine of government along the accepted lines until her chief returned. She did nothing of the kind. Instead, she started a clean-up campaign which shook the political and criminal life of the city to its roots. When she asked the police authorities to close the gambling and disorderly resorts, she was told politely that it was impossible, that there were a hundred men on the police force itself who were financially interested in these resorts and who were openly breaking the law. She fired them and then cleaned up the city. She did so many other sensational things that by the time Mayor Brown got back he hardly knew his old home town. And at the next election "Big Bertha" was elected mayor of Seattle.

Why the reform wave she started didn't last is best explained by the fact that Seattle is still a frontier community; while it takes momentary delight in any kind of cleansing campaign, it likes to remain an outpost, with all the rip-roaring accompaniments of faro, chuck-a-luck, raw red liquor, and a chorus of Diamond Lils. Its friends the lumberjacks, who save up their summer wages to live in furnished rooms in Seattle during the winter, like excitement. So do the miners, cow-punchers, apple-knockers, sheep-herders, and hop-pickers who flock into the city when their work is done. So do other visitors who come to town from all over the Northwest to spend their money and acquire a headache. As early as 1861 there was a dance-hall "down on the sawdust" where men in town for a time could dance with imported beauties and drink American rye. And that famous Seattle character Mother Damnable had a reputation for hospitality long before gold was discovered in the Klondike. During the Alaska boom days gambling-halls blossomed in rich profusion below Yesler Way, the saloon with the silver and gold horseshoe bar was known clear up to the Northern Lights, and Seattle boasted that Billy the Mug's was the toughest joint on the Coast. And now, although hard times have hit the skid-row, the same district is still full of tawdry replicas of the old gaudy palaces, and when there is another boom, they will return in all their sinister glory.

Seattle's political mood at present is not one of reform, but of wise-cracking sophistication. And this is typified in a character more extravagantly impossible than the politicians who cavorted so entertainingly before the public in "Of Thee I Sing." Victor Aloysius Meyers was the inconspicuous leader of a jazz orchestra in a downtown café when fame turned upon him her dazzling calcium flare. A pleasant, merry, roistering young man with a nimble wit, he was a favorite with newspaper men, and when an exceedingly large group of candidates had filed to run for the office of mayor, a reporter on one of the papers said, "I guess every one is going to run for mayor but Vic Meyers." "Why not Vic Meyers?" asked another. "Let's get him to run too!"

A hurried telephone call to Victor informed him that if he would go down to City Hall and file for mayor, they would put his name all over the front page of the last edition and he would get more publicity than Aimee McPherson. Victor scrammed, and next day began his momentous campaign for mayor of Seattle. In a series of speeches which were delivered in everything from churches to dance-halls, he told the voters that his reason for entering the campaign was that his wife had just presented him with a son, and he wanted to do something for the baby. "You have heard of gag rule," he said. "Well, this is a gag campaign." He rode on a beer-truck in a street parade at a time when the Noble Experiment was still popular, and when asked by irate good citizens what his stand was on prohibition, he replied, "I think a small saloon would pay." He went to a luncheon club dressed as Mahatma Gandhi, and he included in his platform a pledge to put a flower box on every water-hydrant and free cracked ice on street-cars after midnight. When one of his opponents ponderously declared that he would help relieve unemployment by abolishing one-man street-cars and requiring both a motorman and a conductor on each car, Vic went him one better. "Not only a motorman and a conductor," said he, "but a hostess on each car to serve coffee, dispense good cheer, and introduce passengers. Let's have more jobs for beautiful women."

Vic did not win the election, but he became locally famous. He led the official Democratic orchestra which played when Governor Roosevelt visited Seattle, and he later filed on the state Democratic ticket as candidate for lieutenant-governor. Among the many, his was the best-known name, so he got the nomination. The rest is history. The Democratic landslide tobogganed him into office to become the state's second-in-command, although, as he quaintly said, he didn't know how to spell "lieutenant." He presided over the Senate with rare aplomb, quieting that body when it was in feverish debate by declaring a recess and calling for a few selections from the quartet; he recognized from the rostrum Tacoma's senator, Mrs. Malstrom, as "Ah there, Katherine"; and he suitably represented the dizziest aspects of the Seattle Spirit in the state Capitol. All this while the populace prayed that history might not be repeated. For the preceding two Democratic governors died while in office and were succeeded by the next in line.

These effervescent fizzings of the Seattle Spirit make life happy and bright in the Queen City, and they have helped the citizens to take things easily and yet overcome all obstacles that lay in the path of building the breezy metropolis. Geographic and mental hazards have been surmounted, the harbor has been improved, the canal built, the city regraded, and the rails and sails brought triumphantly together. Now the cable-cars swoop over the high hills to beautiful parks and interlocking lakeside boulevards such as few cities can boast. It is said that the only summer visitor who failed to enthuse over the views seen on a tour of the city was Calvin Coolidge. Years ago his taciturnity chilled the reception committee because they were unprepared for it. He was only Vice-President at the time, so his silence was not then regarded as golden. Perhaps he was absorbing the minute details of his trip and the names and idiosyncrasies of his companions so that years later he would be able to say, as did that ubiquitous advocate of a memory course whose conversation used to be displayed in full-page advertisements in the magazines, "I remember you perfectly. You are Mr. Addison Sims of Seattle, telephone number, Elliott 4914."

Out on Lake Washington is the State University, with one of the most beautiful campuses in the country, a heritage from the Alaska-Yukon-Pacific Exposition of 1909. In front of the City Zoo is a tablet marking the spot where President Harding made his last speech. And in Volunteer Park is a lovely art museum, filled with Oriental treasures, of which Seattle likes to whisper, "The statues in front were stolen from a Chinese monastery and smuggled into this country." Stolen, too, is the totem-pole on Pioneer Place, if one can believe the backbiting remarks of the people of Tacoma, who self-righteously declare their own totem-pole to be a gift from the Indians. Whether these stories are true or not, the Seattle Spirit is quite capable of appropriating whatever it wants and transporting it to the Queen City of Puget Sound. After an article by one of its residents extolling the city had appeared in a national magazine, the editor reported that letters of wrath were numerous. Skagit County complained of the loss of a seed-farm, Bellingham of her fisheries; Wenatchee and Yakima were astonished to find Seattle the center of the apple industry; British Columbia reported gold-fields moved mysteriously south; and Spokane marveled at hearing of Seattle as a mining center. Tacoma objected to the portrayal of Seattle as her kindly big brother, who had made 400 reservations for the opening of Tacoma's tourist hotel, whereas, so the article reported, Tacoma had boycotted the opening of Seattle's tourist hotel, and only three Tacomans had been brave enough to attend. Thus does the bickering between the cities of the Northwest go on. But *Time* summed up the situation when it said, in response to protests over stories emanating from Seattle, "The cause for errors seems to be Seattle's news vigor, reporting the Northwest more actively than any other Northwestern city. Let news vigor increase elsewhere."

Yes, there is news vigor in Seattle and every other kind of vigor required to build a city. Cool and breezy, summer and winter, the Seattle climate makes its people energetic. And it takes energy to overcome the difficulties of constant hill-climbing. Only the vigorous survive. Life to your Seattleite is no flat succession of events. It is a constant going up and coming down. And if the way up is hard, there is always close at hand the reward of an easy and exhilarating descent.

A proud city, rising on her steep bluffs with the blue bay on one side and a chain of lakes on the other, away to the west the jagged snow-capped chain of the Olympics, Seattle has the advantage of living in a room with a view. And when you have once seen the curiously regimented crowd lined up on the broad, high front pavement of the Public Library waiting for the doors to open, you realize the importance of that view. They are not sitting down idly looking at each other, these Seattleites. They are not reading or talking. Instead, everyone faces, as if by orders, to the front; everyone gazes fixedly at the blue waters of the bay below. And just as they watch it, fascinated, from this vantage-point, so they do from everywhere else in town; time and again it is the view to which the eyes of Seattleites unceasingly return. From every terrace of the downtown hills it shows itself, and it is a constant challenge and inspiration and tonic. For it speaks not of calm rural countrysides or pastoral contentment, but of the vast heaving Pacific, and of the Orient, teeming with life, and of far-flung routes of trade. The fresh breeze plays over it and flutters the pennants on the ships in the harbor, and Seattle looks at it and scorns small things and resolves to conquer difficulties and to make herself, more than ever, the "Seaport of Success."

# CHAPTER XVI

## SPOKANE, CAPITAL OF AN INLAND EMPIRE

AFTER a transcontinental speaking-tour a celebrity remarked to some friends in New York that he had found only one city west of the Mississippi where the men wore dinner clothes as if they were used to them. That city was Spokane. And yet this urbane metropolis has developed from a raw frontier town of a few crude shacks built around the falls of the Spokane River within the memory of men now living—and not such old men either. In fact, its whole history as a white settlement embraces only two generations.

Previous to 1871, when the first white settlers came to Spokane Falls, the site of the future city was an Indian camp-ground. The red men gathered there in the broad, open, sunlit Spokane Valley, hobbled their cayuses in the rich bunch-grass, and lived under the shade of the tall pines because it was a most favorable spot for collecting the Indian's staple article of diet, the salmon. Out of the sea and up the Columbia came these luscious red-meated fish, into the tributary rivers of the upper country, swimming the rapids, leaping over small cataracts. But the falls of the Spokane were too much for them; there they were compelled to stop and were easily caught by the Spokane Indians, who banqueted on them in summer and dried them for use in the winter.

Almost the same route between the Pacific and the Spokane country was followed by the early fur traders. In 1810 David Thompson of the Northwest Fur Company, the Hudson's Bay Company's rival in Canada, established Spokane House, a trading-post at the juncture of the Spokane and the Little Spokane Rivers, about ten miles from the Falls. To this attractive post came the trappers of the interior to trade their furs, to replenish their supplies, to dance with Indian girls in the ball-room, to watch horse-racing, to live in the hotel de luxe of their day—a vacation which was described as luxurious but inexpensive.

In 1812 David Stuart was sent from the mouth of the Columbia by John Jacob Astor's Pacific Fur Company to found a trading-post in the same neighborhood. It is recorded that he brought, for trading with the Indians, guns, ammunition, spears, hatchets, knives, beaver traps, copper and brass kettles, white and green blankets; blue, green, and red cloth, calicoes, beads, rings, thimbles, hawksbells, beef, pork, flour, rice, biscuits, tea, sugar, rum, and wine. On the long trip over the Columbia plateau he lived on Indian cayuses, which he bought for five shillings each, an article of diet which became a staple in the sandy waste lands. After the Northwest Company took possession of Astoria at the mouth of the Columbia, the British flag floated over Spokane House. In 1821 the company was absorbed by the Hudson's Bay Company, and three years later Spokane House was abandoned for a location nearer the Columbia at Colville.

After the white men abandoned their post, the Spokane Indians continued to inhabit the valley, their main village and the home of their chief, Spokane Garry, so named by Governor George Simpson of the Hudson's Bay Company, being near the site of Spokane House. To the south and east were the Yakima, Cayuse, and Walla Walla Indians; to the north there was a small tribe of Cœur d'Alenes; further north lived a few hundred Pend' Oreilles; and to the east the great tribe of the Nez Percé Indians extended across Idaho to the plains of Montana.

Lewis and Clark in their western explorations never touched Spokane Falls, and, in fact, few white men showed any interest in this happy hunting-ground of the Indians. But in 1853, when Isaac I. Stevens came to be governor of Washington Territory, he visited all the Indian tribes in order to make treaties between them and the Great White Father at Washington, and he explored the country thoroughly. Of the Palouse and Big Bend districts, later to be agricultural tributaries of the city of Spokane, he wrote: "This country's better supplied with wood than has been generally imagined. If the voyageur traveling over this country, whatever routes he takes, be asked what sort of a country it is, he will tell you an excellent country for traveling—wood, water and grass everywhere."

But although Lewis and Clark did not visit Spokane Falls, they had penetrated the country near it, and in their contact with the Indians they had interested them in the marvelous book of the white man, the Bible. Christianity had first been introduced among the Flatheads between 1812 and 1820 by a wandering band of Iroquois from the Caughnawaga Catholic Mission near Montreal, who remained and intermarried. From the seeds of religion planted by Ignace La Mansse, the Iroquois leader, long before any missionary organization had planned to enter the Oregon field, the Flatheads came to desire that the "black robes," the Catholic priests, of whom they had been told, should come to bring them the message of Christianity. In 1831 five Nez Percés and two Spokane Indians journeyed eastward to St. Louis to get "the book" that would solve all their troubles and make them as great as the white man. All but one of them died on this trip, but he returned to tell the wonders of the white man's civilization. Moved by this touching story, Catholics sent Father Peter de Smet and others to be missionaries to the Northwest Indians. Methodists sent Jason Lee, and the Congregational, Presbyterian, and Dutch Reformed churches jointly sent Samuel Parker, Dr. Marcus Whitman, and Cushing Eells. "Father" Eells began the first mission among the Spokane Indians, "who spoke in such harsh gutturals that it sounded like husking corn." By 1848 no Indians had been converted, though they listened respectfully, and the work among the Spokanes was abandoned because of the murderous hostility of the Cayuses. Father Joseph Cataldo of the Jesuit Order, who had gone to the Cœur d'Alene mission in 1864, established St. Michael's mission near Spokane. For $2.60 an acre he bought 40 acres of land, and there Gonzaga University was opened in 1887.

The mining that was to mean so much to Spokane began early. Before 1854 settlers at Walla Walla had purchased gold from Spokane Indians, and in that year gold was discovered at Orofino, Elk City, and Florence, Idaho. It happened very simply. When the horses of traders were staked for the night to the high bunch-grass, they sometimes pulled it loose and wandered away. On this certain morning the owners were surprised to find glittering particles of gold where roots of grass had been. These gold-strikes marked the beginning of the great fortunes in Portland made by Ainsworth, Reed, and Thompson from the Oregon Steam Navigation Company, for transportation to the diggings was by way of Portland and the Columbia and Snake rivers. The boats landed at Wallula, Washington, or Umatilla, Oregon, or at the head of navigation on the Snake River, Lewiston, Idaho. In times of high water they were sometimes able to advance some miles beyond Lewiston on the Clearwater.

In the heyday of the strikes there were probably 20,000 men in northern Idaho. In 1861 there were 2,000 in Florence; flour sold for a dollar a pound; whisky for $25 a gallon; a meal of hard bread, bacon, and unsweetened coffee for $3; a kettle, $30; a lot with a cabin, $1,000. Joaquin Miller ran a stage line from Florence to Walla Walla, presumably with profit, for transportation charges were high. On a single trip from the Cascades above Portland to Lewiston one river steamboat took in $18,000, with $1,200 more over the bar. But all the profits went to Portland, for as yet there was nothing at Spokane but a small store.

Meanwhile, in 1858 Lieutenant John Mullan, who built the road from Spokane eastward to the head-waters of the Missouri River, reported that one of his French-Canadian trappers had brought into camp several ounces of pure, heavy free gold that he had found in the head-water of the Cœur d'Alene, and continued,

The members of my expedition were very largely old miners from California, and their universal verdict was that the entire country from Cœur d'Alene Lake on toward and including the eastern slope of the Rocky Mountains, was one vast gold-bearing country, and I was always nervous as to the possible discovery of gold along the line of my road; and I am now frank to say that I did nothing to encourage its discovery at that time, for I feared that any general discovery would lead to a stampede of my men from my own expedition and thus destroy the probable consummation of my work during the time within which I desired to complete the same. I then regarded it as of first importance to myself and the public to open a base line from the plains of the Spokane on the west to the plains of the Missouri on the east, from which other lines could be subsequently opened and by means of which the correct geography of the country could be delineated.

The beginning of Spokane goes back to 1871, when J. J. Downing and S. R. Scranton, two stock-raisers and horse-traders from Montana, who, it is said, were also under suspicion as horse thieves, traveling

west looking for a likely town-site, discovered Spokane Falls and
were fascinated by its possibilities. One filed on a 160-acre claim on
the north side of the falls, the other on the south; thus, between them
they owned all the land around the cataract. They started a sawmill,
using first an overshot water-wheel and later a turbine. Two years
later two other adventurous land-seekers, James N. Glover and J. N.
Matheny, of Salem, Oregon, came to the upper country by boat and,
buying cayuses at Lewiston, Idaho, set out to explore the new land.
When he saw Downing's sawmill at the Falls, Glover decided that
this was the place where he wanted to settle. "Directly I arrived,"
he wrote, "Downing came to me for a deal, and I really was in good
humor for a deal, for I was never so infatuated with a place in all
my life." After buying the property for $2,000 and putting Scranton
in charge of it, Glover continues,*

Mr. Matheny and I then returned to Oregon, riding cayuses to Lewiston, and taking stage there for Wallula by way of Walla Walla. At
Salem I contracted for a new sawmill, and had it shipped to Portland
and thence by boat to the mouth of the Palouse River on the Snake. In
the meantime I had formed a partnership with C. F. Yeaton and J. N.
Matheny, and sent them ahead with the machinery, a millwright and a
few other men to build the mill and install the machinery.

When Glover returned to Spokane, he found that Scranton was wanted
by the constables for some infraction of the law, and Glover, realizing
that Scranton was not the type of man who would make a suitable
business partner, bought him out. So this original settler of Spokane
went to Santa Ana, California, later returning to the Blue Mountains
near Dayton, Washington, and running a shingle sawmill there until
he died.

But James Nettle Glover was easily the most important factor
in the early upbuilding of Spokane, and he continued to be a leader
when the village became a metropolis. Born in Lincoln County, Missouri, on March 15, 1837, he went west with his family when he
was 12. After a six months' wagon trip they arrived at Salem, Oregon,
and there they took a donation claim of 640 acres where much of his

* Nelson W. Durham, *History of Spokane* (Chicago, S. J. Clarke Publishing Company, 1912), which is the source of many of the other quotations in this chapter.

boyhood was spent. When he was 20 years old Glover took Oregon apples to the mines at Yreka, California, and opened a fruit-store there. Later he worked as a carpenter. By the time he was 25, he had saved $15,000, and he began to dabble in mining, along with his business of shipping Oregon apples to San Francisco. He became interested in "the upper country" and the mines of Idaho, and this interest brought him to Spokane Falls.

Glover's first enterprise was a store for trading with the Indians, who, he said, were cautious buyers and always watched the scales very closely: "My first stock of goods was made up of cheap blankets, shawls, calicoes, beads, paints (I did a big business in paints), tobacco, sugar, tea and coffee, cutlery, and all sorts of groceries. I never carried powder and lead, and with the exception of an old shot-gun, had no firearms. I frequently loaned the shot-gun to Indians and they would occasionally bring in a deer for its use."

In 1876 Glover bought out Matheny and Yeaton, who were glad to leave, and became the first citizen of Spokane indeed. At this time, said he,

the present business district was a beautiful prairie of bunch grass and sunflowers, and when the flowers were in bloom they made a sea of gold. I kept a horse staked out there all the time for emergency. One bright beautiful morning in June, 1875, an Indian named George, half brother to Curley Jim, rode up in great excitement, his horse in a foam of perspiration, and told me that he had seen a squad of white men coming up from White Bluff prairie down the Hangman Creek slope. He described them and I knew they were surveyors. I told him to rest a moment till I could put a saddle on my horse, when I would go with him. We went down the road . . . and pretty soon I met Till Sheets and his party of two linemen and two blazers. I introduced myself and he said: "So you are the man they call Jim Glover? I'm trying to locate you. I had a contract from the Government to survey three townships on Crab Creek. After I completed that work I said to my men that Jim Glover is at Spokane Falls and don't know whether he is afoot or ahorseback. I told them that if they would give me their time I would board them and would run a base line and show Mr. Glover where he is." *

The line being run, it was made certain that Glover was rightfully located on government land, much to his delight:

* *Ibid.*

From the beginning I had refused to deal in liquors, but when I bought my second bill of goods from Barney Goldsmith he asked me if we had any rattlesnakes up at the Falls. I replied that there were none at the Falls but I had seen two or three in the rocks west of there. Mr. Goldsmith then said that as I had been a pretty good customer he was going to make me a present of a barrel of whiskey. I accepted, but afterwards I regretted I had done so, as I had heard the Indians could smell liquor a great distance. When the barrel of whiskey arrived I built a little closet in my store just big enough to hold it, and boxed the barrel in, and nailed it up solid. I never tapped that barrel till Surveyor Sheets came in, but then I felt so grateful that I ripped the boards away and gave him and his men all they could drink.*

With his claim validated by the survey, Glover platted the town of Spokane, naming the streets after Washington, Stevens, Sprague, Howard, Lincoln, Madison, Monroe, Jefferson.

This was the period when the Indian uprisings were finally settled. For years the Indians and the whites had fought each other. In 1847 the Cayuses massacred Marcus Whitman and his family at Walla Walla while he was treating them for measles and typhoid, the immediate reason being that they thought he was trying to poison them. In 1855, when Governor Stevens concluded land treaties with some 6,000 Indians at Walla Walla, the Walla Walla Indians planned to kill him but were dispersed. Yakima Indians murdered several white men. Seattle was attacked, and there was a plan to unite all the Indians in eastern Washington to drive out the white men. Colonel E. J. Steptoe at Fort Walla Walla put down an uprising in 1858, and in the same year Colonel George Wright began a campaign of reprisal with 700 cavalry near Spokane. His terms after repulsing an attack by Chief Garry were unconditional surrender. Colonel Wright's campaign resulted in quieting the Indians for many years, but in 1877 Chief Joseph of the Nez Percés fought the whites to save his ancestral Wallowa Valley, which had been taken from him through treaties negotiated by various interior Indian tribes with Governor Stevens. When the government forces, headed by General Oliver O. Howard, moved in on Joseph's territory, the Indians held a council of war near what is now Grangeville, Idaho, and then massacred the people of Cottonwood, Idaho. After other massacres on the Salmon River

* *Ibid.*

and at Camas Prairie, United States cavalry under General Nelson A. Miles drove the Indians into the mountains, marching 1,500 miles, losing 105 officers and men, and definitely quelling the Indians for all time.

Glover's relations with the Indians during these years were quite friendly, however:

From 1873 to 1877 my trade was almost entirely with Indians who brought in furs. I have bought as high as $1,000 in one night. The Indians are peculiar in their ways of doing business, doing their trading almost invariably at night. My first business in this line was in December, 1873. They came in one evening about sunset, a swarm of them. Up to that time a trading post seventeen miles up the river had enjoyed a monopoly of the Indian trade. This time there was about a foot of snow on the ground, and forty or fifty Indians came into my place a little after dark, with their furs packed on their ponies. They always wanted to have a long smoke before getting down to business. Then they would ask prices and this would be followed by the actual business of bartering wares for furs. The skins I bought were chiefly marten—as handsome a fur as could be bought anywhere. For these I paid from $2.50 to $5.00. . . . I bought some of the most beautiful buffalo hides I have ever seen, forty-five of them for $4 to $4.50. I shipped them by wagon to Wallula and thence by boat by way of Portland to Victoria, paying the freight and receiving only $5.25 a robe. If it had not been for the profit on my merchandise, I would have lost on the transaction. I never could learn the reason, but these fur-bearing animals disappeared like magic and after 1877 my Indian trade in furs fell off to nothing.*

When the first settlement was made, Spokane was merely a trading-place of trappers and hunters, who sold their pelts to the Hudson's Bay Company and the Astors. The successive traders at Spokane House before the Oregon Country became a part of the United States. The town did not develop very rapidly until the Northern Pacific arrived in 1881.

But in the meantime Spokane was slowly growing. In 1877 L. W. Rima arrived to open the town's first jewelry store, certainly

an act of sublime confidence, for assuredly the immediate prospect of a demand for diamonds and gold watches could not have been alluring. . . . In April, 1878, came A. M. Cannon and J. J. Browne from Port-

* *Ibid.*

land, then the metropolis of the broad Northwest, with a population of about 15,000, exclusive of Chinese, of whom the town held several thousand, lured there by railroad construction. The newcomers were to play conspicuous parts in the great drama of city building and it may well be doubted if two men, better fitted by courage, enthusiasm, and knowledge of western life and western conditions, could have been found either east or west to take up that work and carry it forward to success and brilliant achievement. Both men had limited means and were in a sense soldiers of fortune. Mr. Cannon had led an adventurous life since early manhood. When a young man he had gone to Chicago and made and lost a considerable fortune on the grain exchange. From Chicago he drifted to the Pacific coast by way of Kansas City and Denver. In Portland he engaged in the business of selling sewing machines, but suffering there from sciatic rheumatism he made up his mind to seek health and fortune in "the upper country," concerning which he had enticing reports, both in respect to its scenic beauty and its natural resources. Mr. Browne's activities had been divided between the law and education, and he had served a term as County Superintendent of Schools at Portland. He was attending court at the Dalles, Oregon, when Mr. Cannon, on his way to Spokane, encountered him and persuaded him to join the scouting expedition.*

These men plotted the town-site in 1878, and three years later, when the town had a population of about 1,000, it was incorporated.

Seeing an opportunity to get some good citizens and town-boosters, Glover sold the two men nearly a half-interest in his properties for $3,000. And since they had little money, he accepted a cash payment of $50. Cannon engaged in the store business for a while and then astonished his neighbors by opening a bank. He told the surprised Glover, "You know better than I do that I haven't got a dollar, but Mrs. Pope, a sister-in-law, had a thousand dollars and agreed to loan it to me. There's no business now here for a bank but the N. P. is coming this way with its grade and construction and there will be all sorts of time-checks and other checks to cash, and I thought I might as well get in and be ready to take care of it."

Realizing that the railroad that was building west would bring the town new commercial importance, Glover himself soon organized the First National Bank of Spokane, with a capital of $500,000. It was not long before his friend Cannon had to call on the new financial power for help for his bank was in difficulties. When Glover went over

* *Ibid.*

to examine the books, he said he "found a most desolate and woe-begone situation. Twenty-five cents was all the cash on hand. I asked Cashier Bennett why he had not bought a drink with the two bits and he replied that it belonged to the bank." But Glover advanced $5,000 for the collateral Cannon had on hand, and so the first bank of Spokane was saved from disaster.

Francis A. Cook came in 1879, and Glover gave him a lot on which to open the town's first newspaper, the *Weekly Times*. But they quarreled, for Cook held that Spokane should be spelled as it is pronounced, without the final *e,* and Glover, Browne, and Cannon felt so strongly that this was false doctrine that they sent to Portland for a printing plant and set up a rival paper under an editor named Carlisle, the Spokane *Chronicle.* All these activities were inspired by the growth that the coming of the railroad was bringing to Spokane Falls, and those who were the leaders of the town dreamed of a day when the old Indian fishing-ground would become a great city for the white man. It was said that Father Joseph Cataldo had as much influence as anyone in getting the railroad officials to route their line through Spokane. This vigorous Catholic priest insisted that the Spokane Valley route was far superior to the one 50 miles south, and his advice probably had great weight, for in later years railroad engineers preferred the southern route.

Every move of the Northern Pacific was closely watched, and excitement knew no bounds when, on Saturday, June 25, 1881, came the event that the town's citizens had long awaited. On that historic day the first train of the Northern Pacific Railroad rolled into Spokane and the frontier capital of the Inland Empire was at last connected with the effete East.

To General John W. Sprague, western head of the railway at Tacoma, the enthusiastic citizens sent this telegram:

The track of the N. P. R. R. is completed to our town and we give it a most hearty welcome. Having here a water power equal to any other in America and a country capable of producing many million bushels of grain annually, with fine building stone, lime, lumber, undeveloped mines, etc., we need but adequate railroad facilities to make another Minneapolis. And to you and your associates who have this day connected us with the outside world by rail, and have done and are doing so much for the development of this great country, we extend our most sincere and cordial congratulations.

To which General Sprague replied: "Thanks for your complimentary telegram. I congratulate the citizens of Spokane Falls on completion of the railroad to their fine town. May your prosperity exceed your most sanguine anticipations." To Portland also the citizens sent greetings, wiring Mayor P. P. Thompson: "Today we welcome to Spokane Falls the track and train of the N. P. R. R., thus connecting the future manufacturing center of the great Northwest with Portland, its commercial metropolis. Spokane Falls again sends greetings and congratulations to Portland." And the Mayor replied: "Portland congratulates Spokane Falls on being connected by railway with the navigable waters of the Columbia, and will, within one year, be connected with Portland by rail. Your prosperity is assured."

Spokane was now a fine, clean little city of 1,200 people, with broad streets and so well situated on a gravelly plateau sloping easily to a high wooded bluff at the south that Henry Villard had called it "the handsomest town-site I have met since leaving the East." Nor did the citizens hide their light under a bushel. With the coming of the first railroad assiduous efforts were made to attract settlers, and the talents of the town's most gifted writers were employed in extolling the advantages of Spokane and the Inland Empire. This is a fair sample of the descriptive circulars of the day:

For the most part the inhabitants are eastern people of means and mostly, full of enterprise, energy and thrift, and a stranger, invited to one of the social gatherings, and judging by the manners, the sentiments expressed, or by the dress of the ladies and gentlemen, could not distinguish any difference between this and the best society of eastern or western cities.

Spokane Falls never segregated that class generally found in isolated western settlements, and today can boast of having a society equal to almost any town or city of its size in the east. . . . The people have leisure, means and disposition at hand for the embellishment of their homes and grounds, and the exception is to find citizens not engaged in planting trees and shrubbery, cultivating flowers, rearranging the box houses into tasty modern cottages, or converting them into really fine and handsome residences. Fences have been placed about most of the lots, lawns laid out, and every advantage taken of the natural surroundings to beautify. Within all these houses the modern civilizers,—music, pictures, books, newspapers are found in profusion. There are four churches and five congregations. The Catholics have located a college here (Gonzaga), which is to be a companion institution to the one in San José, California. It is also the location of the Rodney Morris School, Episcopalian, and special pride of that denomination. Less than one hundred citizens have subscribed $5,575 for a bridge across the river; $3,700 for a Catholic College; $4,000 for a Methodist College; and several thousand dollars for churches, schools and other public enterprises.

A rapturous description of scenic beauties is included:

The beauty of Ladore, the poesy of Minnehaha, and the majesty of Niagara are mingled in the falls of the Spokane, as, breaking abruptly from the level upland, they bound forward over a steep incline and are divided into several distinct cataracts by promontories of basaltic rock, around which the suds-white waters rush with busy pertinacity, their speed augmented by the impulse of the nearby mountains that is still strong within them as they surge, swell, rush, roar, sing, leap, dance, and do everything else but tarry, in their wild endeavor to meet the waters of the Columbia and move on with them toward the distant ocean.

It is no exaggeration to say that Eastern Washington presents the combined landscapes of Switzerland and Italy, the highlands of Scotland and the English lake region, the whole forming a panorama capable of expressing every type and emotion of scenic beauty. No region can excel it in variety and grandeur; its undulating surface displays the rolling prairie and the elevated plateau, the picturesque dingle and the dense forest, the brooklet and the mighty river, the ribbon-like fall and the seething cascade, the sloping motion-giving hill and the towering mountain, whose crest is enwreathed with garlands of perpetual snow. There is no end to the anomalies of nature in this great stretch of country, of which Spokane Falls is alike the threshold, the gem and a sub-specimen; and the tourist to whom the fashionable haunts of the Atlantic states and the charming scenery of Europe are familiar, and who presumes from this fact that he has enjoyed all the scenic beauties of nature worth beholding, will readily learn how fallaciously he has reasoned should his footsteps ever guide him to this part of the great Northwest.

Those who travel in quest of pleasure or health will find here an area which in serenity of climate, richness of color, variety of pastoral scenery, luxuriance of mountain shrubbery, extent of forests, nobleness of rivers and grandeur of snow shrouded mountains, will compare with any in the world.... This grand scene, illumined by the mellow light of the evening sun, produces a picture which cannot be excelled in color, breadth or motion. It presents, at a coup d'œil, contrasts of light and shade, tranquillity and energy, action and repose, yet all blended harmoniously together.

After this flowing and highly imaginative picture of the Spokane countryside, the prospective settler was told of the fortune that awaited him:

It is hardly possible for one coming here to miss it. A thousand chances are open. Trade is nowhere better. The times are good and money plenty and cheap. Wages are high and land can be got for the asking. The opportunity for business enterprise includes the establishment of wholesale houses at suitable points. It is safe to say that every immigrant that finds his way to the Spokane country is certain to have some others who will join him here. This alone will bring thousands.

And it is a good country to come to, because it is one of not only great possibilities, but probabilities. There is about it something real, solid, hopeful. To those in Eastern states, unused to the bustle of frontier life, and ignorant of the causes at work to produce these effects, our pen pictures may seem flashy and highly tinted, but . . . during the next quarter of a century, here will be the theatre of the most stupendous public and private enterprise which the world ever saw. Fortunes will be made and children of another generation will enjoy the luxuries of limitless wealth. Careful investments cannot fail to be profitable. Cities yet unborn will be built and populated where now the prairie is unbroken. The history of the development of the states of Ohio, Indiana, Illinois will be repeated here. There is no other country as the Spokane, so near the markets and so fertile, where land can be had for the asking. There is, in fact, no other prairie country in the great Northwest that is not already cultivated, and in the light of this fact, what argument is there against its rapid settlement? It is now time to look at the matter without hesitation. The doubtful period is past. Others have gone through the period of anxiety and the thorns of pioneering are removed. There is nothing now but to come and occupy the land, rejoice in its prosperity and watch its career, so well begun.

And the country did grow. The rolling hills of the Palouse country, where the soil was so rich and black that it turned to gumbo mud in which horses floundered and wagons sank in the rainy season, began to blossom forth with wheat-fields. The fertile shore-lands of the Snake began to show a few scattered patches of green, the Big Bend country became a grazing-place for live stock. And Spokane was not the only town in the locality. Cheney, the railroad division point, named after Benjamin P. Cheney of Boston, a director of the

Northern Pacific, was an enterprising town, full of "go-aheaditive-ness," which put on very superior airs when Mr. Cheney donated $10,000 to found the academy that in later years became the State Normal School. Indeed, the obstreperous Cheney-ites became so obsessed with their own importance that, through a campaign of skul-duggery, they stole from Spokane the ballot-boxes of the election to choose a county-seat and declared Cheney to be the legal site of the court-house. Since the boxes and all the records and some of the county officials had been transferred to the rival city while Spokane was disporting itself at a wedding dance, nothing could be done about it. And Cheney retained the county-seat for several years, when another election triumphantly returned it to the city at the Falls.

Sprague, named after General Sprague of Tacoma, was another rival, and of it a contemporary historian wrote:

Two months ago you could have bought the whole townsite for $500. Now, ordinary lots bring this. The reason for this rapid rise and the up-building of the town is that the company shops and headquarters buildings are located at this point. These buildings are about as extensive as those of the Central Pacific at Sacramento, California, and here will be employed between 200 and 300 men. The headquarters, or general office building, about completed, is the finest owned by the company in the Northwest.

The Northern Pacific continued to push its line westward. By 1882 the track was laid to Clark's Forks, 500 miles from Portland, and at Wallula, on the Columbia, it had connected with the Oregon Railway and Navigation Company. Moreover, Henry Villard had promised to build branches from Spokane. In New York he told Army officers that he would build a road from Spokane Falls to the Columbia north of Colville, because the Canadian Pacific would come within 200 miles of Colville and would get river traffic from that point. Spokane was held to be the logical connecting-point between San Francisco, Portland, and the great north country. Lured by all this railroad development and the promise of free land, settlers came in droves. It was announced from Spokane that a typical settler, who had arrived with $500, had filed on a government claim, fitted out his farm, built a home, paid for everything, and in two years had a surplus of $639.

But with every Columbia River steamboat line and every train bringing loads of people, it was found necessary, as in other frontier communities, to discourage the idler and the ne'er-do-well. In a pamphlet issued from "The Steam Press of Himes, the Printer," in Portland—that same George Himes who later became the distinguished secretary of the Oregon Historical Society—we find this warning:

Idlers will go from bad to worse, and adventurers will not prosper. Individuals unwilling to work or accustomed to live by their wits are not wanted. It requires health, labor, courage and persistence to succeed here. In this region money don't grow on trees and most honest people get it only by the sweat of their brow. Still there is enough filthy lucre in these parts to supply a moderate amount to every industrious, energetic person who is rightly anxious to work without being particular as to the kind or the wages. Idlers, spendthrifts, intemperate men, slow going, sleepy headed customers, may as well stay where they are, for neither the people nor the country will welcome them or fling fortunes into their laps. If you are wide awake and full of go ahead, come along and reap your share of the prosperity. If you have always been left in the lurch, or had your eyes almost cheated out of you wherever you have lived, don't come here to experiment, for the result would likely be the same.

But, despite the warnings, men of every class and type, including the adventurous and the ne'er-do-well, were drawn to Spokane. For the town became the capital city of the Cœur d'Alene gold-rush. The Cœur d'Alene country came into prominence when A. J. Prichard walked into the office of the Spokane *Review* in 1883 and threw a buckskin poke full of nuggets and coarse gold on the editor's desk. Greatly excited, the editor, Frank Dallam, published an extra with head-lines in his largest type, and the rush was on. Prichard was a freethinker, and he invited liberals and atheists to join him in taking possession of the new country. At least fifty came and Prichard obtained powers of attorney from hundreds of others, locating the best claims for them; these claims of non-resident owners were afterwards "jumped" by new-comers, creating endless litigation. At this time Henry Villard was pushing the Northern Pacific through the Spokane country, and in order to show his bondholders what riches he was tapping, he published a very optimistic circular which resulted in a midwinter rush in 1883, when the new-comers endured much hardship and suffering. The pamphlet declared that

The claims are very rich.... Nuggets have been found that weigh $60, $100, $166, and $200. The ore taken from veins shows a great amount of free gold; in fact it fairly glistens.... The mines surpass in richness and volume the most fabulous quartz and placers ever discovered, even the famous deposits of Potosi being inferior to those which underlie the mountains of the Cœur d'Alenes. As the mines of the old world, some of which have been worked since the eleventh century, are still employing thousands of men, the conclusion to be drawn regarding the Cœur d'Alenes, a region far superior in every way, is that they are inexhaustible, and although thousands may work there, there will still be room for thousands more.

After this exploitation by the Northern Pacific a tremendous boom began, and Spokane and other small towns started to compete for the business of the Cœur d'Alene. The mining town of Eagle is thus described in 1884 : *

The buildings are composed of logs and shake. Great tents with gaudily painted signs loom up in endless variety, from within which come the sound of revelry and strains of music, the click of chips and metallic clink of hard cash as it passes over the bar. The streets and public places are thronged day and night with miners and prospectors waiting for the snow to disappear. Then there are the packers and transient population, a tough looking crowd, but very orderly, who stand around enjoying the luxury of a sun bath.

On the corners are knots of men talking mines and mining, and criticizing the specimens that pass from hand to hand. The stores are thronged with men discussing the localities and merits of the last new thing in strikes. The report of a pistol shot will bring a hundred men to their feet in an instant, and the saloons will disgorge twice as many more in the same moment, all on the alert to catch a sensation. Then there are the arrival of pack trains and toboggans in a more or less advanced stage of dilapidation from hard usage on the trails.... We have two banks, several stores and more saloons and lodging houses than you can shake a stick at.

By 1884 Spokane was a town of between one and two thousand people, of whom it was said, "What they were lacking in numbers they made up in energy, perseverance and pluck." They established a stage line to the Cœur d'Alene and tried to take the mining business away from Rathdrum, Idaho. Thousands were now riding to the

* *Ibid.*

mines or walking, carrying their packs, but there were quite as many disappointed treasure-seekers returning. For a moment, indeed, it began to look as if the possibilities of new strikes had been exhausted. But at the beginning of deflation, in 1885, an event occurred which made the Cœur d'Alene country once and for all. Two men in the mining district, T. J. Cooper and O. O. Peck, had grub-staked a miner, N. S. Kellogg, with $18.75 worth of food and tools and a Mexican burro. After 60 days of wandering he brought back some peculiar-looking ore samples which were regarded as worthless; but one experienced miner, Phil O'Rourke, saw that they were similar to the sulphide ores that had made Colorado rich. So O'Rourke and "Dutch Jake" Goetz turned their supplies and packhorses over to Kellogg, who served notice on Cooper and Peck that he had a new grub-stake. Then the three began to search for the source of the ore that Kellogg had found, and suddenly they stumbled on a vein of pure, lustrous silver-bearing galena, a vein which later became famous as the Bunker Hill Ledge.

Kellogg wrote out the location notices, and next morning he ran into the old white burro that Cooper and Peck had given him, which had wandered away on his first trip. The three men loaded the burro and went up the gulch. Then Kellogg thought he had better not be named as a locator or Cooper and Peck might claim a part-interest in the mine. Accordingly, the former notice was thrown away and a new one made out in O'Rourke's name. When the party arrived at the mining camp of Murray, the news of the discovery threw the inhabitants into a furore. Among those who hurried to the scene of the strike were Cooper and Peck, who found the old location notice that Kellogg had thrown away and learned that their burro had been used by the prospectors on their last trip. So Cooper and Peck sued for an interest in the discovery, and the judge held that "the real discoverers of the Bunker Hill were Phil O'Rourke, Kellogg, and the jackass." The locators appealed the case, but while it was waiting for trial, along came Simeon G. Reed, the Oregon transportation king, and made so large an offer for the mine that they gave Cooper and Peck $76,000 for a clear title. Reed was said to have paid $1,250,000 cash for the property. He soon sold it to Darius O. Mills and others of San Francisco, and John Hays Hammond, who was later to be-

THE FALLS OF THE SPOKANE

Lithograph after a drawing by J. M. Stanley, in Isaac I. Stevens, *Supplementary Report of Explorations for a Route for the Pacific Railroad from St. Paul to Puget Sound*, 1855.

THE NORTHERN PACIFIC BUILDING WESTWARD OVER THE PLAINS

Engraved after a drawing by A. R. Waud, *Harper's Weekly*, 1875.

EARLY SPOKANE

The Northwest Magazine, 1887.

come famous as chief engineer in Cecil Rhodes' South African gold-mines, became superintendent.

Prospectors continued to make rich strikes in the Idaho mountains. The great Hercules Mine was opened up by a barber and a milk-wagon driver, financed by the small earnings of a school-teacher. They were the laughing-stock of all the practical miners, for the formation looked hopeless, and they began to think so too when they ran into "white ashes" and stopped, only to begin again, feverishly, when experts pointed out that the white ashes composed one of the largest silver-lead veins ever uncovered in Idaho.

Under the impetus of all these rich strikes Spokane had come to be an important mining center. And it was honored with a visit from Henry Villard, General U. S. Grant, and the other distinguished members of an official Northern Pacific inspection party. At this time the town was a real bit of the wild and woolly West. J. D. Sherwood describes it as it was in 1884: *

There were cowboys from the Big Bend who gave us interesting exhibitions of horse breaking and pony racing, miners loading their pack trains; Canadian boatmen from the Upper Columbia buying merchandise to smuggle across the line; Chinamen selling fine gold washed from the sands of the Columbia; lumber-jacks and ranchers all buying and trading or blowing in their savings for a good time. . . . Shooting scrapes were not uncommon. I remember one night about ten o'clock hearing considerable hilarity in a saloon opposite. Looking in, I saw a man butting his friends with his head, apparently having great fun over it. A few minutes later he butted some surly cuss who pulled a gun and shot him dead. One summer afternoon the town was enjoying a German picnic . . . ; suddenly a messenger reported a man had been killed by Indians. . . . A posse of volunteers was formed which started in hot pursuit. The picnic was then resumed without further interruption. . . .

A thing quite common, which always gathered crowds on the streets, was a squaw fight in which two squaws would go for each other tooth and nail, until their fierce hair-pulling contest was stopped by the police who lodged the maidens in the Skookum House as the jail was then called. At certain seasons of the year the Indians assembled in Spokane for their pow-wows. Their faces painted yellow and red, attired in colored blankets, they presented a picturesque appearance. . . . They would play cards for days and gamble away all their chattels, including their ponies and

* *Ibid.*

the blankets on their back. The Indians were generally quiet and peaceful unless furnished with liquor which they were always eager to buy. To sell them whiskey had always been a criminal offense but they often managed to obtain lemon or vanilla extract from some unthinking grocer which contained enough alcohol to produce the same dangerous effect.

By 1889 Spokane had 15,000 people and was bright with electric lights, the power for which came from the Falls. The lead- and silver-mines, farm-lands, and grazing-lands had all been developed, and all poured their treasure into the capital of the Inland Empire. And just as the old Indian trails naturally intersected at Spokane Falls, so did the railroads, making Spokane the hub of a wheel of branches extending in every direction. In 1881, as president of the Oregon Railway and Navigation Company, Henry Villard began to extend his system northward to tap the upper country. There was an old railroad known as "the Dr. Baker road," because it was built by a man of that name, between Wallula and Walla Walla. The first 10 miles had originally been of wood; subsequently the wooden rails were shod with strap iron; finally steel rails were laid. It was a money-maker from the start, charging $450 per ton for a 31-mile haul. In 1881 Villard completed his line from Portland to Wallula and purchased this road. He built on to Dayton in 1883, to Pullman in 1885, and in 1889 to Spokane. So Spokane was given a second connection with Portland and valuable branches into the rich farming country of the Inland Empire, where, incidentally, Villard had acquired 150,000 acres of land.

Meanwhile, the Northern Pacific had acquired branch lines into the Palouse country to Pullman, Moscow, and Genesee—lines which were to be extended in 1891 to Lewiston, Idaho, at the head of navigation on the Snake River. The people of Spokane had subscribed $250,000 to help build the Seattle, Lake Shore and Eastern, and this road had been built, from Spokane, 40 miles into the Big Bend country. And Spokane's greatest railroad-builder had arrived from the East.

He was Daniel Chase Corbin. Born in Newport, New Hampshire, on October 1, 1836, a brother of Austin Corbin who was president of the Long Island Railroad in New York, he left New England at 19 and went to Iowa as a surveyor of government lands. Later he engaged in land transactions in Omaha and Denver and transported freight in wagons from the Mississippi to Denver and Salt Lake. He was cashier of a bank in Helena, Montana, and became interested in the Far West when he attended the ceremony that marked the driving of the last spike on the Northern Pacific. When the Bunker Hill and Sullivan Mine was discovered, he came to the Cœur d'Alene and erected one of the first concentrating-mills. He was more or less of a sight-seer on his first trip, so he left the Northern Pacific at Rathdrum and took a stage to Lake Cœur d'Alene. The road was covered with mud two or three feet deep, and this suggested to Corbin that a railroad from the Northern Pacific line to the lake would be profitable. At the lake he took a steamer to the mines, and by the time he reached there, he had a transportation scheme mapped out in his mind. In 1886 Corbin built his railroad and bought the steamboat line, and in 1888 he sold it all to the Northern Pacific.

After consummating this deal Corbin went east, but Spokane had no intention of losing such a citizen. James N. Glover soon wrote asking him to return and build for a group of Spokane men a 90-mile railroad toward British Columbia. Gifts of $100,000 were made, and Corbin completed this road, the Spokane Falls and Northern, to Colville in 1889, building branches into Canada in 1891. This property also was sold to the Northern Pacific in 1893, and the road was later operated by the Great Northern. In addition to these lines, the Washington Central had built 100 miles into the Okanagan country, and the Northern Pacific had pushed its road straight through the Cascades to Tacoma, making it unnecessary to reach Puget Sound by the roundabout way of Portland.

Under the influence of railroad-building and mining, Spokane was flourishing. If we can judge from the newspaper accounts of the day, the social life was exceptionally, even overpoweringly, rich. As "Lady Albion" wrote for a local journal: *

Water, earth and air unite to crown Spokane the ideal, the peerless queen of cities.... The Hill is very aristocratic and receives on Wednesdays, when carriages and coupes, hansoms and gurneys, climb the spacious streets and throng the wide avenues with their fair freight. The heavy portière is lifted and the smiling visitor glides into the perfumed presence

* *Ibid.*

of the mistress of the mansion, where, clad in classic robe or dainty empire gown, she nestles mid downy pillows, silken soft. Coals glow in the brazier, and anon a gentle aroma floats through the room from the Russian samovar where the tea is brewing, while fingers like rose leaves stray softly, yet busily, among the dainty cups.

Art, too, had its devotees, and Miss Maria J. C. à Becket, who had "a natural gift for rifle-shooting, and shooting rapids in a canoe," was leader of the artist colony: "Few painters are more indefatigable. All through last winter she rose early, went to church, breakfasted, then painted without rest till a six o'clock dinner; resumed work after that and often remained in front of the easel till one or two o'clock in the morning."

But all these higher things of life were built on the solid and stolid foundation of business activity. Flour- and sawmills flourished, mines and farms prospered, and Vice-President Thomas F. Oakes of the Northern Pacific declared that Spokane had produced more freight during the past six months than any other point on the road's 3,500 miles of line. Then came the great fire of 1889, when the city was laid in ashes, to rise again more substantially built than ever. Sixteen months later, in 1891, $5,000,000 had been spent on rebuilding, and Spokane was as bright and shiny as a new shoe. In this year new mining discoveries were made in Kaslo and Slocan in the Kootenay district of British Columbia, and they poured their dividends into Spokane to help make up for losses suffered in the great fire.

In 1893 came the panic which closed banks and financial concerns and threw the Northern Pacific into the hands of the receiver. Next year Spokane learned that the Government was about to establish an Army post in the vicinity, and she set out to get it. Forty thousand dollars, $15,000 in cash, must be given to bring the post to the city, and despite the depression Spokane determined to win the plum. When all sources of funds seemed exhausted and there was still more than $4,000 lacking, the women of the city arranged for a community Christmas tree, selling tickets which entitled every holder to a present. The donations included such a strange assortment as a mince-pie, rheumatism medicine, a colt, pickles, cigarette tobacco, curling-irons, a harmonica, music and painting lessons, a month's board, a month's shaves, dental and surgical services, a shot-gun, a bull pup, and a case of beer. When the receipts were counted, $4,500 had been raised, and the location of Fort George Wright at Spokane was assured.

The late Nineties was a time of extraordinary agricultural development. In a single week 5,000 settlers passed through St. Paul on their way to the Northwest, and many of these came to Spokane. Land was cheap, irrigation was beginning, Palouse and Big Bend wheats had established themselves in world markets, and Washington apples were already making a name for themselves in the East. In the early Nineteen Hundreds a number of Indian reservations were thrown open to settlement, and the rush to get land was so great that nearly 300,000 people made application at the Government Land Office. From all this activity the city reaped a benefit.

Spokane was now a center to which mining men and promoters flocked from all over the country, and the spacious lobby of the Hotel Spokane was thronged with them. They entertained lavishly, spent their money in Spokane, and invested heavily in its business property. And Spokane played host to the men of the mining camps in ways that gave her a reputation as one of the widest-open towns in the West. Among the attractions were a group of so-called variety theaters, in one of which the well-known vaudeville-circuit owner John W. Considine got his start. The theaters were of the "box-rushing" variety, so-called because gaudily painted ladies met the miners there, got them drunk, and often relieved them of their bank-rolls. So open did this business become that the girls of the various houses paraded on the main streets in open carriages preceded by brass bands. Gambling also flourished, and "Dutch Jake" Goetz, of Bunker Hill and Sullivan fame, owned one establishment where a thousand men could play faro at once, could play and eat steak at the same time without leaving the table. When Jake owned the Cœur d'Alene, a large theater containing three bar-rooms, gambling-rooms, and a Turkish bath, he once got the idea of relieving the boredom of Sunday afternoons by turning over one of the bars for revival meetings; so there, "mingling with the hymns of salvation and the message of religion were the clink of glasses, the maudlin utterances of tipsy men, the noise of shuffling feet and the calls of 'ham and eggs,' 'one egg sherry.' ... The crowd was entertained with selections on the big mechanical pipe-organ while the electric fountain silently winked its myriad of electric lights." * And through the crowd "Dutch Jake," mightily pleased with himself, bustled about inviting all comers to have a drink with him at the bar.

Typical of those who made large fortunes in the Cœur d'Alene and returned to Spokane to build beautiful homes on its tree-shaded streets and tall buildings in its business district was Charles Sweeney. Having come to Spokane in the Eighties and opened a general-merchandise store, he caught the mining excitement and went into the mountains of the Cœur d'Alene country. In 1886 he had opened the Last Chance mine in Wardner, Idaho, and had made very slight profits from it. He continued to work it but lost it in the panic of 1893. His faith in the possibilities of the property continued strong, however, and so he went to F. Lewis Clark, receiver for the First National Bank, which had acquired the mine, and made arrangements whereby the two men took over the Last Chance. As they pushed forward work in the mine, they uncovered rich veins of lead. The price of this metal soon advanced, and they were shortly making very large profits. In 1903 they organized the Federal Mining and Smelting Company, with a capital of $30,000,000 and bought the Standard and Mammoth mines, and continued to buy until they controlled much valuable property in the Cœur d'Alene. At Everett, on Puget Sound, they bought the Puget Sound Reduction Company's smelter, and from the Rockefellers they acquired in the same neighborhood the Monte Cristo Mine, which had not paid up to that time and which has not paid since. They brought into their mining operations, centered in Spokane, John T. Gates, John D. Rockefeller, and other Eastern investors, and they bought much Spokane real estate and banking property. Within five years the Last Chance, Standard, and Mammoth properties had paid $13,000,000 in dividends, and the money had been largely expended in Spokane.

But despite her mines and her agriculture and her lumber, the city at the hub of the Inland Empire did not prosper as much as she thought she should. No second Minneapolis grew up around the falls which produced more electric power than the city's factories could use. And the reason for this comparative lack of growth was, the people of Spokane believed, that iniquitous device of the Northern

* Nelson W. Durham, *op. cit.*

Pacific known as terminal rates. By this arrangement the railroad gave lower rates on freight from the East to its terminals on Puget Sound and in Portland than it did to Spokane. In fact, Spokane was compelled to pay charges on freight from the East which equaled the charge to tide-water at Tacoma plus the charge for hauling the freight back to Spokane. This inequality was justified by the railroad officials on the ground that at Tacoma, Seattle, and Portland they had to meet the competition of ships carrying freight from New York to the Pacific Coast, and so they were compelled to reduce rates to these terminal points. Since there was no competition at Spokane, the railroad could charge more for the short haul to that city than for the long haul to the Coast. This discrimination kept Spokane factories from competing with those in the Coast cities and confined the area in which her wholesalers could sell to the Inland Empire. And throughout this region all the inhabitants were compelled to pay tribute to the Northern Pacific in the form of freight-rates higher than those paid by the people of the Pacific Coast even though the haul from the East was hundreds of miles shorter. The right of the railroads to establish such tariffs had been upheld in 1887 by Judge Matthew P. Deady of the United States court in Portland, who decided that water competition was a factor which justified the charging of higher rates to interior points than to seaports, thus suspending the fourth section of the Interstate Commerce Law.

This injustice rankled the spirits of Spokane citizens, and they sought relief. But their efforts were vain, for the Northern Pacific remained obdurate. Judge with what joy, therefore, they hailed the coming of their deliverer! He was none other than James J. Hill, advancing with his Great Northern to the Pacific Coast and spreading the doctrine of lower freight-rates and abolishment of that unfair, unjustified, and un-American discrimination, the equal charge for the long and the short haul. Hill's arrival in Spokane was the signal for such rejoicing as had never been seen in the Inland Empire. Moses come to lead his people out of Egypt was no more venerated a figure than was the canny gentleman with the glib tongue from St. Paul. The city was overcome by the honor conferred upon it. Everyone agreed that Spokane's troubles were now over. For James J. Hill was certain to set everything right.

On his first visit with the leading citizens, February 14, 1892, Hill was interrogated as follows:

Mr. Hill, if you had come into the country eight years ago and had been the only transcontinental carrier here, would you have pursued the policy of the old road's, adjusting the tariff so that the merchandise brought here from the east would go clear through to the coast, only to be hauled back to the consumer far in the interior, thereby entailing an unnecessary haul of 500 to 1,000 miles twice over a great mountain range?

The answer came with emphasis:

No, I would not. For one reason, I think it would be illegal. I think you people here made a mistake in going before the Interstate Commerce Commission; you should have made a test case, allowed some shipper to refuse to pay more than is paid by the shippers on the tidewater, and then carried the grievance straight into the United States Court. I don't think that a jury of twelve men could have been found to decide that such a charge was legal. In that manner you could have settled this matter in short order—in a day, once the case got before the court.

Now I don't want to appear in the light of blowing my own horn, and yet I like to discuss these matters with the people in frankness and fairness. I regard the shipper as a business partner; we have transportation for sale, and the shipper desires to buy transportation, and the policy of our company has been and will be to make transportation out of the consumer, and to do it more cheaply than water carriers can do the service. ... We shall start in with the lumber rate from Puget Sound of forty cents per hundred, eight dollars per ton. We can make that rate pay, and a number of ships will have the lumber going to foreign countries. If the market demands it, we might be able to do still better. When I talked in this manner before the City of Seattle, some of my friends said that I had made a mistake. Judge Burke was one of these, and when I assured him the rate would be made he declared it would mean wonderful prosperity of the lumber industry of the Pacific Coast.

Continuing, Hill pointed out the absurdity of the railroads having to reduce rates to meet the lower charges of water competition:

The people have an exaggerated idea about the cheapness of water carriage. Why, you might build a canal ten feet deep right alongside the Great Northern Railway from one end to the other and we would still do the business. You appear surprised, but consider that with such a line as we are building a train crew of five men can take along, at a speed of 15 miles per hour, 800 tons of merchandise. To do that on a canal would require three to five canal boats, and three to five crews of men, and even then they would plod along at about a three-mile gait.

But Hill was not without doubts as to whether the Great Northern could come to Spokane at all. The citizens blanched and quailed when he intimated that the road might be compelled to pass by a few miles away. But such, indeed, was the possibility unless certain friendly acts were performed by the people of Spokane. Said Hill,

You have no idea how hard your city is to get into and out of. There is little or no trouble in building in here on a one and one-quarter per cent grade, but that is a quarter of a per cent higher than we desire to go. With the exception of this short section, of a few miles on either side of your city, the maximum grade from the Columbia River to the Upper Kootenay is only six-tenths of one per cent. Now, have you any notion what the increase of a quarter per cent in a grade means? I will explain it to you. We are surveying, building and equipping our road so that we can run trains of thirty loaded cars over it. This makes a total weight of one thousand tons, the cars themselves weighing four hundred.

The extra quarter of one per cent is equivalent to having to lift one thousand tons thirteen feet in the air for each mile of road traversed. This takes more power, and in the end costs a very great deal of money, while the single object we have always had in view in building our road has been to make it the cheapest operated transcontinental railroad in America. So you can see that here is one thing that requires careful figuring. So as to avoid it, and yet come into Spokane, instead of sliding off down the inviting easy valley of the Little Spokane, it necessitates a cut through the summit two miles long, averaging forty feet in depth.

Again, getting out of the city is no easy matter. The river runs below here in a deep cañon and its course is very tortuous, and the places where it can be crossed to advantage very few. Of course the men can lay rails anywhere, but we did not come out in this country to do that. We came to give you people the lowest possible freight rates, which are absolutely necessary for the development of your country, and to do that we must have a cheaply operated road. The rates you people are paying at present are in many cases absolutely prohibitive, and very much higher than they ought to be.

I hear your coal costs you $8 per ton. It ought not to be more than half that. . . . We propose, too, to give you people a rate on flour so low that the whole grain crop of the Palouse country and the Big Bend will be drawn here and converted into flour. . . . Our policy is to put the rate so low that the business man can see opportunities of making money by manufacturing or producing something and shipping it over our line. This is the way we have built up other cities in the past and is the manner in which we shall contribute to the upbuilding of Spokane. There is no earthly reason why we should not supply the entire country from eastern Montana to the Coast,—aye, even China and Japan, with flour and meats.

After privately explaining the difficulties involved, it was arranged that Hili should have opportunity to discuss the matter before all the people at a mass-meeting and hear from them whether or not they wanted the Great Northern to come to Spokane, and how badly —this to be expressed in financial terms. The *Review* describes the appearance of the railroad Messiah before the people of the chosen city:

Mr. Hill has met the citizens of Spokane in mass convention, and if there ever was a public meeting marked by enthusiasm it was this.... As a drawing card John L. Sullivan isn't in it with James J. Hill.... He was received with prolonged cheers.... At the close of his speech he sat down amid a perfect storm of cheers, and it was quite clear that Mr. Hill had made every person in the audience a warm friend.

"As far as we have gone we have undertaken and have succeeded in building a railroad that is capable of doing more business than any transcontinental road that has been or will be built hereafter," said Mr. Hill. "...We expect that we can bring you from Chicago to Spokane in sixty hours (*applause*) ... from New York to the Pacific Ocean in four days. (*Applause.*) So far we have spared neither effort nor money to make our road what it should be, and I assure you we cannot afford to drop a missing link at this point.... Better for us that we keep away than put a weak link in the chain.

"Now, we could build a railroad through your city for a considerably smaller amount, over one-third, than what it would cost us to build the kind of road that we must have. It will cost us as much to go through the city as to build the most expensive thirty miles of our line of railroad, except where there are some special reasons for cost. What we desire to do is to come here and put our line on a permanent basis, bearing in mind the future growth that must follow where we build. (*Applause.*) As far as possible we must avoid crossing your streets at grade. That will do with a city of twenty-five thousand, but it will not do with a city of a hundred thousand, and if we come here you must grow to a hundred thousand or we will be disappointed. (*Applause.*)

"It will cost us ... one million dollars to go through your city, and I assure you that it is certainly more than twice as much as I expected it would cost when we undertook to make a survey to Spokane...."

Yesterday in going over the places where we could find a reasonable amount of room convenient to the business of the city, I felt more than discouraged. As I told you in September, we had no idea of coming here with a stub line. I will not build two lines where one will do. If we come into Spokane ... it follows that we must also establish here our machine and car shops (*applause*); with that follows an increase of wages alone of $500,000 a year.

"Some gentlemen whom I have met have raised the point as to what would be our policy in regard to the present method of making tariff. I say frankly that our policy will be to back the country the Great Northern Railroad goes through. You can make a distributing point of Spokane and compete with, if not surpass, other distributing centers (*applause*) and we should not feel that we are doing ourselves justice if we cannot bring goods here to sell at a competing point less than any city west or south of here. (*Applause.*)

"Now, what we ask of Spokane is that from the time we come to the city limits it would give us the right of way, so that the building of the road shall not cost anything. (*Applause.*) I want to be frank with you because I cannot afford to be otherwise than frank. Whether we agree or not we must part with the mutual respect and confidence of each other. The right of way we ask you to furnish because our expense in establishing shops here would be a million dollars. That amount of money would cover the distance from the east to the west side of the city limits, —five miles. And for that reason I feel that we are not asking or imposing a condition improper when we ask you to furnish the right of way to build the Great Northern Railway.

"We must begin work within a few days on one line or the other. I am going to the coast now and then shall return home, coming by way of Spokane. I hope matters will be arranged so that we can go to work here at once, and that it may be arranged without delay I would suggest that you, through your mayor, appoint a committee to take this matter up. I do not want you to wait. If a number of your citizens will consider the matter, and will guarantee us a right of way we should be ready to commence work in three days. (*Great applause.*) ... I do not come here asking for bonuses and gifts. The best line for us is ten miles north of here. It is only by the addition of an enormous expense that we shall come into this city. We shall come here, however, feeling absolute confidence that we shall be able to carry your products to the market for less money than any other railroad.... Every man, woman and child in the community depends on railroads and we want as many people to depend on our road as possible. We want to arrange our affairs and business so that the community and our business will be as partners, equally interested in the growth of this country." (*Tremendous applause.*)

While the citizens' committee was beginning its labors of providing a million-dollar right of way for the Great Northern, Hill went on with his discussions of the railroad's policies, meeting leading citizens in the office of L. C. Dillman:

As to our position in regard to terminal rates and what I said about your being able to compete with any city west or south, you could not do it if you had to pay more for the service than they have to pay. (*Cheers.*) Bear this in mind, that as long as there is a city and as long as our railroad is located on the ground, you are nearer to us than any one else. You are one of us. We can get more profit out of the business than by carrying it at our expense three or four hundred miles. We are not a charity road. This is a business proposition from beginning to end; as far as we are concerned we will make every proposition of that kind.

Whether you want to or not, you are going to pay us a lot of money. People living here will get rich; our road is here in partnership with you people and you cannot hurt us without hurting yourselves and falling. We have got to bring the goods, the materials, the groceries, nails, etc. You have to distribute it. We are not traders. Our province is to carry. We must gather the material of this country or we cannot carry it. Here is the situation: We must stand or fall with you. You cannot extend your business without extending ours and vice versa. This country cannot grow unless you are a distributing and collecting center. We are partners. When we are all gone, the railroad company will be here, and the city will be here, in partnership still, and on this basis we are coming here.

Hypnotized by the oratorical flow of Hill's speech, the Spokane men told him that this was the first time they had heard of low rates out of Spokane east. Whereupon the Empire Builder replied:

Well, it is a simple proposition and I will make it clear by a homely illustration. Supposing you and I are running opposition stage lines to some point thirty miles from here and two passengers come along, and you offered to take them both for five dollars, but I make this arrangement: I say to the passengers: "Can you guarantee me any passengers back?" They say they can, and I agree to take them for three dollars, and I get two passengers on the home trip; each man rides for one dollar and fifty and I make a dollar more than you would have made. (*Laughter and applause.*) ... Just as certain as you secure the right of way for me, the railroad will be built, and just as certain as it is built on the plans we have laid out we shall carry the trade of this city. Just as certain as water runs down hill low rates will bring the people. It would be cruel, barbarous for the road to come within eight or ten miles of this city and not run its main line here. Better be one hundred miles away than ten miles.

So excited did the populace become during Hill's visit that any remark questioning the beneficence of the great man or his Great Northern was regarded as an act of high treason, and the Spokane *Review* editorialized as follows:

Whatever doubts were entertained respecting the policy and intentions of Mr. Hill will disappear when the public has read the intensely interesting interview in another part of this paper. He there declares without reservation or evasion, his belief that the present tariff so far as it applies to Spokane, is illegal and cannot run the gauntlet of the courts. This is a remarkable declaration for a man in the position of Mr. Hill. It means something. It is the forerunner of lower rates for Spokane, and it should stimulate a renewed activity of earnest and liberal efforts of the citizens in the work of obtaining the right of way for the road. . . . The occasion calls for the supreme effort of encouragement. No man who, at this critical juncture in the history of the city, fails to come forward with the most liberal tokens of assistance need ever afterwards be considered a true friend of the city. The occasion is one when lack of generosity and public spirit will be little less than a crime; and the man who now puts himself up as a barrier to the city's prosperity must take the chances of the loss of the respect of the community.

It is hoped that no such will be found in the entire city, and that the minor obstructions encountered by the committee will vanish at the first touch. The Great Northern is knocking at the gate of the city. The future will not be altogether pleasant for the man who shall attempt to bar its entrance. There are some things far better than money. One of these is the respect of the community in which one dwells.

The total effect of Hill's oratory, warmth of handclasp, and common touch was to dazzle Spokane. Even the reporter for the *Review* was not immune to Hill's charms. He wrote that

Mr. Hill speaks with the directness and conviction of a man who is thoroughly conversant with every detail of his subject. He talks with an agreeable manner and at times a pleasant twinkle comes into his brown eyes. He expressed his admiration for Spokane and the public spirited citizens with whom he had been engaged for the past three days in the work of obtaining the right of way. . . . After this writer had prepared this interview for publication, it was submitted to Mr. Hill for verification. . . . He directed a few minor changes, chiefly in the nature of making his remarks clear and more emphatic.

Having made a deep impression on Spokane and seen the Soliciting Committee suggested by him busily at work extracting the shekels from business men's pockets, Hill departed for Seattle, promising soon to return. When he came back a few days later, the city was ready to present him with the right of way, and a few of the community leaders met him at a private gathering. "Gentlemen," said A. M. Cannon to the crowd in Dillman's office, "I want to introduce to you again the greatest railroad man in the world, James J. Hill." And Hill responded:

Gentlemen, the great compliment Mr. Cannon pays me I don't believe I am deserving of, but the railroad I am connected with I believe I can say, without boasting, is the lowest grade long railroad in the world. While you may now think I am a "low grade" crank, yet I assure you that the time is coming when you will believe in low grades just as much as I do. Without low grades it is impossible to make a low rate and a low rate is what you want.

While over on the Sound I had a great many people to see; a great many people apparently had to see me. (*Laughter.*) Some of them were engaged in manufacturing, some in merchandising, and some were up at their old tricks—booming. (*Laughter.*) ... In referring to the future of Spokane Falls I have made some statements that would lead you to infer that I would do certain things. I want to say to you frankly and clearly that I have made my last statement with full knowledge of what my words mean. We don't hold out statements to you for the purpose of inducing you to do anything. When I say that we shall enable you to compete in and control your field everywhere, it is true, and you will realize its truth; you will realize its benefits to you. What you have done is but an earnest of what you can do in the future.

In the first opening up of the country, Spokane Falls had grown to be a city of twenty-five to thirty thousand people. The settlement of this country has brought in a great many people and a great deal of money. The Cœur d'Alene mines and their surroundings have given you great stimulus; but if any city is to maintain its growth, it must have business; it must be a place where men do things that result in profit to them. A city can grow only through the business that is transacted in it. The time has come when you must throw up your arms and lay hold of the business that is more remote. You cannot grow and develop unless you do this. The days that are coming will enable you people to compete with any city west or south of you. (*Cheers.*) You are now the only city in Eastern Washington that can call itself a distributing point, the place where the products of that section are exchanged, and there is no reason why you should not always remain a distributing center, controlling the business of Eastern Washington. In that way your city will grow and extend its interests, reaching great wealth and prosperity.

When we come to Spokane I hope we shall make our influence felt at once. So soon as our line is open to the Pacific Coast, we shall feel ourselves independent. Any policy that retards the growth of Spokane will retard our growth. Any policy that will prevent you from distributing a ton of freight will rob us of that ton of freight. Our business is that of transportation; that is all we have to do. The more you do of that, the more we and you are benefited. . . . I would not have you imagine that we run a railroad for any charitable purpose, we do not run it because of any affection for our fellow beings. We run it solely for business reasons, because we expect to make money in good round sums. . . .

Spokane is situated on the eastern edge of Washington and has the advantage of being nearest to the greatest market of the world. (*Cheers.*) The forty million pepole on the other side of the mountain consume more than any other people in the world; they are able to do it. You are nearer though than the people on the Coast, and it costs less to carry goods from you to them, or to bring goods from the east to you, than to the people furthest west. With that advantage we feel that we shall be able to control the business through you, so far as it is possible, by means of land transportation. If any other line of road should come here which will do the work for less than we do, then I say in the name of everything good and everything worthy, give your business to them and we will take a second or third place. But it will be a long time before that can happen. We have measured every hill in those mountains and we know that we are at the bottom of the hill. (*Applause.*) You are also at the top of the hill with us.

It is probable that when Hill promised to cut rates, he intended to keep his promise; for it must have been part of his plan to ruin the Northern Pacific so that he could step in and control it, and his road was so well built and operated at so low a cost that the Northern Pacific could not compete with it. But it was not necessary for Hill to lay low the rival road. The panic of 1893, which arrived the year his railroad reached Spokane, did that for him, and he was enabled to get control by the financier's method of peaceful penetration. So rates on the Great Northern were not lowered, and Hill appeared to have suffered a lapse of memory on the promises made Spokane. He kept the right of way, however, even though he continued to gouge the donors on freight-rates.

Spokane had appealed to the Interstate Commerce Commission, and in November, 1892, the Commission had upheld the right of the railroads to charge higher rates to interior points than to coastal points farther away, but had directed them to lower their rates to Spokane. The railroads ignored this order to reduce rates, however, and in 1897 the United States Supreme Court ruled that the Commission had no power to prescribe freight-rates. Immediately the railroads raised their tariffs until it was possible to ship goods more cheaply from the East to the Orient than to Spokane.

Public indignation grew, and it became so widespread and violent among the farmers that Hill was alarmed. In August, 1902, he set out to stop public criticism of the railroads and the demands for lower rates, which threatened to become legislative enactments, by staging two railroad conferences in the State of Washington. These were held at Davenport, in the Big Bend country, and Colfax, in the Palouse country, and there to meet the embittered grain-farmers came Hill, Charles S. Mellen, president of the Northern Pacific, and A. L. Mohler of the Oregon Railway and Navigation Company. While the farmers spoke feelingly of the high cost of raising grain, Hill was eloquent on the extraordinary outlays of money required to handle freight. In his attempt to quiet the feelings of the agriculturists he said, "You might just as well try to set a broken ankle by statute as to reduce rates by statute. You can legislate until the barn door has fallen off its hinges with rust, and you will not succeed." But the railroads showed that they were frightened when President Mellen announced to the meetings that they had decided to reduce rates on grain about 10 per cent.

In 1906 the Hepburn Act gave the Interstate Commerce Commission power to fix rates, and Spokane filed the first complaint under the new law. In their appeal for relief the citizens engaged as chief counsel the celebrated Boston jurist Brooks Adams. His handling of this historic "long and short haul" case brought it wide attention, and the plea that he made for Spokane was typical of the complaints of all the shipping centers of the intermountain country, including El Paso at the south, which had much the same case against the Southern Pacific.

When the railroads declared that they had to keep the rates to

A WASHINGTON WHEAT-FIELD

Courtesy of the Spokane Chamber of Commerce.

LUMBERING IN THE INLAND EMPIRE

Courtesy of the Spokane Chamber of Commerce.

THE CAPITAL OF THE INLAND EMPIRE

Courtesy of the Spokane Chamber of Commerce.

the Coast lower than to Spokane so as to meet water competition, Spokane inquired why it would not be well for the railroads to make a low rate to Spokane from Chicago, where there was no water competition. Why not make the rate to Spokane so low that the jobbers from Spokane could sell up to the very door of Tacoma? For, the lawyers pointed out, if you take a carload of freight from Chicago and carry it to Tacoma and bring it back, you have the haul through to Tacoma and the haul back. If you merely haul that carload to Spokane, you do not haul it as far by 400 or 500 miles, and then, if there are any goods in the car for Coast points, you take the less-than-carload haul alone. Why wouldn't that be the most effective way to meet water competition—meet it from the interior and not from the seaboard?

But the railroads replied that they hauled a very small percentage of the Eastern goods used in this territory through to the Coast and back again, "and to make the Pacific Coast terminal rate apply to Spokane, is, in our opinion, unnecessary. We can quite effectually meet this indirect water competition by rates which are very considerably higher than the rates to the terminals." So they had decided to grant rates which would permit the Tacoma jobber to sell 250 miles toward Spokane and the Spokane jobber to sell only 100 miles toward Tacoma, because "we figured that over very carefully and the best earnings result from the plan which we are working."

During the hearings the railroad attorneys described the manner in which the lives of the citizens of Spokane and other cities were regulated at the whim of the railroads, which were conceived to be sovereign powers granting exclusive territory and other favors as an act of grace. While admitting that they charged more for Eastern freight to Spokane than to the Coast, the railroad officials claimed that they had given Spokane an absolutely preferential right to sell goods in practically the whole of the Palouse country:

Under those circumstances Spokane has grown up and prospered and is able to-day to absolutely undersell any other jobber in the entire Palouse country and for a distance of 113 or 114 miles west of the lines of the Northern Pacific and Great Northern ... and to express the matter concretely ... Spokane to-day, as the result of an arrangement ... has actually benefited from ocean competition, in that ocean competition has given her merchants an opportunity to compel the railroads to carve out for her special benefit the beautiful Inland Empire and to lay that empire at the feet of the jobbers.

When asked why such a zone should not be carved out for the people of Walla Walla or Pendleton, rival distributing points, the railroads admitted that, like all their other rates, it was an arbitrary arrangement. And it was shown that the transportation kings could, if they would, create another city in the Inland Empire whose power to compete with Spokane would be based on the rates they decreed.

The railroad attorneys declared that the loss in earnings that the Northern Pacific would suffer by giving a terminal rate to Spokane and all territory west of Spokane and a corresponding rate east of Spokane would be about $1,200,000 per annum, and the loss of the Great Northern would be about $600,000. But Spokane attorneys showed that about 70 per cent of the freight shipped in carload lots came from states that were not subject to water competition, and consequently that a rank discrimination existed against Spokane and in favor of Seattle, Tacoma, and Portland upon this freight. Spokane contended that because of the discriminatory rates more than twice as much money was invested in manufacturing in Tacoma as in Spokane, a city of the same size. But the Coast communities replied that terminal rates were made in heaven and should not be removed by earthly power. "The Pacific Ocean," it was averred, "is the only natural advantage which Providence has given Portland, and that advantage must not be abridged, even if its continuance throws upon others the burden of the highway tax which Portland might otherwise be constrained to pay."

In defending their rates the railroads insisted that they must pay interest on their enormous investments. But, as Mr. Adams pointed out, the Great Northern valued its entire property, then deducted the cost of operation, taxes, and depreciation from the gross receipts, and calculated the balance as a species of rental upon the sum total.

In drawing up their schedules these defendants entered thereon all land to which they claimed title, however acquired, whether by private gift, government grant, condemnation proceedings under eminent domain, or amicable purchase, and whether the land bought was paid for with money contributed by stockholders from their own funds, or with money appropriated to the purpose out of surplus earnings, after operating expenses, taxes, depreciation, fixed charges and dividends had been defrayed. The entire acreage thus obtained the defendants caused their own officials to appraise at its supposed present market value, thus charging the unearned increment to capital, and it was upon this valuation that the rental the public owed the companies for the use of the land as a highway was calculated.

Among the lands given the Great Northern was a tract worth $12,000,000 in Minnesota and the property acquired by the railroad in Spokane, the latter donated on condition that the road give the city terminal rates. Although this condition was never fulfilled, the land appeared on the schedule as part of that on which the public was compelled to pay rental at its then market value,

a claim of surpassing effrontery even for these defendants. . . . Far from the Great Northern having a claim against the public for rental of this property, the grantors of the Spokane right of way have a claim for the mesne profits of these lands during fifteen years against the Great Northern. . . .

Mr. Hill was as well advised as to the rate condition as any man in the United States at the time he made his public promise to the people of Spokane. . . . He was not induced by artifice, fraud or deception to visit Spokane and make this solemn covenant, nor was he duped into making the declarations and promises. . . . The good people of Spokane had faith in Mr. Hill. They believed his declarations and relied upon his promises. They did not dream that the master mind of Mr. Hill was a real representation of Dr. Jekyll and Mr. Hyde. They did not then know or believe that he was an Ananias. The people of Spokane did what they agreed to do, but Mr. Hill proved to be a past master in the rôle of confidence man. . . .

The magnificent audacity and nerve of the defendants, the Northern Pacific Railway Company and the Great Northern Railway Company, their officers, agents and representatives, are shown by the presentation of gigantic figures and inflated estimates of cost of reproduction, in the face of the fact that they thereby admit that the rates now existing to Spokane have been exorbitant, if based upon original cost or value at any given time, and yet show, when required to do so, that the properties of said companies have not been assessed at as much as twenty per cent of their values.

These two defendants openly and brazenly admit that the public has been buncoed for all the years that have passed and gone since their existence and since they have been doing business; and without any com-

punction of conscience advertise to the world that the public has been
paying almost unlimited amount of taxes that these public service corporations ought to have been paying in the past. This conduct and the
result of the presentation of these facts to this Commission are almost
beyond comprehension. . . .

The business of railway companies is to treat everyone fairly and all
communities reasonably. To do so would require the defendants to build
up the interior and all points along their railroads, instead of building up
points at the end of their line and terminals like Seattle, Tacoma and
Portland. . . .

The gross and net earnings have more than doubled since Mr. Hill
represented that his road could afford to and would reduce rates to
Spokane to or below terminal rates. The earnings per mile have more
than doubled within the same period. Millions and millions of dollars
from earnings of the Great Northern and Northern Pacific have been
spent in permanently improving their properties. Other roads have been,
or are being built from their earnings, and these two companies still have
in their treasuries, surplus enough to provide against all contingencies
for many, many years in the future—over sixty-eight millions of dollars,
according to the balance sheets in their 1906 annual reports—to which
should be added stocks and bonds on hand. . . .

What would Spokane be to-day had she been fairly treated for the
last ten years and not discriminated against by the railroads? What would
she be to-day if she had enjoyed terminal rates for the last seven or even
five years? What will she be five years from now if she shall continuously,
during that period be put and kept on an equality with her neighbors?
What would she be to-day if Mr. Hill had kept his promise, made in
1892, to give her rates as good or better than Seattle, Tacoma, and Portland? What could she now do with the more than $10,000,000 that have
been unlawfully, illegally, unreasonably and inexcusably exacted from
her? . . .

The three most striking examples of the potency of monopolistic
processes in the United States are the Standard Oil, the United States
Steel, and Mr. Hill's combination in the Northwest. All three have employed the same methods, but they have differed in this: The Standard
Oil and United States Steel are private enterprises which have succeeded
by energy and thrift; Mr. Hill alone has obtained and employed sovereign
powers for the purpose of wholesale confiscation. Coming into a poor
and sparsely settled country many years ago, Mr. Hill has consistently
used a national highway to enrich foreign speculators, precisely as a
Roman proconsul might have plundered a conquered province. Also, he
has ignored public responsibilities. While the Pennsylvania was spending
hundreds of millions in providing for a future expansion which intelligent

men foresaw, Mr. Hill was engaged in dividing his surplus among his stockholders by dividends of watered and undervalued stock, deliberately enfeebling his railways, until last winter the country tributary to them starved amidst the snow. Also the discontent among Mr. Hill's staff is notorious. His niggardly management is hated alike by the public and the employees. On the other hand, the profits to the syndicate which Mr. Hill organized have been dazzling.

The secret of Mr. Hill's success has lain in his ability to maintain the monopolistic price.... Mr. Hill's policy shows genius. To thoroughly succeed the first business of the monopolist is to suppress competition, so that he may be able to extract from his victim all that that victim can pay. His next is to graduate his demands to conform to the limit of his victim's endurance. Mr. Hill ... secured a monopoly in the Northwest.... He then set himself to establish his scale of prices, his problem being to keep all his equipment moving at the highest velocity for the highest price. To do so he graduated his charges to conform to the resisting power of every community and every class in the community. He has often boasted that his average rates are low. Mr. Hill has made low rates to secure business if he needed that business and it could be had on no better terms; perhaps no railroad in the country has made lower. But if the rate be for a necessary of life to be sold to a population under servitude to his monopoly his charge will be the limit of what the purchaser can pay.

Many years ago, Mr. Clough, the vice-president of the Great Northern, and Mr. Hill's confidential adviser, explained, in the first suit between these parties, the process by which the company reached the monopoly price. I have thus quoted from his testimony ... :

*Q.* So you carry shingles and lumber from Seattle to St. Paul for 50 cents a hundred, to keep these people from starvation, ... and you charge $4.75 a ton to haul wheat from Spokane over to Puget Sound?

*A.* That is a fair rate as compared with other rates on the system.

*Q.* Well, are you in doubt as to whether you make money on that basis or not?

*A.* No, we are not making too much....

*Q.* In other words, then, you have to have so much money?

*A.* We have to have so much money, yes, sir. And we have to get it from our patrons, there is nobody that gives it to us.

*Q.* And therefore you go for the people that you think have got in a place where they can't help themselves?

*A.* We try to arrange our sales as far as possible so that business will move....

The substance of success has lain in making the price just low enough to permit the community to buy all that the monopoly has to sell; that is to say, in this instance, to keep its rolling stock constantly moving.

This implies, of course, discrimination carried out scientifically as between individuals, classes, and localities, and this is the system which Mr. Hill has practiced, as far as practicable, and herein has lain his success....

His success has been so complete as to be embarrassing. One of his chief preoccupations has been to devise means of converting the surplus taxes he has thus collected from the people to his own use, without divulging the amount of his exactions. Sometimes, when the surplus has grown unwieldy, he has distributed it in huge blocks, as when he distributed the certificates for the ore lands which he had bought with surplus, or as when, at an earlier day when his ideas were smaller, he issued $10,000,000 of bonds for one-tenth of their face value. But ordinarily he has preferred to invest his surplus in additions to his lines, thus giving him the power to make a cumulative increment of capital out of public money, and collect an income on this increment. The advantage of this method of financiering is palpable. Every dollar of public money thus confiscated is forthwith protected as being a vested interest, and on that vested interest Mr. Hill may divide 7 per cent forever. Furthermore, he may collect thereon as much additional tax as the public can pay, and he is free to invest that surplus also in subsidiary monopolies.

In another statement Mr. Adams pointed out that there was no evidence to show that Mr. Hill and his partners ever put any cash into the original enterprise of the St. Paul and Pacific Railroad Company, but by a dizzy record of absorptions, reorganizations, issuance of stocks and bonds, the benefits conferred on Great Northern stockholders, as stockholders of St. Paul, Minneapolis and Manitoba Railway stock, amounted to between four and five hundred million dollars. And he estimated that $100,000,000 of surplus had been capitalized in the property and in the properties and securities of the proprietary companies. "The defendants," he said, "themselves have proved that by the imposition of the monopolistic price upon those who use their railways, they draw annually from the citizens of Spokane, who live under monopoly, about $1,000,000 more than they draw from the same number of persons for the same or cheaper service, who live where competition prevails,...an imposition of an undue burden very considerably over $10 annually upon every man, woman and child in Spokane."

Summarizing Hill's methods, after an exhaustive study of the official financial documents, Frederick O. Downs, of the Boston bar, had this to say:

Where he pays the public for money loaned, Mr. Hill pays as little as he can.

Where he pays the operating expenses, he pays as little as he can.

Where he pays his staff, he pays as little as he can.

Mr. Hill's object is to get enough business to keep the line moving.

He charges all that his patrons will stand and give him business enough to keep it moving.

He depresses all expenditures that operate to reduce his revenue.

He gives the stockholders the results.

He has paid dividends in the Great Northern Company $69,000,000.

He has put back into the property as much more.

Where he paid six per cent dividends, he might have paid twelve.

Where he pays seven per cent dividends, the company earns fourteen.

Mr. Hill is not an advocate of excessive dividends but he believes that stockholders should have fourteen per cent annually. That is what he works for, that is the return which in one way or another he gives them.

Adams completed the case for Spokane with this stinging indictment:

The railways, while admitting a surplus of several millions, have proved that they extract from Spokane about one-third more money for the transport of the same quantity and the same class of goods, over the same road, that they charge the coast, although the coast cities are four hundred miles further from the initial point, and lie beyond the Cascade Mountains, whose grades are costly to overcome. In substance the only defense made is that the railways who are already so wealthy that they do not dare openly to divide their profits would lose were they to grant relief. The true reason for their resistance is that Spokane is the key to the Northwest. Hold Spokane and Mr. Hill holds his monopoly. Surrender Spokane, and Mr. Hill's highways must pass under national sovereignty.... Mr. Hill saw that Spokane was the natural capital of the interior Northwest, and controlled all territory to the east; but that to the west he met the sea.... They had a monopoly in Spokane, and therefore they took more money from Spokane, not because they could not have earned good dividends by carrying their zones to the Pacific, based on the rates fixed by competition, but because the people of the interior were in their power. Mr. Hill has often boasted that he could work his railway at a profit at far less than terminal rates.... Mr. Clough recognized, as freely as Mr. Hill, the discrimination against Spokane. He justified it only on the ground that they could get no more from those not under servitude, asseverating that if the whole of the traffic of the railroad company should be carried proportionate distances at proportionate rates, the outcome would be very disastrous to the railroad company.... To carry out Mr. Hill's promises, made in 1892, would be to erect popular sovereignty in Spokane and to release the Northwest from servitude to monopoly. That is why Mr. Hill broke his word. Mr. Hill is a man of genius, as his whole life has shown, but even genius has limitations, and Mr. Hill's limitation is an inability to comprehend that the American citizen has any rights which he is bound to respect.... Had Mr. Hill in the Northwest been the agent of the Government, entrusted with the administration of a great public work, he would have been a benefactor to his country and his age. As a sovereign he has proved a greedy despot."

On March 2, 1909, the Interstate Commerce Commission decided in favor of Spokane on certain commodities. Wrangling over rates between the city and the railroads continued, however; the Commission again ordered rate cuts on June 29, 1910; and on Tuesday, July 26, 1911, a sweeping order was given providing that Spokane should receive the long-sought terminal rates. On that day pandemonium broke loose. Spokane citizens celebrated with bells, whistles, horns, a parade, rallies, red lights, and street dances. But the joy was premature, for the railroads appealed the decision to the Supreme Court, a long drawn out contest followed, and it was not until 1918 that Spokane finally won her case and was given the same rates as Seattle and Tacoma.

Meanwhile, railroad construction had continued around Spokane. In 1902 F. A. Blackwell built an electric road from Cœur d'Alene to Spokane, and in 1904, with Jay P. Graves, he built the Spokane and Interurban to Colfax. In 1904 Daniel C. Corbin built another road, the Spokane International, to connect the city with the Canadian Pacific at Yahk in British Columbia, and to further this project the city gave the necessary right of way and terminals. In 1906 the Graves traction interests were consolidated as the Inland Empire Railway system, and in 1909 it was sold to the Great Northern. In 1907 Blackwell built the Idaho and Washington Northern to Metaline Falls, Idaho, and at Spirit Lake, Idaho, laid out a model town in the midst of the forest.

In 1904 the incorporation of the Spokane and Seattle Railroad, by John S. Baker of Tacoma and James D. Hoge of Seattle, excited some comment, and it was later discovered that this proposed line had the backing of James J. Hill, who built it down the north bank of the Columbia, connecting Spokane and Portland. Very soon thereafter there began to be rumors that the Chicago, Milwaukee and St. Paul would build through Spokane on its way to the Coast. President Albert J. Earling visited the city and said the road would like to come there as much as Spokane would like to have it, but made no promises. At about this time, however, there arrived in Spokane a mystery man whose railroad operations kept the newspapers of the Northwest in head-lines for several years.

Robert Edmund Strahorn, the new railroad promoter, was born in Center County, Pennsylvania, May 15, 1852. As a child he had little opportunity for schooling, and he early went with his parents to northern Illinois. In 1870 he engaged in newspaper work in Denver, working as reporter and editor until 1877. He was a correspondent on Indian wars for the New York *Times* and the Chicago *Tribune,* after which he did publicity work for the Denver and Rio Grande Railroad. From 1877 to 1884 he managed the publicity bureau of the Union Pacific and Kansas Pacific in Denver and Omaha, and did confidential work in extending the lines of the Union Pacific. He carried on town-site and irrigation enterprises in Oregon, Washington, and Idaho, and in 1890 returned east to sell municipal bonds in Boston. In 1898 he came to Spokane to develop waterworks, electric plants, and irrigation schemes, and in 1905 he blossomed forth as the promoter of the North Coast Railroad to bring Spokane and Walla Walla closer to Portland, Tacoma, and Seattle.

At this time Edward Hungerford described him as the North Coast Railroad's "president, general attorney and confidential secretary to the president and general attorney." One stenographer served as the entire staff of the railroad and its board of directors. When Strahorn began to buy real estate and took title to a hundred pieces of the most valuable business property in Spokane, the town was mad with excitement. Who was this mystery man and who was backing him? He made surveys, built tracks, organized the Spokane Union Terminal project to eliminate grade crossings in entering the city, and paid for everything with his personal check. A thousand miles had been surveyed, a hundred miles completed into the Yakima Valley, and bridges had been built across the Columbia and the Snake when it became known that Strahorn had proposed his scheme years before to E. H. Harriman and obtained that gentleman's support. By this means Harriman had found a way to challenge Hill's control of the Spokane country.

And Strahorn made a master stroke when he induced the Chicago, Milwaukee and St. Paul, which had intended to pass 40 miles south, to come into his scheme, thus connecting the Milwaukee and the Union Pacific at Spokane. In 1910 the Harriman lines in the Northwest and Strahorn's North Coast Railroad were consolidated as the Oregon–Washington Railroad and Navigation Company, and Strahorn was made vice-president. And he was the toast of Spokane when, September 14, 1914, he wielded the silver hammer to drive home the last spike which connected two railroad systems and brought them into a new $500,000 station in the heart of the city. After that but one more transportation event was to befall. Spokane's latest railroad development was the extension of the Great Northern system to California, completed in 1931, giving the city an outlet to the south over the Spokane, Portland and Seattle Railroad.

So Spokane, with its lines stretching in every direction, became a great railroad center—the most important west of Omaha. And she won those terminal rates for which she waged such a hard fight—rates which have increased her manufacturing and trade territory but which, curiously enough, have turned out to be something of a disadvantage. For under the decision of the Interstate Commerce Commission in Spokane's case, railroads are not permitted to charge less for a short than for a long haul. Consequently, it is impossible for the northern routes to give lower rates to Portland, Tacoma, and Seattle than to Spokane. Neither can the more southerly routes give lower rates to Los Angeles, San Diego, and San Francisco than to Denver and El Paso. Apparently this is a most fair and equitable arrangement for the intermountain cities. But what has been the result? In 1914 the Panama Canal, long advocated by Westerners, who were, paradoxically, heavy holders of the securities of northern railroad lines, was opened, and while its effect was not fully felt until after the World War, the Canal began to take the business away from the transcontinental railways. As John Leeds Kerr, railroad economist, points out, from 1920 up to and including 1933 the major portion of the trade from the Atlantic ports of the United States to Asia changed from rail to water. So did the through business between Atlantic and

Pacific cities. And, moreover, the lower freight-rates on raw materials from the Eastern states to the Pacific ports *via* the Canal made possible the upbuilding of factories in all the port cities which competed with those of the interior. Thus, the railroads were robbed of the major part of their east and west traffic, and the railroad centers, such as Spokane and El Paso, felt the pinch.

It was an odd coincidence that the peak of traffic density on the northern railroad lines passing through Spokane was reached in 1918, the very year she won her fight for terminal rates. On the Northern Pacific it was 1,453,000 tons per traffic mile in that year. By 1930 it had declined to 798,000 tons, and in 1932 it was 461,000. This has meant that the railroad business, which is a major industry in Spokane, employing thousands of men in shops, yards, and headquarters, has declined so markedly as to be a cause of grave concern. Indeed, it is quite likely that the city would be benefited should the Interstate Commerce Commission reverse its ruling, give the railroads "fourth-section relief," and again permit a lower rate for the long haul to the Coast than for the short haul to the interior cities. For if they could compete with the Panama Canal, the railroads would prosper, and Spokane would share in that prosperity: every shipload of freight diverted to the railroads would mean some fifty cars passing through the city, with all the traffic and all the repairs and purchase of supplies coincident with that traffic adding enormously to her pay-roll. It is possible that the Commission will grant this relief to the railroads, and if it does, Spokane might find it as agreeable as she found the reverse in 1918.

Because of cheap transportation of raw materials to the Coast through the Panama Canal, Spokane has suffered from increased competition of factories in the Coast cities; and it has also suffered from the fact that the lumber companies have been disposed to cut timber on the Coast near tide-water, where it can be shipped through the Canal by boat, rather than in the interior near Spokane. But this is a temporary setback, and as the Coast lumber is exhausted, the timber around Spokane will again be drawn upon. Recent increases in the demand for silver and other metals have revived the mining around Spokane; much prospecting is being done in the Salmon River district, which is almost unexploited; quantities of gold are being mined in the

Sunshine Mine near Kellogg; the Spokane Mining Exchange has become a center of feverish activity. Reviving agriculture will add to the city's prosperity as the price of wheat rises and the demand for apples increases. And the city will benefit immeasurably from the construction of the Grand Coulée Dam on the upper Columbia.

This mammoth engineering scheme centers around a strange geological formation, a sort of miniature Grand Canyon and a dry falls 400 feet high, cut by glacial rivers of past ages in the midst of the arid Columbia plateau, 12,000 square miles in extent. The Grand Coulée power and irrigation project, authorized by President Franklin Roosevelt in conjunction with the State of Washington, will utilize the waters of the Columbia at this point to generate 2,100,000 horse-power of electrical energy, and later, as the need for farming-land increases, to irrigate a vast dry area of 1,200,000 acres, which only needs water to make it fertile. Within 60 years it is estimated that this project will add a population of 1,500,000 to the Inland Empire.

So Spokane looks forward optimistically to the future. And in the meantime she has a number of assets which never fail. She is the only city of the first class in a vast stretch of over 2,000 miles between Minneapolis, St. Paul, and the Coast, the capital of a district producing one-quarter of the nation's lead, one-tenth of its wheat, one-quarter of its apples, and the trading center of 500,000 people. Far more important as a center of metropolitan activity than her population would indicate, Spokane has one of the greatest concentrations of government agencies in the West; she is the headquarters for every movement of importance in the Inland Empire, she is the home of the National Apple Show and the National Sportsman's Show; and she proudly entertains her many visitors in one of the most interesting and attractive hotels in the country, the Davenport.

Spokane is a city of beautiful homes, of parks and playgrounds, and of a metropolitan business district which is a fitting center for the wide-spreading Inland Empire. A strangely picturesque city, it is built around the tremendous gash that has been cut through its heart by the Spokane River, and in the middle of its downtown section the waters tumble over the rocks to produce the beautiful and powerful Spokane Falls. Up on the heights there is a beautiful crown of hillside estates with architecturally distinctive houses and lovely gardens.

Downtown the gracefully curved colonnade of the stately white-stone Masonic Temple speaks of the taste and wealth of present-day Spokane, and the tall turreted red-brick Spokesman Review building recalls the days when the city was getting its stride in the gay Nineties.

A vigorous, lively business center, Spokane has also close at hand a multitude of forests and lakes and mountains in which her people and her visitors can play and enjoy the dry, invigorating climate—the climate that is her heritage from the Indians. For long ago, when a malign Indian goddess lived in the falls of the Spokane and enmeshed fishermen in the strands of her flowing hair, before she was annihilated by the great Indian god Coyote, the clouds in the Spokane country were often filled with rain. In those times there was fog and mist and dampness; but one day, when the rain poured and the lightning flashed, an Indian god went up into heaven and slew the god of Thunder, and since then Spokane has been a place of sunshine and dry air and the gentle, spicy Chinook wind— cool in summer, warm in winter—that blows from the west. In grateful thanks for this good gift of the red men, Spokane has remembered their generosity by adopting a smiling Indian girl with a blazing sun on her bosom as the symbol of the city. But the most important factor in Spokane's success is her good citizens, who not only know how to wear dinner clothes, but who, as Governor Alva Adams of Colorado once said, "are young, enthusiastic, and patriotic. Not satisfied to sit and wait for tribute, their capital and enterprise go out into tributary territory, where they plow virgin fields, dig canals, build railroads, transform the desert, mine gold, silver, copper, and lead in the mountains. They are builders, creators, developers." If men make cities, and such men do, Spokane's future is assured.

# BIBLIOGRAPHY

ANY intimate study of the history of the Western states must make use of the files of old newspapers and periodicals and the reminiscences collected in various local libraries and historical societies. These, together with conversations with "old-timers," are the best source of fresh and interesting material. For the stories of the development of the different communities, the local histories, such as those published by S. J. Clarke and Company of Chicago, are most valuable; and for a comprehensive view of the beginnings and early progress of the Western states, the works of the prolific historian Bancroft must be consulted. The *Works of Hubert Howe Bancroft* (San Francisco, A. L. Bancroft and Company, 1883-90) include: Vols. XVIII-XXIV, *History of California* (1888-89); Vols. XXVII-XXVIII, *History of the Northwest Coast* (1889); Vols. XXIX-XXX, *History of Oregon* (1884); Vol. XXXI, *History of Washington, Idaho and Montana* (1886-88). There is also the *Chronicles of the Builders of the Commonwealth,* seven volumes (San Francisco, History Company, 1891-92).

An excellent one-volume *History of the Pacific Coast* is now published (1934) by the author, John Walton Caughey, of the University of California at Los Angeles. The following suggestions for additional reading are in no sense complete, but they list a few of the most valuable sources of information.

## CHAPTERS I, II, III, IV

The story of the surveying and building and financing of the early railroads, told in the first four chapters of this book, has used much manuscript material from the collection of the late Archer Butler Hulbert at Colorado College. It has also drawn from the various reports and pamphlets published by the Union Pacific Railroad. Among these are "Union Pacific Railroad Company, Progress of Their Road West from Omaha" (undated) and "Union Pacific Railroad, Guide to Union Pacific Railroad Lands" (undated). There is also an early history of the road, Henry Kirk White, *History of the Union Pacific* (Chicago, University of Chicago Press, 1895); and a more recent one, Nelson Trottman, *History of the Union Pacific* (New York, Ronald Press, 1923).

General Grenville M. Dodge has written a number of valuable reports and speeches published in small volumes. His *How We Built the*

*Union Pacific* (published by the author, undated) is a good story of the author's part in this work. The best and most comprehensive story both of the building of the Union Pacific and of the life of General Dodge is J. R. Perkins, *Trails, Rails and War* (Indianapolis, Bobbs-Merrill, 1929).

F. H. Hodder, "The Railroad Background of the Kansas-Nebraska Act," *Mississippi Valley Historical Review*, xii (June, 1925), 3-22, explains the relations of Senator Douglas to this legislation.

A spirited story of General William J. Palmer's early railroad surveys in Colorado is contained in William A. Bell, *New Tracks in North America*, two volumes (London, Chapman and Hall, 1869). The complete technical account of the surveys is William J. Palmer, *Report of Surveys for the Kansas Pacific*.

For the story of General Palmer, begun in these chapters and continued in later chapters, the best sources of information are: *General William J. Palmer* (privately printed at Colorado Springs, undated); *William Jackson Palmer, Pathfinder and Builder* (privately printed by George Foster Peabody, Saratoga Springs, New York, 1931); William Jackson Palmer, *Letters, 1853-1868* (privately printed, Philadelphia, 1906).

Cy Warman, *Story of the Railroads* (New York, D. Appleton and Company, 1926) is a good popular account of railroad-building.

More complete and technical accounts are contained in John Moody, *The Railroad Builder* (New Haven, Yale University Press, 1921); Slason Thompson, *Short History of American Railroads* (New York, D. Appleton and Company, 1925); Charles Frederick Carter, *When Railroads Were New* (New York, Simmons-Boardman Publishing Company, 1926).

Glenn Danford Bradley, *Story of the Santa Fe* (Boston, Richard C. Badger, 1920) is the only good history of the Atchison, Topeka and Santa Fe Railroad.

The story of the beginning of the Central Pacific and the later story of the Southern Pacific are best covered, though incompletely, in Stuart Daggett, *Chapters on the History of the Southern Pacific* (New York, Ronald Press, 1922).

Some effective muck-raking of the railroads has been done by Charles Edward Russell in his *Stories of the Great Railroads* (Chicago, Charles H. Kerr and Company, 1912).

## CHAPTER V

A fruitful reference on town-building and the development of Western resources is Albert D. Richardson, *Beyond the Mississippi* (Hartford, American Publishing Company, 1867).

The building of the towns of Colorado, a number of which grew out of railroad enterprises, is covered in the histories of Colorado: Milo Lee Whitaker, *Pathbreakers and Pioneers of the Pueblo Region* (Pueblo, Franklin Press, 1917); Jerome C. Smiley, *Semi-Centennial History of the State of Colorado* (Chicago, Lewis Publishing Company, 1913); Frank B. Hall, *History of the State of Colorado* (Chicago, Blakely Printing Company, 1918); Eugene Parsons, *The Making of Colorado* (Chicago, A. Flanagan Company, 1908); F. C. Grable, *Colorado, the Bright Romance of American History* (Denver, Kistler Press, 1911); James H. Baker, *History of Colorado* (Denver, Linderman and Company, 1927).

Details of the financing of the various Colorado enterprises of General Palmer are contained in Annual Reports, National Land and Improvement Company, Central Colorado Improvement Company, and Colorado Springs Company (Colorado Springs, 1872-1910).

## CHAPTER VI

The contemporary newspaper accounts of the building of Greeley have been collected in James F. Willard, *Union Colony at Greeley, 1869-1871* (Boulder, 1918). The most complete story of the colony is contained in David Boyd, *Greeley and the Union Colony* (Greeley, Greeley Tribune Press, 1890). A well-written story of experiences in Greeley is J. Max Clark, *Colonial Days* (Denver, Smith-Brooks Publishing Company, 1902).

Considerable attention is given the colony in William M. Thayer, *Marvels of the New West* (Norwich, Conn., Henry-Bill Publishing Co., 1887).

## CHAPTER VII

L. R. Hafen has written a good account of Denver's early attempts to get a transcontinental railroad in "Pioneer Struggles for a Railroad Across the Rockies," *Colorado Magazine* (State Museum, Denver), March, 1926.

A. K. McClure describes the city as he saw it in *Three Thousand Miles through the Rockies* (Philadelphia, J. B. Lippincott, 1869). There is a *History of the City of Denver,* published by L. Baskin and Company, Chicago, in 1880.

An authoritative technical report and history of the long and complicated building of the Moffat Tunnel has been written by Edgar Carlisle McMechen, *The Moffat Tunnel of Colorado* (Denver, Wahlgreen Publishing Company, 1927).

The best story of the early mining days around Denver and the other districts of Colorado is the very interesting volume of George Findley Willison, *Here They Dug the Gold* (New York, Brentano, 1931).

## CHAPTERS VIII, IX

The material on the California gold-rush and San Francisco is practically limitless. A few volumes, however, can be arbitrarily selected as furnishing a view of California and of the early development of San Francisco. An authentic and colorful biography of the city is Charles Caldwell Dobie's *San Francisco, a Pageant* (New York, D. Appleton-Century Company, 1933). It covers almost everything of importance concerning the early history, development, and later history of San Francisco.

The early history of the city is well handled in Herbert E. Bolton, *Outpost of Empire* (New York, Alfred A. Knopf, 1931), and Zoeth Skinner Eldredge, *Beginnings of San Francisco* (New York, John C. Rankin and Company, 1912).

An interesting book about the days of the gold-rush is Frank Soulé, M. D. Gihon, and James Nesbit, *Annals of San Francisco* (New York, D. Appleton and Company, 1855).

Josiah Royce wrote a philosophical account of the development of the state in *California* (Boston, Houghton Mifflin Company, 1886).

A readable and scholarly history of California after the Mexican period is Robert Glass Cleland, *A History of California, the American Period* (New York, Macmillan Company, 1927).

Gertrude Atherton's *California* (New York, Liveright, 1927) is an entertaining volume. John Steven McGroarty, *California, Its History and Romance* (Los Angeles, Grafton Publishing Company, 1911) is an interesting journalistic account. Valeska Bari tells of the development of California in *The Course of Empire* (New York, Coward-McCann, 1931).

A résumé of life in San Francisco before the earthquake and fire is contained in the volume by Will Irwin, written while the city was still in ashes, *The City That Was* (New York, B. W. Huebsch, 1906). And a short account of how the city was rebuilt is contained in Rufus Steel, *The City That Is* (San Francisco, 1909).

Aurelia Ransome Neville gives her reminiscences of San Francisco in *The Fantastic City* (Boston, Houghton Mifflin Company, 1932).

A local history worth consulting is Bailey Millard, *History of the San Francisco Bay Region* (San Francisco, American Historical Society, 1924).

Hubert Howe Bancroft gives his estimate of the city and his ideas on city-building in general in his *Some Cities and San Francisco* (New York, Bancroft Company, 1907).

Early San Francisco is described by a contemporary in Samuel Bowles, *Our New West* (Hartford, Hartford Publishing Company, 1869).

Incidents of the gold-rush and mining days are recounted in James A. B. Scherer, *The First Forty-Niner* (New York, Minton, Balch and Company, 1925), and in the *Diary of Johann August Sutter* (San Francisco, Grabhorn Press, 1932).

C. B. Glasscock writes of the Comstock Lode in *The Big Bonanza* (Indianapolis, Bobbs-Merrill, 1931), and George D. Lyman in *The Saga of the Comstock Lode* (New York, Charles Scribner's Sons, 1934).

The careers of the men who built the railroads and headed the industrial enterprises are set forth by Hubert Howe Bancroft in his *Chronicles of the Builders* (San Francisco, History Company, 1891-92). Additional material is contained in the manuscripts of reports made to Bancroft by his assistants, now available in the Bancroft Historical Library of the University of California. Other sources concerning the California railroads and their builders are George T. Clark, *Leland Stanford* (Stanford University Press, 1931); Charles Edward Russell, *Stories of the Great Railroads* (Chicago, Charles H. Kerr Company, 1912); Henry Root, *Reminiscences* (privately printed, San Francisco, 1921); George Wharton James, *Heroes of California* (Boston, Little, Brown and Company, 1910); Glenn D. Bradley, *Story of the Santa Fe* (Boston, Richard G. Badger, 1910); Robert Lardin Fulton, *Epic of the Overland* (San Francisco, A. M. Robertson, 1924); an article on Theodore Dehone Judah, in the *California Historical Quarterly*, San Francisco, September, 1925.

## Chapters X, XI

The best small volume on Los Angeles is Charles Dwight Willard, *History of Los Angeles* (Los Angeles, Kingsley, Barnes and Neuner, 1901).

A most valuable volume, paper bound and profusely illustrated, is issued by the publicity department of a local bank: L. L. Hill, *La Reina, Los Angeles in Three Centuries* (Los Angeles, Security First National Bank, 1931).

More detailed accounts are given in William A. Spalding, *History of Los Angeles* (Los Angeles, J. R. Finnell and Sons); Charles F. Lummis, *Los Angeles and Her Makers* (Los Angeles, Out West Magazine Company, 1909); and J. W. Guinn, *History of California and Los Angeles* (Los Angeles, 1915).

The real-estate boom is convincingly described by T. S. Van Dyke in his *Millionaires of a Day* (New York, Fords, Howard and Hulbert, 1890).

The story of the harbor is told in Ella A. Ludwig's *History of the Harbor District of Los Angeles* (Los Angeles, Historic Record Company, 1928); and the fight for building the harbor at San Pedro is graphically described by Charles Dwight Willard in *The Free Harbor Contest at Los Angeles* (Los Angeles, 1899).

The early history of Southern California is given in C. E. Chapman,

*History of California, the Spanish Period* (New York, Macmillan Company, 1921).

Interesting reminiscences of the city are told by Harris Newmark in *Sixty Years in Southern California* (Boston, Houghton Mifflin Company, 1930).

An extensive bibliography of material on Southern California is published (1931) by the Los Angeles County Library.

## CHAPTER XII

A scholarly account of the early missions is contained in F. W. Blackmar, *Spanish Institutions of the Southwest* (1891).

Local histories of San Diego include Theodore Strong Van Dyke, *City and County of San Diego* (San Diego, Le Berthon and Taylor, 1888), and William E. Smythe, *History of San Diego, 1542-1908* (San Diego, History Company, 1908).

Something of the atmosphere and charm of the city is conveyed in Eugene Neuhaus, *The San Diego Garden Fair* (San Francisco, Paul Elder, 1916), and Ernest Peixotto, *Romantic California* (New York, Charles Scribner's Sons, 1910).

The development of the Imperial Valley and the career of George Chaffey is well covered in J. A. Alexander, *Life of George Chaffey* (London, Macmillan and Company, 1928).

H. Austen Adams describes the contribution of the man who has been called San Diego's leading citizen in *The Man John D. Spreckels* (San Diego, Frye and Smith, 1924).

Gilson Gardner's *Lusty Scripps* (New York, Vanguard Press, 1932) is a journalistic account of the life of Edward Wyllis Scripps.

## CHAPTERS XIII, XIV, XV, XVI

The early stages of the building of the Northern Pacific are covered in Eugene V. Smalley, *History of the Northern Pacific* (New York, G. P. Putnam's Sons, 1883). Some phases of the complicated story of the development of the Northern Pacific and the Oregon Railway and Navigation Company are considered in James Blaine Hedges, *Henry Villard and the Railways of the Northwest* (New Haven, Yale University Press, 1930.)

The lives of the three most prominent figures in the Northwestern railroad building, as well as much information about the roads they built, are contained in: *Memoirs of Henry Villard*, two volumes (Boston, Houghton Mifflin Company, 1904); George Kennan, *E. H. Harriman*, two volumes (Boston, Houghton Mifflin Company, 1922); and Joseph

Gilpin Pyle, *Life of James J. Hill*, two volumes (Garden City, N. Y., Doubleday, Page and Company, 1917).

Something of the activities of Ben Holladay are told by LeRoy R. Hafen in his *Overland Mail* (Cleveland, Arthur H. Clark Company, 1926).

In studying the early history of the cities of Oregon and Washington and of their leading citizens one must consult the *Chronicles of the Builders* by Hubert Howe Bancroft, already referred to.

Further details on local history can be obtained from the following volumes published by S. J. Clarke Publishing Company, Chicago: Clarence B. Bagley, *History of Seattle*; Joseph Gaston, *History of Oregon*; Herbert Hunt, *Tacoma, Its History and Its Builders*; Nelson W. Durham, *History of the City of Spokane* (1912). Another history of Tacoma is by W. P. Bonney, *The History of Pierce County* (Chicago, Pioneer Historical Publishing Company, 1927).

Roberta Frye Watt has written one of the most interesting histories of a city that has ever been printed in her *Story of Seattle* (Seattle, Lowman Hanford and Company, 1932).

The histories of Oregon include Sidona V. Johnson, *Short History of Oregon* (Chicago, A. C. McClurg Company, 1904); Harvey Whitefield Scott, *History of the Oregon Country* (Cambridge, Riverside Press, 1924); Charles Henry Carey, *History of Oregon* (Chicago, Pioneer Historical Publishing Company, 1922); Charles Hiram Chapman, *Story of Oregon and Its People* (Chicago, O. P. Barnes, 1909); Julian Hawthorne, *Story of Oregon* (New York, American Historical Publishing Company, 1892).

The histories of Washington include Edmond Stephen Meany, *History of the State of Washington* (New York, Macmillan Company, 1909); Clinton A. Snowden, *History of Washington* (New York, Century Company, 1909); Herbert Hunt, *Washington, West of the Cascades* (Chicago, S. J. Clarke Publishing Company, 1917); William Farrand Prosser, *A History of the Puget Sound Country* (Chicago, Lewis Publishing Company, 1903).

The story of the long- and short-haul rate cases in which Spokane sought the right for equal overland freight-rates with Pacific Coast ports, and which represented the perennial fight between all the intermountain cities and the Pacific ports, is contained in the documents presented before the United States Interstate Commerce Commission in the City of Spokane and others vs. the Northern Pacific Railway Company and Great Northern Railway Company, 1907.

There are two sources of detailed information about the rather complex early transportation situation in Oregon: John Tilson Ganoe, "History of the Oregon and California Railroad," *Quarterly of the Oregon Historical Society*, xxv, and I. L. Poppleton, "Oregon's First Monopoly—the Oregon Steam Navigation Company," *ibid.*

# INDEX